THE ROUTLEDGE INTERNATIONAL HANDBOOK OF SOCIAL PSYCHOLOGY OF THE CLASSROOM

The Routledge International Handbook of Social Psychology of the Classroom presents the first comprehensive and integrated compilation of theory and research on topics related to the social cohesion of the classroom. Many of these topics have been studied independently; for example, motivation, self-concept, class management, class climate, and teacher expectations are generally studied separately by different groups of researchers. This handbook brings the evidence from different fields in social psychological classroom research together in one place for the first time to explore how these topics relate and how each factor influences students and their learning.

With chapters by established international leaders in their fields, as well as emerging new talent, this handbook offers cutting edge research and surveys the state of the art in the social psychology of the classroom.

Major areas covered include:

- motivation;
- belief, self-concept, and personality;
- emotional engagement;
- teacher–student relationships;
- teacher expectation;
- classroom management;
- culture and identity.

The Routledge International Handbook of Social Psychology of the Classroom provides a review of current theories related to the social psychology of the classroom, including how these theories apply to classrooms and learners. Current evidence clearly shows that areas explored by social psychology – and brought together for the first time in this volume – can have a very significant impact on classroom learning and student achievement (J. Hattie, *Visible Learning: A Synthesis of over 800 Meta-Analyses Relating to Achievement*, Routledge 2009). This handbook is a must for all academics whose research relates to the social psychology of the classroom. It is also an invaluable resource for teachers and teacher education students who want to understand why they are effective instructors and yet still encounter students in their classes who are not responding as expected.

Christine M. Rubie-Davies is a Professor in the Faculty of Education and Social Work, the University of Auckland, New Zealand.

Jason M. Stephens is a Senior Lecturer in the School of Learning, Development and Professional Practice, Faculty of Education and Social Work, the University of Auckland, New Zealand.

Penelope Watson is a Lecturer in the School of Learning, Development and Professional Practice, Faculty of Education and Social Work, the University of Auckland, New Zealand.

The Routledge International Handbook Series

THE ROUTLEDGE INTERNATIONAL HANDBOOK OF SOCIAL PSYCHOLOGY OF THE CLASSROOM

Edited by Christine M. Rubie-Davies,
Jason M. Stephens, and Penelope Watson

Routledge
Taylor & Francis Group

LONDON AND NEW YORK

First published 2015
by Routledge
2 Park Square, Milton Park, Abingdon, Oxon OX14 4RN

and by Routledge
711 Third Avenue, New York, NY 10017

Routledge is an imprint of the Taylor & Francis Group, an informa business

British Library Cataloguing in Publication Data
A catalogue record for this book is available from the British Library

Library of Congress Cataloging in Publication Data
A catalog record for this book has been requested

ISBN: 978-0-415-85696-6 (hbk)
ISBN: 978-1-315-71692-3 (ebk)

Typeset in Bembo
by Book Now Ltd, London

Printed and bound in Great Britain by
TJ International Ltd, Padstow, Cornwall

CONTENTS

ILLUSTRATIONS

Figures

Tables

CONTRIBUTORS

Mohamed Alansari is a University Doctoral Scholar and graduate teaching and research assistant in the Faculty of Education and Social Work at the University of Auckland. His research interests include student and teacher perceptions of the classroom climate, student motivation to learn, and self-expectation beliefs. His work mostly focuses on the tertiary environment.

Jennifer Archer is a Senior Lecturer in the School of Education at the University of Newcastle, Australia. Her PhD in educational psychology is from the University of Illinois at Urbana-Champaign. Her research interest is in motivation theory, including achievement goals, attributions, and self-efficacy. In recent years, she has been examining ways in which the social context of schools and classrooms enhance or reduce students' motivation to learn.

Elisha Babad is a Professor in the School of Education at The Hebrew University of Jerusalem in Israel. His research interests include the social psychology of the classroom, teacher–student interaction and the self-fulfilling prophecy effect, the 'teacher's pet' phenomenon, student evaluation of instruction, and verbal and nonverbal communication.

Betty Becker-Kurz, PhD, is an Assistant Professor at the Department of Personality Psychology and Educational Psychology at the University of Munich in Germany. Her research interests include teacher and student emotions and motivation, multilevel data analyses, and emotional contagion and its role in transmission within academic contexts.

Nathan Berger is a doctoral candidate in the School of Education at the University of Newcastle, Australia. He has an MTeach in secondary social science and an MEd in educational research. His doctoral thesis is a social psychological examination of factors shaping career and education aspirations through childhood and adolescence.

C. Malik Boykin is Chancellor's Fellow and doctoral student of Social and Personality Psychology at UC Berkeley. He attained a master's degree in social-organizational psychology from Teachers College Columbia University, where he worked as a project manager at the Institute of Urban Minority Education.

Maureen E. Brinkworth is a Postdoctoral Researcher at Harvard's Graduate School of Education. She is interested in how social perspective taking impacts different aspects of secondary classrooms, particularly the relationships between teachers and students. Her recent work has focused on developing interventions to improve teacher–student relationships.

Rochelle M. Burnaford completed her PhD at the University of South Florida in 2012, and has been an adjunct faculty member at Diablo Valley College in Pleasant Hill, California since 2013. She greatly enjoys her time in the classroom, and interactions with students.

Elizabeth Canning is a doctoral student in the Department of Psychology at the University of Wisconsin-Madison, USA. She is interested in social-psychological interventions that help to improve motivation, interest, and performance in educational contexts.

Helena D. Cooper-Thomas is a Senior Lecturer and Director of Postgraduate Studies in Industrial Work and Organizational Psychology at the University of Auckland, New Zealand. Helena's research interests focus on how people adjust to new situations, including employees, expatriate adjustment, and students.

Eddie Denessen is an Associate Professor at the Behavioural Science Institute and the Department of Education at Radboud University Nijmegen, the Netherlands. His research interests include educational inequality, cultural contexts of education, diversity and differentiation in education, and relations between teacher attitudes and teacher behavior.

Jeffrey Dorman is an Associate Professor at the Faculty of Education and Social Work, Monash University, Australia, prior to which he was Reader at Australian Catholic University, Brisbane. His research interests include school and classroom learning environments, instrument design and validation, structural equation modelling, and multilevel modelling.

Alaster Scott Douglas is Assistant Director of Education and Reader in Education and Professional Practice at the University of Roehampton, London, UK. He has been the recipient of funded research projects on differentiated teaching practices in UK and USA classrooms and the education and learning of student teachers.

Tracy Durksen is a doctoral candidate in the Department of Educational Psychology at the University of Alberta in Canada, and a visiting PhD scholar at the University of New South Wales, Australia. Her research focuses on the role of professional learning in teachers' motivation and emotions across career stages.

Hunter Gehlbach is an Associate Professor at Harvard's Graduate School of Education. His primary interests lie in using social psychological principles and research to improve schools. Much of his work focuses on social perspective taking, specifically, teachers' and students' capacities to understand one another's thoughts, feelings, and motivations.

Sindu George is a doctoral student in Educational Psychology at the Faculty of Education and Social Work, Monash University, Australia. She has completed master's degrees in Chemistry and in Education. Her research interests include teacher motivation, teachers' classroom behaviors, and teacher education.

Robyn M. Gillies, PhD, is Professor of Education at the University of Queensland. Her research focuses on the social and cognitive aspects of learning through social interaction, including small-group interactions, inquiry-based learning, classroom discourses, and classroom processes related to learning outcomes.

Anne Gregory, PhD, is an Associate Professor in the Department of Applied Psychology at Rutgers University. Her research interests include teacher–student relationships and teacher professional development. She helps schools disrupt the persistent trend of African American adolescents being suspended and expelled from school at higher rates than other groups.

Judith Harackiewicz is Professor of Psychology at the University of Wisconsin-Madison, USA. She conducts laboratory research on interest and achievement motivation, as well as intervention studies in educational contexts. She is interested in promoting academic motivation for high school and college students in STEM disciplines.

Patricia L. Hardré has a doctorate in instructional design and technology, with emphases in cognition and instruction and motivation for learning and performance. She is currently a Professor at the University of Oklahoma, and has worked in educational research, program design, management and evaluation for more than 20 years.

Shane T. Harvey, PGDipPsych(Clin), PhD, is Director of the Psychology Clinic at Massey University, New Zealand. His background as an educational psychologist with Group Special Education (Ministry of Education) led to a PhD, research and publications investigating the nature of teachers' emotional skills and the impact their skills had on students' emotions.

Sophia Hiss is a doctoral student at the USC Rossier School of Education. Her research examines the impact of peer victimization in online settings examining general victimization and racial discrimination. She is also interested in how adolescents cope with victimization and possible buffers that mitigate the negative outcomes associated with victimization online.

Robert Klassen is Professor and Chair of the Psychology and Education Research Centre at the University of York, UK, and an Adjunct Professor at the University of Alberta in Canada. His research focuses on identifying psychological characteristics of effective teachers and on developing evidence-based tools to assist in the selection candidates for teacher training.

Mareike Kunter, has been a Professor for Educational Psychology at the Goethe University Frankfurt, Germany since 2010. Her research interests are professional competence of teachers, teacher career development, classroom instruction, and motivation at school. Her work has been published in many journal articles, book chapters, and books.

Rebecca Lazarides is a Postdoctoral Researcher at the Department of Educational Psychology, Institute of Education, Technical University Berlin, Germany. Her research focuses on girls' and boys' motivation, interest and career choice in math and science as well as parents' and teachers' influences on gendered motivation and interest.

Zheng Li, PhD, is a recently completed doctoral student in the Faculty of Education and Social Work, the University of Auckland in New Zealand. Her research interests relate to teacher expectation effects, teacher beliefs and classroom climate, especially in tertiary institutions. She has examined the moderating and mediating effects of teacher expectations on student outcomes.

Clark McKown, PhD is Associate Professor of Behavioral Sciences at Rush University Medical Center in Chicago, Illinois. His research examines origins and consequences of social status differences in childhood. He and his colleagues have created and evaluated new assessment methods and ways to conceptualize approaches to reduce destructive inequities.

Panayota Mantzicopoulos, PhD, is a Professor of Educational Psychology in the Department of Educational Studies at Purdue University. Her research focuses on children's developmental outcomes and their links with experiences in formal and informal learning contexts.

Rodolfo Mendoza-Denton is Associate Professor of Psychology at the University of California, Berkeley. He has a BA in psychology from Yale University and a PhD, also in psychology, from Columbia University. His research interests lie in processes related to stigma, education, intergroup relations, and cultural psychology.

Amori Yee Mikami, PhD, is an Associate Professor in the Department of Psychology at the University of British Columbia. Her research focuses on peer relationships among children and adolescents, especially those with disruptive behavior problems. Dr Mikami is a Michael Smith Foundation for Health Research Scholar.

Zoe A. Morris is a doctoral student at Monash University in Australia. Her doctoral project explores the conceptualization of professional boundaries amongst preservice and early career teachers. She is a registered educational and developmental psychologist and has broad interests including professional issues, ethics, well-being and mental health.

Katherine Muenks is a doctoral student in educational psychology in the Department of Human Development and Quantitative Methodology at the University of Maryland, College Park. Her research interests centre on achievement motivation.

Amanda Naus, BSc/BBS, is a Master's student at Massey University, Palmerston North, New Zealand, majoring in psychology and accounting. Her research interests include the impact information has on biasing people's responses to others and memory malleability. Amanda is also a volunteer worker for Victim Support and enjoys playing squash.

Helen Patrick, PhD, is a Professor of Educational Psychology in the Department of Educational Studies at Purdue University. Her research focuses on classroom environments, including associations of teachers' instructional practices with student motivation, learning and engagement.

Colette E. Patt, PhD, is the Science Diversity Programs director at the University of California, Berkeley. She also directs Berkeley's National Science Foundation–UC Alliance for Graduate Alliance and the Berkeley Edge Program. Her current research focuses on retention and advancement of students in science doctoral programmes.

Laura Pesu is a doctoral candidate at the Department of Psychology, University of Jyväskylä, Finland. In her research, she focuses on the development of students' self-concept of ability and talent perception, particularly the role of parents and teachers in this development.

Elizabeth R. Peterson is a Senior Lecturer in the School of Psychology at the University of Auckland and currently teaches in the Developmental Programme. Her research focus is on understanding the factors, processes, and pathways that optimize human learning and development and that promote happy, healthy, well rounded and resilient young people.

Robert C. Pianta, PhD, is Dean of the Curry School of Education at the University of Virginia, and Founding Director of the School's Center for Advanced Study of Teaching and Learning. He is the lead developer of the CLASS coding system and the MyTeachingPartner coaching protocol.

Paul Richardson is Associate Professor, Faculty of Education and Social Work, Monash University, Australia, and Associate Dean (Research). Paul investigates beginning teachers' career choice, development, and professional socialization; literacy; adolescent identity; teaching and learning in higher education; and qualitative research methods.

Chad A. Rose, PhD, is an Assistant Professor in the Department of Special Education at the University of Missouri. His research focuses on bullying and victimization among students with disabilities, bully prevention efforts within a multi-component framework, and the intersection of social/emotional learning and bully prevention for students with disabilities.

Robert Rosenthal is Distinguished Professor of Psychology, University of California, Riverside and Emeritus Professor at Harvard. He has received many honours including Fellow in the American Academy of Arts and Sciences (2009), and Gold Medal Award for Life Achievement in the Science of Psychology (2003), American Psychological Foundation.

Emily Q. Rosenzweig is a PhD student in the Department of Human Development and Quantitative Methodology at the University of Maryland, College Park. Emily studies the educational applications of students' motivation and self-regulated learning, focusing on how to develop effective motivation-focused interventions.

Cary J. Roseth is Associate Professor of Educational Psychology at Michigan State University. His research focuses on the development of conflict resolution in early childhood and on the effects of cooperation, competition, and individualistic goal structures on children's academic achievement and peer relations.

Christine M. Rubie-Davies is a Professor of Education at the University of Auckland, New Zealand. She has published widely in the field of teacher expectations, teacher beliefs as moderating expectation effects, and relations of teacher beliefs and expectations with student academic and social outcomes.

Erik A. Ruzek, PhD, is a Research Scientist at the Center for Advanced Study of Teaching and Learning at the University of Virginia. He studies relations between teachers' instructional practices and students' motivation, engagement, and learning. He combines multiple methodologies to measure classroom climates and their effects on student outcomes.

Allison M. Ryan is Associate Professor in the Combined Program in Education and Psychology at the University of Michigan, Ann Arbor. Her research focuses on development of achievement beliefs and behaviors in early adolescence, peer relationships, classroom contexts that support motivation and peer relationships, and transition to middle school.

Pamela Seccombe is an Educational Psychologist, Ministry of Education, Dunedin, New Zealand. She recently completed study at Massey University after having previously taught in secondary schools and involving herself in Playcentres with young children. She has a special interest in supporting socially withdrawn children in early childhood and school settings.

Johanna Seiz is a PhD Student at the department for educational psychology at the Goethe University Frankfurt since 2012. Her research interests are classroom management, motivation in the classroom and professional competence of teachers.

Ulrike Stadler-Altmann is Professor of Didactics and School Pedagogic at the Faculty of Educational Sciences, Free University of Bozen – Bolzano (South Tyrol). Her research interests include school development, learning and self-concept of students, teacher education, teachers training and gender studies. Her work spans both primary and secondary schools.

Jason M. Stephens is a Senior Lecturer in the School of Learning, Development and Professional Practice at the University of Auckland. His research focuses on academic motivation and moral development during adolescence, particularly as it relates to the problem of academic dishonesty.

Jasmine Taylor is a PhD student in psychology at the University of Auckland. Her research focuses on identifying conditions that facilitate engagement for the undergraduate tertiary-level learner. She is also interested in issues of identity, motivation, first-year experience, and the particular challenges of engagement within commuter campuses.

Marek Tesar is a Lecturer in childhood studies and early childhood education at the University of Auckland. His focus is on the philosophy and sociology of childhood, and the history of education/childhood. His research is concerned with the construction of childhoods, notions of the place/space of childhoods, and newly qualified teachers.

Michael Townsend is Professor of Educational Psychology, Institute of Education, Massey University, Auckland, New Zealand. Since completing his MA (University of Canterbury) and PhD (University of Illinois) his research has focused on learning and motivation. A major research theme is the role of social interactions in learning and in psychological wellbeing.

Brendesha M. Tynes is Associate Professor Education and Psychology at USC Rossier School of Education. Her research focuses on the role of the internet in child and adolescent development and academic performance, including STEM, mental health and problem behavior. She is also interested in digital and media literacy interventions.

Detlef Urhahne is a Professor at the Department of Educational Psychology, University of Passau, Germany. Current themes of research are teacher education, motivation and emotion, e-learning, science learning, and high-ability studies.

Jaana Viljaranta is a Postdoctoral Researcher at the Department of Psychology, University of Jyväskylä, Finland. Her research examines students' learning motivation, especially the role of interest and task values in relation to academic skill development and educational plans. She has been a PATHWAYS Fellow since 2012.

Penelope W. StJ. Watson is a Lecturer in the School of Learning, Development, and Professional Practice, Faculty of Education and Social Work, the University of Auckland, New Zealand. Her areas of research interest are stereotype threat and gender stereotyping.

Melinda Webber, PhD, is a Senior Lecturer in the School of Learning, Development and Professional Practice at the Faculty of Education and Social Work, University of Auckland, New Zealand. She is also a qualitative researcher on the Starpath Project. Her research interests focus on racial-ethnic identity development and Māori student success.

Kathryn R. Wentzel is a Professor of Human Development in the Department of Human Development and Quantitative Methodology at the University of Maryland, College Park. Her research interests focus on teachers, peers and parents as motivators of adolescents' classroom behavior and academic accomplishments.

Allan Wigfield is Professor in the Department of Human Development and Quantitative Methodology at the University of Maryland. His research focuses on how children's motivation develops across the school years in different areas and on classroom interventions to improve children's reading motivation.

Ammon J. Wilcken is Assistant Professor of Education, Brigham Young University, Hawaii. His research interests include motivation to learn, relationship quality in school, and helping teachers apply principles of cooperative learning in elementary schools. His teaching interests include elementary methods courses in math, literacy, science and educational psychology.

Frank C. Worrell, PhD is a Professor in the Graduate School of Education at the University of California, Berkeley. His research interests include talent development, the relationship of cultural identities to academic and psychological functioning, and the translation of research into practice.

Mingjing Zhu is a doctoral candidate at the Faculty of Psychology and Educational Sciences, University of Munich, Germany. Research interests include teacher judgments of student achievement, motivation and emotion, and domain-specific learning and instruction.

FOREWORD

Thomas L. Good

It is my pleasure to provide a foreword for the *Routledge International Handbook of Social Psychology of the Classroom*. This volume, edited by Christine Rubie-Davies, Jason Stephens, and Penelope Watson, provides a magnificent summary of research that has important implications for an area that the editors are appropriately calling the Social Psychology of the Classroom. This volume provides a definitive synthesis of a diverse and complex literature that is thoughtfully written in ways to make it broadly accessible to not only those who work in this theoretical and empirical area but also to those who work in different traditions.

The editors note that the impetus for this handbook was stimulated by two publications (Babad 2009; Hattie 2009), and of course these two authors trace the roots of their interest to earlier eras of research. The publication of the book *Pygmalion in the Classroom* (Rosenthal and Jacobson 1968) generated a tremendous amount of excitement about the possible relationships between teacher expectation for student performance and students' actual performance. This important work created much controversy and generated countless theoretical and empirical arguments that continue to date. Now roughly fifty years later, we know that expectation effects exist in many situations and that they can have notable influence on student achievement in certain circumstances.

I share my own orientation to this research tradition. As a graduate student at Indiana University I was searching for a dissertation topic when I read *Pygmalion in the Classroom* and as a result I was motivated to conduct research to see if teachers interacted differently with students they believed to have more or less ability. This work provided evidence that students perceived to be more talented received more opportunity and challenge (Good 1968). Subsequently, at the University of Texas, Jere Brophy and I replicated and extended these findings in a new study (Brophy and Good 1970). These data illustrated that at least in this context, teachers interacted differently with students they believed to be more and less capable, thus providing support for Rosenthal and Jacobson's hypothesis that teacher beliefs influenced teacher–student interactions.

In 1974, Jere and I reviewed a broad literature in our book *Teacher–Student Relationships: Causes and Consequences* (Brophy and Good 1974). Here we drew upon a diverse literature that described student characteristics other than student achievement. We explored many student variables including gender, race, socioeconomic status, physical attractiveness, and the way these student characteristics influenced teacher perceptions and teacher–student relationships. We illustrated that teachers reacted differently to students on the basis of these characteristics, but reciprocally we also demonstrated that students influenced teachers as well. In our book we hypothesized and presented some data to illustrate that warm and supportive teacher–student relationships were central to classrooms that promoted and obtained student achievement.

I provide this brief historical note to illustrate that I have long been interested in the research that is reviewed so well in this handbook and to suggest that I know this literature very well, but also to let the reader know of my potential bias and the possibility that I may overstate the value of the contribution of work that is well summarized in this handbook. I do not think that is the case, but the reader has been warned of this possibility. In making the case for the value of this area of research, I would remind readers that in the 1960s, social scientists did not believe that teachers had much influence on individual student achievement or the achievement of the class as a whole. Then it was commonly believed that differential student achievement was largely attributable to factors such as heredity and social and economic status. If a student was assigned to teacher *a*, *b*, or *c* it made little difference to a parent, as teachers were not seen as having any effect on student achievement. Today the situation is radically different as it is well recognized that teachers and teaching is the most important determinant of student achievement of those factors that can be altered.

At the time Robert Rosenthal and Lenore Jacobson wrote their seminal book in 1968, it raised the important possibility that student performance could be enhanced by schooling more powerfully than had been believed previously. Later, Bruce Biddle, Jere Brophy, and I presented a logical argument (and provided some data) that individual teachers make a difference in student learning (Good *et al.* 1975). This of course suggests that teachers are a variable and that teachers vary in the extent to which they support and encourage student learning. These early works provided a foundation for asking questions: Do teachers make a difference? How do teachers make a difference? Can teachers learn to raise their low expectations? Can teachers encourage students to take charge of their own learning? Chapters in the *Handbook* provide ways to think about these questions and many other issues that have relevancy for policy and improving instruction.

This handbook expands upon these early research traditions in important ways. More than ever, policymakers recognize that it is the differences in teachers and the classroom climates they create with students that promote student achievement and develop those dispositions needed for success in life. The individual authors of the *Handbook* provide careful and reasoned accounts of what we know about teacher expectations, teacher actions, student dispositions, student actions, and many other variables that interact with one another in complex ways. When teachers understand these various factors and can meaningfully coordinate them, it allows for productive and exciting classrooms. If teachers do not understand how to combine these various influences, they necessarily create less productive classrooms.

The editors appropriately suggest that the *Handbook* is of direct benefit to researchers and students studying for research careers. However, I think the editors are too modest in suggesting the scope of the audience. Recently, I have been writing with Alyson Lavigne on the failures of school reform (Lavigne and Good 2014; Lavigne and Good 2015) and we have concluded that policymakers in designing reform consistently underestimate the complexity of life in classrooms and the emotions (both tedium and joy) that surround classroom learning. Knowledge contained in this handbook would go a long way in helping policymakers understand that positive change is difficult and that the basis for change fundamentally rests upon positive teacher–student relationships. Further, I believe that classroom principals who want to build effective programs of staff development would find the *Handbook* a beneficial resource.

To close, the editors and authors collectively have prepared a handbook that artfully summarizes research related to the social psychology of the classroom by building upon fifty years of research in this area. Equally important, the *Handbook* provides a solid base for conceptualizing future research that has the capacity for further describing, understanding, and improving teacher–student relationships in the classroom.

References

Babad, E. (2009) *The Social Psychology of the Classroom*, New York: Routledge.

Brophy, J.E. and Good, T.L. (1970) 'Teachers' communication of differential expectations for children's classroom performance: some behavioral data', *Journal of Educational Psychology*, 61: 365–374.

Brophy, J.E. and Good, T.L. (1974) *Teacher–Student Relationships: Causes and Consequences*, New York: Holt, Rinehart, and Winston.

Good, T. (1968) 'Student achievement level and differential opportunity for classroom response', unpublished doctoral dissertation, Indiana University.

Good, T., Biddle, B. and Brophy, J. (1975) *Teachers Make a Difference*, New York: Holt, Rinehart, and Winston.

Hattie, J. (2009) *Visible Learning: A Synthesis of over 800 Meta-Analyses Relating to Achievement*, London: Routledge.

Lavigne, A.L. and Good, T. (2014) *Teacher and Student Evaluation: Moving Beyond the Failure of School Reform*, New York: Routledge.

Lavigne, A. and Good, T. (2015) *Improving Teaching Through Observation and Feedback*, New York: Routledge.

Rosenthal, R. and Jacobson, L. (1968) *Pygmalion in the Classroom: Teacher Expectation and Pupils' Intellectual Development*, New York: Holt, Rinehart, and Winston.

ACKNOWLEDGMENTS

We would like to acknowledge every author who has contributed to this volume. Obviously without their chapters this book would not exist. However, we would like to thank each one for their patience, persistence, and unwavering willingness to try to meet our sometimes demanding deadlines, as well as for their superb chapters. We are also extremely grateful to the many independent reviewers who gave of their time so willingly to read through the chapters they were sent and who provided incredibly supportive and helpful feedback to the authors which only served to make every chapter stronger. We would like to thank both Professors Tom Good and Elisha Babad, who despite their extremely busy schedules, agreed to write the Foreword and the reflective piece at the end. They are both international leaders in their respective fields and we are honored that they agreed to contribute.

We are also greatly indebted to our School, Learning, Development and Professional Practice, in the Faculty of Education and Social Work where we are based, and our Dean, Professor Graeme Aitken. Our School and our Faculty both provided us with funding that enabled us to run our conference successfully and supported us financially in producing our book. Graeme was encouraging, helpful and a source of many ideas throughout this whole process.

Of course, books such as this only ever come to fruition with the help of a number of people in the background supporting those whose names appear on the front cover. We would like to acknowledge the incredible expertise and affable manner of Eddy van Til who provided much of the background organization for the Social Psychology of the Classroom International Conference and who kept us on track throughout. It is to Eddy that we, in large part, owe the success of the original conference. To Janet Rivers, our editorial assistant who has an eye for detail that is the envy of us all. Always pleasant, always obliging, always efficient and incredibly professional, Janet is to be applauded. Finally, we would like to acknowledge Bruce Roberts and his team at Routledge who saw potential in an initial idea for a book and who have nurtured it to fruition.

INTRODUCTION

This book arose from the interests of three academics at the University of Auckland into the social psychological aspects of classrooms – the editors of this volume. By the social-psychological aspects, we mean aspects of classrooms such as student self-beliefs that result from teacher–student interactions, teacher–student relationships, class climate, teacher expectations, stereotyping, and teacher management of classes. The genesis of the book began with a volume entitled *The Social Psychology of the Classroom* by Elisha Babad (2009), which the first editor had the very great pleasure of reviewing for Routledge several years ago now. Babad's book was the inspiration for a journey into more closely examining and reflecting upon the contribution of the social psychological aspects of classrooms for students' learning. It led to the introduction of a successful undergraduate and then a postgraduate course in the field at the editors' university and has resulted in the hiring of academics specifically in the area of the social psychology of the classroom.

A second stimulus was John Hattie's book (2009), *Visible Learning: A Synthesis of over 800 Meta-Analyses*. In reading this book, and examining the empirical evidence for the contribution of various pedagogical and teacher contributions to student learning, what becomes obvious to those interested in the social-psychological contributions of classrooms is that every one that Hattie explores in his book contributes more than the important threshold of $d = 0.4$, which Hattie argues is the level that defines visible learning, learning gains so obvious that teachers can see them happening. It is argued in the book that $d = 0.4$ is the mean effect of all interventions, teacher, school, and student contributions to learning and that therefore, if any contribution to learning does not have an effect size above $d = 0.4$, then it is not worth doing. For example, the effect of positive teacher–student relationships on student achievement is $d = 0.72$ – clearly worth fostering.

For many years, within educational psychology, and particularly within teacher education programs, the focus has mostly been on the cognitive, behavioral, and pedagogical aspects of classrooms and yet, using the evidence presented by Hattie, many of these practices and processes have only minimal effects on student achievement. For example, in many countries, pre-service teachers are taught to sort students, that is, they are taught that it is "best" for students if they are placed in ability groups (be they within class or across class), that they learn more effectively in such grouping arrangements. This is despite the evidence that Hattie presents that within class ability grouping has a $d = 0.16$ effect on learning whereas tracking or streaming has only a $d = 0.12$ effect. The practice is also encouraged despite evidence that, from a social-psychological perspective, no students benefit (e.g. Hallam *et al.* 2004; Liem *et al.* 2013). From an achievement perspective, the outcomes of those assigned to lower-ability groups are negatively impacted. There are several studies showing that when students are challenged, all can learn and be successful at much higher levels than may previously have been predicted (Weinstein *et al.* 1991; Linchevski and Kutscher 1998).

Further, the contribution of relationships to student learning is often not to the forefront. Perhaps it is easier to alter practices and processes than it is to change how teachers relate to students. Indeed, a search of a range of teacher education programs across several institutions did not reveal a single course dedicated to the social-psychological aspects of learning, despite their large effects on student achievement. Hence, a major thrust for this book is to bring these aspects to the forefront, to dedicate a book to providing evidence for the importance of caring for students, to interacting positively with them, and to the corresponding benefits for their learning that result.

Most of the authors in this volume contributed to *The Social Psychology of the Classroom International Conference* in 2013, which was organized by the editors. It was designed to test the interest among other educational psychologists internationally in having an intense focus on the social psychology of the classroom. The enormous success of that event showed the passion among academics from many countries in the world to promoting the enhancement of student learning through emphasizing teacher–student relationships. Delegates from Europe, the United States, Asia, and the Pacific attended. The conference led, in turn, to this handbook, a unique collection of chapters in which the significance is highlighted of the social psychology of the classroom.

Like other handbooks of this nature, this one was written primarily for university academics (lecturers, professors, and graduate students). As such, each chapter offers a concise introduction to its topic and an overview of the major theoretical and empirical contributions related to it. And each chapter concludes with a section concerning the challenges to be resolved and suggestions for future directions. In doing so, each chapter lays the groundwork for not only understanding the literature, but also provides a road map or blueprint for moving forward. As such, we hope that each chapter will be of great use to both seasoned and beginning investigators as they seek to understand the history, issues, results, and unresolved questions of a particular social psychological aspect of the classroom.

Additionally, we hope that this handbook might also serve as a valuable guide for teachers, teacher educators, and educational policy-makers. As noted above, in myriad ways the social psychology of the classroom is an important and powerful force in students' academic engagement and achievement. The chapters in this volume shed light on the often hidden (or ignored) aspects of teaching and learning, and offer educators at all levels insights and ideas for confronting some of the most difficult challenges they face. Finally, policy-makers in charge of crafting and steering the future of education will find this handbook a helpful resource in their deliberations.

Each part of the handbook addresses a specific topic central to the field of the social psychology of the classroom, and is described below.

Part I: Student motivation

To open the six chapters discussing the factors affecting student motivation, an overview of motivational theories and their development is presented along with insights on expectancy-value theory, self-efficacy theory, achievement goal orientation theory, and regulatory focus theory. A 'big picture' approach is offered as a contrasting perspective in the second chapter with suggestions for a framework for the conceptualization and application of a fine-tuned systemic approach reflecting authentic contexts of practice. Relationships between social class and students' adoption of academic achievement goals, and between student needs and attitudes are probed to add further insights on student motivation. The role that parents play in forming children's and adolescents' scholastic competence beliefs and values is explored, and the part concludes with an investigation of the role that meaning systems might play in the development of motivation.

Part II: Responding to student culture

Part II invites educationalists concerned with the social psychology of the classroom to consider responses to culture. Literature on racial identity and ethnic identity, cultural ecological theory, and stereotype threat is reviewed in relation to academic achievement and achievement gaps among racial and ethnic groups. Stereotype threat is further explored along with status-based rejection sensitivity within the context of devalued social identity. The value of adopting an interpersonal approach, in researching the associations between stigma, prejudice, and learning and learning outcomes is revealed. Providing a unique perspective, a specifically New Zealand view reveals how race and ethnicity can influence the social and academic identities of Māori students. Aspects of mental health, academic motivation, and their association with online and face-to-face discrimination are explored, and the part concludes with insights about the effects of countervailing forces on avoiding or embracing adaptive academic behaviors for minority students.

Part III: Student beliefs and peer relationships

The three chapters constituting this part reveal complimentary aspects of the importance of student beliefs and peer relationships in the social psychology of the classroom. A consideration of the origins of social forces affecting racial-ethnic achievement gaps and social network inequities in elementary school classrooms provides an important focus in opening this part. Recent research that aims to promote students' development and learning through social collaboration in dialogic exchanges is reviewed, and the part closes with a review of stereotype threat literature and suggestions for the construct's future research.

Part IV: Teacher–student relationships

The association between students' relationships with teachers and motivational processes and outcomes is explored in the opening chapter of this part. Giving further perspectives on the importance of teacher–student relationships to motivational constructs, connections between the quality of these relationships and student engagement and achievement is next probed. This part continues with an argument for addressing the dearth of empirical research on teacher–student relationships at tertiary level, and an investigation of a trio of perceptual biases that can impair teacher–student relationships. Insights on the teacher's significant role in recognizing and responding appropriately to specific types of social withdrawal in their students contributes a further aspect to the importance of teacher–student relationships. In a further chapter, relationships between teacher emotions and how this relate to the class climate is explored, and the association between teacher and student emotions is also included. Part IV concludes with an exploration of Foucault's and Havel's philosophical work on power and the production of subjectivities in the early years classroom.

Part V: Classroom climate and classroom management

Issues and perspectives fundamental to classroom climate and management form the foci for the five chapters included in Part V. To commence this part the importance of integrating the strengths of two research methodologies (observation, and student reports) to advance classroom research is highlighted. The importance of individual teacher characteristics (such as teachers' beliefs) for classroom management behavior is disclosed, with important arguments for the place that teachers' social cognitive processes may occupy in teacher education and professional development. An overview of research on the influence of the constructed environment on education, and an exposé of the link between class climate and teacher and student emotions, add the concluding perspectives to this part.

Part VI: Teacher expectations, judgment, and differentiation

Offering a focus on seminal literature related to this part, the extensive research career of Robert Rosenthal is documented in the opening chapter along with much of his contribution to inter-personal expectancy effects and nonverbal research. Fuelled by the concern that ethnic minority students too frequently experience higher rates of discipline sanctions than other groups, the second chapter in this part sheds light on teacher authority and the quality of peer interaction in classrooms. The value of employing sociocultural activity theory in researching classroom prac-tices, and viewpoints about teacher judgment and student motivation further augment this part. Findings of an intervention to train teachers in practices demonstrated by high expectation teachers (those teachers who have high expectations of *all* their students) follow, revealing the importance of teacher beliefs as moderators of expectation effects. Completing this penultimate part of the handbook, further evidence supporting the idea that teacher expectation effects are a function of teacher characteristics rather than student factors is presented in the context of a college foreign language classroom.

Part VII: Teacher motivation, professionalism, and well-being

Providing the flipside to issues surrounding *student* motivation (Part I), the concluding part of the handbook presents perspectives on *teacher* motivation, professionalism, and well-being. Recent advances in research on teacher motivation and emotions are discussed, and a framework is pro-posed to facilitate the application of motivation research to that predicting teacher effectiveness. An overview of the field of self-efficacy, the major issues, limitations of the current research, and prospects for future research directions rounds out this part. Adding further insights, the central importance of teachers' emotional skills, motivation and well-being for effective teaching practice is incorporated into this part. Literature from the fields of education, psychology, and medicine, informing an investigation of contemporary professional boundaries and their relationship with teacher and student well-being, brings this part to a close.

Part VIII: The final word

It seemed fitting, since Elisha Babad first coined the term 'the social psychology of the classroom', to have him write the final chapter of this handbook, in which he looks back to where and how this important area of psychological research developed, how he views the current state of play, and where he sees future developments in the field.

*****

In assembling the chapters in this book, it is the editors' intent to highlight the social-psychological aspects of the classroom as being important for student learning. Learning can be accelerated when students are in a supportive, caring environment where they have warm relationships with their teachers and where teachers respect diversity. It is hoped that, by bringing together in one volume the many aspects of the social-psychological contributions to student learning, more attention will be paid by researchers to exploring these areas in more depth and by those directors of teacher education programs in developing courses for pre-service teachers. It is certainly time to consider other avenues as having the potential to raise student achievement, rather than those that focus on technocratic processes and effective instruction, without considering the people involved. It is also time for policy-makers to consider the effects that policies of high-stakes assessment have on how classrooms and interactions become structured. It is perhaps not surprising that these accountability practices have not resulted in the desired achievement lifts. Students and teachers are people with emotions, beliefs, and ideals; they all need to be valued and supported if achievement is to lift.

References

Babad, E. (2009) *The Social Psychology of the Classroom*, New York: Routledge.

Hallam, S., Ireson, J. and Davies, J. (2004) 'Primary pupils' experiences of different types of grouping in school', *British Educational Research Journal,* 30: 515–533.

Hattie, J. (2009) *Visible Learning: A Synthesis of over 800 Meta-Analyses Relating to Achievement*, London: Routledge.

Liem, G.A.D., Marsh, H.W., Martin, A.J., McInerney, D.M. and Yeung, A.S. (2013) 'The big-fish-little-pond effect and a national policy of within-school ability streaming: Alternative frames of reference', *American Educational Research Journal,* 50: 326-370. doi: 10.3102/0002831212464511

Linchevski, L. and Kutscher, B. (1998) 'Tell me with whom you're learning, and I'll tell you how much you've learned: Mixed ability versus same-ability grouping in mathematics', *Journal for Research in Mathematics Education,* 29: 533–554.

Weinstein, R.S., Soule, C.R., Collins, F., Cone, J., Mehlhorn, M. and Simontacchi, K. (1991) 'Expectations and high school change: Teacher–researcher collaboration to prevent school failure', *American Journal of Community Psychology,* 19: 333–363.

PART I

Student motivation

1

CHILDREN'S ACHIEVEMENT MOTIVATION IN SCHOOL

Allan Wigfield, Katherine Muenks, and Emily Q. Rosenzweig

Motivation theorists are interested in the 'whys' of human behavior: what moves people to act (Wigfield *et al.* in press). Achievement motivation refers to motivation to accomplish activities that have standards of performance. Researchers studying school achievement motivation look at how students' motivation influences their engagement in academic activities, the choices students make about which academic activities to do, their persistence at continuing the activities, and their degree of effort. Motivation researchers taking a social cognitive perspective focus on students' self-beliefs, values and goals as important determinants (Eccles and Wigfield 2002; Maehr and Zusho 2009; Schunk and Pajares 2009; Wigfield *et al.* 2009). Many motivation researchers also are interested in how educational contexts influence these constructs (e.g. Nolen and Ward 2008).

In this chapter we discuss children's achievement motivation in school, focusing on constructs from three major social cognitive theories of motivation: expectancy-value theory, self-efficacy theory, and achievement goal theory.[1] To connect this work to social psychological research on motivation, we also introduce the construct of regulatory focus and consider its connections to students' motivation. We then briefly discuss the development of each construct, and describe some educational interventions that have focused on achievement motivation.

Theoretical background to the field

In this section we provide overviews of several major current theories of motivation: expectancy-value theory, self-efficacy theory, and achievement goal orientation theory, and also regulatory focus theory, which focuses on differences in the ways in which individuals strategically focus their goal-directed behavior.

Expectancy-value theory

Expectancy-value theorists focus on how students' beliefs and values influence their performance and choice in school. Eccles and her colleagues (Eccles-Parsons *et al.* 1983; Wigfield and Eccles 2000) defined expectancies for success as children's beliefs about how well they will do on an *upcoming* task in the near or longer term future. Ability beliefs are children's evaluations of their *current* competence or ability, both in terms of their assessments of their own ability and also how they think they compare to other students.

Numerous studies have shown that students' ability beliefs and expectancies for success predict their school performance and activity choice (Wigfield *et al.* 2009). For instance, researchers have found that self-concept of ability measured in elementary school predicts how many mathematics courses students elect to take in high school (Simpkins *et al.* 2006). Additionally, students' self-concept of their ability in mathematics measured in high school predicts their plans to pursue a mathematics-related career or course of study in college (Nagy *et al.* 2008; Watt 2006).

Eccles and her colleagues defined different values for achievement tasks: attainment value, intrinsic value, utility value, and cost (Eccles-Parsons *et al.* 1983; Eccles 2005; Wigfield *et al.* 2009). Attainment value is the importance of the task to the individual, intrinsic value the enjoyment one gets from the task, and utility value how much a task relates to current and future goals, such as career goals. Cost refers to what the individual has to give up to do the task.

Eccles and her colleagues have found that students' task values predict their course-taking plans and enrollment decisions in different subjects, even after controlling for prior performance levels (Eccles *et al.* 2004; Eccles-Parsons *et al.* 1983). For instance, Eccles *et al.* (2004) found that early adolescents' college plans, task values, and ability beliefs related to whether or not they enrolled in college. Durik *et al.* (2006) found that students' self-concept of ability, interest, and perceived importance of literacy measured in fourth grade related positively to these variables measured in tenth grade. These variables predicted students' increased likelihood of desiring a career where reading skills are critical, such as becoming a lawyer. Additionally, Musu-Gillette *et al.* (2014) found that change in students' mathematics values and ability beliefs related to choice of a mathematics major in college: Students maintaining positive values and ability beliefs were more likely to choose mathematics-related majors.

Self-efficacy theory

Self-efficacy is defined as an individual's 'perceived capabilities to learn or perform behaviors at designated levels' (Schunk and Pajares 2005: 85) and was originally introduced as part of Bandura's (1986) social cognitive theory. Much research has shown that students' self-efficacy beliefs about particular school-related tasks predict important academic outcomes, such as motivation, achievement, and self-regulation in school (Bandura 1997).

The term 'self-efficacy' can be distinguished from other constructs pertaining to competence beliefs, such as ability beliefs and expectancies for success (Wigfield and Eccles 2000). As just discussed, ability beliefs refer to an individual's evaluation of his or her *current* competence, whereas self-efficacy beliefs are related to future performance on a task. Expectancies for success are conceptually similar to self-efficacy beliefs, as they refer to an individual's expectation that he or she will perform well in the future. However, within expectancy-value theory, both ability beliefs and expectancies for success are generally measured at a domain-specific level (e.g. pertaining to mathematics in general), whereas self-efficacy is often measured at a task-specific level (e.g. pertaining to a specific mathematics problem; Wigfield and Eccles 2000).

Bandura (1997) posits that self-efficacy beliefs are constructed from four sources of information: mastery experience, vicarious experience, verbal persuasion, and physiological states. Mastery experiences are instances when the individual has succeeded on the task in the past. This source of efficacy information is especially powerful. Vicarious experiences also contribute to a sense of personal self-efficacy: If an individual sees other people successfully performing an activity, he or she may have a stronger belief in his or her own capabilities. Verbal persuasion occurs when individuals are told that they are capable of performing an action. Finally, physiological and affective states generate emotional arousal, which can influence individuals' sense of self-efficacy.

Research has shown that self-efficacy beliefs predict various school-related outcomes, including task performance, interest, persistence, and self-regulatory processes (Schunk and Pajares 2009).

Collins (1982) selected children who judged themselves to be of high or low efficacy for three levels of mathematical ability (i.e. low, medium, and high) and found that, within each level of ability, children with high mathematical efficacy solved difficult problems more accurately and used more strategies than children with low mathematical efficacy. Collins (1982) also found that efficacy beliefs rather than actual ability predicted interest in mathematics and positive attitudes towards mathematics. Pintrich and De Groot (1990) found that seventh-grade students' self-efficacy predicted their self-reported use of cognitive and metacognitive strategies, controlling for prior achievement. The relation between self-efficacy and achievement was fully mediated by the use of these cognitive strategies. Additional studies suggest that learners who are more efficacious also choose to engage in more challenging tasks, set higher goals, monitor their time, engage in self-evaluation, and persist longer on difficult tasks than learners who are less efficacious (Schunk and Pajares 2009).

Achievement goal orientation theory

Goal orientations are students' broad approaches to school activities. Researchers have focused primarily on two broad goal orientations towards learning: mastery and performance (see Maehr and Zusho 2009; Elliot 2005). A mastery orientation means that the child focuses on improving their skills, mastering material, and learning new things. A performance orientation means that the child focuses on maximizing favorable and minimizing negative evaluations of their competence.

In the 1990s, researchers differentiated approach and avoidance components of performance and mastery goal orientations. Elliot and Harackiewicz (1996) and Skaalvik (1997) defined performance-approach goals as students' desires to demonstrate competence, and performance-avoidance goals as students' desires to avoid looking incompetent. For example, a student who wants to receive an 'A' in a course so that parents, teachers, and friends can see how smart she is has a performance-approach goal, while a student who wants to avoid receiving a 'C' in a course so that she will not appear incompetent has a performance-avoidance goal. Elliot (1999; Elliot and McGregor 2001) and Pintrich (2000) added to this distinction, proposing that mastery-approach goals meant students wanting to master new material, whereas mastery-avoidance goals meant students not wanting to lose competence. For example, a student who works hard to finish her homework to improve her reading skills has a mastery-approach goal, while a student who avoids skipping her homework in order not to lose the skills she possesses has a mastery-avoidance goal.

Elliot et al. (2011) reconceptualized the extant goal orientation models to distinguish between the standards of information people use to judge their competence under mastery and performance orientations. They distinguished self-standards, or individuals' sense of how their performance relates to the trajectory of their competence growth; task standards which come from characteristics of the tasks being done; and other standards, or how one's performance compares to that of others. There are approach and avoidance aspects of each of these information standards. The model is therefore a three (standard of evaluation) by two (approach/avoid) model of goal orientations. Elliot et al. reported empirical support for these new distinctions, and concluded that evaluation standards should be included in models of goal orientations.

Much research has examined the relations of mastery and performance goal orientations to motivation and achievement (see Hulleman and Senko 2010; Maehr and Zusho 2009). Mastery-approach orientations relate positively to students' self-efficacy, intrinsic motivation to learn, and use of deep cognitive strategies when processing academic information (Hulleman and Senko 2010). It is unclear if mastery-approach goals predict achievement; they do in some studies of 5- to 17-year-olds, but not as much in college students (Keys et al. 2012). Senko and Miles (2008) found that mastery-oriented college students achieved lower grades than other students, in part because they focused on their own interests rather than course requirements.

Performance-avoidance goals have strong negative consequences for student motivation and learning, relating to poorer performance, more willingness to cheat, higher anxiety, and so on (e.g. Anderman and Murdock 2007; Hulleman and Senko 2010). By contrast, performance-approach goals relate positively to academic self-concept, task value, and performance (Senko *et al.* 2011). Elliot *et al.* (2011) found that the new goals they identified related differentially to college students' exam performance, intrinsic motivation, and self-efficacy. For example, approach goals based on judging one's competence relative to others related positively to exam performance and avoid goals related to this standard did so negatively. Task-approach goals (when competence judgments are based on characteristics of the task) related positively to students' intrinsic motivation and self-efficacy. Approach and avoid goals based on self-standards generally were not related to these outcomes. These intriguing findings need further exploration.

Debate continues about the relative merits of mastery and performance goal orientations. Researchers agree that mastery goals are beneficial for students, and so should be focused on in school. Researchers also agree that performance-avoidance goals are debilitating. The debate, then, centers on the relative merits of performance-approach goals. Because these goals relate positively to certain important achievement outcomes such as grades, some theorists believe that performance-approach goals are beneficial to students. Other theorists think that mastery goals are more positive because of their influence on intrinsic motivation and striving to improve. Roeser (2004) and Maehr and Zusho (2009) discuss this debate further.

Regulatory focus theory

Beyond the influence that a particular goal or goal orientation may have on an individual's approach to achievement, the *type* of motivation used in pursuing that goal may also influence students' classroom behavior and performance. One such aspect of motivation, studied most frequently in the social psychological literature, is regulatory focus. Regulatory focus theory (Higgins 1997; Molden and Miele 2008) addresses the ways in which individuals strategically regulate their goal-directed behavior. Higgins (1997) argued that all individuals pursue goals in order to fulfill one of two sets of needs: one set driven by a concern for growth and nurturance, and the other by a concern for safety and security. Pursuing one of these sets of needs induces one of two distinct regulatory orientations: promotion or prevention. When individuals are predominantly focused on growth concerns, they hold promotion orientations. During goal pursuit, these individuals represent their goals as ideals they hope to attain and seek opportunities for gain that will move them closer to these ideals. In contrast, when individuals are focused on security concerns, they hold a prevention orientation, representing their goals as responsibilities that they must uphold and protecting against potential losses that threaten these responsibilities.

In any given achievement context, individuals are likely to adopt a promotion versus a prevention orientation based on whether growth versus security concerns are more salient for them. Salience often is driven by environmental cues that temporarily activate potential gains or losses students could experience in that environment (Miele *et al.* 2009). For example, if teachers remind students of a valuable reward they could gain by completing an upcoming homework assignment, this might induce students to adopt promotion orientations when completing that assignment. Salience is also determined by individuals' histories of goal pursuit, which leads them to be partial towards detecting either potential threats or opportunities for gain across environments when overt cues towards one orientation or the other are not present. Such predispositions are called *chronic* regulatory orientations.

Most research on the effects of promotion versus prevention orientation has been done in adults on general cognitive processes that might underlie educational performance, such as recognition memory or error detection. That research has demonstrated robust links between regulatory focus and performance on different types of cognitive tasks (Molden and Miele 2008). Promotion-oriented individuals do better on tasks requiring creative, flexible and abstract processing. This 'eager' process-ing style also leads promotion-oriented individuals to focus on speed when solving problems or completing tasks, as opposed to accuracy. By contrast, prevention-oriented individuals perform better on tasks that require analytical, narrow, or perseverant information processing, and prefer accuracy to speed (Förster and Higgins 2005; Liberman *et al.* 2001). Thus it is likely that prevention-oriented individuals may perform better on educational tasks that require using analytical, careful strategies, such as proofreading a writing assignment. Promotion-oriented individuals may perform better on tasks which require flexible, quick strategies, such as completing many mathematics problems within a short time frame.

Building on this suggestion, some research has begun to demonstrate that regulatory focus affects educational outcomes. Miele *et al.* (2009) found that prevention-oriented college students showed better reading comprehension of a passage, and spent more time on it, than did promotion-oriented students. In another study, individuals with strong prevention orientations performed better both on college course examinations and on Scholastic Aptitude Test questions; this test is used for college entrance decisions in the United States. However, on tests with strict time constraints, promotion-oriented students began to show improvements in their performance, and the individuals with two orientations tested equally well (Rosenzweig and Miele 2014). The research exploring regulatory focus in the classroom is in its infancy, but it does seem that regulatory focus is important for under-standing and predicting students' achievement outcomes.

Theoretical constructs: Summing up

Researchers have identified a number of important beliefs, value, goal, and regulatory focus constructs that have an effect on students' achievement. We discussed these constructs individually and many researchers often have studied each separately. There is increasing interest currently in how these constructs interrelate and relate to various achievement outcomes (e.g. Hulleman and Harackiewicz 2009; Wigfield and Cambria 2010). For instance, having positive ability beliefs, achievement values, and mastery goals for activities may be the most adaptive motivational pat-tern for optimal achievement. Future research should explore how these ability beliefs, values, and goal orientations relate to regulatory focus.

Improving achievement motivation: Empirical findings

A critical question with respect to the motivation constructs we are discussing is how they change over time, and whether motivation-focused interventions can enhance students' motivation. We provide a brief overview of these topics in this section.

Development of ability-related beliefs and values

Eccles, Wigfield, and their colleagues showed two important things with respect to the develop-ment of ability-related beliefs and values. First, they found that ability beliefs and values can be empirically distinguished in children as young as first grade (Eccles *et al.* 1993). Second, children's ability beliefs and their values are distinct in different academic subject areas. Thus, quite early on, children differentiate their beliefs from their values and have distinct ability beliefs and values for different subject areas. This likely occurs because of the feedback they get from parents and teachers about their performance in each subject area, and what areas the socializers emphasize.

Additionally, a substantial body of research shows that children's ability beliefs and values decline across the elementary and secondary school years (Wigfield *et al.* in press). Many young children are optimistic about their competencies in different areas, and this optimism changes to greater realism and (sometimes) pessimism for many children as they get older (Jacobs *et al.* 2002). Children's valuing of achievement also declines (Jacobs *et al.* 2002). Although the overall pattern of these findings is one of decline, most of the research is normative, describing mean-level change across all children. Recent research has shown that the story is more complex, with some groups of children showing strong declines, others little change, and still others some increases (Musu-Gillette *et al.* 2014; Archambault *et al.* 2010). The implications of these different patterns of change for achievement outcomes await further explication.

This decline has been explained with respect to children's understanding of their performance and changes in the school environments children experience. First, as they get older, children both receive more information about their performance and learn to interpret that information more accurately, which can affect their ability beliefs and values. Students who begin to understand they are doing poorly in school are more likely to develop lower ability beliefs and values for the subjects in which they are doing poorly. Because they are with same-aged peers in school, they also learn to compare themselves more systematically with others, which can lead to decreases in motivation for some children, especially those doing less well (Wigfield *et al.* 2009).

Development of self-efficacy: Effect of mastery experience and socialization

Schunk and Pajares (2009) discussed the processes that affect the development of self-efficacy, which include early mastery experiences at home, peer interactions, and the evaluative information children receive in school. Parents who provide warm, supportive environments and encourage their children to explore their surroundings help foster mastery experiences in children and thus increase their self-efficacy. Children also develop their self-efficacy by being a part of peer networks that allow them to engage in vicarious experiences. Schunk and Pajares (2009) emphasize the importance of school environments for developing and supporting a high sense of efficacy, or possibly undermining it if support is not provided.

Like expectancies and values, research suggests that students' self-efficacy beliefs decline over time. School-related practices that focus on competition and normative grading, such as ability grouping, may decrease children's self-efficacy if they begin to fall behind their peers. Additionally, Deatrick *et al.* (2013) found that elementary- and middle-school students' beliefs in their ability to self-regulate their engagement in mathematics learning tasks declined over time (see also Caprara *et al.* 2008). Although children's self-efficacy beliefs decline on average, children's self-efficacy beliefs do appear to become more accurate over time (Schunk and Pajares 2009).

Development of goal orientations: Distinguishing the two orientations

Nicholls *et al.* (1990) found that mastery and performance goal orientations are evident as early as second grade. There is some debate in the literature as to how these goal orientations develop: Are they influenced more by individual or situational factors? Some work suggests that there are individual differences, such as lay theories of intelligence, which influence one's goal orientation (Dweck and Master 2009). Children who believe that intelligence is a fixed, unchanging trait (i.e. an entity theory) tend to adopt a performance orientation, while children who believe that intelligence is malleable and changeable (i.e. an incremental theory) tend to adopt a mastery orientation. These beliefs about intelligence may develop through social feedback from parents and teachers (Dweck and Master 2009).

However, other work suggests that children's goals are more strongly influenced by particular situational contexts, such as the classroom environment. Children tend to focus more on performance goals (Maehr and Zusho 2009) and less on mastery goals (Anderman and Midgley 1997) as they get older, perhaps because schools begin to focus more on evaluation and performance outcomes. Additionally, classroom environments that are cooperative as opposed to competitive may encourage children to adopt mastery goals (Ames and Archer 1988). It therefore seems that goal orientations can be influenced by both individual and situational characteristics.

Development of regulatory focus: Socialization influences and individual differences

Children's past family and cultural socialization experiences are critical to the development of their chronic regulatory orientations. Increased maternal warmth and nurturance have been linked to children developing a strong chronic promotion orientation, whereas more frequent maternal punishment is associated with a prevention orientation (Higgins and Silberman 1998; Manian *et al.* 2006).

In addition to parental socialization, broader cultural values may influence how regulatory orientations develop. Molden and Miele (2008) suggest that schools which emphasize responsibilities or aspirations through incentive programs may encourage children to adopt a stronger prevention or promotion orientation, respectively. Furthermore, individuals who grew up in East Asian cultures, which tend to value interdependence and responsibility towards others, have been shown to hold stronger prevention orientations, whereas members of European–American cultures, which value independence and fulfilling aspirations, tended to adopt stronger promotion orientations (e.g. Aaker and Lee 2001).

Individual differences in promotion versus prevention biases have been reliably measured in children as young as six, but these preferences likely do not stabilize until late adolescence, when children's self-regulatory and self-evaluation capacities have matured (Higgins and Silberman 1998; Manian *et al.* 2006). Therefore, classroom interventions that attempt to target and alter chronic regulatory focus could be effective, viable ways to enhance achievement; we discuss this issue next.

Intervening to facilitate students' achievement motivation

As discussed above, many children's achievement beliefs and values decline as they get older, and they tend to shift towards less adaptive goal orientations. These declines have led to the creation of interventions to improve motivation and achievement (Guthrie *et al.* 2012; Maehr and Midgley 1996; Wentzel and Wigfield 2007). This is an important new direction in the field, because most intervention studies designed to improve students' achievement have focused on cognition. Motivation interventions are of several types: those focused on groups, on classrooms, and on schools. We provide some representative examples of each that are relevant to the constructs on which we focus; Wentzel and Wigfield (2007) and Wigfield *et al.* (in press) provide additional examples.

Individual- and group-level interventions

Interventions to improve self-efficacy often are done at the individual student level. For example, Bandura and Schunk (1981) found that when 7- to 10-year-old children were encouraged to set proximal subgoals, as opposed to distal goals or no goals, their mathematics self-efficacy and performance increased. Similarly, Schunk and Rice (1989) found that elementary-school students whose teachers gave them process goals for reading comprehension tasks (i.e. 'Try to learn how to use the steps to answer the questions about what you read') demonstrated higher self-efficacy and reading comprehension than students whose teachers gave them product goals (i.e. 'Try to answer the questions about what you read') or general goals (i.e. 'Try your best'). Other instructional practices, such as exposing students to social models and encouraging students to verbalize their strategy use, have been shown to increase students' self-efficacy (Schunk and Pajares 2009).

Value-focused interventions also have been effective at the group level. Hulleman and Harackiewicz (2009) and Hulleman *et al.* (2010) had high-school students in a treatment group write every three to four weeks how what they had learned in science was relevant to them. Treatment group students who initially expected to do poorly in science earned higher science grades. Additionally, students' perceived value mediated the effects of the intervention on general interest and performance, suggesting that value-focused interventions can improve achievement outcomes. Similar work has recently demonstrated that college students experience large gains in achievement, and that such gains persist over several years, when they are asked to do a brief written affirmation of their personal values during class time (e.g. Cohen *et al.* 2009; Miyake *et al.* 2010).

Classroom-level interventions

Guthrie, Wigfield, and their colleagues (Guthrie *et al.* 2004, 2012) studied Concept Oriented Reading Instruction (CORI), a reading comprehension instruction program that integrates reading strategy instruction with specific motivational practices to foster students' reading engagement, motivation, and comprehension. The motivational practices used in CORI were derived from multiple motivational theories, including expectancy-value, goal, and self-efficacy theory. In studies of elementary- and middle-school students they found that CORI students had higher reading comprehension, engagement, and achievement than control group students.

With respect to regulatory focus, it is relatively easy to induce a temporary promotion or prevention orientation in individuals (Molden and Miele 2008). Therefore it may be possible to develop classroom-level interventions aimed at helping students adopt a particular, adaptive regulatory orientation before beginning a particular task in the classroom. For example, teachers could remind students of potential point losses they might experience on an upcoming, untimed test. This might induce students to adopt prevention orientations for that test, leading them to be more vigilant and possibly perform better.

School-level interventions

Maehr and Midgley (1996) worked with teachers and administrators at an elementary and a middle school to try to change the overall school goal structure from performance oriented to mastery oriented. They found it easier to change the goal structure at the elementary school; however, there was evidence that students' motivation improved at both schools.

In summary, it is encouraging that motivation interventions have been successful in improving both students' motivation and achievement. One important question for future research is how elaborate these interventions need to be to change students' motivation. Yeager and Walton (2011) reviewed a number of brief social and psychologically based intervention programs that have been effective in improving both children's and motivation and performance. They describe why these programs are effective even though they are brief; more systematic investigations of the effects of both complex and simple motivation interventions are needed to understand better how extensive interventions need to be to be effective.

Future research directions

We close our chapter with some issues that we believe need research attention over the next few years.

How do different classroom contexts influence students' motivation?

Other chapters in this handbook discuss various characteristics of how teachers and classrooms affect students' motivation. An important issue with respect to this work is how variation in classroom contexts affects students' motivation. Perry *et al.* (2006) review research on how contextual features of different classrooms have an effect on students' motivation. They take a sociocultural approach to student motivation and learning, arguing that students' participation in different classroom environments and interactions with others co-creates motivation. One of their important conclusions is that the complex nature of classrooms means that classroom practices designed to enhance students' motivation may have different meanings in different classrooms (see also Hickey 2008; Nolen and Ward 2008). This conclusion is echoed by Kaplan *et al.* (2012), who argued that the complexity inherent in classroom environments makes it difficult to use general principles derived from research on motivation for improving students' classroom outcomes. An implication of these points is that researchers doing intervention studies should think carefully about the effects their interventions may have in different kinds of classrooms with different kinds of students. We are convinced, however, that there is strong evidence showing that students' motivation for different school subjects can be improved through both brief and complex interventions.

How does motivation vary in different groups of children?

This book is an international handbook, and so the question of how motivation varies in different groups of children is especially relevant. Researchers have focused on gender and ethnic differences in motivation (Murdock 2009; Wigfield *et al.* in press). This work shows that boys' and girls' competence-related beliefs and values tend to follow gender stereotypic patterns, with boys having more positive beliefs and values in domains such as mathematics and sports, and girls in reading/English and music. However, more recent studies show that these patterns may be changing (Jacobs *et al.* 2002.)

Researchers interested in ethnic differences in motivation have moved away from making group comparisons to trying to understand broader cultural and societal issues that have an effect on student motivation in different groups. These include the perceived societal opportunity structure for different groups, discrimination, and cultural frame (Murdock 2009; Wigfield *et al.* in press). The complex influences of these factors on students' motivation needs further research attention. A clearer understanding of motivation in different groups also will inform motivation interventions.

Conclusion

In conclusion, research on achievement motivation continues to burgeon. We are especially encouraged at the success of the research work on motivation interventions, and urge researchers to continue these efforts. As we think about the international audience for this handbook, we also urge researchers from around the world to study children's motivation in all its varieties, to provide a more complete understanding of this essential construct.

Note

1 Other motivation constructs, such as intrinsic motivation and interest, are relevant to a discussion of children's motivation in school, but we do not discuss them because of space limitations. See Deci and Ryan (2012) and Schiefele (2009) for discussion of these constructs.

References

Aaker, J.L. and Lee, A.Y. (2001) '"I seek pleasures and "we" avoid pains: the role of self-regulatory goals in information processing and persuasion', *Journal of Consumer Research*, 28: 33–49.

Ames, C. and Archer, J. (1988) 'Achievement goals in the classroom: students' learning strategies and motivation processes', *Journal of Educational Psychology*, 80: 260–267.

Anderman, A.H. and Murdock, T.B. (2007) *Psychology of Cheating*, San Diego: Elsevier Academic Press.

Anderman, E.M. and Midgley, C. (1997) 'Changes in achievement goal orientations, perceived academic competence, and grades across the transition to middle-level schools', *Contemporary Educational Psychology*, 22: 269–298.

Archambault, I., Eccles, J.S. and Vida, M.N. (2010) 'Ability self-concepts and subjective value in literacy: joint trajectories from grades 1–12', *Journal of Educational Psychology*, 102: 804–816.

Bandura, A. (1986) *Social Foundations of Thought and Action: A Social-Cognitive View*, Englewood Cliffs, NJ: Prentice-Hall.

Bandura, A. (1997) *Self-Efficacy: The Exercise of Control*, New York: W.H. Freeman.

Bandura, A. and Schunk, D.H. (1981) 'Cultivating competence, self-efficacy, and intrinsic interest through proximal self-motivation', *Journal of Personality and Social Psychology*, 41: 586–598.

Caprara, G.V, Fida, R., Vecchione, M., Del Bove, G., Vecchio, G.M., Barbaranelli, C. and Bandura, A. (2008) 'Longitudinal analysis of the role of perceived self-efficacy for self-regulated learning in academic continuance and achievement', *Journal of Educational Psychology*, 100: 525–534.

Cohen, G.L., Garcia, J., Purdie-Vaughns, V., Apfel, N. and Brzustoski, P. (2009) 'Recursive processes in self-affirmation: intervening to close the minority achievement gap', *Science*, 324: 400–403.

Collins, J.L. (1982, March) 'Self-efficacy and ability in achievement behavior', paper presented at the annual meeting of the American Educational Research Association, New York.

Deatrick, E.E., Waiters, B.L., Creek, T., Snyder, E., Butz, A.R. and Usher, E.L. (2013, April) 'Making the transition: changes in elementary and middle school mathematics motivation', paper presented at the Spring Research Conference, Lexington, KY.

Deci, E.L. and Ryan, R. (2012) 'Motivation, personality, and development within embedded social contexts: an overview of self-determination theory', in R. Ryan (ed.) *Oxford Handbook of Human Motivation* (pp. 85–107), New York: Oxford University Press.

Durik, A.M., Vida, M. and Eccles, J.S. (2006) 'Task values and ability beliefs as predictors of high school literacy choices: a developmental analysis', *Journal of Educational Psychology*, 98: 382–393.

Dweck, C. and Master, A. (2009) 'Self theories and motivation: students' beliefs about intelligence', in K.R. Wentzel and A. Wigfield (eds) *Handbook of Motivation at School* (pp. 123–140), New York: Routledge.

Eccles, J.S. (2005) 'Subjective task values and the Eccles *et al.* model of achievement-related choices', in A.J. Elliott and C.S. Dweck (eds) *Handbook of Competence and Motivation* (pp. 105–121), New York: Guilford.

Eccles, J.S., Midgley, C., Buchanan, C.M., Wigfield, A., Reuman, D. and MacIver, D. (1993) 'Developmental during adolescence: the impact of stage/environment fit', *American Psychologist*, 48: 90–101.

Eccles, J.S., Vida, M.N. and Barber, B. (2004) 'The relation of early adolescents' college plans and both academic ability and task-value beliefs to subsequent college enrollment', *The Journal of Early Adolescence*, 24: 63–77.

Eccles, J.S. and Wigfield, A. (2002) 'Motivational beliefs, values, and goals', *Annual Review of Psychology*, 53: 109–132.

Eccles-Parsons, J.S., Adler, T.F., Futterman, R., Goff, S.B., Kaczala, C.M., Meece, J.L. and Midgley, C. (1983) 'Expectancies, values, and academic behaviors', in J.T. Spence (ed.) *Achievement and Achievement Motivation* (pp. 75–146), San Francisco: W.H. Freeman.

Elliot, A.J. (1999) 'Approach and avoidance motivation and achievement goals', *Educational Psychologist*, 34: 169–189.

Elliot, A.J. (2005) 'A conceptual history of the achievement goal construct', in A.J. Elliot and C.S. Dweck (eds) *Handbook of Competence and Motivation* (pp. 52–72), New York: Guilford.

Elliot, A.J. and Harackiewicz, J.M. (1996) 'Approach and avoidance goals and intrinsic motivation: a mediational analysis', *Journal of Personality and Social Psychology*, 70: 461–475.

Elliot, A.J. and McGregor, H. (2001) 'A 2 × 2 achievement goal framework', *Journal of Personality and Social Psychology*, 80: 501–509.

Elliot, A.J., Murayama, K. and Pekrun, R. (2011) 'A 3 × 2 achievement goal model', *Journal of Educational Psychology*, 103: 632–648.

Förster, J. and Higgins, E.T. (2005) 'How global versus local perception fits regulatory focus', *Psychological Science*, 16: 631–636.

Guthrie, J.T., Wigfield, A. and Klauda, S.L. (2012) *Adolescents' Engagement in Academic Literacy*, available from http://www.cori.umd.edu/research-publications/2012_adolescents_engagement_ebook.pdf

Guthrie, J.T., Wigfield, A. and Perencevich, K. (eds) (2004) *Motivating Reading Comprehension: Concept Oriented Reading Instruction*, Mahwah, NJ: Lawrence Erlbaum Associates.

Hickey, D.T. (2008) 'Sociocultural theories of motivation', in E.M. Anderman and L. Anderman (eds) *Psychology of Classroom Learning* (pp. 847–851), Farmington Hills, MI: Thomson Gale Publishers.

Higgins, E.T. (1997) 'Beyond pleasure and pain', *American Psychologist*, 52: 1280–1300.

Higgins, E.T. and Silberman, I. (1998) 'Development of regulatory focus: promotion and prevention as ways of living', in J. Heckhausen and C. Dweck (eds) *Motivation and Self-Regulation Across the Life-Span* (pp. 78–113), Cambridge: Cambridge University Press.

Hulleman, C.S., Godes, O., Hendricks, B.L. and Harackiewicz, J.M. (2010) 'Enhancing interest and performance with a utility value intervention', *Journal of Educational Psychology*, 102: 880–895.

Hulleman, C.S. and Harackiewicz, J.M. (2009) 'Promoting interest and performance in high school science classes', *Science*, 326: 1410–1412.

Hulleman, C.S. and Senko, C. (2010) 'Up around the bend: forecasts for achievement goal theory and research in 2020', in T.C. Urdan and S.A. Karabenick (eds) *Advances in Motivation and Achievement* (Vol. 16a, pp. 71–104), Bingley, UK: Emerald Group.

Jacobs, J., Lanza, S., Osgood, D.W., Eccles, J.S. and Wigfield, A. (2002) 'Ontogeny of children's self-beliefs: gender and domain differences across grades one through 12', *Child Development*, 73: 509–527.

Kaplan, A., Katz, I. and Flum, H. (2012) 'Motivation theory in educational practice: knowledge claims, challenges, and future directions', in K.R. Harris, S. Graham, and T. Urdan (eds) *APA Educational Psychology Handbook* (Vol. 2, pp. 165–194), Washington, DC: American Psychological Association.

Keys, T.D., Conley, A.M., Duncan, G.J. and Domina, T. (2012) 'The role of goal orientations for adolescent mathematics achievement', *Contemporary Educational Psychology*, 37: 47–54.

Liberman, N., Molden, D.C., Idson, L.C. and Higgins, E.T. (2001) 'Promotion and prevention focus on alternative hypotheses: implications for attributional functions', *Journal of Personality and Social Psychology*, 80: 5.

Maehr, M.L. and Midgley, C. (1996) *Transforming School Cultures*, Boulder, CO: Westview Press.

Maehr, M.L. and Zusho, A. (2009) 'Achievement goal theory: past, present, and future', in K.R. Wentzel and A. Wigfield (eds) *Handbook of Motivation at School* (pp. 77–122), New York: Routledge.

Manian, N., Papadakis, A.A., Strauman, T.J. and Essex, M.J. (2006) 'The development of children's ideal and ought self-guides: parenting, temperament, and individual differences in guide strength', *Journal of Personality*, 74: 1619–1646.

Miele, D.B., Molden, D.C. and Gardner, W.L. (2009) 'Motivated comprehension regulation: vigilant versus eager metacognitive control', *Memory and Cognition*, 37: 779–795.

Miyake, A., Kost-Smith, L.E., Finkelstein, N.D., Pollock, S.J., Cohen, G.L. and Ito, T.A. (2010) 'Reducing the gender achievement gap in college science: a classroom study of values affirmation', *Science*, 330: 1234–1237.

Molden, D.C. and Miele, D.B. (2008) 'The origins and influences of promotion-focused and prevention-focused achievement motivation', in S. Karabenick and T. Urdan (eds) *Advances in Motivation and Achievement* (Vol. 15, pp. 81–118), Bingley, UK: Emerald Group.

Murdock, T. (2009) 'Achievement motivation in racial and ethnic context', in K.R. Wentzel and A. Wigfield (eds) *Handbook of Motivation at School* (pp. 433–462), New York: Routledge.

Musu-Gillette, L., Wigfield, A., Harring, J. and Eccles, J.S. (2014) 'Trajectories of change in students' self-concepts of ability and values in math and college major choice', manuscript submitted for publication.

Nagy, G., Garrett, J., Trautwein, U., Cortina, K. S., Baumert, J. and Eccles, J.S. (2008) 'Gendered high school course selection as a precursor of gendered careers: the mediating role of self-concept and intrinsic value', in H.M.G. Watt and J.S. Eccles (eds) *Gender and Occupational Outcomes* (pp. 115–143). Washington, DC: American Psychological Association.

Nicholls, J.G., Cobb, P., Yackel, E., Wood, T. and Wheatley, G. (1990) 'Students' theories of mathematics and their mathematical knowledge: multiple dimensions of assessment', in G. Kulm (ed.) *Assessing Higher Order Thinking in Mathematics* (pp. 137–154), Washington, DC: American Association for the Advancement of Science.

Nolen, S.B. and Ward, C.J. (2008) 'Sociocultural and situative approaches to studying motivation', in M.L. Maehr, S. Karabenick and T. Urdan (eds) *Advances in Motivation and Achievement* (Vol. 15, pp. 425–461), Bingley UK: Emerald Group.

Perry, N.E., Turner, J.C. and Meyer, D.K. (2006) 'Classrooms as contexts for motivating learning', in P.A. Alexander and P.H. Winne (eds) *Handbook of Educational Psychology*, 2nd edn (pp. 327–349), Mahwah, NJ: Erlbaum.

Pintrich, P.R. (2000) 'An achievement goal theory perspective on issues in motivation terminology, theory, and research', *Contemporary Educational Psychology*, 25: 92–104.

Pintrich, P.R. and De Groot, E.V. (1990) 'Motivational and self-regulated learning components of classroom academic performance', *Journal of Educational Psychology*, 82: 33–40.

Roeser, R.W. (2004) 'Competing schools of thought in achievement goal theory', in S. Karabenick and T. Urdan (eds) *Advances in Motivation and Achievement* (Vol. 13, pp. 265–299), Bingley, UK: Emerald Group.

Rosenzweig, E.Q. and Miele, D.B. (2014) 'The influence of regulatory focus on academic test performance', University of Maryland, College Park, manuscript submitted for publication.

Schiefele, U. (2009) 'Situational and individual interest', in K.R. Wentzel and A. Wigfield (eds) *Handbook of Motivation at School* (pp. 197–222), New York: Routledge.

Schunk, D.H. and Pajares, F. (2005) 'Competence perceptions and academic functioning', in A.J. Elliot and C.S. Dweck (eds) *Handbook of Competence and Motivation* (pp. 85–104), New York: Guilford Press.

Schunk, D.H. and Pajares, F. (2009) 'Self-efficacy theory', in K.R. Wentzel and A. Wigfield (eds) *Handbook of Motivation in School* (pp. 35–54), New York: Routledge.

Schunk, D.H. and Rice, J.M. (1989) 'Learning goals and children's reading comprehension', *Journal of Reading Behavior*, 21: 279–293.

Senko, C., Hulleman, C.S. and Harackiewicz, J.M. (2011) 'Achievement goal theory at the crossroads: old controversies, current challenges, and new directions', *Educational Psychologist*, 46: 26–47.

Senko, C. and Miles, K.M. (2008) 'Pursuing their own learning agenda: how mastery-oriented students jeopardize their class performance', *Contemporary Educational Psychology*, 33: 561–583.

Simpkins, S.D., Davis-Kean, P.E. and Eccles, J.S. (2006) 'Math and science motivation: a longitudinal examination of the links between choices and beliefs', *Developmental Psychology*, 42: 70.

Skaalvik, E. (1997) 'Self-enhancing and self-defeating ego orientation: relations with task and task avoidance orientation, achievement, self-perceptions, and anxiety', *Journal of Educational Psychology*, 89: 71–81.

Watt, H.M. (2006) 'The role of motivation in gendered educational and occupational trajectories related to maths', *Educational Research and Evaluation*, 12: 305–322.

Wentzel, K.R. and Wigfield, A. (2007) 'Motivational interventions that work: themes and remaining issues', *Educational Psychologist*, 42: 261–271.

Wigfield, A. and Cambria, J.M. (2010) 'Children's achievement values, goal orientations, and interest: definitions, development, and relations to achievement outcomes', *Developmental Review*, 35: 1–30.

Wigfield, A. and Eccles, J.S. (2000) 'Expectancy-value theory of motivation', *Contemporary Educational Psychology*, 25: 68–81.

Wigfield, A., Eccles, J.S., Fredricks, J., Simpkins, S., Roeser, R., and Schiefele, U. (in press) 'Development of achievement motivation and engagement', in R. Lerner (series ed.) and M.E. Lamb and C. Garcia Coll (vol. eds.), *Handbook of Child Psychology*, 7th edn, Vol. 3, *Social, Emotional, and Personality Development*, New York: John Wiley.

Wigfield, A., Tonks, S. and Klauda, S.L. (2009) 'Expectancy-value theory', in K.R. Wentzel and A. Wigfield (eds) *Handbook of Motivation at School* (pp. 55–76), New York: Routledge.

Yeager, D.S. and Walton, G.M. (2011). 'Social-psychological interventions in education: they're not magic', *Review of Educational Research*, 81: 267–301. doi:10.3102/0034654311405999

2

SEEING THE BIG PICTURE

A systemic perspective on motivation, and its implications for social and psychological research

Patricia L. Hardré

Teaching and learning, and motivation and achievement are integrated in a complex dynamic (Dai and Sternberg 2004). To fully understand how teachers and learners are motivated, research on this dynamic must consider these complex factors together, in their authentic nature and contexts (Hardré 2007). It also needs to take into account features of the context and culture, both those within educational systems and those which infringe authentically from outside.

The international educational community is demonstrating an increasing awareness of the powerful implications of social psychology for educational research and instruction at all levels and for all disciplines (e.g. Dai and Sternberg 2004; Smith and Conrey 2009). We recognize that our learning environments are complex and dynamic, not always traditional classrooms. They include myriad physical and virtual spaces, such as laboratories, libraries, clinics, garages, art studios, homes, dorm rooms, and boardrooms. We have also come to recognize that learning environments are not discrete, but overlapping, integrated, and dynamically connected (Hardré *et al.* 2012, 2013). The whole field will benefit if ways of conceptualizing educational research on learning adapt to address changes in education itself.

Much of educational research remains oversimplified, framed in narrowly defined, artificially bounded ways; built on single-theory, discrete-outcome foundations (e.g., goal theory, self-determination theory, social cognitive theory). In such studies, a few specific factors or variables are identified and separated out from their authentic context, tested or correlated, and mapped to broad claims about their central importance to the success and future of motivation and learning. The characteristics and constructs featured in these studies clearly present important elements of the complex motivational dynamic; however, too many of these studies leave findings artificially separate from the larger systemic whole. This separation of elements from complex systemic and organizational dynamics, temporarily, to examine them in detail is consistent with the centuries-long standards of scientific research, to which educational and social sciences research are often held. However, some of this single-theory and narrowly defined research has neglected to reintegrate those elements into their authentic dynamic to complete the process of developing understanding. A systemic approach to educational and motivational research offers promise to support such reintegration, but to be used, it must first be understood.

Patricia L. Hardré

What is 'systemic' research?

Synthesizing definitions from several dictionaries, the term 'systemic' used alone means: reflecting, pertaining to, or affecting the larger entity or group to which it belongs. That entity or group can be biological, social, educational, professional, economic, political, or some combination. However, the term 'systemic' is used frequently, and sometimes loosely, across disciplines and fields of practice in scholarship and education. To investigate and capture a synthesis of how 'systemic' approaches have been used, and currently were being used, in educational and motivational research, this author conducted systematic library and internet searches linking the terms ('systemic' + 'research' + 'education').

That library search produced thousands of instances referring to educational research as systemic, and the internet search produced millions of instances. There is not space in this chapter to detail all of these documents and their nuanced differences; however, following is a brief synthesis of their convergent and divergent patterns. In the vast majority of these cases, 'systemic' was linked to reform, and to the use of large bodies of research findings to enact change in educational institutions and systems. Some documents reported original research findings and the authors supplied their own applications or extensions as 'systemic implications.' In other instances, the documents were reviews or syntheses of research supporting development of a 'systemic research agenda' focused on building bodies of inquiry to fill existing gaps for educational practice or to address critical problems for a particular discipline or profession. In only a very small percentage of these articles and documents, 'systemic' referred to the design of a study or body of research, and the general patterns among these are detailed in the following paragraphs.

Articles using 'systemic' approaches tended to be more prevalent in specific disciplines, such as educational policy and leadership (e.g. Fowler and Walberg 1991), and health professions such as family therapy (e.g. Oka and Whiting 2013). Other fields featuring and advocating for systemic research in education included applied professions such as agriculture (e.g. Alrøe and Kristensen 2002) and distance learning (e.g. Passi and Mishra 2004). Action research, applied research conducted by teachers to address teaching needs, was frequently termed 'systemic' based on its link to professional application (e.g. Stones 1986). Others used the term to refer to explicitly linked research agendas facilitated through interdisciplinary and professional networks (e.g. Hubert *et al.* 2012). Rural education research has historically integrated contextual elements systemically, based on recognition of the authentic embeddedness of rural schools within their communities (e.g. Herzog and Pittman 1995; Quaglia and Cobb 1996) (though not all of these studies used the term 'systemic').

A tiny subset of these documents (less than 1 percent) conceptualized 'systemic research' as a specialized type of research study design, and even these presented a huge spectrum of variations. One often-cited article used 'systemic' and 'analytic' as terms to describe complementary approaches to research, as an alternative conceptualization to the traditional data-type classifications of 'quantitative' and 'qualitative' research (Salomon 1991). This conceptualization made the most profound published break from traditional categories to signal 'systemic' as a unique direction in research design. Other researchers readily adopted the new terms, equating 'systemic' with applied qualitative research of education *in situ* (Corno 1995), essentially fusing the distinction of applied research from other professional fields with the qualitative framework and elements of classroom action research.

While some theorists have aligned systemic research with particular belief systems or compared it to existing methodological types, it may be seen as a distinct, fluid, and context-responsive method of its own, a method that may bridge and overlap others. It is this conceptualization of 'systemic research' that is used to frame this chapter. While it may take the forms and include the strategic approaches of a number of familiar research designs, systemic research is an adaptive approach to educational inquiry, distinguished by its attention to multilevel and multifaceted elements of all relevant contexts of the people and activities under study.

Over the past two decades, education has trended toward greater scholarly acceptance of a plethora of new research methods outside of traditional epistemological and methodological frameworks. Based on Salomon's systemic–analytic departure from qualitative–quantitative distinctions, a number of theorists have found systemic research, with its attention to multilevel and embedded elements, a natural fit to theories such as those asserting the implicit influence of underlying beliefs on research strategies and outcomes (e.g. Schommer-Aikins 2004).

The historic nature of research use for educational change and reform as the collection of findings from many discrete independent research studies is laudable. However, making research useful requires reformers to link together many vastly different studies, any subset of which were conducted in divergent participant groups and contexts, or experimentally controlled so they became divorced from context. Unless studies are part of an intentionally linked and methodologically aligned research agenda, these studies may have used different instruments for measurement, as well as different analysis methods and procedural protocols. Educational research that is truly systemic supplies and accounts for its context, so that accurate linkages can be made authentically from relevant information. Systemic research that meets these criteria of methodological alignment, consistent instrumentation, and accounting for context, can indeed help to bridge the research-to-practice gap and inform the next generation of research.

Operationalizing systemic research

The systemic perspective accounts for the complexity of individuals and groups interacting within an environment (Maehr 1989). It arises from an understanding of educational environments as intellectually, socially and emotionally interactive spaces (Maehr and Midgley 1996). Factors in systems are interdependently connected to each other, and embedded within larger systems, so that change in one factor necessarily results in change in other factors (Salomon 1991). Learning and development are the unique products of these dynamically interactive, embedded elements which form a unique integrated whole. This conceptualization of educational research across institutions and learning environments is similar to Bronfenbrenner's (1979) conceptualization of ecological systems applied to child development, and which other scholars have applied to social issues and human behaviors (e.g. Woodside *et al.* 2006). However, such an approach has not consistently and systematically been applied to motivational research in education, and to the interactions among natural and design characteristics of learning environments, broadly defined.

Learning environments in the twenty-first century are diverse and complex; however, to simplify illustration here, consider, for example, a traditional school learning environment, whether for children, college students or adult trainees. Schools and classrooms are local, interpersonal, social and academic microsystems which exist inside school districts or agencies, communities, and local and national political entities. All of these layers of systems influence the work that schools do, from context, methods, and curriculum, to standards and outcomes assessment. Students are also influenced from outside by peer groups, families and cultures-of-origin, and bring to school these influences on their motivation, learning and development. Similarly, in college, adult, vocational, continuing education, training, and development opportunities are created in response to needs or changes in business and professional practice, and to industrial and technological advances, all of which constitute layers in their systemic frameworks for inquiry. In both examples, and across all levels of education, these various and sometimes conflicting systems create interactions and send messages that influence motivation, learning, and development, for both teachers and learners. Figure 2.1 shows this conceptual relationship, though simplified for depicting those complex influences.

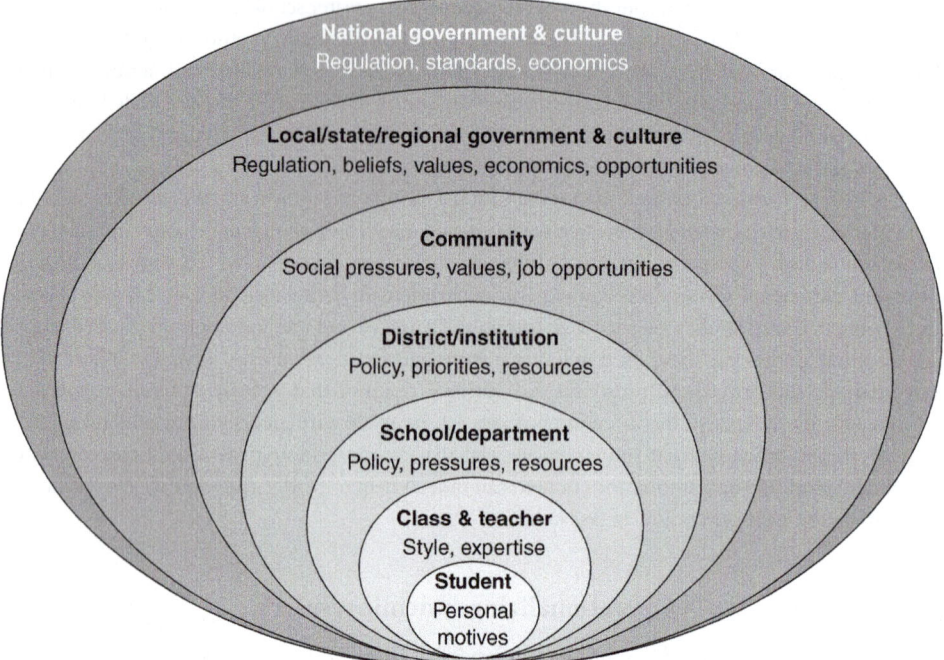

Figure 2.1   School-within-system culture concept model.

This simple concept graphic needs to be elaborated with all the students in a class, all of the classes in a school, all of the schools in a district, all the districts in a state or nation. Then add the influences of nations on one another; changes in district and government administration and leadership; cultural values, economics and job markets; and digital tools and virtual learning environments, and it begins to approach an authentic mapping of systemic educational influences. Systemic research takes key components of this dynamic into account, informed by theory and existing research precedent, using the broad perspective of systemic dynamics.

General comment

Nature of motivation

Human motivation is complex, internal, and interactive. It is also highly contextualized and place-based; that is, people have different motivations in some contexts than in others (different in traditional classrooms versus digital environments; different in clinical versus laboratory settings; Anderman and Young 1994; Lee and Tsai 2005). Motivation is highly task-based: people have different motivations for simple procedures versus complex problem solving, for tasks they see as easy versus difficult, and for routine versus novel tasks (Beck 2004). It is also very socially sensitive: people respond to feedback differently in private versus in groups; motivation and engagement may be different for written versus verbal communication and performance, and in competitive versus cooperative group situations (Dweck, 1996). Learners respond motivationally to role models they have, examples they see, and social pressures they face (Hardré *et al.* 2012). This means that learners who seem highly motivated in one setting or task may need support for another, and that research conclusions about individuals and groups will vary when context and task parameters change.

[handwritten: general comment ↗]

How motivation supports learning

Motivation is essential to learning, as demonstrated by research in both behavioral-affective and cognitive-developmental research. Motivation for learning drives choices related to what is being learned: choices to use and apply it, to transfer it to address daily needs, to frame career goals, to make profound life changes (Linnenbrink and Pintrich 2004). Behaviorally and affectively, motivation to learn causes students to pay attention, so they engage with information, and then to engage in practice activities, so they develop skills accurately (Deci and Ryan 2000). It promotes investment of effort to learn and master skills, tenacity, and resilience to overcome challenges, and even initial failure to achieve eventual success (Bandura 1997). Strong, productive motivation supports learning skills well enough to transfer to authentic practice and retain them over time (Latham 2007). Motivation energizes the willingness to exercise creativity, put forth effort and initiative, take risks, and innovate, resulting in adaptive application of learned skills (Hardré and Siddique 2013). From the cognitive-developmental perspective, motivation helps learners to attend to new knowledge and then activate and link prior knowledge, developing complex schema for later retrieval (Hardré and Kollmann 2013). As basic knowledge forms the foundation for more complex types of knowledge, motivation supports learning and integration that progressively build toward mastery, so learners can develop rich, adaptive skills and problem solve rather than just doing rote tasks (Beck 2004). This is the power of motivated learning: it enables learners to take and use what they are given, process it actively, use it effectively, and transfer it authentically (Dai and Sternberg 2004). Motivation influences how people process information and develop skills now, as well as how they position themselves for future learning and life choices (Dweck *et al.* 2004).

[handwritten margin notes: → What it does; → What motivation does; → Motivation + creativity]

A systemic perspective on motivation

Motivation for learning and development is personal and internal, yet embedded in a complex 'social fabric' (Weiner 1990: 621) of interpersonal, organizational, and cultural elements. The classroom motivational environment is a function of its dominant attitudes and values, such as the valuing (or devaluing) of outcome goals and relevant supports, such as aptitude, effort, achievement, creativity, challenge, risk-taking, and various post-school career options (Hardré 2008). Students' motivation results from interactions among their psychological needs and preferences (Pietsch *et al.* 2003); perceptions of the content and skills being taught (Pintrich 2003); self-perceptions of competence, self-efficacy, ability, and probable success (Ozer and Bandura 1990; Schoenfelder 2006); value for and investment in learning (Hardré and Reeve 2003); and how learning links to their future goals and aspirations (Anderman and Young 1994; Liem *et al.* 2008). Students' academic motivation depends in part on the nature and quality of the school's cultural and social contexts, including factors such as role modeling, autonomy support, competence information, encouragement to promote efficacy, error and constructive feedback as learning supports, task relevance and value messages (Hardré 2011; Hardré, Chen *et al.* 2006; Salili *et al.* 2001; Smith and Conrey 2009).

Motivational messages are communicated explicitly and implicitly, intentionally and unintentionally, in daily class and school-based interactions (Dweck 1996; Ryan and Powelson 1991). Teachers seek to motivate students, individually and in groups, based on their beliefs about learning and motivation, and about the subjects and students they teach (Hardré 2008; Hardré and Sullivan 2009). Motivating also has reciprocal effects, as teachers who see students motivated tend to persist (Linnenbrink and Pintrich 2002; Radel *et al.* 2010). Teachers' efforts to support learners' motivation are complicated by implicit tensions between long-term benefits of intrinsic motivation (e.g. personal growth, internal aspirations, passion to learn) and short-term management and productivity benefits from extrinsic motivation (e.g. compliance with rules, current grades) (Deci and Ryan 2000; Druckman and Bjork 1994).They are also influenced by administrative and organizational policy and philosophy (Battistich *et al.* 1995; D'Amico *et al.* 1996; Hardré *et al.* 2013).

Schools are social and cultural systems, a composite of shared and divergent beliefs and expectations of community members (Ley *et al.* 1996). Motivational beliefs and strategies infuse the school systemic so that teachers and staff tend to adopt community-sanctioned motivational beliefs and practices (Capper, 1993; Hardré, Huang *et al.* 2006). School policy and practice drive motivational opportunities in schools, influencing students' goals and performance standards, choices, control and self-determination, aspirations and possible futures, and definitions and expectations of success (Maehr and Midgley 1996; Wang and Guthrie 2004), including the role of standardized tests and grades (Duke 2004). As people function within a system, over time they more fully adopt its patterns and practices – for better or worse (Keyton 2011; Kohn 1993). Student motivation and achievement influence school performance overall (Duke 2004). The whole system is embedded in a complex of larger entities and communities, creating interactions among diverse factors, difficult to sort but critical to examine (Weiner 1990). Systemic motivational research acknowledges the complexity of the teaching–learning interaction and its unique, dynamic, multilevel influences, and requires the study of interdependent relationships and patterns of change.

Approaching motivational research systemically

Though researchers tend to agree that education is indeed complex, too often in practice educational research treats individuals, classrooms and schools as overly simplistic, ignoring complex systemic relationships among factors, as if people existed in sterile environments without myriad, multilevel influences. Historically, few researchers and practitioner-scholars have fully acknowledged and investigated systemic influences. Researchers who recognize and acknowledge the value and fit of a systemic approach to motivational research in education may ask, 'How can this be achieved?'

A systemic approach to research requires acknowledging the nature and effects of those influences that surround the individuals and systems under study. It does not require that the design and data collection include *all* of these influences, but researchers need to consider the relevant systemic factors, and evaluate their direct and indirect (often nuanced) effects, on the variables or phenomena under study, rather than ignoring them. Systemic data analysis should include the comparative examination, synthesis, and convergence of multisource data, reflecting various perspectives of stakeholders, so its results reflect the diversity of perspectives within the system (Hardré 2007).

Research using the ideal of experimental controls, producing certainty of outcomes and apparent objectivity, artificializes the authentic nature of motivation and learning. Too often, researchers who extract constructs and factors for experimental study never reintegrate them into the authentic context to derive meaningfulness from their findings. For an area of research with the complexity and multilevel influences of motivation, systemic research is theoretically and intuitively appropriate. Considering educational motivation systemically and fluidly integrates elements that include its various time-based components (past experiences, present interactions and experiences, future expectations and aspirations, present and future goals); its multiple levels of value-based influences (political, organizational, institutional, local, culture, individual); and its various social elements (past and present role models, teachers and mentors, parents and authority figures, family and culture-of-origin, peers and working teams, aspirant identities and professional goals).

Examples of systemic considerations

Systemic motivational research cannot be absolutely comprehensive, as including all relevant influences on any learner's motivation would be prohibitive in scope for most researchers' agendas. However, it needs to include more than the simplest, most sterile map of factors, and demonstrate that the researchers have taken into account relevant influences of the larger educational system or learning environment on the motivational dynamic. To provide a sense of the balance needed in systemic motivational research, below are some examples of how studies in various groups and contexts can gain systemic authenticity:

- In a study setting out to understand the overall academic motivation of high-school students, who may change teachers four to eight times a day, systemic inclusion of whole-school policy and practice is crucial.
- In a school or district that is under pressure to raise test scores, with implications for teacher and administrator employment, a study of curriculum change or instructional flexibility would need to take that pressure into account, because it is likely to influence decisions beyond the direct effects of teacher style and autonomous choice.
- A study of college and university faculty productivity (such as grants, publications and conference presentations) should take into account available supports (financial, staff, graduate assistants), conflicting demands on faculty time and resources (teaching, service), and performance assessment, all of which influence goals and constrain choices.
- Research on the motivation of employees in industrial jobs should take into account not just their individual differences and immediate supervisors, but also the broader context of the company's organizational structure, values, and culture.
- Investigations of college motivation and retention in applied professional fields (such as engineering, architecture, and health sciences) should include how well students understand the relevance of what they are learning to their eventual career goals and demands.
- Studies of K-12 teachers' skill development in university-based learning environments assessing transfer-to-practice need to account for social and organizational supports for teachers and students in their schools.
- Studies of motivation in community-based health educational programs (with goals such as reducing youth risk behaviors for HIV-AIDS) will benefit if they include community cultural and social values, and use multilevel data (e.g. from youth, parents, and community leaders).
- Motivation research in rural schools is more contextually authentic when it acknowledges rural schools' 'place-based-ness', linked to motivating values (e.g. family responsibility) and potential constraints on identity development (e.g. social and geographic isolation).
- Balancing inclusion of influential cultural characteristics with community and organizational specifics, East Asian educational studies often include systemic characteristics of family and cultural values on motivation.
- Studies of learning and motivation in digital and distance learning environments should take into account personal and interpersonal motivating characteristics and perceptions (such as access to assistance, technological competence, and the larger user context outside the system itself).

While not all studies that take systemic perspectives use that term to describe their methods, they are distinct from nonsystemic research in that they frame their background, methods, and findings with attention to relevant system characteristics and apparent or plausible influences. Which factors to include and emphasize can be framed based on theory and previous research precedents and findings.

Systemic research may take on any overall design (e.g. experimental, quasi-experimental, descriptive, ethnographic, narrative) and use any combination of data types (e.g. quantitative, qualitative, mixed) and data sources (e.g. surveys, performance observations, interviews, metadata). In identifying systemic research studies in motivation, it is important to underscore that the inclusion of systemic elements needs to be nontrivial; that is, systemic research treats system characteristics as central in the methods and in deriving meaning from the study findings. Hundreds of published articles mention the context of 'an urban school,' a 'research university,' or a 'large corporation' in describing their location or participant group, but these contexts are rarely mentioned again, and their defining characteristics not at all. Systemic research makes context a substantive component of design, analysis, and the development of meaning from data.

Summary, challenges, and future directions

There are critical differences in how the term 'systemic' is used across scholarly studies, reviews, reports, and other documents, dividing between systemic study, systemic agenda, and systemic application. The term 'systemic' can refer to an individual research study design, to a study series or research agenda, or to an applied synthesis of a body of work. In referring to a single study design, 'systemic' indicates design with attention to multilevel, embedded contexts and influential elements, relevant to the research questions and factors under study. It is not merely a term for a subgroup of qualitative methods, but a unique approach that may include multiple data types and will necessarily include multiple data sources. Systemic research for motivation in education offers potential for integrating nuances of system characteristics and factors, to examine their possible influences on measured variables and outcomes. As has been observed by many scholars, examining the constructs that influence learning and development in their authentic contexts holds promise to bridge the research-to-practice gaps and recontextualize what we think we know about why learners and teachers (of all ages and groups) think and behave as they do.

Challenges to systemic research include that it is more complex than traditional approaches. Rigorous and reasoned measurement and analysis design and methods need to match the systemic perspective and frameworks. Researchers need systematic and accepted ways of identifying and validating what systemic factors to include in explicit design of scholarly research studies. International leaders and funding agencies in education have stressed the need and taken up the call for systemic research. Still, it has not been fully engaged and accepted, as the field of educational research has lacked clarity on how systemic approaches apply to the study of traditional, theory-based subspecialties such as motivation.

References

Alrøe, H.F. and Kristensen, E.S. (2002) 'Towards a systemic research methodology in agriculture: rethinking the rule of values in science', *Agriculture and Human Values,* 19: 3–23.

Anderman, E. and Young, A. (1994) 'Motivation and strategy use in science: individual differences and classroom effects', *Journal of Research in Science Teaching,* 31: 811–831.

Bandura, A. (1997) *Self-efficacy: The Exercise of Control,* New York: W.H. Freeman.

Battistich, V., Solomon, D., Kim, D., Watson, M. and Schaps, S. (1995) 'Schools as communities, poverty levels of student populations, and students' attitudes, motives, and performance: a multilevel analysis', *American Research Journal,* 32: 627–658.

Beck, R.C. (2004) *Motivational Theories and Principles,* 5th edn, New York: Pearson.

Bronfenbrenner, U. (1979) *The Ecology of Human Development: Experiments by Nature and Design,* Cambridge, MA: Harvard University.

Capper, C.A. (1993) 'Rural community influences on effective school practices', *Journal of Educational Administration,* 31: 20–38.

Corno, L. (1995) 'Comments on Winne: analytic and systemic research are both needed', *Educational Psychologist,* 30: 201–206.

Dai, D.Y. and Sternberg, R.J. (2004) 'Beyond cognitivism: toward an integrated understanding of intellectual functioning and development', in D.Y. Dai and R.J. Sternberg (eds) *Motivation, Emotion and Cognition: Integrative Perspectives on Intellectual Development and Functioning* (pp. 3–40), Mahwah, NJ: Lawrence Erlbaum.

D'Amico, J., Matthes, W., Sankar, A., Merchant, B. and Zurita, M. (1996) 'Young voices from the rural Midwest', *Journal of Research in Rural Education,* 12: 142–149.

Deci, E.L. and Ryan, R.M. (2000) 'Self-determination theory and the facilitation of intrinsic motivation, social development, and well-being', *American Psychologist,* 55: 68–78.

Druckman, D. and Bjork, R.A. (1994) *Learning, Remembering, Believing: Enhancing Human Performance,* Washington, DC: National Academy Press.

Duke, D. (2004) *The Challenges of Educational Change,* New York: Pearson.

Dweck, C.S. (1996) 'Social motivation: goals and social-cognitive processes', in J. Juvonen and K. Wentzel (eds) *Social Motivation: Understanding Children's School Adjustment* (pp. 181–193), Cambridge, UK: Cambridge University Press.

Dweck, C.S., Mangels, J.A. and Good, C. (2004) 'Motivational effects on attention, cognition and performance', in D.Y. Dai and R.J. Sternberg (eds) *Motivation, Emotion and Cognition: Integrative Perspectives on Intellectual Development and Functioning* (pp. 41–56), Mahwah, NJ: Lawrence Erlbaum.

Fowler, Jr., W.J. and Walberg, H.J. (1991) 'School size, characteristics, and outcomes', *Educational Evaluation and Policy Analysis,* 13: 189–202.

Hardré, P.L. (2007) 'Preventing motivational dropout: a systemic analysis in four rural high schools', *Leadership and Policy in Schools,* 6: 231–265.

Hardré, P.L. (2008) 'Taking on the motivating challenge: rural high school teachers' perceptions and practice', *Teacher Education and Practice,* 21: 72–88.

Hardré, P.L. (2011) 'Motivating math learning for rural students: teacher and student perspectives', *Math Education Research Journal,* 23: 213-233.

Hardré, P.L., Chen, C.H., Huang, S.H., Chiang, C.T., Jen, F.L. and Warden, L. (2006) 'Influences on high school students' academic motivation in an Asian nation', *Asia-Pacific Journal of Education,* 26: 189–207.

Hardré, P.L., Garcia, F., Apamo, P., Mutheu, L. and Ndege, M. (2012) 'Information, affect and action: motivating hope toward reducing risk behaviors for HIV-AIDS in Kenya and Tanzania', *Sex Education,* 12: 1–24.

Hardré, P.L, Huang, S.H., Chen, C.H., Chiang, C.T., Jen, F.L. and Warden, L. (2006) 'High school teachers' motivational perceptions and strategies in an East Asian nation', *Asia-Pacific Journal of Teacher Education,* 34: 199–221.

Hardré, P.L. and Kollmann, S.L. (2013) 'Dynamics of instructional and perceptual factors in ID competence development', *Journal of Learning Design,* 6: 34–48.

Hardré, P.L., Ling, C., Shehab, R.L., Nanny, M., Nollert, M., Refai, H., Ramseyer, C., Herron, J. and Wollega, E.D. (2013) 'Teachers in an interdisciplinary learning community: engaging, integrating and strengthening K-12 education', *Journal of Teacher Education,* 64: 410–426. doi: 10.1177/0022487113496640

Hardré, P.L. and Reeve, J. (2003) 'A motivational model of rural students' intentions to persist in, versus drop out, of high school', *Journal of Educational Psychology,* 95: 347–356.

Hardré, P.L. and Siddique, Z. (2013) 'SUCCESS in engineering education: applying an ID motivational framework to promote engagement and innovation', *Journal of Applied Instructional Design,* 3: 7–14.

Hardré, P.L. and Sullivan, D.W. (2009) 'Motivating adolescents: teachers' beliefs, perceptions and classroom practices', *Teacher Development,* 13: 1–16.

Herzog, M.J. and Pittman, R.B. (1995) 'Home, family and community: ingredients in the rural education equation', *Phi Delta Kappan,* 77, 113-118.

Hubert, B., Ison, R., Sriskandarajah, N., Blackmore, C., Cerf, M., Avelange, I., Barbier, M. and Steyaert, P. (2012) 'Learning in European agricultural and rural networks: building a systemic research agenda', *Farming Systems Research into the 21st Century: The New Dynamic,* Dordrecht: Springer Science and Business Media. doi: 10.1007987-94-007-4503-2_9

Keyton, J. (2011) *Communication and Organizational Culture,* 2nd edn, Thousand Oaks, CA: Sage.

Kohn, A. (1993) *Punished by Rewards,* New York: Houghton-Mifflin.

Latham, G. P. (2007) *Work Motivation: History, Theory, Research, and Practice,* Thousand Oaks, CA: Sage.

Lee, M. and Tsai, C. (2005) 'Exploring high school students' and teachers' preferences toward the constructivist, internet-based learning environments in Taiwan', *Educational Studies,* 31: 149–167.

Ley, J., Nelson, S. and Beltyukova, S. (1996) 'Congruence of aspirations of rural youth with expectations held by parents and school staff', *Journal of Research in Rural Education,* 12: 133–141.

Liem, A.D., Lau, S. and Nie, Y. (2008) 'The role of self-efficacy, task value, and achievement goals in predicting learning strategies, task disengagement, peer relationship and English achievement outcome', *Contemporary Educational Psychology*, 33: 486–512.

Linnenbrink, E.A. and Pintrich, P.R. (2002) 'Achievement goal theory and affect: an asymmetrical bidirectional model', *Educational Psychologist*, 37: 69–78.

Linnenbrink, E.A. and Pintrich, P.R. (2004) 'Role of affect in cognitive processing in academic contexts', in D.Y. Dai and R.J. Sternberg (eds) *Motivation, Emotion and Cognition: Integrative Perspectives on Intellectual Development and Functioning* (pp. 57–88), Mahwah, NJ: Lawrence Erlbaum.

Maehr, M. (1989) 'Thoughts about motivation', in C. Ames and R. Ames (eds) *Research on Motivation in Education: Goals and Cognitions* (Vol. 3, pp. 299–267), New York: Academic Press.

Maehr, M.L. and Midgley, C. (1996) *Transforming School Culture*, Boulder, CO: Westview Press.

Oka, M. and Whiting, J. (2013) 'Bridging the clinician/researcher gap with systemic research: The case for process research, dyadic and sequential analysis', *Journal of Marital and Family Therapy*, 39: 17–27. doi: 10.1111/j.1752–0606.2012.00339.x

Ozer, E.M. and Bandura, A. (1990) Mechanisms governing empowerment effects: a self-efficacy analysis', *Journal of Personality and Social Psychology*, 58: 472–486.

Passi, B.K. and Mishra, S. (2004) 'Selecting research areas and research design approaches in distance education: process issues', *International Review of Research in Open and Distance Learning*, 5.

Pietsch, J., Walker, R. and Chapman, E. (2003) 'The relationship among self-concept, self efficacy and performance in mathematics during secondary school', *Journal of Educational Psychology*, 95: 589–603.

Pintrich, P.R. (2003) 'A motivational science perspective on the role of student motivation in learning and teaching contexts', *Journal of Educational Psychology*, 95: 667–686.

Quaglia, R.J. and Cobb, C.D. (1996) Toward a theory of student aspirations. *Journal of Research in Rural Education*, 12, 127–132.

Radel, R., Sarrazin, P., Legrain, P. and Wild, T. (2010) 'Social contagion of motivation between teacher and student: analyzing underlying processes', *Journal of Educational Psychology*, 102: 577–587.

Ryan, R.M. and Powelson, C. (1991) 'Autonomy and relatedness as fundamental to motivation and education', *Journal of Experimental Education*, 60: 49–66.

Salili, F., Chiu, C.Y. and Lai, S. (2001) 'The influence of cultures and context on students' motivation orientation and performance', in F. Salili, C.Y. Chiu and Y.Y. Hong (eds) *Student Motivation: The Culture and Context of Learning* (pp. 221–247), New York: Kluwer Academic/Plenum Publishers.

Salomon, G. (1991) 'Transcending the qualitative-quantitative debate: the analytic and systemic approaches to educational research', *Educational Researcher*, 20: 10–18.

Schoenfelder, E. (2006) 'Classroom effects on student motivation: goal structures, social relationships, and competence beliefs', *Journal of School Psychology*, 44: 331–349.

Schommer-Aikins, M. (2004) 'Explaining the epistemological belief system: introducing the embedded systemic model and coordinated research approach', *Educational Psychologist*, 39: 19–29.

Smith, E.R. and Conrey, F.R. (2009) 'The social context of cognition', in P. Robbins and M. Aydede (eds) *The Cambridge Handbook of Situated Cognition* (pp. 454–466), New York: Cambridge University Press.

Stones, E. (1986) 'Towards a systemic approach to research in teaching: the place of investigative pedagogy', *British Educational Research Journal*, 12: 167–181.

Wang, H.Y. and Guthrie, J.T. (2004) 'Modeling the effects of intrinsic motivation, extrinsic motivation, amount of reading and past reading achievement on text comprehension between U.S. and Chinese students', *Reading Research Quarterly*, 39: 162–186.

Weiner, B. (1990) 'History of motivational research in education', *Journal of Educational Psychology*, 82: 616–622.

Woodside, A.G., Caldwell, M. and Spurr, R. (2006) 'Advancing ecological systems theory in lifestyle, leisure, and travel research', *Journal of Travel Research*, 44: 259–272.

3

THE RELATIONSHIP BETWEEN SOCIAL CLASS AND STUDENTS' ACADEMIC ACHIEVEMENT GOALS

Three hypotheses

Nathan Berger and Jennifer Archer

Educational and social psychologists have done little to explore the relationship between social class and goal pursuit (Massey *et al.* 2008). In the case of achievement goals, considerable attention to the construct has produced more than 1,000 papers and theses since the early 1980s (Hulleman *et al.* 2010), but with little focus on social class. However, related research into intrinsic/extrinsic motivation suggests that achievement goals might differ along class lines (for example, Ginsburg and Bronstein 1993). Given that parental socioeconomic status has been consistently linked with student academic achievement throughout childhood and adolescence (Sirin 2005), lack of attention to social class in achievement goal research is surprising. It is timely that the achievement goal construct receives attention given mounting concern about the influence of social class on academic outcomes (Strenze 2007).

While examination of social class largely has been the preserve of sociologists, some integrative theories of social class have appeared in the psychology literature (e.g. see Kraus *et al.* 2012). These theories delineate how the material and social contexts in which individuals develop shape their psychological experience of their world (Kraus and Stephens 2012). There are synergies between this new theorizing and the extant literature on the antecedents of goal adoption. In this chapter, we extend the psychological understanding of how a person's cognition, behavior, and affect may be shaped by his or her social status. We argue that social class may influence goal adoption in academic contexts and thereby influence achievement. Given the scarcity of class-related achievement goal research, we instead draw upon theory to formulate three hypotheses that we hope will prompt scholarly discussion and encourage a new research agenda.

Before we review the achievement goal and social psychological literature, which in turn inform development of our hypotheses, we briefly address the specific conceptualization of social class used in this chapter.

Conceptualizing social class

What is social class? Kraus *et al.* (2011) argue that social class is one of the most pervasive sources of rank in social hierarchy. While it is generally agreed that social class determines access to materials, services and institutions (Snibbe and Markus 2005), researchers are far less clear about the basis by which social class position or rank is derived, with various definitions and conceptions used in the literature. Hout (2008) outlines three prevalent and potentially overlapping conceptualizations of social class: how people earn their money, how much money they have, and what they do with their money. Most researchers in their statistical and descriptive work prefer the first conceptualization, not least because it is readily operationalized as socioeconomic status (usually in some combination with measures of educational attainment and income). Indeed, socioeconomic status often is the preferred term because of the difficulty in quantifying more abstract notions such as social and cultural capital (Marks 1999).

However, Conley (2008) criticized purely structural and economic conceptions as largely neglecting the social psychological aspects of class. We suggest there is a need for a more sophisticated understanding of the influence of social structures on individual life courses, and this presents an opportunity for social psychological researchers. In this chapter, we use the term social class because it is the term used by Kraus *et al.* (2012) in their social cognitive theory of social class. We note that some readers may be uncomfortable with this approach. However, we argue that the term socioeconomic status, with its emphasis on income and occupation, does not encompass sufficiently the psychological orientations that we are exploring here.

Academic achievement goals

We now review the achievement goal literature and the development of the construct to date. As Elliot (2005) pointed out, the achievement goal construct was developed in the United States in separate and collaborative work by Ames (1984), Dweck (1986), and Nicholls (1984). While much of this early work was theoretical, research since then has applied the constructs to a variety of educational contexts, including universities and schools in the United States and elsewhere (e.g. Ames and Archer 1988; Elliot and Harackiewicz 1996; Mansfield 2010).

Goals were conceptualized as the purposes students have in pursuing a learning task; purposes which guide their cognition, behavior, and affect (Ames 1992). Two contrasting goal constructs were identified: students wanting either to develop competence or to demonstrate competence in achievement tasks (Ames 1992). Students adopting the former goal wanted to master a task and evaluated their competence based on self-referenced perceptions of growth. Students taking the latter goal orientation wanted to be seen to outperform others and judged their ability according to normative or comparative criteria (Ames 1992; Mansfield 2010). A variety of labels has been applied to these constructs. The terms used by Ames and Archer (1988) have become the most widely used: mastery goals for students approaching a task to develop competence and performance goals for students approaching a task to demonstrate competence to others (Elliot *et al.* 2011).

Early work tended to construe mastery and performance goals as dichotomous. However, Elliot and Harackiewicz (1996) incorporated the approach–avoid valence of other psychological theories to create a bifurcated performance goal, thus providing a trichotomous achievement goal construct. Elliot (1999) extended the distinction to mastery goals, creating a 2 × 2 achievement goal model. Given the somewhat protracted and piecemeal development of achievement goals, and despite Elliot's call for greater clarity (2005; Elliot *et al.* 2011), a snapshot of the literature at any particular point reveals a plurality of goal constructs. There are individual and disciplinary differences in the use of various achievement goal constructs (Elliot 2005). Nevertheless, achievement goals have become an important and widely used approach to understanding student motivation.

Research has linked mastery goals to deep processing of information, enjoyment of tasks, and persistence in the face of failure (Elliot 1999), while performance goals, particularly performance-avoid goals, have been shown to promote maladaptive strategies such as surface processing, cheating, procrastinating, disruptiveness, and negative affect about school (Patrick *et al.* 2011). Mastery goals originally were seen as more desirable than performance goals. However, it has been demonstrated that students can pursue multiple goals (Ames and Archer 1988). Performance-approach goals are not always undesirable, particularly in competitive settings where mastery goals also are encouraged (Harackiewicz *et al.* 2002; Midgley *et al.* 2001). Huang (2012), in a meta-analysis of 151 studies, found that approach goals (both mastery and performance) are associated with higher academic achievement, while avoid goals are associated with lower academic achievement.

In addition to mastery and performance goals, a third goal was identified in early goal research because a mastery orientation or a performance orientation did not describe the motivation, or lack of it, displayed by many students. For these students, the goal was not to achieve competence (mastery) or to demonstrate competence (performance) but to complete tasks with a minimum of effort. It was not a goal as such, more a way of categorizing the behavior of students who did not adopt achievement goals. Nicholls *et al.* (1985) called it an academic alienation goal. Meece *et al.* (1988) developed a similar goal labeled work avoidant that subsequently was used by Archer (1994), Dowson and McInerney (2001), and others.

The desire of the work-avoidant student to exert little effort can be distinguished from what may appear to be a similar desire in a performance-avoid student. For performance-avoid students, success with little apparent effort provides evidence of high ability, while failure with little effort does not provide evidence of low ability. For work-avoidant students, their interests and source of self-worth lie in areas other than schoolwork. Their proclaimed lack of effort and lack of interest in academic work are not hedges to conceal lack of ability.

In all, achievement goals have been shown to influence students' achievement-related behavior and thereby their academic achievement. Experimental and observational studies have also shown that the achievement goals people adopt are amenable to external influence. Goal orientations can be induced experimentally in laboratory settings (Elliot and Harackiewicz 1996) and can be induced by teachers in classrooms using situational cues (Ames and Archer 1988; Urdan *et al.* 1998). Children's perceptions of the goal orientations of their parents are significant predictors of their own goals. Perceived parental support of school positively predicts students' adoption of a mastery goal (Friedel *et al.* 2007; Wentzel 1998). Gutman (2006) found that parents who endorsed mastery goals had children with higher grade-point averages. These studies demonstrate links among external influences, students' goal adoption, and students' achievement.

According to Elliot and Church's (1997) hierarchical model of achievement goals, demographic variables such as social class, gender and race are among several antecedents of goal adoption. Research into achievement motivation, the theoretical precursor of the achievement goals, saw some exploration of socioeconomic status as a moderator variable (see Stein 1971; Willig *et al.* 1983). However, research into goals largely has been limited to exploring the effects of gender and race on goals (see Gutman 2006; Lepper *et al.* 2005). Kaplan and Maehr (1999) conducted one of the few studies into the possible relationship between socioeconomic status and achievement goals. The study found no significant difference in achievement goal orientations between socioeconomic status groups; however, the groups were defined by eligibility for free or reduced-cost school meals. This method of measuring a student's socioeconomic status has been criticized as a less than perfect proxy (Harwell and LeBeau 2010; Hobbs and Vignoles 2010). Further research is required using more sophisticated conceptualizations of social class to determine whether there exists a relationship between class and students' achievement goal orientations (Gonzalez *et al.* 2002).

The emerging psychology of social class

Psychologists largely have left examination of social class to sociologists (Lott 2002). This is surprising given the influence of socioecological contexts on people's cognition, behavior, and affect (Bronfenbrenner 1986). Kraus and Stephens (2012) argued that socioecological contexts are organized by social class because people tend to live, work, and associate with others of similar class backgrounds. The conditions of a particular social class socialize its members into common intrapsychic and interpersonal patterns (Kraus and Stephens 2012). We argue that social class can be categorized within Elliot's hierarchical model of achievement motivation both as a demographic variable and a neurophysiological predisposition (Elliot 1999; Elliot *et al.* 1997). Social class is an antecedent to goal adoption. While an integrated psychological understanding of social class is relatively new, it is sufficiently developed to allow us to hypothesize how an individual's class context may encourage or discourage the adoption of achievement goals. Before developing these hypotheses, we briefly review one psychological theory of social class.

The social cognitive theory of social class proposed by Kraus *et al.* (2012) characterizes people in lower classes as having what they call contextualistic social cognitive tendencies; that is, an 'external orientation to the environment motivated by managing external constraints, outside threats, and other individuals' (549). Because people in lower classes possess relatively few material and economic resources, they often experience situations over which they have little personal choice or control. The cumulative effect of this is to render them responsive to changes in the social environment and dependent on others for material, economic and social support (Kraus and Stephens 2012; Piff *et al.* 2012). People in lower classes, compared with people in higher classes, are more likely to attribute their behavior to external rather than internal forces. In addition, they are more likely to favor a conjoint model of agency in situations where decisions or choices are to be made (Stephens *et al.* 2011; Kraus *et al.* 2012). Preference for conjoint agency means they make decisions that favor similarity to and identification with others (Stephens *et al.* 2007).

Vulnerability to changes in the environment prompts heightened vigilance to potential threats (Kraus *et al.* 2012). One threat in educational contexts is a threat to social identity. To examine this, Stephens *et al.* (2012) conducted a quasi-experimental study with two groups of first-year university students from working class backgrounds. Each group was primed with a different message purported to be from the college dean: one emphasizing independent learning as the norm in college, and the other emphasizing interdependent processes as the norm. Compared with a group of middle-class students, working-class students in the independent earning condition performed worse on an academic task, whereas students in the interdependent condition performed just as well. If it is accepted that people in lower classes have a preference for working with others, a threat to social identity (in this case, the expectation that students will work independently) may have negative consequences.

In contrast to the tendency of people in lower classes to see their lives constrained by environmental factors, Kraus *et al.*'s (2012) social cognitive theory characterizes people in higher classes as having what they call a solipsistic social cognitive tendency. This represents 'an individualistic orientation to the environment motivated by internal states, goals, and emotions' (549). Possessing greater material and economic resources, people in higher classes are less vulnerable to changes in the environment, have greater means to exert personal control over situations, and are more likely to downplay external influences on their behavior. As a result, they are more independent, more self-focused, and more self-interested than people in lower classes (Kraus *et al.* 2012; Kraus and Stephens 2012; Piff *et al.* 2012). People in higher classes see themselves in charge of their lives: they have agentic self-concepts. This way of seeing the world is reflected in a disjoint model of agency in situations requiring decisions (Stephens *et al.* 2011, Kraus *et al.* 2012). That is, the choices made by people in higher classes display a preference for uniqueness or individuality (Stephens *et al.* 2007).

Stephens *et al.* (2007) demonstrated the individualistic mindset held by people in higher classes in a series of experimental studies. In one study, university students from middle-and working class backgrounds were asked to choose one pen from a group of five as a reward for participating in a survey. The pens were arranged to ensure participants were presented with two color options, with more of one color than the other. Students from middle class backgrounds were more likely to select a pen of the minority color, whereas students from working class backgrounds were more likely to select a pen of the majority color (Stephens *et al.* 2007). These choices were interpreted as symbolic of the middle-class desire to be unique and independent of others (Kraus and Stephens 2012). This finding aligns with other research that suggests higher-class people are more likely to take risks at the expense of others (Côté 2011; Côté *et al.* 2013). In the pen study, the students gained by diminishing the availability of the scarce resource. Following this reasoning, students from upper class backgrounds are likely to be comfortable working independently, taking cognitive risks in pursuit of academic outcomes, sometimes to the detriment of other students, and behaving in ways that make them stand out from others.

To recap, Kraus and colleagues (2012) argue that people in higher classes engage in self-focused thinking and behavior, and seek to change undesirable environments, while people in lower classes exhibit other-focused thinking and behavior and try to cope with undesirable environments rather than try to change them (Piff *et al.* 2012; Townsend *et al.* 2014). These 'solipsistic' (self-focused) and 'contextualistic' (other-focused) mindsets are somewhat analogous to mastery and performance goal orientations. However, it would be simplistic to argue that people in higher classes are oriented toward mastery goals while people in lower classes are oriented towards performance goals. There is considerable evidence for the adoption of multiple goals, and potential within both solipsistic and contextualistic mindsets for people to demonstrate adaptive and maladaptive behavior.

Using ideas generated by the social cognitive theory of social class, as well as ideas generated by ourselves and others, we propose three hypotheses about the way in which social class affects students' adoption of achievement goals.

Relationship between achievement goals and social class

The first hypothesis focuses on the extent to which students from lower class backgrounds, compared with students from upper class backgrounds, adopt achievement goals. The second and third hypotheses make connections between solipsism and mastery goals on the one hand, and contextualism and performance goals on the other. An additional factor in the third hypothesis is the adoption of multiple goals. Particular combinations of goals might help to explain differing levels of achievement; in particular, adaptive orientations by students from higher class backgrounds and maladaptive orientations by students from lower class backgrounds.

Hypothesis 1

In achievement situations, students from lower class backgrounds are less likely to endorse academic achievement goals, either mastery or performance, than students from higher class backgrounds.

We argue that students from lower class backgrounds, compared with students from upper class backgrounds, are more likely to adopt a work-avoidant goal than a mastery goal or a performance goal. For students like these, school essentially is a social venue, a place to meet up with friends, find romantic partners, battle with teachers, and engage in extracurricular activities. Many students do academic work only if threatened with punishment or loss of privileges even if teachers try to make the work interesting and relevant. They often do not take a long-term perspective of schooling

(Kauffman and Husman 2004); that is, they do not ask themselves how they will use what they are learning when they leave school. Given little academic engagement with schoolwork and a short time perspective, the achievement gap between high- and low- socioeconomic-status students is not surprising.

A small exploratory study by Berger (2013) provides some support for this hypothesis. Students from two schools completed a questionnaire about goals for schooling. One school was assessed as moderately disadvantaged (or low socioeconomic status) while the other was assessed as moderately advantaged (or high socioeconomic status) according to the schools' Index of Community Socio-Educational Advantage (ICSEA) scores reported on the Australian Government's My School website (www.myschool.edu.au). ICSEA is a comprehensive measure of the educational advantage of each Australian school and is calculated using data on parents' occupation, school education, and tertiary education, as well as indictors of the remoteness of the school and its percentage of students from Indigenous and non-English-language backgrounds. Scores assigned to schools range from 500 to 1300, where the lowest values represent schools with students from 'extremely disadvantaged back-grounds' and the highest values represent schools with students from 'very advantaged backgrounds' (Australian Curriculum, Assessment and Reporting Authority 2011: 2).

Students in the low-socioeconomic-status school endorsed fewer academic achievement goals, both mastery and performance, than students in the high-socioeconomic-status school. Interview data with some of these students (reported in Archer and Berger 2013) supported the questionnaire findings. Students in the high-socioeconomic-status school provided clear evidence of a mastery orientation towards at least some of their current studies and the intention to continue these stud-ies when they moved to university. There was no evidence of such an intention with students in the low-socioeconomic-status school. Students in the high-socioeconomic-status school also spoke about the benefits of the 'healthy' competition that existed within their cohort, an indication of a performance-approach orientation. Again, there was no evidence of such an orientation in the low-socioeconomic-status school. A mastery goal orientation coupled with a future time perspec-tive is exemplified in this quote from one of the students in the high-socioeconomic-status school: 'I like what Uni represents. Uni represents ongoing education, a furthering of your education, developing what we've already learnt here and, you know, furthering our minds' (Female, 17 years old).

It is useful here to refer to research using the intrinsic/extrinsic motivation construct. There are similarities between achievement goals and intrinsic and extrinsic motivation. Intrinsic motivation has overlap with a mastery achievement goal because the focus is the task itself. Extrinsic motivation is a broader construct covering a range of motivations that do not spring from the task itself. For example, a student may undertake a task because he will get paid to do it. There can be some overlap between extrinsic motivation and a performance goal. For example, a student may choose an easy task rather than a hard task because he does not want to look incompetent in front of his peers.

Ginsburg and Bronstein (1993: 1473) found that 'children from more economically disadvantaged environments . . . are rated by teachers as less intrinsically motivated, and are more dependent on external sources to guide and evaluate their academic behavior'. We consider the implications of dependence on external sources in Hypothesis 2. For Hypothesis 1, we argue that the lower intrinsic motivation of students from economically disadvantaged environments provides support for a lower mastery orientation in students with lower class backgrounds.

Hypothesis 2

In achievement situations, students from lower class backgrounds are more likely to endorse a performance-avoid goal than other achievement goals.

The contextualistic mindset encourages people in lower classes to orient towards others, to engage in behaviors which promote similarity to peers, to express an external locus of control, and to react to potential threats in the environment (Kraus *et al.* 2012; Stephens *et al.* 2007; Stephens *et al.* 2012). This mindset might encourage a performance goal because of the goal's focus on comparisons with others (Mansfield 2010). In addition, because people from lower class backgrounds are more vigilant to potential threats, and more concerned about their similarity with peers, we argue they may want to avoid unfavorable judgments about their academic ability relative to others. That is, they would be more likely to adopt a performance-avoid rather than performance-approach goal. A maladaptive combination of lower mastery goals and high performance-avoid goals might help to explain the lower academic achievement of students from lower class backgrounds.

To return to the statement from the Ginsburg and Bronstein study quoted in the previous section, 'children from more economically disadvantaged environments . . . are rated by teachers as less intrinsically motivated, and are more dependent on external sources to guide and evaluate their academic behavior' (1993: 1473). When students rely on teachers to evaluate their work because they lack the confidence to do it themselves, they may feel vulnerable to teachers' negative evaluations. There is an interesting link here to the self-regulation literature: one of the characteristics of students who are capable of high levels of self-regulation is their ability to evaluate their own work (Zimmerman and Schunk 2001).

Berger's (2013) data lend further preliminary support to the argument that students from lower class backgrounds are likely to endorse performance-avoid goals. Approach and avoidance items from Elliot and Murayama's (2008) AGQ-R were added to create dichotomous mastery (Cronbach $\alpha = 0.85$) and performance (Cronbach $\alpha = 0.85$) scales with six items each. A paired-samples *t*-test showed a significant difference between the mastery ($M = 19.65, SD = 5.77$) and performance ($M = 21.65, SD = 5.13$) scales for students attending a low socioeconomic school, $t(56) = -3.89$, $p < 0.001$. Low-socioeconomic-status students were more oriented towards performance than mastery goals. The previously discussed research on threats to social identity by Stephens *et al.* (2012) shows that environmental threats can encourage a performance-avoid goal which has a negative effect on achievement. Finally, Berger (2013) found the most highly endorsed performance goal at a low-socioeconomic-status school was performance-avoid.

Hypothesis 3

In achievement situations, students from higher class backgrounds are likely to have higher mastery goals and higher performance-approach goals than students from lower class backgrounds.

As described earlier, the self-focused mindset of people from higher classes generates a focus on their internal states, goals and emotions, and reduces a focus on external influences on their behavior (Kraus *et al.* 2012). In a similar manner, students adopting a mastery goal have 'self-established achievement standards' (Mansfield 2010) and evaluate their competence against these standards rather than the performance of others.

In addition to the arguments put forward to support Hypothesis 1, we provide more arguments about why students from higher class backgrounds are more likely to have higher mastery orientations than students from lower class backgrounds. Because students from higher class backgrounds want to be independent of others, and are more likely to take risks at others' expense (Côté 2011; Côté *et al.* 2013; Kraus *et al.* 2012), they are more likely to want to demonstrate superior ability relative to others. That is, they are more likely to adopt a performance-approach goal. The combination of high mastery and performance-approach goals is highly adaptive (Harackiewicz *et al.* 2000; Midgley *et al.* 2001) and may help to explain the consistently higher academic attainment of students from higher socioeconomic backgrounds (Strenze 2007).

Again, research using the intrinsic/extrinsic motivation construct would support the first part of the hypothesis that students from higher class backgrounds are likely to have higher mastery goals than students from lower class backgrounds: the more democratic parenting styles of people in higher classes develop in children an internal sense of control, higher intrinsic motivation, and less need for external regulation (Ginsburg and Bronstein 1993, Lepper *et al.* 2005). The study by Berger (2013) also provides empirical support for the second part of the hypothesis. Students at the high-socioeconomic-status school endorsed higher performance-approach goals than students at the low-socioeconomic-status school.

Future directions

In this chapter we have argued that researchers have paid little attention to the relationship between people's social class and their psychological experience of the world, in this case, their attitudes towards schooling (Lott 2002; Massey *et al.* 2008). While some research using intrinsic/extrinsic motivation has suggested differences along class lines (Ginsburg and Bronstein 1993; Stein 1971; Willig *et al.* 1983), research into achievement goals largely has been limited to exploring the effects of gender and race on students' goals. Given the scarcity of empirical studies linking achievement goals to social class, we used an emerging psychological theory of social class to formulate three hypotheses about goal adoption in different class contexts. The social cognitive theory of social class provides an explanation for how the material and social contexts in which people develop shape their thinking and behavior (Kraus *et al.* 2012, Kraus and Stephens 2012). We argue that social class is one antecedent to goal adoption. While we acknowledge the speculative and theoretical nature of the three hypotheses proposed in this chapter, we argue they provide useful directions for future research into the achievement goal construct.

The hierarchical achievement goal model presented by Elliot and Church (1997) provides a useful means for exploring the influence of social class on goal adoption. However, there are several conceptual and methodological challenges to overcome. Research has shown that parents can influence the achievement goal orientations of their children (Friedel *et al.* 2007; Gutman 2006; Wentzel 1998). We argue that parental influence represents a means by which social class differences may manifest in the classroom. While our hypotheses are focused at the school level, much of the research into the psychology of social class has used adults, typically undergraduate students. The research presents social class differences as the outcome of a developmental process. The use of university students has made possible much of the work; however, it has limited the research agenda to the variables that can be conveniently studied with undergraduate students (Henry 2008). Because of this, the developmental processes of socialization into the social cognitive aspects of a social class have not been examined.

While we argue the psychology of social class is a useful way of theorizing how social class might influence adoption of achievement goals, it is possible the hypotheses proposed here would manifest differently according to a student's developmental stage. That is, students' class-related attitudes and behaviors could be expected to strengthen as they move through school. Given growing concern about socioeconomic status-related gaps in educational attainment that widen through primary and secondary schooling, goal researchers could design longitudinal studies which are capable of examining developmental trajectories and the relative influence of social class on achievement-related goals over the course of schooling.

The second methodological challenge is related to the first. Psychologists often prefer to conduct experimental studies to make claims about causality. It is near impossible to conduct experimental studies in schools, for both practical and ethical reasons. A challenge posed by the three hypotheses is how to design suitable school-based studies. Is it possible to design research that can disentangle the many overlapping influences on student achievement? For example, we know already that teachers have expectations about social class that can lead them to treat students differently, creating self-fulfilling prophecies that produce different outcomes (Côté 2011; Stephens *et al.* 2013). On a practical level, moving from easily accessible university students and laboratories to school students and classrooms is expensive and time consuming, especially so if studies adopt a longitudinal design. If school-based research or longitudinal designs are not necessary for 'publishing in top-cited journals then there is little incentive to invest such expense' (Henry 2008: 53).

Finally, an impediment to investigation of social class from a psychological perspective is the sensitivity of the topic: 'research on social class is bound to be provocative, controversial, and infused with ideology' (Côté 2011: 64). Psychological researchers need to be careful not to reinforce, even unwittingly, cultural stereotypes of social classes. However, there is much to be gained from an increased understanding of the way in which people from different social classes make sense of and negotiate their worlds. We encourage social psychologists to accept the challenge.

References

Ames, C. (1984) 'Competitive, cooperative and individualistic goal structures: a cognitive-motivational analysis', in C. Ames and R. Ames (eds) *Research on Motivation in Education: Student Motivation* (Vol. 1, pp. 177–207), New York: Academic Press.

Ames, C. (1992) 'Classrooms: goals, structures, and student motivation', *Journal of Educational Psychology*, 84: 261–271.

Ames, C. and Archer, J. (1988) 'Achievement goals in the classroom: students' learning strategies and motivation processes', *Journal of Educational Psychology*, 80: 260–267.

Archer, J. (1994) 'Achievement goals as a measure of motivation in university students', *Contemporary Educational Psychology*, 19: 430–446.

Archer, J. and Berger, N. (2013) 'Exploring the motivations and future plans of senior students in a high and a low SES school', paper presented at the Australian Association for Research in Education Conference, Adelaide, South Australia.

Australian Curriculum, Assessment and Reporting Authority (2011, February) *My School Fact Sheet: About ICSEA*, Sydney: Author.

Berger, N. (2013) 'Exploring the motivational goals of Preliminary HSC students from divergent socioeconomic backgrounds', unpublished master's thesis, the University of Newcastle, Newcastle, New South Wales, Australia.

Bronfenbrenner, U. (1986) 'Ecology of the family as a context for human development: research perspectives', *Developmental Psychology*, 22: 723-742.

Conley, D. (2008) 'Reading class between the lines (of this volume): a reflection on why we should stick to folk concepts of social class', in A. Lareau and D. Conley (eds) *Social Class: How Does It Work?* (pp. 366–373), New York: Russell Sage Foundation.

Côté, S. (2011) 'How social class shapes thoughts and actions in organizations', *Research in Organizational Behavior*, 31: 43-71.

Côté, S., Piff, P.K. and Willer, R. (2013) 'For whom do the ends justify the means? Social class and utilitarian moral judgment', *Journal of Personality and Social Psychology*, 104: 490–503.

Dowson, M. and McInerney D.M. (2001) 'Psychological parameters of students' social and work avoidance goals: a qualitative investigation', *Journal of Educational Psychology*, 93: 35–42.

Dweck, C. (1986) 'Motivational process affects learning', *American Psychologist*, 41: 1040–1048.

Elliot, A. (1999) 'Approach and avoidance motivation and achievement goals', *Educational Psychologist*, 34: 169–189.

Elliot, A. (2005) 'A conceptual history of the achievement goal construct', in A. Elliot and C. Dweck (eds) *Handbook of Competence and Motivation* (pp. 52–72), New York: Guilford Press.

Elliot, A. and Church, M.A. (1997) 'A hierarchical model of approach and avoidance achievement motivation', *Journal of Personality and Social Psychology*, 72: 218–232.

Elliot, A. and Harackiewicz, J.M. (1996) 'Approach and avoidance achievement goals and intrinsic motivation: a mediational analysis', *Journal of Personality and Social Psychology*, 70: 461–475.

Elliot, A. and Murayama, K. (2008) 'On the measurement of achievement goals: critique, illustration, and application', *Journal of Educational Psychology*, 100: 613–628.

Elliot, A.J., Murayama, K. and Pekrun, R. (2011) 'A 3 × 2 achievement goal model', *Journal of Educational Psychology*, 103: 632–648.

Friedel, J.M., Cortina, K.S., Turner, J.C. and Midgley, C. (2007) 'Achievement goals, efficacy beliefs, and coping strategies in mathematics: the role of perceived parent and teacher goal emphases', *Contemporary Educational Psychology*, 32: 434–458.

Ginsburg, G.S. and Bronstein, P. (1993) 'Family factors related to children's intrinsic/extrinsic motivational orientation and academic performance', *Child Development*, 64: 1461–1474.

Gonzalez, A.R., Doan Holbein, M.F. and Quilter, S. (2002) 'High school students' goal orientations and their relationship to perceived parenting styles', *Contemporary Educational Psychology*, 27: 450–470.

Gutman, L.M. (2006) 'How student and parents goal orientations and classroom goal structures influence the math achievement of African Americans during the high school transition', *Contemporary Educational Psychology*, 31: 44–63.

Harackiewicz, J.M., Barron, K.E., Pintrich, P.R., Elliot, A.J. and Thrash, T.M. (2002) 'Revision of achievement goal theory: necessary and illuminating', *Journal of Educational Psychology*, 94: 638–645.

Harackiewicz, J.M., Barron, K.E., Tauer, J.M., Carter, S.M. and Elliot, A.J. (2000) 'Short-term and long-term consequences of achievement goals: predicting interest and performance over time', *Journal of Educational Psychology*, 92: 316–330.

Harwell, M. and LeBeau, B. (2010) 'Student eligibility for a free lunch as an SES measure in education research', *Educational Researcher*, 39: 120–131.

Henry, P.J. (2008) 'College sophomores in the laboratory redux: influences of a narrow data base on social psychology's view of the nature of prejudice', *Psychological Inquiry*, 19: 49–71.

Hobbs, G. and Vignoles, A. (2010) 'Is children's free school meal "eligibility" a good proxy for family income?', *British Educational Research Journal*, 36: 73–690.

Hout, M. (2008) 'How class works: objective and subjective aspects of class since the 1970s', in A. Lareau and D. Conley (eds) *Social Class: How Does It Work?* (pp. 25–64), New York: Russell Sage Foundation.

Huang, C. (2012) 'Discriminant and criterion-related validity of achievement goals in predicting academic achievement: a meta-analysis', *Journal of Educational Psychology*, 104: 48–73.

Hulleman, C.S., Schrager, S.M., Bodmann, S.M. and Harackiewicz, J.M. (2010) 'A meta-analytic review of achievement goal measures: different labels for the same constructs or different constructs with similar labels?', *Psychological Bulletin*, 136: 422–449.

Kaplan, A. and Maehr, M. (1999) 'Achievement goals and student well-being', *Contemporary Educational Psychology*, 24: 330–358.

Kauffman, D.F. and Husman, J. (2004) 'Effects of time perspective on student motivation: introduction to a special issue', *Educational Psychology Review*, 16: 1–7.

Kraus, M., Piff, P. and Keltner, D. (2011) 'Social class as culture: the convergence of resources and rank in the social realm', *Current Directions in Psychological Science*, 20: 246–250.

Kraus, M., Piff, P., Mendoza-Denton, P.R., Rheinschmidt, M. and Keltner, D. (2012) 'Social class, solipsism, and contextualism: how the rich are different from the poor', *Psychological Review*, 119: 546–572.

Kraus, M. and Stephens, N. (2012) 'A road map for an emerging psychology of social class', *Social and Personality Psychology Compass*, 6: 642–656.

Lepper, M.R., Corpus, J.H. and Iyengar, S.S. (2005) 'Intrinsic and extrinsic motivational orientations in the classroom: age differences and academic correlates', *Journal of Educational Psychology*, 97: 184–196.

Lott, B. (2002) 'Cognitive and behavioral distancing from the poor', *American Psychologist*, 57: 100–110.

Mansfield, C. (2010) 'Motivating adolescents: goals for Australian students in secondary schools', *Australian Journal of Educational and Developmental Psychology*, 10: 44–55.

Marks, G.N. (1999) 'The measurement of socioeconomic status and social class in the LSAY project', Technical Paper No. 14, LSAY Technical Reports, Australian Council for Educational Research. Available from http://research.acer.edu.au/lsay_technical/28

Massey, E.K., Gebhardt, W.A. and Garnefski, N. (2008) 'Adolescent goal content and pursuit: a review of the literature from the past 16 years', *Developmental Review*, 28: 421–460.

Meece, J.L., Blumenfeld, P.C. and Hoyle, R.K. (1988) 'Students' goal orientations and cognitive engagement in classroom activities', *Journal of Educational Psychology*, 80: 514–523.

Midgley, C., Kaplan, A. and Middleton, M. (2001) 'Performance-approach goals: good for what, for whom, under what circumstances, and at what cost?', *Journal of Educational Psychology*, 93: 77–86.

Nicholls, J. (1984) 'Achievement motivation: conceptions of ability, subjective experience, task choice, and performance', *Psychological Review*, 91: 328–346.

Nicholls, J., Patashnick, M. and Nolen, S.B. (1985) 'Adolescents' theories of education', *Journal of Educational Psychology*, 77: 683–692.

Patrick, H., Kaplan, A. and Ryan, A. (2011) 'Positive classroom motivational environments: convergence between mastery goal structure and classroom social climate', *Journal of Educational Psychology*, 103: 367–382.

Piff, P., Martinez, A., Stancato, D., Kraus, M. and Keltner, D. (2012) 'Class, chaos, and the construction of community', *Journal of Personality and Social Psychology*, 103: 949–962.

Sirin, S.R. (2005) 'Socioeconomic status and academic achievement: a meta-analytic review of research', *Review of Educational Research*, 75: 417–453.

Snibbe, A.C. and Markus, H. (2005) 'You can't always get what you want: educational attainment, agency, and choice', *Journal of Personality and Social Psychology*, 88: 703–720.

Stein, A.H. (1971) 'The effects of sex-role standards for achievement and sex-role preference on three determinants of achievement motivation', *Developmental Psychology*, 4: 219–231.

Stephens, N., Fryberg, S. and Markus, H. (2011) 'When choice does not equal freedom: a sociocultural analysis of agency in working-class American contexts', *Social Psychological and Personality Science*, 2: 22–41.

Stephens, N., Fryberg, S., Markus, H., Johnson, C. and Covarrubias, R. (2012) 'Unseen disadvantage: how American universities' focus on independence undermines the academic performance of first-generation college students', *Journal of Personality and Social Psychology*, 102: 1178–1197.

Stephens, N., Markus, H. and Phillips, L.T. (2013) 'Social class culture cycles: how three gateway contexts shape selves and fuel inequality', *Annual Review of Psychology*, 65: 611–634.

Stephens, N., Markus, H. and Townsend, S. (2007) 'Choice as an act of meaning: the case of social class', *Journal of Personality and Social Psychology*, 93: 814–830.

Strenze, T. (2007) 'Intelligence and socioeconomic success: a meta-analytic review of longitudinal research', *Intelligence*, 35: 401–426.

Townsend, S., Eliezer, D., Major, B. and Mendes, W. (2014) 'Influencing the world versus adjusting to constraints: social class moderates responses to discrimination', *Social Psychological and Personality Science*, 5: 226–234.

Urdan, T., Midgley, C. and Anderman, E.M. (1998) 'The role of classroom goal structure on students' use of self-handicapping strategies', *American Educational Research Journal*, 35: 101–122.

Wentzel, K. (1998) 'Social relationships and motivation in middle school: the role of parents, teachers, and peers', *Journal of Educational Psychology*, 90: 202–209.

Willig, A.C., Harnisch, D.L., Hill, K.T. and Maehr, M.L. (1983) 'Sociocultural and educational correlates of success-failure attributions and evaluation anxiety in the school setting for Black, Hispanic, and Anglo children', *American Educational Research Journal*, 20: 385–410.

Zimmerman, B. and Schunk, D. (eds) (2001) *Self-Regulated Learning and Academic Achievement: Theoretical Perspectives* (2nd edn), Mahwah, NJ: Lawrence Erlbaum.

4

MOTIVATED LEARNING

The relationship between student needs and attitudes

*Jasmine Taylor, Helena D. Cooper-Thomas,
and Elizabeth R. Peterson*

Students' motivation is complex and multiply determined, affecting the nature and depth of students' involvement with their learning. One core element in this motivational complexity is students' needs. Arising from the demands of learning, these needs may be basic, held by virtue of students' human nature, or contextual, existing as a result of the specific tasks and environments that students find themselves in as learners. The satisfaction, or deprivation, of students' needs has important ramifications for students' motivation, achievement, development, and general well-being. It is therefore appropriate that this handbook include a chapter considering the meaning and effect of needs for students.

This chapter addresses not only student needs, but also the relationship between students' needs and attitudes. Attitudes are psychological dispositions towards an object that are evaluative in nature. Attitudes are valenced (positive to negative), indicate an individual's position with respect to attitude content, and are strong predictors of attitude-relevant behavior (Ajzen and Fishbein 2005). As such, the relationship between student needs and attitudes, as well as other outcomes, should be of interest to students, educators, and researchers alike.

Consequently, this chapter starts by considering major need theories and their implications for students. Specifically, we focus on need theories relevant to motivation, including self-determination theory; social needs such as belonging, and one's intellectual and social integration into like-minded communities; as well as the safety, meaning, and availability necessary for engagement. Next, we consider learners' attitudes and the nature of need–attitude relationships more generally. Here we draw heavily from the organizational 'fit' literature, which includes the most developed and extensive research on need–attitude relationships, and therefore contributes substantially to the consideration of needs and attitudes for students. We bring the chapter to a close by considering measurement issues, as well as challenges and further directions for research.

Research background and major empirical findings

One of the most prominent contributions to our understanding of human motivational needs is self-determination theory (Deci and Ryan 2012). Self-determination theory proposes that individuals have three fundamental psychological needs – autonomy, competence, and relatedness. Environments that fulfill these needs facilitate intrinsically motivated actors who identify with their actions and experience vitality in their personal development. Self-determination theory rests on the concept of human beings as creatures who learn not simply because they are reinforced or constrained to, but who have 'evolved to be inherently active, intrinsically motivated, and oriented toward developing naturally through integrative processes' (Deci and Ryan 2012: 417).

On the basis of this understanding of human nature, Deci, Ryan, and colleagues initially distinguished between intrinsic and extrinsic motivation. Intrinsic motivation arises from within an individual, and relates to activities that are experienced as valuable and interesting in their own right. For example, a student may spend time reading about situational moderators of gene expression because they are intellectually drawn to the topic and wish to explore it, independent of whether that reading was associated with any formal learning task. Intrinsic motivation is an innately valuable human state, but also has educational relevance – being associated with deeper learning, better performance, and greater persistence by students (Reeve *et al.* 2008).

Deci and Ryan's work has established that intrinsic motivation requires two factors to flourish: a sense of autonomy, of being able to choose how one will think and act; and competence, the ability to follow through on what one wishes to do. Without one or both of these conditions, intrinsic motivation diminishes or disappears completely. As learning is inherently related to motivation, autonomy and competence can therefore be seen as learning needs, as well as motivational ones.

One effect worth noting here is that external rewards have been repeatedly found to decrease, rather than increase, intrinsic motivation (e.g. Deci *et al.* 1999). This effect is most substantial when the reward is contingent on task completion (associated with a decreased sense of autonomy and competence) or performance (associated with a decreased sense of autonomy). In addition, while lowered levels of autonomy signal a shift to more externally controlled motivation, a sufficiently lowered sense of competence is able to elicit amotivation, where individuals are not motivated to perform the task at all. This has important implications for those seeking to motivate students, or for teachers who wish to encourage individuals in what is intrinsically interesting to them.

In contrast to an internal impetus, extrinsically motivated actions arise from external, second-order considerations. These activities are undertaken not for their own sake, but to achieve other ends. For example, a student may not be particularly interested in essay work, but may nonetheless be motivated to complete essay-based assignments to develop their writing skill, refine their views on the essay topic, or achieve good grades.

Extrinsic motivation can have a variety of origins. However, when it comes to individuals' performance and well-being, not all of these are equal. In particular, the degree to which individuals identify with the reason for their action greatly affects the motivational experience and characteristic outcomes. Specifically, when people's actions directly reflect their 'core values and practices' (integrated motivation; Deci and Ryan 2012: 421) or they otherwise believe in the value of what they are doing (identified motivation), these are experienced as more autonomous, and are associated with greater task involvement, depth of learning, and personal well-being. For example, a student who is deeply concerned with justice may consider their law class project focusing on underserved areas as expressing their values, and resourcing them for the work they wish to be involved in throughout their life. That is, they may experience the project as being integrated with who they are (integrated motivation). Similarly, someone who is interested in mental processes may identify with the work involved in their dissertation research on the way the brain visualizes objects (identified motivation). Educators should therefore pay attention to ways in which learners can come to identify with their studies and the rationale for engaging with learning materials.

The idea that people's identities are important for their motivated action is evident throughout the literature on engagement. For example, Kahn (1992) argued that engagement was characterized by individuals being psychologically present within their work, such that their personal skills, abilities, and characteristics could be drawn on without hesitation in their employment roles. While mental activity such as self-regulation is generally considered to consume psychological resources and energy, fully autonomous action has been found to be psychologically energizing (Deci and Ryan 2012) and, similarly, engagement with work can aid recovery (Sonnentag *et al.* 2012). In addition to positively directing action, this psychological energy is associated with greater personal well-being (Ryan and Frederick 1997).

However, extrinsic motivation can also be rooted in felt obligation or constraint (introjected motivation). In this situation, behavior is more associated with what one feels one *should* do, rather than what one wants to do. Whereas integrated and identified action is associated with positive outcomes for learning and well-being, introjected motivation is substantively associated with the negative outcomes of externally controlled (nonautonomous) behavior. For example, a student who gets the impression that they need to complete a reading log to avoid disappointing others, but has no other convincing need or motivator for the activity, would be more likely to participate at a surface level and experience lower task enjoyment, reading comprehension, and well-being than a classmate who found the task intrinsically motivating or had a personal appreciation of the value of keeping the log.

In short, for tasks that originate externally, two things appear to make a substantive difference for individuals' motivation experience and outcomes; first, the degree of autonomy that is experienced in an action, and second, the associated integration of an individual's behavior with one's self. Educators and the parents of younger students play an important role in supporting their students' internalization and integration of their actions, and the positive outcomes with which this is associated. Effective strategies for giving students a sense of choice in an educational environment include providing reasons the action is valuable, introducing and working on tasks in nonpressuring ways, acknowledging the reality of students' negative and apathetic feelings about a task, and interacting in caring and responsive ways to support students' sense of interpersonal relatedness (Reeve *et al.* 2008).

While autonomy and competence are sufficient to fuel intrinsic motivation, social relationships and settings are also crucial to foster and sustain extrinsic motivation. This is because extrinsically motivated tasks arise in a social order and take their value from the purpose that social order bestows on them. For example, students may come to value assignments because these are acknowledged as a fair means of assessing learning, stimulate students to pursue learning and assimilate knowledge, and contribute to their final course grade or degree qualification. The extent to which students buy into, or feel related to, the social structure in which they learn will affect how completely they take on the logic of the social structure as their own, such as recognizing the value of assignments in the example above. This is known as relatedness. Relatedness refers to the state of possessing warm and supportive human ties, where individuals are meaningfully socially connected to the people or communities which structure the task. Relatedness has been found to reliably function as a third motivational need, and Deci and Ryan found it necessary in addition to autonomy and competence to account for changes in the establishment and continuation of extrinsic motivation (Deci and Ryan 2012).

Within educational environments, intrinsic motivation is recognized as the most autonomous and desirable motivation. However, in practice, most educational tasks do not emanate first and foremost from students' desire to learn a particular topic in the particular way that it is being taught. As a result, students' sense of relatedness should be seen as crucial for stimulating their motivation. Educators may foster this by creating warm relational conditions and socially compelling learning environments that generate roles or tasks that the learner (a) wants to work within and (b) believes implicates them to act and behave as a motivated learner.

The importance of feeling personally implicated is recognized by Schlenker *et al.* (2013) in their triangle model of university student engagement (where engagement was measured as responsibility, commitment, and determination to achieve academic goals). They proposed and found evidence that a sense of personal obligation is important for engendering engagement in addition to prescription (task) clarity and personal control (or, the combination of felt competence and autonomy). As one would expect given the importance of relatedness for fostering extrinsic motivation, personal obligation was considered to arise under multiple conditions related to one's self-identity and also other-imposed identities. These included personal self-concept, social roles, and verbal and enacted claims to these concepts and roles, all of which are shaped by the social relationships and settings that foster or hinder relatedness.

The effect of relatedness may go beyond implicating students in their educational tasks, however. Relatedness is conceptually similar to belonging, an established human need. Belonging consists of:

> a pervasive drive to form and maintain at least a minimum quantity of lasting, positive, and significant interpersonal relationships [characterized by] frequent, affectively pleasant interactions with a few other people . . . in the context of a temporally stable and enduring framework of affective concern for the other's welfare.
>
> *(Baumeister and Leary 1995: 497)*

Belonging is positively associated with human health, psychological well-being, and levels of life and relationship adjustment – including moderating the effect of other sources of stress (Baumeister and Leary 1995). Its effects are evident in the positive implications of need satisfaction, as well as the acute and chronic effects of need deprivation.

Research from self-determination theory and related fields has confirmed the importance of social relationships (i.e. relatedness, belonging, and similar concepts) to human motivation. Consequently, social relationships are also likely to be a key factor in motivating learners. The importance of social relations has been acknowledged for a long time, with the sociologist Durkheim (1897/1951) noting this in his book *Suicide*. In this work, he proposed that humans have a fundamental need to be integrated socially and intellectually within human communities. Durkheim's account of social integration is akin to that of Baumeister and Leary's concept of belonging (1995), comprising warm interactions based in ongoing interpersonal relationships characterized by value and care. However, Durkheim suggested that humans have an additional need to be in relationships with at least some similar-minded people, with whom they can express, and be affirmed in, their ideas and perspectives. Without either intellectual or social integration, he claimed that humans experience great psycho-social distress – to the extent that it could bring an individual to commit suicide.

Durkheim's work on social and intellectual integration has been applied to both organizational settings and higher education (e.g. Pascarella and Terenzini 2005; Tinto 1993). For example, in tertiary environments, Tinto proposed that individuals' levels of integration into the social and academic (intellectual) structures of an institution, or membership within any part of the environment which provided academic or social structure for the individual in question, would predict both an individual's commitment to the educational institution as a whole, and to the goal of acquiring the qualifications with which his or her enrolment at the institution was associated. In contrast, those who did not manage to integrate into at least one of these spheres were theorized to demonstrate lower commitment and be more likely to leave the program or institution.

Whether it is called relatedness, belonging, or integration, individuals' need for social and intellectual connection with others is fundamental. Durkheim's account is sobering, as it highlights the possibilities that accompany ultimate need deprivation. However, in doing so, this work also underscores the value of creating space for students' perspectives and wider life experiences. Educational settings often comprise people with disparate histories, perspectives and approaches to the world. Social contexts are crucial for signalling who 'fits' and who does not (Cooper-Thomas and Wright 2013). Consequently, if all individuals are to thrive in these environments, they need to feel welcome and accepted for who they are, and able to bring their frameworks for understanding into learning spaces for consideration and strengthening. The effect of failing to create responsive spaces – either in particular contexts, or systematically over time – is evident in the lower levels of achievement and other educational outcomes of marginalized minority students, such as New Zealand Māori (Bishop 2005). For educators, providing an inclusive social context involves paying particular attention to the content and structure of the material, and the way these represent, misrepresent, or are silent with respect to students' persons and communities.

Physical and emotional safety is not only important for ensuring students' well-being; it is also fundamental for facilitating engagement (Kahn 1990). When individuals feel secure, they are able to draw on the resources of their whole person, such as prior knowledge, experiences, emotions, and skills, while also being open with their questions and limitations. For learners, feeling safe enables them to inhabit their personal identities, as well as their identity as a learner, rather than having to pick one over the other. Consequently, secure learners do not feel the need to either withdraw from educational activities or keep their 'learning' disconnected from other elements of their life.

While feeling safe is necessary, it is not sufficient for engagement. From his observations of what facilitated engagement in different work settings, Kahn (1990) concluded that individuals also need to feel that the activity is meaningful and that they have the physical, mental, and emotional resources (i.e. availability) necessary to engage. In educational settings, meaning is the primary motivator. Whether meaning originates internally from a students' personal interest in the topic or activity (intrinsic motivation, as discussed above), or from the way the educational task is tied to an individual's identity (integrated or identified motivation), connection between the learner and the learning content is fundamental. Successful educators create contexts where students can recognize the link between the content or direction of the material and their current or future (aspirational) selves.

In terms of availability, learners who have competing claims on their time, attention, or personal capacities are compromised in their ability give educational activities the attention they need. For example, students who are worried about their home life may find that they are unable to concentrate on class activities. Educators and institutions who prioritize identifying and resolving these conflicts, or helping their students to do so, will remove barriers for student engagement.

Attitudes

Given the nature of human needs – as opposed to wants – the condition of students' needs being or failing to be met should have a substantial effect on their outcomes. Among other things, need satisfaction and deprivation might reasonably be expected to relate to individuals' attitudes, such as their perceptions of well-being; behaviors, such as their proactive pursuit of learning opportunities; and their actual context-relevant performance. We focus on attitudes here.

As noted above, attitudes are psychological dispositions held towards an object, based on an individual's evaluation of that object. Attitudes are ubiquitous as outcome constructs within social science research and are regularly used to assess stakeholders' experience with education. This is in part due to the ease with which attitudes can be assessed through self-report, and the way that attitudes are believed to be indicative of more objective outcomes such as applied effort, academic performance, and retention. Attitudes do indeed predispose people to act in ways that are consistent with the content and valence of that attitude (Erdogan *et al.* 2012; Ajzen and Fishbein 2005). For example, a students' attitude towards chemistry experiments is likely to affect their interest and depth of participation in these.

Attitudes can be held at many different levels – towards a specific action, subtask, idea, group, or environment as a whole – and are most strongly related to individual behavior when the behavior and attitude are matched on content and specificity (Ajzen and Fishbein 2005). For example, an attitude towards essay writing in general may predict an individual's involvement in essay-writing tasks across the ten essays set in a year, but for any one essay, that general-level attitude may not predict the particular degree of involvement for that particular essay. The relationship between more general attitudes and behavior is seen most clearly when a number of potentially attitude-relevant behaviors is considered, rather than a single target behavior (ibid.). Moreover, greater experience, involvement, and interaction with a specific issue or topic will lead to a stronger relationship between the general attitude towards that issue and relevant behaviors (ibid.).

While a wide diversity of attitudes has attracted interest, among the most common attitudes in the research literature are satisfaction, commitment, and the intent to stay in or leave a setting. Satisfaction is a positive sense of contentment and satiation. It is a valued human state, associated with higher levels of performance, more creative thinking, and lowered tendencies to withdraw from or act counterproductively at work (Judge and Kammeyer-Muller 2011). Commitment is an attitude that reflects individuals' willingness to be and remain involved with a task, environment, person, or group. While commitment can originate from a variety of causes, it is most predictive of positive behavioral outcomes when it is grounded in an individual's emotional attachment to that to which they are committed (affective commitment; Meyer and Allen 1991). In a similar way, attitudes towards staying or leaving reflect people's desires and intentions to remain in or leave a setting. These are the strongest single predictor of leaving behavior, but do not account for all of the variation (Hom *et al.* 2012).

Need–attitude relationship

While attitudes have been considered in many domains, organizational literature has been the most explicit about assessing the need–attitude relationship. This has been particularly true of organizational fit research, which focuses on the process and outcomes of compatibility or incompatibility, or 'fit' and 'misfit', between people and their working environments. Many elements affect individuals' compatibility with their environment; however, person and environmental needs are a key contributor. Consequently, while developed to understand individuals as workers and not specifically as students, organizational fit research can be useful in informing the development of theory about, and examination of, individuals' learning needs.

Compatibility between a person and their environment can occur at many levels, and holds different relationships with outcomes depending on the level and type of (mis)fit being assessed. Specifically, fit is typically conceptualized as supplementary or complementary. Both supplementary and complementary fit are positively related to valued attitudes, behavior, and performance, both for the individual and environment in which they are based. In educational settings, we might therefore expect that meeting individuals' needs by either supplementary or complementary means will have a similar positive effect on students' attitudes, behavior, and performance.

Supplementary fit occurs where a person and environment are similar in some important respect, with similar goals and values being the most common compatibilities assessed. Goal- and value-based supplementary fit possess strong resemblance to people's need for intellectual integration – or interaction with and acceptance by those who share their views of life and the world (Durkheim 1897/1951). To the extent that similarities foster warm interactional environments characterized by care, they may also cultivate a sense of belonging (Baumeister and Leary 1995) and relatedness (Deci and Ryan 2012), and function more generally to meet individuals' needs in this regard.

A meta-analysis of organizational fit research indicated that holding similar values to an organization was moderately strongly associated with higher job satisfaction, organizational commitment, and lower intent to quit, while sharing organizational goals was moderately positively related to job satisfaction (Kristof-Brown *et al.* 2005). We might therefore expect that students who find their values reflected in their education may be more satisfied, committed, and less likely to be looking for ways to 'exit' the environment – whether by being absent or by reducing effort. In a similar way, educational environments that effectively establish shared learning goals may foster more satisfied learners.

Supplementary fit has also been examined with respect to personality; however, it is not clear that similarity rather than difference should *always* be more beneficial within a working environment (or any other task-based, cooperative setting, such as school; van Knippenberg and Schippers 2007). For example, having a team comprising a mix of introverted and extroverted people may result in greater idea strength and productivity than a team of all extroverts. In a well-managed classroom environment, diverse personalities may lead to more complex, robust discussions and learning opportunities in the same way that diverse histories and personal characteristics can add to a learning environment. However, this relies on the classroom teacher being both willing and able to incorporate different approaches into class activities, and in ways that ensure these differences do not negatively affect students' sense of belongingness. It is perhaps unsurprising, then, that Kristof-Brown and colleagues (2005) found a positive, but small, average effect size of .07 of personality-based supplementary fit on an organization's performance.

Complementary fit, in contrast, refers to the compatibility that occurs when a person or environment directly functions to meet the other's needs. Complementary fit can work in two directions. 'Need–supply' fit refers to when individual's specific work-related needs are met ('supplied') by their work environment, such as providing the degree of autonomy or support that an individual needs to operate well – emotionally, mentally, behaviorally, or in terms of productive output (Kristof-Brown and Guay 2011). In a similar way, a student who works best within unstructured environments where their creativity is given free reign may find they learn best in a Montessori school where their need for autonomy is supplied.

The degree to which individuals' needs are met in their jobs has been moderately strongly related to job satisfaction (positively), intent to quit (negatively), moderately related to organizational commitment (positively), strain (negatively), and somewhat related to job performance (Kristof-Brown *et al.* 2005). Similarly, we might expect that when students have their educational and other needs met in learning environments, they will feel more satisfied and committed, will perform better, and will feel less strain and a lower desire to leave the educational setting.

The second kind of complementary, or 'demands–abilities', fit is also said to occur where a person's abilities meets the needs or 'demands' of the work (or task) environment (Kristof-Brown and Guay 2011). For example, a student in a computing class who translates a line of computer code would meet the environmental task need ('demand') for this computer program analysis. While the focus of 'demands–abilities' fit is on environmental needs, a good match between a task need and personal capacity is beneficial for individuals.

Being well matched to one's job demands has been moderately positively associated with job satisfaction, organizational commitment, somewhat with job performance, and moderately negatively with intent to quit and with strain (Kristof-Brown *et al.* 2005). We might therefore expect that learning activities aimed neither too far above nor too far below individuals' competencies would be less negatively stressful for students, and associated with greater satisfaction, commitment, performance, and willing participation. This expectation aligns with evidence that individuals who encounter both optimal challenge and personal competence in a task experience 'flow', where the task holds their full attention and elicits maximum cognitive resources (Csikszentmihalyi 2000).

Overall, then, meeting individuals' needs has a positive effect on core attitudes towards the relevant task and environment. Interestingly, research on 'fit' with a work environment suggests that having needs met directly (needs–supplies fit) has a stronger influence on individuals' attitudes than indirect need satisfaction, such as that achieved through supplementary or 'demands–abilities' fit. Similarly, we might expect that, in an educational environment, more direct need fulfillment will lead to better attitudinal outcomes for learners as well.

Measuring need–attitude relationships:
Approaches, issues and insights

When it comes to research, our contribution towards knowledge can only be as robust as our conceptualization, research design, and analytic approach. The following section covers some key considerations for the need–attitude researcher, and what we know as a result of measurement approaches used to date.

First, it is important to match need and attitude context. Within organizational research, individuals' degree of fit with their job, organization, or peer group, for example, consistently demonstrates the strongest relationships with job, organization, or peer group-related attitudes respectively (Kristof-Brown *et al.* 2005). The relationship between attitudes and associated behaviors works the same way – specific attitudes strongly predict attitude-specific behavior, while general attitudes predict general types of behavior well (but may predict a specific attitude of the general type poorly; Ajzen and Fishbein 2005). Similar patterns may well exist within educational settings. For example, feeling secure in a classroom environment may have implications for attitudes towards a teacher, peers, or class activities, as well as activities in other classes, other educators, and with learning more generally; however, we might expect that the strongest relationship would exist with respect to the attitudes students hold about that classroom in particular.

Second, the relationship between a need, the degree to which it is met, and an attitude may not be linear. While early organizational fit theory allowed for nonlinear relationships between fit components, quantitative measurement has traditionally fallen into two types – direct measures of an individual's perceived fit, where people answer questions directly about their degree of fit; and indirect measures, where person and environment values on the relevant content dimensions are assessed separately and compared[1] (Jansen and Kristof-Brown 2006). In practice, indirect measures assume a direct correspondence between person and environment as the most appropriate indication of fit, and the relationship between both direct and indirect measures and associated outcomes have been primarily assessed within linear, regression equations. Recently, however, nonlinear (polynomial regression) methods have become more popular, allowing for more nuanced testing of need–attitude relationships. Briefly, for readers who are interested, polynomial regression allows for person, environment, person*environment (interaction), person^2, and environment^2 (quadratic) variables to be assessed simultaneously, creating a much more detailed picture of the person–environment dynamic. For readers interested in theoretical progress in person–environment fit conceptualization and measurement, Edwards (2008) provides an excellent review.

Many interesting insights have come out of polynomial analyses. First, the strength of relationship between need fulfillment and attitudes (among other outcomes) appears to differ depending on the level of need being supplied. More technically, the correspondence between need and supply has a stronger relationship with an individual's outcomes (e.g. satisfaction) when the person and environment values are high than when person and environment values are low (Kristof-Brown and Guay 2011; Kristof-Brown *et al.* 2005). If this was found to apply to students, for example, we might find that a match between the level of autonomy needed and supplied to a student in a particular context had a greater positive effect on the student's satisfaction, well-being, and achievement if they needed and were supplied with a large amount of autonomy, than if the student needed and was supplied with very little autonomy.

Second, the effect of needs not being met appears to be asymmetric as well. That is, in general, the effect of the environment being deficient for an individual has a greater negative effect on outcomes than the environment supplying more than what is desired. This appears to support a threshold, or deficiency, model of need–attitude (and other outcome) relationships, where individuals' needs represent a baseline, with additional amounts of desired environmental characteristics having comparatively little effect once that baseline is met, at least for those variables and environments studied. If this was also found to be true for students, for example, we may find that the experience of having insufficient structure has a stronger, negative effect on students' understanding and satisfaction than having too much structure.

Third, sometimes what individuals need, and what an environment is like, may be more important than the way the environment corresponds with those needs. A meta-analysis of organizational fit research using polynomial techniques showed that simple person and environment measures themselves are the strongest predictors of outcomes, rather than their interaction or quadratic functions (Yang *et al.* 2008). However, the meta-analysis did suggest that the relationship between needs and the degree to which they were met is still important. This was found to be particularly true (1) for predicting contextual performance and job attitudes, compared to task performance and (2) for predicting these in immediate task environments compared to other settings (Yang *et al.* 2008). This suggests that need fulfillment may be of particular relevance for determining attitudes, and that individuals' immediate task environment may be the most influential context for these relationships. In other words, a classroom, tutorial room, or similar may be a more important context for determining whether students' needs are met or not than the wider institutional context.

Finally, the direction of need–attitude relationships should not be assumed. While theory and data analytic models tend to place need fulfillment as predictors of attitudes, it is possible that the affective quality of positive attitudes may result in context-relevant needs being met, in addition to being an outcome of met needs. Cross-lagged analyses on university student need and attitude data which we, the authors, conducted (Taylor *et al.* 2013) provided some support for this scenario. Specifically, our analysis found that students' social and academic needs both predicted later satisfaction and commitment and were themselves largely predicted by earlier levels of these attitudes.

Challenges and future directions

Student needs are not yet well understood. We have a sense of their importance for students' attitudes, as well as students' well-being, motivation, growth, and achievement. We know that supporting students' experience of autonomy, competence, and relatedness are important; that they require physical, emotional, and psychological safety; that availability and meaning are important; and that experiencing a deep sense of belonging to and within a learning community both intellectually and socially is deeply beneficial. What we do not have, however, is a more detailed and nuanced picture of student needs – which needs exist, who they exist for, why particular needs are important, when they are relevant, which outcomes they relate to, under what conditions these previous things are true and, importantly, how to facilitate these needs being met for relevant students in timely and effective ways.

Moving forward, we could benefit from research that examines the detailed what, who, why, when, and how of need relationships and outcomes for students. As well as treating these elements independently, research should examine how they interact as systems. This integrative approach will hopefully enable blind spots to be detected and avoided; for example, where 'positive' effects of apparent need fulfillment at one time point, or in one domain, have negative repercussions in others. Simply because it is easily overlooked, particular attention should also be paid to the influence of time, and the way this influences individual, contextual, and other (e.g. educational policy) changes. Keeping a greater perspective in mind will allow us to form a more coherent, and therefore useful, picture of the influence and importance of individuals' needs as learners across their lives.

Note

1 'Subjective' fit measurement involves person and environment assessments taken by the individual in question, while 'objective' measurements involve the environment and occasionally the person component being measured by objective data or someone external to the employee themselves.

References

Ajzen, I. and Fishbein, M. (2005) 'The influence of attitudes on behavior', in D. Albarracín, B. Johnson and M. Zanna (eds) *The Handbook of Attitudes* (pp. 173-222), Mahwah, NJ: Lawrence Erlbaum Associates.

Baumeister, R.F. and Leary, M.R. (1995) 'The need to belong: desire for interpersonal attachments as a fundamental human motivation', *Psychological Bulletin,* 117: 497–529.

Bishop, R. (2005) 'Pathologizing the lived experiences of the indigenous Māori people of Aotearoa/ New Zealand', in C.M. Shields, R. Bishop and A.E. Mazawi (eds) *Pathologizing Practices: The Impact of Deficit Thinking on Education* (pp. 55–84), New York: Peter Lang.

Cooper-Thomas, H.D. and Wright, S. (2013) 'Person–environment misfit: the neglected role of social context', *Journal of Managerial Psychology,* 28: 21–37.

Csikszentmihalyi, M. (2000) *Beyond Boredom and Anxiety*, San Francisco, CA: Jossey-Bass.

Deci, E.L., Koestner, R. and Ryan, R.M. (1999) 'A meta-analytic review of experiments examining the effects of extrinsic rewards on intrinsic motivation', *Psychological Bulletin,* 125: 627–668.

Deci, E.L. and Ryan, R.M. (2012) 'Self-determination theory', in P.A.M. Van Lange, A.W. Kruglanski and E.T. Higgins (eds) *Handbook of Theories of Social Psychology* (Vol. 1, pp. 416–437), Thousand Oaks, CA: Sage.

Durkheim, E. (1951) *Suicide*, trans J.A. Spaulding and G. Simpson, Glencoe: The Free Press. (Originally published as *Le suicide: Etude de Sociologie*, Paris, Felix Alcan, 1987.)

Edwards, J.R. (2008) 'Person–environment fit in organizations: an assessment of theoretical progress', *The Academy of Management Annals,* 2: 167–230.

Erdogan, B., Bauer, T.N., Truxillo, D.M. and Mansfield, L.R. (2012) 'Whistle while you work: a review of the life satisfaction literature', *Journal of Management,* 38: 1038–1083.

Hom, P.W., Mitchell, T.R., Lee, T.W. and Griffeth, R.W. (2012) 'Reviewing employee turnover: focussing on proximal withdrawal states and an expanded criterion', *Psychological Bulletin,* 138: 831–858.

Jansen, K.J. and Kristof-Brown, A. (2006) 'Toward a multidimensional theory of person–environment fit', *Journal of Managerial Issues,* 18: 193-212.

Judge, T.A. and Kammeyer-Muller, J.D. (2011) 'Happiness as a societal value', *Academy of Management Perspectives,* 25: 30–41.

Kahn, W.A. (1990) 'Psychological conditions of personal engagement and disengagement at work', *Academy of Management Journal,* 33: 692–724.

Kahn, W.A. (1992) 'To be fully there: psychological presence at work', *Human Relations,* 45: 321–349.

Kristof-Brown, A. and Guay, R.P. (2011) 'Person–environment fit', in S. Zedeck (ed.) *Handbook of Industrial/ Organizational Psychology* (Vol. 3, pp. 3–50), Washington DC: American Psychological Association.

Kristof-Brown, A.L., Zimmerman, R.D. and Johnson, E.C. (2005) 'Consequences of individuals' fit at work: a meta-analysis of person–job, person–organization, person–group and person–supervisor fit', *Personnel Psychology,* 58: 281–342.

Meyer, J.P. and Allen, N.J. (1991) 'A three-component conceptualisation of organizational commitment', *Human Resource Management Review,* 1: 61–89.

Pascarella, E.T. and Terenzini, P.T. (2005) *How College Affects Students: A Third Decade of Research* (Vol. 2), San Francisco, CA: Jossey-Bass.

Reeve, J., Ryan, R., Deci, E.L. and Jang, H. (2008) 'Understanding and promoting autonomous self-regulation: a self-determination theory perspective', in D.H. Schunk and B.J. Zimmerman (eds) *Motivation and Self-regulated Learning: Theory, Research, and Applications* (pp. 223–244), New York: Lawrence Erlbaum.

Ryan, R.M. and Frederick, C. (1997) 'On energy, personality, and health: subjective vitality as a dynamic reflection of well-being', *Journal of Personality,* 65: 529–565.

Schlenker, B.R., Schlenker, P.A. and Schlenker, K.A. (2013) 'Antecedents of academic engagement and the implications for college grades', *Learning and Individual Differences,* 27: 75–81.

Sonnetag, S., Mojza, E.J., Demerouti, E. and Bakker, A.B. (2012) 'Reciprocal relations between recovering and work engagement: the moderating role of job stressors', *Journal of Applied Psychology,* 97: 842–853.

Taylor, J., Cooper-Thomas, H. and Peterson, E. (2013) 'Which comes first? Predicting satisfaction, commitment and need fulfilment among university students', paper presented at EARLI (European Association for Research on Learning and Instruction bi-annual conference), Munich, Germany.

Tinto, V. (1993) *Leaving College: Rethinking the Causes and Cures of Student Attrition*, 2nd edn, Chicago: The University of Chicago Press.

van Knippenberg, D. and Schippers, M.C. (2007) 'Work group diversity', *Annual Review of Psychology*, 58: 515–541.

Yang, L., Levine, E., Smith, M., Ispas, D. and Rossi, M.E. (2008) 'Person–environment fit or person plus environment: A meta-analysis of studies using polynomial regression analysis', *Human Resource Management Review*, 18: 311–321.

5

THE ROLE OF PARENTS IN STUDENTS' MOTIVATIONAL BELIEFS AND VALUES

Rebecca Lazarides, Judith Harackiewicz, Elizabeth Canning,
Laura Pesu, and Jaana Viljaranta

Motivational beliefs and values are salient determinants of performance, persistence, and behavioral choices (e.g. Eccles 2005; Eccles 2009; Eccles and Wigfield 2002). According to Eccles and colleagues' expectancy-value theory (Eccles *et al.* 1983), competence beliefs are motivational beliefs that refer to individuals' evaluations of their competence in different areas (Eccles and Wigfield 2002: 118). Positive estimates of one's own ability and competence are crucial for producing successful learning processes (e.g. Marsh *et al.* 2005; Schunk and Pajares 2005). Other crucial predictors of individuals' achievement and choice behavior are subjective task values, which are defined as 'the quality of the task that contributes to the increasing or decreasing probability that an individual will select it . . .' (Eccles 2005: 109). Students' interest in tasks or activities (intrinsic value/interest) and students' perceptions of a task as useful and relevant (utility value) are such values that influence domain-specific attitudes and career intentions and are therefore addressed in this chapter (e.g. Harackiewicz *et al.* 2008, 2012; Nagy *et al.* 2006; Watt *et al.* 2012). There are two other components of subjective task value – students' personal importance of doing well on the task (attainment value) and the negative aspects of engaging in the task, such as performance anxiety or lost opportunities (cost) (Eccles *et al.* 1998). Given the high importance of individuals' competence beliefs and values, it is noticeable that both competence beliefs (e.g. Jacobs *et al.* 2002; Wigfield *et al.* 1997) and values (e.g. Fredricks and Eccles 2002; Watt 2004) decline significantly from childhood to adolescence.

Parents tend to play a decisive role in the motivational development of children and adolescents and shape children's early achievement-related orientations and perceptions (e.g. Eccles and Jacobs 1986; Frome and Eccles 1998; Pomerantz *et al.* 2005; Pekrun 2001; Simpkins *et al.* 2015; Wild and Lorenz 2009) as well as children's development of competence beliefs and values across domains (e.g. Eccles 1993; Eccles *et al.* 1998; Fredricks and Eccles 2002). As the decline in motivation is particularly steep in mathematics and science (e.g. Wigfield *et al.* 2006), empirical work has often focused on the role that parents play in students' motivational development in these two subjects (e.g. Eccles and Jacobs 1986; Harackiewicz *et al.* 2012; Jacobs 1991). Recent motivational theories have drawn on a few specific parent-related factors that are central for children's motivation. Eccles and colleagues (Eccles *et al.* 1998: 1054), for example, proposed the importance of parents' general beliefs and behaviors (e.g. gender-role stereotypes, efficacy beliefs, parenting styles) and child-specific beliefs (e.g. ability-related expectations, perceptions of a child's interest) as predictors of children's competence beliefs and values. Self-determination theory (Deci and Ryan 1985) highlights the importance of parental behaviors that support students' feelings of competence, autonomy, and relatedness. Self-determination theory suggests that behaviors that satisfy these three intrinsic psychological needs facilitate the development of students' intrinsic motivation (e.g. Deci *et al.* 1991; Ryan and Deci 2000), which is theoretically related to the constructs of interest and intrinsic value (see Eccles 2005: 114).

In this chapter, we provide an overview of the roles that parents play in shaping children's and adolescents' competence beliefs and values, particularly in the domains of mathematics and science. Parents are important for their children's development in many spheres of life (e.g. Wild and Lorenz 2009; Youniss 1982). However, given the thematic focus of this book, we concentrate in this chapter on parents' influences on students' school-, classroom-, and learning-related competence beliefs and values. Thereby each section of this chapter focuses on how parents influence the following specific parts of the Eccles and colleagues expectancy-value model (Eccles *et al.* 1983): competence beliefs, utility value, and intrinsic value. Thus we do not focus on attainment value and cost. This is due to a lack of research on how parents affect adolescents' attainment value and cost. The chapter aims to combine research and educational practice by reviewing empirical findings but also by focusing on interventions that target parents' beliefs and behaviors. In the first section, we outline effects of parental beliefs on children's mathematics-related self-concept of ability. In the second section, we present an intervention study that facilitates parents' utility beliefs and related behaviors in science and mathematics and thereby enhances students' perceptions of the utility value of these disciplines. In the third section, we present empirical results on the effects of parents' beliefs and behaviors on their children's interest and intrinsic value in mathematics and science.

Parental beliefs and children's mathematics-related self-concept

Previous literature has strongly suggested that students' achievement-related beliefs play an important role in academic environments by directing behavior and effort in learning situations (e.g. Atkinson 1964; Bandura 1986, 1997; Eccles *et al.* 1983; Wigfield *et al.* 2006). There have been several ways to define these achievement-related beliefs, such as 'perceived competence' (Harter 1982) and 'self-concept of ability' (e.g. Nurmi and Aunola 2005). Despite the different definitions used, all of them, in general, refer to students' own understanding of their abilities and competencies in academic situations (for a review, see Bong and Skaalvik 2003). More precisely, task-specific achievement-related beliefs refer to students' perceptions and understanding of their abilities in a particular subject area, such as mathematics or reading (Wigfield and Eccles 2000). Although a large number of different constructs have been defined, different theories seem to share the same basic idea about the role of these beliefs and expectancies in educational settings: students who believe that they are capable and that they can and will do well on a task are much more likely to be motivated than students who do not believe in their abilities and expect to fail on a certain task (Bandura 1997; Eccles *et al.* 1998; Pintrich and Schunk 2002). In this section, we use the term self-concept of ability when referring to subject-specific ability beliefs.

Parental effects on children' ability self-concept in Eccles' expectancy-value theory

The expectancy-value model of achievement motivation developed by Eccles and colleagues (Eccles *et al.* 1983; Wigfield and Eccles 1992, 2000) offers a broad framework for understanding how children's self-concept of ability develops in a wider social and cultural context. In general, children's self-concepts are shaped by various kinds of interactions with other people (see

Dermitzaki and Efklides 2000). For example, experiences in early learning situations (see Bong and Skaalvik 2003) and comparisons with classmates and the skill level in the classroom (Marsh 1987; Skaalvik and Skaalvik 2002; Trautwein *et al.* 2009) have an effect on the development of self-concept of ability.

However, Eccles' expectancy-value model (Eccles *et al.* 1983) suggests that parents, teachers, and other important adults play a significant role in the formation of children's self-concept of ability. Research on parental beliefs has shown that positive beliefs in children's skills and success have a positive effect on children's subject-specific self-concept of ability (Eccles Parsons *et al.* 1982; Lau and Pun 1999; MacGrath and Repetti 2000; Phillips 1987), and this effect may be stronger, even, than the effect of children's previous success in academic situations. Thus, parental beliefs have been reported to be positively related to children's self-concept of mathematics ability (Eccles Parsons *et al.* 1982; Jacobs 1991). And the other way around, in the realm of mathematics, it has been shown that parents who think their children will not succeed in mathematics and believe that this subject is difficult for their children have children whose mathematics-related self-concept is particularly low (Eccles *et al.* 1982).

According to the expectancy-value model (Eccles *et al.* 1983), the links between parental beliefs and youths' achievement-related behaviors can be explained by multiple mechanisms (Eccles *et al.* 1983; Simpkins *et al.* 2012). The model proposes that parents' beliefs predict parents' behaviors, which then predict youths' motivational beliefs (Eccles *et al.* 1998). There is some empirical support for this assumption, at least in the case of mathematics (Simpkins *et al.* 2012). However, only a few empirical studies have tried to identify these parental behaviors by determining which parents' beliefs are transferred to their children. The expectancy-value model (Eccles *et al.* 1983) proposes that role modeling, communicating expectations, and providing differential experiences are examples of these kinds of behaviors (Eccles *et al.* 1983; Simpkins *et al.* 2012). In addition to parental behaviors, parents' perceptions might affect children's self-concept of ability by acting as a mediator between children's grades and their self-perceptions. According to Frome and Eccles (1998), parents' perceptions of their children's success influence children's interpretations of how their grades represent their abilities.

Parental beliefs, mathematics self-concept, and age of children

Although the role of parental beliefs in the formation of children's self-concept of mathematics ability is widely acknowledged, it is likely that the role of parental beliefs with respect to students' self-concept varies with age (e.g. Gniewosz *et al.* 2012). Furthermore, recent studies have suggested that the influence of parents on children's self-concept of ability might be small compared with the influence of teachers, at least during the early years of children's school careers (Pesu *et al.* 2014). According to Pesu and colleagues, it seems that the role of teachers' beliefs is emphasized in relation to children's ability self-concepts. They found that teachers' beliefs had a stronger effect on first graders' self-concept of mathematics ability than parents' beliefs did. Moreover, Spinath and Spinath (2005) discovered that the influence of teacher evaluations on children's general ability self-perceptions increases, whereas the influence of parents' perceptions decreases in Grades 1–4 in elementary school.

These results are not surprising as previous research has shown that feedback given by teachers, such as grades, is a good predictor of students' self-concept of ability (Wigfield and Eccles 2000). Eccles (1993) pointed out that parents rely heavily on objective feedback (e.g. school grades) when forming their impressions of their children's abilities. It might be that during the early school years, parents are forming their impressions of their children's skill levels on the basis of feedback gathered from teachers and school grades. Thus, the early school years may provide an important period for the development of not only children's self-concepts of ability but also parents' belief systems concerning their children. This could be one explanation for recent results that have emphasized the role of teachers in addition to the role of parents in the development of children's self-concept of ability.

However, there are also studies that have shown that the role of parental beliefs increases during the later school years. Gniewosz *et al.* (2012), for example, found that the effects of maternal competence beliefs on students' mathematics-related self-concept of ability increased during the secondary school transition, whereas the effect of grades decreased. However, the effect of maternal competence beliefs decreased and the effect of grades increased after the school transition. Gniewosz *et al.* pointed out that because of the instability created by school transitions (such as changes in the school and classroom environments), students instead obtain information about their abilities through a source that is stable and valid, such as through parental competence appraisals.

Future directions

Although the role of parental beliefs in the formation of children's mathematics self-concept is widely recognized, more research on this topic is needed. One important limitation of previous research is that it is mainly mothers' beliefs that have been studied, whereas fathers' beliefs and their effect on children's self-concepts have not been studied as much. However, it may be the case that parental beliefs play a different role (Frome and Eccles 1998; MacGrath and Repetti 2000). Another understudied area is how the nature of parent–child relationships moderates parental effects on children. Lane (2012), for example, highlighted the idea that children are more likely to adopt the attitudes of adults whom they like or with whom they strongly identify. Therefore, we assume that the quality of parent–child relationships may have an effect on the effects of parental beliefs on children's self-concept of mathematics ability. As a conclusion, the perceptions children have of themselves direct their behavior and choices (see e.g. Jacobs 1991). Thus, parents may play an important role in widening or narrowing the road that children see ahead of them. All possible information about the ways in which parents contribute to children's futures is therefore more than welcome.

Parents' beliefs and students' perceptions of subject utility value

According to Eccles' expectancy-value model, parents play a pivotal role in influencing their children's motivational beliefs (Jacobs and Eccles 2000). A large body of survey research and longitudinal studies support this idea, showing that parents' beliefs in educational domains are closely linked to the beliefs and behaviors of their children and that parental involvement is a strong predictor of students' attitudes, values, and academic choices (Jodl *et al.* 2001; Simpkins *et al.* 2012). These studies have suggested that parents may be able to influence their children's perceptions of the utility of different school topics.

Harackiewicz *et al.* (2012) tested an intervention intended to influence students' perceptions of utility value by intervening with parents in a randomized field study. Specifically, they tested whether an intervention targeted at parents could promote parents' and students' perceptions of utility value and subsequently increase mathematics and science course enrollment. Their utility-value intervention consisted of two brochures mailed to parents and a website that explained the utility value of various STEM (science, engineering, technology, mathematics) topics. The intervention was targeted entirely at parents, with the intention that they would then communicate the utility-value information to their teens. This represents an indirect utility-value intervention in which parents were given utility-value information, were encouraged to communicate that information to their teens, and were guided on how to do so. Participants in the randomized experiment were 188 (88 girls, 100 boys) adolescents from 108 different high schools and their parents. The first brochure, entitled 'Making

Connections: Helping Your Teen Find Value in School' was mailed to parents in October of the tenth-grade year. The brochure provided information about the utility of mathematics and science in daily life and for various careers (e.g. how physics and chemistry help us understand how cell phones work and how video game designers use physics to make design decisions). In addition to the utility-value information, the brochure included guidance for parents about how to talk to their children about the connections between mathematics, science, and their children's lives. For instance, the brochure suggested that instead of telling teens how relevant math and science is to their lives and their futures, parents should help teens to discover the connections that are most meaningful to them. The brochure also explained the normalcy of teen resistance to such conversations and suggested utilizing other trusted resources such as mentors, teachers, and coaches.

The second brochure, entitled 'Making Connections: Helping Your Teen with the Choices Ahead' was sent to each parent separately in January of the eleventh-grade year and included a password-protected website entitled 'Choices Ahead'. As with the first brochure, the second one emphasized the connections between mathematics and science to peoples' lives as well as the importance of conveying these connections to students. The second brochure was different from the first in that it placed an increased emphasis on the relevance of STEM courses for preparing students for college and future careers.

The website contained clickable links to a number of different resources about STEM fields and careers in addition to interesting science sites that described the relevance of STEM topics to every-day life. The website also highlighted excerpts from interviews with current college students who expressed the importance of their high-school mathematics and science courses for their college preparation. Parents were also given the option of e-mailing specific links from the website to their teens. Parents in the control group did not receive either of the brochures or access to the website.

Parents reported their perceptions of the utility of mathematics and science for their teens (e.g. 'Math and science are important for my teen's life') at two separate points: once when the students were in the ninth grade (prior to the intervention) and once when the students were in the eleventh grade (after the intervention materials were issued). After the twelfth grade, students and parents each completed a survey assessing the extent to which parents and teens had engaged in conversations about the importance of mathematics and science, and teens provided self-reports of their perceptions of the utility value of mathematics and science. The main hypothesis was that students whose parents had received the intervention would enroll in more advanced mathematics and science courses.

The results of this relatively simple intervention were dramatic. Harackiewicz *et al.* (2012) found that students whose parents received the intervention enrolled in significantly more mathematics and science courses in the eleventh and twelfth grades than teens whose parents were in the control group. The difference was equivalent to nearly an extra semester of mathematics or science over a two-year period. For most students, these extra courses consisted of advanced elective courses. They also found, consistent with previous findings (Jodl *et al.* 2001; Simpkins *et al.* 2006), that parental education was a significant predictor of STEM course-taking in high school. The two effects were independent, and the size of the intervention effect ($\beta = .16$) was comparable to the effect of parental education ($\beta = .17$).

Additional analyses indicated that the intervention significantly increased mothers' perceptions of STEM utility value for their teens as well as students' reports of conversations with parents about the importance of mathematics and science. Thus, the intervention was effective at changing parental values and was also effective in promoting conversations with teens about the value of STEM disciplines. Process analyses indicated that the direct effects of the intervention on mothers' perceptions of STEM utility value and students' reports of conversations with their parents were associated with students' perceptions of STEM utility value after graduation. Overall, these results suggest that an intervention that targeted parents had direct effects on their teens' STEM course-taking in high school and had indirect effects on their teens' perceptions of STEM utility value.

Future directions

The results of this randomized intervention study suggest that parents, a largely untapped resource, can and should be viewed as powerful instruments in the promotion of students' STEM-related motivation. However, more research is needed to understand the dynamics involved in parent–teen conversations and their effect on course-taking. For instance, parent–teen relationship quality, parental background in mathematics and science, and gender (both parental gender and teen gender) could each influence the quality and content of parent–teen conversations. The intervention effects reported here might be stronger for some groups than other, and it will be important to explore such moderators in future research. Overall, however, the findings are promising, given that a relatively minimal intervention had such dramatic effects. Indeed, these results suggest that parents are willing and able to influence their children's motivation in STEM courses – they just need the support and resources to do so.

Parent beliefs and students' interest in mathematics and science

Interest and intrinsic value

Academic interest is viewed as a motivational factor that contributes significantly to students' domain-specific competence beliefs (e.g. Denissen *et al.* 2007; Marsh *et al.* 2005), achievement (e.g. Fisher *et al.* 2012; Koeller *et al.* 2001), mastery goals (Harackiewicz *et al.* 2002, 2008; Hidi and Harackiewicz 2000; Hulleman *et al.* 2008), course choice in high school, and career interests (e.g. Nagy *et al.* 2006; Watt *et al.* 2012). Theoretically, interest is characterized as an interactive relation between a person and particular objects in his or her environment (Hidi and Harackiewicz 2000: 152; Krapp 2007: 8) and it includes affective and cognitive components (e.g. Krapp 1999: 26). Interest research distinguishes two interacting types of interest, namely, situational interest and individual interest (Hidi 1990; Krapp *et al.* 1992). Situational interest has been conceptualized as a psychological state that is suddenly evoked by features of the (learning) environment (Hidi 1990: 551). Individual interest has been delineated as a slowly developing and relatively stable affective–evaluative orientation toward certain domains (Schiefele 2009: 198) that develops from situational interest through four phases (Hidi and Renninger 2006: 113). In their four-phase model of interest development, Hidi and Renninger (2006) conceptualized situational interest as a basis for an emerging individual interest. Thereby the early phases of interest development are characterized as consisting of focused attention and positive feelings. The later phases consist of positive feelings as well as both stored value and knowledge (Hidi and Renninger 2006: 114). In Eccles and colleagues' expectancy-value theory, the concept of interest is related to intrinsic value, which is described as the enjoyment one gains or expects to gain while engaging in a task (Eccles 2005: 111). Thus 'interest' in expectancy-value theory as 'situational interest' in the four-phase model refers to positive feelings while engaging in a task as a main characteristic of interest. Another approach is the person–object theory of interest of Krapp (1999), which also distinguishes between situational interest and individual interest and which conceptualizes interest as consisting of values and feelings. Krapp (1999) relates interest to the concept of intrinsic motivation (Deci and Ryan 1985) by emphasizing its self-intentional and intrinsic character. This means that an interest-related goal is compatible with one's preferred values and ideals of the growing self (Krapp 1999: 16).

Although the conceptualization of interest differs across theoretical approaches, it is typically assumed that socializers' attitudes and behaviors are important determinants of students' interest (e.g. Hidi and Renninger 2006; Jacobs and Eccles 2000; Krapp 1999). Hidi and Renninger (2006: 112) state that 'without support from others, any phase of interest development can become dormant, regress to a previous phase, or disappear altogether . . .'. Referring to the theory of self-determination (Deci and Ryan 1985), Krapp (1999) assumes that learning environments facilitate interest if they foster feelings of competence, autonomy, and social relatedness. Based on these theoretical assumptions, the next sections focus on parents' behaviors, expectancies, and beliefs as predictors of students' interest, perceptions of intrinsic value, and intrinsic motivation in mathematics and science.

Parents' beliefs and students' interest

Eccles *et al.* (1998: 1057f) outlined several dimensions of parental beliefs that are assumed to be important for children's interest and motivation: (1) causal attributions for children's performance; (2) perceptions of task difficulty for their children; (3) expectations of their children's ability and success; (4) value beliefs regarding particular tasks and activities; (5) achievement standards across domains; and (6) beliefs about external barriers to success and strategies that can be applied to overcome these barriers. In this section, we focus on children-specific parental beliefs about their childrens' abilities (3) as well as on parental beliefs about difficulty and value beliefs (2, 4) of certain tasks and domains. These beliefs have been shown to be related to students' interest. Tenenbaum and Leaper (2003), for example, demonstrated that mothers' perceptions of science as difficult for their children led to low levels of interest in science when their children were in secondary school. Mothers' high ratings of science as an interesting domain were associated with high levels of interest in science in secondary school. No such effect occurred with regard to fathers' beliefs.

There is also empirical evidence that mothers' expectations about their children's mathematics ability are significantly related to children's own interest in mathematics (Eccles 1993). Lazarides and Ittel (2013) showed that when secondary students perceived that their parents valued and enjoyed mathematics, this significantly predicted mathematics interest, but only for girls. Thus, some research has led to the conclusion that the effect of parental values on students' interest might depend on parents' and students' gender. Furthermore, empirical findings have prompted the idea that parental values affect differently students' level of interest in early secondary school and their interest development. Frenzel *et al.* (2010), for example, found that when parents valued mathematics as an important and interesting domain, this contributed to students' level of interest at the ages of 5–9 but did not prevent the decline in interest during secondary school.

Concerning the mechanisms through which parents' beliefs and values have an effect on their children's values, in their model of parent socialization, Eccles and colleagues (1998) explain that parents transfer their values to their children through their behaviors. In contrast to these assumptions, cross-sectional studies have not found significant relations between parenting practices (e.g. involvement in school) and children's values (Jodl *et al.* 2001; Noack 2004). However, longitudinal research has shown that parents' child- and mathematics-specific value beliefs directly influence their subsequent child-specific behavior and, through this, subsequently affect their children's values (Gniewosz and Noack 2012a, b; Simpkins *et al.* 2012). Simpkins and colleagues (2012) furthermore showed that youths' valuing of mathematics in turn predicted their subsequent activities and mathematics courses in high school. Given that parents' behaviors play an important role in shaping whether their children value mathematics, the next section points out several parental behaviors that are associated with students' interest, intrinsic motivation, and task values.

Parents' behaviors and students' interest

Jacobs and Bleeker (2004: 7) outlined several ways by which parents may transfer their beliefs and values about a specific domain to their children: (1) by playing the role of 'interpreters of reality' through the messages they provide regarding their perceptions of their children's experiences; (2) by providing particular opportunities such as toys, games, or activities; (3) by being involved in activities with their children; and (4) by acting as role models by engaging in valued activities.

In line with these assumptions, research has provided evidence that certain parental behaviors are central prerequisites for a positive development of students' academic interest, values, and intrinsic motivation. Some examples are parental encouragement and praising children's learning success (e.g. Ginsburg and Bronstein 1993; Ferry *et al.* 2000), engaging in cognitively demanding parent–child conversations (Daniels 2008; Tenenbaum 2009), engaging in joint activities (e.g. Noack 2004), providing cognitive stimulation at home (e.g. Gottfried *et al.* 1998), providing autonomy-supportive behaviors (e.g. Aunola *et al.* 2013), or intrinsic motivational practices (e.g. Gottfried *et al.* 1994, 2009).

Regarding parents' role as interpreters of reality, Ferry and colleagues (2000), for example, showed, in a cross-sectional study, that when parents encouraged learning and career plans in mathematics and science, this facilitated students' positive outcome expectancies, which in turn predicted students' interests in mathematics and science. Lazarides and Ittel's results (2012, 2013) revealed that parents' encouragement and interest in students' learning significantly predicted students' interest in mathematics.

Concerning the effects of parents providing opportunities on students' interest in mathematics and science, Gottfried and colleagues (1998) revealed that the provision of a cognitively stimulating home environment by parents (e.g. providing learning materials, and exposing children to and engaging in cognitively stimulating conversations) positively influenced subsequent intrinsic motivation in mathematics from childhood through early adolescence. Daniels' longitudinal findings (2008) suggested that parent–child conversations about learning, personal problems, and future or career plans had a positive effect on seventh graders' subsequent interest in mathematics. Noack (2004) highlighted that whether students would place a high value on mathematics (importance, utility, and intrinsic quality) was predicted best by their perception of maternal values and joint leisure activities between students and their mothers (e.g. excursions, conversations, and solving mathematical and other problems). Jacobs and Bleeker (2004) revealed that such relations may depend on parents' gender, and their results showed that only mothers' mathematics and science purchases (for example, science books, math games) and activities led to higher subsequent interest in mathematics by their children. With regard to the effects of parents providing mathematics and science activities and students' interest, Jacobs and Eccles (2000) assume that parents' behaviors are also influenced by their children's behaviors and suggest that future research should take into account the complexity of such interactive relationships.

Studies drawing on parents' involvement in their children's learning activities often focus on parental autonomy support. Aunola and colleagues (2013) demonstrated positive effects of maternal support behaviors on feelings of autonomy (encouraging independent problem solving) on first graders' subsequent mathematics interest. In their study, maternal support of competence (high ability expectations) and relatedness (warmth/affection in interactions) also predicted mathematics interest. Gottfried and colleagues (2009) showed that parents' use of task-extrinsic motivational practices were associated with low initial intrinsic motivation in mathematics and science in elementary school and were not related to students' motivational development from childhood throughout adolescence. Parental task-extrinsic practices apply to parents' behaviors that, for example, emphasize external control, diminish autonomy, and devaluate competence (Gottfried *et al.* 1994: 104). Parents' task-intrinsic motivational practices were positively related to children's initial intrinsic motivation in mathematics and science and inhibited the developmental decline in intrinsic motivation. Parental task-intrinsic practices hereby refer to encouraging enjoyment, curiosity, involvement, and persistence in learning processes (Gottfried *et al.* 2009: 730).

Research on parents as role models has often focused on the effects of parents' education and occupation on students' career choices rather than on students' motivation (e.g. Eccles 1993; Dryler 1998). Dryler's results (1998), for example, showed that students' career plans in technology and engineering were strongly influenced by their parents' occupation. Boys' career plans were thereby particularly strongly influenced by their fathers' occupations.

Future directions

While parents' beliefs and behaviors have been identified as crucial for children's beliefs and later career choices, research has suggested that the effect of parents' values on students' interest might depend on parents' and students' gender. However, studies have rarely focused on the effects of mothers' and fathers' beliefs and behaviors on daughters' and sons' beliefs and behaviors separately. Furthermore, there is a need to differentiate between the effects of parents' beliefs and behaviors on children's current level of interest and the development of children's interest. Beyond that, Jacobs and Eccles (2000) point out that reciprocal effects should be taken into account by examining the effect of children's behaviors on parents' behaviors and vice versa (see also Simpkins *et al.* 2015).

Predictors of parents' beliefs and behaviors

Research has suggested that parents' beliefs and behaviors depend to a large degree on social-contextual and child-specific factors such as family demographic characteristics, age and gender of the child, or children's ability level (Eccles 1998; Eccles and Harold 1993; Gottfried *et al.* 1998; Grolnick *et al.* 1997). Family demographic characteristics, such as parents' education, parents' financial resources, or parents' occupation, influence how successfully parents translate their child-specific beliefs and values and their support of their children's talents (Eccles 1993; Eccles and Harold 1993). Gottfried and colleagues (1998) demonstrated that cognitive stimulation at home depended on *families' socioeconomic* status such that families with higher socioeconomic status are more likely to provide a cognitively stimulating home environment. Grolnick and colleagues (1997) revealed that families with a higher socioeconomic status tend to be more involved in school. Eccles (1993) reported that parents from low-risk neighborhoods are more likely to support their children's talents than parents from high-risk neighborhoods. The latter, thus, were more likely to be putting their efforts toward protecting their children from danger. However, Grolnick and colleagues (1997) highlighted that mothers' personal involvement was not associated with socioeconomic status, suggesting that affective parental involvement does not depend on parents' occupation and education. Another important factor that influences parents' beliefs and behaviors is *students' age*. Parents' gender-stereotyped expectancies of their child's ability in mathematics increase with the child's age (Frome and Eccles 1998). Conversely, parents' school involvement decreases dramatically after children's transition to secondary school (Eccles and Harold 1993). A large amount of research has examined the relations between *students' gender* and parents' beliefs and behaviors (e.g. Crowley *et al.* 2001; Eccles 1993; Eccles and Jacobs 1986; Gunderson *et al.* 2012; Jacobs and Bleeker 2004; Simpkins *et al.* 2015). Preference tends to be given to boys with regard to, for example, parents' promotion of mathematics- and science-related activities and their purchasing of mathematics and science items (Jacobs and Bleeker 2004); parents' explanatory talks in mathematics and science disciplines (Crowley *et al.* 2001); parents' child-specific beliefs about ability, talent, and students difficulty with a given task as well as their expectations of children's interest in science (e.g. Eccles *et al.* 1990; Eccles and Jacobs 1986;

Tenenbaum and Leaper 2003); and parental encouragement to participate in mathematics and science disciplines (e.g. Simpkins *et al.* 2012). Parents of girls, however, tend to be more strongly involved in girls' mathematics and science activities (e.g. Grolnick *et al.* 1997; Jacobs and Bleeker 2004), and tend to perceive girls as more diligent (Stöckli 1997).

Conclusions

The research presented in this chapter showed how various dimensions of parents' beliefs guide parents' behaviors, and how parents' behaviors then affected children's own beliefs. Children's beliefs, in turn, were shown to influence their later course choices and career interests (e.g. Gniewosz and Noack 2012a, b; Lazarides and Watt 2015; Simpkins *et al.* 2012; Watt *et al.* 2012). This chapter thereby highlights the importance of such empirical research results for educational practice. Theory-based interventions yield highly positive effects on parents' supportive behaviors in mathematics and science, and by this, influence students' later choices. Harackiewicz and colleagues (2012) emphasized that a utility-value intervention that targeted parents' ability to communicate the importance of mathematics and science to their teens facilitated students' utility-value beliefs and thus enhanced later high-school mathematics and science enrollment. More research is needed to examine the effects of such interventions in various subgroups, for example, in different gender groups. Furthermore, there is a need to investigate how to include both mothers and fathers in research, as parental effects on students' beliefs may differ depending on the gender of the parent (e.g. Frome and Eccles 1998; MacGrath and Repetti 2000; Tenenbaum and Leaper 2003). The research presented in this chapter indicates that the importance of parents for children's mathematics-related beliefs and behaviors might depend on children's gender (e.g. Gottfried *et al.* 2009; Lazarides and Ittel 2013) or age group (Gniewosz *et al.* 2012; Pesu *et al.* 2014; Spinath and Spinath 2005). This chapter elucidated the idea that different dimensions of parental beliefs and behaviors have an effect on students' beliefs and behaviors through complex developmental mechanisms that depend on multiple characteristics of parents, children, and the social context. Further research needs to address these mechanisms in greater detail; for example, by analyzing parental effects on their children's attainment value and cost. Such research is needed to provide a detailed understanding of parent–child motivational processes.

References

Atkinson, J. W. (1964) *An Introduction to Motivation*, Princeton, NJ: Van Nostrand.

Aunola, K., Viljaranta, J., Lehtinen, E. and Nurmi, J.E. (2013) 'The role of maternal support of competence, autonomy and relatedness in children's interests and mastery orientation', *Learning and Individual Differences*, 25: 171–177.

Bandura, A. (1986) *Social Foundations of Thought and Action: A Social Cognitive Theory*, Englewood Cliffs, NJ: Prentice-Hall.

Bandura, A. (1997) *Self-efficacy: The Exercise of Control*, New York: Freeman.

Bong, M. and Skaalvik, E. M. (2003) 'Academic self-concept and self-efficacy: how different are they really?', *Educational Psychology Review*, 15: 1–40.

Crowley, K., Callanan, M.A., Tenenbaum, H.R. and Allen, E. (2001) 'Parents explain more often to boys than to girls during shared scientific thinking', *Psychological Science*, 12: 258–261.

Daniels, Z. (2008) *Entwicklung schulischer Interessen im Jugendalter [Interest Development in Adolescence]*, Münster: Waxmann.

Deci, E.L. and Ryan, R.M. (1985) *Intrinsic Motivation and Self-determination in Human Behavior*, New York: Plenum.

Deci, E.L., Vallerand, R.J., Pelletier, L.G. and Ryan, R.M. (1991) 'Motivation and education: the self-determination perspective', *Educational Psychologist*, 26: 325–346.

Denissen, J.J., Zarrett, N.R. and Eccles, J.S. (2007) 'I like to do it, I'm able, and I know I am: longitudinal couplings between domain-specific achievement, self-concept, and interest', *Child Development*, 78: 430–447.

Dermitzaki, I. and Efklides, A. (2000) 'Aspects of self-concept and their relationship to language performance and verbal reasoning ability', *The American Journal of Psychology*, 113: 621–637.

Dryler, H. (1998) 'Parental role models, gender and educational choice', *The British Journal of Sociology*, 49: 375–398.

Eccles, J.S. (1993) 'School and family effects on the ontogeny of children's interests, self-perceptions, and activity choices', in J. E. Jacobs (ed.) *Nebraska Symposium on Motivation* (Vol. 40, pp. 145–208), Lincoln, NE: University of Nebraska Press.

Eccles, J.S. (2005) 'Subjective task value and the Eccles *et al.* model of achievement-related choices', in A.J. Elliot and C.S. Dweck (eds) *Handbook of Competence and Motivation* (pp. 105–121), New York: Guilford Press.

Eccles, J.S. (2009) 'Who am I and what am I going to do with my life? Personal and collective identities as motivators of action', *Educational Psychologist*, 44: 78–89.

Eccles, J.S., Adler, T.F., Futterman, R., Goff, S.B., Kaczala, C.M., Meece, J. and Midgely, C. (1983) 'Expectancies, values and academic behaviors', in J.T. Spence (ed.) *Achievement and Achievement Motives: Psychological and Sociological Approaches* (pp. 75–146), San Francisco, CA: Freeman.

Eccles, J.S. and Harold, R. (1993) 'Parent–school involvement during the early adolescent years', *The Teachers College Record*, 94: 568–587.

Eccles, J.S. and Jacobs, J.E. (1986) 'Social forces shape math attitudes and performance', *Signs*, 11: 367–380.

Eccles, J.S., Jacobs, J. E., and Harold, R. D. (1990). 'Gender role stereotypes, expectancy effects, and parents' socialization of gender differences', *Journal of Social Issues*, 46(2): 183–201.

Eccles, J.S. and Wigfield, A. (2002) 'Motivational beliefs, values, and goals', *Annual Review of Psychology*, 53: 109–132.

Eccles, J.S., Wigfield, A. and Schiefele, U. (1998) 'Motivation to succeed', in N. Eisenberg (ed.) *Handbook of Child Psychology*, 5th edn (Vol. 3, pp. 1017–1095), New York: Wiley.

Eccles Parsons, J.S., Adler, T.F., and Kaczala, C.M. (1982) 'Socialization of achievement attitudes and beliefs: parental influences', *Child Development*, 53: 310–321.

Ferry, T.R., Fouad, N.A. and Smith, P.L. (2000) 'The role of family context in a social cognitive model for career-related choice behavior: a math and science perspective', *Journal of Vocational Behavior*, 57: 348–364.

Fisher, P.H., Dobbs-Oates, J., Doctoroff, G.L. and Arnold, D.H. (2012) 'Early math interest and the development of math skills', *Journal of Educational Psychology*, 104: 673-81.

Fredricks, J.A. and Eccles, J.S. (2002) 'Children's competence and value beliefs from childhood through adolescence: growth trajectories in two male-sex-typed domains', *Developmental Psychology*, 38: 519–533.

Frenzel, A.C., Goetz, T., Pekrun, R. and Watt, H.M.G. (2010) 'Development of mathematics interest in adolescence: influences of gender, family, and school context', *Journal of Research on Adolescence*, 20: 507–537.

Frome, P.M. and Eccles, J.S. (1998) 'Parents' influence on children's achievement-related perceptions', *Journal of Personality and Social Psychology*, 74: 435–452.

Ginsburg, G.S. and Bronstein, P. (1993) 'Family factors related to children's intrinsic/extrinsic motivational orientation and academic performance', *Child Development*, 64: 1461–1474.

Gniewosz, B., Eccles, J. and Noack, P. (2012) 'Secondary school transition and the use of different sources of information for the construction of the academic self-concept', *Social Development*, 21, 537–557.

Gniewosz B. and Noack, P. (2012a) 'What you see is what you get: the role of early adolescents' perceptions in the intergenerational transmission of academic values', *Contemporary Educational Psychology*, 37: 70–79.

Gniewosz, B. and Noack, P. (2012b) 'The role of between-parent values agreement in parent-to-child transmission of academic values', *Journal of Adolescence*, 35: 809–821.

Gottfried, A.E., Fleming, J.S. and Gottfried, A.W. (1994) 'Role of parental motivational practices in children's academic intrinsic motivation and achievement', *Journal of Educational Psychology*, 86: 104–113.

Gottfried, A.E., Fleming, J.S. and Gottfried, A.W. (1998) 'Role of cognitively stimulating home environment in children's academic intrinsic motivation: a longitudinal study', *Child Development*, 69: 1448–1160.

Gottfried, A. E., Marcoulides, G. A., Gottfried, A. W. and Oliver, P. H. (2009) 'A latent curve model of parental motivational practices and developmental decline in math and science academic intrinsic motivation', *Journal of Educational Psychology*, 101: 729–739.

Grolnick, W.S., Benjet, C., Kurowski, C.O. and Apostoleris, N.H. (1997) 'Predictors of parent involvement in children's schooling', *Journal of Educational Psychology*, 89: 538–548.

Gunderson, E.A., Ramirez, G., Levine, S.C. and Beilock, S.L. (2012) 'The role of parents and teachers in the development of gender-related math attitudes', *Sex Roles,* 66: 153–166.

Harackiewicz, J.M., Barron, K.E., Tauer, J.M. and Elliot, A.J. (2002) 'Predicting success in college: a longitudinal study of achievement goals and ability measures as predictors of interest and performance from freshman year through graduation', *Journal of Educational Psychology,* 94: 562–575.

Harackiewicz, J.M., Durik, A.M., Barron, K.E., Linnenbrink-Garcia, L. and Tauer, J.M. (2008) 'The role of achievement goals in the development of interest: reciprocal relations between achievement goals, interest, and performance', *Journal of Educational Psychology,* 100: 105–122.

Harackiewicz, J.M., Rozek, C.S., Hulleman, C.S., and Hyde, J.S. (2012) 'Helping parents to motivate adolescents in mathematics and science an experimental test of a utility-value intervention', *Psychological Science,* 23(8): 899–906.

Harter, S. (1982) 'The perceived competence scale for children', *Child Development,* 53: 87–97.

Hidi, S. (1990) 'Interest and its contribution as a mental resource for learning', *Review of Educational Research,* 60: 549–571.

Hidi, S. and Harackiewicz, J.M. (2000) 'Motivating the academically unmotivated: a critical issue for the 21st century', *Review of educational research,* 70: 151–179.

Hidi, S. and Renninger, K.A. (2006) 'The four-phase model of interest development', *Educational Psychologist,* 41: 111–127.

Hulleman, C.S., Durik, A.M., Schweigert, S.B. and Harackiewicz, J.M. (2008) 'Task values, achievement goals, and interest: an integrative analysis', *Journal of Educational Psychology,* 100: 398–416.

Jacobs, J.E. (1991) 'Influence of gender stereotypes on parent and child mathematics attitudes', *Journal of Educational Psychology,* 83: 518–527.

Jacobs, J.E. and Bleeker, M. (2004) 'Girls' and boys' developing interests in math and science: do parents matter?', *New Directions for Child and Adolescent Development,* 106: 5–21.

Jacobs, J.E. and Eccles, J.S. (2000) 'Parents, task values, and real-life achievement-related choices', in C. Sansone and J.M. Harackiewicz (eds) *Intrinsic and Extrinsic Motivation: The Search for Optimal Motivation and Performance* (pp. 405–439), New York: Academic Press.

Jacobs, J.E., Lanza, S., Osgood, D.W., Eccles, J.S. and Wigfield, A. (2002) 'Changes in children's self-competence and values: gender and domain differences across grades one through twelve', *Child Development,* 73: 509–527.

Jodl, K.M., Michael, A., Malanchuk, O., Eccles, J.S. and Sameroff, A. (2001) 'Parents' roles in shaping early adolescents' occupational aspirations', *Child Development,* 72: 1247–1265.

Koeller, O., Baumert, J. and Schnabel, K. (2001) 'Does interest matter? The relationship between academic interest and achievement in mathematics', *Journal for Research in Mathematics Education,* 32: 448–470.

Krapp, A. (1999) 'Interest, motivation and learning: an educational-psychological perspective', *European Journal of Psychology of Education,* 14: 23–40.

Krapp, A. (2007) 'An educational-psychological conceptualisation of interest', *International Journal for Educational and Vocational Guidance,* 7: 5–21.

Krapp, A., Hidi, S. and Renninger, K.A. (1992) 'Interest, learning and development', in K.A. Renninger, S. Hidi and A. Krapp (eds) *The Role of Interest in Learning and Development* (pp. 3–25), Hillsdale, NJ: Erlbaum.

Lane, K.A. (2012) 'Being narrow while being broad: the importance of construct specificity and theoretical generality', *Sex Roles,* 66: 167–174.

Lau, S. and Pun, K-T. (1999) 'Parental evaluations and their agreement: relationship with children's self-concepts', *Social Behavior and Personality,* 27: 639–650.

Lazarides, R. and Ittel, A. (2012) 'Mathe und mädchen: eine frage der erziehung. Unterricht und familie prägen fachspezifische geschlechterunterschiede' ['Math and girls: a question of education. Classroom and family shape domain-specific gender differences'], *Schule im Blickpunkt [Focal Point School],* 45: 13–15.

Lazarides, R. and Ittel, A. (2013) 'Mathematics interest and achievement: what role do perceived parent and teacher support play? A longitudinal analysis', *Journal of Gender, Science and Technology,* 5: 207–231.

Lazarides, R. and Watt, H.M.G. (2015) 'Girls' and boys'-perceived mathematics teacher beliefs, math classroom learning environments and gendered math career intentions', *Contemporary Educational Psychology,* 41: 51–61.

MacGrath, E.P. and Repetti, R.L. (2000) 'Mothers' and fathers' attitudes toward their children's academic performance and children's perceptions of their academic competence', *Journal of Youth and Adolescence,* 29: 713–723.

Marsh, H.W. (1987) 'The big-fish-little-pond effect on academic self-concept', *Journal of Educational Psychology,* 79: 280–329.

Marsh, H.W., Trautwein, U., Lüdtke, O., Köller, O. and Baumert, J. (2005) 'Academic self-concept, interest, grades, and standardized test scores: reciprocal effects models of causal ordering', *Child Development*, 76: 397–416.

Nagy, G., Trautwein, U., Baumert, J., Köller, O. and Garrett, J. (2006) 'Gender and course selection in upper secondary education: effects of academic self-concept and intrinsic value', *Educational Research and Evaluation: An International Journal on Theory and Practice*, 12: 323–345.

Noack, P. (2004) 'The family context of preadolescents' orientations toward education: effects of maternal orientations and behavior', *Journal of Educational Psychology*, 96: 714–722.

Nurmi, J.-E. and Aunola, K. (2005) 'Task-motivation during the first school years: a person-oriented approach to longitudinal data', *Learning and Instruction*, 15: 103–122.

Pekrun, R. (2001) 'Familie, schule und entwicklung' [Family, school and development] in S. Walper and R. Pekrun (eds) *Familie und Entwicklung: Aktuelle Perspektiven der Familienpsychologie* (pp. 84–105), Göttingen: Hogrefe.

Pesu, L., Viljaranta, J. and Aunola, K. (2014) 'The role of academic performance, and parents' and teachers' expectations in children's self-concept of ability development during the first grade', manuscript in progress.

Phillips, D.A. (1987) 'Socialization of perceived academic competence among highly competent children', *Child Development*, 58: 1308–1320.

Pintrich, P.R. and Schunk, D.H. (2002) *Motivation in Education. Theory, Research and Applications*, 2nd edn, Upper Saddle River, NJ: Pearson Education.

Pomerantz, E.M., Grolnick, W.S. and Price, C.E. (2005) 'The role of parents in how children approach achievement', in A.J. Elliot and C.S. Dweck (eds) *Handbook of Competence and Motivation* (pp. 259–278), New York: Guilford.

Ryan, R.M. and Deci, E.L. (2000) 'Self-determination theory and the facilitation of intrinsic motivation, social development, and well-being', *American Psychologist*, 55: 68–78.

Schiefele, U. (2009) 'Situational and individual interest', in K.R. Wentzel and A. Wigfield (eds) *Handbook of Motivation at School* (pp. 197–222), New York: Routledge.

Schunk, D.H. and Pajares, F. (2005) 'Competence perceptions and academic functioning', in A.J. Elliot and C.S. Dweck (eds) *Handbook of Competence and Motivation* (pp. 85–104), New York: Guilford.

Simpkins, S.D., Davis-Kean, P., and Eccles, J.S. (2006) 'Math and science motivation: a longitudinal examination of the links between choices and beliefs', *Developmental Psychology*, 42: 70–83.

Simpkins, S.D., Fredricks, J.A. and Eccles, J.S. (2012) 'Charting the Eccles' expectancy-value model from mothers' beliefs in childhood to youths' activities in adolescence', *Developmental Psychology*, 48: 1019–1032.

Simpkins, S.D., Fredricks, J.A. and Eccles, J.S. (2015) *The Role of Parents in the Ontogeny of Achievement-related Motivation and Behavioral Choices*. Monographs of the Society for Research on Child Development, In press.

Skaalvik, E.M. and Skaalvik, S. (2002) 'Internal and external frames of reference for academic self-concept', *Educational Psychologist*, 37: 233-244.

Spinath, B. and Spinath, F.M. (2005) 'Development of self-perceived ability in elementary school: the role of parents' perceptions, teacher evaluations, and intelligence', *Cognitive Development*, 20: 190–204.

Stöckli, G. (1997) *Eltern, Kinder und das andere Geschlecht. Selbstwerdung in sozialen Beziehungen* [Parents, Children and Gender. Individuation in Social Relationships], Weinheim: Beltz.

Tenenbaum, H.R. (2009) '"You'd be good at that": gender patterns in parent–child talk about courses', *Social Development*, 18: 447–463.

Tenenbaum, H.R., and Leaper, C. (2003) 'Parent–child conversations about science: the socialization of gender inequities?', *Developmental Psychology*, 39: 34–47.

Trautwein, U., Lüdtke, O., Marsh, H.W. and Nagy, G. (2009) 'Within-school social comparison: how students perceive the standing of their class predicts academic self-concept', *Journal of Educational Psychology*, 101: 853–866.

Watt, H.M.G. (2004) 'Development of adolescents' self-perceptions, values, and task perceptions according to gender and domain in 7th- through 11th-grade Australian students', *Child Development*, 75: 1556–1574.

Watt, H.M.G., Shapka, J.D., Morris, Z.A., Durik, A.M., Keating, D.P. and Eccles, J.S. (2012) 'Gendered motivational processes affecting high school mathematics participation, educational aspirations, and career plans: a comparison of samples from Australia, Canada, and the United States', *Developmental Psychology*, 48: 1594–1611.

Wigfield, A. and Eccles, J.S. (1992) 'The development of achievement task values: a theoretical analysis', *Developmental Review*, 12: 1–46.

Wigfield, A. and Eccles, J.S. (2000) 'Expectancy-value theory of achievement motivation', *Contemporary Educational Psychology*, 25: 68–81.

Wigfield, A., Eccles, J.S., Schiefele, U., Roeser, R.W. and Davis-Kean, P. (2006) 'Development of achievement motivation', in N. Eisenberg (ed.) *Handbook of Child Psychology: Vol. 3, Social, Emotional, and Personality Development*, 6th edn (pp. 933–1002), New York: Wiley.

Wigfield, A., Eccles, J.S., Yoon, K.S., Harold, R.D., Arbreton, A., Freedman-Doan, K. and Blumenfeld, P.C. (1997) 'Changes in children's competence beliefs and subjective task values across the elementary school years: a three-year study', *Journal of Educational Psychology*, 89: 451–469.

Wild, E. and Lorenz, F. (2009) 'Familie' [Family], in E. Wild and J. Möller, J. (eds) *Pädagogische Psychologie [Educational Psychology]* (pp. 236–259), Heidelberg: Springer.

Youniss, J. (1982) *Parents and Peers in Social Development: A Sullivan–Piaget Perspective*, Chicago: University of Chicago Press.

6

THE ROLE OF MEANING SYSTEMS IN THE DEVELOPMENT OF MOTIVATION

Helen Patrick and Panayota Mantzicopoulos

One of the central social psychological issues within classrooms involves why some children are excited to learn and exert effort to do so, whereas others are not – that is, why children's motivation varies so much. Motivational differences are explained well by psychological factors, particularly beliefs about how people construe learning, the learning context, and themselves. These motivational beliefs even moderate the effects of physical or physiological characteristics, such as gender or learning difficulties. Accordingly, motivation researchers primarily examine individuals' beliefs and perceptions. We argue, however, that motivational beliefs develop in ways that are consistent with the *larger systems of meaning* that exist within and beyond school. We illustrate how school- and society-level meanings undergird children's developing science motivation, using data from the Scientific Literacy Project (2009), a program of integrated science inquiry and literacy during children's first year of school (i.e. kindergarten in the United States). Although we address learning science in kindergarten, we believe our research is relevant to motivation for learning other disciplines and in other grade levels.

Conceptualizing motivation

Individuals' motivation is observable from their behaviors: choices made, energy exerted, extent of persistence, care taken, and thoughtfulness applied. Specifically, when motivated, people take on challenges, apply effort, continue with a problem, topic, or issue even after making errors or incurring set-backs, and are thoughtful and strategic. Unsurprisingly, motivation is associated with learning and achievement. Accompanying individuals' motivated behavior are particular beliefs about what it is they are motivated to do. They include thinking that the activity process or its outcome (or both) is worthwhile, important, interesting, or enjoyable, and that they are good at the activity or will become skilled with practice. These beliefs fuel the effort, persistence, and challenge-seeking (Graham and Weiner 2012; Wigfield and Cambria 2010).

The predominant theories of motivation are social-cognitive. That is, they emphasize that behavior is influenced by perceptions and beliefs. Motivated behavior, according to social cognitive theories, depends in large part on how individuals construe: (1) the *task or subject* (e.g. enjoyment, interest, usefulness, importance, difficulty); (2) their own *ability or skills* (e.g. perceived competence, self-efficacy); (3) their *goals and desires*; and (4) the *reasons* for their success or failure (e.g. their own efforts, luck) (Graham and Weiner 2012; Wigfield and Cambria 2010). Motivational theories differ with respect to the beliefs that are emphasized, although conceptually similar beliefs may feature in different theories – albeit with different terminology.

Motivation to learn science

The widespread concern that too few people with sufficient ability are choosing careers in science, technology, engineering, and mathematics (STEM) is a motivational issue – many people who potentially could, choose not to. Most research on science motivation addresses the secondary and tertiary years, probably because career- and vocational-related decisions are central at this time (Aschbacher *et al.* 2010; Britner 2008; Sadler *et al.* 2012). Research also comes from the middle or intermediate grades (e.g. Britner and Pajares 2006; Vedder-Weiss and Fortus 2011), given the importance of adolescence for identity development. However, there is a dearth of research about motivation for science in the early school years.

Why consider young children's motivation for learning science?

Young children are inherently curious and seem to ask questions almost incessantly. Many questions involve the natural world, such as why trees have leaves (Piaget 1955), what stars are for, and why we cannot reach the sky (Perez-Granados and Callanan 1997). Children also tend to be very positive about learning science when they begin school, and express similar confidence in their ability to learn reading and mathematics (Mantzicopoulos *et al.* 2013).

There is considerable evidence that students in the middle- and high-school grades have typically lost much of their initial interest in science and optimism in being good at it (e.g. Vedder-Weiss and Fortus 2011). For example, longitudinal research shows a linear decline in science motivation from the age of 9 years to ages 10, 13, and 16 (Gottfried *et al.* 2001). Similarly, comparisons of third through twelfth graders' science attitudes showed that the third and fourth graders were the most positive, the ninth to twelfth graders were least positive, and fifth to eighth graders' attitudes were between the other two groups. The younger children (i.e. Grades 3-4) also saw themselves as more able or competent at science than did the older students (Greenfield 1996).

Science motivation seems to fare poorly in elementary school when compared with motivation for other subjects, although there are strikingly few studies in the early grades. Children in kindergarten through third grade believe, on average, that they are better at mathematics than life science, and also better at mathematics, reading, and life science than physical science (Andre *et al.* 1999). They also like life science as much as mathematics and reading, but like physical science less than those subjects (Andre *et al.* 1999). The researchers did not report results separately by grade level, however, and therefore it is not known whether motivation differs between kindergarten and third grade.

In short, children's science motivation is generally high before beginning school and at the start of their school careers, but much lower five or six years later. Very little is known about the development of children's science motivation in the early school years; however, the pattern of shying away from science is identifiable well before high school. We believe it is important to examine science motivation early in children's schooling.

Overview of our science motivation research in the early school years

The Scientific Literacy Project addressed kindergarteners' learning of and motivation for science. We had many objectives, including promoting children's conceptual understanding of science, increasing children's engagement with informational text, developing integrated inquiry and literacy materials, and developing measures. Space precludes discussion of these topics here; however, we have reported on them elsewhere (e.g. Mantzicopoulos *et al.* 2008, 2009, 2013; Samarapungavan *et al.* 2008, 2011). In this chapter, we focus on motivation, and draw from Scientific Literacy Project data to illustrate the necessity of considering undergirding meaning systems in order to understand student motivation.

We examined children's motivation in two United States public school contexts in the same district: (1) within regular kindergartens where teachers invited us to observe and record their 'typical science lessons', and (2) within kindergartens that implemented the year-long Scientific Literacy Project activities. Both contexts were comparable in terms of students' demographics, ethnic diversity and achievement. We were interested not only in whether students' motivation for learning science differed between the two instructional contexts, but also in understanding reasons for any motivational differences – that is, the 'how' and 'why' of motivation development.

Co-constructing meaning and motivation about science

Throughout the three-year period of enacting the Scientific Literacy Project and investigating its efficacy, we observed science lessons and talked with children and their teachers. During this time we became increasingly aware of the co-evolution of meaning and motivation as coordinated, complimentary systems – a point we illustrate later. We believe that without understanding the context of individuals' participation in an activity or domain, particularly the inherent meanings involved, we cannot understand the nature of their motivation.

Through children's participation in school activities, they experience particular patterns of discourse and activity structures from which they create meaning. That is, as children engage with specific content (e.g. science) they simultaneously participate in constructing meaning within the shared practices and activities of the classroom (Roth and Lee 2007). Embedded in the collective, meaning structures involve knowledge about disciplinary content, epistemic norms, procedures, and the discipline itself: what science is, how one learns science, who can learn science, how valuable science is and why, what is expected from students and teachers during the learning process, and what satisfactory progress and skilled performance look like. Thus, what it means to 'do science' is fundamentally expressed through 'doing science'. Meaning systems are created jointly by teachers and students, and therefore exist in the collective social world of the classroom (Kelly and Crawford 1997). Meanings extend beyond the classroom too; classroom activity and the discourse associated with it reflect the meanings that exist in systems within which the classrooms are embedded. These include, in the case of science, norms and beliefs about who can and should learn, or teach, science; what is needed in order to learn it, and what science should be learned and when. Meaning-making also emerges at the individual level, as children reconstruct and appropriate socially shared knowledge (Hicks 1996; Rogoff 1992; Vygotsky 1978).

Motivation, we argue, is also situated in these shared practices; the culture-specific meaning systems form an integral, inseparable aspect of students' motivation. For example, *the extent to which students want to learn science, how enthusiastically they approach learning it, or how competent they feel doing science (i.e. motivational beliefs) reflects inherently the meanings they ascribe in that context to science.* Motivation and meaning are then reconstituted at the individual level, as teachers and children enter into dialogic interactions with the socially negotiated norms, beliefs, and values of their classroom. Both new meanings and motivation are continually co-created from these processes as individual participants appropriate socially derived constructions into new motivation structures that, over time, take the shape of relatively stable entities. Thus, understanding students' motivation for learning and teachers' motivation for teaching particular content requires an understanding of situated meanings.

Illustrating the convergence between meaning systems and motivation

The classrooms we worked in provided us with rich evidence of the emergence of meaning processes and motivation. We saw motivation and meaning-making emerging first at the collective classroom level through discourse processes situated in the social activity of the classroom, and then at the individual level for children and teachers. The children's expressed beliefs about their science competence and their enthusiasm for and liking of science reflected their experiences of what learning science meant to them. Their accounts of learning science reflected what we saw enacted day after day, throughout the year, in their classrooms and was also consistent with the teachers' accounts of their own meanings around teaching kindergarten science. Thus, the classroom discourse and activity patterns were mirrored in children's and teachers' co-construction of the meanings of science, in addition to the motivational beliefs that evolved from and were situated in their shared science practices. We illustrate this process through a multilevel approach that considers: (a) classroom-level observational data and teacher interviews; and (b) data collected from children.

Overview of evidence

Classroom-level data

While observing science lessons, we attended closely to the behavior and talk that unfolded across the year; these formed the basis of the children's co-constructions of what science is, who can do it, and whether it is interesting or worth learning about. We noted, for example, what teachers said about specific topics, in addition to science in general; how science was connected to students' experiences; how the language of science was used by teachers and children; the extent to which students' and teachers' access to materials and opportunities to talk influenced the course of lessons; what questions were encouraged from children and how teachers responded to children's questions; and what types of behavior and products were encouraged.

We also talked with the teachers to learn their views about teaching science. These included their objectives for kindergarten, instructional practices best suited for kindergarteners, their objectives for teaching science, how and what they typically taught about science, and the reasons for their instructional practices (see Mantzicopoulos *et al.* 2009, 2013 for details).

Individual-level data

We interviewed children individually to learn the meanings they had developed about science and learning science. We wanted to know norms and beliefs the children had appropriated about who can and should learn science; what is needed to learn it; and what science should be learned and when. To do this we asked children whether they learn science at school. Then, depending on their answer, we asked either what science they learned about or what they might learn about if they were to learn science. In asking children to tell us 'what happens' (or might happen) when they have science and what sorts of things they learn (or might learn) about, we prompted them to draw from their personal involvement with science, rather than on general notions about what science means. Thus, they shared their situated meanings about what experiences, processes, and knowledge counted for them as science. Our interviews, therefore, served as a window into how the children had appropriated the social discourses associated with their science experiences.

We also used the Puppet Interview Scales of Competence in and Enjoyment of Science (PISCES; Mantzicopoulos *et al.* 2008) to assess children's motivation. Questioned individually, children indicated which of two puppets' statements expressed what they themselves thought. Statements were dichotomous, one positive and one negative (e.g. 'I can't do science yet' versus 'I can do science'), and fully counterbalanced. Items formed two distinct scales, measuring perceived competence for learning science and science interest and enjoyment.

The wider educational context within which all classrooms were situated

The teachers in both the Scientific Literacy Project and non-Scientific Literacy Project classes faced the same demands and expectations from school administrators in terms of what they taught, and their descriptions of how they structured science teaching were similar (i.e. before teachers began using the Scientific Literacy Project activities).

All teachers told us that although they were technically supposed to teach the state science standards, no one ever asked about them or required documentation. In contrast, reading and, to a lesser extent, mathematics was of paramount importance: teachers were required to document 90 minutes of reading and 60 minutes of mathematics instruction each day (kindergarten was half day) and children who were slow to learn letters and sounds had to be tested every two weeks. Teachers' typical comments about science included the following:

> We don't really have to [teach science], it's not on the report card. And so I think, in teachers' minds, we think 'OK, I'm going to be grading them on that, so I better get that taught'. [But with science], because it's not on their report card, that's why I think you can slide it.

> The only two areas that we have listed on our lesson plans are reading and math. We have guided reading and guided math. We have practice reading and practice math. We have manuscript, we have printing, and we have problem-solving.

Constructing meanings of science and motivation in typical classrooms

Activity and discourse

The science lessons that we observed in the typical kindergarten classrooms (details in Mantzicopoulos *et al.* 2009, 2013; Samarapungavan *et al.* 2011) looked very much like descriptions of science reported over a decade ago. Based on data from 320 K-2 teachers who participated in the National Survey of Science and Mathematics education, Fulp (2002) documented that the majority of teachers felt unprepared to teach science, and thus taught science infrequently, covered a few isolated topics, made few connections between these topics and between science and other subjects, and did not use inquiry-oriented practices. In our sample of regular kindergarten classrooms, teachers never used the term 'science' with their students, in contrast to other subjects such as reading or mathematics. Content that teachers indicated to us as being science was referred to in class as learning about, for example, 'germs' or 'the ocean' or 'plants'. Science lessons almost exclusively involved children sitting on the carpet listening to the teacher reading a story, or working at their desks, often on art activities.

The following excerpt from a unit on butterflies shows that although the lesson involves science, that content is not emphasized; the focus is neatness and fine motor skills.

Ms Milne: We're going to make our butterfly book, and your butterfly book is going to look something like this [*holds up her finished book*]. But your butterfly book doesn't look like this yet. And I put brand new sharpened colored pencils in everybody's can because some of these [*pointing to areas for coloring*] are really small. // [*She hands out a sheet of paper with an outline of a butterfly*]

What I want you to do, and I want you to listen very carefully, I want you to take scissors! And do you see that big black line that goes all the way around the outside of your butterfly? I want you to cut along that outside line. Now when you get up to his antennas, you're going to have to make a little bit of a curve. Do your very best to stay on the line. [*Children begin cutting out the butterfly shapes*] //

Jackie: Do not cut his antennas off.

Ms Milne: Nope, don't cut his antennas off, you'll have to cut around them. // I like how I see lots of you staying on the lines.

The second excerpt typifies the science book reading we observed in the regular science classrooms. It occurred during the first of Ms Reeve's lessons about plants. The book was an informational text with clear, attractive photographs and used vocabulary specific to plants (e.g. stem, bloom, pollen).

Ms Reeve: We're gonna start talking about flowers and plants this week. And today I'm going to read a story about the life cycle of a flower, and the title of our story is *Sunflower Life Cycle* and this story is by Jeff Bauer. I want everyone to sit on their pockets with their legs crossed and their hands in their laps, and their voices . . . [*pauses to let children respond*]

Children: [*Chorus*] Off.

Ms Reeve: All right. [*Starts reading*] 'Look at this beautiful field of bright sunflowers. This book will tell you all about them. Sunflowers are plants. So is everything in this garden. Plants are living things. But they do not move around like animals. Plants stay in one place and grow. Some plants have flowers. Some plants have vegetables or fruits. Both animals and people depend on plants for food.'

[*Talks to children*] So animals depend on the flowers to get nectar, that's what they eat [*points to photos of a humming bird and a butterfly drinking nectar from flowers*]. And we depend on the vegetables and fruits that grow, like tomatoes and watermelon, because that's what we eat. [*Continues reading*] 'There are millions of kinds of plants in the world. Do you know what makes all of them alike?' They all need three things. Do you guys know what they need?

Travis: [*Calls out*] Water.

Ms Reeve: Shhhh, I want you to raise your hand. Miley, what's one thing?

Miley: You put the seed in the dirt and you cover it up.

Ms Reeve: Well, that's the first step to growing a flower. But what do they need? What do they have to have in order to live? Bernard?

Bernard: Water.

Ms Reeve: Huh?

Bernard: Water.

Ms Reeve: They need water. [*Points to Serena*]

Serena: Um . . . [*long pause*] They need, um . . .

Ms Reeve: What the – what's that big yellow thing up in the sky?

Serena: Uh, sun.

Ms Reeve   They need water, they need the sun, and they need – Andrea?

Andrea: They need dirt.

Ms Reeve:	They need dirt, or soil.
Austin:	[*Calls out*] Or, or, or food.
Ms Reeve:	[*Resumes reading*] 'They all began as tiny seeds! Let's take a look at the life cycle of a sunflower to see how a plant grows. These are sunflower seeds. They get planted in the spring. They need warmth and rain to grow into flowers.' So, can you plant flowers in the winter outside?
Children:	[*Chorus*] No.
Ms Reeve:	No. Well, one, it's really cold and they could freeze. And there's not a whole lot of rain. And if you do water a flower outside in the cold, it'd freeze, right? [*Children make sounds of agreement*]
Briana:	[*Calls out*] Like this. [*She pretends to be frozen solid*]
Ms Reeve:	[*To Briana*] Alright. [*Continues reading*] 'Rainwater wets the ground. It softens a seed until it bursts open.'

As the excerpt showed, teacher talk predominated, and the students had few opportunities for dialog. The teacher prompted for simple yes/no answers and then provided causal explanations ('It's really cold and they could freeze … there's not a whole lot of rain … if you do water a flower outside in the cold, it'd freeze'), without giving children the opportunity to think for themselves.

Our observations were consistent with the teachers' descriptions of their typical science lessons. For example, they said:

> When we did butterflies – I have a book called *Katrina*. It's about a butterfly, and it's a song, so I would teach the kids the song and we would all make the butterfly paper.

> I would do [i.e. make] a bee, and they would too. And they could see the three body parts, and they would add the wings, and the six legs, and the antennae. So they actually do a little bee and then we hang 'em up in the classroom.

In summary, there was little if any language of science used in regular science classes. The dialog was predominantly teacher-controlled and generally followed an I-R-E (i.e. teacher initiates question, child responds, teacher evaluates) pattern (Mehan 1985). Students were rarely asked to contribute ideas of their own; their role was generally passive. The science within the lessons was typically not the focus of attention, and when it was, the emphasis was usually on facts. Therefore, it would be understandable if the children did not realize that these lessons were science, and if they did, if they interpreted them as part of art.

Children's expressed meanings of science

We spoke individually with 70 children who received only the typical science instruction. Of those, 12 said they learned science at school, although 7 children spoke only about school activities or behaviors not related to science. For example:

> (What do you learn in science?) Be quiet. Behave. That's very important. (What happens when you have science?) Be quiet. Centers. Play, and sometimes you get to work on [the] 'puter [i.e. computer].

Of the 70 children, 24 made at least one science-relevant response; 5 said they learned science at school and 19 said they knew about science from other sources (e.g. an older sibling). Examples of explanations are:

You make stuff. (Like what stuff?) Electric stuff, like electric robots. (Anything else that science is about?) Um, that's all I know.

Science is learning about stuff, like being a doctor when you grow up, or how to be a science teacher. The science teacher teaches you how to be a science person.

Twelve of the 24 children who made a relevant statement about science described it as the enterprise of making solutions—mostly dangerous mixtures or potions. For example:

Science is like when you have potions and stuff and they turn into different things.

When a person has stuff and they pour it together and it blows up. You wear a mask to see and you use a towel to clean up.

More than half of the 24 children with science narratives noted that science is appropriate for older students or adults but not necessarily for children their age. For example, they said:

We're too young! Kindergarteners are too young for science. My brother does science. He likes science, and he is good at science. (How old is your brother?) 12!

You have to be big to do science. If you're little, you'd get hurt.

One child said that he did not know about science because in kindergarten they are expected to work on reading:

ABCs, numbers, read, and read little books and we make sure we go to school. Because if you are in third grade you can learn science and math.

Other children mentioned science topics, however their descriptions sounded like art activities and were not unlike the teachers' accounts of their lessons. Examples of these children's accounts are:

Bugs. We just color them in, that's all.

Dolphins, whales, the boat, alligators, sharks. (What do you do in science?) We kind of make them with paper and we paint them.

Children's motivational beliefs about science

Children in the regular science classes reported, on average, low levels of science competence ($M = 0.27$ on a scale from 0 to 1). They also reported moderate levels of liking science ($M = 0.47$). An important finding in terms of gender differences in the leaky STEM pipeline is that girls liked science significantly less than boys did ($M = 0.39$ and 0.59, respectively). For more information, see Patrick *et al.* (2009).

Summary

Most children did not have a notion of science that included anything science-related, and most did not recognize that their teachers were engaging them in science lessons most weeks. Those children who said they knew about science referred most often to fictional, stereotypical portrayals of dangerous or magical potions. Children often noted that science did not relate to them and was not appropriate for kindergarteners. As illustrated in the classroom excerpts, children had few, if any, opportunities to think about and rework these stereotypical meanings about science at school. Because motivation (co)evolves as the child actively (re)creates and transforms meaning, we reason that this is why these children also expressed low perceptions of competence and liking of science.

Constructing meanings of science and motivation in Science Literacy Project classrooms

Activity and discourse

The Science Literacy Project lessons addressed central themes in science (e.g. ways that living things adapt to their environment), and were grouped by topics into units, thus allowing themes to be revisited and extended with different content. Each lesson involved reading and talking about an informational science book, conducting an investigation or observation, and/or recording observations (Mantzicopoulos *et al.* 2009, 2013; Samarapungavan *et al.* 2011). Children's observations were either recorded as a class using an idea board, or individually in science notebooks in ways most suitable for the activity and each child (e.g. drawing, writing, or pasting photos). Children were encouraged to ask questions and offer suggestions or thoughts, and teachers used dialogic reading strategies while reading with the children. The lessons were explicitly labeled as science. The language of science was also used routinely, whether in terms of process (e.g. *prediction, recording*) or vocabulary (e.g. living things *excrete*). The ubiquity and accessibility of science in children's everyday lives was emphasized throughout; for example, dissolving drink powder in water, puddles of water drying up in the sun, and playground equipment were identified as being science. Furthermore, children were reminded frequently that they were scientists, because they were asking questions and learning about the world around them. Meanings of what science is, as well as motivation-related meanings such as agency, relevance, community, competence and value were co-constructed during the lessons and became part of the shared context. The following excerpt from the introductory unit *What is Science?* illustrates this interconnection between meaning and motivation.

Ms Burke: First, boys and girls, I wanna tell you something. We're gonna start to learn about science. Have any of you guys heard that word before

Children: [*Interrupting*] No …

Ms Burke: SCIENCE?

Children: No.

Ms Burke: No? Well I want to tell you that science is the study of the WORLD around us. Things that are outside; things that are inside; things about us. It's a study about what's around us, OK? //

    We're going to try and take guesses about things. We're gonna predict what might happen if we do some experiments.// We're gonna what would happen if? We're gonna ask all those kinds of questions as scientists, and we're gonna try and answer those questions by doing the experiment or by doing the activity. And then we're gonna say, 'Well, guess what? We guessed right,' or 'We didn't guess right – this is what happened.' But you know what's cool about science? You don't always have to be right. //

    We're gonna investigate what happens when we make lemonade. [*Shows materials to the class*] Here is the pitcher of water – here is the mix – here's the spoon and here's the ice. Now, scientists usually start by asking questions. What kind of questions might you have about making lemonade?

Katya:	Sometimes Pete makes lemonade.
Ms Burke:	Pete makes lemonade at home?
Katya:	Aha [*nods*]. Pete is my step dad. //
Ms Burke:	What's gonna happen to the lemonade mix when we put it in the water? Is that a question we could have?
Children:	Yeah.
Ms Burke:	What else do you wonder about? What might you ask a question about?
Andrew:	I think the ice is going to turn into water.
Ms Burke:	Do you think the ice is gonna turn into water? You know what! That could be a PREDICTION – you think the ice is gonna turn into water so, and a prediction just means a guess! //
Allie:	It's gonna float!
Tyrone:	Float!
Ms Burke:	That's your prediction … I'll put [*writing on the idea board*] *Ice will float* … Now boys and girls, how can we find out about our questions? //
Natasha:	You put that [*points to ice*] in there [*points to water*].
Ms Burke:	OK! Let's do it. Should we put the mix in first?
Felicia:	No! Let's do the bag [*points to bag of ice*]. //
Ms Burke:	You want to do the ice first? OK. Let's see what happens when the ice goes in [*puts ice in the pitcher of water*].
Children:	It's floating! It's floating!
Ms Burke:	So we already have an observation that we can put down – what we're seeing – ice floats – That's an observation. Let's put down [*writes 'Ice floats' on the idea board*]. We're recording our observation.

As the excerpt showed, the teacher defined science concisely and immediately identified that they, through studying the world around them, would be scientists. This was accompanied with establishing community and connectedness with a discipline. They, just as scientists do, would begin with asking questions. The language of science (e.g. predict, investigate, observation, recording) was used naturally in the context of a familiar activity. As part of learning what science is the teacher noted that science is 'cool' and 'you don't always have to be right'. Meanings of agency were also explicitly situated in the discourse, in that everyone was able to participate in making predictions and observations, and suggest different steps in the investigation.

Children's expressed meanings of science

As we did for the children in regular science classes, we asked children about learning science after they had engaged in 20 weeks of Scientific Literacy Project lessons, spread across the school year. Of the 123 children we questioned, 109 made comments that indicated some understanding of science. Some statements reflected content-specific knowledge, such as:

> I learn that fish have gills and they hide and food eaters hide to catch prey sometimes. . . .
> Prey comes to it instead of hiding.

> Learn about living things. (What else do you learn?) That living things need food and water.

Other explanations indicated an understanding of the process of doing science, including asking questions, making predictions, conducting investigations, and recording observations. The following are examples:

We learn how to predict and be a scientist. We predict what's going to happen, and if it happens, our prediction is right.

(What do you learn?) Science experiments. One of them, we had a bumpy ramp and a smooth ramp where two trains went down and we wanted to see which one went faster. Smooth was faster.

You have these journals that you keep notes in.

In contrast to the many students in the typical science classes, none of the Scientific Literacy Project children's descriptions referred to potions, robots, or danger. Furthermore, no child suggested that science was not appropriate for them.

Children's motivational beliefs about science

Children who experienced the Scientific Literacy Project reported, on average, they were quite competent at science ($M = 0.86$ on a 0–1 scale). They also liked science ($M = 0.89$), with girls having similar responses to boys ($M = 0.92$ and 0.88, respectively; Patrick *et al.* 2009).

Summary

The Scientific Literacy Project children expressed high motivation for science. Their understanding of science appeared to have been constructed from their activities during science lessons. In talking about learning science they expressed a legitimacy and naturalness for their engagement. Their descriptions of participating in science lessons reflect competence through their appropriation and use of correct science language, and an appreciation for what they learned. It is these meanings about competence and value that also emerged as children responded to the measure of science motivation.

Conclusions and implications

After analyzing all types and levels of data, we gained an understanding of the development of the children's motivation for learning science. In particular, we identified reasons for how and why children in the two instructional contexts may have constructed such different perspectives towards themselves as science learners, and such different sets of motivational beliefs.

The teachers with whom we worked 'knew' that science is not important in kindergarten, because they were not accountable for teaching it, children did not receive a grade for it, and it was all but squeezed out of the week because of time mandated for reading and mathematics. The science experiences of the children in the regular classes were typically superficial in terms of science content, conceptually unconnected, and often more art or fiction than science. Consistent with their experiences, children did not recognize these lessons as being science. Children tended to see science as not applying to them, and did not view it as part of what they should be learning at school. Furthermore, they expressed a superficial understanding of science. In many instances children's descriptions of science resembled the way it is often portrayed in television shows, movies, and books – as a dangerous venture involving unusual people (usually men, often the villain) who mix potions or create dastardly inventions. Their classroom science lessons did not alter these stereotypical views of science.

In contrast, the children who participated in the Scientific Literacy Project lessons engaged regularly in doing science throughout the year and knew they were doing so. They had developed rich, personal, cohesive, and relatively authentic experiences learning and doing science, which were reflected in their ownership of the knowledge and the relatively deep, connected meanings of science they had developed. Their jointly created meanings of what science is were infused with meanings of competence and value. This was despite their teachers' views of science at the beginning of the year, which were the same as those expressed by the other teachers.

The motivational beliefs that children expressed were connected integrally to the meanings they had developed for the discipline. For example, part of being interested in a topic or subject is an understanding of what that topic is – its inherent meaning. We believe that the Scientific Literacy Project lessons provided a context within which children and teachers co-constructed different, richer, more elaborated understandings of what science is, compared to those constructed by the children and teachers in the regular science classes. The children's expressed expectancies and values reflected their experiences of what learning science meant to them. Children's accounts of learning science reflected what we saw enacted day after day, throughout the year, in their classrooms and was also consistent with the teachers' accounts of their own meanings around teaching kindergarten science. That is, through changing the discourse and activity patterns in Scientific Literacy Project classrooms from what the norm was in kindergarten – and still was in the regular classrooms – not only children's co-construction of the meanings of science differed, but also the motivational beliefs that evolved from and were situated in their shared science practices. Thus, what emerged along with meaning was a collective sense of competence, value, agency, and purpose, which became reconstituted at the individual level. These individual (re) constructions came into being as children considered and (re)worked the socially negotiated meanings and beliefs of their classroom and appropriated them into new, personally relevant meanings and beliefs of competence, value, and purpose.

Our findings that individuals' development and appropriation of situated meaning is integral to any understanding of their motivated behavior has implications for education. Namely, if the intent is for children to see science as appropriate for them to learn, within their capabilities, interesting, and important, these meanings must be palpable within and intrinsic to the context. The findings also have implications for research. For example, when students are asked questions designed to measure their motivational beliefs, such as how much they want to learn science or how good they are at doing science, their responses reflect inherently the meanings they ascribe to, among other things, what science is, what it means to 'do science', and what learning science involves. We argue that *without knowing what study participants refer to when they rate their motivation for a discipline or activity, we cannot be certain what the results mean.*

Acknowledgments

The research reported here was supported by a grant (#R305K050038) from the United States Department of Education, Institute of Education Sciences. The opinions expressed are the authors' and do not represent views of the United States Department of Education. We greatly appreciate the involvement of the teachers and children in this project. We also thank Allan Wigfield for his feedback on an earlier version of this chapter.

References

Andre, T., Whigham, M., Hendrickson, A. and Chambers, S. (1999) 'Competency beliefs, positive affect, and gender stereotypes of elementary students and their parents about science versus other school subjects', *Journal of Research in Science Teaching*, 36: 719–747.
Aschbacher, P.R., Li, E. and Roth, E.J. (2010) 'Is science me? High school students' identities, participation and aspirations in science, engineering, and medicine', *Journal of Research in Science Teaching*, 47: 564–582.
Britner, S. (2008) 'Motivation in high school science students: comparison of gender differences in life, physical, and earth science classes', *Journal of Research in Science Teaching*, 45: 955–970.

Britner, S. and Pajares, F. (2006) 'Sources of science self-efficacy beliefs of middle school students', *Journal of Research in Science Teaching,* 43: 485–499.

Fulp, S.L. (2002) '2000 national survey of science and mathematics education: status of elementary school science teaching'. Available at http://2000survey.horizon-research.com/reports/elem_science.php

Gottfried, A.E., Fleming, J.S. and Gottfried, A.W. (2001) 'Continuity of academic intrinsic motivation from childhood through late adolescence: a longitudinal study', *Journal of Educational Psychology,* 93: 3–13.

Graham, S. and Weiner, B. (2012) 'Motivation: past, present, and future', in K.R. Harris, S. Graham and T. Urdan (eds) *APA Educational Psychology Handbook: Volume 1. Theories, Constructs, and Critical Issues* (pp. 367–397), Washington, DC: American Psychological Association.

Greenfield, T.A. (1996) 'Gender, ethnicity, science achievement, and attitudes', *Journal of Research in Science Teaching,* 33: 901–933.

Hicks, D. (1996) 'Contextual inquiries: a discourse oriented study of classroom learning', in D. Hicks (ed.) *Discourse, Learning, and Schooling* (pp. 104–141), New York: Cambridge University Press.

Kelly, G.J. and Crawford, T. (1997) 'An ethnographic investigation of the discourse processes of school science', *Science Education,* 81: 533–559.

Mantzicopoulos, P., Patrick, H. and Samarapungavan, A. (2008) 'Young children's motivational beliefs about learning science', *Early Childhood Research Quarterly,* 23: 378–394.

Mantzicopoulos, P., Patrick, H. and Samarapungavan, A. (2013) 'Science literacy in school and home contexts: kindergarteners' science achievement and motivation', *Cognition and Instruction,* 31: 62–119.

Mantzicopoulos, P., Samarapungavan, A. and Patrick, H. (2009) '"We learn how to predict and be a scientist": early science experiences and kindergarten children's social meanings about science', *Cognition and Instruction,* 27: 312–369.

Mehan, H. (1985) 'The structure of classroom discourse', in T.A. Van Dijk (ed.) *Handbook of Discourse Analysis* (Vol. 3, pp. 119–131), London: Academic Press.

Patrick, H., Mantzicopoulos, P. and Samarapungavan, A. (2009) 'Motivation for learning science in kindergarten: is there a gender gap and does integrated inquiry and literacy instruction make a difference?', *Journal of Research in Science Teaching,* 46: 166–191.

Perez-Granados, D.R. and Callanan, M.A. (1997) 'Parents and siblings as early resources for young children's learning in Mexican-descent families', *Hispanic Journal of Behavioral Sciences,* 19: 3–33.

Piaget, J. (1955) *The Language and Thought of the Child,* Cleveland, OH: The World Publishing Company.

Rogoff, B. (1992) 'Three ways to relate person and culture: thoughts sparked by Valsiner's review of *Apprenticeship in Thinking*', *Human Development,* 35: 316–320.

Roth, W. and Lee, Y. (2007) '"Vygotsky's neglected legacy": cultural-historical activity theory', *Review of Educational Research,* 77: 186–232.

Sadler, P.M., Sonnert, G., Hazari, Z. and Tai, R. (2012) 'Stability and volatility of STEM career interest in high school: a gender study', *Science Education,* 96: 411–427.

Samarapungavan, A., Mantzicopoulos, P. and Patrick, H. (2008) 'Learning science through inquiry in kindergarten', *Science Education,* 92: 868–908.

Samarapungavan, A., Patrick, H. and Mantzicopoulos, P. (2011) 'What kindergarten students learn in inquiry-based science classrooms', *Cognition and Instruction,* 29: 416–470.

Scientific Literacy Project (2009) Available at: http://www.purduescientificliteracyproject.org

Vedder-Weiss, D. and Fortus, D. (2011) 'Adolescents' declining motivation to learn science: inevitable or not?', *Journal of Research in Science Teaching,* 48: 199–216.

Vygotsky, L.S. (1978) *Mind and Society: The Development of Higher Mental Processes,* Cambridge, MA: Harvard University Press.

Wigfield, A. and Cambria, J. (2010) 'Students' achievement values, goal orientations, and interest: definitions, development, and relations to achievement outcomes', *Developmental Review,* 30: 1–35.

PART II

Responding to student culture

7

RACIAL AND ETHNIC IDENTITY

Frank C. Worrell

Racial identity and ethnic identity are two of the most frequently examined cultural identities in the psychological literature on minority populations. Although frequently discussed with regard to educational outcomes, the relationship of these two constructs to academic achievement is at best ambiguous, and is generally predicated on the fact that academic achievement differs across racial and ethnic groups (Worrell 2014). In this chapter, after a brief review of the literature on the achievement gap, I highlight two major theoretical models – cultural ecological theory and stereotype threat – that implicate racial and ethnic identity in academic achievement. Next, I define racial identity, provide a brief overview of the theoretical models specifically associated with this construct, as well as their operationalization in the extant literature, and summarize the empirical findings relating racial identity to academic achievement. Third, I present a similar overview for ethnic identity. Finally, I close with some suggestions for future research that will allow educational researchers to get a more complete understanding of if and how racial and ethnic identity contribute to academic achievement outcomes.

Given this handbook's focus, the review of the empirical literature is generally confined to studies that used school-age rather than college-age populations. This decision is not intended to suggest that racial identity and ethnic identity are not important to college students. Rather, the focus on the school-age population is related to the fact that students in college have not been derailed academically, and that a focus on these issues in the classroom implicates elementary and secondary education to a greater extent than it does tertiary education. It is also important to note that the extant literature has been complicated by the interchangeable use of the terms, racial identity and ethnic identity, in the literature, as well as the interchangeable use of the instruments operationalizing these constructs (Worrell 2013; Worrell and Gardner-Kitt 2006). In this chapter, racial identity and ethnic identity will be discussed separately for several reasons. First, they have different theoretical underpinnings and the ways in which the constructs have been operationalized are directly related to the underlying theoretical models. Second, there are multiple theories and operationalizations of both constructs. Third, there are no studies suggesting that the two constructs are identical, although they are similar (Worrell and Gardner-Kitt 2006). Finally, although many recent scholars have used the term race/ethnicity as the construct that they are measuring, there are as yet no theoretical models with instruments developed to specifically assess this combined construct.

The achievement gap

Racial identity and ethnic identity have become prominent in academic discourse in response to substantial differences in academic performance among racial and ethnic groups. These differences are reflected in statistics from the United States, where racial and ethnic disparities in educational performance and outcomes are particularly stark. For example, high-school graduation rates are considerably lower for Hispanic Americans (62%), African Americans (83%), and American Indians/Alaska Natives (78%) than for European Americans (92%) and Asian Americans/Pacific Islanders (89%; Aud *et al.* 2010), and these disparities in educational attainment and performance are present from the early elementary grades through tertiary education (Aud *et al.* 2013), and are particularly stark at the highest levels of performance (Plucker *et al.* 2013). Moreover, educational disparities across racial and ethnic groups are not limited to the United States, and can be found in most multiethnic societies. For example, in New Zealand, Māori (16.3%) and Pasifika (28%) students complete secondary school at far lower rates than their Asian (65%) and Pākehā (49%) peers (Webber 2011). And it is these disparities in achievement that lead researchers to conclude that cultural identities may play a role in classroom performance.

Models linking cultural identities and school performance

There are two major theoretical models that link cultural identities to academic performance. Ogbu's (1978, 1985, 1989, 1992, 2003, 2004) cultural ecological theory is one of the models. The other model is Steele's (1997, 2010; Steele and Aronson 1995) stereotype threat. Interestingly, neither cultural ecological theory nor stereotype threat assesses racial or ethnic identity directly, although both theories implicate individuals' sense of identification with their racial or ethnic group in academic performance outcomes.

Cultural ecological theory

Based on research on the educational performance of groups in six different countries, Ogbu (1982; Ogbu and Simons 1998) postulated that there are three types of minorities: autonomous, voluntary, and involuntary. Autonomous minorities are typically smaller in number than the dominant group and although different on some cultural characteristic (e.g. language or religion), they are not readily distinguishable from the dominant group and typically become indistinguishable from the dominant group over a relatively short period of time. Voluntary (or immigrant) minorities are those who *choose* to emigrate to a new society for educational or socioeconomic advancement. They maintain their culture of origin, assume that they can return home if they choose to do so, and focus on the additional opportunities that brought them to the new country in the first place. Given the voluntary nature of their presence, Ogbu argued that even when discriminated against, they are less likely to be derailed as their *dual consciousness* acts as protective factor. The third type of minority is the involuntary minority. These are groups who became members of the host society involuntarily (Ogbu 1985) through conquest or slavery, for example. Examples of involuntary minorities include African Americans and Native Americans in the United States and Māori in New Zealand. It is crucial to note involuntary minority status is not necessarily numerical, but is determined in part by the subordinate position that the group holds in the power structure of the society it inhabits (Ogbu and Simons 1998).

These minority groups encounter three types of discontinuities between home and school: universal discontinuities, which every group experiences; primary discontinuities, which occur when voluntary minorities begin attending school in their new country; and secondary discontinuities, which 'develop *after* members of two populations have been in contact', especially in contact situations involving structural inequities between dominant and subordinate groups (Ogbu 1982: 298). Secondary discontinuities are experienced most by involuntary minorities and can result in involuntary minority group members being less committed to adopting the patterns of behavior associated with success in society or in school.

Ogbu contended that these secondary discontinuities were not irrational. They are based on several beliefs of involuntary minorities: (a) academic credentials having less instrumentality for success for members of these groups; (b) tremendous mistrust of the dominant group; and (c) schooling being perceived by involuntary minorities as a way to subordinate and control them while taking away their culture of origin. Ogbu (1989) did point out that not all members of involuntary minorities held these viewpoints. He theorized that there were at least eight patterns that African Americans in the United States adopted, only two of which – ambivalents and encapsulated – were associated with lack of success in school; ambivalents were postulated to be unable to resolve the conflict they felt between succeeding in school and being loyal to their racial–ethnic group, and encapsulated youth perceive success in schools as 'acting White' (Ogbu, 1989: 200), and consequently reject this option.

Cultural ecological theory has been contested in the literature and both sides of the debate are summarized in an edited volume (see Ogbu 2008). The full debate is beyond the scope of this chapter, but I summarize a few empirical studies from the United States that provide some support for Ogbu's broad claims. In 2003, Oyserman *et al.* interviewed African American, American Indian and Latino middle-school students and classified them on the basis of the interviews into four groups on the basis of their espoused racial–ethnic schemas: aschematic, in-group only, minority, and dual. Students with the in-group-only schema – that is, they were connected only to their group – seemed to reflect Ogbu's encapsulated group. These students had significantly and substantively lower ($d = .78$) academic achievement than students with the dual schema. Moreover, this finding was replicated in the United States with a sample of Native Americans and in Israel with a sample of Palestinians (Oyserman *et al.* 2003), both of which are stigmatized groups in their respective societies.

In another study, Taylor and Graham (2007) found that as students moved from the elementary- to the middle-school grades, African American and Latino males began to adopt students with low achievement as role models, in part due to the belief that as minority males, there were greater barriers to opportunities for them. In a third study, Ford *et al.* (2008) addressed the notion of 'acting White' directly. They asked African American students in the fourth to twelfth grades if they had heard the terms, 'acting Black' and 'acting White', and if yes, what did the terms mean. About 80 percent of the students were familiar with the terms, and the students reported that acting Black was associated with underachievement, lack of education, and pretending not to be smart, whereas acting White was associated with doing well in school, taking advanced classes, and completing homework. These findings suggest that even if some of the tenets of cultural ecological theory are not supported, there are some students who associate racial and ethnic identification with academic achievement. Questions for the literature include how widespread are these views and how much do they contribute to actual achievement and the achievement gap.

Stereotype threat

Steele's (1997) notion of stereotype threat is the second prominent model that associates academic performance with racial and ethnic identity, and is premised on the risk of confirming a widely held *negative* stereotype about one's group. To the extent that individuals belong to a group stereotyped as unintelligent, those individuals are vulnerable to stereotype threat in situations where the stereotype of low intelligence is salient (e.g. academic assessment situations for stigmatized minorities). The idea is that fear of confirming the stereotype results in heightened emotion, which interferes with cognition and thus impedes academic performance and leads, paradoxically, to confirming the stereotype that the individual was afraid of confirming in the first place.

The stereotype threat phenomenon has been replicated in many – albeit mostly laboratory based – studies (Steele and Aronson 1995) and in several countries, and the majority of work to date has been conducted with university samples in selective institutions. However, there are several studies that have included students in elementary- and secondary-school settings. A few of these studies have been studies that have looked for stereotype threat, but the majority of the studies with these age groups are intervention studies intended to mitigate stereotype threat. In 2003, McKown and Weinstein showed in a sample of elementary-school students that the awareness of broadly held stereotypes increases across the elementary-school grades, alongside the ability to infer the stereotype of a particular individual. These researchers also demonstrated that stereotype threat results in lowered effort and performance in elementary-school students from stigmatized groups, suggesting that under some circumstances, stereotype threat can manifest itself in student performance before middle school.

Several researchers have conducted interventions with school-aged students intended to mitigate against stereotype threat. For example, Cohen *et al.* (2006) randomly assigned middle-school students to two groups, with one group writing about why positive values were important to them personally, and the second group writing about why positive values might be important to someone other than themselves. These researchers hypothesized that the self-affirmation group would enhance the integrity of their identity and thus be less vulnerable to stereotype threat. Results indicated that African Americans in the self-affirmation group closed the achievement gap by 40 percent, but there was no effect on African American peers in the other person affirmation (control) group or European Americans in either group. Moreover, the academic gains were maintained up to two years following the initial intervention (Cohen *et al.* 2009). Although these studies are used to provide support for stereotype threat's effects, it should be noted that stereotype threat was not assessed directly in either study. Moreover, a replication of the study by Simmons (2011) with high-schoolers assigned to a continuation school did not yield the same benefits, suggesting that even if this intervention mitigates against threat, it may need to be done before students are too much at risk.

Summary

Both stereotype threat and cultural ecological theory posit that racial–ethnic group identification has implications for academic performance through disengagement from the learning process, and there are studies that provide some support for the claims. It is important to note that neither model assesses racial identity or ethnic identity directly. Nonetheless, the differences in achievement between dominant and subordinate groups in many countries suggest that these claims should be investigated further. In the next section, I focus attention on racial identity and ethnic identity as constructs that have been operationalized and studied directly rather than inferred.

Racial identity and academic achievement

Racial identity has been defined as 'a sense of group or collective identity based on one's perception he or she shares a common racial heritage with a particular racial group' (Helms 1990a: 3). Although this construct is most frequently studied in African Americans, beginning with the seminal doll studies in the mid-1900s (e.g. Clark and Clark 1950), the study of racial identity was subsequently extended to European Americans (e.g. Helms 1990b), and many contemporary scholars use the terms racial identity and ethnic identity interchangeably in their research across multiple groups. Contemporary theorizing (e.g. Cokley and Vandiver 2012) describes racial identity as a series of attitudes that should together make up an individual's racial identity profile.

There are four major models of Black racial identity in the literature with instruments that operationalize them. These include the original nigrescence model (Cross 1971) and the Racial Identity Attitude Scale (RIAS; Helms and Parham 1990, 1996; Parham and Helms 1981); Africentric theory (Baldwin 1981) and the African Self-Consciousness Scale (Baldwin and Bell 1985); the multidimensional model of racial identity (Sellers *et al.* 1998) and the Multidimensional Inventory of Black Identity (Sellers *et al.* 1997); and the expanded nigrescence model (Cross and Vandiver 2001) and the Cross Racial Identity Scale (CRIS; Vandiver *et al.* 2000; Worrell *et al.* 2004). No study has examined the relationship between African Self-Consciousness Scale scores and academic achievement, and this model will not be discussed further.

Original nigrescence model (NT-O)

The original nigrescence model (NT-O) (Cross 1971) postulated that African American identity goes through a series of five stages – pre-encounter, encounter, immersion–emersion, internalization, and internalization–commitment – and that movement through the stages reflected movement from less healthy to more healthy identity attitudes. The RIAS (Parham and Helms 1981) was developed to assess the first four stages of NT-O, and the relationship between scores on the RIAS and academic achievement in school-aged samples has been examined in two studies. Witherspoon *et al.* (1997) examined the relationship of racial identity attitudes based on the RIAS to both academic self-concept and academic achievement in a sample of 86 African American high-school students. They found that academic achievement had negative correlations with encounter (−.28) and immersion (−.31) scores, both of which reflect pro-Black and anti-White attitudes. No other relationships with the academic variables were greater than $|.20|$. Given the reliability estimates for RIAS scores in this study ($.42 \leq \alpha \leq .64$, $Mdn = .49$), these findings need to be regarded with caution.

In another study, Ford and Harris (1997) examined RIAS scores in a sample of 149 middle- and high-school students: 44 students classified as gifted by their school district, 67 students that the authors classified as potentially gifted, and 38 general education students. Ford and Harris also classified the students into achievers and underachievers, and examined differences in racial identity attitudes by both gifted/potentially gifted/general education and achiever/underachiever classifications. They reported that the potentially gifted group had significantly higher pre-encounter scores than the gifted group, and that the gifted education group had significantly higher internalization scores than the regular education group. They also reported significant differences in internalization scores among the achievement groups as follows: male underachievers ($M = 3.3$); male achievers and female achievers ($M = 3.6$); and female underachievers ($M = 3.8$). These results do not show a consistent relationship between racial identity and achievement. For example, if internalization scores are related to higher achievement, they should be higher for the gifted group, as well as the male and female achiever groups. Thus, it is not clear that the differences in racial identity are related to achievement.

Multidimensional model of racial identity (MMRI)

The MMRI (Sellers *et al.* 1997, 1998) is another major theory of Black racial identity and it is operationalized with a seven-subscale instrument, the Multidimensional Inventory of Black Identity (MIBI). The subscales are centrality, public regard, private regard, assimilation, oppressed minority, nationalist, and humanist. However, the four studies examining the relationship between

MIBI scores and academic achievement in school-aged students have used only variations of three subscales: centrality, private regard, and public regard. Centrality assesses how important race is to an individual's self-concept; Fuligni *et al.* (2005) used a 7-item version of centrality and both Chavous *et al.* (2008) and Byrd and Chavous (2011) used 3-item versions. Private regard assesses individuals' positive feelings toward their own ethnic group. Fuligni *et al.* used an 8-item version of this scale, Byrd and Chavous used a 6-item version, and Butler-Barnes *et al.* (2012) used a 4-item version. Finally, Byrd and Chavous also used a 2-item version of public regard, which assesses individuals' perceptions of how society views their group, in a single study. Additionally, the versions of the subscales used by Fuligni *et al.* had to be adapted for general use, as these authors examined the scores in adolescents of Chinese, European, and Mexican backgrounds, and the MIBI was developed to assess racial identity in African Americans.

In spite of the differences in versions of scales used, the findings are remarkably similar. Bivariate correlations indicate that centrality ($-.06 \leq r \leq .07$), private regard ($-.09 \leq r \leq .23$), and public regard ($r = .10$) scores are not meaningfully correlated with academic achievement. Fuligni *et al.* (2005) did report that private regard scores were moderately and meaningfully correlated ($r = .32$) with identification with school, although not with school self-concept ($r = .03$), but these authors did not report correlations by subgroup. In the other three studies, the authors reported interactions involving racial identity attitudes with implications for achievement or achievement-related factors, but all of these findings need to be replicated.

Expanded nigrescence model (NT-E)

Only one dissertation study has used the CRIS, which operationalizes the expanded nigrescence model, NT-E, to predict academic achievement in school-aged students. In 2005, Gardner-Kitt examined the relationship between CRIS scores and academic achievement in more than 100 middle- and high-school students and reported that none of the six racial identity attitudes assessed by the CRIS was meaningfully related to academic achievement ($-.19 \leq r \leq .20$), although anti-White attitudes predicted engaging in problem behaviors in school ($r = .35$). It is worth noting that the studies of the relationship between racial identity attitudes and achievement in college samples have also yielded similar findings.

Ethnic identity and academic achievement

There are three ethnic identity instruments in the extant literature: the Multigroup Ethnic Identity Measure (MEIM; Phinney 1992), the Ethnic Identity Scale (Umaña-Taylor *et al.* 2004), and the revised version of the MEIM (MEIM-R; Phinney and Ong 2007). All three scales have been used in studies examining academic achievement in school-aged samples. As with racial identity, results are generally consistent with most researchers finding no meaningful bivariate correlations (i.e. $r > .30$) between ethnic identity scores and achievement (e.g. Breskin 2009; Jo 1999; Landron 2009; Rust 2008; Sobansky 2004; Tan and Jordan-Arthur 2012).

Direct relationships between achievement and ethnic identity have been found in two studies. Yasui *et al.* (2004) reported a substantial correlation ($r = .57$) between ethnic identity scores and achievement for African American adolescents but not for European American adolescents ($r = .24$). In another study, Worrell (2007) found that ethnic identity was negatively related to school achievement ($sr^2 = -.41$), but not related to summer program achievement ($sr^2 = .19$) in a sample of African Americans, and not related to achievement in either context for Asian Americans, European Americans, and Hispanic Americans ($-.20 \leq sr^2 \leq .07$). A few indirect relationships have also been observed. For example, Gardner-Kitt (2005) found that ethnic identity was related to academic orientation, which in turn predicted academic achievement. Finally, in a study in which academic achievement was not assessed directly (Webber, 2011; Webber *et al.* 2013), ethnic identity scores were found to be related to embedded achievement, a construct which assesses the belief that success in school is related to ethnic identity.

Summary

As the previous review of the literature shows, the preponderance of evidence indicates that racial and ethnic identity are not directly related to academic achievement. Moreover, although some studies have indicated that racial and ethnic identity may have mediated or moderated influences on achievement, none of these studies has been replicated. These findings highlight the fact that the purported relationship of cultural identities to academic performance in school-aged populations is based primarily on theory (Graham, 2004; Hudley and Irving, 2012; Ogbu and Simons, 1998; Steele, 2010; Tatum 1997) and less on empirical research. They do not necessarily mean that the achievement is not affected by racial and ethnic identity, but they do indicate that if these relationships exist, we have yet to fully understand how racial and ethnic identity affect achievement. In the next section, I lay out a research agenda for addressing this issue.

Future research

There are several actions that are needed to determine if and how racial and ethnic identity are related to academic achievement. First, with regard to both cultural ecological theory and stereotype threat, it will be important to assess the accuracy of the claims that these models make (e.g. low-effort syndrome, disidentification) as well as the amount of variance that they account for in academic performance. It is not sufficient for research to claim that it is countering an effect that has never been quantified. Second, in all studies that include racial and ethnic identity, it will be important to report the correlations between these constructs and achievement so that there is sufficient literature on which to make strong claims (e.g. through meta-analyses). Third, relatedly, researchers need to be clear about the construct that they are investigating (i.e. racial identity or ethnic identity) and use a measure that was designed to operationalize that specific construct.

Fourth, with regard to racial identity especially, researchers need to use the same instruments to operationalize these constructs across studies. For example, when racial identity is assessed in relationship to achievement using different versions of a measure in different studies, it is difficult to determine what the true nature of the relationship between achievement and racial identity is, and if differences that occur across studies are the result of actual differences in the relationship or merely differences due to the operationalization. Fifth, there is a critical need for studies that pay attention to and account for a variety of contexts (e.g. cultural, socioeconomic). Along these lines, the extant literature suggests convincingly that the relationship between cultural identities and academic achievement is dependent on context, and understanding the role of contexts – through qualitative research, mixed-method studies, and quantitative studies with comprehensive descriptions of contexts – is necessary to advance the knowledge base in this area.

References

Aud, S., Fox, M. and KewalRamani, A. (2010) *Status and Trends in the Education of Racial and Ethnic Groups* (NCES 2010–015), U.S. Department of Education, National Center for Education Statistics, Washington, DC: U.S. Government Printing Office.

Aud, S., Wilkinson-Flicker, S., Krstapovich, P., Rathburn, A., Wang, X. and Zhang, J. (2013) *The Condition of Education 2013* (NCES 2013–037), Washington, DC: U.S. Department of Education, National Center for Educational Statistics. Retrieved from https://nces.ed.gov/pubsearch/pubsinfo.asp?pubid=2013037

Baldwin, J.A. (1981) 'Notes on an Africentric theory of Black personality', *The Western Journal of Black Studies,* 5: 172–179.

Baldwin, J.A. and Bell, Y.R. (1985) 'The African Self-Consciousness Scale: an Africentric personality questionnaire', *The Western Journal of Black Studies,* 9: 61–68.

Breskin, L. (2009) 'The relationship among ethnic identity, academic achievement, attitude toward gender, and education', doctoral dissertation, available from ProQuest Dissertations and Theses database (UMI No. 3358330).

Butler-Barnes, S.T., Williams, T.T. and Chavous, T.M. (2012) 'Racial pride and religiosity among African American boys: implications for academic motivation and achievement', *Journal of Youth and Adolescence,* 41: 486–498.

Byrd, C.M. and Chavous, T.M. (2011) 'Racial identity, school racial climate, and school intrinsic motivation among African American youth: the importance of person–context congruence', *Journal of Research on Adolescence,* 21: 849–860.

Chavous, T.M., Rivas-Drake, D., Smalls, C., Griffin, T. and Cogburn, C. (2008) 'Gender matters, too: the influences of school racial discrimination and racial identity on academic engagement outcomes among African American adolescents', *Developmental Psychology,* 44: 637–654.

Clark, K.B. and Clark, M.P. (1950) 'Emotional factors in racial identification and preference in Negro children', *Journal of Negro Education,* 19: 341–350.

Cohen, G.L., Garcia, J., Apfel, N. and Master, A. (2006) 'Reducing the racial achievement gap: a social-psychological intervention', *Science,* 313: 1307–1308.

Cohen, G.L., Garcia, J., Purdie-Vaughns, V., Apfel, N. and Brzustoski, P. (2009) 'Recursive processes in self-affirmation: intervening to close the minority achievement gap', *Science,* 324: 400–403.

Cokley, K.O. and Vandiver, B.J. (2012) 'Ethnic and racial identity', in E.M. Altmaier and J.C. Hansen (eds) *The Oxford Handbook of Counseling Psychology* (pp. 291–325), New York: Oxford University Press.

Cross, W.E. Jr. (1971) 'The Negro-to-Black conversion experience: toward a psychology of Black liberation', *Black World,* 20: 13–27.

Cross, W.E. Jr. and Vandiver, B.J. (2001) 'Nigrescence theory and measurement: introducing the Cross Racial Identity Scale (CRIS)', in J.G. Ponterotto, J.M. Casas, L.A. Suzuki, and C.M. Alexander (eds) *Handbook of Multicultural Counseling,* 2nd ed. (pp. 371–393), Thousand Oaks, CA: Sage.

Ford, D.Y., Grantham, T.C. and Whiting, G.W. (2008) 'Another look at the achievement gap: learning from the experiences of gifted Black students', *Urban Education* 43: 216–238.

Ford, D.Y. and Harris, J.J. III. (1997) 'A study of the racial identity and achievement of Black males and females', *Roeper Review,* 20: 105–110.

Fuligni, A.J., Witkow, M. and Garcia, C. (2005) 'Ethnic identity and the academic adjustment of adolescents from Mexican, Chinese, and European backgrounds', *Developmental Psychology,* 41: 799–811.

Gardner-Kitt, D. (2005) 'Black student achievement: the influence of racial identity, ethnic identity, perception of school climate, and self-reported behavior', *Dissertation Abstracts International,* 66(4-B): 2292.

Graham, S. (2004) '"I can, but do I want to?" Achievement values in ethnic minority children and adolescents', in G. Philogène (ed.) *Racial Identity in Context: The Legacy of Kenneth B. Clark* (pp. 125–147), Washington, DC: American Psychological Association.

Helms, J.E. (1990a) 'Introduction: review of racial identity terminology', in J.E. Helms (ed.) *Black and White Racial Identity: Theory, Research, and Practice* (pp. 3–8), New York: Greenwood.

Helms, J.E. (1990b) 'Toward a model of White racial identity development', in J.E. Helms (ed.) *Black and White Racial Identity: Theory, Research, and Practice* (pp. 49–66), New York: Greenwood.

Helms, J.E. and Parham, T.A. (1990) 'Black Racial Identity Attitude Scale (Form RIAS-B)', in J.E. Helms (ed.) *Black and White Racial Identity: Theory, Research, and Practice* (pp. 245–247), New York: Greenwood Press.

Helms, J.E. and Parham, T.A. (1996) 'The development of the Racial Identity Attitude Scale', in R.L. Jones (ed.) *Handbook of Tests and Measurements for Black Populations* (Vol. 2, pp. 167–174), Hampton, VA: Cobb & Henry.

Hudley, C. and Irving, M. (2012) 'Ethnic and racial identity in childhood and adolescence', in K.R. Harris, S. Graham, T. Urdan, S. Graham, and J.M. Royer (eds.) *APA Educational Psychology Handbook,* Vol. 2: *Individual Differences and Cultural and Contextual Factors* (pp. 267–292), Washington, DC: American Psychological Association.

Jo, H. (1999) 'The influence of African American urban students' ethnic identity and coping strategies on academic involvement and psychological adjustment', doctoral dissertation, available from ProQuest Dissertations and Theses database (UMI No. 9839651).

Landron, A. (2009) 'A comparative analysis of school membership and ethnic identity between dual language and English as a second language instruction', doctoral dissertation, available from ProQuest Dissertations and Theses database (UMI No. 3116609).

McKown, C. and Weinstein, R.S. (2003) 'The development and consequences of stereotype consciousness in middle childhood', *Child Development*, 74: 498–515.

Ogbu, J.U. (1978) *Minority Education and Caste: The American Education System in Cross-Cultural Perspective*, New York: Academic Press.

Ogbu, J.U. (1982) 'Cultural discontinuities and schooling', *Anthropology and Education Quarterly*, 13: 290–307.

Ogbu, J.U. (1985) 'Research currents: cultural-ecological influences on minority school learning', *Language Arts*, 62: 860–869.

Ogbu, J.U. (1989) 'The individual in collective adaptation: a framework for focusing on academic under-performance and dropping out among involuntary minorities', in L. Weis, E. Farrar and H.G. Petrie (eds) *Dropouts from School: Issues, Dilemmas, and Solutions* (pp. 181–204), New York: SUNY Press.

Ogbu, J.U. (1992) 'Understanding cultural diversity and learning', *Educational Researcher*, 21: 5–14.

Ogbu, J.U. (2003) *Black American Students in an Affluent Suburb: A Study of Academic Disengagement*, Hillsdale, NJ: Lawrence Erlbaum Associates.

Ogbu, J.U. (2004) 'Collective identity and the burden of "acting White" in Black history, community, and education', *The Urban Review*, 36: 1–35.

Ogbu, J.U. (Ed.) (2008) *Minority Status, Oppositional Culture, and Schooling*, New York: Routledge.

Ogbu, J.U. and Simons, H.D. (1998) 'Voluntary and involuntary minorities: a cultural-ecological theory of school performance with some implications for education', *Anthropology and Education Quarterly*, 29: 155–188.

Oyserman, D., Kemmelmeier, M., Fryberg, S., Brosh, H. and Hart-Johnson, T. (2003) 'Racial-ethnic self-schemas', *Social Psychology Quarterly*, 66: 333–347.

Parham, T.A. and Helms, J.E. (1981) 'The influence of Black students' racial identity attitudes on preference for counselor's race', *Journal of Counseling Psychology*, 28: 250–258.

Phinney, J.S. (1992) 'The Multigroup Ethnic Identity Measure: a new scale for use with diverse groups', *Journal of Adolescent Research*, 7: 56–176.

Phinney, J.S. and Ong, A.D. (2007) 'Conceptualization and measurement of ethnic identity: current status and future directions', *Journal of Counseling Psychology*, 54: 271–281.

Plucker, J.A., Hardesty, J. and Burroughs, N. (2013) *Talent on the Sidelines: Excellence Gaps and America's Persistent Talent Underclass*, Storrs, CT: Center for Education Policy Analysis, Neag School of Education, University of Connecticut.

Rust, J.P. (2008) 'Biculturalism, cultural identity, self-esteem, and academic achievement of African American high school students', doctoral dissertation, available from ProQuest Dissertations and Theses database (UMI No. 3302119).

Sellers, R.M., Rowley, S.A.J., Chavous, T.M., Shelton, J.N. and Smith, M.A. (1997) 'Multidimensional inventory of Black identity: a preliminary investigation of reliability and construct validity', *Journal of Personality and Social Psychology*, 73: 805–815.

Sellers, R.M., Smith, M.A., Shelton, J.N, Rowley, S.A. and Chavous, T.M. (1998) 'Multidimensional model of racial identity: a reconceptualization of African-American racial identity', *Personality and Social Psychology Review*, 2: 18–39.

Simmons, C.M. (2011) 'Reducing stereotype threat in academically at-risk African American students: a self-affirmation intervention', doctoral dissertation, available from ProQuest Dissertations and Theses database (UMI No. 3498889).

Sobansky, R.R.B. (2004) 'Ethnic identity and psychological well being among youth in residential treatment: exploring links with school success and psychological distress', doctoral dissertation, available from ProQuest Dissertations and Theses database (UMI No. 3116609).

Steele, C.M. (1997) 'A threat in the air: how stereotypes shape intellectual identity and performance', *American Psychologist*, 52: 613–629.

Steele, C.M. (2010) *Whistling Vivaldi and Other Clues to How Stereotypes Affect Us*, New York: Norton.

Steele, C.M. and Aronson, J. (1995) 'Stereotype threat and the intellectual test performance of African Americans', *Journal of Personality and Social Psychology*, 69: 797–811.

Tan, T.X. and Jordan-Arthur, B. (2012) 'Adopted Chinese girls come of age: feelings about adoption, ethnic identity, academic functioning, and global self-esteem', *Children and Youth Services Review*, 8: 1500–1508.

Tatum, B.D. (1997) '*Why are All the Black Kids Sitting Together in the Cafeteria' And Other Conversations about Race*, New York: Basic Books.

Taylor, A.Z. and Graham, S. (2007) 'An examination of the relationship between achievement values and perceptions of barriers among low-SES African American and Latino adolescents', *Journal of Educational Psychology*, 99: 52–64.

Umaña-Taylor, A.J., Yazedjian, A. and Bámaca-Gómez, M. (2004) 'Developing the ethnic identity scale using Eriksonian and social identity perspectives', *Identity: An International Journal of Theory and Research*, 4: 9–38.

Vandiver, B.J., Cross, W.E., Jr., Fhagen-Smith, P.E., Worrell, F.C., Swim, J.K., and Caldwell, L.D. (2000) *The Cross Racial Identity Scale*, State College, PA: Author.

Webber, M. (2011) 'Identity matters: racial-ethnic representations among adolescents attending multi-ethnic high schools', unpublished doctoral dissertation, University of Auckland, New Zealand.

Webber, M., McKinley, E. and Hattie, J. (2013) 'The importance of race and ethnicity: an exploration of New Zealand Pākehā, Māori, Samoan, and Chinese adolescent identity', *New Zealand Journal of Psychology*, 42: 17–28.

Witherspoon, K.M., Speight, S.L. and Thomas, A.J. (1997) 'Racial identity attitudes, school achievement, and academic self-efficacy among African American high school children', *Journal of Black Psychology*, 23: 344–357.

Worrell, F.C. (2007) 'Ethnic identity, academic achievement, and global self-concept in four groups of academically talented adolescents', *Gifted Child Quarterly*, 51: 23–38.

Worrell, F.C. (2013) 'African American racial identity and learning', in L. Meyer (ed.) *Oxford Bibliographies in Education*, New York: Oxford University Press.

Worrell, F.C. (2014) 'School and academic interventions', in F.T.L. Leong (ed.) *APA Handbook of Multicultural Psychology*, Vol. 2: *Applications and Training* (pp. 543–559), Washington, DC: American Psychological Association.

Worrell, F.C. and Gardner-Kitt, D.L. (2006) 'The relationship between racial and ethnic identity in Black adolescents: the Cross Racial Identity Scale (CRIS) and the Multigroup Ethnic Identity Measure (MEIM)', *Identity: An International Journal of Theory and Research*, 6: 293–315.

Worrell, F.C., Vandiver, B.J. and Cross, W.E., Jr. (2004) *The Cross Racial Identity Scale: Technical Manual*, 2nd edn, Berkeley, CA: Author.

Yasui, M., Dorham, C.L. and Dishion, T.J. (2004) 'Ethnic identity and psychological adjustment: a validity analysis for European American and African American adolescents', *Journal of Adolescent Research*, 19: 807–825.

8

STIGMA

Implications for student achievement and mentoring

C. Malik Boykin, Rodolfo Mendoza-Denton, and Colette E. Patt

Academic achievement disparities as a function of group membership remain a pervasive problem in education. These disparities are observed in educational systems around the world, and they share an important common feature that provides a clue to their etiology. The clue is this: where there are group-based disparities, the lower-performing group is almost universally a societally stigmatized and historically low-status group in that particular cultural context (Martinez and Mendoza-Denton 2011; Ogbu 1978; Walton and Spencer 2009). The fact that group differences in academic performance are so strongly tied to the relative status differences within a given cultural setting argues strongly against biological accounts or explanations for achievement differences, as some scholars have contended (e.g. Herrnstein and Murray 1994). Rather, these patterns suggest a *causal* effect of status and stigmatization on academic performance.

This chapter provides a brief introduction into some ways through which the experience of being a member of a stigmatized societal group can affect academic outcomes. Crocker *et al.* (1998: 504–5) define stigma as being, 'in essence . . . a devaluing social identity,' further noting that 'the person who is stigmatized is a person whose social identity, or membership in some social category, calls into question his or her full humanity – the person is devalued, flawed, or spoiled in the eyes of others.' As this quotation makes clear, processes relating to prejudice – the attitudes, feelings, or evaluations that people have about others based on their perceived group membership (Dovidio and Gaertner 2010) – often go hand in hand with those relating to stigma. Indeed, prejudice and stigma can be thought of as reflecting different vantage points of the same phenomenon. Nevertheless, we note from the outset that this chapter focuses on processes related to stigma, rather than prejudice – that is, the psychological implications of being the *target* of others' prejudices, and not of being the perpetrator of prejudice. We focus on two processes in particular: stereotype threat and status-based rejection sensitivity. We discuss each in turn, subsequently turning to a discussion of the importance of mentoring relationships in promoting academic achievement among stigmatized minority students.

Research background and empirical findings

Stereotype threat

Research on stereotype threat (see Steele 1997; Steele and Aronson 1995) has provided compelling evidence that the negative stereotypes that are often associated with stigmatized group membership can influence academic performance through a disruptive process of worry or concern that one may be viewed or treated through the lens of that stereotype. Stereotypes – and by extension stereotype threat – are highly sensitive to both content and context. An elderly woman behind the wheel, for example, may grow concerned that other drivers assume she cannot park, and this preoccupation itself may lead her to make mistakes, have to realign the car for parking, and become flustered – thus confirming the stereotype.

Latino and African American students in the United States context are particularly vulnerable to stereotype threat in the domain of academics, because the stereotype of these students centers on a presumption of low intelligence or ability. In the classic demonstration of this effect, Steele and Aronson (1995) presented African American and European American college students with the same 'test,' yet this test was framed in different ways. In one condition (the 'ability-diagnostic' condition), the students were told that the researchers were interested in measuring their verbal ability, and were thus being tested with items diagnostic of that ability. In the other condition, the students were told that these (same) questions were being used to understand the psychological processes associated with problem solving, but that the researchers would not be evaluating the participants' ability. The researchers expected that the former manipulation, which stresses ability, would automatically prime the African American students with the already highly accessible stereotype of low ability pertinent to their group, making it highly applicable within this context. The latter manipulation, by contrast, was intended to lift the students' concern that ability was under suspicion or scrutiny, thereby situationally lifting stereotype threat.

The results showed that the African American students underperformed relative to White students in the 'ability-diagnostic' condition, yet performed as well as the White students in the 'non-diagnostic' condition when controlling for prior levels of performance (i.e. SAT scores). In other words, African American participants' performance on the same set of questions was affected by a small, but psychologically critical, framing of the test.

Stereotype threat effects have been widely replicated for a wide range of stigmatized groups. Hoff and Pandey (2004) found that lower-caste individuals in India performed more poorly on a problem-solving task simply as a function of a public roll-call by surname, which reveals a person's caste in this setting. Croizet and Claire (1998) as well as John-Henderson and colleagues (2013) found that framing a test as ability diagnostic versus nondiagnostic among participants of low and high socioeconomic status led to stereotype threat effects that were analogous to the effects found by Steele and Aronson (1995). Quinn *et al.* (2004) have shown that revealing a mental health diagnosis depresses cognitive performance in 'reasoning ability' tasks. Across all of these studies, performance differences are attenuated when the threat of the stereotype is lifted, providing evidence for stereotype threat as an important contributing factor to achievement differentials.

It is important to note that while stereotype threat processes are robust in experimental studies, they have not been demonstrated as conclusively in real-world educational settings (e.g. see Sackett *et al.* 2004, 2008). This is to be expected, given that school performance is multiply determined and reflects both psychological and structural influences (e.g. socioeconomic status, educational access; see Fryer and Levitt 2004). Nonetheless, Walton and Spencer (2009) have argued that an important portion of variance in summary performance indicators, such as classroom grades and standardized test scores, can be attributed to the threat of confirming stereotypes. These researchers reasoned that if stereotype threat in fact undermines the real-world achievement of stigmatized minorities, then students' prior achievement indicators should *underestimate* these students' performance specifically in contexts where the stereotype threat is removed. To test this hypothesis, the researchers meta-analyzed findings examining the performance of stigmatized students in contexts that manipulated the presence or absence of stereotype threat ('threat' versus 'safe' conditions). The findings demonstrated that, in conditions where stereotype threat had been situationally removed (e.g. by explicitly invalidating the stereotype for achievement in the tested domain, or by refuting its relevance to the testing situation), students' prior performance was indeed biased towards underprediction in post-manipulation performance by approximately a fifth of a standard deviation. This effect was evident across all levels of prior performance. These findings provide evidence that the group-level achievement gaps reflected in performance indicators such as grades or standardized test scores are attributable, in part, to stereotype threat effects.

Status-based rejection sensitivity

A program of research on status-based rejection sensitivity provides a complementary yet alternative explanation to stereotype threat effects. Stemming from a literature on human attachment processes (Bowlby 1969, 1973, 1981), the status-based rejection sensitivity model emphasizes that, quite independently of worrying about one's own behavior, people are concerned about their level of acceptance and rejection in groups that they can potentially belong to, such as a classroom, a school community, or a broader community of scholars. Within this framework, then, the active psychological ingredient that can affect academic achievement is not an assessment of one's performance relative to a stereotype, but rather one's assessment of the tenor and temperature of the relationships in the academic spaces one navigates.

The status-based rejection sensitivity model (Mendoza-Denton *et al.* 2002) postulates that discrimination – rejection, exclusion, mistreatment, or marginalization – on the basis of status characteristics (such as race, class, sexual orientation, or gender) leads people to develop anxious expectations that they will be treated similarly in future contexts that afford the possibility of such rejection. Importantly, given that the source of the rejection is a personal characteristic that is nevertheless shared by a group of people, one does not need to personally have experienced discrimination to realize that one might be targeted in the future (Mendoza-Denton *et al.* 2002). Anxious expectations, once activated in the system, elicit anticipatory anxiety and physiological stress responses in the face of potential discrimination (e.g. increases in cortisol; Page-Gould *et al.* 2008), and dispose people to have strong, affect-laden reactions to the rejection once it is perceived (Mendoza-Denton *et al.* 2002).

In contrast to research on stereotype threat, status-based rejection sensitivity research focuses on *within-group* variability – that is, individual differences – to test the psychological processes that mediate the link between the threat of discrimination and achievement outcomes. The approach provides an alternative to group-level comparisons in outcomes (e.g. among men versus women, White students versus Black students, and so on) and serves as a reminder that far from being monolithic, cultural groups themselves exhibit variability that is important to recognize and work with in educational settings (Mendoza-Denton 2010).

Given the centrality of race as an enduring source of stigma in the United States context, the first empirical demonstration of status-based rejection sensitivity focused on the effects of race-based rejection sensitivity (*RS-race*) on the academic achievement of college students (Mendoza-Denton *et al.* 2002). This research showed that race-based rejection sensitivity among first-year, African American college students was related to how students experienced the first few weeks of college. More specifically, over the first 21 days of college, race-based rejection sensitivity was related to a muted sense of enthusiasm at being in the university, as well as a reduced sense of closeness with students' professors. These differences were relatively subtle over the first 21 days of college, yet they mediated differences in the sense of legitimacy students afforded towards the university at the end of the first year of college. Over time, individual differences in race-based rejection sensitivity negatively predicted students' academic trajectories over their first five semesters of college.

Importantly, individual differences in status-based rejection sensitivity interact with other intra-individual, as well as contextual, variables in ways that uncover when and how these processing dynamics are expressed. Mendoza-Denton and colleagues (2009), for example, conducted a study in which women were asked to complete an academic task in one of three offices, each of which was decorated differently. The first office contained an empty case of 'Big Daddy IPA' beer, pictures of bikini-clad models on motorcycles, and books suggesting that the occupant (the purported evaluator of the academic task) was chauvinist. The second office included a 'Race for the Cure' banner (associated in the United States with breast cancer awareness) and a certificate from a coeducational fraternity promoting equality across gender; the decor was meant to suggest that the evaluator held progressive attitudes. Finally, the 'ambiguous' office included an empty case of iced tea and a certificate from 'Volunteers of America, Ivy League Undergraduate Division.' Although there were no cues in the office that explicitly revealed the occupant's attitudes towards women, his gender and his position as an evaluator of participants' aptitude were expected to activate discrimination concerns specifically among women high in gender-based rejection sensitivity (*RS-gender*).

The results showed that among participants in the 'progressive' office, no differences emerged as a function of gender-based rejection sensitivity, suggesting that the rejection-sensitivity dynamic is only activated in contexts where the threat of discrimination is relevant. However, in the 'ambiguous' office, women high in RS-gender were especially likely to underperform. Moreover, consistent with the 'ironic effects' of prejudice (Shelton *et al.* 2005), when cues of chauvinism were clear, women high in RS-gender were, in a way, liberated from ambiguity, and their performance did not suffer. The context manipulation did not significantly affect the performance of women low in RS-gender because they are, overall, not as vigilant about gender-based rejection cues in the environment.

Status-based rejection sensitivity also interacts with identity processes to predict academic achievement in ways that underscore how a sense of acceptance and trust is integral to the educational enterprise. Some prior research suggests that being strongly identified with one's ethnic group, for example, prevents the development of affiliative ties with academic institutions. In contrast, Mendoza-Denton *et al.* (2008) showed that this is the case only among students who feel that the institution is likely to devalue or exclude members of their ethnic group – in other words, students high in race-based rejection sensitivity. In contrast, for students low in race-based rejection sensitivity, ethnic identity was not only unrelated to institutional identification, but it was related to *increased* academic achievement over time.

Mendoza-Denton *et al.* (2010) tackled the well-established observation that minority students sometimes disengage their self-esteem from academic endeavors, a coping strategy enacted in response to perceived discrimination (Crocker *et al.* 1998). Mendoza-Denton *et al.* randomly assigned African American students to receive either positive or negative feedback, with their race being either known or unknown by their evaluator. The results revealed that participants higher in race-based rejection sensitivity who thought their race was known tended to mistrust the academic feedback they were given, regardless of whether such feedback was positive or negative. By contrast, participants who were low in race-based rejection sensitivity tended to trust in the fairness of their evaluators, and thus their self-esteem rose or fell depending on the valence of feedback. Importantly, the engagement of these minority students occurred *even* when they thought that their evaluators knew their race, suggesting that knowledge of race in and of itself does not have to be a hindrance to student engagement. The research highlights the importance of creating and maintaining learning environments in which all students can experience a sense that they are valued and accepted within the institution. How can institutions foster a sense among students that they are valued and accepted?

Challenges and future directions: Role of mentorship

At the heart of our analysis is the idea that, beyond the 'three R's' that have been the historical pillars of a sound education – 'reading, 'riting and 'rithmetic' – a fourth R is of critical importance to people's intellectual development. This fourth R is *relationships*, and reflects an acknowledgment of acceptance and trust as critical components in the educational enterprise. When students are mindful of a history of stigmatization and rejection against groups they belong to, this fourth R may be of magnified importance to their success.

Research on wise feedback (Cohen *et al.* 1999; see also Yaeger and Walton 2011) illustrates this point. Cohen and colleagues invited African American and European American students to write an essay that participants thought would be considered for publication in a university-wide outlet, and were given feedback on the essay by a European American university professor (the purported editor of the magazine). In the 'criticism only' condition, students received critical feedback on their essay in the form of red markings along the margins (e.g. 'unclear', 'awkward'), two checkmarks for good points, plus specific suggestions, not unlike the emotion-free, 'objective' feedback that is highly valued within academic circles. In the 'criticism plus high standards' condition, students received the same critical feedback as in the 'criticism only' condition, but the professor also wrote, "Remember, I wouldn't go through the trouble of giving you this feedback if I weren't committed to the quality of this journal. I want to uphold the highest standards for what I consider a suitable entry." Finally, in a 'criticism plus high standards plus assurance' condition, the professor additionally wrote, "Remember, I wouldn't go through the trouble of giving you this feedback if I didn't think, based on what I've read in your letter, that you are capable of meeting the higher standard I mentioned".

The results from this study showed that African American students' motivation to revise the essay, based on the professor's feedback, was strongest in the 'wise' feedback condition – that is, criticism plus high standards plus assurance. By contrast, the 'criticism only' condition led to the lowest task motivation, lack of identification with the writing task, and the greatest ratings of perceived bias among the African American students. These results suggest that there may be negative motivational consequences, particularly for stigmatized students, in the face of the affectively neutral, 'objective' feedback that is prized within the United States educational context. Indeed, the African American students found motivation from learning that the professor believed in them. Cohen and Steele (2002) reported generalizability of these findings to other stigmatized groups, such as women working in the natural sciences.

Although mentoring relationships in academic contexts can take many forms, both formal and informal (Jacobi 1991), they are differentiated from strictly academic relationships in that they include psychosocial support, career-related support, and role modeling (Berk *et al.* 2005; Wang *et al.* 2010). As such, mentoring relationships are centrally characterized by a socioemotional component. A common thread that emerges in research on mentorship is the importance of the quality of the relationship between mentors and their protégées and/or mentees (Eby *et al.* 2010; Jacobi 1991; Kram 1985).

At the same time, the literature suggests that the formation of high-quality close relationships in the mentor–protégé dynamic can be elusive in intergroup contexts. In a study assigning 476 minority adolescents to either same-race or cross-race mentors, for example, Rhodes and colleagues (2002) found that male students in cross-race mentorship pairs experienced a diminished scholastic identity while their female cross-race paired counterparts reported a diminished valuation of both schooling and their own self-worth. These patterns were not present in the same-race mentorship conditions. In an analysis of focus group and survey data exploring career mentoring, Thomas (1989) uncovered patterns of unspoken race and gender taboos. These taboos underlay cross-group avoidance and thus hindered the development of cross-racial professional mentorship relationships.

These discouraging findings mirror a much broader literature showing that intergroup interactions are marked by anxiety and negative affect (Goff *et al.* 2008; Plant and Devine 1998; Mendes *et al.* 2002). As such, intergroup contexts generate high levels of self-regulation, expressive concerns, and threat (Dovidio and Gaertner 1998; Fazio *et al.* 1995; Mendes *et al.* 2003).

But does this mean that intergroup mentoring relationships are doomed to fail? Not necessarily. Campbell and Campbell (1997) found compelling results when they compared 339 undergraduate students assigned mentors with a control group of 339 undergraduates who were not assigned mentors, and subsequently matched on several demographic and performance measures. The mentor pool comprised 126 faculty, professors, administrators, academic deans, and staff members who volunteered and agreed to meet with their assigned students throughout the year. The results of this study suggested that the mentored students achieved higher GPAs than their un-mentored counterparts (2.45 vs. 2.29) and were 55 percent more likely to matriculate to the next academic year.

An encouraging association was discovered by Rhodes and colleagues (2002) such that cross-race mentor and student pairs who were matched with regards to shared interests or geographical identity did not show the same deleterious effects of other cross-race pairs. Work by Ensher and Murphy (1997) found corroborating evidence for this dynamic in their investigation of the effects of perceived similarities on mentor–mentee relationships within a summer internship program. Mentorship pairings were either same-race or cross-race with mostly European American mentors coupled with minority mentees in the cross-race pairings. Within the cross-race pairs, they found the closeness, social support, and task-oriented benefits of mentorship in instances where the mentor–protégé pairs identified points of commonality. This highlights Trompenaars and Wooliams' (2004) assertion that individuals within a given cultural framework vary greatly from each other on their personal preferences, ideas, and identities. Cultures have central tendencies around which individuals personal tendencies are distributed. This variation allows the opportunity and potential for individuals from differing cultures and ideologies to find overlapping similarities with others. In other words, as we are all different, we are also simultaneously similar, and thus finding ways to discover and explore our similarities, while making room for and respecting each other's differences, could help build the necessary bridges to form meaningful cross-cultural and cross-racial mentorship bonds.

This approach to thinking about mentorship is consistent with research using the Teacher Student Response Quality paradigm (Boykin and Noguera 2011). Through an analysis of several studies, Boykin and Noguera established that African American and Latino students glean especially positive and achievement-gap closing benefits when they perceive their teachers as being sincere, empathetic, and caring about their success and personal well-being. If we switch our focus to one that builds upon the assets that students bring to the learning environment, we should know the students' assets and thus know the students. These assets – whether defined as social, motivational, experiential, cultural, or ideological – provide bridges to both relational and academic understanding.

The above patterns support Aron and McLaughlin-Volpe's (2001) conception that cross-group relationships can be facilitated when individuals find overlapping identities and interests with an out-group member. This constructive contact can be the catalyst for the process of *self-expansion* among individuals who are dissimilar in one salient quality. The idea of self-expansion was originally proposed within the domain of romantic relationships to describe how people come to incorporate the attributes of their romantic partners into their own self-concepts, even when those attributes are not necessarily descriptive of the self. In the domain of cross-group friendships, Page-Gould *et al.* (2010) hypothesized and found that when someone has a close friend of another ethnicity, the closer that relationship, the longer it took participants in a reaction-time task to say that their friend's ethnicity did not in fact describe them. This suggests greater overlap between the self-concept and the attributes of one's friend. In subsequent studies, the researchers found that the latency of participants' responses in this task helped explain the degree of comfort experienced by participants in a novel intergroup situation (both an imagined one and a real-live interaction). Such self-expansion and contact can also generalize more broadly in the development of warmer feelings towards the group to which the out-group member belongs. Importantly, if the self-expansion model is correct, in the context of a mentoring relationship, a protégé may slowly grow to incorporate the most salient of a mentor's identities – the professional or academic identity – providing a pathway to continued academic engagement.

Conclusions

Many of us are familiar with the *golden rule*, the axiom that states that we should treat others the way that we would like to be treated. While noble in intent, the *golden rule* nevertheless assumes that others wish to be treated the way *we* want to be treated, and that they share our wants, needs, and values. Maltbia and Power (2011) have introduced an alternative *platinum rule* to the lexicon of intercultural work. The *platinum rule* states that you should treat others the way they would like to be treated. As such, the *platinum rule* respects variability in perspective and calls individuals to understand the needs and wants of others. A sense of understanding the wants, needs, and values of protégés could help to strengthen the essential relational component represented in the fourth 'R' we have proposed in this chapter.

With this in mind, mentors should be willing to leverage their status to give voice to mentees who are less willing to engage. This does not imply pushiness or creating an environment where mentees feel coerced into speaking, but it does mean taking an interest in understanding what engagement style works best for mentees. Even a conversation about how they most prefer to engage in the context of the mentorship could add value to the engagement. Relationships are co-constructions with negotiable rules of engagement. The very act of negotiating the rules of engagement gives insight into ideas, needs, and values of mentees on which trust and understanding can be built. Our point here is to highlight that both individual level differences and the cultural environment in which they were reared impact behavior in significant ways. Environment, individual differences, and behaviors are related in ways we must make room for within relationships among students and educators from many different groups.

This material is based upon work supported by the National Science Foundation under grant numbers 1306709 and 1306747.

References

Aron, A. and McLaughlin-Volpe, T. (2001) 'Including others in the self: extensions to own and partner's group memberships', in C. Sedikides and M.B. Brewer (eds) *Individual Self, Relational Self, and Collective Self: Partners, Opponents, or Strangers?* (pp. 89–109), Philadelphia: Psychology Press.

Berk, R.A., Berg, J., Mortimer, R., Walton-Moss, B. and Yeo, T.P. (2005) 'Measuring the effectiveness of faculty mentoring relationships', *Academic Medicine,* 80: 66–71. doi: http://dx.doi.org/10.1097/00001888–200501000–00017

Bowlby, J. (1969) *Attachment and Loss:* Vol. I. *Attachment,* New York: Basic Books.

Bowlby, J. (1973) *Attachment and Loss:* Vol. II. *Separation: Anxiety and Anger,* New York: Basic Books.

Bowlby, J. (1980) *Attachment and Loss:* Vol. III. *Loss: Sadness and Depression,* New York: Basic Books.

Boykin, A.W. and Noguera, P. (2011) *Creating the Opportunity to Learn: Moving from Research to Practice to Close the Achievement Gap,* Alexandria, VA: ASCD.

Campbell, T.A. and Campbell, D.E. (1997) 'Faculty/student mentor program: effects on academic performance and retention', *Research in Higher Education,* 38: 727–742.

Cohen, G.L. and Steele, C.M. (2002) 'A barrier of mistrust: how negative stereotypes affect cross-race mentoring', in J. Aronson (ed.) *Improving Academic Achievement: Impact of Psychology Factors on Education* (pp. 305–331), New York: Academic Press.

Cohen, G.L., Steele, C.M. and Ross, L.D. (1999) 'The mentor's dilemma: providing critical feedback across the racial divide', *Personality and Social Psychology Bulletin*, 25: 1302–1318. doi: http://dx.doi.org/10.1177/0146167299258011

Crocker, J., Major, B. and Steele, C. (1998) 'Social stigma', in D. Gilbert, S. Fiske and G. Lindzey (eds) *Handbook of Social Psychology*, 4th edn (pp. 504–553), Boston: McGraw-Hill.

Croizet, J.C. and Claire, T. (1998) 'Extending the concept of stereotype threat to social class: the intellectual underperformance of students from low socioeconomic backgrounds', *Personality and Social Psychology Bulletin*, 24: 588–594.

Dovidio, J.F. and Gaertner, S.L. (1998) 'On the nature of contemporary prejudice: the causes, consequences, and challenges of aversive racism', in J. Eberhardt and S.T. Fiske (eds) *Confronting Racism: The Problem and the Response* (pp. 3–32), Newbury Park, CA: Sage.

Dovidio, J.F. and Gaertner, S.L. (2010) 'Intergroup bias', in S.T. Fiske, D.T. Gilbert and G. Lindzey (eds) *The Handbook of Social Psychology*, 5th edn (Vol. 2, pp. 1084–1121), New York: Wiley.

Eby, L.T., Rhodes, J.E. and Allen, T.D. (2010) 'Definition and evolution of mentoring', in T.D. Allen and L.T. Eby (eds) *The Blackwood Handbook of Mentoring: A Multiple Perspectives Approach*, (pp. 7–20), Chichester: John Wiley.

Ensher, E.A. and Murphy, S.E. (1997) 'Effects of race, gender, perceived similarity, and contact on mentor relationships', *Journal of Vocational Behavior*, 50: 460–481.

Fazio, R., Jackson, J., Dunton, B. and Williams, C. (1995) 'Variability in automatic activation as an unobtrusive measure of racial attitudes: a bona fide pipeline?', *Journal of Personality and Social Psychology*, 69: 1013–1027.

Fryer, R.G. Jr. and Levitt, S.D. (2004) 'Understanding the Black–White test score gap in the first two years of school', *The Review of Economics and Statistics*, 86: 447–464.

Goff, P.A., Steele, C.M. and Davies, P.G. (2008) 'The space between us: stereotype threat and distance in interracial contexts', *Journal of Personality and Social Psychology*, 94: 91–107.

Herrnstein, R.J. and Murray, C. (1994) *The Bell Curve: Intelligence and Class Structure in American Life*, New York: Free Press.

Hoff, K. and Pandey, P. (2004) 'Belief systems and durable inequalities: an experimental investigation of Indian caste', World Bank Policy Research Working Paper 3351.

Jacobi, M. (1991) 'Mentoring and undergraduate academic success: a literature review', *Review of Educational Research*, 61: 505–532.

John-Henderson, N.A., Rheinschmidt, M.L., Mendoza-Denton, R. and Francis, D.D. (2013) 'Performance and inflammation outcomes are predicted by different facets of SES under stereotype threat', *Social Psychological and Personality Science*. doi:10.1177/1948550613494226

Kram, K. E. (1985). *Mentoring at Work*. Glenview, IL: Scott, Foresman & Co.

Maltbia, T. and Power, A. (2011) *A Leader's Guide to Leveraging Diversity: New Frontiers in Learning*, Oxford: Butterworth-Heineman.

Martinez, A.G. and Mendoza-Denton, R. (2011) 'The prospect of plasticity: malleability views of group differences and their implications for intellectual achievement, mental/behavioral health, and public policy', *Social Issues and Policy Review*, 5: 137–159.

Mendes, W.B., Blascovich, J., Lickel, B. and Hunter, S. (2002) 'Challenge and threat during social interactions with White and Black men', *Personality and Social Psychology Bulletin*, 28: 939–952.

Mendes, W.B., Reis, H., Seery, M.D. and Blascovich, J. (2003) 'Cardiovascular correlates of emotional expression and suppression: do content and gender context matter?', *Journal of Personality and Social Psychology*, 84: 771–792.

Mendoza-Denton, R. (2010) 'Relational diversity in higher education: a psychological perspective', *Psychological Science Agenda*, 24. Available at: http://www.apa.org/science/about/psa/2010/11/relational-diversity.aspx

Mendoza-Denton, R., Downey, G., Purdie, V., Davis, A. and Pietrzak, J. (2002) 'Sensitivity to status-based rejection: implications for African-American students' college experience', *Journal of Personality and Social Psychology*, 83: 896–918.

Mendoza-Denton, R., Goldman-Flythe, M., Pietrzak, J., Downey, G. and Aceves, M. (2010) 'Group value ambiguity: understanding the effects of academic feedback on minority students' self-esteem', *Social Psychological and Personality Science*, 1: 127–135. doi: 10.1177/1948550609357796

Mendoza-Denton, R., Pietrzak, J. and Downey, G. (2008) 'Distinguishing institutional identification from academic goal pursuit: interactive effects of ethnic identification and race-based rejection sensitivity', *Journal of Personality and Social Psychology*, 95: 338–351.

Mendoza-Denton, R., Shaw-Taylor, L., Chen, S. and Chang, E. (2009) 'Ironic effects of explicit gender prejudice on women's test performance,' *Journal of Experimental Social Psychology,* 45: 275–278. doi: 10.1016/j.jesp.2008.08.017

Ogbu, J.U. (1978) *Minority Education and Caste: The American System in Cross-Cultural Perspective,* New York: Academic Press.

Page-Gould, E., Mendoza-Denton, R., Alegre, J.M. and Siy, J.O. (2010) 'Understanding the impact of cross-group friendship on interactions with novel out-group members', *Journal of Personality and Social Psychology,* 98: 775–793. doi: 10.1037/a0017880

Page-Gould, E., Mendoza-Denton, R. and Tropp, L. (2008) 'With a little help from my cross-group friends: reducing intergroup anxiety through cross-group friendship', *Journal of Personality and Social Psychology,* 95: 1080–1094.

Plant, E.A. and Devine, P.G. (1998) 'Internal and external motivation to respond without prejudice', *Journal of Personality and Social Psychology,* 75: 811–832.

Quinn, D., Kahng, S. and Crocker, J. (2004) 'Discreditable: stigma effects of revealing mental illness history on test performance', *Personality and Social Psychology Bulletin,* 30: 803–815.

Rhodes, J.E., Reddy, R., Grossman, J.B. and Lee, J.M. (2002) 'Volunteer mentorship relationships with minority youth: an analysis of same versus cross-race matches', *Journal of Applied Social Psychology,* 32: 2114–2133.

Sackett, P.R., Borneman, M.J. and Connelly, B.S. (2008) 'High-stakes testing in higher education and employment: appraising the evidence for validity and fairness', *American Psychologist,* 63: 215–227.

Sackett, P.R., Hardison, C.M. and Cullen, M.J. (2004) 'On interpreting research on stereotype threat and test performance', *American Psychologist,* 60: 271–272.

Shelton, J.N., Richeson, J.A., Salvatore, J. and Trawalter, S. (2005) 'Ironic effects of racial bias during inter-racial interactions', *Psychological Science: A Journal of the American Psychological Society/APS,* 16: 397–402.

Steele, C.M. (1997) 'A threat in the air: how stereotypes shape intellectual identity and performance', *American Psychologist,* 52: 613–629.

Steele, C.M. and Aronson, J. (1995) 'Stereotype threat and the intellectual test performance of African Americans', *Journal of Personality and Social Psychology,* 69: 797–811.

Thomas, D.A. (1989) 'Mentoring and irrationality: the role of racial taboos', *Human Resources Management,* 28: 279–290.

Trompenaars, F. and Wooliams, P. (2004) *Business Across Cultures,* Chichester: Capstone Publishing.

Walton, G.M. and Spencer, S.J. (2009) 'Latent ability: grades and test scores systematically underestimate the intellectual ability of negatively stereotyped students', *Psychological Science,* 20: 1132–1139.

Wang, S., Tomlinson, E.C. and Noe, R.A. (2010) 'The role of mentor trust and protégé internal locus of control in formal mentoring relationships', *Journal of Applied Psychology,* 95: 358–367.

Yeager, D.S. and Walton, G.M. (2011) 'Social-psychological interventions in education: they're not magic', *Review of Educational Research,* 81: 267–301. doi:10.3102/0034654311405999

9

OPTIMIZING MĀORI STUDENT SUCCESS WITH THE OTHER THREE 'R'S

Racial–ethnic identity, resilience, and responsiveness

Melinda Webber

One can almost guarantee that race, ethnicity, and culture will play a complex role in the educational well-being of students in New Zealand. Yet explanations for why and how they matter have continued to elude educational researchers. Racial–ethnic identity is a fundamental aspect of Māori students' identity because it includes the attitudes and feelings associated with their ethnic and/or racial group membership. To this end, this chapter supports the contention that adolescents develop both racial *and* ethnic identities simultaneously, and thus the use of the term racial–ethnic identity.

For most, if not all of us, our socialization as racial–ethnic beings begins early in life within our *whānau* (family), and much of this socialization continues during the compulsory years of schooling, from preschool to high school, and even further during the tertiary years and beyond. Racial–ethnic identity therefore emerges in institutional, cultural, and personal contexts; is neither static nor one dimensional; and its meanings, as expressed in schools, neighborhoods, peer groups, and families, vary across time, space, and place. But perhaps, more critically, what is relevant in the field of social psychology is *how* racial–ethnic identity and the concomitant cultural behaviors matter to student, in this case Māori, educational engagement.

The achievement gap between Māori and non-Māori remains a serious issue in New Zealand schools, with many students failing to reach their educational potential. While the New Zealand Qualifications Authority (2012) reported an improvement in achievement for the National Certificate of Educational Achievement (NCEA) for students from all ethnicities over the period from 2004 to 2011, the achievement gap between Māori and non-Māori remained. In 2011, the percentage of New Zealand Pākehā (New Zealanders of European/British ancestry) students in Year 11 who achieved NCEA Level 1 was 84 percent, while only 64 percent of Māori students achieved this same qualification. Also of concern is that many Māori students are leaving school without completing any qualifications. In 2007, approximately one in ten Māori students left school without qualifications (McNaughton 2011), which is three times as high as the number of New Zealand Pākehā students without qualifications. It is clear that the New Zealand education system is not working effectively for many Māori students.

The New Zealand Ministry of Education (2011) has acknowledged that identity, language, and culture are critical ingredients in the educational success of Māori and have stated that schools and teachers need a greater 'understanding [of] the importance of Māori identity, language and culture in effective teaching and learning' (2011: 34). Through the national strategy, *Ka Hikitia – Managing for Success: The Māori Education Strategy 2008–2012*, the Ministry of Education has recognized the widespread aspirations of Māori to live and succeed as Māori. *Ka Hikitia* – the words mean to step up, to lengthen one's stride, to lift up – encourages schools and teachers to pay attention to cultural components, personalizing education so that Māori students enjoy educational success in ways that affirm their cultural identity (Ministry of Education 2008: 9). In addition, *Te Kotahitanga*, a research-based professional development program designed to raise Māori educational achievement, has also emphasized the importance of teachers and school leaders becoming more culturally responsive. Moreover, strong evaluative evidence from *Te Kotahitanga* has shown that creating an environment where Māori student's identity is valued and affirmed can have an empowering effect on their learning (Ministry of Education 2011).

In the past two decades, educational research has signaled the need to better understand the relationship between Māori identity and the educational outcomes of Māori students (Bishop *et al.* 2009; Durie 1998; Macfarlane 2004; Webber 2012). The underpinning assertion has promoted positive Māori identity and cultural efficacy as critical resilience factors for improving the educational outcomes of Māori. That is, a positive sense of Māori identity, experienced as cultural competence, cultural efficacy, and racial–ethnic group pride, may help to buffer or ameliorate the negative experiences of Māori students at school. This chapter argues that Māori adolescents must develop a strong, positive racial–ethnic identity to protect themselves from the prejudice, racism, and discrimination they experience, either directly or indirectly, in their lives. I further contend that Māori adolescents with salient racial–ethnic identities, positive attitudes toward their group, and an awareness of racism, are more likely to have the resilience to deal with adversity in the form of racist experiences, and are therefore more likely to have better academic outcomes. I also argue that teachers must be responsive to racial–ethnic identity; that is, they must use pedagogies and practices that accentuate the academic potential of Māori students, their families, and their communities. Finally, I close with some suggestions for future research.

The main theoretical framework underpinning this chapter is Henri Tajfel's social identity theory. According to Tajfel (1981), the social groups to which we belong help define who we are and thus constitute an essential part of the self. Racial–ethnic identity can be considered a social identity in that racial–ethnic groups can be seen as social groups. One fundamental assumption of social identity theory is that people strive to maintain or increase their self-esteem. Therefore, racial–ethnic identity can be one type of group identity that will influence the self-concept and self-esteem of its members. While racial–ethnic identity is only one of the many components that comprise a sense of self, it is the 'single component [that] is consistently positively related to an individual's self-esteem' (Umana-Taylor 2004: 139). Since self-esteem rests not only on individual attributes, but also on the attributes of the groups with which one identifies (Mackie and Smith 1998), an important question is how Māori students cope when they belong to a group that is often negatively stereotyped. This chapter postulates a relationship among Māori student racial–ethnic identity, self-esteem, and resilience in the face of racial discrimination. These socioemotional aspects of the educational experience will be shown to have a significant effect on the ways Māori students respond to adversity and opportunities to learn in the school context.

The first 'R': Racial–ethnic identity

Racial–ethnic identity in its broadest sense comprises three key components – race, ethnicity, and culture. The three components interact together to give Māori students a sense of individual and collective identity. The first component is race, and although the term race is no longer useful as a biological construct, we cannot avoid the fact that socially constructed perceptions of race, and consequently racism, are an everyday occurrence for many Māori. As such, notions of race essentialize and stereotype Māori, their social statuses, their social behaviors, and their social ranking. In the form of racism, race continues to play an important role in determining how Māori construe, indeed construct, their racial–ethnic identities and their academic achievement at school (Webber 2012).

The second component is ethnicity, which is most closely associated with the issues of authenticity and membership. Ethnic boundaries operate to determine who is a member, and who is not, by the use of criteria such as language, knowledge of descent, participation in cultural activities and the like. Therefore, racial–ethnic identities for Māori students are largely dependent on their developing knowledge, and eventual mastery of, the third component: culture. Culture dictates the appropriate and inappropriate content of a particular ethnicity and designates the language, religion, belief system, art, music, dress and traditions that constitute ethnic group membership. These elements of culture are part of a 'toolkit', as Swidler (1986: 273) called it, used to create the meaning and way of life seen to be unique to particular ethnic groups. Thus, culture can be seen as the substance of ethnicity and the mechanism by which individuals 'demonstrate' their authenticity as group members. However, humans, as individuals or groups, are not born 'with propensities for any particular culture, culture traits, or language, only with the capacity to acquire and to create culture' (Smedley and Smedley 2005: 17).

As such, developing a positive and strong racial–ethnic identity is complex. Primarily, Māori student's racial–ethnic identity is negotiated, defined, and produced through their social interactions with others, most importantly their family and peers. It is within these interactions that they learn about culture – the acts, languages, stories, and customs associated with 'being Māori'. However, racial–ethnic identity is also influenced by external racial, social, economic, and political messages that shape the feasibility and attractiveness of certain identity choices. These three components influence the construction of racial–ethnic identity, and the meanings Māori students attach to it.

As reported in recent studies, there are a number of key influences on the ways Māori students construct their racial–ethnic identity (Hollis 2013; Rata 2012; Webber 2011, 2012). The first is their sense of connectedness and belonging to the Māori label. Māori students, across a range of studies, have consistently asserted that Māori identity is associated with knowing what 'being Māori' means, knowing where you come from and knowing what connects you to others as Māori. Hollis's (2013) model of positive Māori youth development identified relationships, involvement in cultural activities, cultural factors (including access to environments to learn about culture and respecting and valuing culture), education/work, health/healthy lifestyles, sociohistorical factors (including history, social attitudes towards Māori and Māori youth, community, and media), and personal characteristics (such as resilience and having goals/aspirations) as factors contributing towards positive Māori identity development. Hollis's (2013) research also argued that key indicators of positive Māori identity development included:

- *Collective responsibility* – Māori students were contributing towards the collective (*whānau*, community, and society) and acknowledging their place amongst their *whānau* and the wider collective.
- *Successfully navigating the world* – Māori students were able to navigate Māori and non-Māori environments with confidence.
- *Cultural efficacy* – knowing *te reo* (Māori language) and *tikanga* (Māori protocols and traditions), being proud of being Māori and wanting to share that with others.
- *Health* – physical, emotional, and intellectual.
- *Personal strengths* – individual strengths, including confidence, achieving their desired goals, personal responsibility, and curiosity.

One of the two most important ways that Māori students construct a positive sense of connectedness to their identity as Māori is through participation in Māori cultural activities (Rata 2012) and socialization messages from their families and peers (Webber 2011). Rata's research shows that a school's cultural environment can enhance, or constrain, Māori identities, which in turn can increase, or decrease, psychological well-being and engagement in learning. Overall, Rata's (2012) results suggest that any school interventions designed to increase Māori students' cultural engagement could consequently enhance their Māori identity, which could then increase their psychological well-being. Māori students who are psychologically well are more likely to feel confident in their ability to learn because 'when students … develop healthy, positive, and strong racial identities … they are freer to focus on the need to achieve' (Ford *et al.* 2006: 16).

Families also play a crucial role in helping Māori students to learn about who they are, and who they are not, by means of socialization into the cultural aspects of their racial–ethnic identity (Webber 2011). This form of 'cultural socialization' can be evidenced in parental practices, including: teaching them about their racial–ethnic heritage and histories; promoting cultural customs and traditions; and promoting cultural, racial, and ethnic pride, either deliberately or implicitly (Webber 2011). Family practices like these are likely to promote racial–ethnic pride in Māori students, orient them to race-related barriers, and prepare them to succeed in both their Māori and non-Māori endeavors. Parents who expose children to their heritage and actively discuss issues relevant to ethnic group membership, including the dual messages of pride in group membership and preparation for experiences with racism, may be initiating a child toward a positive racial–ethnic identity.

The second 'R': Resilience in the face of racism

How might racial–ethnic identity influence academic achievement? As documented by the literature on stereotype threat and stereotype lift (Steele 2004), simply being reminded of one's membership in a group that is stereotyped in terms of academic performance influences one's subsequent academic performance. One's racial–ethnic identity may either promote or undermine academic achievement depending on whether the content of the identity is positive or negative with regard to achievement. When a positive stereotype exists, for example, the stereotype of Asian academic ability, then making the group membership salient has a positive influence on academic performance (Shih *et al.* 1999). When a negative stereotype exists, such as the case for working-class (Croizet and Claire 1998), gender, and minority groups (including Māori) (Rubie-Davies *et al.* 2006; Steele, 2004), then making group membership salient can have a negative influence on academic performance.

Previous research in the New Zealand context has shown that many of the social expectations for Māori are of laziness, irresponsibility, low intelligence, and even violence (Borrell 2005; McIntosh 2005). Additionally, other New Zealand research has shown that teachers have lower academic expectations for Māori students than for other ethnic groups (Rubie-Davies *et al.* 2006). The influence of negative stereotypes and low academic expectations on Māori student educational outcomes can be significant because they affect Māori student psychosocial functioning and the ways they behave in the world. When these negative reflections are received in a number of mirrors, including the media, the classroom, and the street, the outcome can be devastating. In a study investigating the negative factors affecting Māori student racial–ethnic identity, I found that Māori students were acutely aware of the negative generalizations and stereotypical constructions of Māori people and culture in the mainstream media and in their own local communities, including the school community. Of particular concern, given the school age of the Māori participants in the study, was the perceived notion that Māori were 'not very smart', 'dumb' and/or unlikely to 'pass school and [subsequently] drop out' (Webber 2012: 23). A number of the students also commented on the perceived likelihood of Māori students being profoundly affected by experiences of real or perceived discrimination, resulting in low school engagement and achievement. One student in the study (Webber 2012: 23) clearly stated that 'when you hear stuff like that often enough it is more likely to come true'.

Racism was perceived by the Māori students in this 2012 study as encounters where they were racially discriminated against, treated badly, mocked, not given respect, or considered inferior because of the misrepresentations of Māori culture and people in society. All of the students acknowledged that experiences of racism were a common phenomenon at school and shaped who they interacted with. All of the students had experienced or witnessed racist behavior at school. These encounters were mostly experienced with peers, teachers, the media and other adults outside of the school context (like shopkeepers) and were mostly verbal. Also, the venues in which racism was experienced represented the social settings and contexts where the Māori students led their lives – in schools and their communities, among peers, and with adults and authority figures.

The Māori students felt that they were consistently negatively stereotyped. Comments by the Māori students alluded to discriminatory comments including, 'we are [seen as] dumb, dirty and poor', 'they think we are like the stupid people and we don't know anything' (2012: 23). Another Māori student stated (2012: 23):

> Māori are normally the ones on TV being violent and misbehaving. They stereotype that and think that everyone behaves like that. If someone reads in the newspaper that most Māori fail, they will probably expect nearly every Māori person to fail. I think that boys are probably portrayed the worst, like whenever you see stuff on TV … people robbing some stores … Māori, oh man … like that I think portrays it even more.

The students' sentiments about racism seemed to center on the perceptions, beliefs, or comments they recalled their teachers, school staff, and other adults making about them 'as Māori'. These comments are tantamount to what Pierce (1974) referred to as racial micro-aggressions – subtle insults (verbal, nonverbal, and visual) and insinuations directed towards Māori students, often automatically or subconsciously. In isolation, racial micro-aggressions may seem innocuous and non-threatening, but the damage comes from the cumulative burden of a lifetime of micro-aggressions, which can have a detrimental influence on Māori students' perceptions of themselves, their confidence, and ultimately their academic performance. Pierce (1974: 516) states that 'one must not look for the gross and obvious. The subtle cumulative mini-assault is the substance of today's racism'. When examining achievement disparities across racial groups, one has to contemplate whether Māori students who have been the target of racial micro-aggressions for years have experienced subpar performance as a result of these subtle assaults on their intelligence because of their race. Indeed, a growing group of scholars have investigated the effect of racial stereotyping on academic performance and found it can lead to levels of anxiety and doubt that can negatively influence school performance (Steele 2004; Steele and Aronson 1998).

Repeated experiences with racism, stereotyping, and discrimination can have one of two effects – the student can withdraw from the context in which they feel stereotyped (for example, rejecting either their racial–ethnic or academic identity), or be resilient and persist and try to compensate for the stigma (Steele 2004). One way of compensating is to work to disconfirm the stereotype. This strategy is illustrated in the following quotation from a Māori student from my study (2012: 25) who stated, 'Nobody should be like judged just because of what they are … Yeah; it makes you want to just to be at the top of all this stuff … just to show them up'.

Māori students must develop a strong, positive racial–ethnic identity to protect themselves from the prejudice, racism, and discrimination they experience, either directly or indirectly, in their lives. Māori adolescents with salient racial–ethnic identities, positive attitudes toward their group, and an awareness of racism, are more likely to have the resilience to deal with adversity in the form of racist experiences, and are therefore more likely to have better academic outcomes (Webber 2011, 2012).

Additionally, the most resilient and persistent Māori students are those who have a well-developed awareness of the role that racism and discrimination could play in their educational lives. They also have strong role models (usually parents) for taking action against encounters with racism and oppression (O'Connor 1997). There is clear evidence that having a strong, positive sense of racial–ethnic identity may protect Māori students from the negative psychological and academic effects of perceiving racial–ethnic group barriers or experiencing interpersonal discrimination and racism based on their ethnic group membership (Webber 2011, 2012).

Positive racial–ethnic identity enables Māori students to be more resilient in the face of racism. The term resilience can be used to refer to better-than-expected developmental outcomes, competence when under stress, and/or competence when dealing with threats to well-being (Kirby and Fraser 1997). What these definitions share in common is that they all argue that resilience occurs in the presence of adversity. These conceptualizations of resilience also all share the notion that resilience is influenced by a child's environment, and that the interaction between individuals and their social ecologies will determine the degree of positive outcomes experienced. Furthermore, cultural variation is understood to exert an influence on children's resilience (Arrington and Wilson 2000).

Research supports the idea that students with a strong identification with their racial–ethnic group tend to do better in the school environment (Lerner and Galambos 1998; Yasui and Dishion 2007). Māori students with strong cultural ties use their racial–ethnic identity group as a support structure, calling on family members and their cultural beliefs and traditions when facing adverse circumstances in the environment. New Zealand research has strongly suggested that a strong racial–ethnic identity can serve as a buffer to protect Māori students from negative environmental conditions because it has a powerful influence on the way Māori students view their world and make meaning of it (Rata 2012; Webber 2012). As such, racial–ethnic identity can be considered a protective factor in times of adversity. It is thought that protective factors moderate a person's reaction to stress or adversity and interact with the sources of risk to reduce the probability of negative outcomes. According to Rutter (1979), protection from risk does not mean risk is completely avoided; rather, a resilient individual engages with risk and copes with it. Protective factors for Māori students emanate from three sources: the individual, the family, and the environment or social context (Webber 2011). Students who lack individual competencies, or family and community protective factors, have a greater likelihood of maladaptive outcomes in adulthood (Masten and Coatsworth 1998; Werner 2000). As such, Māori student resilience is not a condition of Māori students alone, but also exists as a characteristic of their home, school, and community settings. Therefore, careful attention must be paid to the ways families and schools advocate for and model stronger, more competent and better functioning in adverse situations.

Māori students must also learn resiliency skills that enable them to become culturally flexible (Carter 2010) so that they can effectively navigate diverse social environs such as schools, communities and neighborhoods with confidence. Ultimately, culturally flexible Māori students are resilient, and possess the ability to interact in, participate in, and navigate different social and cultural settings. Resilient Māori students embrace multiple forms of cultural knowledge and make efforts to expand their own understanding of their racial–ethnic identity, as a means of maintaining their psychological well-being in the face of racism. Moreover, culturally flexible Māori students must develop inclusive perspectives about others who differ in myriad social aspects or racial–ethnic identity (Carter 2010).

The third 'R': Racial–ethnic identity responsiveness

The effective fusion of racial–ethnic identity responsiveness and pedagogy is built upon a comprehensive and informed set of knowledge and skills that many practitioners fail to recognize in their attempts to engage Māori learners in the teaching and learning process. Being responsive to the racial–ethnic identity of Māori students is more than just a way of teaching or a simple set of practices embedded in curriculum lessons and units. Racial–ethnic identity responsiveness seeks to move away from the 'methods fetish' (Bartolome 1994: 173) because better addressing Māori student achievement cannot be reduced to finding the 'right' teaching methods, strategies, or prepackaged curricula. Rather, genuine responsiveness to racial–ethnic identity embodies a professional, political, cultural, and ethical disposition that supersedes mundane teaching acts. It is instead centered on fundamental beliefs about teaching and learning and accentuates the academic potential of Māori students, their families, and their communities. Racial–ethnic identity responsiveness requires an unyielding commitment to seeing Māori student success become less rhetoric and more of a reality.

Racial–ethnic identity responsiveness is situated in a framework that recognizes the rich and varied cultural wealth, knowledge, and skills that Māori students and their families bring to schools, and seeks to develop dynamic teaching practices, strengths-based teacher–student relationships, place-based learning content, multiple means of assessment, and a philosophical view of teaching that is dedicated to nurturing Māori student academic, social, emotional, cultural, and psychological well-being. Importantly, racial–ethnic identity responsiveness attempts to disrupt deficit-based explanations of Māori student achievement and instead focuses on the ways that teachers can recognize and respect the intricacies, differences, and complexities of race, ethnicity, and culture. Such responsiveness assumes that if teachers are able to make connections between the racial, ethnic, and cultural beliefs, knowledge, and practices that Māori students bring from home, and the content, pedagogy, and relationships that they use in their classrooms, the academic performance and overall schooling performance of Māori students will improve.

Race, ethnicity, and culturally responsive pedagogies for Māori are becoming more comprehensive and concrete in the New Zealand context and a number of New Zealand researchers have identified place-based learning as an effective teaching approach for Māori students (Kidman *et al.* 2011; Macfarlane *et al.* 2014; Macfarlane and Macfarlane 2012). As a means to engage, and in many cases re-engage, Māori students' in their education, one thing is obvious: there is a need to approach Māori students from a strong, culturally inclusive position. Māori students need to see the relevance of the learning and connect with the curriculum content and activities for learning to be meaningful. According to Penetito (2009) and Kidman *et al.* (2011), the objective of place-based learning is to develop in Māori students a love of their environment, of the place where they are living, of its social history, and of the biodiversity that exists there. Place-based learning should also enable them to develop an appreciation of the ways in which Māori people have responded and continue to respond to their local, natural, and social environments. As such, effective place-based learning should provide Māori students with the answers to two essential questions: 'What is this place?' and 'What is my relationship to it?' Kawagley (1995) has further argued that place-based learning should place an emphasis on teaching *through* rather than *about* culture. Kawagley also asserts that place-based learning should use the local context and culture as the primary lens for the conveyance of academic subject matter. The culture he refers to is that which is embedded in Māori communities. Therefore, place-based learning, as a responsive racial–ethnic identity approach suitable for Māori, should promote Māori distinctiveness by emphasizing Māori collective strengths, their lived and shared experiences, and their connectedness to the land, history, and environment.

Place-based learning can be local and unique, and Māori students from homes that maintain Māori cultural practices can be valuable resources for teachers and other students. Place-based learning is designed to provide students with skills to become lifelong learners, and Lewicki (2007) asserts that place-based learning strategies can:

- support students to become passionately interested in a topic of their choice;
- assist in the development of precision observation and analytical skills;
- allow students to demonstrate tenacity.

Therefore, place-based learning is critical when considering an approach to working with Māori students that is responsive to racial–ethnic identity because place-based learning reflects their lived realities. This is important because, as Penetito (2010: 35) purports, there are two basic requirements for Māori students to feel good about school:

> [F]irstly if it holds up a mirror to them and they can see themselves growing and develop-ing in a way that is personally meaningful for them; and secondly, if it helps them to project themselves into the immediate world around them as well as into the world at large.

Conclusion and suggestions for future research

The educational success of Māori students is a multifaceted phenomenon that encompasses far more than academic achievement and school completion. Other important aspects of the edu-cational experience include factors connected to the acquisition of positive academic and social identities, including Māori students' feelings about the role of their racial–ethnic identity at school; the resilience strategies they employ to buffer their experiences with racism and low teacher expectations; and their connectedness to the learning content in the school context. These socioemotional aspects of the educational experience have important consequences for the ways Māori students respond to opportunities to learn. Effective teachers must recognize the important influence the 'other' three 'R's, discussed in this chapter, have on Māori student success. Educating Māori students must involve encouraging them to take their language, their cultures and their knowledge with them on the learning journey. It should encourage access to knowl-edge of the world, not at the expense of their cultural knowledge, but rather alongside the acquisition of their own knowledge.

Several further research actions are needed to better understand the ways racial–ethnic identity affects Māori student engagement and academic achievement at school. First, with regard to the relationship between racial–ethnic identity and Māori engagement at school, it is important that future research assess the size of the relationship between these two variables as well as the amount of variance they account for in terms of academic achievement. Second, future racial–ethnic identity research with Māori should investigate the conditions under which racial–ethnic identity is protective (that is, promotes resilience) or not. Relatedly, researchers need to be clearer about the aspects of racial–ethnic identity that relate to Māori student motivation for academics, academic achievement, and school connectedness.

References

Arrington, E. and Wilson, M. (2000) 'A re-examination of risk and resilience during adolescence: incorpo-rating culture and diversity', *Journal of Child and Family Studies*, 9: 221–230.

Bartolomé, L. (1994) 'Beyond the methods fetish: toward a humanizing pedagogy', *Harvard Educational Review*, 64: 173–195.

Bishop, R., Berryman, M., Cavanagh, T. and Teddy, L. (2009) 'Te kotahitanga: addressing educational disparities facing Māori students in New Zealand', *Teaching and Teacher Education*, 25: 734–742.

Borrell, B. (2005) 'Living in the city ain't so bad: cultural identity for young Māori in South Auckland', in J. Liu, T. McCreanor, T. McIntosh and T. Teaiwa (eds), *New Zealand Identities: Departures and Destinations* (pp. 191–206), Wellington: Victoria University Press.

Carter, P. (2010) 'Race and cultural flexibility among students in different multiracial schools', *The Teachers College Record,* 112: 1–2.

Croizet, J. and Claire, T. (1998) 'Extending the concept of stereotype and threat to social class: the intellectual underperformance of students from low socioeconomic backgrounds', *Personality and Social Psychology Bulletin,* 24: 588–594.

Durie, M. (1998) *Te Mana, Te Kawanatanga: The Politics of Māori Self-Determination,* Auckland: Oxford University Press.

Ford, D., Grantham, T. and Moore, J. (2006) 'Essentializing identity development in the education of students of color', in H.R. Milner and E.W. Ross (eds), *Race, Ethnicity and Education* (pp. 3–18), Westport, CT: Praeger.

Hollis, H. (2013) 'Te kete whanaketanga – rangatahi: a model of positive development for Māori youth', unpublished MA thesis, University of Auckland, New Zealand.

Kawagley, A. O. 1995. *A Yupiaq Worldview: A Pathway to Ecology and Spirit,* Prospect Heights, IL: Waveland Press.

Kidman, J., Abrams, E. and McRae, H. (2011) 'Imaginary subjects: school science, indigenous students, and knowledge-power relations', *British Journal of Sociology of Education,* 32: 203–220.

Kirby, L. and Fraser, M. (1997) 'Risk and resilience in childhood', in M. Fraser (ed.), *Risk and Resilience in Childhood: An Ecological Perspective* (pp. 10–33), Washington, DC: NASW Press.

Lerner, R. and Galambos, N. (1998) 'Adolescent development: challenges and opportunities for research, programs, and policies', *Annual Review of Psychology,* 49: 413–446.

Lewicki, J. (2007) 'Place based learning measures up: tips on local learning: successful educational projects that focus on the community share key characteristics,' *Edutopia Journal* [The George Lucas Educational Foundation]. Retrieved from: http://www.edutopia.org/place-based-learning-measures

Macfarlane, A. (2004) *Kia Hiwa Ra – Listen to Culture: Māori Students' Plea to Educators,* Wellington: New Zealand Council for Educational Research.

Macfarlane, A. and Macfarlane, S. (2012) 'Weaving the dimensions of culture and learning: implications for educators', in B. Kaur (ed.), *Understanding Teaching and Learning: Classroom Research Revisited* (pp. 213–224), Rotterdam: Sense Publishers.

Macfarlane, A., Webber, M., Cookson-Cox, C. and McRae, H. (2014). '*Ka Awatea:* an *iwi* case study of Māori students' success' [unpublished manuscript], University of Auckland, New Zealand. Retrieved from http:www.maramatanga.co.nz/projects_publications.

McIntosh, T. (2005) 'Māori identities: fixed, fluid, forced', in J. Liu, T. McCreanor, T. McIntosh and T. Teaiwa (eds), *New Zealand Identities: Departures and Destinations* (pp. 38–51), Wellington: Victoria University Press.

Mackie, D. and Smith, E. (1998) 'Intergroup relations: insights from a theoretically integrative approach', *Psychological Review,* 105: 606–616.

McNaughton, S. (2011) 'Educational outcomes in adolescence for Māori and Pasifika students', *Improving the Transition: Reducing Social and Psychological Morbidity During Adolescence – a Report from the Prime Minister's Chief Science Advisor* (pp. 97–109), Auckland: Office of the Prime Minister's Science Advisory Committee.

Masten, A. and Coatsworth, J. (1998) 'The development of competence in favorable and unfavorable environments: lessons from research on successful children', *American Psychologist,* 53: 205–220.

Ministry of Education (2008) *Ka Hikitia – Managing for Success: Māori Education Strategy 2008–2012,* Wellington: Ministry of Education.

Ministry of Education (2011) *A summary of Te Kotahitanga: Maintaining, Replicating and Sustaining Change in Phase 3 and 4 Schools 2007–2010,* Wellington: Ministry of Education.

New Zealand Qualifications Authority (2012) *New Zealand Qualifications Authority Annual Report on NCEA and New Zealand Scholarship Data and Statistics (2011)* Wellington, NZ: New Zealand Government. Retrieved from http://www.nzqa.govt.nz/assets/About-us/Publications/stats-reports/ncea-annual-report-2011.pdf.

O'Connor, C. (1997) 'Dispositions toward (collective) struggle and educational resilience in the inner city: a case analysis of six African American high school students', *American Educational Research Journal,* 34: 593–629.

Penetito, W. (2009) 'Place-based education: catering for curriculum, culture and community', *New Zealand Annual Review of Education,* 18: 5–29.

Penetito, W. (2010) *What's Māori About Māori Education?* Wellington: Victoria University Press.

Pierce, C. (1974) 'Psychiatric problems of the Black minority', in S. Arieti (ed.), *American Handbook of Psychiatry* (pp. 512–523), New York: Basic Books.

Rata, A. (2012) 'Te pitau o te tuakiri: affirming Māori identities and promoting well-being in state secondary schools', unpublished PhD thesis, Wellington: Victoria University of Wellington.

Rubie-Davies, C., Hattie, J. and Hamilton, R. (2006) 'Expecting the best for students: teacher expectations and academic outcomes', *British Journal of Educational Psychology,* 76: 429–444.

Rutter, M. (1979) 'Protective factors in children's responses to stress and disadvantage', in M. Kent and J. Rolf (eds), *Primary Prevention of Psychopathology: Social Competence in Children* (pp. 49–74), Hanover, NH: University Press of New England.

Shih, M., Pittinsky, T. and Ambady, N. (1999) 'Stereotype susceptibility: identity salience and shifts in quantitative performance', *Psychological Science,* 10: 80–83.

Smedley, A. and Smedley, B. (2005) Race as biology is fiction, racism as a social problem is real: anthropological and historical perspectives on the social construction of race', *American Psychologist,* 60: 16–26.

Steele, C. (2004) 'A threat in the air: how stereotypes shape intellectual identity and performance', in J. Banks and C. Banks (eds), *Handbook of Research on Multicultural Education* (pp. 682–699), San Francisco: Jossey-Bass.

Steele, C. and Aronson, J. (1998) 'How stereotypes influence the standardised test performance of talented African American students', in C. Jencks and M. Phillips (eds), *The Black-White Test Score Gap* (pp. 401–427), Washington, DC: Brookings Institute.

Swidler, A. (1986) 'Culture as action: symbols and strategies', *American Sociological Review,* 51: 273–286.

Tajfel, H. (1981) *Human Groups and Social Categories: Studies in Social Psychology,* New York: Cambridge University Press.

Umana-Taylor, A. (2004) 'Ethnic identity and self-esteem: examining the role of social context', *Journal of Adolescence,* 27: 139–146.

Webber, M. (2011) 'Identity matters: racial-ethnic representations among adolescents attending multi-ethnic high schools', unpublished PhD thesis, University of Auckland, New Zealand.

Webber, M. (2012) 'Identity matters: the role of racial-ethnic identity for Māori students in multiethnic secondary schools', *Set: Research Information for Teachers,* 2: 20–25.

Werner, E. (2000) 'Protective factors and individual resilience', in J. Shonkoff and S. Meisels (eds), *Handbook of Early Childhood Intervention* (pp. 115–132), New York: Cambridge University Press.

Yasui, M. and Dishion, T. (2007) 'The ethnic context of child and adolescent problem behavior: implications for child and family interventions', *Clinical Child and Family Psychology Review,* 10: 137–179.

10

IN-SCHOOL VERSUS ONLINE DISCRIMINATION

Effects on mental health and motivation among diverse adolescents in the United States

Brendesha M. Tynes, Sophia Hiss, Allison M. Ryan, and Chad A. Rose

Racial discrimination is a common stressor and a growing threat to adolescent health. Within their lifetime, 57–94 percent of African American, Latino, and Asian youth have experienced in-school, face-to-face discrimination that was associated with their racial and ethnic background (Benner and Kim 2009; Dotterer *et al.* 2009; Flanagan *et al.* 2009; Harris-Britt *et al.* 2007; Huynh and Fuligni 2010; Martin *et al.* 2011; Medvedeva 2010; Neblett *et al.* 2008; Pachter *et al.* 2010). Much of the research in the area of face-to-face, or offline, racial discrimination focuses on the perceived frequency of these experiences within the classroom, including unfair treatment because of race (Chavous *et al.* 2008), where respondents may be treated with less respect or teased because of their race or ethnicity (Rivas-Drake *et al.* 2009; Shin *et al.* 2011). Some scholars have extended this body of research by exploring the experiences ethnic minority youth of tracking, unfair discipline, perceptions of lower levels of intelligence, or receiving less academic praise than their white counterparts (Benner and Kim 2009; Cogburn *et al.* 2011; Dotterer *et al.* 2009).

While much is known about adolescents' experiences of offline discrimination, less is known about adolescents' experiences in online contexts. Because of a reported increase in online hate activity, it is critical that scholars explore the nature of online forms of discrimination (Simon Wiesenthal Center 2009) as well as associations with mental health and behavior. With up to 95 percent of adolescents between the ages of 12 and 17 accessing the internet (Lenhart *et al.* 2011), growing numbers of youth are potentially vulnerable to racially driven hate activity. In the first study of online racial discrimination and adjustment, Tynes *et al.* (2008) found that 29 percent of African American and 42 percent of multiracial/other high-school students reported experiencing racial discrimination in online contexts. Findings also show that 71 percent of the entire sample witnessed vicarious online discrimination through text message, social networking sites, online games, and other internet-based sites. Similarly, Shin *et al.* (2011) assessed the nature and frequency of bullying among Asian American high-school students, and determined that almost one quarter of the respondents experienced online victimization. Among the identified victims, 29 percent reported their victimization was the result of their point of origin (i.e. home country), while 23 percent were victimized because of their skin color.

African American adolescents who perceive higher levels of discrimination tend to exhibit lower levels of self-esteem (Seaton and Yip 2009), exhibit more conduct problems (Brody *et al.* 2006), and report higher levels of depressive symptoms (Cogburn *et al.* 2011; Gaylord-Harden and Cunningham 2009; Neblett *et al.* 2008). Perceived discrimination is also associated with increased depressive symptoms for Latino and Asian American youth (Grossman and Liang 2008; Juang and Alvarez 2010; Lorenzo-Blanco *et al.* 2011; Umaña-Taylor and Updegraff 2007). Thus, adolescents who experience racial discrimination tend to have increased psychological distress and behavioral problems.

Increasing evidence from studies on school-based discrimination shows that these experiences are associated with academic adjustment. Negative classroom experiences can make a strong impression on teens, particularly when unfair treatment stems from individuals whose opinions they may value, such as peers or teachers (Wong *et al.* 2003). These incidents appear to distance students from others in their school environment. For example, studies show that those who experience more discrimination tend to feel lower school belonging than their peers who did not have these experiences (Cogburn *et al.* 2011; Dotterer *et al.* 2009). With students feeling less a part of school culture, they are at risk of experiencing academic problems. Studies link discriminatory incidents with lowered academic motivation in both Latino and African American samples, with students less likely to 'try hard in school' (Alfaro *et al.* 2009; Thompson and Gregory 2011). African American males who reported more perceived discriminatory events less frequently endorsed attitudes of school importance, with students less likely to agree that school is 'necessary for future success' (Chavous *et al.* 2008; Cogburn *et al.* 2011). Clearly, the academic outcomes of adolescents' experiences of racial bias are harmful and disruptive to their education as a whole.

While less explored than adolescent experiences of offline discrimination, adolescents' experiences with online racial discrimination are adversely related to their health, independent of other types of discrimination and stress. In a previous study we found that racial discrimination online was positively associated with depressive symptoms and anxiety, even after adjusting for offline racial discrimination and perceived stress (Tynes *et al.* 2008). However, our sample size for African Americans and Latinos was relatively small. In the current study, we investigate the associations of both adolescents' experiences of online and offline discrimination with their psychological adjustment (specifically depressive symptoms and anxiety) in a larger and more diverse sample. Further, we examine the associations of online and offline discrimination experiences with utility values. Given that much research has shown that offline discrimination experiences are associated with psychological and academic motivation, such as utility values for school, it is important to control for offline discrimination experiences when examining online discrimination experiences. This will establish if there are unique associations between online discrimination and adjustment. Further, it will be informative to see if online discrimination experiences affect not only more general psychological adjustment but also are associated with academic motivation which we know matters for school success (Eccles *et al.* 2006).

Method

Data were from wave 1 of the ongoing Teen Life Online and in Schools (TLOS) project. This project is a longitudinal study funded through a National Institute of Child Health and Human Development grant examining the risk and protective factors associated with online experiences of diverse youth in 12 public Midwestern middle, K–8, 6–12 and high schools. Six schools were in a major metropolitan area, and six were in small urban communities. Participants included 777 adolescents (43.9 percent male, 53.7 percent female, and 0.02 percent did not report) in grades 6–12 ($M = 9.0$, $SD = 1.9$), with ages ranging from 10 to 18 years. Based on youth self-report, the ethnic–racial distribution of the sample was 43.6 percent African American ($n = 339$), 30.0 percent Latino ($n = 233$), 7.3 percent East Asian ($n = 57$), 9.3 percent multiracial ($n = 72$),

3.0 percent Native American (n = 24), 0.9 percent South Asian (n = 7), 0.6 percent Middle Eastern (n = 5), and 5.1 percent unidentified (n = 40). Because the number of Middle Eastern, Native American, and South Asian participants was small, these groups were combined to create an 'other' ethnic group in analyses (n = 93), 12.0 percent. The TLOS project oversampled for African American and Latino participants, as many large-scale studies in the online victimization literature are nationally representative and thus majority White (Jones *et al.*, 2012; Mitchell *et al.*, 2011). This project aims to fill the gap in the literature in understanding the online experiences of young people of color.

Procedure

Research assistants recruited students from classrooms chosen by administrators. Classes chosen were primarily technology classes, English classes, and homeroom. Research assistants gave a brief ten-minute presentation to all classes to describe the study and distribute English and Spanish versions of consent forms. Parental consent was required for participation in the project, and the average response rate among the twelve schools was 49.8 percent. This figure is based on the total number of consent forms returned from those distributed to students, not on active refusals. At an agreed date, researchers returned to each school to administer surveys through a web link to all students who had obtained parental consent.

Online surveys were sent to email addresses that were provided by participants and were accessed during the allotted classroom time. In the event that participants did not have a valid email address before the administration of the survey, temporary email addresses were provided to access the survey. Surveys were also accessed by some students through a web link. Survey administration occurred over one to two class periods. Research assistants were present to inform students of confidentiality, answer questions, and troubleshoot any technical difficulties. Before beginning the survey, students were informed of confidentiality, they were told that they would be asked about their online experiences and their feelings about themselves, and they were told they could stop participating at any time. All students were provided with resources such as local counseling services and internet safety websites to report online predators following their completion of the survey. Students received $15 gift certificates for participation and schools were provided with a stipend. Recruitment and consent procedures were approved by the institutional review board of the principal investigator's institution.

Variables

Academic motivation

Our measure of academic motivation has 12-items and included expectancies of success for school as well as utility values (see Wigfield and Eccles 1995 and Wong *et al.* 2003). For these analyses, only the utility values scale was used. A sample item of utility values is 'In general, how useful is what you learn in school?' Items were scored on a scale where 1 = not at all useful to 5 = very useful. Higher values indicated higher academic motivation. For this scale, Cronbach's alpha was 0.85 in the current sample.

Depressive symptoms

We used the Center for Epidemiologic Studies Depression Scale (CESD) (Roberts and Sobhan 1992) to measure depressive symptoms. The full measure contains 20 items, but the current study used a shortened 12-item measure. Participants were asked how often they felt or behaved a certain way in the past week, where 0 = rarely or less than one day and 3 = most of the time or the past 5 to 7 days. Prior research has found that the CESD does not have a single factor and that a three-factor model may be more appropriate (McArdle *et al.* 2001). To examine this, we conducted an exploratory factor analysis. The best model was a three-factor model and item 7 ('I felt that everything I did was an effort') was dropped from the analyses because of the very low loading (0.015). The first factor included items 5, 6, 11, 17, and 20 that measure negative affect (e.g. 'I felt depressed'), the second factor included reverse-coded items 4, 8, 12, and 16 that measured happiness (e.g. 'I felt hopeful about the future'), and the third factor contained only two items, 15 and 19, that measured interpersonal conflict (e.g. 'I felt that people dislike me'). A confirmatory factor analysis of the three-factor model showed a good model fit (χ^2 = 167.85, *df* = 41, RMSEA = 0.069, CFI = 0.933) with a root mean square error of approximation (RMSEA) less than 0.08 and a comparative fit index (CFI) greater than 0.90 (Hu and Bentler 1999; Kline 1998). In the following analyses, only the items of the first factor were included, and the mean score of the factor was used for analyses with a higher score indicating more depressive symptoms. Cronbach's alpha for this factor was 0.70.

Anxiety

Anxiety was measured using a four-item scale, the Profile of Mood States–Adolescents tension subscale (Terry *et al.* 1999). Participants were asked to what degree they were experiencing a particular feeling either panicky, anxious, worried, or nervous at the time of the survey. Participants responded using a scale from 0 = not at all to 4 = extremely. For this scale, a higher score indicated more anxiety. Cronbach's alpha was 0.80 in this sample.

Online discrimination

Online discrimination was measured using individual discrimination subscale on the Online Victimization Scale (Tynes *et al.* 2010). The four-item scale asked how often a particular type of incident has happened to each participant while online in the past year (e.g. 'People have excluded me from a site because of my race or ethnic group online'). Items were scored on a scale from 0 = never to 5 = every day. Cronbach's alpha for this scale was 0.70 in this sample.

In-school discrimination from adults

Face-to-face discrimination from adults was measured by the Perceived Discrimination Scale by Adults and Peers (Way 1997) which consists of three independent subscales of five questions each. The subscale used in this study measured how often participants feel adults in their school discriminate against them due to their race or ethnicity (e.g. 'How often do you feel that adults in school don't listen to your thoughts on things because of your race or ethnicity?'). The measure used a five-point scale where 0 = never and 4 = all the time. Cronbach's alpha for this scale was 0.93 in this sample.

School racial discrimination climate

To construct a school-level variable of school climate, the perceived discrimination from adults score was averaged for each participant in a school creating a school-mean discrimination variable. Schools in which many students report experiencing discrimination had a higher mean than schools in which only a few or no students reported discrimination from adults in that school. To facilitate interpretation of the results, we group mean centered the variable by school. That is to say a score of zero on this variable would indicate a school with the average score among those in the sample.

Results

To understand the data, we explored a number of descriptive statistics to examine preliminary relationship in the data. First, we examined means and standard deviations to better understand the average values and the variance in the data (see Table 10.1). The mean score on the academic utility values measure was high on the scale and showed a reasonable amount of variance (M = 4.12, SD = 0.91). The online discrimination variable (M = 0.36, SD = 0.70) and school climate variable (M = 0.41, SD = 0.18) were low scores on each of their respective scales and the variance in-school scores was low. However, the small variance for school climate is likely due to the small number of schools in the data.

The results of the correlations are also in Table 10.1. In-school discrimination from adults is moderately positively correlated with school climate (r = 0.247) and online discrimination (r = 0.325), but school racial climate is only slightly positively correlated with online discrimination (r = 0.082), indicating that students who experience face-to-face discrimination may not experience discrimination online. Finally, the direction of the correlation between each of the discrimination variables and the outcome variables was in the expected direction.

To examine the contribution of racial discrimination on psychological well-being and student motivation, we performed three separate hierarchical multiple regression analyses. In each analysis, variables were added to the model in a progressive sequence of steps to examine the unique contribution of each variable or set of variables. In each model, demographic variables (gender, grade level, and racial categories) were entered in the first step. In the second step, the two face-to-face discrimination variables, in-school discrimination from adults and school discriminatory climate, were entered, and in the final step we entered online discrimination to examine whether this variable was predictive when controlling for all other variables in our study for each regression analysis. Since the analyses examine both individual and school-level variables, hierarchical linear modeling (HLM) was considered, but the number of schools, 12, was too low for sufficient power.

Anxiety

The first hierarchical analysis examined anxiety experienced by participants. Results for these analyses are listed in Table 10.2. The first step included the demographic variables and accounted for 3.9 percent of the variance in anxiety, and the variables contributed significantly to the model ($F_{(5, 641)}$ = 5.22, $p < 0.001$). In this step, the variable for gender was significant, with females reporting higher anxiety scores on average (β = 0.19, $p < 0.05$). In the second step of the anxiety analyses, we added school racial climate and in-school discrimination from adults. These variables accounted for 4.3 percent of the variance in anxiety ($F_{(2, 639)}$ = 15.10, $p < 0.001$) and discrimination from adults had a significant coefficient (β = 0.21, $p < 0.001$), indicating that participants who experienced more in-school discrimination from adults reported more anxiety. The final

Table 10.1 Means, standard deviations, and correlations among race and discrimination variables

		1	2	3	4	5	M	SD
1	In-school discrimination from adults	–					0.41	0.74
2	School climate	0.247	–				0.41	0.18
3	Online discrimination	0.325	0.082	–			0.36	0.70
4	Utility values	−0.137	−0.124	−0.132	–		4.12	0.91
5	Depressive symptoms	0.255	0.106	0.287	−0.159	–	0.64	0.59
6	Anxiety	0.197	0.053	0.219	−0.054	0.450	0.71	0.84

Note: *p < 0.05; **p < 0.01; ***p < 0.001.

Table 10.2 Summary of hierarchical regression analysis predicting anxiety (N = 647)

		B	(SE)	β	R^2	ΔR^2
Step 1	Female	0.32*	(0.07)	0.19	0.039	
	Grade	0.02	(0.02)	0.04		
	Latino	−0.01	(0.08)	0.00		
	Multiracial	0.17	(0.11)	0.06		
	Other	0.05	(0.10)	0.02		
Step 2	Female	0.33***	(0.07)	0.19	0.082	0.043***
	Grade	0.01	(0.02)	0.02		
	Latino	0.03	(0.08)	0.02		
	Multiracial	0.15	(0.11)	0.05		
	Other	0.09	(0.10)	0.04		
	School racial climate	0.02	(0.22)	0.00		
	In-school discrimination from adults	0.24***	(0.05)	0.21		
Step 3	Female	0.35***	(0.07)	0.20	0.111	0.029***
	Grade	0.00	(0.02)	0.00		
	Latino	0.02	(0.08)	0.01		
	Multiracial	0.14	(0.11)	0.05		
	Other	0.10	(0.10)	0.04		
	School racial climate	0.07	(0.22)	0.01		
	In-school discrimination from adults	0.17***	(0.05)	0.15		
	Online discrimination	0.22***	(0.05)	0.18		

Note: For analyses of race, African American is the reference group.
*$p < 0.05$; **$p < 0.01$; ***$p < 0.001$.

step showed that higher levels of online racial discrimination were associated with more anxiety for participants ($\beta = 0.18, p < 0.001$) and uniquely accounted for 2.9 percent of the variance in anxiety ($F_{(1, 638)} = 20.63, p < 0.001$). The full model explained 11.1 percent of the variance in anxiety for participants.

Depressive symptoms

The second hierarchical analysis examined depressive symptoms experienced by participants. Results for these analyses are listed in Table 10.3. The first block of variables accounted for 4.9 percent of the variance in depressive symptoms ($F_{(5, 652)} = 6.72, p < 0.001$) and the coefficients for females ($\beta = 0.20, p < 0.001$) and grade level ($\beta = 0.10, p < 0.01$) were significant. The positive coefficients indicate that female and older participants reported more depressive symptoms than their male and younger counterparts. In the second step, higher levels of in-school discrimination from adults were associated with more depressive symptoms ($\beta = 0.26, p < 0.001$). School climate and discrimination from adults were able to account for 6.3 percent of the variance in depressive symptoms ($F_{(2, 650)} = 12.01, p < 0.001$). The final step showed that higher levels of online racial discrimination were associated with more depressive symptoms for participants ($\beta = 0.23, p < 0.001$) and uniquely accounted for 4.7 percent of the variance ($F_{(1, 649)} = 15.62, p < 0.001$). The full model explained 16.1 percent of the variance in depressive symptoms for participants.

Academic motivation

The final hierarchical analysis examined utility values for education reported by participants. Results for these analyses are listed in Table 10.4. In the first step, demographic variables accounted for 4.9 percent of the variance in utility values of participants ($F_{(5, 626)} = 6.50, p < 0.001$). Specifically, females reported higher levels of utility values than their male peers ($\beta = 0.12, p < 0.01$) and as student

Table 10.3 Summary of hierarchical regression analysis predicting depression (*N* = 647)

		B	(SE)	β	R²	ΔR²
Step 1	Female	0.23★★★	(0.05)	0.20	0.049	
	Grade	0.03★★	(0.01)	0.10		
	Latino	−0.03	(0.06)	−0.03		
	Multiracial	0.04	(0.08)	0.02		
	Other	0.02	(0.07)	0.01		
Step 2	Female	0.25★★★	(0.04)	0.21	0.114	0.063★★★
	Grade	0.02	(0.01)	0.07		
	Latino	0.00	(0.06)	0.00		
	Multiracial	0.03	(0.08)	0.01		
	Other	0.06	(0.07)	0.01		
	School racial climate	0.02	(0.15)	0.01		
	In-school discrimination from adults	0.21★★★	(0.03)	0.26		
Step 3	Female	0.26	(0.04)	0.22	0.161	0.047★★★
	Grade	0.02	(0.01)	0.05		
	Latino	−0.01	(0.05)	0.01		
	Multiracial	0.01	(0.07)	0.05		
	Other	0.06	(0.15)	0.02		
	School racial climate	0.06	(0.22)	0.01		
	In-school discrimination from adults	0.15★★★	(0.03)	0.18		
	Online discrimination	0.20★★★	(0.03)	0.23		

Note: For analyses of race, African American is the reference group.
★*p* < 0.05; ★★*p* < 0.01; ★★★*p* < 0.001.

Table 10.4 Summary of hierarchical regression analysis predicting utility values of school (*N* = 632)

		B	(SE)	β	R²	ΔR²
Step 1	Female	0.22★★	(0.07)	0.12	0.049	
	Grade	−0.06★★	(0.02)	−0.13		
	Latino	−0.22★	(0.09)	−0.11		
	Multiracial	−0.26★	(0.12)	−0.09		
	Other	0.03	(0.11)	0.01		
Step 2	Female	0.21★★	(0.07)	0.11	0.073	0.024★★★
	Grade	−0.03	(0.02)	−0.06		
	Latino	−0.29★★	(0.09)	−0.14		
	Multiracial	−0.25★	(0.12)	−0.08		
	Other	−0.02	(0.11)	−0.01		
	School racial climate	−0.49★	(0.24)	−0.10		
	In-school discrimination from adults	−0.15★★	(0.05)	−0.12		
Step 3	Female	0.20★★	(0.07)	0.11	0.08	0.007★★★
	Grade	−0.03	(0.02)	−0.05		
	Latino	−0.28★★	(0.09)	−0.14		
	Multiracial	−0.25★	(0.12)	−0.08		
	Other	−0.02	(0.11)	−0.01		
	School racial climate	−0.52★	(0.24)	−0.11		
	In-school discrimination from adults	−0.11★	(0.05)	−0.09		
	Online discrimination	−0.13★	(0.06)	−0.09		

Note: For analyses of race, African American is the reference group.
★*p* < 0.05; ★★*p* < 0.01; ★★★*p* < 0.001.

grade level increased, their utility values decreased (β = −0.13, *p* < 0.01). Racial differences also emerged in this model. Both the Latino (β = −0.11, *p* < 0.05) and multiracial (β = −0.09, *p* < 0.05) participants reported lower utility values than their African American peers. In the second step, higher levels of in-school discrimination from adults (β = −0.12, *p* < 0.01) and more discriminatory school environments ($\beta = -0.10, p < 0.05$) were associated with lower utility values, and these two variables also accounted for 2.4 percent of the variance in utility values ($F_{(2, 624)} = 7.01, p < 0.001$). The final model showed that higher levels of online racial discrimination were associated with lower utility values for participants ($\beta = -0.09, p < 0.05$) but only uniquely accounted for 0.7 percent of the variance in the outcome ($F_{(1, 623)} = 6.75, p < 0.001$). The full model explained 8.0 percent of the variance in utility values for participants.

Discussion

The current study explored adolescent experiences with discrimination at school compared with online discrimination and how these experiences relate to depressive symptoms, anxiety, and academic motivation as expressed by utility values. Hierarchical regression results revealed that in-school discrimination from adults was related to each of the outcome variables, indicating that those who experienced this type of discrimination experienced more anxiety, more depressive symptoms, and lower utility values for school. We also found that online racial discrimination has a unique contribution over and above offline experiences, as this variable was significant in the final step of each model after all offline variables had been accounted for in that model. However, the racial environment of the school was a significant predictor only for utility values and not the two psychological outcomes. This finding highlights the importance of context as those who attended school with a more discriminatory environment reported lower values for the learning activities in that school environment.

These findings parallel extant literature that has found associations between discrimination and adjustment for youth of color (Coker *et al.* 2009; Fisher *et al.* 2000). Coker *et al.* (2009), for example, found for African American and Latino fifth graders, discrimination was associated with depressive symptoms and conduct disorder (attention deficit hyperactivity disorder and oppositional defiant disorder were also found for Latinos). In addition, Russell *et al.* (2012) found that youth who experienced bias-based harassment because of race, sexual orientation, disability or religion reported lower mental health status and increased substance use levels. Consequently, it appears that being victimized because of these social identities is particularly detrimental for health.

In addition to mental health outcomes, in-school discrimination from adults as well as a climate of discrimination was related to lower academic motivation. This is consistent with prior research (Cogburn *et al.* 2011; Eccles *et al.* 2006). Our findings build on this work by showing that online experiences of discrimination are also associated with lower academic utility values. Our findings indicate that discriminatory experiences outside the school walls can dampen adolescents' academic utility values. This suggests that when adolescents experience hateful and derogatory messages about their worth, it can decrease their beliefs that their work at school has value. Academic motivation has important implications for achievement and choices about what courses to take in school (Eccles *et al.* 2006). Thus, these findings are concerning and contribute to an understanding of the breadth of consequences for online discriminatory experiences.

A key strength is that we examined school-based (or offline) discriminatory experiences in tandem with online discriminatory experiences. This provided insights into the extent that students report having both experiences. We found a small correlation indicating that these two constructs are orthogonal – some students will experience both or neither, while others may experience just one form of discrimination. When adolescents do experience either form of discrimination, they are at risk of decreased levels of psychological adjustment and academic motivation. Thus, it is important to continue to study both forms of discrimination and adolescent development. An avenue for future work may be to investigate potentially interactive effects between the two forms of discrimination. For example, an interesting question to examine would be whether a lack of discrimination in school would minimize the negative effects of online discrimination on academic motivation. Other school-based protective factors could also be explored. For example, if a student has a supportive teacher, does that minimize the effects of online discrimination? Or students' support from peers could be examined. To date, much more is known about students' family, peer and school experiences. However, given the large amount of time that students spend online we must start to integrate online and in-person experiences. Such work integrating online and in-person experiences could be informative and contribute to a more comprehensive understanding of adolescent development.

Acknowledgments

This work was supported by the Eunice Kennedy Shriver National Institute of Child Health & Human Development of the National Institutes of Health under Award Number R01HD061584. The content is solely the responsibility of the authors and does not necessarily represent the official views of the National Institutes of Health.

References

Alfaro, E.C., Umaña-Taylor, A.J., Gonzales-Backen, M.A., Bamaca, M.Y. and Zeiders, K.H. (2009) 'Latino adolescents' academic success: the role of discrimination, academic motivation, and gender', *Journal of Adolescence*, 32: 941–962.

Benner, A.D. and Kim, S.Y. (2009) 'Intergenerational experiences of discrimination in Chinese American families: influences of socialization and stress', *Journal of Marriage and Family*, 71: 862–877.

Brody, G.H., Chen, Y.F., Murry, V.M., Ge, X., Simons, R.L., Gibbons, F.X., Gerrard, M. and Cutrona, C.E. (2006) 'Perceived discrimination and the adjustment of African American youths: a five-year longitudinal analysis with contextual moderation effects', *Child Development*, 77: 1170–1189.

Chavous, T.M., Rivas-Drake, D., Smalls, C., Griffin, T. and Cogburn, C. (2008) 'Gender matters, too: the influences of school racial discrimination and racial identity on academic engagement outcomes among African American adolescents', *Developmental Psychology*, 44: 637–654.

Cogburn, C.D., Chavous, T.M. and Griffin, T.M. (2011) 'School-based racial and gender discrimination among African American adolescents: exploring gender variation in frequency and implications for adjustment', *Race and Social Problems*, 3: 25–37.

Coker, T.R., Elliott, M.N., Kanouse, D.E., Grunbaum, J., Schwebel, D.C., Gilliland, J., Tortolero, S.R., Peskin, M.F. and Schuster, M.A. (2009) 'Perceived racial/ethnic discrimination among fifth-grade students and its association with mental health', *American Journal of Public Health*, 99: 878–884.

Dotterer, A.M., McHale, S.M. and Crouter, A.C. (2009) 'Sociocultural factors and school engagement among African American youth: the roles of racial discrimination, racial socialization, and ethnic identity', *Applied Developmental Science*, 13: 61–73.

Eccles, J.S., Wong, C.A. and Peck, S.C. (2006). 'Ethnicity as a social context for the development of African-American adolescents', *Journal of School Psychology*, 44: 407–426.

Fisher, C.B., Wallace, S.A. and Fenton, R.E. (2000) 'Discrimination distress during adolescence', *Journal of Youth and Adolescence*, 29: 679–695.

Flanagan, C.A., Syvertsen, A.K., Gill, S., Gallay, L.S. and Cumsille, P. (2009) 'Ethnic awareness, prejudice, and civic commitments in four ethnic groups of American adolescents', *Journal of Youth and Adolescence*, 38: 500–518.

Gaylord-Harden, N.K. and Cunningham, J.A. (2009) 'The impact of racial discrimination and coping strategies on internalizing symptoms in African American youth', *Journal of Youth and Adolescence*, 38: 532–543.

Grossman, J.M. and Liang, B. (2008) 'Discrimination distress among Chinese American Adolescents', *Journal of Youth and Adolescence*, 37: 1–11.

Harris-Britt, A., Valrie, C.R., Kurtz-Costes, B. and Rowley, S.J. (2007) 'Perceived racial discrimination and self-esteem in African American youth: racial socialization as a protective factor', *Journal of Research on Adolescence*, 17: 669–682.

Hu, L.T. and Bentler, P.M. (1999) 'Cutoff criteria for fit indexes in covariance structure analysis: conventional criteria versus new alternatives', *Structural Equation Modeling: A Multidisciplinary Journal*, 6: 1–55.

Huynh, V.W. and Fuligni, A.J. (2010) 'Discrimination hurts: the academic, psychological, and physical well-being of adolescents', *Journal of Research on Adolescence*, 20: 916–941.

Jones, L.M., Mitchell, K.J., and Finkelhor, D. (2012) 'Trends in youth internet victimization: findings from three youth internet safety surveys 2000–2010', *Journal of Adolescent Health*, 50: 179–186.

Juang, L.P. and Alvarez, A.A. (2010) 'Discrimination and adjustment among Chinese American adolescents: family conflict and family cohesion as vulnerability and protective factors', *American Journal of Public Health*, 100: 2403–2409.

Kline, R.B. (1998) *Principles and Practice of Structural Equation Modeling*, New York: Guilford Press.

Lenhart, A., Madden, M., Smith, A., Purcell, K., Zickuhr, K. and Raine, L. (2011) 'Teens, kindness and cruelty on social network sites', *Pew Internet* and *American Life Project*. Online. Available at: http://www.pewinternet.org/files/old-media/Files/Reports/2011/PIP_Teens_Kindness_Cruelty_SNS_Report_Nov_2011_FINAL_110711.pdf (accessed 19 March 2014).

Lorenzo-Blanco, E.I., Unger, J.B., Ritt-Olson, A., Soto, D. and Baezconde-Garbanati, L. (2011) 'Acculturation, gender, depression, and cigarette smoking among U.S. Hispanic youth: the mediating role of perceived discrimination', *Journal of Youth and Adolescence*, 40: 1519–1533.

McArdle, J.J., Johnson, R.C., Hishinuma, E.S., Miyamoto, R.H. and Andrade, N.N. (2001) 'Structural equation modeling of group differences in CES-D ratings of native Hawaiian and non-Hawaiian high school students', *Journal of Adolescent Research*, 16: 108–149.

Martin, M.J., McCarthy, B., Conger, R.D., Gibbons, F.X., Simons, R.L., Cutrona, C.E. and Brody, G.H. (2011) 'The enduring significance of racism: discrimination and delinquency among Black American youth', *Journal of Research on Adolescence*, 21: 662–676.

Medvedeva, M. (2010) 'Perceived discrimination and linguistic adaptation of adolescent children of immigrants', *Journal of Youth and Adolescence*, 39: 940–952.

Mitchell, K.J., Finkelhor, D., Wolak, J., Ybarra, M.L. and Turner, H. (2011) 'Youth internet victimization in a broader victimization context', *Journal of Adolescent Health*, 48: 128–134.

Neblett, E.W., White, R.L., Ford, K.R., Philip, C.L., Nguyên, H.X. and Sellers, R.M. (2008) 'Patterns of racial socialization and psychological adjustment: can parental communications about race reduce the impact of racial discrimination?', *Journal of Research on Adolescence*, 18: 477–515.

Pachter, L.M., Szalacha, L.A., Bernstein, B.A. and Coll, C.G. (2010) 'Perceptions of Racism in Children and Youth (PRaCY): properties of a self-report instrument for research on children's health and development', *Ethnicity and Health*, 15: 33–46.

Rivas-Drake, D., Hughes, D. and Way, N. (2009) 'A preliminary analysis of associations among ethnic-racial socialization, ethnic discrimination, and ethnic identity among urban sixth graders', *Journal of Research on Adolescence*, 19: 558–584.

Roberts, R.E. and Sobhan, M. (1992) 'Symptoms of depression in adolescence: a comparison of Anglo, African, and Hispanic Americans', *Journal of Youth and Adolescence*, 21: 639–651.

Russell, S.T., Sinclair, K.O., Poteat, V.P. and Koenig, B.W. (2012) 'Adolescent health and harassment based on discriminatory bias', *American Journal of Public Health*, 1023: 493–495.

Seaton, E.K. and Yip, T. (2009) 'School and neighborhood contexts, perceptions of racial discrimination, and psychological well-being among African American adolescents', *Journal of Youth and Adolescence*, 38: 153–163.

Shin, J.Y., D'Antonio, E., Son, H., Kim, S.A. and Park, Y. (2011) 'Bullying and discrimination experiences among Korean-American adolescents', *Journal of Adolescence*, 34: 873–883.

Simon Wiesenthal Center (2009) *iReport online terror + hate: The first decade*. Online. Available at. http://www.wiesenthal.com/atf/cf/%7BDFD2AAC1-2ADE-428A-9263-35234229D8D8%7D/IREPORT.PDF (accessed 19 March 2014).

Terry, P.C., Lane, A.M., Lane, H.J. and Keohane, L. (1999) 'Development and validation of a mood measure for adolescents', *Journal of Sports Sciences*, 17: 861–872.

Thompson, A.R. and Gregory, A. (2011) 'Examining the influence of perceived discrimination during African Americans' early years of high school', *Education and Urban Society*, 43: 3–25.

Tynes, B.M., Giang, M.T., Williams, D.R. and Thompson, G.N. (2008) 'Online racial discrimination and psychological adjustment among adolescents', *Journal of Adolescent Health*, 43: 565–569.

Tynes, B.M., Rose, C.A. and Williams, D.R. (2010) 'The development and validation of the Online Victimization Scale for Adolescents', *Cyberpsychology: Journal of Psychosocial Research on Cyberspace*, 4: 1–15.

Umaña-Taylor, A.J. and Updegraff, K. (2007) 'Latino adolescents' mental health: exploring the interrelations among discrimination, ethnic identity, cultural orientation, self-esteem, and depressive symptoms', *Journal of Adolescence*, 30: 549–567.

Way, N. (1997) 'Adult and peer discrimination measure', unpublished document.

Wigfield, A. and Eccles, J. (1995) 'Middle grades schooling and early adolescent development: Interventions, practices, beliefs, and contexts', *Journal of Early Adolescence*, 15: 5–8.

Wong, C.A., Eccles, J. S. and Sameroff, A. (2003) 'The influence of ethnic discrimination and ethnic identification on African American adolescents' school and socioemotional adjustment', *Journal of Personality*, 71: 1197–1212.

11

COUNTERVAILING FORCES IN MINORITY IDENTITY

Enacting and avoiding 'good student' behaviors

Rochelle M. Burnaford

Across many countries, racial and ethnic minority groups (e.g. African Americans, Latinos) have shown consistently lower rates of academic achievement than their majority counterparts, attributed in part to differences of socioeconomic status (Carnoy and Rothstein 2013). Psychologists have attempted to explain this gap in a number of ways. For example, stereotype threat research has documented the effects of priming both negative and positive stereotypes (Spencer *et al.* 1999; Steele and Aronson 1995; Walton and Cohen 2003). The stereotype threat literature has further shown evidence for the effect of direct and indirect primes of cultural stereotypes about one's group on performance in a variety of domains (e.g. Inzlicht and Ben-Zeev 2000). Other research has demonstrated the influence of self-fulfilling prophecies on a target's achievement. That is, if someone (e.g. a teacher) expects that a racial/ethnic minority student will not achieve academically at the same level as their European American peers, the student is less likely to be successful in that class (Rosenberg 1965).

However, researchers have largely ignored processes that may stem from minority group identity itself, perhaps in part because there is a fear that such research would be labeled as victim blaming. I do not argue that such processes are inherent to minority groups in particular, but that group identity shapes behavior through self-regulation and social exclusion. Further, the way that minority group identity is constructed, sometimes in opposition to majority culture (Ogbu 2004), can lead minority group members to avoid academic behavior. On the other hand, identity and self-concept research on the construction of possible selves demonstrates that members of minority groups can and do successfully attain positive academic selves by engaging in good student behaviors.

Over the course of this chapter I will first provide evidence for the ways in which *any* group identity may lead individuals to avoid certain behaviors. Then I contrast this with the ways in which possible selves prompt people to enact behaviors in pursuit of an individual goal. Finally, I will use current research to illustrate that these two processes create countervailing forces for minority students by simultaneously pushing them to avoid good student behaviors and maintain group belonging, or to enact such behaviors to attain a future possible self.

Research background

Social identity theory and self-esteem

Work in social identity may help to explain disparate rates of academic behaviors between minority and majority groups. Social identity theorists (e.g. Hogg and McGarty 1990; Tajfel and

Turner 1979) posit that identity is made up of two parts: one's social identities (i.e. collective selves such as race, gender or political affiliation) and one's personal identities (e.g. individual selves, such as an academically successful self, a healthy self). Both elements can shape behavior. However, if one identity is made more salient than the other, then that salient identity will have greater influence on behavior. For example, if students are reminded of their identification with being a successful student, they might be more likely to spend time studying or pay attention in class. On the other hand, if the same students' group identification with being part of the popular clique is more salient, they might be more likely to pay attention to friends than to class work. Therefore, both identities can shape behaviors in our daily lives.

Additionally, social identity theorists argue that feeling positive about our in-groups is often coupled with antagonistic attitudes towards out-groups as a way to maintain or enhance group and self-esteem. For example, group members may engage in discriminatory or prejudicial behaviors to maintain their own group's superiority (Branscombe *et al.* 1999). Additionally, negative effects of group membership can include an individual's own in-group members in a process termed the "black sheep effect" (Marques *et al.* 1988). According to research, group members can be subject to disparagement for violating an in-group norm when the behavior is perceived to threaten the group or the self in some way. Further, social identity theorists have shown that such effects are strongest when someone is highly identified with a given social group (Luhtanen and Crocker 1992). That is, the more value one places on a given group identity, the more vehemently they will defend its integrity. Coupled with the black sheep effect, we can expect that the more value a social identity has to the self, the more likely a person will be to attack fellow group members for deviant behavior. Additionally, it follows that those individuals who violate their group norms may anticipate repercussions of norm violating behavior.

Identity misclassification

Whereas group norms are general expectations that guide behavior, research on identity misclassification has investigated reactions to specific behaviors that are perceived as a violation of a valued social identity (Bosson *et al.* 2005). The identity misclassification model argues that when individuals choose to perform behaviors that violate a valued social role, they risk being labeled as 'falsely accused deviants' (Becker 1963), in that their behavior is seen as deviating from the group norm. When an individual is strongly identified with a given social group, they are more vulnerable to threats to that identity because of the group's importance to the self (Crocker and Wolfe 2001). Researchers using the identity threat model have found that engaging in out-group behaviors poses threats to an individual's essential need to belong (e.g. Baumeister and Leary 1995; Swann 1990). Our essential need to belong is defined as our need to maintain quality social bonds through membership and standing within valued social groups. Consequently, fears about what one's peers may think can motivate one to refrain from certain behaviors when such behaviors are associated with relevant out-groups as a way to maintain valued group belonging. In other words, to prevent possible threats to a valued identity, individuals may avoid behaviors that are *out-group identity-infused* (Oyserman 2007).

Identity-based motivation

Based in part on social identity theories, Oyserman (2007) developed a model of identity-based motivation. She argues that we are motivated to engage in specific behaviors which she calls *identity-infused behaviors*, because they reinforce a valued identity. Identity-infused behaviors are associated with membership in a given social group. Consequently, performance of identity-infused behaviors is a direct expression of a group identity, and can foster feelings of belonging and inclusion in the group (Oyserman *et al.* 2007). The identity-based motivation model also incorporates behaviors that we are motivated *not* to do. Specifically, when a set of behaviors is associated with a relevant out-group, an individual will be motivated to avoid such behaviors (Oyserman *et al.* 2014). Avoidance of out-group identity-infused behaviors as well as engagement with in-group identity-infused behaviors may, therefore, both act as an assertion of group membership because it allows the individual to maintain their status as a good group member. Given this logic, group members must not only enact group-specific behaviors but also avoid out-group associated behaviors to prove and maintain group status. Therefore, individuals may avoid out-group identity-infused behaviors despite negative consequences if there is a greater desire to maintain group membership status. Indeed, identity misclassification research provides initial support for such an argument by showing that individuals engaged in what are arguably out-group identity-infused behaviors (e.g. men asked to braid hair) feel threats to their sense of belonging and coherence (e.g. Bosson *et al.* 2005).

Processes of out-group identity infusion may be especially problematic for minority group members in school. Oyserman (2007) and Ogbu (2004) argue that academic behaviors have become European identity-infused in the United States due to the country's history of racial inequality. Where there is inequality in social power, majority group identity is more likely to be associated with domains relevant to a desirable achievement. Such an association is most often found in domains that are vital for social power and advancement, such as academic performance (Oyserman 2007). Hence, behaviors that increase chances for academic success (such as spending time studying) have a great potential to be considered majority-group infused because they provide a means for advancement and offer greater income security. Consequently, historical and social processes that lead to academic behaviors becoming associated with European identity may be similar in any culture where Europeans have historically held, or continue to maintain dominance.

But our social identities (group memberships) are not our only sources of self-regulatory influences. Our personal identities, elements of our self-concept, can also motivate behavior through the construction of possible selves (Markus and Nurius 1986; Oyserman and James 2009). As with our social identities, our possible selves can also produce goal-oriented behaviors, such as studying hard to achieve an academically successful self. While anyone can imagine a successful possible self, only those who engage in specific strategies conducive to their goal will be able to achieve it (Oyserman *et al.* 2004). That is, if one both aspires to achieve academically *and* can describe and enact specific behaviors toward that end, one will be able to attain the possible self who is academically successful. Attainment of positive possible selves is also contingent on avoidance of negative possible selves, much like avoiding out-group identity behaviors. Research has found, paradoxically, that having more negative (to be avoided) possible selves increases likelihood of becoming a negative possible self (Oyserman and Markus 1990). Essentially this research demonstrates that when an individual's negative possible selves are not counterbalanced with positive possible selves, and especially the behaviors needed to attain them, one's ability to avoid negative possible selves is weakened. That is, it is not enough merely to avoid the negative self; one must also simultaneously strive for the positive self. Therefore, to achieve an academically successful possible self, minority students must engage in behaviors that not only avoid their negative possible selves (e.g. high-school dropout) but also actively pursue the academically successful possible self.

The processes outlined above may create countervailing forces for minority students who seek to both avoid out-group identity-infused behaviors *and* engage in the behaviors needed to achieve their academically successful possible self. That is, specific behaviors required to achieve their academically successful possible self are out-group identity-infused and create a countervailing tension between achievement of the academically successful self, and maintenance of social group membership. Therefore, minority individuals must choose to either maintain group belonging and status by avoiding academic behaviors or to achieve the positive academic self by engaging in them, and risk social exclusion.

Social exclusion of the possible self

Minority students who choose to pursue their academically successful self at the cost of their group membership risk social exclusion, or ostracism, by their minority peers. Evolutionarily, social exclusion was a way for social groups (e.g. tribes) to police fellow group members and to maintain group security (Gruter and Masters 1986). Today, social psychological research has shown that group norm violations affect those who engage in norm violating behaviors (e.g. Bosson *et al.* 2005), as well as perception of such individuals (e.g. Wenegrat *et al.* 1996). In fact, researchers have connected the use of social exclusion to the black sheep effect by showing that in-group members will show a preference for those who abide by group norms and actively reject those who violate them (Marques *et al.* 1998). It further stands to reason that groups could use social exclusion as a means to police specific out-group identity-infused behaviors because the individual risks being misclassified as an out-group member (Bosson *et al.* 2005; Oyserman 2007). In light of the fact that being excluded from valued social groups can have drastic effects on one's self-esteem, sense of meaningful existence, and mood (Williams 1997), specific behavioral strategies for attaining academic possible selves may be more difficult to enact when they are out-group identity-infused. That is, group members may avoid out-group identity-infused behaviors despite the fact that they represent achievement of a desired possible self in order to protect both group and self-esteem. Thus, despite conceiving an academically successful possible self, this self is more difficult to achieve for minorities when they are motivated to avoid academic behaviors because of out-group identity-infusion processes.

In what follows I will present evidence for the countervailing forces on minority students in school that push them to either enact or avoid good student behaviors. First, I will briefly discuss how minority students may achieve positive academic possible selves. This will be followed by contrasting research indicating that processes of social exclusion may thwart minority students' attempts to achieve such possible selves.

Major findings: Identity-based motivation model and academic achievement

One counter-argument to this is that minority students who *do* find or have peers who are supportive of academic success are far more able to succeed academically (e.g. Wentzel *et al.* 2012). I do not seek to contradict such research. However, I would argue that while some minority students may be able to achieve academically in part because of supportive and like-minded peers, we cannot ignore the ways in which research shows us that minority group identity may make academic achievement more difficult. Additionally, if engagement with academically minded peers prevents or results in exclusion from membership in one's cultural group, this again supports the idea that countervailing forces, the choice between cultural group inclusion or academic success, are still in play. That is, I would argue that even if a minority student's supportive peers are from the same racial/ethnic group, they may still be subject to social exclusion from the group at large.

Enacting behavior: Pursuing academic selves

Research has long evidenced that minority students do *not* report lower levels of interest in academic achievement (e.g. Graham 1994), despite the continued persistence of the academic achievement gap. That is, minority students still conceptualize academically successful possible selves (Oyserman *et al.* 2004), but somehow their possible selves are not translating into self-regulatory behavior as effectively as their majority peers. For example, Oyserman and Markus (1990) found that delinquent versus non-delinquent adolescents held different patterns of possible self-expectations and fears. Non-delinquents were more likely than delinquent adolescents to both expect positive selves (e.g. success in school) and fear negative selves (e.g. not having friends). Essentially, it is not enough to simply avoid a negative self; one must also expect a future positive possible self. This balance conceptualization of both positive and negative academic selves may act to maximize self-regulatory control over academic behaviors.

Research on the effects of balance in possible selves has evidenced the ways in which balance in possible selves promotes behavioral strategies that work to increase self-regulatory behavior. Oyserman et al. (2006) used an intervention designed to promote balance in possible selves and behavioral strategies among at-risk students. After a two-year intervention process, they found that students who held a balance between positive and negative academic possible selves (e.g. college graduate versus high-school dropout) were more likely to be successful in regulating behavior to achieve their goal. Additionally, those who were able to describe specific good student behavioral strategies to attain their positive possible selves and avoid negative possible selves (e.g. I will pay attention in class; I will not skip class) were more able to enact such behaviors and consequently improve their academic achievement. Therefore, for minority students to be academically successful, it is vital that they are able to elucidate not only the negative identities (e.g. delinquent) they fear, but also the positive academic possible selves that they wish to strive for. Possible selves research additionally stipulates that these goals must contain very specific good student behavioral strategies (Oyserman et al. 2006; Oyserman and Markus 1990) However, the identity misclassification and identity-based motivation models suggest that engaging in these good student behaviors to attain the academically successful possible self may have different consequences (e.g. social exclusion) for minority versus majority group students (Burnaford and Bosson 2014; Oyserman 2007).

Avoiding behavior: Fear of social exclusion

Processes of social exclusion are used to enforce group norms and behaviors (Williams 1997). Further, individuals risk social exclusion by becoming 'falsely accused deviants' (Becker 1965) when they engage in behavior that violates a valued social role. Finally, behaviors that are group identity-infused are means of expressing membership (Oyserman et al. 2007). As such, group members who engage in *out-group* identity-infused behaviors run the risk of being excluded from a valued social group. The implications of these processes may be more significant for minority youth if academic behaviors are majority (European) identity-infused. Oyserman (2007) argued that academic behaviors are European identity-infused because of the historical power differentials between European American and minority groups.

To test whether this was the case, Burnaford and Bosson (2014) assessed whether people do associate good student behaviors (e.g. paying careful attention in class) with European American identity. Items were embedded among other behaviors that students might engage in (e.g. partying, exercising, eating). Participants were asked to rate how associated they thought each behavior was with several different racial/ethnic groups (European American, African American, Asian American, Latino). Participants were further instructed that a strong association between the identity and the behavior meant that they though it was very likely for them to see a member of that racial/ethnic group exhibit the given behavior, whereas a weak association meant that they thought it was unlikely for them to see a member of that racial/ethnic group exhibit that behavior. As expected, participants rated the good student behaviors as more associated with European American identity than with African American or Latino identity. We can then conclude that

Oyserman's (2007) argument was correct and that academic behaviors have become European identity-infused.

The association of academics with European American identity is particularly problematic for minority students. Specifically, if academic behaviors are European American identity-infused, then highly identified minority students may be motivated to avoid these behaviors in order to maintain status in their valued group. To test this, Burnaford and Bosson (2014) assessed a mediational model of the link between race/ethnicity, strength of identification with racial group, and good student behaviors. They found that highly identified African American students reported lower rates of good student behaviors, and that this effect was partially mediated by concerns about being teased for engaging in academic behaviors (e.g. 'If I study too hard, my friends are likely to tease me'). This indicates that minorities may be sensitive to the potential for social exclusion following engagement in out-group identity-infused behaviors.

To examine whether such fears may influence subsequent behaviors, Burnaford and Bosson (2014) manipulated racial/ethnic identity threat using a false feedback paradigm. African American and European American participants were given a bogus Rorschach-style test, and then told either that they had performed similarly to European American students or similarly to African American students. Following this, participants were asked to take part in an ostensibly separate study in which they would 'practice for an upcoming test' by using a sample problem from the test. The problem asked them to combine the numbers two, three, five, and seven to make 36 (Oyserman *et al.* 1995: 1224). Each attempt and the amount of time spent making attempts were counted as measures of motivation. Results indicated that when racial/ethnic identity was threatened, African American students made fewer attempts and spent less time practicing than African American students whose racial/ethnic identity had been affirmed, and European American students whose racial/ethnic identity had been threatened. These results indicate that minority students may reduce motivation to engage in academic behaviors if they feel that their sense of belonging to their racial/ethnic group has been threatened by performing similarly to the out-group (European American).

The question still remained, though, as to whether minority individuals would not only recognize social exclusion based on engaging in out-group identity-infused behaviors, but also whether they would exclude fellow group members if they were thought to have enacted such behaviors. To test this, Burnaford (2012) told minority (African American and Latino) participants they had scored similarly either to other minority students or similarly to European American students on a survey of academic behaviors. Participants were then told that an ostensible fellow participant, who had information about them, including their survey score, did not choose them for a subsequent task. When asked why they thought the ostensible participant had excluded them, participants who received identity-threatening feedback were more likely to believe the exclusion was because of their feedback than those who had received identity-affirming feedback. In a follow-up study designed to assess whether minority participants would actually exclude fellow group members for out-group identity-infused behaviors, Burnaford (2012) found that minorities (African Americans and Latinos) who were highly identified with their racial/ethnic group were more likely to choose an identity affirmed partner for a subsequent task over identity threatened partner, regardless of the nature of the task.

Together, these studies suggest that not only are racial/ethnic minority students aware of exclusion for engaging in out-group identity-infused behaviors, but when group membership is important to their sense of self they will also exclude fellow group members for such behaviors. As a consequence, the minority achievement gap may in part be explained by social exclusion processes that dissuade minority students from engaging in good student behaviors, thus preventing them from attaining their positive academic possible selves.

Conclusion

Possible self- and social exclusion processes act as countervailing forces for minority students, each predicting either enactment or avoidance of good student behaviors. Social identity and self-categorization theories would suggest that which force is successful will depend in part on whether the (possible) self or the group is more salient (Turner *et al.* 1987). For minority students, especially those of low socioeconomic status, this creates additional challenges, as role models of academic success are scarcer in these communities (Fordham and Ogbu 1986; Ogbu 2004). The lack of positive academic role models makes conception of future academically successful selves more difficult for minority adolescents. One of the reasons that the intervention used by Oyserman and her colleagues (2004) was so successful is that it began with an initial session that brought minority adolescents together in an attempt to make academic possible selves congruent with identity. That is, minority adolescents had the opportunity to experience how their peers desired and engaged in behavior to achieve their academic possible selves. This supports research from Wentzel and colleagues (2012) suggesting that when minority students have supportive peer groups, they are much better equipped to succeed academically. However, often in adolescence, desire for future achievement is far less immediate than the lure of belonging to present social groups. If a minority student does not have academically supportive peers, they may be subject to countervailing forces on their academic behavior.

One distinct challenge for researchers is to address how identity processes of social exclusion might be changed for minority groups who avoid out-group identity-infused behaviors and hence good student behaviors. Future research should examine the ways in which minority students are able to either deflect or ignore social exclusion to the benefit of their academic selves. Additionally, while some individuals may be fortunate enough to find supportive peers, this may not be the case for a large part of the minority student body. Therefore research should also address the ways in which cultural conceptualizations can be changed to include academically successful possible selves as part and parcel of minority identity.

Over the course of this chapter, I have reviewed theories of social identity and how social identity is linked to self-esteem and behavior. As a result of this link, we are motivated to engage in identity-infused behaviors and avoid out-group identity-infused behaviors. Additionally, elements of our self-concept can also drive behavior in the pursuit of future possible selves. The research reviewed here suggests that these processes have important consequences for minority academic achievement. Specifically, minority students are subject to countervailing forces to enact good student behaviors and pursue a possible self or to avoid good student behaviors, averting social exclusion and maintaining social group status. Each of these forces can exert influence simultaneously on the choices of minority students. However, research has yet to directly compare them or ascertain exactly how to produce academic engagement in the direct face of a threat to social group membership.

References

Baumeister, R.F. and Leary, M.R. (1995) 'The need to belong: desire for interpersonal attachments as a fundamental human motivation', *Psychological Bulletin,* 117: 497–529.

Becker, H.S. (1963) *Outsiders: Studies in the Sociology of Deviance,* Oxford: Free Press Glencoe.

Bosson, J.K., Prewitt-Freilino, J.L. and Taylor, J.N. (2005) 'Role rigidity: a problem of identity misclassification?', *Journal of Personality and Social Psychology,* 89: 552–565.

Branscombe, N.R., Ellemers, N., Spears, R. and Doosje, B. (1999) 'The context and content of social identity threat', in N. Ellemers, R. Spears and B. Doosje (eds) *Social Identity: Context, Commitment, Content* (pp. 35–58), Oxford: Blackwell Science.

Burnaford, R.M. (2012) 'Race, ethnicity, and exclusion in group identity', unpublished doctoral dissertation. University of South Florida, Tampa, FL.

Burnaford, R.M. and Bosson, J.K. (2014) 'Race and motivation: how threats to identity impact the academic motivation of minority students', unpublished manuscript.

Carnoy, M. and Rothstein, R. (2013, January 15) 'International tests show achievement gaps in all countries', *Economic Policy Institute* blog. Available at http://www.epi.org/blog/international-tests-achievement-gaps-gains-american-students/

Crocker, J. and Wolfe, C.T. (2001) 'Contingencies of self-worth', *Psychological Review,* 108: 593–623.

Fordham, S. and Ogbu, J.U. (1986) 'Black students' school success: coping with the "burden of acting White"', *The Urban Review,* 18: 176–206.

Graham, S. (1994) 'Motivation in African Americans', *Review of Educational Research,* 64: 55–117.

Gruter, M. and Masters, R.D. (1986) 'Ostracism as a social and biological phenomenon: an introduction', *Ethology and Sociobiology,* 7: 149–158.

Hogg, M.A. and McGarty, C. (1990) 'Self-categorization and social identity', *Social Identity Theory: Constructive and Critical Advances,* 10: 27.

Inzlicht, M. and Ben-Zeev, T. (2000) 'A threatening intellectual environment: why females are susceptible to experiencing problem-solving deficits in the presence of males', *Psychological Science,* 11: 365–371.

Luhtanen, R. and Crocker, J. (1992) 'A collective self-esteem scale: self-evaluation of one's social identity', *Personality and Social Psychology Bulletin,* 18: 302–318.

Markus, H. and Nurius, P. (1986) 'Possible selves', *American Psychologist,* 41: 954–969.

Marques, J., Abrams, D., Paez, D. and Martinez-Taboada, C. (1998) 'The role of categorization and in-group norms in judgments of groups and their members', *Journal of Personality and Social Psychology,* 75: 976–988.

Marques, J.M., Yzerbyt, V.Y. and Leyens, J.-P. (1988) 'The "black sheep effect": extremity of judgments towards ingroup members as a function of group identification', *European Journal of Social Psychology,* 18: 1–16.

Ogbu, J.U. (2004) 'Collective identity and the burden of "acting White" in Black history, community, and education', *The Urban Review,* 36: 1–35.

Oyserman, D. (2007) 'Social identity and self-regulation', in A.W. Kruglanski and E.T. Higgins (eds) *Social Psychology: Handbook of Basic Principles,* 2nd edn (pp. 432–453), New York: Guilford Press.

Oyserman, D., Bybee, D. and Terry, K. (2006) 'Possible selves and academic outcomes: how and when possible selves impel action', *Journal of Personality and Social Psychology,* 91: 188–204.

Oyserman, D., Bybee, D., Terry, K. and Hart-Johnson, T. (2004) 'Possible selves as roadmaps', *Journal of Research in Personality,* 38: 130–149.

Oyserman, D., Fryberg, S.A. and Yoder, N. (2007) 'Identity-based motivation and health', *Journal of Personality and Social Psychology,* 93: 1011–1027.

Oyserman, D., Gant, L. and Ager, J. (1995) 'A socially contextualized model of racial identity: possible selves and school persistence', *Journal of Personality and Social Psychology,* 69: 1216–1232.

Oyserman, D. and James, L. (2009) 'Possible selves: from content to process', in K. Markman, W.M.P. Klein and J.A. Suhr (eds) *The Handbook of Imagination and Mental Stimulation* (pp. 373–394), New York: Psychology Press.

Oyserman, D. and Markus, H. (1990) 'Possible selves and delinquency', *Journal of Personality and Social Psychology,* 59: 112–125.

Oyserman, D., Smith, G.C. and Elmore, K. (2014) 'Identity-based motivation: implications for health and health disparities', *Journal of Social Issues,* 70: 206–225.

Rosenberg, M. (1965) *Society and the adolescent self-image,* Princeton, NJ: Princeton University Press.

Spencer, S.J., Steele, C.M. and Quinn, D.M. (1999) 'Stereotype threat and women's math performance', *Journal of Experimental Social Psychology,* 35: 4–28.

Steele, C.M. and Aronson, J. (1995) 'Stereotype threat and the intellectual test performance of African Americans', *Journal of Personality and Social Psychology,* 69: 797–811.

Swann, W.B. Jr. (1990) 'To be adored or to be known: the interplay of self-enhancement and self-verification', in R.M. Sorrentino and E.T. Higgins (eds) *Foundations of Social Behavior* (Vol. 2, pp. 408–448), New York: Guilford.

Tajfel, H. and Turner, J.C. (1979) 'An intergrative theory of intergroup conflict', in W. G. Austin and S. Worchel (eds) *The Social Psychology of Intergroup Relations* (pp. 33–47), Monterey, CA: Brooks/Cole.

Turner, J.C., Hogg, M.A., Oakes, P.J., Reicher, S.D. and Wetherell, M.S. (1987) *Rediscovering the Social Group: A Self-Categorization Theory,* Oxford: Basil Blackwell.

Walton, G.M. and Cohen, G.L. (2003) 'Stereotype lift', *Journal of Experimental Social Psychology,* 39: 456–467.

Wenegrat, B., Castillo-Yee, E. and Abrams, L. (1996) 'Social norm compliance as a signaling system: II. Studies of fitness-related attributions consequent on a group norm violation', *Ethology and Sociobiology*, 17: 417–429.

Wentzel, K.R., Baker, S. A. and Russell, S.L. (2012) 'Young adolescents' perceptions of teachers' and peers' goals as predictors of social and academic goal pursuit', *Applied Psychology: An International Review*, 61: 605–633.

Williams, K.D. (1997) 'Social ostracism', in R. Kowalski (ed.) *Aversive Interpersonal Behaviors* (pp. 133–170), New York: Springer.

PART III

Student beliefs and peer relationships

12

ORIGINS AND CONSEQUENCES OF SOCIAL STATUS DIFFERENCES IN MIDDLE CHILDHOOD

Clark McKown

Inequality is an inevitable feature of collective life. For any socially valued outcome, it is nearly certain that across culture, geography, and community, in every era of human history, some have had more than others. Height, attractiveness, earnings, and intellectual ability vary between individuals, as do social acceptance, social support, and all manner of valued outcomes. And while there are few sure things, it is a safe wager that even a cursory review of history, perusal of the daily news, or forecast of days to come will reveal a bounty of inequality.

Insofar as inequality has always been and will always be part of collective life, it is as much a law of the social world as gravity is a law of the physical world. It is interesting, then, that the law of social inequality coexists with an apparent contradiction: social conditions, influenced by human action, can magnify or attenuate inequality. The availability of high-quality and sufficient nutrition quality can influence the distribution of characteristics as seemingly immutable as height and lifespan. Economic conditions between countries and across time are associated with the magnitude of income inequality. Inequality can also be influenced by local social conditions. Teacher practices can magnify or attenuate social status differences between students.

As long as humans have had the power to shape environments, there has always therefore been a puzzling tension between the inevitability and the malleability of inequality. This tension lies at the heart of public policy debates past, present, and (no doubt) future. On one side, those who hold inequality to be inevitable tend to advocate laissez-faire policies and see public efforts to mitigate inequality as counterproductive exercises in social engineering that run afoul of nature's design. On the other side, those who believe inequality is malleable tend to advocate a muscular approach to collective intervention designed to reduce inequality, and see laissez-faire approaches as a form of collective neglect that is fundamentally unfair (Lakoff 2009).

There is no easy resolution to this tension as it expresses itself in the public discourse. However, there may be a path to lessening inequality and its harms that acknowledges both its ubiquity and malleability. A key premise of this chapter is that whether inequality is inevitable or not, feasible actions to reduce it and its harmful consequences can be identified and enacted. A second premise of this chapter is that the best solutions to reduce inequality and its consequences are rooted in empirically supported models of inequality's origins.

The purpose of this chapter is to examine the origins and consequences of two highly consequential forms of inequality, found in schoolhouses throughout the United States and beyond. The first is the racial–ethnic achievement gap. This is an instance of one broad class of social inequality: between-group inequality. The second inequality considered in this chapter is variability in children's classroom social network positions, which is an instance of a second broad class of social inequality: within-group inequality.

The chapter will review what is known about the origins of the racial–ethnic achievement gap and variability in social network position. In so doing, a central goal of the chapter is to identify malleable features of the school environment that have been or could be the targets of intentional efforts to reduce the magnitude and consequences of social inequalities. These inequalities exist in schools and pertain to children. However, it is the ambition of this chapter that the ways of understanding these inequalities could be fruitfully applied to other forms of social inequality.

The racial–ethnic achievement gap

In the United States, mean racial–ethnic differences in performance on tests of academic achievement have decreased, but persist. Much of the historical focus on the American racial–ethnic achievement gap has been on African American–European American performance gaps. Depending on the sample and measure, European American students score an average of 0.5–1.0 standard deviation higher on achievement tests than their African American classmates (Jencks and Phillips 1998; Lee 2002; Reardon and Galindo 2009; Reardon and Robinson 2007; Vanneman *et al.* 2009). Mean group differences in achievement and attainment cascade throughout the lifespan, leading to mean differences in economic and other opportunities (Levin 2009).

A clear and comprehensive understanding of the gap's origins may set the stage for effective remedies. To that end, my colleagues and I articulated social equity theory, a model of the social processes that give rise to racial–ethnic achievement gaps (McKown 2013; McKown and Strambler 2008). Here is social equity theory in its most compact form:

$$\Delta_g = \sum_{c=1}^{k} (D + S \mid i)$$

In this formulation, Δ_g reflects mean differences between identifiable groups in a socially valued outcome – in this case, the mean difference between children from different American racial–ethnic groups on measures of academic achievement. Δ_g is equal to the sum, across k key developmental contexts (c) of direct influences (D) and signal influences (S), and signal influences are contingent on children's ability to understand a particular class of social cues ($S \mid i$).

The terms 'direct influence' (D) and 'signal influence' (S) have particular meanings. Both involve social transactions between individuals, or between an individual and a setting. Direct influences are social transactions that produce positive social outcomes for all children. When those transactions are more available to one racial–ethnic group than another, this directly influences group mean difference in achievement. Signal influences – most clearly described in the stereotype threat literature – are events or experiences that signal to members of stigmatized racial–ethnic groups that they are not intellectually capable. Signal influences depend on children's ability to detect and interpret those environmental signals as signifiers of low expectations about their racial–ethnic group.

As we have noted elsewhere (McKown 2013; McKown and Strambler 2008), there is substantial evidence that direct influences occur in schools, at home, among peers, and in communities. There is also evidence that signal influences occur in schools. In our own work, for example, we have found that elementary-school teachers expect less of African American and Latino students than European American and Asian American peers with similar records of achievement (McKown and Weinstein 2008), and that African American students' achievement is more likely than European American students' achievement to confirm teacher underestimates of ability (McKown and Weinstein 2002). Because this chapter is focused on social processes in schools, we will provide examples of direct and signal influences, with an emphasis on those that are likely to occur in schools. However, social equity theory makes a strong assumption that the entirety of the racial–ethnic achievement gap can be explained only by accounting for social processes that occur both within and outside of the schoolhouse.

A kaleidoscopic array of social processes in school influence achievement. Key examples include the quality of instruction, the supportiveness and warmth of teacher–student relationships (Gregory and Weinstein 2004; Hamre and Pianta 2001, 2005), and teacher expectations (Weinstein 2002). We know that these social resources influence academic outcomes – the better the quality of the instruction, the more supportive the student relationships with teachers, and the more the teacher expects, the more students learn and the better they perform on achievement tests. Those social processes therefore engender one of the characteristics of a direct influence – they are social processes that promote academic growth and achievement.

For these social processes to exert a direct influence on the racial–ethnic achievement gap, they must be available differently to students from different racial–ethnic groups. In fact, they are. On average, European American students are the beneficiaries of better teachers and more challenging instruction (Clotfelter *et al.* 2004; Lee and Burkham 2002). In addition, European American students enjoy better relationships with their teachers (Gregory and Weinstein 2004; Hamre and Pianta 2005; Saft and Pianta 2001; Weinstein 2002) than do African American students with similar records of achievement and behavior. Teachers in general expect more of European American students than African American students with similar records of achievement (Baron *et al.* 1985; McKown and Weinstein 2008).

Of course, many additional social processes, both at school and elsewhere, surely exert direct influences on racial–ethnic achievement gaps. We have explored in greater depth elsewhere the role of parents, peers, and neighborhoods (McKown 2013; McKown and Strambler 2008). Instructional quality, teacher–student relationships, and teacher expectations are offered as illustrative examples of school-based direct influences highly likely to contribute to racial–ethnic achievement gaps.

Another class of social process contributes to the racial–ethnic achievement gap. In social equity theory, these are referred to as 'signal influences'. Signal influences are social processes that signal to a member of a stereotyped group that their ability is devalued because of their racial–ethnic group membership. The concept of a signal influence draws heavily from research on stereotype threat. Among adults, the context of academic performance can signal to members of academically stereotyped groups that their group's intellectual abilities are devalued, which in turn propagates a self-fulfilling prophecy. For example, characterizing a test as diagnostic of ability can interfere with cognitive performance for members of stereotyped groups (Steele and Aronson 1995).

For signal influences to affect academic performance, individuals from stereotyped groups must be capable of interpreting social cues as signaling a stereotyped expectation. Adults are aware of others' stereotypes (Pinel 1999, 2002; Vorauer *et al.* 2000; Vorauer and Kumhyr 2002; Vorauer *et al.* 1998). It is less clear that children have a sufficiently developed social understanding to make such an interpretation. Children's understanding of the existence and nature of broadly held stereotypes emerges in the elementary years (McKown and Weinstein 2003; McKown and Strambler 2009). Furthermore, among African American and Latino children who are aware of broadly held stereotypes, when the conditions of testing are described as diagnostic of academic ability, performance is worse than when the very same task is described as a problem-solving task (McKown and Weinstein 2003; McKown and Strambler 2009). For European American and Asian American students, *and* for African American and Latino students who are *not* aware of broadly held stereotypes, how the test is described does not affect test performance (McKown and Weinstein 2003; McKown and Strambler 2009). These findings suggest that signal influences are contingent on children's ability to interpret social signals as communicating a stereotyped expectation.

Social equity theory lends itself to developing and testing strategies designed to reduce the racial–ethnic achievement gap. In fact, educational field trials have provided evidence supporting the proposition that addressing direct and signal influences can reduce racial–ethnic achievement gaps.

In terms of direct influences, for example, Success for All, a literacy curriculum that combines intensive focus on phonics and adherence to particular instructional practices, has been shown to reduce the achievement gap. The longer students are exposed to the curriculum, the greater the reduction in the gap (Slavin and Madden 2001). Similarly, KIPP (Knowledge is Power Program) charter schools engage in practices that may reduce direct influences – they have extended hours, culturally appropriate instructional practices, individualized mentoring, and structured instruction. The KIPP model has shown promising evidence of promoting racial–ethnic minority achievement (Educational Policy Institute 2005). These lines of evidence suggest that the quality of instruction is a direct influence on the achievement gap, with differential allocation of instructional quality contributing to African American–European American differences in learning and achievement.

In terms of signal influences, there is growing evidence that children can be inoculated against signal influences. For example, teaching middle-school girls to believe that intelligence depends on effort and that academic difficulties are situational reduced the effects of stereotype threat on mathematics test performance (Good *et al.* 2003). Drawing from self-affirmation theory (Steele 1988), Cohen *et al.* (2006) found when African American students wrote a paragraph about their values and their importance, they showed lower levels of stereotype activation and received higher grades than their African American peers in a control condition.

Classroom social status differences

The American racial–ethnic achievement gap is an example of one kind of social inequality – between-group inequality. This is substantially different than another class of social inequality – within-group inequality. The former is reflected in mean between-group differences on measures of socially valued outcomes. The latter is reflected in variation within a population on socially valued outcomes. Social equity theory was formulated as a way to understand factors that influence between-group inequality. It does not address within-group inequality. Indeed, even if all between-group inequalities were eliminated, within-group inequality would persist.

Within-group inequality is arguably even more inevitable than between-group inequality. It is implausible, and probably undesirable, that everyone in a population should have the same level of intelligence or the same personality characteristics, for example. However, there are some measurable within-group inequalities that confer different levels of risk for individuals who are in possession of different levels of the characteristic. Furthermore, some of those inequalities may respond to interventions designed to reduce those inequalities and their negative outcomes. Although not commonly framed in this way, the mental health professions are predicated on the assumption that different levels of anxiety, depression, psychosis, inattention, and other characteristics confer different functional risks. Accordingly, many therapies, from biological agents to psychosocial interventions, have been developed to address those at greatest risk. The mental health endeavor is thus dedicated to reducing harmful forms of within-group inequality.

In schooling and classroom life, there are forms of within-group inequality that confer risk to children on the tail of the distribution. One form of inequality that confers differential risk is student level of social acceptance and social network integration.

Social acceptance is the extent to which an individual child enjoys positive peer regard and is free of negative peer regard. It is frequently assessed using sociometric methods in which children nominate classmates they like the most and those they like the least. The number of most-liked and least-liked peer nominations each child receives can be transformed into a 'social preference' score which reflects overall peer acceptance (Coie *et al.* 1982). Sociometric methods have a long history, originating in the work of Moreno (1933). Furthermore, the risks and outcomes associated with different levels of social acceptance have been extensively studied. Peer rejection is a predictor of behavioral maladjustment (Cowen *et al.* 1973; Parker *et al.* 1995; Roff *et al.* 1972), low academic achievement (O'Neil *et al.* 1997), truancy and delinquency (Kupersmidt *et al.* 1990), and mental illness (Bagwell *et al.* 2001; French and Waas 1985; McDougall *et al.* 2001).

Social network methods have been more recently applied to the study of individual students and the settings they navigate. Social networks are operationalized as the pattern of ties between members of a defined group such as a class. Social networks can be measured using the same peer nomination procedures used to assess social preference. However, valid social network analysis requires nearly complete peer nomination information. An alternative method, social cognitive mapping, is much more robust to missing data, and can be used to create social network maps (Neal 2008).

Social network data can be used to characterized children's social network position and the network overall in ways that complement and extend what can be learned from sociometric data. Most importantly for the purposes of this chapter, social network data can be used to characterize the magnitude of the social inequality in a classroom (Cappella *et al.* 2013). For example, using social network data, social inequality could be defined as the level of concentration of positive social ties to a few children, the magnitude of the difference in the number of social ties between the most networked and the least networked members, or the magnitude of the distribution of positive social network ties in a classroom (Gest and Rodkin 2011).

One recent definition of social network equity is derived from individual student 'degree centrality', or the number of connections each child has divided by the number of possible connections (Cappella *et al.* 2013). The investigators proposed that a classroom's social network equity can be formally defined as the network centrality standard deviation divided by the network centrality mean. They multiplied this ratio by −1 so that a more positive score reflected higher network equity.

This method provides a metric to characterize the social hierarchy. Higher social network equity means that more students are more similarly tied to others in the social network, whereas lower social network equity means that some students enjoy many ties, while others enjoy few. Cappella and colleagues demonstrated that social network equity is consequential, with higher social network equity early in the school year associated with higher behavioral engagement at the end of the year, particularly for children with behavioral difficulties, and particularly when teachers had good command of classroom organization.

There is also emerging evidence that a classroom's social network characteristics are influenced by teacher practices. Gest and Rodkin (2011) found, for example, that teacher grouping practices are significantly associated with the extent to which classroom networks are dense in positive ties and friendships. They also found that in classrooms in which teachers seek to promote new friendship ties, social status hierarchies are not as steep, particularly for girls.

It is important to note that individual student characteristics and behaviors can affect social acceptance and social network position. The literature has clearly established that children who are disruptive and aggressive are less well accepted by their peers (e.g. Dodge 1983; Newcomb *et al.* 1993). Therefore, individual student characteristics, and the group composition of those characteristics, inevitably play a role in shaping both individual student acceptance and the shape of the social network. Nevertheless, existing research suggests that, all other things being equal, teacher actions can influence the classroom pattern of positive social network ties.

Thus, in elementary-school classrooms, how teachers group for instruction, and their attitudes about and behaviors towards peer relationships, affect classroom social networks. The social network hierarchy, in turn, affects individual student outcomes, particularly among socially vulnerable children. Much work remains to be done to fully understand what characteristics of the social network are the best indicators of the overall network's social 'health' and what teacher practices can most efficiently be deployed to promote greater social network equity. Nevertheless, social network inequality is clearly an important and highly consequential feature of the classroom landscape and there appears to be great promise that intentional adult actions can be taken to reduce this form of inequality and its sting.

A few interventions have been developed to improve children's social network position or the overall level of equity in the classroom social network. One promising intervention, peer mediation, was developed to foster the social integration of high-functioning and mainstreamed children on the autism spectrum. In peer mediation classrooms, teachers nominate children with strong social skills and teach them to identify socially isolated children and help them socially engage. The peer media- tion intervention leads to increased numbers of social network connections for children with autism-spectrum disorders, and is more effective than teaching mainstreamed children with autism- spectrum disorders specific social strategies (Kasari *et al.* 2012).

Another intervention, called 'Making Socially Accepting Inclusive Classrooms' (MOSAIC), was designed to increase the positive social integration of children with attention deficit hyperactivity disorder (ADHD; Mikami *et al.* 2013). In MOSAIC classrooms, teachers use contingency manage- ment strategies, but feedback to children with ADHD is given privately when feasible. In addition, all students are expected to be inclusive and can lose points for exclusionary behavior. Teachers also point out commonalities between students with and without ADHD and provide public praise for reputation-disconfirming behavior of children with ADHD. The peer preference of children with ADHD significantly improves in MOSAIC classrooms.

Both peer mediation and MOSAIC were designed to benefit children with identified disor- ders known to interfere with social functioning. However, the principles engendered in both of these interventions – creating conditions for positive peer influence, and supporting student skills and behaviors – are, in theory, relevant to all classrooms in which any children are not well- connected to the social network or not well-regarded by peers. Applying these principles in all classrooms has the potential to aid socially isolated or ostracized children and create greater social network equity.

There is evidence that other intervention strategies, designed to enhance academic achievement for all students, may enhance positive social connectedness for those who are not well-liked. Specifically, many forms of cooperative learning structure student workgroup participation in a way that enhances interdependence. In cooperative learning, students work in small groups together on a common task in which they serve as resources for one another (Aronson and Patnoe 1997). Teachers assign children to academically and sometimes ethnically heterogeneous work groups. Group mem- bers work together on tasks that are meaningfully connected to the class learning objectives. In cooperative learning groups, for each student to succeed, the other students in the group must suc- ceed. In other words, group structure maximizes interdependence, with different cooperative learning models enhancing interdependence differently. All cooperative learning methods have demonstrated evidence of efficacy for increasing cross-race and cross-status liking (Pettigrew and Tropp 2000) and enhancing academic achievement (Aronson and Patnoe 1997; Johnson and Johnson 1982, 1985; Johnson *et al.* 1984).

A variant on cooperative learning called 'complex instruction' directly addresses social and aca- demic status differences (Cohen and Lotan 1997). In complex instruction classrooms, teachers assign students roles within a cooperative group. Teachers work to increase the status of marginally involved group members by publicly pointing out the low-status group member's strengths and potential contributions to the group, and encouraging other group members to take advantage of the low- status member's skills and talents. This method seems likely to promote positive network connections. However, no research currently supports this claim.

Differences, commonalities, and future directions

The American racial–ethnic achievement gap and classroom social network equity are different forms and expressions of inequality. Whereas the achievement gap is a between-group form of inequity, social network inequality is a within-group form of inequality. Whereas the achievement gap is about academic outcomes, social network equity is about the quality and kind of children's peer relationships. Thus, in many ways, these forms of inequality are distinct.

Despite the very real differences between these forms of social status inequality, there are striking similarities. As this chapter demonstrates, every classroom creates, with the teacher's guidance and consent, social conditions that can either contribute to or attenuate social inequalities. In the case of the racial–ethnic achievement gap, educators can and have reduced direct and signal influences, and in so doing, have measurably reduced academic inequity. In the case of peer preference and social network equity, researchers have fruitfully quantified network equity, and a small but growing body of research suggests that teacher practices can influence the magnitude of social inequality for children with and without diagnosed conditions.

And here is where the work on the achievement gap and social acceptance perhaps converge. It is conceivable that classrooms high in social network equity produce more equitable academic outcomes across racial–ethnic lines. For example, greater peer caring and better developed social-emotional learning skills may create a more positive racial climate, reducing signal influences. The common ground these two forms of social inequality share is highlighted by substantial commonality in evidence-based or promising remedies. Indeed, some of the interventions previously described – particularly cooperative learning – have great potential to reduce the racial–ethnic achievement gap and reduce social network inequity!

For both the achievement gap and social network equity, research and practice have come a long way. We know the antecedent conditions that promote equity and the role of children's understanding in creating or reducing inequalities. For both forms of inequality, however, there is important work to be done. Although research supports the component propositions of social equity theory, no empirical tests of the whole theory have been undertaken. Although researchers are beginning to define social network equity, more work is needed to understand the key characteristics of social network equity and its consequences. For both forms of inequality, more work is needed to create efficient means of reducing unnecessary inequity.

Inequality is an inevitable feature of the social world, and it should not fall solely on the shoulders of educators to remedy the ills of an unfair world. Nevertheless, the magnitude and effect of inequality is not a foregone conclusion and the conditions of learning, which are largely within educators' sphere of influence, can have a substantial effect on social and academic inequalities. Teachers and educational leaders therefore play an important role in creating conditions of learning and interacting that maximize fairness and promote equitable outcomes.

References

Aronson, E. and Patnoe, S. (1997) *The Jigsaw Classroom: Building Cooperation in the Classroom*, 2nd edn, New York: Longman.

Bagwell, C.L., Schmidt, M.E., Newcomb, A.F. and Bukowski, W.M. (2001) 'Friendship and peer rejection as predictors of adult adjustment', in C.A. Erdley (ed.) *The Role of Friendship in Psychological Adjustment* (pp. 25–49), San Francisco, CA: Jossey-Bass.

Baron, R.M., Tom, D.Y. and Cooper, H.M. (1985) 'Social class, race, and teacher expectations', in J.B. Dusek (ed.) *Teacher Expectancies* (pp. 251–270), Hillsdale, NY: Erlbaum.

Cappella, E., Kim, H.Y., Neal, J.W. and Jackson, D.R. (2013) 'Classroom peer relationships and behavioral engagement in elementary school: the role of social network equity', *American Journal of Community Psychology*, 52: 367–379.

Clotfelter, C., Ladd, H. and Vigdor, J. (2004) 'Do school accountability systems make it more difficult for low performing schools to attract and retain high quality teachers?', *Journal of Policy Analysis and Management*, 23: 251–271.

Cohen, G.L., Garcia, J., Apfel, N. and Master, A. (2006) 'Reducing the racial achievement gap: a social-psychological intervention', *Science*, 313: 1307–1310.

Cohen, E.G. and Lotan, R.A. (eds) (1997) *Working for Equity in Heterogeneous Classrooms*, New York: Teachers College Press.

Coie, J.D., Dodge, K.A. and Coppotelli, H. (1982) 'Dimensions and types of social status: a cross-age perspective', *Developmental Psychology*, 18: 557–570.

Cowen, E.L., Pederson, A., Babigian, H., Isso, L.D. and Trost, M.A. (1973) 'Long-term follow-up of early detected vulnerable children', *Journal of Consulting and Clinical Psychology*, 41: 438–446.

Dodge, K.A. (1983) 'Behavioral antecedents of peer social status', *Child Development*, 54: 1386–1399.

Educational Policy Institute (2005) *Focus on Results: An Academic Impact Analysis of the Knowledge is Power Program (KIPP)*, Virginia Beach, VA: Education Policy Institute.

French, D.C. and Waas, G.A. (1985) 'Behavior problems of peer-neglected and peer-rejected elementary-age children: parent and teacher perspectives', *Child Development*, 56: 246–252.

Gest, S.D. and Rodkin, P.C. (2011) 'Teaching practices and elementary classroom peer ecologies', *Journal of Applied Developmental Psychology*, 32: 288–296.

Good, C., Aronson, J. and Inzlicht, M. (2003) 'Improving adolescents' standardized test performance: an intervention to reduce the effects of stereotype threat', *Journal of Applied Developmental Psychology*, 24: 645–662.

Gregory, A. and Weinstein, R.S. (2004) 'Connection and regulation at home and in school: predicting growth in achievement for adolescents', *Journal of Adolescent Research*, 19: 405–427.

Hamre, B. and Pianta, R. (2001) 'Early teacher–child relationships and the trajectory of children's school outcomes through eighth grade', *Child Development*, 72: 625–638.

Hamre, B. and Pianta, R. (2005) 'Can instructional and emotional support in the first-grade classroom make a difference for children at risk of school failure?', *Child Development*, 76: 949–967.

Jencks, C. and Phillips, M. (eds) (1998) *The Black-White Test Score Gap*, Washington, DC: Brookings Institution Press.

Johnson, D.W. and Johnson, R.T. (1982) 'Effects of cooperative, competitive, and individualistic learning experiences on cross-ethnic interaction and friendship', *Journal of Social Psychology*, 118: 47–58.

Johnson, D.W. and Johnson, R.T. (1985) 'Relationships between black and white students in intergroup cooperation and competition', *The Journal of Social Psychology*, 124: 421–428.

Johnson, D.W., Johnson, R.T, Tiffany, M. and Zaidman, B. (1984) 'Cross-ethnic relationships: the impact of intergroup cooperation and intergroup competition', *Journal of Educational Research*, 78: 75–79.

Kasari, C., Rotheram-Fuller, E., Locke, J. and Gulsrud, A. (2012) 'Making the connection: randomized controlled trial of social skills at school for children with autism spectrum disorders', *Journal of Child Psychology and Psychiatry*, 53: 431–439.

Kupersmidt, J.B., Coie, J.D. and Dodge, K.A. (1990) 'The role of poor peer relationships in the development of disorder', in J.D. Coie (ed.) *Peer Rejection in Childhood* (pp. 274–305), New York: Cambridge University Press.

Lakoff, G. (2009) *The Political Mind: A Cognitive Scientist's Guide to Your Brain and Politics*, New York: Penguin Books.

Lee, J. (2002) 'Racial and ethnic achievement gap trends: reversing the progress toward equity?', *Educational Researcher*, 31: 3–12.

Lee, V.E. and Burkam, D.T. (2002) *Inequality at the Starting Gate: Social Background Differences in Achievement as Children Begin School*, Washington, DC: Economic Policy Institute.

Levin, H.M. (2009) 'The economic payoff to investing in educational justice', *Educational Researcher*, 38: 5–20.

McDougall, P., Hymel, S., Vaillancourt, T. and Mercer, L. (2001) 'The consequences of childhood peer rejection', in M.R. Leary (ed.) *Interpersonal Rejection* (pp. 213–247), New York: Oxford University Press.

McKown, C. (2013) 'Social equity theory and racial-ethnic achievement gaps', *Child Development*, 84: 1120–1136.

McKown, C. and Strambler, M.J. (2008) 'Social influences on the ethnic achievement gap', in S. Quintana and C. McKown (eds) *Handbook of Race, Racism, and the Developing Child* (pp. 366–396), Hoboken, NJ: John Wiley.

McKown, C. and Strambler, M.J. (2009) 'Developmental antecedents and social and academic consequences of stereotype-consciousness in middle childhood', *Child Development*, 80: 1643–1659.

McKown, C. and Weinstein, R.S. (2002) 'Modeling the role of child ethnicity and gender in children's differential response to teacher expectations', *Journal of Applied Social Psychology*, 32: 159–184.

McKown, C. and Weinstein, R.S. (2003) 'The development and consequences of stereotype-consciousness in middle childhood', *Child Development,* 74: 498–515.

McKown, C. and Weinstein, R.S. (2008) 'Teacher expectations, classroom context, and the achievement gap', *Journal of School Psychology,* 46: 235–261.

Mikami, A.Y., Griggs, M.S., Lerner, M.D., Emeh, C.C., Reuland, M.M., Jack, A. and Anthony, M.R. (2013) 'A randomized trial of a classroom intervention to increase peers' social inclusion of children with attention-deficit/hyperactivity disorder', *Journal of Consulting and Clinical Psychology,* 81: 100–112.

Moreno, J.L. (1933) 'Psychological and social organization of groups in the community', *Proceedings and Addresses. American Association on Mental Deficiency,* 38: 224–242.

Neal, J.W. (2008) '"Kracking" the missing data problem: applying Krackhardt's cognitive social structures to school-based social networks', *Sociology of Education,* 81: 140–162.

Newcomb, A.F., Bukowski, W.M. and Pattee, L. (1993) 'Children's peer relations: a meta-analytic review of popular, rejected, neglected, controversial, and average sociometric status', *Psychological Bulletin,* 113: 99–128.

O'Neil, R., Welsh, M., Parke, R.D., Wang, S. and Strand, C. (1997) 'A longitudinal assessment of the academic correlates of early peer acceptance and rejection', *Journal of Clinical Child Psychology,* 26: 290–303.

Parker, J.G., Rubin, K.H., Price, J.M. and DeRosier, M.E. (1995) 'Peer relationships, child development, and adjustment: a developmental psychopathology perspective', in D.J. Cohen (ed.) *Developmental Psychopathology* (Vol. 2, pp. 96–161), Oxford: John Wiley.

Pettigrew, T.F. and Tropp, L.R. (2000) 'Does intergroup contact reduce prejudice? Recent meta-analytic findings', in S. Oskamp (ed.) *Reducing Prejudice and Discrimination* (pp. 93–114), Mahwah, NJ: Lawrence Erlbaum.

Pinel, E. (1999) 'Stigma-consciousness: the psychological legacy of stereotypes', *Journal of Personality and Social Psychology,* 76: 114–128.

Pinel, E. (2002) 'Stigma-consciousness in intergroup contexts: the power of conviction', *Journal of Experimental Social Psychology,* 38: 178–185.

Reardon, S.F. and Galindo, C. (2009) 'The Hispanic–white achievement gap in math and reading in the elementary grades', *American Educational Research Journal,* 46: 853–891.

Reardon, S.F. and Robinson, J.P. (2007) 'Patterns and trends in racial/ethnic and socioeconomic academic achievement gaps', in H.F. Ladd (ed.) *Handbook of Research in Education Finance and Policy* (pp. 497–516), New York: Routledge.

Roff, M., Sells, S.B. and Golden, M.M. (1972) '*Social Adjustment and Personality Development in Children,* Oxford: University of Minnesota Press.

Saft, E.W. and Pianta, R.C. (2001) 'Teachers' perceptions of their relationships with students: effects of child age, gender, and ethnicity of teachers and children', *School Psychology Quarterly,* 16: 125–141.

Slavin, R.E. and Madden, N. A. (2001) 'Reducing the gap: success for all and the achievement of African American students', paper presented at the Annual Meeting of the American Educational Research Association, Seattle, WA.

Steele, C.M. (1988) 'The psychology of self-affirmation: sustaining the integrity of the self', in L Berkowitz (ed.) *Advances in Experimental Social Psychology* (Vol. 20, pp. 261–302), San Diego, CA: Academic Press.

Steele, C.M. and Aronson, J. (1995) 'Stereotype threat and the intellectual test performance of African Americans', *Journal of Personality and Social Psychology,* 69: 797–811.

Vanneman, A., Hamilton, L., Anderson, J.B. and Rahman, T. (2009) *Achievement Gaps: How Black and White Students in Public Schools Perform in Mathematics and Reading on the National Assessment of Educational Progress,* (NCES No. 2009–455), Washington, DC: U.S. Department of Education.

Vorauer, J.D., Hunter, A.J., Main, K.J. and Roy, S.A. (2000) 'Meta-stereotype activation: evidence from indirect measures for specific evaluative concerns experienced by members of dominant groups in intergroup interaction', *Journal of Personality and Social Psychology,* 78: 690–707.

Vorauer, J.D. and Kuhmyr, S.M. (2002) 'Is this about you or me? Self- versus other-directed judgments and feelings in response to intergroup interactions', *Personality and Social Psychology Bulletin,* 27: 706–719.

Vorauer, J.D., Main, K.J. and O'Connell, G.B. (1998) 'How do individuals expect to be viewed by members of lower status groups? Content and implications of meta-stereotypes', *Journal of Personality and Social Psychology,* 75: 917–937.

Weinstein, R.S. (2002) *Reaching Higher: The Power of Expectations in Schooling,* Cambridge, MA: Harvard University Press.

13

ACADEMIC TALK IN THE CLASSROOM

Developments in research

Robyn M. Gillies

Academic talk in the classroom and its capacity to promote intellectual development and academic attainment has become the focus of attention in recent years. Numerous studies have demonstrated the key role social collaboration plays in the construction of knowledge, understanding, and learning (Forman 1989; Mercer 2008; Resnick 1987, 1991; Wells 2007) and how such interaction has the capacity to build the mind (Resnick *et al.* 2010). While both individual and social constructivism (Piaget 1950; Vygotsky 1978) advocate the importance of social interaction in the development of children's reasoning and cognition, it is only in the past thirty years that empirical studies have begun to emerge that have demonstrated how children learn from each other and how teachers, in turn, can use this information to construct opportunities in classrooms to ensure the benefits attributed to such social collaboration occur.

Concurrently, research has also focused on teachers' talk and the capacity it has to promote or inhibit student talk, with many teachers still preferring to act as the 'sage on the stage' rather than allowing children to engage in dialogic discussions with each other. In a study of teachers' classroom discourse over a twenty-year period in the United Kingdom, Galton *et al.* (1999) observed that children are rarely asked cognitively challenging questions where they are required to think about the issues and justify their responses. The general pattern of teachers' verbal behaviors tended to fall into two categories where teachers asked questions of a factual or closed nature or made statements that required minimal or unelaborated responses. Ways of responding often mirrored the initiation–response–evaluation pattern of questioning used in many classrooms, where authority resides with the teacher and discourse is often regimented for teacher control (Mehan 1979). This behavior was so entrenched that Galton *et al.* observed that over the twenty-year period, teachers' propensity to provide students with facts or ideas and give directions had increased from about 57 percent to more than 80 percent of teachers' total classroom talk. Similar patterns of teacher discourse have been observed in secondary classrooms with more than 80 percent of teachers' total classroom talk given to directing or lecturing either the whole class or individual students within their classes, while less than 20 percent of their total talk involved interacting with students in small groups (Galton 2002). The consequence is that students are socialized into becoming passive recipients of knowledge rather than active in its creation. They rarely ask questions, engage in sustained conversations, or elaborate on information unless they are required to do so (Chinn *et al.* 2000; Melroth and Deering 1999). As a consequence, Galton *et al.*, Chinn *et al.*, and Meloth and Deering argue that direct intervention by teachers to facilitate student discussion is warranted if children are to learn to dialog effectively with each other.

There is no doubt that teachers play a critical role in creating experiences for students where they have opportunities to collaborate, discuss ideas, share understandings, challenge and rebut different proposals, and consider alternative propositions before reaching a decision; these are important skills that students must demonstrate if they are to talk and reason effectively together (Rojas-Drummond and Mercer 2003). However, helping children to engage in dialogic exchanges where they demonstrate these discourses requires a concerted effort on the part of teachers to ensure that students are not only taught such dialoguing skills but that teachers, also, understand the role their own dispositions play in promoting or inhibiting responses from students (Gillies *et al.* 2012). This chapter discusses these developments in the context of recent research on academic talk in classrooms and its capacity to promote student development and learning through social collaboration and teacher guidance.

Research on academic talk

Children learn from interacting with others. However, how this learning occurs is explained from two different theoretical perspectives, personal and social constructivism. The first perspective, personal constructivism, emphasizes the intrapersonal dimensions of learning; that is, learning is mediated through interacting with others (Piaget 1950). According to this perspective, interactions that expose children to different points of view are likely to give rise to a state of cognitive conflict as children are challenged to keep their own points of view in mind while taking account of other incompatible ones. This dilemma creates a state of intrapersonal cognitive tension and disequilibrium which, if it is to be resolved, forces the child to 'decenter' and consider what others have to say. In so doing, children are forced to re-examine their own points of view and reassess their validity, and, second, they learn that they must justify and clearly communicate the reasons for their opinions if their opinions are to be accepted as valid by others. While interacting with others is a trigger for social and cognitive change, the change itself is achieved by the individual who is motivated to resolve perturbing feedback and return to a state of cognitive equilibrium.

The second theoretical perspective on how children learn, social constructivism (Vygotsky 1978), emphasizes the interpersonal dimensions of learning; that is, more capable peers and adults mediate children's learning by focusing attention on relevant information in the child's environment and providing the tools for problem solving such as speech and other cultural artifacts (e.g. memory strategies) and ways of reasoning. Children are introduced to new ways of thinking and patterns of thought when they engage in dialogic exchanges with more competent others; so, eventually, these skills are incorporated into the child's mental system where they become internalized as part of the child's cognitive repertoire. Damon (1984) argued that this occurs because when peers interact together their dialog is essentially a cooperative exchange of ideas that, through repeated exchanges, eventually helps them to not only acquire new information but also new ways of thinking implicit in the communication. It is through these new ways of thinking that they learn to acquire strategies that are specifically suited to solving cognitively challenging tasks.

While both individual and social constructivism (Piaget 1950; Vygotsky 1978) highlight the importance of social interaction in the development of children's reasoning and cognition, it is only in the past three decades that research has begun to emerge that has demonstrated how children learn from each other and how teachers, in turn, can use this information to construct experiences in classrooms to promote children's development of thinking, reasoning, problem solving, and learning.

Cognitive acceleration

Building on the notion that children learn when they are cognitively challenged, Adey *et al.* (2007) reported on a series of cognitive acceleration programs they conducted over a twenty-year period in science and mathematics in primary- and high-school classrooms. The students were confronted with cognitively challenging situations but in the context of socially mediated learning where the teachers guided the students' thinking and learning. The effects of these programs on students' cognitive development and academic achievements were significant when compared to peers of the same age who received the regular curriculum. Furthermore, the gains recorded generalized to national public examinations up to three years after the original intervention, with gains not only in mathematics and science, the original targeted subject domains, but also in English, thus demonstrating clear transfer effects (see Adey and Shayer 1990, 1993, 1994).

Adey and Shayer (2011) attribute the success of these cognitive acceleration programs to three common features. First, they challenge children's thinking; second, they emphasize that knowledge and understanding are socially constructed through collaboration with others, building on their ideas and cognitively reorganizing and reconstructing information to co-construct new knowledge and understandings; and, finally, they encourage students to reflect on their learning and to think about the processes involved. In so doing, learning is consolidated as students learn to think metacognitively about the learning and thinking processes they employed (Wiggins 1998). These three features, Adey and Shayer argued, are inextricably intertwined because when students' thinking is challenged, they are motivated to reconcile the cognitive dissonance they experience by reflecting on what they need to do to solve the dilemmas they are confronting. Piaget (1950) believed that peer interactions where students have opportunities to reflect on what others have to say provides the context for students to revise their current cognitive perspectives and understandings, and so construct new understandings and cognitions. Teachers promote cognitive growth in children when they use language that challenges children's understandings, confronts discrepancies in their thinking, and requires them to provide reasons for their solutions (Gillies and Boyle 2006).

The success of cognitive acceleration programs in promoting students' cognitive ability and academic achievements, Adey *et al.* (2007) argued, occurs when:

1   Learning activities are cognitively challenging so students are motivated to abandon misconceptions and search for solutions.
2   Learning is collaborative so that students have opportunities to work together, listen to what others have to say, argue and rebut different positions, and receive acknowledgment and criticism from their peers. When children collaborate they often learn new and creative ways of thinking and talking which they had not previously considered. In this context, Mercer (1996) considered talk to be a social mode of thought.
3   Current learning is connected to previous concepts and experiences.
4   Students accept responsibility for their learning so they are more self-reliant and self-regulating of their thinking and learning processes. This involves students articulating the approaches they have taken to problem solving and reasoning so that other students can access other ways of thinking and evaluating issues that they may not have considered previously.

The results obtained by Adey and his colleagues (above) have been replicated in more recent cognitive acceleration programs by Ender and Bond (2008) who found that the Cognitive Acceleration through Science Education (CASE) program led to cognitive growth in participating students and high correlations between cognitive level and results in state-mandated tests. Hu *et al.* (2010) reported long-term transfer effects on students' thinking and academic achievement from participating in a cognitive acceleration program called Learning to Think. Similarly, Oliver *et al.* (2012) found that students who participated in a cognitive acceleration intervention in science in a low-socioeconomic high school showed significant cognitive gains with concomitant improvement in state-wide testing in science.

Accountable talk

Other researchers who have investigated the powerful effects of dialogic interactions on students' thinking and learning include Resnick (1987, 1991, 2010) and Resnick *et al.* (2010). There is mounting evidence that learning occurs in interaction with others where students engage in discursive processes that include actively listening to others' expositions, challenging their perspectives, and interpreting and explaining what is being discussed. In so doing, students learn that knowledge is socially shared and often co-constructed in collaboration with others. Michaels *et al.* (2008), though, argue that academically productive talk, which they called 'accountable talk', only emerges when students learn that they are expected to listen to others, build on their ideas, engage in providing explanations and justifications for their propositions, and be prepared to challenge what is said when evidence is not supported or available. When students engage in this type of dialogic exchange, they are socialized into communities of practice in which they learn that discussion is respectful of others' ideas but grounded on knowledge and accepted standards of reasoning. The teacher's discourse in this type of interaction often switches between providing authoritative knowledge to ensure that students acquire discipline-correct concepts to being more dialogic where students are challenged and scaffolded to explore new ideas, ask questions, interpret findings, formulate hypotheses, and share their understandings.

Wolf *et al.* (2006), in a study of the use of accountable talk in reading comprehension instruction in elementary- and middle-school students, found that when teachers ask questions that require students to link information and ideas, provide knowledge, and engage in rigorous thinking about the topic, the students, in turn, provide more reasons to support their ideas and they also elaborate on their logic. The authors argued that a classroom discourse that includes listening to others, questioning others' knowledge, and exploring one's own thoughts has a positive relationship with the academic rigor of reading comprehension and the quality of the talk that emanates.

This type of dialogic exchange, Resnick (2010) argues, requires teachers to be able to manage classroom discussions, including challenges to students' explanations and reasons, while simultaneously revoicing or paraphrasing students' attempts to articulate their thoughts and ideas so all students are helped to understand and share important concepts in different texts and tasks and through interpretative questions. The teacher's role is to ensure that students are guided through their directed conversations towards acquiring deeper subject-matter knowledge. In short, dialogic discourse is heavily scaffolded by the teacher (Michaels and O'Connor 2011).

Dialogic teaching

Robin Alexander (2010) drew parallels between accountable talk and his work on dialogic teaching, arguing that both were discourse pedagogies that emphasized reciprocal dialogs; they occurred in a social or group environment that was supportive of students' discussions; there was a clear purpose to the interaction; and the focus was to build on the ideas of others to co-construct and create new knowledge to help students learn. Dialogic teaching, Alexander argues, is not just any talk. It requires interactions which encourage students to think in different ways; questions which probe for more detailed responses; answers that are well reasoned and justified; feedback which is informative as well as encouraging; contributions that elaborate on information or ideas; discussion and argument that probe and challenge accepted positions; professional engagement with discipline knowledge; and a classroom environment that invites open discussion.

While students have much to gain when teachers engage in dialogic teaching, Mercer *et al.* (2009) found that such teaching rarely occurs. In a study of the classroom dialog of twelve teachers they observed teaching science, only three engaged students in extended discussions, with the majority using talk to maintain order and control rather than as a tool for learning. Follow-up interviews with these teachers indicated that they were relatively unaware of the patterns of teacher talk in their classrooms, leading the authors to suggest that initial teacher training and professional development should include more specific training in the effective use of talk for learning.

Lehesvuori *et al.* (2011) reported on a study where twenty-one preservice physics teachers were introduced to a communicative approach to teaching science that involved dialogic teaching in addition to authoritative teacher talk. In dialogic teaching, exchanges between teacher and students are linked together in coherent lines of inquiry rather than left disconnected. Dialogic teaching in science is supportive and reciprocal and involves students and teachers interacting with each other to discuss ideas. In essence, the dialog is multidimensional. In contrast, authoritative talk usually involves the teacher expressing a particular scientific point of view in a unidimensional way. The aim of the intervention was to heighten the participants' awareness of these different dialogic practices and to determine if they were able to use these ways of communicating in their preservice field practice. The results demonstrated that training in dialogic teaching and authoritative talk did heighten participants' awareness of different dialogic options that were available for communicating with students. The authors also reported that the dialogic approach to teaching created a classroom climate where students had opportunities to discuss and pose questions themselves. Reznitskaya (2012) argued that 'by making their classroom interactions more dialogic, teachers can engage students in a collaborative deliberation of complex questions and support the development of students' thinking' (446).

Mercer (1996) and colleagues (Mercer *et al.*, 1999; Rojas-Drummond and Mercer, 2003) reported on a similar dialogic discourse which they called 'exploratory talk' where students were taught how to engage critically and constructively with each other's ideas by learning how to reason and justify their assertions and opinions as they collaborated on group-based tasks. The results from these studies showed that not only did the use of exploratory talk enable students to become more effective in using language as a tool for reasoning and sharing knowledge but it also led to higher levels of individual achievement, and significant improvements in students' capacities to solve follow-up reasoning and problem-solving tests. The results led Mercer *et al.* (1999) to conclude that

> the use of exploratory talk helps to develop children's individual reasoning skills. It appears that even nonverbal reasoning, like that involved in solving the Raven's problems, may be mediated by language and developed by adult guidance and social interaction amongst peers without the provision of any specific training in solving such problems.
>
> *(106)*

The authors further concluded that 'our results support the view that the induction of children into cultural language practices influences their use of language as a cognitive tool' (106).

The Philosophy for Children approach

Others who have found that dialogic interactions promote the development of critical and creative problem solving and enhanced cognitive ability include Trickey and Topping (2004, 2006) and Topping and Trickey (2007a, b). Using the Philosophy for Children (P4C) approach (Lipman, 1988), which teaches students how to hold a dialog, the authors investigated the effects of the approach on students' academic, social, and cognitive abilities. Because P4C not only teaches students how to communicate cognitively with each other but also how to use social and emotional communication skills, the authors argued that engagement in P4C could also be expected to have socioemotional effects as well as cognitive ones. Indeed, this was so, with Trickey and Topping (2006) finding that participation in P4C over a seven-month period led to significant gains in self-esteem, including a significant reduction in dependency and anxiety and greater self-concept among participating students in comparison to their control peers.

In a follow-up study that investigated the effects of P4C implemented for one hour per week across a sixteen-month period on 10- to 12-year-old students, Topping and Trickey (2007a) found that students who participated in P4C showed significant standardized gains in verbal and nonverbal reasoning ability that was consistent across schools and largely irrespective of student ability or gender. The study showed that it is possible to intervene effectively in the cognitive development of primary-aged children by using P4C for one hour per week. Furthermore, these gains were maintained when students were followed up two years later when they had transferred to secondary school even though they had not received further instruction in P4C (Topping and Trickey 2007b). In contrast, students in the control group showed a persistent deterioration in their scores from pre- to post-test and at follow-up. In short, Trickey and Topping and Topping and Trickey demonstrated that instruction in P4C leads to social, emotional and cognitive gains and these gains are maintained and transfer across contexts and schools.

Types of student interactions that promote understanding and learning

Given that there is a large body of research that reports on how different dialogic approaches can enhance students' social, emotional, and cognitive development, it is also important to understand what specific types of student interactions contribute to learning when students work collaboratively together. In a series of studies, Webb and colleagues (Webb *et al.* 1995; Webb and Farivar 1999; Webb and Mastergeorge 2003a) found that providing elaborated help in response to requests for help was positively related to achievement, whereas unelaborated responses were not. Webb and colleagues also found that receiving explanations when they were not requested was usually negatively related to achievement, possibly because recipients may not perceive that they need help, may not realize the relevance of the help, or may not have opportunities to apply the help to problems at hand.

Drawing on previous studies about how students respond to help while working in collaborative groups, Webb and Mastergeorge (2003a) identified a cluster of student verbal behaviors that are necessary for effective helping. For students seeking help, there were three types of behaviors that were associated with successful learning. These included: asking precise questions to indicate specifically what they do not understand; continuing to seek help until they receive it; and, applying the help received to the problem they are working to solve. On the other hand, those who provide help must provide detailed explanations of the topic under discussion, provide opportunities for those being helped to apply the help received, and ensure that those being helped understand how to use the help they have been given.

In a follow-up study, Webb and Mastergeorge (2003b) investigated the behaviors and experiences of students in four Grade 7 classrooms who needed assistance in solving mathematics problems as they worked collaboratively. The authors found that students who received detailed explanations during their collaborative group work were able to solve problems without further assistance. The study also confirmed previous findings that help-seekers are more likely to be successful on follow-up learning activities when they ask for specific information rather than just the answer, persist in seeking assistance, and apply the help to the problem they are discussing. Help-giving behaviors that were identified as also important included providing detailed explanations and continuing to do so rather than resorting to descriptions of the procedures for solving the problem. More recently, Webb (2009) and colleagues (Webb *et al.* 2008) have extended this research to include the teacher's role in promoting collaborative dialog in the classroom.

Others who have investigated the role of student interactions in learning during small cooperative group activities include Gillies (2003, 2004) and colleagues (Gillies and Ashman, 1998, 2000); they found that students, including students with learning difficulties, who worked in structured cooperative groups where they had been taught how to cooperate provided more elaborated help to each other than peers who had not participated in these types of groups. Interestingly, Gillies (2000) found that these results were maintained one year after the experience of working in structured groups had ceased, with students who had worked in structured cooperative groups providing more explanations and reasons and obtaining higher learning outcome scores than their untrained peers.

Enhancing academic talk

While it has been demonstrated that children who work in structured cooperative groups provide more elaborated help to each other than their untrained peers, it is also recognized that this help does not emerge unless students have been explicitly taught how to provide it. King (2008) argued that it is rare for students working together to engage spontaneously in effective helping interactions or match the way they communicate to the task unless they are provided with some specific prompts or guidance from the teacher. Engaging in discussion and debate is a complex process and if left to develop naturally, students may fail to develop skills that will help them to engage in productive academic talk (Baines *et al.* 2009).

However, when teachers are taught how to scaffold and challenge students' thinking as they work in cooperative groups, Gillies and Khan (2008, 2009) found that students, in turn, provide significantly more elaborative help to group members, and this has a positive effect on the learning that occurs. Similar results were obtained by Gillies *et al.* (2012) who found that children who had been taught how to ask cognitively challenging questions during inquiry-based science are more verbally interactive, provide more explanatory responses, and obtain higher scores on follow-up reasoning and problem-solving tasks than untrained peers. Teaching students to ask and answer questions is critically important if students are to learn to talk and reason effectively together (Gillies *et al.* 2014).

Types of academic talk

In an examination of the types of academic talk that contribute to enhanced explanatory responses, reasoning, and problem solving, Gillies *et al.* (2014) examined the discourse of twenty-one groups of students who were provided with one of three linguistic tools – cognitive questioning (King 1999), Philosophy for Children (Lipman 1988), and collaborative strategic reading (Vaughn *et al.* 2001) – to scaffold the questioning process and promote small-group discussion during cooperative inquiry-based science. The results revealed that the students used a variety of discourses that included using analogy to construct meaning, questioning to elicit information, and providing reasons, elaborations, and statements to clarify issues. In many instances, students appropriated various stratagems from their teacher or each other for talking and thinking together to promote shared understandings and learning.

Teacher's role

There is no doubt that teachers play a key role in promoting those interactional behaviors that challenge children's thinking and scaffold their learning. Gillies and Boyle (2005) found that when teachers are explicit in the types of thinking they want children to engage in, it encourages children to be more focused and explicit in the types of help they provide. Gillies and Boyle (2006) examined the types of the discourse that ten Grade 4–6 teachers used after they had participated in training in how to embed cooperative learning into their curricula and use communication skills to promote children's thinking and to scaffold their learning. They found that the teachers used a range of mediated-learning interactions that included challenging the children's perspectives, asking more cognitive and metacognitive questions, and scaffolding the children's learning. In turn, the children modeled many of these types of helping discourses in their interactions with each other, which Gillies and Khan (2008) and Gillies *et al.* (2012) found contributed to higher scores on follow-up reasoning and problem-solving activities than the scores of peers whose teachers were not been taught how to use these skills.

Challenges and future directions

While there is a large volume of research that indicates that students benefit by being active in their learning, there is still considerable resistance from teachers in implementing approaches to learning that enable students to engage in dialog. This resistance appears to emanate from different sources. First, many teachers find it a challenge to their own organizational structures in their classrooms. Encouraging students to work together in small groups where they discuss tasks involves careful planning and some disruption to the class routine and, in some instances, requires closer guidance and monitoring from the teacher. While many teachers are willing to do this, others appear to regard it as an additional imposition on their already busy schedules.

Second, old habits die hard. Teachers have a propensity to talk and, as Galton *et al.* (2009) found, this pattern of behavior has not changed in over thirty years, so structuring situations where children have opportunities to discuss tasks they are working on is often not embraced.

Third, students often do not have the verbal skills that will enable them to engage in productive discussion and learning. Given these difficulties, recommendations that students be trained in those skills that will enable them to interact successfully with others is widespread (Baines *et al.* 2009; Gillies 2004).

Finally, teachers not only often lack understanding of the corpus of studies that attest to the benefits students derive from interacting with each other but they also often do not know how to establish learning environments that encourage students to think in different ways and question and probe for answers to resolve problems at hand. Knowing how to engage in dialogic teaching that emphasizes reciprocal dialogs between teachers and students in environments that support the co-construction of knowledge and ideas is a challenge that many teachers find difficult.

Many of the difficulties teachers encounter in implementing approaches to teaching that encourage students to engage in dialog can be overcome with targeted professional development programs. Buczynski and Hansen (2010) reported that elementary teachers who participated in an inquiry science professional development program increased their science content knowledge, and reported implementing inquiry practices in their classrooms. Their students also demonstrated modest gains on a follow-up standardized science achievement test. Lumpe *et al.* (2012) found that elementary teachers who participated in a long-term professional development program displayed significant gains in their science teaching self-efficacy and this had a significant effect on students' science achievement. Similar results were reported by Capps and Crawford (2013), which led them to comment that short-term and intensive professional development in inquiry science supported teachers in enhancing their knowledge and views about inquiry science and the nature of science. In short, Buczynski *et al.*, Lumpe *et al.*, and Capps *et al.* found that teachers' content knowledge of inquiry science and their self-efficacy in teaching science can be enhanced through professional development programs that address these issues. Gillies and colleagues (Gillies 2003, 2006; Gillies and Haynes 2011;

Gillies and Khan 2008, 2009) have provided numerous professional development opportunities for teachers participating in their studies and found that the training teachers receive has a positive effect on their teaching and the learning students demonstrate.

Acknowledgement

This work was supported by an Australian Research Grant: ARC-SKI: Science of Learning Research Centre (project number SR120300D15).

References

Adey, P., Csapo, B., Demetriou, A., Hautamaki, J. and Shayer, M. (2007) 'Can we be intelligent about intelligence? Why education needs the concept of plastic general ability', *Educational Research Review*, 2: 75–95.

Adey, P. and Shayer, M. (1990) 'Accelerating the development of formal thinking in middle and high school students', *Journal of Research in Science Teaching*, 27: 267–285.

Adey, P. and Shayer, M. (1993) 'An exploration of long-term far-transfer effects following an extended intervention programme in the high school science curriculum', *Cognition and Instruction*, 11: 1–29.

Adey, P. and Shayer, M. (1994) *Really Raising Standards: Cognitive Intervention and Academic Achievement*, London: Routledge.

Adey, P. and Shayer, M. (2011, September) 'The effects of cognitive acceleration – and speculation about causes of these effects', paper presented at the AERA research conference, Socializing Intelligence Through Academic Talk and Dialogue. Learning, Research and Development Centre, University of Pittsburgh.

Alexander, R. (2010) 'Speaking but not listening? Accountable talk in an unaccountable context', *Literacy*, 44: 103–111.

Baines, E., Rubie-Davies, C. and Blatchford, P. (2009) 'Improving pupil group work interaction and dialogue in primary classrooms: results from a year-long intervention study', *Cambridge Journal of Education*, 39: 95–118.

Buczynski, S. and Hansen, C. (2010) 'Impact of professional development on teacher practice: uncovering connections', *Teaching and Teacher Education*, 26: 599–607.

Capps, D. and Crawford, B. (2103) 'Inquiry-based professional development: what does it take to support teachers in learning about inquiry and nature of science?', *International Journal of Science Education*. Available at: http://dx.doi.org/10.1080/09500693.2012.760209

Chinn, C., O'Donnell, A. and Jinks, T. (2000) 'The structure of discourse in collaborative learning', *The Journal of Experimental Education*, 69: 77–89.

Damon, W. (1984) 'Peer education: the untapped potential', *Journal of Applied Developmental Psychology*, 5: 331–343.

Ender, L. and Bond, T. (2008) 'Changing science outcomes: cognitive acceleration in a US setting', *Research in Science Education*, 38: 149–166.

Forman, E. (1989) 'The role of peer interaction in the social construction of mathematical knowledge', *International Journal of Educational Research*, 13: 55–70

Galton, M. (2002) 'Continuity and progression in science teaching at key stages 2 and 3', *Cambridge Journal of Education*, 32: 249–265.

Galton, M., Hargreves, L., Comber, C., Wall, D. and Pell, T. (1999) 'Changes in patterns of teacher interaction in primary classrooms: 1976–1996', *British Educational Research Journal*, 25: 23–37.

Galton, M., Hargreves, L. and Pell, T. (2009) 'Group work and whole class teaching with 11- to 14-year-olds compared', *Cambridge Journal of Education*, 39: 119–140.

Gillies, R. (2000) 'The maintenance of cooperative and helping behaviours in cooperative groups', *British Journal of Educational Psychology*, 70: 97–111.

Gillies, R. (2003) 'Structuring cooperative group work in classrooms', *International Journal of Educational Research*, 39: 35–49.

Gillies, R. (2004) 'The effects of communication training on teachers' and students' verbal behaviours during cooperative learning', *International Journal of Educational Research*, 41: 257–279.

Gillies, R. (2006) 'Teachers' and students' verbal behaviours during cooperative and small-group learning', *British Journal of Educational Psychology*, 76: 271–287.

Gillies, R. and Ashman, A. (1998) 'Behavior and interactions of children in cooperative groups in lower and middle elementary grades', *Journal of Educational Psychology*, 90: 746–757.

Gillies, R. and Ashman, A. (2000) 'The effects of cooperative learning on children with learning difficulties in the lower elementary school', *The Journal of Special Education*, 34: 19–27.

Gillies, R. and Boyle, M. (2005) 'The effects of communication training on teachers' scaffolding behaviours during cooperative learning', *Asia Pacific Journal of Teacher Education*, 33: 243–259.

Gillies, R. and Boyle, M. (2006) 'Ten Australian elementary teachers' discourse and reported pedagogical practices during cooperative learning', *Elementary School Journal*, 106: 429–451.

Gillies, R. and Haynes, M. (2011) 'Increasing explanatory behaviour, problem-solving and reasoning within classes using cooperative group work', *Instructional Science*, 39: 349–366.

Gillies, R. and Khan, A. (2008) 'The effects of teacher discourse on students' discourse, problem-solving and reasoning during cooperative learning', *International Journal of Educational Research*, 47: 323–340.

Gillies, R. and Khan, A. (2009) 'Promoting reasoned argumentation, problem-solving and learning during small-group work', *Cambridge Journal of Education*, 39: 7–27.

Gillies, R., Nichols, K., Burgh, G. and Haynes, M. (2012) 'The effects of two strategic and meta-cognitive questioning approaches on children's explanatory behaviour, problem-solving, and learning during cooperative, inquiry-based science', *International Journal of Educational Research*, 53: 93–106.

Gillies, R., Nichols, K., Burgh, G. and Haynes, M. (2014) 'Primary students' scientific reasoning and discourse during cooperative inquiry-based science activities', *International Journal of Educational Research*, 63: 127–140.

Hu, W., Adey, P., Jia, X., Liu, J., Zhang, L., Li, J. and Dong, X. (2010) 'Effects of a "Learn to Think" intervention programme on primary school students', *British Journal of Educational Psychology*, 81: 531–557.

King, A. (1999) 'Discourse patterns for mediating peer learning', in A. O'Donnell and A. King (eds), *Cognitive Perspectives on Peer Learning* (pp. 87–116), Mahwah, NJ: Erlbaum.

King, A. (2008) 'Structuring peer interaction to promote higher-order thinking and complex learning in cooperating groups', in R. Gillies, A. Ashman, and J. Terwel (eds), *The teachers' role in implementing cooperative learning in the classroom* (pp. 73–91), New York: Springer.

Lehesvuori, S., Viiri, J. and Rasku-Puttonen, H. (2011) 'Introducing dialogic teaching to science student teachers', *Journal of Science Teacher Education*, 22: 705–727.

Lipman, M. (1988) *Philosophy Goes to School*, Philadelphia: Temple University Press.

Lumpe, A., Czerniak, C., Haney, J. and Beltyukova, S. (2012) 'Beliefs about teaching science: the relationship between elementary teachers' participation in professional development and student achievement', *International Journal of Science Education*, 34: 153–166.

Mehan, H. (1979) *Learning Lessons: Social Organisation in the Classroom*, Cambridge, MA: Harvard University Press.

Meloth, M. and Deering, P. (1999) 'The role of the teacher in promoting cognitive processing during collaborative learning', in A. O'Donnell and A. King (eds), *Cognitive Perspectives on Peer Learning* (pp. 235–255), Mahwah, NJ: Lawrence Erlbaum.

Mercer, N. (1996) 'The quality of talk in children's collaborative activity in the classroom', *Learning and Instruction*, 6: 359–377.

Mercer, N. (2008) 'Talk and the development of reasoning and understanding', *Human Development*, 51: 90–100.

Mercer, N., Dawes, L. and Staarman, J. (2009) 'Dialogic teaching in the primary science classroom', *Language and Education*, 23: 353–369.

Mercer, N., Wegerif, R. and Dawes, L. (1999) 'Children's talk and the development of reasoning in the classroom', *British Educational Research Journal*, 25: 95–111.

Michaels, S. and O'Connor, C. (2011, September) 'Conceptualizing talk moves as tools', paper presented at the AERA research conference, Socializing Intelligence Through Academic Talk and Dialogue, Pittsburgh, PA.

Michaels, S., O'Connor, C. and Resnick, L. (2008) 'Deliberative discourse idealized and realized: accountable talk in the classroom and in civic life', *Studies in Philosophy of Education*, 27: 283–297.

Oliver, M., Venville, G. and Adey, P. (2012) 'Effects of cognitive acceleration programme in a low socioeconomic high school in regional Australia', *International Journal of Science Education*, 34: 1393–1410.

Piaget, J. (1950) *The Psychology of Intelligence*, London: Routledge and Kegan.

Resnick, L. (1987) 'Learning in school and out', *Educational Researcher*, 16: 13–20.

Resnick, L. (1991) 'Shared cognition: Thinking as a social practice', in L. Resnick, J. Levine and S. Teasley (eds), *Perspectives on Socially Shared Cognition* (pp. 1–20), Washington, DC: APA.

Resnick, L. (2010) 'Nested learning systems for the thinking curriculum', *Educational Researcher*, 39: 183–197.

Resnick, L., Michaels, S. and O'Connor, C. (2010) 'How (well structured) talk builds the mind', in D. Preiss and R. Sternberg (eds), *Innovations in Educational Psychology: Perspectives on Learning, Teaching and Human Development* (pp. 163–194), New York: Springer.

Reznitskaya, A. (2012) 'Dialogic teaching: rethinking language during literature discussions', *The Reading Teacher,* 65: 446–456.

Rojas-Drummond, S. and Mercer, N. (2003) 'Scaffolding the development of effective collaboration and learning', *International Journal of Educational Research,* 39: 99–111.

Topping, K. and Trickey, R. (2007a) 'Collaborative philosophical inquiry for school children: cognitive effects at 10–12 years', *British Journal of Educational Psychology,* 77: 271–288.

Topping, K. and Trickey, R. (2007b) 'Collaborative philosophical inquiry for school children: cognitive gains at a 2-year follow-up', *British Journal of Educational Psychology,* 77: 787–796.

Trickey, R. and Topping, K. (2004) 'Philosophy for children: a systematic review', *Research Papers in Education,* 19: 365–380.

Trickey, R. and Topping, K. (2006) 'Collaborative philosophical enquiry for school children', *School Psychology International,* 27: 599–614.

Vaughn, S., Klingner, J. and Bryant, D. (2001) 'Collaborative strategic reading as a means to enhance peer-mediated instruction for reading comprehension and content-area learning', *Remedial and Special Education,* 22: 66–74.

Vygotsky, L. (1978) *Mind in Society: The Development of Higher Psychological Processes,* Cambridge, MA: Harvard University Press.

Webb, N. (2009) 'The teacher's role in promoting collaborative dialogue in the classroom', *British Journal of Educational Psychology,* 79: 1–28.

Webb, N. and Farivar, S. (1999) 'Developing productive group interaction in middle school mathematics', in A. O'Donnell and A. King (eds) *Cognitive Perspectives on Peer Learning* (pp. 117–150), Mahwah, NJ: Lawrence Erlbaum.

Webb, N., Franke, M., Ing, M., Chan, A., De, T., Freund, D. and Battery, D. (2008) 'The role of teacher instructional practices in student collaboration', *Contemporary Educational Psychology,* 33: 360–381.

Webb, N. and Mastergeorge, A. (2003a) 'Promoting effective helping in peer-directed groups', *International Journal of Educational Research,* 39: 73–97.

Webb, N. and Mastergeorge, A. (2003b) 'The development of students' helping behavior and learning in peer-directed small groups', *Cognition and Instruction,* 21: 361–428.

Webb, N., Troper, J. and Fall, R. (1995) 'Constructive activity and learning in collaborative small groups', *Journal of Educational Psychology,* 87: 406–423.

Wells, G. (2007) 'Semiotic mediation, dialogue and the construction of knowledge', *Human Development,* 50: 244–274.

Wiggins, G. (1998) *Educative Assessment: Designing Assessments to Inform and Improve Student Performance,* San Francisco, CA: Jossey-Bass.

Wolf, M., Crosson, A. and Resnick, L. (2006) *Accountable Talk in Reading Comprehension Instruction,* CSE Technical Report, Learning and Research Development Center, University of Pittsburgh.

14

STEREOTYPE THREAT

Looking back and moving forward

Penelope W. StJ. Watson

Two decades have elapsed since Steele and Aronson's (1995) seminal empirical study of stereotype threat was conducted. Steele and Aronson revealed that stereotype threat (the worry of confirming a negative stereotype leveled at a group to which one belonged) resulted in a taxing of cognitive resources and a consequent reduction in task performance quality for those susceptible to the specific threat (the targets). The authors identified stereotype threat as contributing to a scenario where test outcomes did not reflect actual learning, and revealed implications for educational inequity and impaired futures for negatively stereotyped groups.

Researchers have responded to the findings of that study by further investigating nuanced definitions (e.g. Shapiro and Neuberg 2007), mechanisms and processes (e.g. Schmader et al. 2008), and consequences (e.g. Woodcock et al. 2012) of stereotype threat. Mediators of stereotype threat (e.g. Kray et al. 2001) and its moderators (e.g. Schmader 2002), including the influence of context (e.g. Picho and Stephens, 2012), have also been investigated. A further arm of stereotype threat research has critiqued the validity of the construct itself (Delgado and Prieto 2008) and its role in explaining achievement gaps (Sackett et al. 2004); yet another arm of stereotype threat research has investigated the possibility of related constructs (e.g. Walton and Cohen 2003). As well, meta-analyses (e.g. Nadler and Clark 2011) have pointed out common strengths and new discoveries in stereotype threat research.

The research has largely concentrated on the targets' experiences of stereotype threat (e.g. Schmader 2002), and thus the focus has been on intrapersonal processes. The field offers enduring and rich possibilities for continued study, notably in advancing understanding of the role of intersubjectivity (psychological relations between rather than within individuals) in social psychological processes (Steele 2012). This chapter presents an overview of the major aspects of the stereotype threat literature, and suggests possibilities for future research in the field.

What is stereotype threat?

In the original definition, stereotype threat existed when one was at risk of confirming a negative stereotype associated with one's group as characteristic of one's self (Steele and Aronson 1995). Stereotype threat was experienced by the individual target as a self-evaluative threat, and in an attempt to disprove self-threatening negative stereotypes the disruption of the target's performance or protective disidentification with the stigmatized domain could occur (Steele and Aronson 1995). The stereotype did not need to be endorsed by the target: it was enough for the target of the stereotype to know that it existed in contexts where it could potentially be applied to his group (Steele and Aronson 2005).

In their detailed seminal study, Steele and Aronson (1995) focused on 'immediate situational threat' generated by societal perceptions that African Americans were possessed of lower intellectual ability. Steele and Aronson asked whether stereotype threat might play a role in school achievement gaps between African and White Americans. In four studies the authors showed that salient stereotype threat had the effect of impairing intellectual performance in African Americans, and that its removal improved that performance.

In the first of the studies, Steele and Aronson (1995) compared test results of African American and White American college students from Stanford University across three conditions: a stereotype-threat condition where a test was presented as diagnostic of intellectual ability, and two intellectually non-diagnostic conditions where threat was absent (without and with a challenge). An ANCOVA on the number of test items achieved correctly by participants, with SAT scores used as the covariate, revealed that African American students experienced comparatively greater performance decrement in the diagnostic condition, although this was only of marginal significance. The findings of the subsequent three studies confirmed the findings of the first. As well, it was found that racial stereotype was triggered for the African American participants, and that these participants reported high levels of self-doubt and were strongly motivated to avoid conforming to, or being judged by, the stereotype in the diagnostic test condition. The authors found that salience of stereotype threat (primed by stating race before test completion) had the power to decrease test performance in African Americans, even in the absence of a diagnostic condition.

Steele and Aronson pointed out that there were several mechanisms (some combined) which could mediate (conduct) stereotype threat (e.g. anxiety), and argued effectively against withdrawal of effort as a mediator. They suggested that compromised cognitive processing may occur, and cautioned that 'token status' and 'attributional ambiguity' (uncertainty of prejudicial treatment) should be seen as distinct from stereotype threat.

Further definitions have added nuance to that of the original one; for example, stereotype threat has been identified as situational, occurring in a *specific* context where a negative stereotype about the target's group applied (Steele *et al.* 2002). Importantly, Shapiro and Neuberg (2007) observed that some definitions of stereotype threat had developed in line with original conceptualization, and others had drifted. Shapiro and Neuberg, for example, noted that some researchers (e.g. Kray *et al.* 2001) had focused on self-stereotypes, or the belief that one personally possesses a stereotyped characteristic, while others (e.g. Bosson *et al.* 2004) focused on the belief that group performance could confirm a stereotype, and that further research (e.g. Schmader 2002) had combined both self and group concerns. Shapiro and Neuberg indicated that threat could be manifest, moderated, and mediated by different processes in a variety of ways, depending on how the two dimensions of threat (target: either self or group; and source: either self, out-group, or in-group) intersected. Subsequent studies (e.g. Wout *et al.* 2008) have investigated how stereotype threat differently mediates self and group threats, but there appears to be much room for further research in this field.

Steele *et al.* (2002) established stereotype threat as one of several social identity threats, and acknowledged that people have multiple social identities. Adams *et al.* (2006) distinguished clearly between stereotype threat (as pertaining to stereotypes about domain-specific performance inferiority) and social identity threat (a broader set of concerns of evaluation in terms of a threatened social identity). More recently, Steele (2010) pointed out that threat will render dominant that aspect of a person's social identity to which it is directed at a given time. In this case, the feelings and thoughts generated by threat to a given identity will overwhelm the target's identity as a whole.

A multiplicity of definitions of stereotype threat has therefore existed and moreover may have compromised the effectiveness and universal application of measures and interventions employed in stereotype research (Shapiro and Neuberg 2007).

Shapiro and Neuberg proposed a multithreat framework (rather than one concept of stereotype threat) as a solution to the ambiguity surrounding stereotype threat definitions, and as an aid to tailoring ameliorating interventions to specific stereotype threats. These authors revealed the need to expand the definition of stereotype threat to allow a full exploration of the construct. Such a definition may well take into account the relationship between self and group threat (experienced or posed by target or source), and the relationship between stereotype threat and other social identity threats.

How does stereotype threat work? Mechanisms and processes

Steele and Aronson (1995) asserted that as a social–psychological predicament, stereotype threat could be experienced by the target as a self-evaluative threat. The seminal authors, and later Aronson *et al.* (2002), showed that in the presence of stereotype threat, those engaged in the threatened domain attempted to disprove the stereotype to prevent verifying for themselves or to others that the threat was self-characteristic. Negative stereotypes could be sufficiently self-threatening as to disrupt and therefore compromise the target's performance or cause protective disidentification with the stigmatized domain. As well, in a threatening scenario, subjects were likely to choose tasks which they thought would ensure success, thus avoiding creative risk taking, and had a propensity to underperform in the face of a challenge. Steele and Aronson proposed that stereotype threat causes behavioral responses such as increased self-monitoring and anxiety, which in turn causes performance decrement, but they did not elaborate further on the mechanisms which might be at play. In their work, the stereotype did not need to be endorsed by the target: it was enough for the target of the stereotype to know that it existed in contexts where it could potentially be applied to his or her group (Steele and Aronson 2005).

Other researchers (e.g. Beilock *et al.* 2007; Schmader *et al.* 2008) have investigated the link between behavioral responses and stereotype threat. Beilock *et al.* pinpointed a causal association between stereotype threat and working memory, suggesting that stereotype threat co-opted working memory resources needed to optimize performance, introducing counterproductive task-related thoughts and worries. Phonological loop functions (verbalized thoughts and concerns), and central executive functions (e.g. suppression of worrying thoughts) were suggested to be negatively engaged in this context.

Building on the work of such research, Schmader *et al.* (2008) claimed their integrated process model would explain how stereotype threat disrupted performance; namely, through three interrelated but distinct mechanisms: physiological stress response (which impairs prefrontal processing), intrusive self-monitoring, and negative thought and emotion suppression. The three interrelated disruptive mechanisms compromised available 'executive resources' and ultimately performance quality. Under stereotype threat, working memory was taxed and degraded, and resources were diverted to tasks and concerns unrelated to optimal performance; this supports the ideas of Beilock and colleagues. Schmader and colleagues stringently scrutinized their proposed process model for possible areas of weakness or lack of clarity, distinguishing carefully between increasing 'mere effort' and taxing working memory. Their study also proved valuable in revealing a range of factors which moderated and mediated stereotype threat.

In terms of the wider effect of the third of Schmader and colleagues' three entwined mechanisms, Carr and Steele (2009) explored the meditational relationship between depleted working memory and inflexibility of mindset as a result of suppressing stereotype threat. Importantly, Beilock *et al.* urged future researchers to further investigate links between stereotype threat, cognitive psychology, test anxiety, and performance pressure. A review of previous research (Wheeler and Petty 2001) had called for thorough comparative testing of pathways that mediate stereotype threat and automatic behaviors, and cautioned that tests of stereotype threat-mediating variables had resulted in inconsistent findings. It could be argued then, that research to explain stereotype threat mechanisms is by no means exhausted, and that Beilock and colleagues' recommendations for liaisons between the fields of cognitive and social psychology, and the development of comprehensive theories of skill failure may also provide future opportunities for stereotype threat research.

Contexts and moderating factors

The research on stereotype threat has broadened since Steele and Aronson's seminal study to include a variety of threat-inducing contexts. The effect of stereotype threat on the academic achievement of racial groups other than African Americans, for example, French Arabs (Chateignier *et al.* 2009), has been explored. Gender groups, for example, females in mathematics scenarios (Schmader 2002) and students in groups defined by socioeconomic status (e.g. Croizet *et al.* 2001), have been probed to determine the effects of stereotype threat on academic outcomes. The findings of these subsequent studies supported the premise of the seminal study that threat was triggered by a notion of inferior intellectual ability in a particular academic domain, with negative outcomes for the targets, and that interventions could lessen stereotype threat. The mediation of stereotype threat in nonacademic contexts has also been studied. In gendered domains, threat has been triggered by stereotypes that suggest women are not good leaders (Davies *et al.* 2005), that young men who sing in choirs are homosexual (Watson 2012), and that homosexual childcare workers are both pedophilic and liable to pervert their charges (Bosson *et al.* 2004).

Steele *et al.* (2002) emphasized the importance of understanding how a potential target's social identity in a particular setting could render him open to stereotype threat. Context has triggered identity salience, negatively affecting a sense of belonging for females in mathematics (Good *et al.* 2012), a sense of competence for students in sport (Stone 2002) and a sense of ability for White men, compared to Asians, in mathematics (Aronson *et al.* 1999). The low or minority status of one's group, its cultural or structural marginalization, and its reputation as being of less value than other groups, all had the potential to endow that group with an unfavorable identity (Steele *et al.* 2002). Croizet and colleagues found that manipulating identity salience could ameliorate the effects of stereotype threat in test situations. They found that reducing the self-relevance of a threatening stereotype, and accessing alternative aspects of one's social identity, had the power to remediate the situational effect of stereotype threat; they cautioned, however, that their intervention could only be considered context specific.

Interestingly, and with relevance to the social psychology of the classroom, the interface between teacher expectancy and stereotype threat has been little explored in a direct manner. Research has suggested that there are similarities and links between teacher expectancy effects and stereotype threat, and that interpersonal expectancy effects have been shaped by stereotypes (McKown *et al.* 2010). Correspondingly, teacher expectations influenced by negative stereotypes (e.g. the stereotype that New Zealand Maori students are less likely to achieve academically than their Pakeha (Eurpoean) counterparts) have been shown to negatively influence student academic outcomes (Rubie-Davies *et al.* 2006). Given these ideas, there may be room to explore the role of teacher expectations as a mediator of stereotype threat.

Moderators have altered the strength with which stereotype threat was experienced, and context itself has been studied in this role (e.g. Picho and Stephens 2012). In a study which investigated the applicability of stereotype threat to Ugandan mathematics students, Picho and Stephens found that when exposed to stereotype threat, girls in single sex (compared to coeducational) schools experienced no decline in mathematics performance, and higher identification and self-efficacy in mathematics. Identity salience has also moderated stereotype threat. Murphy *et al.* (2007) found that women who were highly identified with mathematics domains could lose a sense of belonging to mathematics domains if their gender identity was heightened. Further, higher stereotype endorsement (Schmader *et al.* 2004), higher identification with domain (Steele *et al.* 2002), higher identification with gender (Schmader 2002), and solo status (Sekaquauptewa and Thompson 2003), were found to increase the strength of stereotype threat effects. On the other hand, intervention to increase self-affirmation (Taillandier-Schmitt *et al.* 2012) has reduced the effects of stereotype threat.

Recently, Steele (2012) has pointed out that the further investigation of moderators could reveal answers vital for stereotype threat research. In addition, other literature has revealed that negative affect can exacerbate stereotype threat effects (Aronson and Inzlicht 2004), and Kit *et al.* (2008) have suggested how mediators and moderators of stereotype threat may work together to depress test performance. Thus continued exploration of variables that conduct and alter the strength of stereotype threat may generate fruitful clues for its reduction.

The consequences of stereotype threat

Research on stereotype threat has often centered on performance decrement, as this consequence has most saliently contributed to academic achievement gaps associated with ethnicity, socioeconomic status, and gender. However, other consequences have been noted too. Individuals targeted by stereotype threat have experienced distraction (Mrazek *et al.* 2011); reduction of the ability for perceptual thought (Rydell *et al.* 2010); health problems such as increased blood pressure (Blascovich *et al.* 2001); and choice of protective actions such as self-handicapping (Stone, 2002), denial (von Hippel *et al.* 2005), disidentification and abandonment (Woodcock *et al.* 2012), and a reduction in value of the domain (Steele *et al.* 2002). Further, it has been suggested that stereotype threat results in a reduction in a sense of belonging for women in mathematics, science, and engineering fields (Murphy *et al.* 2007), and for students of color to school (Mello *et al.* 2012).

Changes in motivation have also been identified as a consequence of stereotype threat (e.g. Thoman *et al.* 2013). Achievement goal orientation, sense of belonging, and intrinsic motivation were explored over time, revealing that uncertainty and lowered interest in a domain could be experienced by stigmatized students, even if they were highly motivated (Thoman *et al.* 2013). Other recent articles (e.g. Chalabaev *et al.* 2012) offer the potentially controversial view that manipulation of performance approach and performance avoidance goals may improve performance under stereotype threat conditions because of regulatory fit. The motivational experience model of Thoman *et al.* could provide possibilities for investigating the integrated effect of several motivational consequences of stereotype threat. It could also bridge what the authors describe as a divide between motivation and stereotype threat, hitherto considered quite distinct disciplines. Interestingly, performance avoidance goals were suggested to mediate stereotype threat with very similar effects to cognitive processes (Steele and Aronson 2005), and Schmader and colleagues (2008) suggested that their process model (mentioned above) moved beyond a simplistic view in which stereotype threat was confined to being either a cognitive or motivational issue. Importantly, an integration of hitherto discontinuous disciplines could shed light on the long-term consequences that stereotype threat may hold for reduced career choice in gendered fields.

Critiques, and controversies surrounding stereotype threat

Sackett *et al.* (2004) examined misconceptions about Steele and Aronson's (1995) seminal work in the popular media, scientific journals, and psychology textbooks. They found that a significant percentage of the literature interpreted the findings of Steele and Aronson (1995) in such a way as to suggest stereotype threat was the main cause of the academic achievement gap between African and White Americans. However, in this and a subsequent critique (Sackett *et al.* 2004,

2005), the authors clarified, defended, and endorsed the Steele and Aronson study as valuable and robust, encouraging further stereotype threat research, particularly in real-world settings.

The validity and integrity of stereotype threat as a construct has been challenged by Delgado and Prieto's (2008) exploration of possible differential effects of stereotype threat on male and female mathematics performance. The authors recorded variable performance results in mathematics for males and females, and between individuals of high and low anxiety, attributing their findings to variable levels of anxiety rather than stereotype threat itself. As well, Delgado and Prieto asserted that in their study, and in previous studies of stereotype threat, it was not possible to make a clear distinction between results caused by stereotype threat and those caused by stereotype lift.

Further debate has surrounded the choice of a self-report measure to assess threat-induced state anxiety in stereotype threat research (e.g. Quintana and McKown 2008). Other research (Gawronski *et al.* 2007) has assessed arguments that self-report measures did not accurately assess traits or access implicit information. As Steele and Aronson's (1995) seminal study involved the assessment of a situational state (anxiety), the use of a self-report measure was deemed appropriate. Nevertheless, it might be suggested that the value of self-report data could be augmented in future research design by the conjoint use of measures which address stable implicit views, implemented further in real-world rather than laboratory settings.

Other authors have challenged the statistical methods used in stereotype threat research. Wicherts (2005) suggested that the use of ANCOVA was unsuitable in stereotype threat research, foreshadowing the assertions of Stoet and Geary (2012), mentioned below. In other work, Wicherts *et al.* (2005) cautioned that the internal validity of real-life stereotype threat experiments was likely to be problematic. In the light of inconsistent results of stereotype threat research conducted in real-world settings (e.g. that of Stricker and Ward 2004) the authors proposed a method of statistical modeling which would aid generalizability of the research methods in both laboratory and real-world settings. Recent research to explore measurement invariance (e.g. Merkle and Zeileis 2013) has exemplified the need to further refine and test statistical models in real-world contexts.

Controversy has been associated with stereotype threat research. Stricker and Ward (2004) replicated Steele and Aronson's (1995) seminal work in two field studies, finding no stereotype threat effects despite manipulating the placement of a statement of ethnicity and gender. However, Danaher and Crandall (2008) upheld the value of conducting stereotype threat research in real-world settings after their re-examination of Sticker and Ward's findings revealed flawed conclusions. Of particular interest was the performance of the non-stereotype-threatened group (in this case males) which decreased *unless* their sense of category membership was activated prior to the test. Here, it seemed that acknowledgment of membership of the group for whom performance ability was *not* threatened was necessary for successful performance.

Stereotype-threat-related constructs

Danaher and Crandall's findings held relevance not only for studies of stereotype threat, but those of the related construct of *stereotype lift*, which occurred when members of an in-group achieved a performance boost by comparing themselves favorably with a negatively labeled out-group (Walton and Cohen 2003). Walton and Cohen were careful to distinguish between stereotype lift and *stereotype susceptibility*, noting that the latter term, outlined by Shih *et al.* (1999), described the performance boost which occurred as a result of a positive stereotype associated with an in-group. Other research (e.g. Kray *et al.* 2001) has probed the influence of positive stereotyping. Described by Wheeler and Petty (2001) as a motivational complement of stereotype threat, positive self-stereotype (Kray *et al.* 2001) was found to boost confidence, and promote an enhanced performance rather than the performance decrement associated with stereotype threat.

It is worth noting that Delgado and Prieto's findings (mentioned above), while inconclusive in terms of predicting the effect of differential levels of male and female anxiety on performance, served to support the bolstering effects of downward comparison found in stereotype lift by indicating that males benefited where female ability was doubted, exposing the need for further research in this area.

The premise on which Steele and Aronson's (1995) seminal study was based was that African Americans were believed to be possessed of inferior intellectual ability, and it was the triggering of this domain-specific 'threat in the air' (Steele 1997) that activated the stereotype threat responsible for causing performance decrement. There is research, however (e.g. Beilock *et al.* 2007), which has indicated that a cultural stereotype may 'spill over', negatively affecting performance in an unrelated domain. Inzlicht and Kang (2010) reported that stereotype threat spill-over can affect self-control in nonstereotyped domains, supporting the findings of Beilock *et al.*

Thus, there are indications that stereotype threat may be intertwined with social identity threat in a way that pervades more than the threatened part of one's identity. The idea of Steele (2010) that one's emotion, thought, and whole identity are dominated by the currently threatened aspect of one's social identity, provides a clue to future directions in stereotype threat research. Perhaps it is time to look more closely at how social processes rather than intrapersonal processes could be associated with stereotype threat.

Meta-analyses of stereotype threat research

Meta-analyses of stereotype threat studies (e.g. Picho *et al.* 2013) have revealed commonalities, discoveries, and differences with single studies. Nadler and Clark (2011) found that the effects of stereotype threat-nullifying interventions had similar effects across different ethnicities, and the effects of stereotype threat did not alter significantly when in-group numbers varied across ethnic contexts, thus strengthening the generalizability of stereotype threat. The findings of Picho *et al.* echoed the latter scenario, in gendered contexts, and revealed the importance of further research to explore the moderating role of multiple identities on stereotype threat (see Rydell *et al.* 2009), particularly when positive social identities were made salient. However, Nadler and Clark noted that when results of multiple studies were aggregated, the large effect of stereotype threat on intellectual performance reported in single studies became only a moderate one. They also noted that no difference between explicit and implicit test outcomes were reported when results were aggregated, and pressed for the creation of a comprehensive model of stereotype threat. The authors found the effects of the construct to be pervasive, stable across a variety of contexts, and consistent across diverse populations, but along with Picho *et al.* (who suggested that geographical context may moderate stereotype threat effects) urged researchers to continue testing stereotype threat in wider populations.

Stoet and Geary's meta-analysis revealed that mode of analysis caused an important difference in results, where ANCOVAs yielded statistically significantly negative stereotype threat effects but ANOVAs did not. Two further meta-analyses of Walton and Spencer (2009) pointed to environmental rather than content threats as potential test-result depressors for those people stigmatized by negative intellectual stereotypes, and the need to research as yet unidentified and unremediated threats. Nguyen and Ryan's (2008) meta-analysis disclosed women's test performance was more negatively affected by subtle stereotype threat cues, whereas explicit cues negatively affected that of ethnic minorities, and explicit remedial interventions benefitted both groups. Interestingly, the authors revealed that women who were moderately (rather than highly) identified with mathematics were at greatest risk being negatively affected by stereotype threat. Thus, meta-analyses have highlighted common strengths, and the need for further research in the field of stereotype threat.

The future of stereotype threat research

It has been suggested that stereotype threat works alongside other social processes, rather than acting independently to contribute to academic achievement gaps, and in a way that the proportional role of stereotype threat changes with student age (McKown 2013). Researchers (e.g. Subotnik *et al.* 2011) have continued to urge for studies which test the generalizability, contextual relevance, and applicability of stereotype threat studies to real-world settings, motivated by inequuities such as the underrepresentation of students from less advantaged backgrounds, reported in gifted education. Thus, it may be beneficial to explore stereotype threat's relationship with other psychosocial processes, as well as in isolation from those processes.

Importantly, in attempting to explain and reduce stereotype threat, researchers have largely focused on the lot of the target while the contextual environment has been relegated to a peripheral role. In addition, the role of the trigger of salience of stereotype threat has been seen as finite rather than ongoing (Steele *et al.* 2002). Further, although interventions to moderate the effects of situational stereotype threat have been implemented, there has been no guarantee that these could be carried beyond the classroom, or be stable in the long term (Steele *et al.* 2002). Opinions have also varied in terms of the practical possibilities of working to change stereotypical and prejudicial beliefs held by others. It has been thought that building identity-safe environments may be more effective in reducing stereotype threat (as a social identity threat) than attempting to reduce prejudice and stereotyping (Steele 2003); however, Steele (2010) emphasized that changing situational cues and identity contingencies should not replace changes which would diminish disadvantage *per se*.

Recently, Steele (2012) proposed that the further exploration of intersubjectve threat may offer a meaningful way forward for stereotype threat research. In adjunct to this idea, it is interesting to note that social psychological theory has promoted the idea that stereotyping has enhanced prejudice, that prejudice reduction has been reliant upon stereotype change, that prejudice has moderated stereotype endorsement, and that stereotypes have been promoted by prejudice and have functioned as a means by which social inequality has been justified (Sherman *et al.* 2005). Further, Goff *et al.* (2008) asserted that stereotype threat may have been formed as a reaction to self-threat. Such research suggested that stereotype threat, rather than being a tool or cause of prejudice, was instead an unfortunate concomitant.

Blurring group boundaries to counteract implicit prejudice (Hall *et al.* 2009) and increasing successful cross-group friendships to reduce intergroup anxiety (Page-Gould *et al.* 2008) have been suggested as methods to promote positive intersubjective experiences. Research (e.g. Quintana and McKown 2008) has asserted that widespread 'lay theories' strongly influence attitudes and behaviors between groups. Further, Mendoza-Denton *et al.* (2008) pointed out that changing beliefs and expectations may be central to changing stereotypes. An understanding of how and why popular beliefs and stereotypes are formed would therefore seem necessary as a prelude to future research in stereotype threat reduction. In the light of these ideas, the notion of stereotype threat as a coincidental accompaniment of prejudice (Goff *et al.* 2008) seems problematic, and the challenge to explore stereotype threat in intersubjective contexts seems all the more relevant in the future study of the construct.

In conclusion, the fine tuning of definitions of stereotype threat to enhance the specificity of threat-reducing interventions, research beyond purely academic contexts, and the marriage of disciplines rather than their isolation in stereotype threat research, could be suggested as central in shaping future study of the construct. In addition, responses to questions surrounding the variables that moderate stereotype threat, the continued investigation of related constructs and of stereotype threat processes and consequences, and of the continued testing of stereotype threat among a range of populations in real-world settings, also seem needed. Importantly, meta-analyses of stereotype threat have revealed common strengths of the construct, points of difference between aggregated results and single studies, and the need for a comprehensive model of stereotype threat. Further, meta-analyses have also exposed the need to explore the moderating role of multiple identities, and the choice of statistical models which may enable more appropriate analysis of stereotype threat. However, the possibility of exploring stereotype threat in the context of intersubjectivity (Steele 2012) opens the way to probe associations between stereotype threat, prejudice, and other barriers to interpersonal harmony. Revelations of the nature of such associations may add not only to stereotype threat research, but to the broader field of the social psychology of the classroom.

Acknowledgment

I would like to acknowledge the valuable feedback given by my colleagues and reviewers, and in particular the help and inspiration of Christine Rubie-Davies, and John Hattie who fueled my interest in exploring the stereotype threat literature in the initial stages of my doctoral study.

References

Adams, G., Garcia, D.M., Purdie-Vaughns, V. and Steele, C.M. (2006) 'The detrimental effects of a suggestion of sexism in an instruction situation', *Journal of Experimental Social Psychology*, 42: 602–615. doi: 10.1016/j.jesp.2005.10.004

Aronson, J., Fried, C. and Good, C. (2002) 'Reducing the effects of stereotype threat on African Americans by shaping theories of intelligence', *Journal of Experimental Social Psychology*, 38: 113–125. doi: 10.1006/jesp.2001.1491

Aronson, J. and Inzlicht, M. (2004) 'The ups and downs of attributional ambiguity: stereotype vulnerability and the academic self-knowledge of African American college students', *Psychological Science*, 15: 829–836.

Aronson, J., Lustina, M.J., Good, C., Keough, J., Steele, C.M. and Brown, J. (1999) 'When white men can't do math: necessary and sufficient factors in stereotype threat', *Journal of Experimental Social Psychology*, 35: 29–46.

Beilock, S.L., Rydell, R.J. and McConnell, A.R. (2007) 'Stereotype threat and working memory: mechanisms, alleviation and spillover', *Journal of Experimental Social Psychology: General*, 136: 256–276. doi: 10.1037/0096–3445.136.2.256

Blasovich, J., Spencer, S.J., Quinn, D. and Steele, C.M. (2001) 'African Americans and high blood pressure: the role of stereotype threat', *Psychological Science*, 12: 225–229.

Bosson, J.K., Haymovitz, E.L. and Pinel, E.C. (2004) 'When saying and doing diverge: the effects of stereotype threat on self-reported versus non-verbal anxiety', *Journal of Experimental Social Psychology*, 40: 247–255. doi: 10.1016/S0022–1031(03)00099–1

Carr, P.B. and Steele, C.M. (2009) 'Stereotype threat and inflexible perseverance in problem solving', *Journal of Experimental Social Psychology*, 45: 853–859. doi: 10.1016/j.jesp.2009.03.003

Chalabaev, A., Major, B., Sarrazin, P. and Cury, F. (2012) 'When avoiding failure improves performance: stereotype threat and the impact of performance goals', *Motivation and Emotion*, 36: 130–142. doi: I 10.1007/s11031–011–9241–x

Chateignier, C., Dutrévis, M., Nugier, A. and Chekroun, P. (2009) 'French Arab students and verbal intellectual performance: do they really suffer from a negative intellectual stereotype?', *European Journal of Psychology of Education*, 24: 219–234.

Croizet, J.-C., Désert, M., Dutrévis, M. and Leyens, J.-P. (2001) 'Stereotype, social class, gender, and academic under-achievement: when our reputation catches up to us and takes over', *Social Psychology of Education*, 4: 295–310.

Danaher, K. and Crandall, C.S. (2008) 'Stereotype in applied settings re-examined', *Journal of Applied Social Psychology*, 38: 1639–1655. doi:10.1111/j.1559–1816.2008.00362.x

Davies, P.G., Spencer, S. and Steele, C.M. (2005) 'Clearing the air: identity safety moderates the effects of stereotype threat on women's leadership aspirations', *Journal of Personality and Social Psychology*, 88: 276–287. doi:10.1037/0022–3514.88.2.276

Delgado, A. and Prieto, G. (2008) 'Stereotype threat as validity threat: the anxiety–sex–threat interaction', *Intelligence*, 36: 635–640. doi: 10.1016/j.intell.2008.01.008

Gawronski, B., LeBel, E.P. and Peters, K. (2007) 'What do implicit measures tell us? Scrutinizing the validity of three common assumptions', *Perspectives on Psychological Science*, 2:181–193. doi:10.1111/j.1745–6916.2007.00036

Goff, P.A., Steele, C.M. and Davies, P.G. (2008) 'The space between us: stereotype threat and distance in interracial contexts', *Journal of Personality and Social Psychology*, 94: 91–107. doi: 10.1037/0022–3514.94.1.91

Good, C., Rattan, A. and Dweck, C.S. (2012) 'Why do women opt out? Sense of belonging and women's representation in mathematics', *Journal of Personality and Social Psychology*, 102: 700–717. doi: 10.1037/a0026659

Hall, N., Crisp, R. and Suen, M. (2009) 'Reducing implicit prejudice by blurring intergroup boundaries', *Basic and Applied Social Psychology*, 31: 244–254. doi: 10.1080/01973530903058474

Inzlicht, M. and Kang, S.K. (2010) 'Stereotype threat spillover: how coping with threats to social identity affects aggression, eating, decision making, and attention', *Journal of Personality and Social Psychology*, 99: 467–481. doi: 10.1037/a0018951

Kit, K.A., Tuokko, H.A. and Mateer, C.A. (2008) 'A review of the stereotype threat literature and its application in a neurological population', *Neuropsychology Review*, 18: 132–148.

Kray, L.J., Thompson, L. and Galinsky, A.D. (2001) 'Battle of the sexes: gender stereotype confirmation and reactance in negotiations', *Journal of Personality and Social Psychology*, 80: 942–958.

McKown, C. (2013) 'Social equity theory and racial-ethnic achievement gaps', *Child Development*, 84: 1120–1136. doi: 10.1111/cdev.12033

McKown, C., Gregory, A. and Weinstein, R.S. (2010) 'Expectations, stereotypes, and self-fulfilling prophecies in classroom and school life', in J.L. Meece and J.S. Eccles (eds) *Handbook of Research on Schools, Schooling and Human Development* (pp. 256–274), New York: Routledge.

Mello, Z.R., Mallet, R.K., Andretta, J.R. and Worrell, F.C. (2012) 'Stereotype threat and school belonging in adolescents from diverse racial/ethnic backgrounds', *The Journal of At-Risk Issues*, 17: 9–14.

Mendoza-Denton, R., Park, S.H. and O'Connor, A. (2008) 'Gender stereotypes as situation-behavior profiles', *Journal of Experimental Social Psychology*, 44: 971–982. doi: 10.1016/j.jesp.2008.02.010

Merkle, E.C. and Zeileis, A. (2013) 'Tests of measurement invariance without subgroups: a generalization of classical methods', *Psychometrika*, 78: 59–82.

Mrazek, M.D., Chin, J.M., Schmader, T., Hartson, K.A., Smallwood, J. and Schooler, J.W. (2011) 'Threatened to distraction: mind-wandering as a consequence of stereotype threat', *Journal of Experimental Social Psychology*, 47: 1243–1248. doi: 10.1016/j.jesp.2011.05.011

Murphy, M.C., Steele, C.M. and Gross, J.J. (2007) 'Signaling threat: how situational cues affect women in math, science, and engineering settings', *Psychological Science*, 18: 879–885. doi: 10.1111/j.1467–9280.2007.01995.x

Nadler, J.T. and Clark, M.H. (2011) 'Stereotype threat: a meta-analysis comparing African Americans to Hispanic Americans', *Journal of Applied Social Psychology*, 41: 872–890. doi: 10.1111/j.1559–1816.2011.00739.x

Nguyen, H-H.D. and Ryan, A.M. (2008) 'Does stereotype threat affect test performance of minorities and women? A meta-analysis of experimental evidence', *Journal of Applied Psychology*, 93: 1314–1334. doi: 10.1037/a0012702

Page-Gould, E., Mendoza-Denton, R. and Tropp, L. (2008) 'With a little help from my cross-group friend: reducing anxiety in intergroup contexts', *Journal of Personality and Social Psychology*, 95: 1080–1094. doi: 10.1037/0022–3514.95.5.1080

Picho, K., Rodriguez, A. and Finnie, L. (2013) 'Exploring the moderating role of context on the mathematics performance of females under stereotype threat: a meta-analysis', *Journal of Social Psychology*, 153: 299–333. doi: 10.1080/00224545.2012.737380

Picho, K. and Stephens, J.M. (2012) 'Culture, context and stereotype threat: a comparative analysis of young Ugandan women in coed and single-sex schools', *Journal of Educational Research*, 105: 52–63. doi: 10.1080/00220671.2010.517576

Quintana, S.M. and McKown, C. (Eds) (2008) *Handbook of Race, Racism and the Developing Child*, Hoboken, NJ: John Wiley.

Rubie-Davies, C.M., Hattie, J. and Hamilton, R. (2006). 'Expecting the best for students: teacher expectations and academic outcomes', *British Journal of Educational Psychology*, 76: 429–444. doi: 10.1348/000709905X53589

Rydell, R.J., McConnell, A.R. and Beilock, S.L. (2009) 'Multiple social identities and stereotype threat: imbalance, accessibility, and working memory', *Journal of Personality and Social Psychology*, 96: 949–966. doi: 10.1037/a0014846

Rydell, R.J., Shiffrin, R., Boucher, K.L., van Loo, K. and Rydell, M.T. (2010) 'Stereotype threat prevents perceptual learning', *Proceedings of the National Academy of Sciences of the United States of America*, 107: 14042–14047.

Sackett, P.R., Hardison, C.M. and Cullen, M.J. (2004) 'On interpreting stereotype threat as accounting for African American-White differences on cognitive tests', *American Psychologist*, 59: 7–13. doi: 10.1037/0003–066X.59.1.7

Sackett, P.R, Hardison, C.M. and Cullen, M.J. (2005) 'On interpreting research on stereotype threat and test performance', *American Psychologist,* 60: 271–272. doi: 10.1037/0003–066X.60.3.271

Schmader, T. (2002) 'Gender identity moderates stereotype threat effects on women's maths performance', *Journal of Personality and Social Psychology,* 38: 194–201. doi: 10.1006/jesp.2001.1500

Schmader, T., Johns, M. and Barquissau, M. (2004) 'The costs of accepting gender differences: the role of stereotype threat endorsement in women's experience in the maths domain', *Sex Roles,* 50: 835–850.

Schmader, T., Johns, M. and Forbes, C. (2008) 'An integrated process model of stereotype threat effects on performance', *Psychological Review,* 115: 336–356. doi: 10.1037/0033–295X.115.2.336

Sekaquaptewa, D. and Thompson, M. (2003) 'Solo status, stereotype threat, and performance expectancies: their effects on women's performance', *Journal of Experimental Social Psychology,* 39: 68–74.

Shapiro, J. and Neuberg, S. (2007) 'From stereotype threat to stereotype threats: implications of a multi-threat framework for causes, moderators, mediators, consequences and interventions', *Personality and Social Psychology Review,* 11: 107–130. doi: 10.1177/1088868306294790

Sherman, J.W., Stroessner, S.J., Conrey, F.R. and Azam, O.A. (2005) 'Prejudice and stereotype maintenance processes: attention, attribution and individuation', *Journal of Personality and Social Psychology,* 89: 607–622. doi: 10.1037/0022–3514.89.4.607

Shih, M., Pittinsky, T. and Ambady, N. (1999) 'Stereotype susceptibility: identity salience and shifts in quantitative performance', *Psychological Science,* 10: 80–83. Retrieved from http://www.blackwellpublishing.com/journal.asp?ref=0956–7976

Steele, C.M. (2003) 'Through the back door to theory', *Psychological Inquiry,* 14: 314–317.

Steele, C.M. (2010) *Whistling Vivaldi and Other Clues to How Stereotypes Affect Us,* New York: Norton.

Steele, C.M. (2012) 'Extending and applying stereotype threat research: a brief essay', in M. Inzlicht and T. Schmader (eds) *Stereotype Threat: Theory, Process, and Application* (pp. 297–303), New York: Oxford University Press.

Steele, C.M. and Aronson, J. (1995) 'Stereotype threat and the intellectual test performance of African Americans', *Journal of Personality and Social Psychology,* 69: 797–811.

Steele, C.M. and Aronson, J. (2005) 'Stereotypes and the fragility of academic competence, motivation, and self-concept', in A.J. Elliot and C.S. Dweck (eds) *Handbook of Competence and Motivation* (pp. 436–455), New York: Guilford Press.

Steele, C.M., Spencer, S.J. and Aronson, J. (2002) 'Contending with group image: the psychology of stereotype and social identity threat', in M.P. Zanna (ed.) *Advances in Experimental Social Psychology* (pp. 379–440), San Diego, CA: Academic Press.

Stoet, G. and Geary, D.C. (2012) 'Can stereotype threat explain the gender gap in mathematics performance and achievement?', *Review of General Psychology,* 16: 93–102. doi: 10.1037/a0026617

Stone, J. (2002) 'Battling doubt by avoiding practice: the effect of stereotype threat on self-handicapping in white athletes', *Personality and Social Psychology Bulletin,* 28: 1667–1678.

Stricker, L.J. and Ward, W.C. (2004) 'Stereotype threat, inquiring about test takers' ethnicity and gender, and standardized test performance', *Journal of Applied Social Psychology,* 34: 665–693. doi: 10.1111/j.1559–1816.2004.tb02564.x

Subotnik, R.F., Olszewski-Kubilius, P. and Worrell, F.C. (2011) 'Rethinking giftedness and gifted education: a proposed direction forward based on psychological science', *Psychological Science in the Public Interest,* 12: 1–54.

Taillandier-Schmitt, A., Esnard, C. and Mokounkolo, R. (2012) 'Self-affirmation in occupational training: effects on the math performance of French women nurses under stereotype threat', *Sex Roles,* 67: 43–57. doi: 10.1007/s11199–012–0157–z

Thoman, D.B., Smith, J.L., Brown, E.R., Chase, J. and Lee, J.K. (2013) 'Beyond performance: a motivational experiences model of stereotype threat', *Education Psychology Review,* 25: 211–243. doi: 10.1007/s10648–013–9219–1

von Hippel, W., von Hippel, C., Conway, Y.L., Preacher, K.J., Schooler, J.W. and Radvansky, G.A. (2005) 'Coping with stereotype threat: denial as an impression management strategy', *Journal of Personality and Social Psychology,* 89: 22–35. doi: 10.1037/0022–3514.89.1.22

Walton, G.M. and Cohen, G.L. (2003) 'Stereotype lift', *Journal of Experimental Social Psychology,* 39: 456–467. doi: 10.1016/S0022–1031(03)00019–2

Walton, G.M. and Spencer, S.J. (2009) 'Latent ability: grades and test scores systematically underestimate the intellectual ability', *Psychological Science,* 20: 1132–1139. doi: 10.1111/j.1467–9280.2009.02417.x

Watson, P.W. St J. (2012) *Stereotype Threat, Gender, and Adolescent Activity Choice: Who Dares Sings,* Saarbrücken, Germany: LAP.

Wheeler, S.C. and Petty, R.E. (2001) 'The effects of stereotype activation on behavior: a review of possible mechanisms', *Psychological Bulletin,* 127: 797–826. doi: 10.1037//0033–2909.127.6.797

Wicherts, J.M. (2005) 'Stereotype threat research and the assumptions underlying analysis of covariance', *American Psychologist,* 60: 267–269. doi: 10.1037/0003–066X.60.3.267

Wicherts, J.M., Dolan, C.V. and Hessen, D.J. (2005) 'Stereotype threat and group differences in test performance: a question of measurement invariance', *Journal of Personality and Social Psychology,* 89: 696–716. doi: 10.1037/0022–3514.89.5.696

Woodcock, A., Hernandez, P.R., Estrada, M. and Schultz, P.W. (2012) 'The consequences of chronic stereotype threat: domain disidentification and attrition (for some)', *Journal of Personality and Social Psychology,* 103: 635–646. doi: 10.1037/a0029120

Wout, D., Danso, H., Jackson, J. and Spencer, S. (2008) 'The many faces of stereotype threat: group- and self-threat', *Journal of Experimental Social Psychology,* 44: 792–799. doi: 10.1016/j.jesp.2007.07.005

PART IV

Teacher–student relationships

15

TEACHER–STUDENT RELATIONSHIPS, MOTIVATION, AND COMPETENCE AT SCHOOL

Kathryn R. Wentzel

There is no doubt that the nature and quality of children's relationships with their teachers play a central role in motivating and engaging students to learn (Wentzel 2009). Teacher–student relationships that are emotionally close, safe, and trusting, that provide access to instrumental help, and that foster a more general ethos of community and caring in classrooms appear to be highly effective in promoting positive student outcomes. With respect to motivation, these relationship qualities are believed to support the development of students' goals to achieve positive social and academic outcomes, emotional well-being and a positive sense of self, and actual levels of engagement. Empirical evidence that supports these claims (see Wentzel 2009, 2014 for reviews) suggests that emotionally supportive relationships with teachers are related significantly to students' motivational outcomes throughout the school-aged years, including mastery and performance goal orientations, academic values, interest, and self-efficacy. The affective quality of students' relationships with teachers also has been related to a range of motivational processes, including perceived autonomy, perceived control, self-esteem and positive self-regulatory skills. Finally, interventions have documented that improvements in teacher–student relationships can lead to enhanced motivation to achieve on the part of students.

Given the robust nature of this literature, a central issue addressed in this chapter is how and why students' relationships with teachers might be related to motivational processes and outcomes. Toward this end, I highlight various perspectives on teacher–student relationships and motivation, including definitions of constructs and theoretical perspectives that guide current work in this area. A specific model of teacher–student relationships that focuses on relationship provisions in the form of emotional warmth and expectations for goal pursuit is presented, and suggestions for future directions for theory and research are offered.

Definitions and conceptual models

Definitions of motivation

How might teacher–student relationships contribute to student motivation at school? Perhaps the first step in answering this question is to define what is meant by motivation. Motivation is typically defined as a set of interrelated beliefs that explain the initiation, direction, intensity, persistence, and quality of behavior. As I have conceptualized (Wentzel and Brophy 2013), these beliefs can be described as reflecting a set of questions relevant for motivational decision making:

1 What do I want to do?
2 What am I supposed to do?
3 Is this important and enjoyable to do?
4 Can I do it?
5 What causes success and failure?
6 Does anybody care if I do it?

The answers to these questions reflect beliefs about goals (questions 1 through 3), causality and control (questions 4 and 5), and a sense of social belongingness (question 6) that combine to explain why students may or may not be motivated to engage in classroom activities.

With regard to goal-related beliefs (i.e. 'What do I want to do?'), personal goals determine why students do what they do. The content of goals (e.g. Ford 1992) directs efforts toward specific outcomes (e.g. to learn algebra), and goal standards (e.g. Bandura 1986) define acceptable levels of accomplishment (e.g. to learn enough algebra to pass the exam). Goal orientations (Maehr and Zusho 2009) focus on specific reasons for trying to achieve academically, such as to gain mastery or to prove ability. The second question, 'What am I supposed to do?', reflects the possibility that decisions to pursue goals can be influenced by external forces that define what it is you are supposed to do in a given situation. These beliefs about social expectations can be socialized by way of extrinsic rewards and reinforcements, or can develop through exposure to a range of social experiences and interactions with teachers that inform students about what is valued in the classroom, what they are expected to do, and how well. These social experiences also convey to students the potential affective and interpersonal consequences if they do not behave or perform as expected.

Research suggests that most students understand what is expected of them at school but that low-achieving students often choose not to do what is expected because it is not important to them. This distinction between 'should' and 'want' reflects the additional importance of values emanating from personal desires and internalized beliefs about the importance of achieving a goal (question 3: 'Is this important and enjoyable to do?'). Decisions to pursue goals can be influenced by values that reflect the perceived costs and benefits of goal accomplishment, the importance and long-term utility of goal achievement, and the intrinsic pleasure of engaging in goal-directed behavior (Wigfield and Eccles 2000). Deci and Ryan (e.g. 2002) support the notion that motivated action may be either controlled or self-determined. To the extent that it is self-determined, behavior is experienced as freely chosen and emanating from one's self, and can develop naturally through experiences of intrinsic motivation (Harter 1978) or flow experiences (Csikszentmihalyi 1993) or by way of socialization experiences over time (Deci and Ryan 2002).

Students' beliefs about their abilities (e.g. 'I am able to learn math') also can influence what they choose to do and why they persist at certain activities and not others (Bandura 1986; Schunk and Pajares 2009). These beliefs focus on whether we believe we can accomplish a task successfully (question 4: 'Can I do it?'). Students who enter achievement situations with positive self-efficacy perceptions believe that they can accomplish what the situation calls for, whereas people who lack these positive perceptions are unsure that they can succeed or are even convinced that they cannot. As with personal values, beliefs about efficacy to accomplish tasks often distinguish high from low achieving students (Schunk and Pajares 2009; see also Wentzel 1989).

In addition, beliefs about autonomy and control (e.g. 'I am learning algebra because I want to') provide students with a lens for interpreting past events and with a basis for developing expectations for the future (question 5: 'What causes success and failure?'). Work by Weiner (e.g. 1992; see also

Graham and Williams 2009) has focused on the explanations and reasons that students generate to explain their behavior. For the most part, these theorists have focused on causal attributions and beliefs about the level of performance achieved ('Why did I fail that math test?'), and their implications concerning future performance (e.g. 'Will I fail the next test as well?'). A similar perspective has been provided by Dweck (e.g. Dweck and Master 2009), who proposes that individuals hold theories or mindsets about if and why things change. For example, entity theories reflect beliefs that things such as ability and personality are relatively stable, whereas incremental theories reflect beliefs that ability and personality are malleable and can be changed. In both cases, these beliefs represent reasons individuals succeed or fail and therefore, for engaging in or refraining from future goal pursuit.

Finally, although less common in discussions of motivation, students are also motivated by concerns that reflect the nature of their relationships with others (question 6: 'Does anybody care if I do it?') (Ford 1992; Wentzel 2004). These concerns are reflected in beliefs about belongingness and emotional connectedness; that is, feeling like one is a valued and integral member of a social group (Connell and Wellborn 1991). From this perspective, engagement in a socially valued activity is more likely to occur if students believe that others care about them and want them to engage. This belief is central to understanding the role of interpersonal relationships with teachers in motivating students to engage academically and socially at school.

Perspectives on defining teacher–student relationships are presented in the following paragraphs.

Defining teacher–student relationships

Relationships are typically defined as enduring connections between two individuals, uniquely characterized by degrees of continuity, shared history, and interdependent interactions across settings and activities (e.g. Collins and Repinski 1994). In addition, definitions frequently include desirable qualities of a relationship, such as levels of trust, intimacy, and sharing; the presence of positive affect and closeness; and the content and quality of communication (ibid.; Laible and Thompson 2007). Finally, relationships are often defined with respect to their influence and what they provide the individual. In this regard, researchers have focused on the benefits of relationship provisions such as emotional well-being, a sense of cohesion and connectedness, instrumental help, a secure base, and a sense of identity for promoting positive developmental outcomes (Bukowski and Hoza 1989).

From a developmental perspective, relationships are believed to be experienced through the lens of mental representations developed over time and with respect to specific experiences (Bowlby 1969; Laible and Thompson 2007). Mental representations believed to be optimal for the internalization of social influence are those that associate relationships with a personal sense of power and agency, predictability and safety, useful resources, and reciprocity (see Kuczynski and Parkin 2007). Mental representations also provide stability and continuity to relationships over time. In this regard, young children's representations of relationships with parents are believed to provide the foundation for developing relationships outside the family context, with the quality of parent–child relationships (especially levels of warmth and security) often predicting the quality of peer and teacher relationships in early and middle childhood (see Wentzel 2014).

In light of these definitions, teacher–student relationships are typically studied with respect to emotional support as perceived by the student (i.e. based on their mental representation of relationships), and examined with respect to a range of motivation outcomes that reflect the beliefs described earlier. A substantial literature indicates significant and positive associations between students' perceptions that teachers are emotionally supportive and caring and aspects of motivation, including goals, perceived expectations for social and academic outcomes, academic interest, educational aspirations and values, beliefs about causality and control, and a sense of belongingness (see Wentzel 2009). Why then, might students' relationships with teachers be associated with or even influence their motivation to engage in positive school-related outcomes? In the following section, models that explain connections between teacher–student relationships and student motivation are described.

Explanatory models linking teacher–student relationships to student motivation

The prevailing theoretical models that guide work on teacher–student relationships are derived from work on parent–child relationships and typically adopt a causal approach, with the affective quality of teacher–student relationships viewed as the central motivator of student adjustment (e.g. Pianta *et al.* 2003). The basic tenets of attachment theory (Bowlby 1969; Bretherton 1987) reflect this notion. Other perspectives describe teacher–student relationships with respect to specific dimensions and provisions (Wentzel 2004), as specified by models of parent–child interactions (e.g. Baumrind 1971).

Attachment theory perspectives

Attachment theory has provided the strongest impetus for work on teachers' relationships with young children. According to this perspective, the dyadic relationship between a child and caregiver (usually the mother) is a dynamic system of ongoing interactions in which children experience varying degrees of positive affect and responsiveness to their basic needs; predictable and sensitive responses are associated with secure attachments, and more arbitrary and insensitive responses are believed to result in insecure attachments (see Bowlby 1969). Moreover, secure relationships are believed to foster children's curiosity and exploration of the environment, positive coping skills, and a mental representation of one's self as being worthy of love and of others as being trustworthy. In contrast, insecure attachments are believed to result in either wary or inappropriately risky exploratory behavior, difficulty in regulating stress in new settings, and negative self-concepts. Within the context of attachment relationships, children also are believed to develop mental representations of self and others, which are then used as a basis to interpret and judge the underlying intentions, reliability, and trustworthiness of others' actions in new relationships (Bretherton 1987). Therefore, depending on the nature of primary attachments, children will expect to experience new relationships characterized either by positive affect and trust, or by conflict and rejection, or as anxiety-producing, overly dependent, or enmeshed.

Although teacher–student relationships are not typically viewed as primary attachment relationships, attachment theory principles imply that they would be concordant with the quality of parent–child attachments. Therefore, attachment theory has been used as a framework for generating predictions concerning children's relationships with their teachers, especially during the preschool and elementary-school years. The implications of attachment theory for understanding children's motivation for school-related activities are straightforward. A positive sense of self, curiosity and willingness to explore, and trust in others that develops out of the attachment relationship can be viewed as precursors to children's beliefs about emotional connectedness with teachers, efficacy to learn, a sense of personal control and self-determination, and intrinsic interest in classroom activities (e.g. Harter 1978; Raider-Roth 2005).

Evidence from correlational studies confirms that secure and close relationships with teachers are related positively to young children's school-related outcomes (see Wentzel 2014). Work on motivational outcomes at this age is rare, although young students' reports of school liking have been linked to students' attachment to teachers (e.g. Ladd *et al.* 1999). Similarly, attachment to teachers has been related to levels of anxiety and depression in adolescents (Murray and Greenberg 2000). In general, however, these relations have been fairly weak and appear to differ as a function of measurement and design strategies, and specific outcomes being predicted (see Wentzel 2009).

Dimensions of teacher–student relationships

An additional approach has been to consider teacher–student relationships as serving a broader range of functions that contribute to students' competence at school. This approach has been used primarily to study relationships in middle childhood and adolescence. Although the affective tone of teacher–student interactions is a central focus of this work, these perspectives propose that teacher–student relationships should be defined with respect to multiple dimensions that combine with emotional support to motivate students to engage in the social and academic life of the classroom (Connell and Wellborn 1991; Wentzel 2004). Similar to those described in models of effective parenting (e.g. Baumrind 1971; Darling and Steinberg 1993), these dimensions reflect concern for a student's emotional and physical well-being, predictability and structure, and instrumental resources. When applied to the social worlds of the classroom, these dimensions are reflected in teachers' communications of rules and expectations for behavior and performance, provisions of instrumental help, and opportunities for emotional support and interpersonal connectedness.

Support for this perspective is found in students' and teachers' qualitative descriptions of caring and supportive teachers, and from studies relating these dimensions of support to student outcomes. For example, middle-school students describe teachers who demonstrate democratic and egalitarian communication styles designed to elicit student participation and input, who develop expectations for student behavior and performance in light of individual differences and abilities, who model a 'caring' attitude and interest in their instruction and interpersonal dealings with students, and who provide constructive rather than harsh and critical feedback (Wentzel 1998; see also Hayes *et al.* 1994; Oldfather 1993). It is noteworthy that students who perceive their teachers as providing high levels of these multiple supports also tend to pursue appropriate social and academic classroom goals more frequently than students who do not (Wentzel 2002).

Additional evidence comes from studies where multiple dimensions of supports have been assessed simultaneously (see Wentzel 2009 for a review). For example, my colleagues and I (Wentzel *et al.* 2010) documented unique relations of teachers' provisions of clear expectations, classroom safety, instrumental help, and emotional support to students' interest in class and efforts to behave appropriately. Skinner and Belmont (1993) identified significant relations between teachers' provisions of involvement and structure (e.g. clear expectations, instrumental help) and students' engagement in class. Finally, researchers have reported significant main effects of structure and emotional support from teachers on positive behavior at school (Gregory and Weinstein 2004, 2008).

Integration and extension of theoretical perspectives

Adopting a perspective that teachers' multiple social supports are important precursors to school success raises several important conceptual issues. First, work in this area is still in its infancy with respect to understanding the nature and relevance of social supports at school. In addition, conceptual models that describe possible mechanisms are not well-developed, and empirical work that examines the intervening factors that explain why perceived supports are associated with academic outcomes are rare. In response to these issues, I (Wentzel 2004) have described more specifically how teacher–student relationships as defined by multiple dimensions of support can promote student motivation and subsequent performance. Derived from theoretical perspectives on person–environment fit and personal goal setting (e.g. Bronfenbrenner 1989; Eccles and

Midgley 1989), I argue that school-related competence is achieved to the extent that students are able to accomplish goals that have personal as well as social value, in a manner that supports continued psychological and emotional well-being. This perspective proposes that students will come to value and subsequently pursue academic and social goals valued by teachers when the students perceive their interactions and relationships with teachers as: providing clear expectations concerning goals that should be achieved; facilitating the achievement of their goals by providing help, advice, and instruction; being safe and responsive to their goal strivings; and being emotionally supportive and nurturing (see also Ford 1992).

In line with attachment theory and work by Darling and Steinberg (1993), I also assign a unique role to the emotional climate of relationships such that teachers are believed to have the strongest motivational effect on students if they provide instrumental resources within a context of warmth and emotional support. In this view, the roles of relationship warmth and communication of expectations and values in motivating students can be unique but also interrelated. To illustrate, it is well-documented that warmth and expectations each have direct, main effects on adolescents' social and academic functioning at school. Research has yielded the most consistent findings in support of a link between emotional support from teachers and students' pursuit of social goals to be prosocial and socially responsible, concurrently (e.g. Wentzel 1997, 1998, 2002) as well as over time (Wentzel 1997). Perceived emotional support from teachers also has been related to academic aspects of student motivation (Wentzel 1997, 1998, 2002). Students' perceptions of teachers' expectations for social behavior and academic performance also have been related to social goal pursuit as well as to academic goal pursuit (e.g. Wentzel *et al.* 2010, 2012).

Of additional interest, however, is the possibility that teacher warmth and expectations might influence motivation and engagement not only in an additive fashion but also as interactive effects. In this regard, Darling and Steinberg (1993) argued that the effectiveness of domain-specific parenting practices will be determined, in part, by the overall warmth and emotional climate of the parent–adolescent relationship. Applied to the classroom, this notion suggests that teachers' multiple provisions should be more predictive of motivation and engagement outcomes if they are communicated within the context of an emotionally caring relationship. In my ongoing program of research, I have begun to examine this possibility, focusing on the main effects as well as interactive effects of teachers' emotional caring and expectations for adolescents' social and academic outcomes on students' own goals and values. This work suggests that emotional support from teachers moderates the strength of association between expectations and student motivation. Specifically, results from two of my studies support the notion that teacher expectations for academic outcomes are most effective when communicated within a context of emotional warmth and caring (Wentzel 2012; Wentzel *et al.* 2012; see also Wentzel *et al.* 2011).

Future directions and challenges for the field

Although much is now known concerning the role of teacher–student relationships in motivating students at school, many questions remain unanswered. For example, the significance of the teacher–student relationship as a causal predictor of student adjustment is not yet clear. Although some evidence for causal influence has been reported, experimental work is rare. However, intervention studies designed to enhance the quality of school climate have demonstrated that when students begin to experience a greater sense of school community, they also demonstrate more positive social and interpersonal skills (Battistich and Hom 1997; Limber 2012). In addition, school-based interventions are beginning to shed light on the efficacy of training teachers and students to interact with each other in supportive ways to facilitate the development of social and academic skills (Durlak *et al.* 2011; Vazsonyi *et al.* 2004). Training teachers to develop positive relationships with individual students (e.g. MyTeachingPartner, see Hamre *et al.* 2010), and to create positive emotional climates in classrooms (Palomera *et al.* 2008; Reyes *et al.* 2012) also has shown promising results.

In addition, progress toward understanding the developmental significance of students' relationships with teachers requires more systematic attention to the construction of more complex theoretical models; further consideration of what might develop in students as a result of teacher–student relationships, especially with respect to motivational processes; and identification of individual differences in teachers that contribute to the nature and quality of teacher–student relationships. School-level factors, levels of parental involvement and peer networks and groups within a school also are likely to influence teachers' ability to develop supportive relationships with their students.

Finally, individual characteristics such as racial identity, perceived discrimination, and the extent that students are oriented towards gaining social approval are also likely to influence the degree to which students are open to forming relationships with teachers and being influenced by them. Student ability also appears to influence characterizations of supportive teachers. For example, students from high-ability tracks value teachers who challenge them, encourage class participation, and who express educational goals similar to theirs, whereas students from low-ability tracks tend to value teachers who treat them with kindness, who are fair, explain subject matter clearly, and maintain control in the classroom (Daniels and Arapostathis 2005). Academically successful inner-city ethnic minority adolescents report valuing instrumental help from teachers but also warmth and acceptance coupled with high academic expectations (Smokowski *et al.* 2000).

A full discussion of these issues is beyond the scope of this chapter. Two issues, however, are worth noting in greater depth. First, an inordinate focus on emotional support as central to understanding the influence of teacher–student relationships on student outcomes draws attention away from the possibility that teachers might not play a central role in students' emotional functioning relative to parents and peers. Indeed, when school-aged children rate the importance of their relationships with teachers, mothers, fathers, siblings, and friends, they typically report being very satisfied with their relationships with their teachers. However, on affective dimensions such as intimacy, nurturance, and admiration, teachers are routinely ranked by children as the least likely source of support when compared to parents and peers. Rather, they tend to rank teachers as most important for providing instrumental aid and informational guidance (Furman and Buhrmester 1985; Lempers and Clark-Lempers 1992; Reid *et al.* 1989).

This work provides clear support for including provisions of instrumental help as a dimension of teacher–student relationships that is important to students at all ages, but calls into question the relative role of teachers' emotional support in most students' lives. Given the overwhelming evidence that emotional support does make a difference, the question then becomes 'Why?' Several possibilities are viable. First, it might be that affectively positive relationships with teachers are not something that most students seek out but that are welcomed and appreciated nonetheless. It could also be that measures of emotional support mask students' definitions of teacher caring and emotional support, leading to assumptions that affective caring is being assessed when students are really thinking of 'caring' in terms of instrumental help (see Wentzel 1997, 2009). Finally, it is also possible that perceptions that teachers' are emotionally supportive are merely reflections of mental representations of relationships based on parenting. Each of these possibilities deserves careful consideration in future work in this area.

An additional theoretical challenge to the study of teacher–student relationships is to gain greater understanding of what it is that develops or is changed on the part of students as a function of their relationships and interactions with teachers. As noted in this chapter, teacher–student relationships have been related positively to a range of motivational outcomes. These findings, however, tell us little about which aspects of relationships are relevant for promoting which aspects of motivation, or about how and why these relationships affect students' accomplishments at school. With respect to the six defining questions introduced at the beginning of this chapter, is the central role of emotional support to promote a sense of caring ('Does anybody care if I do it?'), an internalization of adult values ('Is this important and enjoyable to do?'), and a sense of self-determination to explore personal goals ('What do I want to do?' and 'What causes success and failure?'), in contrast to the role of instrumental support, which might be central to the development of efficacy beliefs ('Can I do it?') and understanding of expectations for performance ('What am I supposed to do?')? In short, continued work on how the multiple qualities and provisions of teacher–student relationships promote specific motivational outcomes is essential to move the field forward.

Additional theorizing and research concerning pathways by which motivation provides a link between teacher–student relationships and objective outcomes also is needed. For example, the affective quality of relationships with teachers appears to be related to academic achievement by way of young students' engagement in the form of effort, persistence, and attention (Hughes and Kwok 2007; Ladd *et al.* 1999), and their sense of relatedness, autonomy, and competence (e.g. Marchand and Skinner 2007). In older students, relations between perceived emotional support from teachers and achievement appear to be mediated by students' mastery goal orientations and self-efficacy (Patrick *et al.* 2007), and their social goal pursuit tends to mediate relations between perceived teacher supports and students' prosocial behavior (Wentzel 2002). These important and intriguing issues should provide impetus for research in this area for many years to come.

References

Bandura, A. (1986) *Social Foundations of Thought and Action: A Social Cognitive Theory*, Englewood Cliffs, NJ: Prentice-Hall.

Battistich, V. and Hom, A. (1997) 'The relationship between students' sense of their school as a community and their involvement in problem behaviors', *American Journal of Public Health*, 87: 1997–2001.

Baumrind, D. (1971) 'Current patterns of parental authority', *Developmental Psychology Monograph*, 4: 1 (Pt. 2).

Bowlby, J. (1969) *Attachment and Loss. Attachment* (Vol. 1), New York: Basic Books.

Bretherton, I. (1987) 'New perspectives on attachment relations: security, communication and internal working models,' in J. Osofsky (ed.) *Handbook of Infant Development* (pp. 1061–1100), New York: John Wiley.

Bronfenbrenner, U. (1989) 'Ecological systems theory', in R. Vasta (ed.) *Annals of Child Development* (Vol. 6, pp. 187–250), Greenwich, CT: JAI.

Bukowski, W.M. and Hoza, B. (1989) 'Popularity and friendship: issues in theory, measurement, and outcome', in T.J. Berndt and G.W. Ladd (eds) *Peer Relationships in Child Development* (pp. 15–45), New York: John Wiley.

Collins, W.A. and Repinski, D.J. (1994) 'Relationships during adolescence: continuity and change in interpersonal perspective', in R. Montemayor, G. Adams and T. Gullotta (eds) *Personal Relationships During Adolescence* (pp. 7–36), Thousand Oaks, CA: Sage.

Connell, J.P. and Wellborn, J.G. (1991) 'Competence, autonomy, and relatedness: a motivational analysis of self-system processes', in M.R. Gunnar and L.A. Sroufe (eds) *Self Processes and Development: The Minnesota Symposia on Child Development* (Vol. 23, pp. 43–78), Hillsdale, NJ: Erlbaum.

Csikszentmihalyi, M. (1993) *The Evolving Self: A Psychology for the Third Millennium*, New York: HarperCollins.

Daniels, E. and Arapostathis, M. (2005) 'What do they really want? Student voices and motivation research', *Urban Education*, 40: 34–59.

Darling, N. and Steinberg, L. (1993) 'Parenting style as context – an integrative model', *Psychological Bulletin*, 113: 487–496.

Deci, E. and Ryan, R. (2002) *Handbook of Self-Determination Research*, Rochester, NY: University of Rochester Press.

Durlak, J.A., Weissberg, R.P. and Dymnicki, A.B. (2011) 'The impact of enhancing students' social and emotional learning: a meta-analysis of school-based universal interventions', *Child Development*, 82: 405–432.

Dweck, C.S. and Master, A. (2009) 'Self-theories and motivation: students' beliefs about intelligence', in K. Wentzel and A. Wigfield (eds) *Handbook of Motivation at School* (pp. 123–140), New York: Routledge.

Eccles, J.S. and Midgley, C. (1989) 'Stage-environment fit: developmentally appropriate classrooms for young adolescents', in C. Ames and R. Ames (eds) *Research on Motivation in Education* (Vol. 3, pp. 139–186), New York: Academic Press.

Ford, M.E. (1992) *Motivating Humans: Goals, Emotions, and Personal Agency Beliefs*, Newbury Park, CA: Sage.

Furman, W. and Buhrmester, D. (1985) 'Children's perceptions of the personal relationships in their social networks', *Developmental Psychology*, 21: 1016–1024.

Graham S. and Williams, C. (2009) 'An attributional approach to motivation in school', in K. Wentzel and A. Wigfield (eds) *Handbook of Motivation at School* (pp. 11–34), New York: Routledge.

Gregory, A. and Weinstein, R.S. (2004) 'Connection and regulation at home and in school: predicting growth in achievement for adolescents', *Journal of Adolescent Research*, 19: 405–427.

Gregory, A. and Weinstein, R.S. (2008) 'The discipline gap and African Americans: defiance or cooperation in the high school classroom', *Journal of School Psychology*, 46: 455–475.

Hamre, B.K., Justice, L.M., Pianta, R.C., Kilday, C., Sweeney, B., Downer, J.T. and Leach, A. (2010) 'Implementation fidelity of MyTeachingPartner literacy and language activities: association with pre-schoolers' language and literacy growth', Early Childhood Research Quarterly, 25: 329–347.

Harter, S. (1978) 'Effectance motivation reconsidered toward a developmental model', *Human Development*, 21: 34–64.

Hayes, C.B., Ryan, A. and Zseller, E.B. (1994) 'The middle school child's perceptions of caring teachers', *American Journal of Education*, 103: 1–19.

Hughes, J.N. and Kwok, O.M. (2006) 'Classroom engagement mediates the effect of teacher-student support on elementary students' peer acceptance: a prospective analysis', *Journal of School Psychology*, 43: 465–480.

Kuczynski, L. and Parkin, M. (2007) 'Agency and bidirectionality in socialization: interactions, transactions and relational dialectics', in J. Grusec and P. Hastings (eds) *Handbook of Social Development* (pp. 259–283), New York: Guilford.

Ladd, G.W., Birch, S.H. and Buhs, E.S. (1999) Children's social and scholastic lives in kindergarten: related spheres of influence?', *Child Development,* 70: 1373–1400.

Laible, D. and Thompson, R.A. (2007) 'Early socialization: a relationship perspective', in J. Grusec and P. Hastings (eds), *Handbook of Social Development* (pp. 181–207), New York: Guilford.

Lempers, J.D. and Clark-Lempers, D.S. (1992) 'Young, middle and late adolescents' comparisons of the functional importance of five significant relationships', *Journal of Youth and Adolescence*, 21: 53–96.

Limber, S. (2012) 'The Olweus Bullying Prevention Program: an overview of its implementation and research basis', in S. Jimerson, A. Nickerson, M. Mayer and M. Furlong (eds) *Handbook of School Violence and School Safety: International Research and Practice* (pp. 369–381), New York: Routledge.

Maehr, M.L. and Zusho, A. (2009) 'Achievement goal theory: the past, present, and future', in K. Wentzel and A. Wigfield (eds) *Handbook of Motivation at School* (pp. 77–104), New York: Routledge.

Marchand, G. and Skinner, E.A. (2007) 'Motivational dynamics of children's academic help-seeking and concealment', *Journal of Educational Psychology*, 99: 65–82.

Murray, C. and Greenberg, M.T. (2000) 'Children's relationship with teachers and bonds with school an investigation of patterns and correlates in middle childhood', *Journal of School Psychology*, 38: 423–445.

Oldfather, P. (1993) 'What students say about motivating experiences in a whole language classroom', *The Reading Teacher*, 46: 672–681.

Palomera, R., Fernandez-Berrocal, P. and Brackett, M.A. (2008) 'Emotional intelligence as a basic competency in pre-service teacher training: some evidence', *Electronic Journal of Research in Educational Psychology*, 6: 437–454.

Patrick, H., Ryan, A.M. and Kaplan, A. (2007) 'Early adolescents' perceptions of the classroom social environment, motivational beliefs, and engagement', *Journal of Educational Psychology,* 99: 83–98.

Pianta, R.C., Hamre, B. and Stuhlman, M. (2003) 'Relationships between teachers and children', in W. Reynolds and G. Miller (eds) *Handbook of Psychology,* Vol. 7: *Educational Psychology* (pp. 199–234), New York: John Wiley.

Raider-Roth, M.B. (2005) 'Trusting what you know: negotiating the relational context of classroom life', *Teachers College Record*, 107: 587–628.

Reid, M., Landesman, S., Treder, R. and Jaccard, J. (1989) '"My family and friends": six- to twelve-year-old children's perceptions of social support', *Child Development*, 60: 896–910.

Reyes, M.R., Brackett, M.A., Rivers, S.E., White, M. and Salovey, P. (2012) 'Classroom emotional climate, student engagement, and academic achievement', *Journal of Educational Psychology*, 104: 700–712.

Schunk, D. and Pajares, F. (2009) 'Self-efficacy theory', in K.R. Wentzel and A. Wigfield (eds) *Handbook of Motivation at School* (pp. 35–54), New York: Taylor & Francis.

Skinner, E.A. and Belmont, M.J. (1993) 'Motivation in the classroom: reciprocal effects of teacher behavior and student engagement across the school year', *Journal of Educational Psychology*, 85: 571–581.

Smokowski, P.R., Reynolds, A.J. and Bezrucko, N. (2000) 'Resilience and protective factors in adolescence: an autobiographical perspective from disadvantaged youth', *Journal of School Psychology*, 37: 425–448.

Vazsonyi, A., Belliston, L. and Flannery, D. (2004) 'Evaluation of a school-based, universal violence prevention program: low-, medium- and high-risk children', *Youth Violence and Juvenile Justice,* 2: 185–206.

Weiner, B. (1992) *Human Motivation: Metaphors, Theories and Research*, Newbury Park, CA: Sage.

Wentzel, K.R. (1989) 'Adolescent classroom goals, standards for performance, and academic achievement: an interactionist perspective', *Journal of Educational Psychology*, 81: 131–142.

Wentzel, K.R. (1997) 'Student motivation in middle school: the role of perceived pedagogical caring', *Journal of Educational Psychology*, 89: 411–419.

Wentzel, K.R. (1998) 'Social support and adjustment in middle school: the role of parents, teachers, and peers', *Journal of Educational Psychology*, 90: 202–209.

Wentzel, K.R. (2002) 'Are effective teachers like good parents? Interpersonal predictors of school adjustment in early adolescence', *Child Development*, 73: 287–301.

Wentzel, K.R. (2004) 'Understanding classroom competence: the role of social-motivational and self-processes', in R. Kail (ed.) *Advances in Child Development and Behavior* (Vol. 32, pp. 213–241), New York: Elsevier.

Wentzel, K.R. (2009) 'Students' relationships with teachers as motivational contexts', in K. Wentzel and A. Wigfield (eds) *Handbook of Motivation at School* (pp. 301–322), Mahwah, NJ: LEA.

Wentzel, K.R. (2012) 'Teacher-student relationships and adolescent competence at school', in T. Wubbels, J. van Tartwijk, P. den Brok and J. Levy (eds) *Advances in Learning Environments* (pp. 19–36), The Netherlands: SENSE Publishers.

Wentzel, K.R. (2014) 'Socialization in school settings', in J. Grusec and P. Hastings (eds) *Handbook of Socialization*, 2nd edn, New York: Guilford.

Wentzel, K.R., Baker, S.A. and Russell, S.L. (2012) 'Young adolescents' perceptions of teachers' and peers' goals as predictors of social and academic goal pursuit', *Applied Psychology: An International Review*, 61: 605–633.

Wentzel, K.R., Battle, A., Russell, S. and Looney, L. (2010) 'Social supports from teachers and peers as predictors of academic and social motivation', *Contemporary Educational Psychology*, 35: 193–202.

Wentzel, K.R. and Brophy, J. (2013) *Motivation to Learn*, 3rd edn, New York: Taylor & Francis.

Wentzel, K.R., Russell, S., Garza, E. and Merchant, B (2011) 'Understanding the role of social supports in Latina/o adolescents' school engagement and achievement', in N. Cabrera, F. Villarruel and H. Fitzgerald (eds) *Volume of Latina/o Adolescent Psychology and Mental Health: Vol. 3, Adolescent Development* (pp. 195–216), Santa Barbara, CA: ABC-CLIO.

Wigfield, A. and Eccles, J. (2000) 'Expectancy-value theory of achievement motivation', *Contemporary Educational Psychology*, 25: 68–81.

16

THE IMPORTANCE OF TEACHER–STUDENT RELATIONSHIPS FOR STUDENT ENGAGEMENT AND ACHIEVEMENT

Ammon J. Wilcken and Cary J. Roseth

Schools and classrooms are the setting for much of the formal learning that occurs in an individual's life. In schools, educators work to ensure that all students are provided with an opportunity to find success in academic pursuits. However, schools are also a social arena where students learn through their interactions how to work appropriately and effectively with others (Juvonen 2006). For example, in a given day, an individual student is likely to interact multiple times with teachers, peers, and school staff. Historically, the quality of these relationships and student engagement and achievement may have been viewed as distinct and unrelated. However, the past two decades have seen increased attention to how perceptions of relationship quality in school influence academic outcomes (Pianta *et al.* 2012; Skinner and Pitzer 2012; Wentzel 1999). The results of this research suggest that a full account of academic achievement or success in school must include the quality of the teacher–student relationship (Hughes and Kwok 2006; Ryan *et al.* 1994; Wentzel 1997).

While theory and empirical research suggest many outcomes may be influenced by relationship quality (Pianta 1998), the purpose of this chapter is to examine the research connecting teacher–student relationship quality to student engagement and achievement. Specifically, this chapter begins with brief definitions of relationship quality, relatedness, and engagement. Attachment theory and self-determination theory are then discussed as useful theoretical frameworks for understanding how the quality of teacher–student relationships affects engagement and achievement in school. We then highlight limitations in extant research and conclude with directions for the future that appear most promising in the field.

Teacher–student relationship definition

A relationship is built through a history of meaningful interactions between at least two people (Hinde 1979; Pianta 1998). In a school setting, interactions between a teacher and student throughout the school year provide the environment where the quality of the relationship is created. Relationships are dynamic in that they can change in their duration, quality, purpose, and value (Berschied 1999). Thus, the quality of a relationship can move from close and supportive to bitter and conflictual, or vice versa, based on the interactions and perceptions between teachers and students. It should also be recognized that the quality of teacher–student relationships are not necessarily consistent across school years. Students may connect adaptively with one teacher but struggle with another. Thus the principle of dynamic change in relationships may hold especially true in schools where relationships are generally limited to one school year (Pianta 1998).

Engagement definition

While the importance of engagement in school has not been questioned, the field has not settled on a single, coherent description of the construct which remains an issue of concern in the field (Appleton *et al.* 2008; Reschly and Christenson 2012). Generally, engagement is seen as an observable manifestation of student motivation to learn (Connell and Wellborn 1991; Fredericks *et al.* 2004). The most common view is that it can be broken down into some combination of emotional, behavioral, and cognitive engagement (Fredericks *et al.* 2004).

The focus of the current chapter is on behavioral engagement. Engaged students are those who tend to work hard, complete assignments, find academic tasks to be useful, and in general are motivated to learn (Appleton *et al.* 2008; Brophy 2004). The fact that this type of engagement is based on observable behavior has proven to be a boon for researchers. This has allowed for triangulation of data collection because teacher and student responses can be surveyed directly regarding the engagement of individual students with significant correlations found between the two raters (Lee and Reeve 2012; Wilcken 2013). Engagement can also be measured through standardized third-party observations (Pianta *et al.* 2008). These methodological advantages have led to greater construct validity in measuring student behavioral engagement. In addition, engagement is seen as a construct with considerable practical value since it is malleable, thus offering teachers and students a channel for intervention and hope for increased effort and success in school.

Teacher–student relationships and student engagement: Theoretical frameworks

Relationships are thought to influence engagement in school in at least two ways. First, interactions within a relationship provide instruction, correction, modeling, and support for students, forming the basis for the quality of the teacher–student relationship. This has generally been reported by teachers (Pianta 1998; Wu *et al.* 2010). Second, a student's perception of a positive relationship with a teacher provides security and increases willingness to engage in the school environment (Baumeister and Leary 1995; Deci and Ryan 1985). Students' perceptions are generally self-reported, and are described as students' sense of relatedness (Furrer and Skinner 2003; Ryan and Deci 2000; Skinner and Belmont 1993). While relatedness is a construct that is often used interchangeably with relationship quality (see e.g. Roseth *et al.* 2011), there are both theoretical and practical differences between the two that should be noted. Specifically, a more precise view highlights the fact that a sense of relatedness is conceptualized as existing *within* an individual, while the quality of the relationship exists *between* people (Juvonen 2006). For the current chapter, we use the term relatedness when discussing research from the student's internal perception of feeling safe, cared for, and liked by their teacher.

Attachment theory

The connection between the quality of the teacher–student relationship and student engagement is most often based on attachment theory (Pianta 1998; Wu *et al.* 2010). The central theme of attachment theory is that humans have an innate desire to connect with others and that emotional security results from a positive relationship with a caregiver (Bowlby 1969). The perception that one is cared about by others is posited to provide a safe environment for learning and exploring the world (Ainsworth 1989; Baumeister and Leary 1995). Research on teacher–student relationship quality works within an extended attachment framework (Roorda *et al.* 2011) suggesting that a similar 'secure base' occurs between caring and supportive teachers and students (Birch and Ladd 1997; Pianta 1998; Saft and Pianta 2001). This feeling of safety or security promotes internal working models or schemata of how relationships work, which in turn help to promote positive relationships in the future (Ainsworth 1989). For example, children in school who experience positive relationships tend to see school as a safe place and are more likely to engage in the environment. According to theories of engagement and motivation, this increased engagement should lead to enhanced learning opportunities and success in academic outcomes (Appleton *et al.* 2008; Pianta 1998; Skinner *et al.* 1990) as well as positive reciprocal effects on teacher–student interactions where teachers provide more support for engaged students (Skinner and Belmont 1993). In this way, positive relationships facilitate and provide tools that can enhance learning opportunities.

Attachment theory predicts the opposite result for children without secure relationships. When interactions with others include anger, fear, distrust, conflict, and disappointment, there is no feeling of safety that encourages exploration and engagement in the environment (Bowlby 1969). These children are also less likely to trust others, leading to impoverished relationships in the future (Birch and Ladd 1997). In schools, students without a positive relationship with teachers would be less likely to engage in learning tasks. Thus, poor relationship quality constrains interactions in the environment, which is associated with decreased engagement and lower school performance (Hamre and Pianta 2005).

Self-determination theory

Deci and Ryan's self-determination theory (Ryan and Deci 2000; Ryan *et al.* 1994) is a second theory which is often employed to explain connections between relationship quality and student engagement. According to this theory, relatedness is one of three innate needs that when fulfilled are causal of motivational outcomes such as self-regulation, engagement, intrinsic motivation, and self-esteem. Specifically, any environment that provides sufficient support for relatedness (a feeling of connectedness or belonging), autonomy (perception of being in control of one's actions), and competence (perception of achievement and the ability to succeed) will lead to increased motivation. According to self-determination theory, these needs tend to be intertwined but also can have unique effects. For example, a student who feels competent in schoolwork is also more likely to feel in control of their success in school and to perceive that his or her relatedness needs are being fulfilled. However, there are situations where these basic needs could be in conflict. For example, if a student feels that they must give up autonomy to have a positive relationship with their teacher, then self-determination theory would predict a drop in motivation even though relatedness needs could be considered fulfilled (Vansteenkiste *et al.* 2006).

A sense of relatedness has consistently shown associations with important academic outcomes. For example, students who perceive that they have a supportive, close relationship with their teacher are more likely to approach the teacher for help in times of confusion (Marchand and Skinner 2007), feel a sense of security at school, have higher self-esteem (Ryan *et al.* 1994), and are more behaviorally and emotionally engaged in school (Furrer and Skinner 2003). A sense of relatedness is posited to buffer students against the negative effects of hardship, stress, and even failure in school and thus facilitate academic achievement, retention, and school adjustment both concurrently and in the future (Furrer and Skinner 2003; Pianta 1998). One of the ways that relatedness could influence student engagement is through an increased desire in students (and all people) to assimilate practices and values from people who show us care and warmth (Ryan and Deci 2000). In a school setting, this would suggest that students who feel a sense of relatedness with their teacher are more likely to act according to established standards of conduct, give more effort and have higher engagement (Deci and Ryan 2009). Thus, according to self-determination theory, a sense of relatedness can energize individuals toward teacher-desired behaviors and tasks even when the tasks may not be considered exceptionally interesting or intrinsically motivating to students (Deci *et al.* 1991).This position should obviously not encourage teachers to rely on a sense of relatedness alone to get their students engaged. The best course is for well-planned, engaging classroom instruction to be mixed with a sense of support and relatedness (Council of Chief State School Officers 2011).

Research demonstrates that engaged students tend to have academic and social success in school (Fredericks *et al.* 2004; Furlong and Christenson 2008; Martin *et al.* 2010). Researchers also consistently find positive associations between the quality of teacher–student relationships and engagement (Juvonen 2006; Roorda *et al.* 2011; Wentzel 1999) and between students' sense of relatedness and engagement (Furrer and Skinner 2003; Ryan *et al.* 1994; Skinner *et al.* 2008), suggesting that both relationship quality and student relatedness act as influential moderators or facilitators of engagement in school (Juvonen and Wentzel 1996; Skinner *et al.* 2009).

In general, relationships in elementary and middle school have been characterized as either close or conflictual (Birch and Ladd 1997; Hughes 2011; Pianta 1992; Pianta and Stuhlman 2004). Close relationships are those that are viewed as positive, secure, supportive, and warm. Both theory and empirical research indicate that close relationships are significantly associated with many beneficial academic outcomes including greater engagement and academic achievement (Decker *et al.* 2007; Hughes and Kwok 2007; O'Conner and McCartney 2007), more interest and persistence in school (Van Ryzin *et al.* 2009; Wentzel 1999), and higher self-esteem (Wentzel *et al.* 2010). Close relationships may also act as a buffer when risk for failure is high. For example, teacher-reported close relationships with students predict reading gains but only for students whose parents reported less progressive parenting attitudes (Burchinal *et al.* 2002).

Close relationships have also proven to be protective in early stages of schooling. Specifically, kindergarten students who were identified as high risk for academic and social problems were compared across time based on the emotional and instructional support (specific variables that promote close relationships) shown by their teachers. The kindergarten students who had teachers who scored high in emotional support scored at a comparable level on academic indicators in first grade as their peers with low risk for school failure. Conversely, initially high-risk students who had teachers who scored low in emotional support scored lower on average academically than their low-risk peers (Hamre and Pianta 2005).

Conflictual relationships between teachers and students are characterized by impatience, aggression, frustration, arguing, and tension (Birch and Ladd 1997; Goodenow 1993; Hughes and Kwok 2007; Pianta 1998). Students having conflictual relationships with teachers are more likely to have poor relationships later in their education (Pianta and Stuhlman 2004), greater likelihood of not finishing school (Finn 1989), disaffection with school (Decker *et al.* 2007; Pianta *et al.* 1995), and lower achievement (Hughes and Kwok 2006; Hughes *et al.* 2008). Associations between negative outcomes and conflictual relationships in elementary school tend to be more robust than the associations between close relationships and positive outcomes (Jerome *et al.* 2009; Roorda *et al.* 2011).

Student achievement

In general, previous research has shown positive associations between teacher–student relationship quality and student achievement as well as between student engagement and achievement. However, the strength of these associations is often weak and inconsistent. For example, Hamre and Pianta (2001) and Baker (2006) found no significant correlation between teacher-rated closeness and student achievement on standardized tests of mathematics and reading. However, both studies found a significant negative relationship with teacher-rated conflict and standardized test scores with r's ranging from {min}.29 to {min}.21. Furrer and Skinner (2003) found a significant positive correlation ($r = .16$) between student-rated relatedness to teacher and student grades. In terms of engagement, Wu *et al.* (2010) found correlations between teacher-rated engagement and student achievement on a standardized test with r's ranging from .23 to .41. Furrer and Skinner, (2003) reported a correlation of $r = .59$ between teacher-rated engagement and teacher-generated grades. As relational researchers, we predict that relationship quality is actually causing an increase in student engagement. However, all of these results are correlational in design and therefore we cannot make causal claims regarding the direction of the influence.

One reason for the differences in strength of correlation between these constructs could be the diverse methods of measuring student achievement. Previous studies have used either standardized achievement measures (Hughes *et al.* 2008; Wu *et al.* 2010), teacher-generated grades (Furrer and Skinner 2003), or a combination of both (Baker 2006; Decker *et al.* 2007; Hamre and Pianta 2001). Because of shared methods, we would expect correlations to be higher when teachers are the source of academic achievement ratings (i.e. grades) as well as of reports of teacher–student relationship quality and engagement. This is a concern that is discussed more fully in a later section of this chapter.

It is important to recognize in this discussion of the associations between relationship quality and academic achievement that the influence of relationships may not bring about immediate academic change that would show up statistically as main effects. Rather, researchers in the field often speak of the shaping influence of relationships as a mechanism that can change trajectories that get students on the right track so that future success is more likely. It may also be that the best gauge of the influence of relationship quality could be seen in so-called 'sleeper' effects, where earlier patterns of interaction predict later academic outcomes. Hamre and Pianta (2005) show some evidence of this sleeper effect in showing that conflict in preschool significantly predicted behavioral and academic outcomes in eighth grade.

Teacher interventions

Both teacher–student relationship quality and student engagement are viewed as malleable constructs and therefore both are prime opportunities for intervention. There are several programs and models in the motivational field that aim to increase student engagement, such as Check and Connect (Christenson and Reschly 2010). However, we found only one program that is explicitly built on improving engagement through promoting more effective teacher–student interactions. MyTeachingPartner is a web-based program that provides teachers with video models of teacher–student interactions. Teachers observe these models and receive annotated feedback from a mentor explaining what was effective in the interactions and what could be improved. Teachers using MyTeachingPartner also have the opportunity to record their teaching experiences and then to reflect on the quality of interactions they had with students. They receive feedback from their mentor based on standardized observation measures. Teachers move through this process of teaching, reflection, feedback, and reteaching multiple times (Pianta 2012). We see this program as a wonderful development in moving the field from research to practical application for teachers.

Limitations and future directions

We see great promise in the valuable work that has been done previously in helping to explicate the role of social interactions and relationships in academic engagement and achievement.

However, there are limitations that need to be addressed to provide greater clarity for the field. Our concerns lie specifically in three methodological limitations common to research in this area that limit the confidence that we, as researchers and practitioners, can place in the results reported in the majority of previous research. We will detail these limitations briefly and give suggestions for improvements that will place the field on firmer ground.

Single-rater bias

Relationships by their very nature are composed of at least two people. However, variables of relationship quality and engagement and achievement have nearly always reported by a single rater (Decker *et al.* 2007; Furrer and Skinner 2003; Hamre and Pianta 2001; Hughes and Kwok 2006; Hughes *et al.* 2008; Wentzel 1997, 1999). This can lead to shared method variance. This is a measurement issue that can result in artificially high intercorrelations between variables when a single rater gives his or her response regarding distinct but related variables. The concern is that those variables will tend to be associated with each other, such as when teachers report on academic engagement and relationship quality (Campbell and Fiske 1959). Thus, the correlation could be the result of similarities in response patterns within the individual rather than actual associations between the variables. This affects Type I and Type II error and can therefore decrease the validity of the results of previous work (Campbell and Fiske 1959). This is a methodological concern in many fields in social sciences, but this does not excuse us. It is important that we as researchers do not base our claims for the influence of relationships on outcomes such as achievement and engagement largely on data from single raters. It is more appropriate to gather data from both teacher and student.

Lack of longitudinal data

Relationship quality is not established in a day (Pianta 1998). Relationships must develop over time and are dynamic in that they can shift in quality, purpose, and importance (Berscheid 1999). As Reis (2007: p. 5) states: 'Relationships are intrinsically longitudinal: they have beginnings, middles, ends, and aftermaths; they may differ, often substantially so, depending on their current stage; and what happens at one time is almost always influenced by what has happened earlier'. Thus, the dynamic and temporal nature of relationships in school suggests that relationships are not solely the product of current teacher–student interactions but are also cyclical, in that past relationships influence what each member of the dyad expects to occur in the current relationship. These expectations then guide future behavior (Hughes 2011; Pianta 1998). Thus, a history of interactions over time is posited to have a cumulative influence on current interactions and student perceptions of relatedness (Hamre and Pianta 2001).

This understanding of relationships changing over time suggests the importance of longitudinal data collection. However, a review of the literature suggests that with few exceptions (e.g. Wu *et al.* 2010), our understanding of a sense of relatedness and student engagement is based on cross-sectional data. For example, in a meta-analysis report, it was determined that out of ninety-nine studies of relationships and engagement, only nine collected longitudinal data and of these only five continued beyond one year (Roorda *et al.* 2011). To truly understand the influence of relationships in school, it is essential that we work to gather data for longer periods of time with multiple data points. It is likely that this will provide a much more complete picture, first of whether relationship quality exerts the influence that we expect, but also how, why, and under what conditions.

Hierarchical nature of students' relationships

Data gathered from individuals in an educational setting are always nested. Every classroom is a unique context with teachers and students creating a shared environment that influences the learning and development of individual students. The importance of the context is recognized in ecological models of learning and development which posit that developmental growth occurs through the interaction between an individual and the context in which they are embedded (Bronfenbrenner and Morris 1998). While this position is well accepted, it has not always been easy to account statistically for the nested nature of educational data. For example, to control for nested data, one study of teacher–student relationship quality and school functioning took longitudinal data from multiple classrooms but then randomly selected one school year for each student to be used in a cross-sectional analysis (Baker 2006). This type of analysis results in the loss of valuable data and a statistically weaker cross-sectional design. Recent methodological advances in multilevel analysis or hierarchical linear modeling have provided a tool that allows researchers to analyze hierarchical data in a multilevel framework and thus make better use of longitudinal and nested data (Burchinal *et al.* 2002; Lau and Nie 2008; Raudenbush and Bryk 2002).

The statistical rationale for hierarchical or multilevel models for classroom data is that because of shared experiences, individuals within classrooms tend to be more similar when compared with other classrooms (O'Connell and McCoach 2008). Failing to account for the similarity within a classroom can lead to lower variance estimates and thus increase the likelihood of Type I error (Martin *et al.* 2010). For example, results detailed in the current review of literature consistently suggest a significant association between teacher–student relationship quality and engagement (Connell and Wellborn 1991; Furrer and Skinner 2003; Hughes 2011; Wentzel 1999). However, the magnitude of these correlations could be lower than reported if within-group similarities were accounted for. When associations are inflated, the results of these analyses can lead to inaccurate conclusions and inferences (Ma *et al.* 2008). The same analyses conducted using hierarchical linear modeling would be more conservative and appropriate in analyzing the data regarding relationship quality, engagement, and achievement. This allows for greater confidence in the statistical validity of the analyses and the inferences that follow (O'Connell and McCoach 2008). Multilevel models not only help control for this statistical concern, they also allow researchers to explore the influence that context has on individual outcomes. For example, in looking for change in student's engagement over time, a new school year involves several changes in context including a new teacher, new classroom, new peers, and possibly a new school (Eccles *et al.* 1993). By failing to account for these changes in context, changes in engagement may be inaccurately ascribed to changes within the individual (Ma *et al.* 2008).

Our own work has focused on addressing these limitations. Across two years and four data points, we surveyed students' and teachers' perceptions of relational quality and engagement. Results were encouraging in showing significant associations between teacher ratings of closeness and conflict and student ratings of engagement. This is important for the field because the associations were significant even after controlling for nested classrooms and without relying on a single rater for data. This supports previous theory and research and provides more solid footing for engaging in future work. Less encouraging were our results from student ratings of relational quality where there were no significant associations with teacher ratings of engagement or academic outcomes (Wilcken 2013).

Future directions

The first area worthy of further research is an examination of whether the quality of teacher–student relationships can help to protect students from the oft-cited drop in motivation to learn and engagement as students move through school (Eccles *et al.* 1993). While it makes sense intuitively that a close relationship with a teacher could moderate the drop in engagement, there is little longitudinal research examining this issue from the perspective of social psychology. Second, while there is research suggesting that early relationship quality can influence the trajectory of student achievement (Hamre and Pianta 2005), we know very little about whether relationships in later elementary years or middle school can also change student achievement. To see this, we need longitudinal studies that follow students' and teachers' perceptions of relationship quality while also tracking achievement and engagement. Only then can we examine the long-term consequences and influence of relationship quality in school. Finally, we, along with others (e.g. Reschly and Christenson 2012), see the need for improved measures that can more accurately capture the complexity of classroom interactions and student engagement. The validity and reliability of the measures used in the field will allow for greater clarity and should help to clear up some of the conceptual confusion that often characterizes the work in this field.

Conclusion

We believe that it is an exciting time to be working in the field of teacher–student relationships and engagement in school. The work of the past has consistently shown significant connections between these important constructs. We also have the benefit of well-established theories with both attachment theory and self-determination theory providing a solid foundation for further research. As we move forward with increased clarity and methodological rigor by using better methodologies including multiple raters, longitudinal designs, and more conservative statistical models, there is great potential for both theoretical and practical research in the school setting.

References

Ainsworth, M.D.S. (1989) 'Attachments beyond infancy', *American Psychologist,* 44: 709–716.
Appleton, J.J., Christenson, S.L. and Furlong, M.J. (2008) 'Student engagement with school: critical conceptual and methodological issues of the construct', *Psychology in the Schools,* 45: 369–386.
Baker, J.A. (2006) 'Contributions of teacher–child relationships to positive school adjustment during elementary school', *Journal of School Psychology,* 44: 211–229.
Baumeister, R.F. and Leary, M.R. (1995) 'The need to belong: desire for interpersonal attachments as a fundamental human motivation', *Psychological Bulletin,* 117: 497–529.
Berscheid, E. (1999) 'The greening of relationship science', *American Psychologist,* 54: 260–266.
Birch, S.H. and Ladd, G.W. (1997) 'The teacher–child relationship and children's early school adjustment', *Journal of School Psychology,* 35: 61–79.
Bowlby, J. (1969) *Attachment: Attachment and Loss,* Vol. 1, New York: Basic Books.
Bronfenbrenner, U., and Morris, P.A. (1998) 'The ecology of developmental processes', in W. Denton (series ed.) and R.M. Lerner (vol. ed.), *Handbook of Child Psychology: Vol.1, Theory,* 5th edn (pp. 993–1028), New York: Wiley.
Brophy, J. (2004) *Motivating Students to Learn,* Mahwah, NJ: Lawrence Erlbaum Associates.
Burchinal, M.R., Peisner-Feinberg, E., Pianta, R. and Howes, C. (2002) 'Development of academic skills from preschool through second grade: family and classroom predictors of developmental trajectories', *Journal of School Psychology,* 40: 415–436.
Campbell, D.T. and Fiske, D.W. (1959) 'Convergent and discriminant validation by the multitrait-multimethod matrix', *Psychological Bulletin,* 56: 81–105.
Christenson, S.L. and Reschly, A.L. (2010) 'Check & Connect: enhancing school completion through student engagement', in E. Doll and J. Charvat (eds), *Handbook of Prevention Science* (pp. 327–348), Mahwah, NJ: Lawrence Erlbaum Associates.
Connell, J.P. and Wellborn, J.G. (1991) 'Competence, autonomy and relatedness: a motivational analysis of self-system processes', in M. Gunnar and L.A. Sroufe (eds), *Minnesota Symposium on Child Psychology: Vol. 23, Self Processes in Development* (pp. 43–77), Chicago: University of Chicago Press.

Council of Chief State School Officers (2011, April) 'Interstate Teacher Assessment and Support Consortium (InTASC) Model Core Teaching Standards: a resource for state dialogue', Washington, DC: Author.

Deci, E. and Ryan, R. (1985) *Intrinsic Motivation and Self-Determination in Human Behavior*, New York: Academic Press.

Deci, E., and Ryan, R. (2009) 'Promoting self-determined school engagement: motivation, learning, and well-being', in K. Wentzel and A. Wigfield (eds), *Handbook of Motivation in School* (pp. 301–322), Mahwah, NJ: Erlbaum.

Deci, E. L., Vallerand, R. J., Pelletier, L. G. and Ryan, R. M. (1991) 'Motivation and education: the self-determination perspective', *Educational Psychologist*, 26: 325–346.

Decker, D.M., Dona, D.P. and Christenson, S.L. (2007) 'Behaviorally at-risk African American students: the importance of student–teacher relationships for student outcomes', *Journal of School Psychology*, 45: 83–109.

Eccles, J. S., Wigfield, A., Midgley, C., Mac Iver, D. and Feldlaufer, H. (1993) 'Negative effects of traditional middle schools on students' motivation', *The Elementary School Journal*, 93: 553–573.

Finn, J. D. (1989) 'Withdrawing from school', *Review of Educational Research*, 59: 117–142.

Fredericks, J.A., Blumenfeld, P.C. and Paris, A.H. (2004) 'Engagement: potential for the concept, state of the evidence', *Review of Educational Research*, 74: 59–109.

Furlong, M.J. and Christenson, S.L. (2008) 'Engaging students at school and with learning: a relevant construct for all students', *Psychology in the Schools*, 45: 365–368.

Furrer, C. and Skinner, E. (2003) 'Sense of relatedness as a factor in children's academic engagement and performance', *Journal of Educational Psychology*, 95: 148–162.

Goodenow, C. (1993) 'Classroom belonging among early adolescent students: relationships to motivation and achievement', *The Journal of Early Adolescence*, 13: 21–43.

Hamre, B.K. and Pianta, R.C. (2001) 'Early teacher–child relationships and the trajectory of children's school outcomes through eighth grade,' *Child Development*, 72: 625–638.

Hamre, B.K. and Pianta, R.C. (2005) 'Can instructional and emotional support in the first-grade classroom make a difference for children at risk of school failure?', *Child Development*, 76: 949–967.

Hinde, R.A. (1979) *Towards Understanding Relationships*, London: Academic Press.

Hughes, J.N. (2011) 'Longitudinal effects of teacher and student perceptions of teacher–student relationship qualities on academic adjustment', *The Elementary School Journal*, 112: 38–60.

Hughes, J.N. and Kwok, O. (2006) 'Classroom engagement mediates the effect of teacher–student support on elementary students' peer acceptance: a prospective analysis', *Journal of School Psychology*, 43: 265–280.

Hughes, J.N. and Kwok, O. (2007) 'Influence of student–teacher and parent–teacher relationships of lower achieving readers' engagement and achievement in the primary grades', *Journal of Educational Psychology*, 99: 39–51.

Hughes, J.N., Luo, W., Kwok, O., Loyd, L.K. (2008) 'Teacher–student support, effortful engagement, and achievement: a 3-year longitudinal study', *Journal of Educational Psychology*, 100: 1–14.

Jerome, E.M., Hamre, B.K. and Pianta, R.C. (2009) 'Teacher–child relationships from kindergarten to sixth grade: early childhood predictors of teacher-perceived conflict and closeness', *Social Development*, 18: 915–945.

Juvonen, J. (2006) 'Sense of belonging, social relationships, and school functioning,' in P.A. Alexander and P.H. Winne (eds), *Handbook of Educational Psychology*, 2nd edn (pp. 255–674), Mahwah, NJ: Erlbaum.

Juvonen, J. and Wentzel, K.R. (eds) (1996) *Social Motivation: Understanding Children's School Adjustment*, Cambridge: Cambridge University Press.

Lau, S. and Nie, Y. (2008) 'Interplay between personal goals and classroom goal structure in predicting student outcomes: a multilevel analysis of person-context interactions', *Journal of Educational Psychology*, 100(1): 15–29.

Lee, W. and Reeve, J. (2012) 'Teachers estimates of their students' motivation and engagement: being in synch with students', *Educational Psychology: An International Journal of Experimental Educational Psychology*, 32(6): 727–747.

Ma, X., Ma, L. and Bradley, K.D. (2008) 'Using multilevel modeling to investigate school effects', in A. O'Connell and D.B. McCoach (eds), *Multilevel Modeling of Educational Data*, Vol. 1 (pp. 59-110), Charlotte, NC: Information Age Publishing.

Marchand, G. and Skinner, E.A. (2007) 'Motivational dynamics of children's academic help-seeking and concealment', *Journal of Educational Psychology*, 99: 65–82.

Martin, A.J., Malmberg, L.E. and Liem, G.A.D. (2010) 'Multilevel motivation and engagement: assessing construct validity across students and schools', *Educational and Psychological Testing*, 70: 973–989.

O'Conner, E. and McCartney, K. (2007) 'Attachment and cognitive skills: an investigation of mediating mechanisms', *Journal of Applied Developmental Psychology,* 28: 458–476.

O'Connell, A.A., and McCoach, K.B. (2008) 'Pedagogy and context for multilevel models', in A. O' Connell and D.B. McCoach (eds), *Multilevel Modeling of Educational Data,* Vol. 1 (pp. 3–10), Charlotte, NC: Information Age Publishing.

Pianta, R.C. (1992) *The Student–Teacher Relationship Scale,* Charlottesville: University of Virginia.

Pianta, R.C. (1998) *Enhancing Relationships Between Children and Teachers,* Washington, DC: American Psychological Association.

Pianta, R.C., Hamre, B.K. and Allen, J.P. (2012) 'Teacher–student relationships and engagement: conceptualizing, measuring, and improving the capacity of classroom interactions', in S.L. Christenson, A.L. Reschly and Wylie, C. (eds), *Handbook of Research on Student Engagement* (pp. 21–44), New York: Springer.

Pianta, R.C., LaParo, K.M. and Hamre, B.K. (2008) *Classroom Assessment Scoring System™ (CLASS™) Manual, Pre-K,* Baltimore, MD: Brookes Publishing.

Pianta, R.C., Steinberg, M.S. and Rollins, K. (1995) 'The first two years of school: teacher–child relationships and deflections in children's classroom adjustment', *Development and Psychopathology,* 7: 295–312.

Pianta, R.C. and Stuhlman, M.W. (2004) 'Conceptualizing risk in relational terms: associations among the quality of child–adult relationships prior to school entry and children's developmental outcomes in first grade', *Educational and School Psychology,* 21: 32–45.

Raudenbush, S.W. and Bryk, A.S. (2002) *Hierarchical Linear Models* (2nd edn), Thousand Oaks, CA: Sage Publications.

Reis, H.T. (2007) 'Steps toward the ripening of relationship science', *Personal Relationships,* 14: 1–23.

Reschly, A.L. and Christenson, S.L. (2012) 'Jingle, jangle and conceptual haziness: evolution and future directions of the engagement construct', in S.L. Christenson, A.L. Reschly and C. Wylie (eds), *Handbook of Research on Student Engagement* (pp. 21–44), New York: Springer.

Roorda, D.L., Koomen, H.M.Y., Split, J.L. and Oort, F.J. (2011) 'Influence of affective teacher–student relationships on students' school engagement and achievement: a meta-analytic approach', *Review of Educational Research,* 81: 493–529.

Roseth, C.J., Saltarelli, A.J. and Glass, C.R. (2011) 'Effects of face-to-face and computer mediated constructive controversy on social interdependence, motivation and achievement', *Journal of Educational Psychology,* 1–17.

Ryan, R.M. and Deci, E.L. (2000) 'Self-determination theory and the facilitation of intrinsic motivation, social development, and well-being', *American Psychologist,* 55: 68–78.

Ryan, R.M., Stiller, J.D. and Lynch, J.H. (1994) 'Representations of relationships to teachers, parents, and friends as predictors of academic motivation and self-esteem', *Journal of Early Adolescence,* 14: 226–249.

Saft, E.W. and Pianta, R.C. (2001) 'Teachers' perceptions of their relationships with students: effects of child age, gender, and ethnicity of teachers and children', *School Psychology Quarterly,* 16: 125–141.

Skinner, E.A. and Belmont, M.J. (1993) 'Motivation in the classroom: reciprocal effects of teacher behavior and student engagement across the school year', *Journal of Educational Psychology,* 85: 571–581.

Skinner, E.A., Furrer, C., Marchand, G. and Kindermann, T. (2008) 'Engagement and disaffection in the classroom: part of a larger motivational dynamic?', *Journal of Educational Psychology,* 100: 765–781.

Skinner, E.A., Kindermann, T.A., Connell, J.P. and Wellborn, J.G. (2009) 'Engagement as an organizational construct in the dynamics of motivational development', in K. Wentzel and A. Wigfield (eds), *Handbook of Motivation in School* (pp. 223–245), Mahwah, NJ: Erlbaum.

Skinner, E.A. and Pitzer, J.R. (2012) 'Developmental dynamics of student engagement, coping and everyday resilience', in S.L. Christenson, A.L. Reschly and C. Wylie (eds), *Handbook of Research on Student Engagement* (pp. 21–44). New York: Springer.

Skinner, E.A., Wellborn, J.G. and Connell, J.P. (1990) 'What it takes to do well in school and whether I've got it: the role of perceived control in children's engagement and school achievement', *Journal of Educational Psychology,* 82: 22–32.

Van Ryzin, M.J., Gravely, A.A. and Roseth, C.J. (2009) 'Autonomy, belongingness, and engagement in school as contributors to adolescent psychological well-being', *Journal of Youth Adolescence,* 38: 1–12.

Vansteenkiste, M., Lens, W. and Deci, E.L. (2006) 'Intrinsic versus extrinsic goal contents in self-determination theory: another look at the quality of academic motivation', *Educational Psychologist,* 41: 19-31.

Wentzel, K.R. (1997) 'Student motivation in middle school: the role of perceived pedagogical caring', *Journal of Educational Psychology,* 89: 411–419.

Wentzel, K.R. (1999) 'Social influences on school adjustment: commentary', *Educational Psychologist,* 34: 59–69.

Wentzel, K.R., Battle, A., Russell, S.L. and Looney, L. (2010) 'Social supports from teachers and peers as predictors of academic and social motivation', *Contemporary Educational Psychology,* 35: 193–202.

Wilcken, A.J. (2013) 'The role of relationship quality and relatedness to teachers in engagement and achievement in elementary and middle school: a longitudinal study', doctoral dissertation, available from MSU Library, Order Number 9781303060045 1303060043.

Wu, J.Y., Hughes, J.N., and Kwok, O.M. (2010) 'Teacher–student relationship quality type in elementary grades: effects on trajectories for achievement and engagement', *Journal of School Psychology,* 48: 357–387.

17

STUDENT–TEACHER RELATIONSHIPS AT THE TERTIARY LEVEL

Prevailing perspectives, existing research, and future possibilities

Mohamed Alansari

Often researchers talk about student–teacher relationships, or classroom relationships, as an integral part of the learning process. Relationships between students and their teachers have been shown to have a large effect on student achievement (Cohen's d = 0.72, Hattie 2012), and have become a focal point of educational research in the past few decades. Investigating classroom relationships is predicated on the premises that: (1) relationships are foundational to the classroom environment (Babad 2009); (2) these relationships can be conceptualized and measured against student outcomes (Hattie 2009; Moos 1979); and (3), fostering relationships could have a positive influence on student cognitive and affective outcomes at all education levels (Cornelius-White 2007; Kek and Huijser 2011).

Despite the belief that student–teacher relationships are important at all education levels (primary, secondary, or tertiary), there is a lack of empirical studies investigating these relationships at the post-secondary level. The lack of such studies is evident in a number of handbooks and literature reviews (Fraser *et al.* 2012; Freiberg 1999), where studies investigating classroom relationships at the tertiary level were outnumbered by studies investigating classroom relationships at the pre-tertiary level. One possible explanation for the relative void of research may be the difficulty associated with conceptualizing and measuring what constitutes a *relationship* in a post-secondary classroom setting. The current chapter unravels some of the challenges in conceptualizing tertiary student–teacher relationships, explores existing perspectives, and provides future research directions in that area.

Throughout this chapter, it is argued that the existing literature and theoretical frameworks on student–teacher relationships are not inclusive of studies exploring the relationship between tertiary students and their teachers. The chapter begins by exploring the nature of the tertiary learning environment, which has different characteristics from a pre-tertiary learning environment (e.g. a primary or secondary learning environment), and how tertiary classroom relationships are associated with a number of classroom outcomes such as teacher job satisfaction, student satisfaction, and student achievement. Next, this chapter discusses a number of theoretical frameworks used to conceptualize and assess student–teacher relationships, including a number of standardized measurement instruments and observational measures. Although the majority of the existing instruments were developed to measure classroom relationships at the pre-tertiary level, there is some overlap between the scales used at the secondary level and scales used at the tertiary level. Finally, this chapter concludes with recommendations for future research directions and practice, and puts forward a theoretical definition of tertiary classroom relationships for future empirical research.

Both quantitative and qualitative research methods have been employed in previous studies to examine the nature of student–teacher relationships. The majority of these studies have focused on students' perceptions of their relationships with their teachers or on how their relationships with their teachers have influenced their learning. Interestingly, what is common about most of these studies is the loosely defined, subjective view of what constitutes a relationship between students and their teachers. To start with, some students do not expect their actual classroom experiences to match what they would like them to be (e.g. they hope for a large amount of interactivity but do not expect it; Sander *et al.* 2000). Further, tertiary students and teachers often report differing views of how the teaching–learning practices taking place in their classrooms foster their relationships with each other (Fraser *et al.* 1996). Given such findings, it is worthwhile to define the notion and boundaries of the relationship between tertiary students and their teachers when such a relationship is understudied, yet has a great effect on the students' aspirations, learning beliefs and actions (Chepchieng *et al.* 2006).

The challenge

The challenge is for educational and social psychologists to put forward empirical evidence suggesting ways in which the term *relationships* can be conceptualized, validated, and measured at the tertiary level. Tertiary learning environments are rapid and complex because students attend multiple laboratories, tutorials, and lectures every day which vary in terms of class size, duration, subject, and teaching style. Moreover, Lage *et al.* (2000) argued that tertiary learning environments can be seen as 'inverted'. This means that learning practices that have traditionally taken place *inside* the classroom at the primary or secondary level (e.g. group work, class discussions, and learning assessments) now, at the tertiary level, take place *outside* the classroom, which limits student–teacher interaction and hence the feedback students receive on their learning (Wulff *et al.* 1987). Further, Trees and Jackson (2007) supported the argument that fostering positive student–teacher interactions in large tertiary classrooms introduces a set of pedagogical challenges for teachers to ensure students' active participation in these classrooms. Given the varying class sizes, durations, and seating arrangements of tertiary learning environments, the authors argued that 'even the most engaging lecture is limited in how much it can support and facilitate wide-spread student involvement and interaction' (Trees and Jackson 2007: 21).

At the same time, tertiary teachers are involved in a combination of teaching, tutoring, lecturing, and supervision throughout the academic year. In other words, there is as much variability in the nature of the learning environments that tertiary students experience as there is variability in the academic and occupational role of the teacher at that tertiary institution (Startup 1980). Therefore, one would suspect that the nature of the relationship between teachers, lecturers, tutors, or laboratory demonstrators and their students would differ from the one formed during previous years of education, especially given that tertiary classroom relationships are formed between teachers and students who are young adults. Therefore, the emphasis in tertiary relationships is likely to be more on regulating student higher-order thinking processes and how students construct knowledge (Tynjala 1999; Trees and Jackson 2007), and less on regulating student social behavior.

One way of looking at classroom relationships is by first identifying the dimensions by which a student–teacher relationship is defined. Initial conceptualization of such dimensions, or constructs, is often based on the investigators' intuitive understanding of the construct to be assessed (Fraser 1986). As a result, the degree to which the dimensions identified represent all facets of classroom relationships (i.e. content validity) depends heavily on the subjective opinions of the investigators and other experts. Conceptualizing classroom relationships also involves a close examination of the range of practices that could take place in tertiary learning environments which can then be observed and measured. The need for such a close examination is important because ideas and constructs used in pre-tertiary settings may not necessarily be relevant in tertiary learning environments, given the different contexts and teaching–learning practices in different education levels (Fraser 1998).

It must be noted here that the nature of student–teacher interactions could also vary according to the type of tertiary environment investigated (e.g. whether a lecture, tutorial, or laboratory environment is being investigated). Logan *et al.* (2006) attempted to validate a 'traditional' classroom environment instrument often used in secondary schools in a tertiary computer laboratory environment. As a result, the authors highlighted the unsatisfactory statistical performance (i.e. reliability) of the instrument, and discussed the appropriateness of some of the existing constructs used to capture the nature of student relationships with their teachers in tertiary environments and other nontraditional settings such as laboratories and classrooms with major online components. Moreover, they recommended closely examining the learning environment first, and designing a data collection instrument that reflected the nature of the environment second (Logan *et al.* 2006). Similar results were found by Newby and Fisher (1999) where the instruments used in their study to measure student perceptions of their relationship with peers and teachers were modified to suit the nature of the tertiary laboratory environment. Put simply, what we know about pre-tertiary education might not be enough to draw inferences on the nature and dynamics of student–teacher relationships at the post-secondary level.

What do we know about student–teacher relationships at the tertiary level?

Hattie's (2009, 2012) findings mentioned earlier were perhaps predictable – establishing positive relationships between tertiary students and teachers has the potential to foster students' sense of self-worth (Crossman 2007) and satisfaction (Moos 1976), and to increase classroom productivity (Walberg 1979), leading to increased feedback on performance (Booth 1997) and enhanced student outcomes. When interviewed, another sample of university students emphasized the importance of establishing well-grounded relationships with their teachers which allowed them to freely express their beliefs and feelings about learning in the classroom (Crossman 2007). This is further supported by Kek and Huijser's (2011) study that showed tertiary student outcomes such as achievement can be attributed to differences at the student and teacher level, including student–teacher interactions in the learning environment.

In another study by Bieber and Worley (2006), a total of 34 graduate students were interviewed about their university experiences and the positive aspects they could recall which supported their learning. Using a thematic analysis approach, the authors concluded that the experiences that were most memorable and most helpful for student learning were related to the socioemotional climate created in tertiary learning environments, the personal interactions they had with their teachers, and the availability of their teachers to respond to their questions. The authors concluded their study by suggesting that increasing interactions between students and the university teaching staff was an integral part of how students conceptualized the academic life at the university.

Other studies have also revealed positive associations between establishing warm student–teacher relationships and positive classroom outcomes, using samples of participants from different education levels (e.g. primary or secondary). For example, Smith (2013) analyzed self-report data from 267 students (218 secondary students and 49 tertiary students), and showed that perceived positive classroom relationships were significantly associated with higher levels of student satisfaction. Smith (2013) also showed that positive classroom relationships were significantly associated with higher levels of perceived sense of personal agency (i.e. an individual's sense of control of the direction of his or her life). Further, Tatar and Horenczyk (2003), using a sample of 135 teachers from 15 primary schools and 145 teachers from 15 secondary schools, showed that teacher-related factors such as teacher job satisfaction and teacher burnout can be attributed to the ways teachers perceive their relationship with their students (Tatar and Horenczyk 2003). Although the two studies mentioned above were in primary and secondary classrooms, they revealed similar patterns to the studies carried at the tertiary level where positive associations between student–teacher relationships and classroom outcomes were found (e.g. Bieber and Worley 2006; Crossman 2007; Booth 1997). Therefore, it would be worthwhile to investigate whether similar results would be found in tertiary learning environments.

Other empirical studies that have explored student views of their teachers' interpersonal behaviors have established positive and consistent links between the quality of the teacher–student relationships and student achievement and attitudes (Fraser and Walberg 2005). To date, however, the number of qualitative studies examining such patterns is minimal compared with the large number of quantitative studies (e.g. Fisher and Khine 2006; Goh and Khine 2002; Fraser 1989). Even fewer studies have attempted to improve classroom relationships using the feedback gained from exploring the existing teaching–learning practices in these classrooms. Exceptions include intervention studies by Sinclair and Fraser (2002) and Yarrow *et al.* (1997). Both studies, however, were carried out in pre-tertiary classroom settings (primary and middle school). Similar intervention studies have been carried out in secondary classrooms (Wubbels and Brekelmans 2005). The success of such pre-tertiary interventions suggests that similar interventions to improve tertiary classroom relationships may be of benefit to students. However, currently there is a paucity of research that explores teacher–student relationships in a tertiary setting.

Theoretical frameworks

The quest to identify a reflective model, or theoretical framework, to understand the mechanics of student–teacher relationships can be traced back to Moos and colleagues' research on social climates and interactive environments (Moos and Brownstein 1977; see also Moos and Insel 1974; Moos 1979). Moos introduced a three-dimensional framework in which relationships were presented as pivotal to the social climate of the classroom. These were: (1) the relationships dimension; (2) the personal growth dimension; and (3) the system maintenance dimension (see Table 17.1 for sample factors of each dimension with brief description).

The first dimension, relationships, focuses on the interpersonal relationships that take place in the classroom, how these are experienced by students and teachers, and how these relationships foster and contribute to the psychosocial atmosphere of the classroom. The second dimension, personal growth, focuses on student learning experiences in the classroom and how the teaching–learning practices foster students' academic development. Finally, the system maintenance dimension focuses on the managerial aspects of the classroom and how the executive role of the teacher assists the process of teaching and learning in that classroom. These definitions have largely been adapted from those presented by Babad (2009). Further, Moos and colleagues argued that the three dimensions are applicable to most classrooms in different grade levels at the pre-tertiary level (Moos and Brownstein 1977; Moos 1979). However, the influence of each dimension on the learning environment may differ by subject or the education level. That is, it may be that in primary-school learning environments there is more emphasis on the dimensions of system maintenance and relationships, whereas in secondary-school learning environments, the emphasis may be more on the personal growth and the relationships dimensions.

The development of many classroom climate instruments, as well as the variables to investigate when measuring relationships in that environment, has become dependent on Moos' dimensions of the classroom climate (Fraser 2002). Elton (1998) argued that establishing relationships is one of the

Table 17.1 Sample factors (with descriptions) of Moos' dimensions of the classroom climate

Factor	Dimension	Description
Cohesiveness	R	The overall sense of unity and cohesion of the classroom
Favoritism	R	The degree to which students are treated equitably or differentially in the classroom
Friction	R	Students' assessment of the atmosphere of tension in the classroom
Autonomy	PG	The extent to which students feel independent and 'free' in the classroom
Competitiveness	PG	The extent to which the classroom is designed to be competitive and to encourage academic competition
Task orientation	PG	The extent to which classroom tasks are performed with minimal interference and the teacher spends less time in nonacademic tasks
Teacher control	SM	The extent to which the teacher is successful in controlling the classroom effectively
Equity	SM	The extent to which students are treated equally by the teacher
Clarity	SM	The extent to which rules in the classroom are clear

Note: R = relationships, PG = personal growth, SM = system maintenance.

key competencies for excellent university teachers to demonstrate in the classroom alongside reflective practice, classroom organization, assessment, and evaluation competencies (for a discussion on effective university teaching, see Kane *et al.* 2004). As a result, classroom relationships are defined as the extent to which student interactions with peers and teachers contribute to their academic and personal development, as well as the extent to which students are involved in the environment and support each other (Fraser 1998). Fraser and Walberg (2005: 105) explained that the relationships dimension also involves 'the strength and type of personal relationships within an environment and the extent to which people are involved in the environment and help and support each other'.

Interestingly, the way in which classroom relationships have been defined seems to rely heavily on the methodological manner in which these relationships have been assessed. Quantitative researchers, for example, often rely on self-report data by students or teachers, or both, to infer the extent to which specific teaching–learning practices are fostering positive relations in the classroom (Babad 2009). In doing so, researchers often end up choosing a set of classroom behaviors, or processes, and argue that these are indicative of the nature of student relationships with their teachers. That is, the reported frequencies with which certain behaviors are taking place in a classroom are assumed to indicate whether positive or negative relationships are being fostered in that classroom. As a result, a wide variety of validated and robust instruments have been developed to measure classroom relationships (Fraser 1986) at various education levels (Fisher and Khine 2006; Goh and Khine 2002). Examples of well-established tertiary learning environment instruments are the College and University Classroom Environment Inventory (CUCEI, Nair and Fisher 2001); and the Science Laboratory Environment Inventory (SLEI, Fraser and McRobbie 1995). Examples of well-established secondary learning environment instruments include the Learning Environment Inventory (LEI, Walberg *et al.* 1977); the Classroom Environment Scale (CES, Moos and Trickett 1987); the Constructivist Learning Environment Survey (CLES, Taylor *et al.* 1997); and the What Is Happening in this Class questionnaire (WIHIC, Aldridge and Fraser 2000). At the primary school level, well-established learning environment instruments include the My Class Inventory (MCI, Fisher and Fraser 1981); and the Questionnaire on Teacher Interaction (QTI, also suitable for secondary classrooms; Fisher *et al.* 1995).

However, there is insufficient current literature on tertiary learning environments and student–teacher relationships in relation to (1) the basis on which some measures have been either chosen or discarded when researchers want to investigate relationships in tertiary classrooms, and (2) which measures constitute an appropriate set of measures that accurately reflect the nature of the relationship between tertiary students and their teachers. Den Brok and Levy's (2005) review of studies examining relationships in multicultural classes revealed a similar pattern where they considered the available literature on tertiary classroom relationships to be 'insufficient', with the majority of studies focusing on secondary classrooms. The authors argued that, in the studies they reviewed, there was a lack of information regarding the data collection instruments used. Den Brok and Levy (2005) further argued that the theoretical frameworks used to define and measure tertiary classroom relationships were unclear in the studies they reviewed.

Measuring relationships

Development of standardized measurement instruments (SMIs, Liu 2012) has received the attention of many researchers in education and psychology. However, one limitation of standardized measurement instruments is the standardization of the type and number of scales used to measure latent constructs of interest. It can be difficult to generate a set of items that uniquely measures a set of scales that reflect a latent, or unobservable, variable. This raises a debate on which scales to choose and which to drop from a standardized measurement instrument, and whether certain scales are more appropriate for one education level than for another.

Table 17.2 is adapted from Fraser's (1998, 2012) review of nine commonly used standardized measurement instruments, along with the education level each instrument was designed for; it also identifies the scales in each of the instruments used to measure classroom relationships. While there is some overlap in the scales used by the different instruments, and some overlaps in the learning level of each instrument, there is a lack of empirical evidence to argue for the differences in scales used by different instruments. For example, although teacher support is used is an indicator of student–teacher relationships at the secondary level (see the scales used in CES and WIHIC, Table 17.2), Smith (2013) argued that teacher support plays a significant role in how students' relationships with their teachers are formed even at the tertiary level. Therefore, one may argue that teacher support can also be used as an indicator of student–teacher relationships at the tertiary level. Table 17.2 also shows that the number of scales in each instrument ranges from one or two to as many as five, which raises the question of how many scales are required to reliably capture classroom relationships as a valid construct. Further, there seems to be an assumption that secondary and tertiary learning environments are similar, in that the scales used to measure tertiary classroom relationships are all replications of the scales used in the secondary classroom instruments. However, little is known about the similarities and differences between secondary and tertiary classroom climates, and whether secondary classroom climates are sufficiently similar to tertiary classroom climates for the standardized measurement instruments to be used interchangeably for both levels.

While some studies mentioned earlier focused on interaction as an important part of forming relationships, others have developed models in which the teacher is central to the formation of student–teacher relationships. For example, Wubbels and Brekelman (2012) presented a theoretical model in which relationships were seen as a function of interpersonal teacher behaviors, and depending on how such behaviors took place in classrooms, the resulting relationships would arguably differ. Research by Wubbels *et al.* (2006) on primary and secondary classroom relationships showed that classroom interactions could be analyzed on the basis of two dimensions that were controlled, or mainly driven, by the teacher: *proximity* and *influence*. Wubbels *et al.* (2006) established a structured observational measure enabling independent raters to observe and analyze classroom behaviors in terms of (1) the degree of

Table 17.2 Overview of survey instruments and scales designed to measure classroom relationships

Instrument	Level	Scales identified to measure classroom relationships
College and University Classroom Environment Inventory (CUCEI)	Tertiary	Personalization Involvement Cohesion Satisfaction
Science Laboratory Environment Inventory (SLEI)	Secondary/tertiary	Cohesion
Learning Environment Inventory (LEI)	Secondary	Cohesion Friction Favoritism Cliqueness Satisfaction Apathy
Classroom Environment Scale (CES)	Secondary	Involvement Affiliation Teacher support
Individualized Classroom Environment Questionnaire (ICEQ)	Secondary	Personalization Participation
Constructivist Learning Environment Survey (CLES)	Secondary	Personal relevance Uncertainty
What is Happening in This Classroom (WIHIC)	Secondary	Cohesion Teacher support Involvement
Questionnaire on Teacher Interaction (QTI)	Secondary/primary	Helpful/friendly Understanding Dissastisfied Admonishing
My Class Inventory (MCI)	Elementary	Cohesion Friction Satisfaction

closeness between teacher and students (proximity), ranging from cooperative to oppositional behaviors; and (2) the direction and frequency of communication between students and their teacher (influence), ranging from dominant to submissive teacher behaviors. In doing so, Wubbels and colleagues were able to identify patterns of student–teacher relationships based on the interpersonal teacher behaviors observed in that classroom (Wubbels and Brekelmans 1998). Identification of patterns of classroom relationships could then be used to identify potential areas of growth in classroom relationships, through addressing the relevant teacher behaviors that could be improved in that classroom.

Another major contribution to the current literature on learning environments and student–teacher relationships is Pianta's work on classroom interactions and processes (see Pianta and Hamre 2009). However, Pianta's work is concerned with pre-tertiary education only (i.e. early childhood to secondary levels). Through a theoretically and empirically supported framework, a standardized Classroom Assessment Scoring System (CLASS; see Pianta *et al.* 2008) was established as an observational measure of the global state of the classroom. The authors argued that the quality of classroom interactions could be observationally measured through a standardized, yet adjustable, scoring system to suit the nature of various primary and secondary classrooms. Pianta and Hamre (2009) argued that this was because, as students progressed through schooling, the amount of emotional and instructional support provided to these students may change. Therefore, an account of the changes needed to be reflected in the scoring system used. The CLASS instrument measures classroom processes by evaluating the degrees of instructional and emotional support, as well as the overall classroom organization. The model views relationships as an indicator of emotional support, and a function of how well teachers support students' socioemotional well-being in classrooms. Kane *et al.* (2004) further supported the argument that relationships can be seen as functions of specific teacher behaviors in the classroom, and that it is the 'person' of the teacher that will make a difference to how student and teacher relations are formed. Interestingly, although research into excellent tertiary teaching has been well documented in the literature (e.g. Elton 1998; Hativa *et al.* 2001; Horan 1991; McLean 2001), with many of these studies suggesting relationships as an important component of effective tertiary teaching and learning environments, less attention has been given to the study of how these relationships are formed, and how these relationships should be optimized to maximize student learning.

Conclusion

The theoretical, methodological, and empirical literature on student–teacher relationships discussed in this chapter provides a platform for future research directions and practice. The lack of mixed-method studies on student–teacher relationships at the tertiary level signals a need for future research to investigate how such relationships are formed, the ways in which these relationships are similar to or different from the ones formed at the pre-tertiary level, and the types of relationships that optimize student learning. Moreover, understanding how relationships are formed brings researchers and practitioners closer to understanding how these relationships can be improved. As mentioned earlier, there are few studies that have looked at how to use available data on student–teacher relationships to improve classroom teaching behaviors and tertiary learning environments. Feedback information collected through both quantitative and qualitative data collection instruments can be used to inform teachers of their current classroom practices, as well as how to improve these practices to enhance their relationship with their students (Fraser 2012).

It may be that researchers are deterred from exploring this area because of the difficulty in conceptualizing what constitutes a relationship at the tertiary level. However, as argued throughout this chapter, relationships can be measured and therefore defined in terms of the degrees of emotional and instructional support provided, as well as the interpersonal teacher behaviors which are visible and measurable in the classroom. Therefore, this chapter concludes by putting forward a theoretical definition of such relationships for future empirical research. Namely, tertiary classroom or student–teacher relationships are professional connections established by and between students and their teachers to optimize student outcomes. These connections are led by effective teachers who address students' academic needs and foster a positive climate in the classroom.

References

Aldridge, J. and Fraser, B. (2000) 'A cross-cultural study of classroom learning environments in Australia and Taiwan', *Learning Environments Research*, 3: 101–134.

Babad, E. (2009) *The Social Psychology of the Classroom*, New York: Routledge.

Bieber, J. and Worley, L. (2006) 'Conceptualizing the academic life: graduate students' perspectives', *Journal of Higher Education*, 77: 1009–1035.

Booth, A. (1997) 'Listening to students: experiences and expectations in the transition to a history degree', *Studies in Higher Education*, 22: 205–219.

Chepchieng, M., Mbugua, S. and Kariuki, M. (2006) 'University students' perception of lecturer–student relationships: a comparative study of public and private universities in Kenya', *Educational Research and Reviews*, 1: 80–84.

Cornelius-White, J. (2007) 'Learner-centred teacher–student relations are effective: a meta-analysis', *Review of Educational Research,* 77: 113–143.

Crossman, J. (2007) 'The role of relationships and emotions in student perceptions of learning and assessment', *Higher Education Research and Development,* 26: 313–327.

Den Brok, P. and Levy, J. (2005) 'Teacher–student relationships in multicultural classes: reviewing the past, preparing the future', *International Journal of Educational Research,* 43: 72–88.

Elton, L. (1998) 'Dimensions of excellence in university teaching', *International Journal for Academic Development,* 3: 3–11.

Fisher, D. and Fraser, B. (1981) 'Validity and use of My Class Inventory', *Science Education,* 65: 145–156.

Fisher, D., Henderson, D and Fraser, B. (1995) 'Interpersonal behaviour in senior high school biology classes', *Research in Science Education,* 25: 125–133.

Fisher, D. and Khine, M. (2006) *Contemporary Approaches to Research on Learning Environments: Worldviews,* London: World Scientific.

Fraser, B. (1986) *Classroom Environment,* London: Croom Helm.

Fraser, B. (1989) 'Twenty years of classroom climate work: progress and prospect', *Journal of Curriculum Studies,* 21: 307–327.

Fraser, B. (1998) 'Classroom environment instruments: development, validity and applications', *Learning Environments Research,* 1: 7–33.

Fraser, B. (2002) 'Learning environments research: yesterday, today and tomorrow,' in S.C. Goh and M.S. Khine (eds) *Studies in Educational Learning Environments: An International Perspective* (pp. 1–25), London: World Scientific.

Fraser, B. (2012) 'Classroom learning environments: retrospect, context and prospect', in B.J. Fraser, K. Tobin and C. McRobbie (eds) *Second International Handbook of Science Education* (pp. 1191–1239), Berlin: Springer.

Fraser, B., Fisher, D. and McRobbie, C. (1996, April) 'Development, validation and use of personal and class forms of a new classroom environment instrument', paper presented at the annual meeting of the American Educational Research Association, New York.

Fraser, B. and McRobbie, C. (1995) 'Science laboratory classroom environments at schools and universities: a cross-national study', *Educational Research and Evaluation,* 1: 289–317.

Fraser, B., Tobin, K. and McRobbie, C. (eds) (2012) *Second International Handbook of Science Education,* Berlin: Springer.

Fraser, B. and Walberg, H. (2005) 'Research on teacher–student relationships and learning environments: context, retrospect and prospect', *International Journal of Educational Research,* 43: 103–109.

Freiberg, J. (ed.) (1999) *School Climate: Measuring, Improving and Sustaining Healthy Learning Environments,* Philadelphia: Taylor & Francis.

Goh, S. and Khine, M. (Eds) (2002) *Studies in Educational Learning Environments: An International Perspective,* London: World Scientific.

Hativa, N., Barak, R. and Simhi, E. (2001) 'Exemplary university teachers: knowledge and beliefs regarding effective teaching dimensions and strategies', *The Journal of Higher Education,* 72: 669–729.

Hattie, J. (2009) *Visible Learning: A Synthesis of over 800 Meta-Analyses Relating to Achievement,* New York: Routledge.

Hattie, J. (2012) *Visible Learning for Teachers: Maximizing Impact on Learning,* London: Routledge.

Horan, M. (1991) *Attributed of Exemplary Community College Teachers: A Review of the Literature,* ERIC Document Reproduction Service No. ED 346 900.

Kane, R., Sandretto, S. and Heath, C. (2004) 'An investigation into excellent tertiary teaching: emphasising reflective practice', *Journal of Higher Education,* 47: 283–310.

Kek, M. and Huijser, H. (2011) 'Exploring the combined relationships of student and teacher factors on learning approaches and self-directed learning readiness at a Malaysian university', *Studies in Higher Education,* 36: 185–208.

Lage, M., Platt, G. and Treglia, M. (2000) 'Inverting the classroom: a gateway to creating an inclusive learning environment', *The Journal of Economic Education,* 31: 30–43.

Liu, X. (2012) 'Developing measurement instruments for science education research', in B.J. Fraser, K. Tobin and C. McRobbie (eds) *Second International Handbook of Science Education* (pp. 651–665), Berlin: Springer.

Logan, K., Crump, B. and Rennie, L. (2006) 'Measuring the computer classroom environment: lessons learned from using a new instrument', *Learning Environments Research,* 9: 67–93.

McLean, M. (2001) 'Rewarding teaching excellence: can we measure teaching "excellence"? Who should be the judge?', *Medical Teacher,* 23: 6–11.

Moos, R. (1976) 'Social environments of university student living groups: architectural and organizational correlates', *Environment and Behaviour*, 10: 109–126.

Moos, R. (1979) *Evaluating Educational Environments: Procedures, Measures, Findings and Policy Implications*, San Francisco: Jossey-Bass.

Moos, R. and Brownstein, R. (1977) *Environment and Utopia: A Synthesis*, New York: Plenum Press.

Moos, R. and Insel, P. (eds) (1974) *Issues in Social Ecology: Human Milieus*, Palo Alto, CA: National Press Books.

Moos, R. and Trickett, E. (1987) *Classroom Environment Scale Manual*, 2nd edn, Palo Alto, CA: Consulting Psychologists Press.

Nair, S. and Fisher, D. (2001) 'Learning environments and student attitudes to science at the senior secondary and tertiary levels', *Issues in Educational Research*, 11: 12–31.

Newby, M. and Fisher, D. (1999) 'A model of the relationship between university computer laboratory environment and student outcomes', *Learning Environments Research*, 3: 51–66.

Pianta, R.C. and Hamre, B.K. (2009) 'Conceptualization, measurement, and improvement of classroom processes: standardized observation can leverage capacity', *Educational Researcher*, 38: 109–119.

Pianta, R.C., La Paro, K. and Hamre, B.K. (2008) *Classroom Assessment Scoring System* (CLASS), Baltimore, MD: Paul H. Brookes.

Sander, P., Stevenson, K., King, M. and Coates, D. (2000) 'University students' expectations of teaching', *Studies in Higher Education*, 25: 309–323.

Sinclair, B. and Fraser, B. (2002) 'Changing classroom environments in urban middle schools', *Learning Environments Research*, 5: 301–328.

Smith, P. (2013) 'Psychosocial learning environments and the mediating effect of personal meaning upon satisfaction with education', *Learning Environments Research*, 16: 259–280.

Startup, R. (1980) *The University Teacher and His World: A Sociological and Educational Study*, Brookfield, VT: Renouf.

Tatar, M. and Horenczyk, G. (2003) 'Diversity-related burnout among teachers', *Teaching and Teacher Education*, 19: 397–408.

Taylor, P., Fraser, B. and Fisher, D. (1997) 'Monitoring constructivist classroom learning environments', *International Journal of Educational Research*, 27: 293–302.

Trees, A. and Jackson, M. (2007) 'The learning environment in clicker classrooms: student processes of learning and involvement in large university-level courses using student response systems', *Learning, Media and Technology*, 32: 21–40.

Tynjala, P. (1999) 'Towards expert knowledge? A comparison between a constructivist and a traditional learning environment in the university', *International Journal of Educational Research*, 31: 357–442.

Walberg, H. (ed.) (1979) *Educational Environments and Effects: Evaluation, Policy, and Productivity*, Berkeley, CA: McCutchan.

Walberg, H., Singh, R. and Rasher, S. (1977) 'Predictive validity of student perceptions: a cross-cultural replication', *American Educational Research Journal*, 14: 45–49.

Wubbels, T. and Brekelmans, M. (1998) 'The teacher factor in the social climate of the classroom', in B.J. Fraser and K.G. Tobin (eds) *International Handbook of Science Education* (pp. 565–580), Dordrecht, The Netherlands: Kluwer.

Wubbels, T. and Brekelmans, M. (2005) 'Two decades of research on teacher–student relationships in class', *International Journal of Educational Research*, 43: 6–24.

Wubbels, T. and Brekelmans, M. (2012) 'Teacher–students relationships in the classroom', in B.J. Fraser, K. Tobin and C. McRobbie (eds) *Second International Handbook of Science Education* (pp. 1241–1255), Berlin: Springer.

Wubbels, T., Brekelmans, M., den Brok, P. and van Tartwijk, J. (2006) 'An interpersonal perspective on classroom management in secondary classrooms in the Netherlands', in C. Evertson and C. Weinstein (eds) *Handbook of Classroom Management: Research, Practice, and Contemporary Issues* (pp. 1161–1191), Mahwah, NJ: Lawrence Erlbaum Associates.

Wulff, D.H., Nyquist, J.D. and Abbott, R.D. (1987) 'Students' perceptions of large classes', in M. Weirner (ed.) *New Directions for Teaching and Learning: Teaching Large Classes Well* (pp. 17–30), San Francisco: Jossey-Bass.

Yarrow, A., Millwater, J. and Fraser, B. (1997) 'Improving university and primary school classroom environments through preservice teachers' action research', *International Journal of Practical Experiences in Professional Education*, 1: 68–93.

18

PERCEPTUAL BARRIERS TO TEACHER–STUDENT RELATIONSHIPS

Overcoming them now and in the future

Maureen E. Brinkworth and Hunter Gehlbach

Scholars have developed a rich literature describing the qualities of positive teacher–student relationships and the factors that contribute to their development (see Davis 2003; Pianta *et al.* 2003 for reviews). These studies often focus on the facilitators of positive teacher–student relationships, frequently trying to identify mechanisms that could be applied in classrooms to improve them (e.g. Driscoll *et al.* 2011; Gehlbach *et al.* 2012a; Helker *et al.* 2007; Murray and Malmgren 2005; Pianta *et al.* 2002).

This chapter examines teacher–student relationships from a slightly different perspective. Rather than focusing on what might be added to promote positive relationships, we focus on barriers that could be removed to facilitate these relationships. To this end, we review the social psychological scholarship on perceptual biases; specifically, the most pervasive biases which are likely to impede the development of positive teacher–student relationships. After discussing these biases, we offer some steps that scholars and practitioners could take to overcome them.

Although many barriers can impede positive teacher–student relationships, we focus on perceptual biases for two reasons: first, because biases afflict all teachers and students, and research identifying means of attenuating them has the potential to improve most teacher–student relationships; second, because teachers and students perceive one another so often, effective interventions to mitigate harmful biases might be deployed hundreds of times per day.

Genres of biases

Within social cognition – that is, 'the process by which people think about and make sense of people' (Fiske 1995: 151) – scholars have rapidly accumulated knowledge about perceivers' conscious and unconscious motivations. Although we are typically motivated to accurately understand others in our social world, this primary goal can be derailed by one of two competing motives (Gehlbach and Brinkworth 2008).

The first of these competing motives is efficiency. As perceivers, we attempt to understand others quickly, without equivocating. Thus, we subconsciously seek to minimize the cognitive effort involved in understanding our social world; that is, we are all 'cognitive misers' (Fiske 1995: 153). The resultant mental processing has been identified by Kahneman (2011) as System

1 thinking. Automatic, rapid, associative, and affective, System 1 processing is 'thinking fast'. By contrast, when System 2 is activated, people think slowly, deductively, and deliberatively. System 2 thinking provides a check on the intuitive conclusions drawn by System 1. Thinking fast (while avoiding labor-intensive System 2 mental processing) facilitates our adaptation to a complex world. Not surprisingly, System 1 can be tremendously adaptive in educational contexts. Teachers are regularly confronted with classrooms containing dozens of students. In these settings, they cannot carefully consider each student's behavior, language, and personal history while simultaneously exposing students to important content and checking every student's understanding of that content. Thus, teachers and students often avoid complex thinking in favor of shortcuts such as stereotyping (Andre *et al.* 1999; Chang and Demyan 2007; Helwig *et al.* 2001) and the fundamental attribution error (Ross *et al.* 1977), which comprise the first two focal biases that we discuss in this chapter.

Second, in addition to saving cognitive energy, individuals strive to maintain positive perceptions of themselves (Dunning 1999; Greenwald and Pratkanis 1984). To uphold their self-esteem, individuals often maintain and project a public 'self' that is cohesive and consistent to avoid experiencing cognitive dissonance. Festinger (1962) theorized that cognitive dissonance – holding two conflicting cognitions simultaneously – creates feelings of unpleasant arousal. Awareness of these inconsistent cognitions, particularly regarding assessments of one's goodness, may threaten a person's sense of cohesiveness. In classrooms, one particular approach to rationalizing dissonance can be especially problematic. Teachers and students often organize their perceptions of one another into working theories about the other party. At some point, they usually encounter evidence that contradicts these working theories. However, to incorporate this new evidence would require acknowledging that their theory about the other person was wrong – thereby causing uncomfortable cognitive dissonance and threatening their self-esteem. Confirmation bias, people's tendency to develop these theories and cling to them despite contradicting evidence, is our third focal bias in this chapter.

In sum, although we generally try to perceive others as they really are, this motivation may be superseded by a need to think efficiently or to protect one's sense of self (Gehlbach and Brinkworth 2008). Given the complexities of person perception in most classrooms, these ulterior perceptual motivations likely act as barriers to teacher–student relationships. Although we limit our discussion to stereotyping, the fundamental attribution error, and confirmation bias, we hope that this framework offers a lens through which to view a wide array of other biases that might affect teacher–student relationships.

Bias 1: Stereotyping

In perceiving others, stereotyping is a primary cognitive labor-saving strategy. Through stereotyping, individuals categorize and sort complex stimuli into groups, thereby facilitating the mental processing of large numbers of perceptual targets. Though this is considered one of the most essential cognitive processes individuals engage in (Allport 1979/1954), stereotyping often leads to problematic oversimplification.

Stereotypes are commonly understood to be the beliefs individuals have about the attributes of other groups of people. Jussim *et al.* (1995) note that stereotypes can be positive or negative, accurate or inaccurate. However, stereotypes also tend to be over-generalized and resistant to change (Katz and Bialy 1933). These shortcuts are invaluable when people encounter new individuals. They allow people to quickly categorize a person in gross terms (whether they are male or female, large or small, different or the same race as me, and so on) and apply knowledge about the whole group to which that individual belongs. By activating one's associative memory, a person can apply these categorizations and, through System 1 processing, rapidly make the intuitive judgments and assumptions that follow (Morewedge and Kahneman 2010).

However, stereotyping has negative consequences as well. Often people identify others as 'like us' or 'not like us' and form in-groups and out-groups accordingly (Devine 1995). People tend to view their in-group as relatively diverse and more favorable than corresponding out-groups (Devine 1995; Turner *et al.* 1979). Several studies have demonstrated that, given even the smallest excuse to think of themselves as a group, people often do so and then exhibit in-group bias (Billig and Tajfel 1973; Brewer and Silver 1978; Galinsky and Moskowitz 2000). In the more extreme cases, identification of in- and out-groups can lead to an *us versus them* mentality. That such a mentality might develop in classrooms is particularly worrisome given that teachers and students will inevitably see themselves as members of distinct groups. This can easily affect not only the classroom climate but also individual relationships between teachers and students.

When it comes to teacher–student relationships, stereotyping can be a difficult barrier for teachers and students. The most destructive instances of stereotyping can lead to prejudice and differential treatment in the classroom. These practices can profoundly affect how students feel about school and their teachers. Research on discrimination indicates that ethnic minority youth perceive disproportionate levels of harsh discipline and unfair grading compared to their non-minority counterparts (Fisher *et al.* 2000). Students who perceive race or gender discrimination exhibit greater behavior problems and less interest in school (Graham *et al.* 2006). Given evidence that both teachers and students consider respect and fairness to be essential components of positive teacher–student relationships (Brinkworth 2010; Goodman 2009; Wentzel 2002), experiences of prejudice and disrespect undoubtedly jeopardize the prospects for healthy relationships. Unsurprisingly, students who experience prejudice typically feel a diminished sense of belonging in school, perform less well academically, and are at great risk of dropping out of school (Fine 1991).

Though prejudice and discrimination are important problems to consider, stereotyping may affect teacher–student relationships through additional pathways as well. An important aspect of nurturing teacher–student relationships is developing positive affect between teachers and students. To build positive affect with young people, teachers need to express a genuine interest in knowing them personally. Students feel more cared for by teachers who treat them as individuals and express interest in their well-being inside and outside of the classroom (Ferreira and Bosworth 2001; Garza 2009; Muller 2001). By stereotyping a student, teachers may presume to know more about the student than they actually do. Moreover, they will be unlikely to take advantage of opportunities to revise their beliefs about the student (Katz and Braly 1933). This process could work in the opposite direction (i.e. students stereotyping their teachers) just as easily. Regardless of the direction in which it occurs, the presumption of knowing the other party better than one actually does will infuse psychological distance into the relationship – particularly when those presumptions are inaccurate.

In sum, although categorizing and stereotyping perform the essential task of simplifying our social cognitions, they often lead to problematic biases in the classroom. At its most deleterious, stereotyping can result in prejudice and discrimination and can profoundly damage students' attitudes towards school and their teacher–student relationships. However, even in less severe cases, stereotyping may inhibit teachers and students from developing accurate, authentic pictures of each other and may infuse psychological distance into their relationships. Under these conditions, the teacher–student relationships that develop are likely to be lower quality.

Bias 2: Fundamental attribution error

Another bias that can affect teacher–student relationships is the 'fundamental attribution error'. This error occurs as perceivers try to discern what caused an individual of interest to behave in a particular way. Perceivers typically overemphasize the importance of a target's dispositions in explaining that person's behavior. At the same time, individuals tend to underestimate the relative influence of contextual factors (Ross *et al.* 1977). Committing this error can affect teacher–student relationships through multiple pathways.

One problematic pathway is students and teachers misperceiving underlying causes in each other's communications. For instance, Coren (1993) found that students commit the fundamental attribution error when considering information taught in class. After reading scenarios in which a professor delivers content about genetic influences on intelligence and cognitive skills, students tended to attribute the information in the lecture to the educator's beliefs (e.g. that he or she is racist or sexist), rather than the content being part of a standard curriculum (Coren 1993). Such a failure to separate the message from the messenger could have problematic consequences. Students' mistaking factual or objective information for their teacher's personal opinions or beliefs could create inaccurate perceptions that damage teacher–student relationships.

To illustrate the wide range of communication problems the fundamental attribution error can create, first imagine a context of students receiving feedback from their teachers. If students receive numerous corrections from their teachers on an essay that took hours of hard work, the fundamental attribution error may lead to misperceptions that the comments indicate teacher harshness, pessimism, or a lack of caring. In this scenario, the teacher likely feels that he or she is merely enacting his or her role, holding high expectations for students, and providing feedback to promote learning. Given many ways in which teachers provide feedback to students (written, spoken, or nonverbal), inaccurate attributions in these contexts could have a widespread influence on students' perceptions of their teacher. In this way, the fundamental attribution error can lead to misunderstandings which cause psychological distance that can inhibit teacher–student relationships.

A second pathway through which the fundamental attribution error may affect teacher–student relationships is by leading teachers and students to develop inaccurate profiles of each other when trying to understand each other's behavior. For instance, a teacher committing the fundamental attribution error will fail to account for contextual factors that could influence students' behavior and, instead, misattribute that behavior to something intrinsic to the student. As a result, the teacher may develop a potentially inaccurate 'character sketch' of the student. For example, a teacher might erroneously assume that a student is irresponsible and lazy based on repeated late arrivals to class. Yet, these attributions would likely differ if the teacher knew that the student had to care for a younger sibling every morning before arriving. In this example, the fundamental attribution error again causes an overemphasis on dispositional factors and an underappreciation of situational factors, but it also helps shape a negative narrative about the student's character.

This misattribution process could happen for students just as easily. For instance, students might attribute a teacher's decision to spend large portions of class time on standardized test preparation to a lack of creativity, ignoring the situational pressures teachers face to raise test scores. In sum, the fundamental attribution error is likely to lead to faulty character sketches that would cause teachers and students to overestimate the degree to which they actually know each other. The resultant strain on interactions that this misperception would generate will likely cause problems for teacher–student relationships.

The final pathway through which the fundamental attribution error could negatively affect teacher–student relationships involves teachers' assessments of their students' academic abilities and motivation. As a core aspect of their profession, teachers regularly assess students' learning. Though these assessments are intended to indicate students' abilities and work ethic, many contextual factors can play a role in the work that students produce. Due to the fundamental attribution error, a teacher may assume that a student's work on any given assignment or test represents the student's best effort and ability. If the teacher fails to appreciate situational factors

that influence the quality of the work, then he or she may view the student as lacking competence, intelligence, or motivation. Teachers do, in fact, tend to attribute students' serious classroom
problems to internal factors such as intelligence, motivation, and personality before family/home
factors or teaching variables (Medway 1979). Such views of students strain teacher–student relationships. Medway found that teachers provided significantly more negative feedback and
criticism to students when they attributed the students' problems to a lack of effort or motivation.
Given that adolescents who perceive more negative feedback or criticism from their teachers
tend to engage in significantly less prosocial behavior (Wentzel 2002) and are more likely to cause
discipline problems (Murdock 1999), the fundamental attribution error may be particularly problematic for the development of positive teacher–student relationships.

In sum, the fundamental attribution error represents a difficult challenge for developing
teacher–student relationships. When teachers and students attribute each other's actions disproportionately to dispositional factors, it will be more difficult for them to understand each other
accurately. First, students and teachers may misinterpret the degree to which the other party's
statements actually represent that party's beliefs or values. Second, the fundamental attribution
error may lead teachers and students to develop inaccurate character profiles when they misattribute each other's behaviors. Third, teachers may develop faulty views of their students' abilities
and motivation because of attributions that fail to appreciate the contextual factors that may
affect students' work. In combination, these three pathways represent serious impediments to
teachers and students developing positive relationships.

Bias 3: Confirmation bias

Confirmation bias is a heuristic that not only aids in conserving cognitive energy but also helps
to maintain one's self-image as a sensible, consistent person. When people commit confirmation
bias they selectively seek evidence that confirms their pet theories. Simultaneously, confirmation
bias causes people subconsciously to discredit, ignore, misinterpret, or undervalue evidence that
might challenge or disconfirm their theories (Myers 2007; Wason 1960). This System 1 process
often occurs seamlessly as individuals' brains make information that is consistent with their
theories more accessible and easier to activate than other information (Morewedge and
Kahneman 2010). In other words, individuals automatically develop theories about people in
their social environments and then selectively attend to, encode, store, and retrieve information
that reinforces those theories.

Conformation bias can affect teacher–student relationships through its influence on teachers'
expectations of and, subsequently, behaviors towards students. Rosenthal and Jacobson's (1968)
seminal work on self-fulfilling prophecies in the classroom illustrates how confirmation bias can
play an integral role in teachers' interactions with their students. In the classic Pygmalion experiment, teachers were falsely told that a select group of students was on the brink of making a big
academic leap during the coming year. This information provided teachers with a 'theory' about
their students that they could seek to confirm, discredit, or ignore during their work throughout
the school year. The results of the original study as well as follow-ups (e.g. Jussim and Eccles
1992) indicated that teachers confirmed the theory they were given about the students whom
they had been told were poised to make great academic progress. The teachers created a better
academic climate for these students, taught them more, gave them more opportunities to respond
in class, and provided them with higher-quality feedback than other students (Rosenthal 2002).
In the end, in their attempts to confirm their theory, the teachers behaved in ways that led the
selected students to perform better than students in the control group. Following this research, a
number of studies have established that teacher expectation effects are associated with differential

treatment of students (Brophy and Good 1970, 1972; Raudenbush 1984). Thus, if teachers develop negative theories or expectations about their students, confirmation bias may lead them to engage with the students in ways that may create self-fulfilling prophecies and undermine the health of their teacher–student relationships.

In addition to influencing teachers' behaviors, confirmation bias might affect teacher–student relationships simply by making it more difficult for teachers and students to alter negative views they develop about each other. For instance, a teacher may form an impression of a student who disrupts the class repeatedly at the beginning of the school year as disrespectful or uninterested in learning. Once that theory takes root, the teacher may look less favorably upon the student even after the student has improved his or her behavior. For example, if the student raises his or her hand feverishly during class, the teacher might see a signal that the student is again attempting to disrupt the class rather than seeing that the student has finally engaged in the content. Because of confirmation bias, it is unlikely that the teacher's relationship with the student would improve despite the student's shift toward more positive classroom behavior.

Finally, confirmation bias can affect teacher–student relationships by intensifying the strength and effect of other biases. In this way, confirmation bias can be viewed as a sort of 'booster shot' bias. For instance, when confirmation bias combines with stereotyping, teachers or students committing the stereotyping are likely to become even more convinced of their judgments, given the bounty of confirming evidence and dearth of disconfirming evidence that they perceive. Given the achievement gap in many countries between majority and non-majority students, teachers may develop stereotypes that non-majority students will be lower achieving, resulting in teachers having lower expectations for those students (Alexander *et al.* 1987; Dusek and Joseph 1983; Ferguson 2003; Muller 1997). The teacher may attend to information and behave differently when engaging with the stereotyped students in order to confirm the original theory.

In a series of meta-analyses, Tenenbaum and Ruck (2007) found that teachers not only had more positive expectations of European American children than African American and Latino/a children but they also spoke to them more positively and made more positive and fewer negative referrals for them. In a classroom where the teacher stereotypes students in this way and succumbs to confirmation bias, that teacher may interpret greater engagement from their European American students as a sign of greater intellectual curiosity. The teacher may also ignore how his or her own tendency to provide those students with more positive feedback could instigate the greater motivation. Thus, it appears that negative stereotypes combined with confirmation bias can easily lead to differential treatment that can affect teacher–student engagement and students' learning.

Although our discussion of confirmation bias has focused on teachers, students can just as easily succumb to this error. Through parallel processes, students' theories may influence the way they attend to and process information about their teachers, which may, in turn, affect their behavior towards their teachers. In addition, students are just as likely as teachers to stereotype the other party and allow those stereotypes to be reinforced by confirmation bias. In each of these ways, the negative consequences of confirmation bias that can act as a barrier for teacher–student relationships have the potential to influence these relationships from both the teacher and student sides.

Overcoming perceptual biases through perspective taking

We conclude this chapter by presenting ideas of how scholars and educational practitioners might collaborate to improve teacher–student relationships through ameliorating perceptual biases. Our discussion of stereotyping, the fundamental attribution error, and confirmation bias illustrates how person perception can play a critical role in teacher–student relationships. A growing literature on social perspective taking – how individuals discern the thoughts, feelings, and motivations of others (Gehlbach *et al.* 2012b) – suggests three routes through which social perspective taking might enhance teacher–student relationships.

First, interventions might be developed to bolster teachers and students social perspective-taking motivation (Gehlbach *et al.* 2012b). In other words, by encouraging students and teachers to engage in the perspective-taking process more frequently, fewer misunderstandings may arise; when miscommunications do occur, each party may try harder to give one another the benefit of the doubt. Second, teachers and students could be taught skills and strategies to improve their perspective-taking abilities (Gehlbach and Brinkworth 2012). By enhancing the accuracy with which each party perceives the other, more sensitively calibrated interactions with the other party might ensue (Galinsky and Moskowitz 2000). However, a third pathway also exists in which individuals could enhance their social perspective-taking accuracy without actually improving their underlying ability. Analogous to test-taking strategies that help students avoid making careless errors, teaching teachers and students to identify and counteract biases could help improve teacher–student relationships. We focus our discussion on exploring this third opportunity: using social perspective taking as a lever through which to mitigate biases between teachers and students, thereby improving their relationships.

The social perspective-taking literature provides initial indications that certain social perspective-taking approaches can diminish the ill-effects of stereotyping. When Galinsky and Moskowitz (2000) induced participants to take the perspective of others by writing a brief essay about 'a day in the life' of another person, they found that social perspective taking leads to a decrease in stereotypic thinking. Vescio *et al.* (2003) also found that getting subjects to engage in perspective taking reduced prejudice and improved attitudes towards a frequently stereotyped out-group. So how might future research test ways to see if these approaches can help teachers and students perceive each other more accurately and improve their teacher–student relationships?

Galinsky and Moskowitz (2000) as well as Ames (2004) suggest that when individuals perceive themselves and others as having overlapping, similar characteristics, the tendency to stereotype is reduced. Thus, teachers may wish to go out of their way early in the year to identify qualities that they have in common with their students (e.g. a 'get-to-know-you' survey) and potentially share that information with their students. Scholars could evaluate a practice like this one through field experiments that investigate whether certain types of similarities are more important than others, whether learning about dissimilar beliefs and values is detrimental, and whether this practice alters teachers' and students' perceptions of which individuals constitute their 'in-group'.

Initial research also suggests that certain social perspective-taking approaches might help mitigate the fundamental attribution error. For instance, certain cognitive styles or systems of thought seem to give rise to the fundamental attribution error more than others. Specifically, the Chinese locate causality in situational factors to a greater degree than Americans (Morris and Peng 1994). Nisbett *et al.* (2001) attribute this to the cognitive style that is nurtured in East Asian societies. Unlike those raised in Western societies, East Asians are taught to perceive their social world by paying more attention to the situation than the actor (Nisbett *et al.* 2001).

Thus, retraining teachers' and students' attributions so that they make more situational inferences could diminish the number of fundamental attribution errors in Western classrooms and teacher–student relationships might be enhanced. Fortunately, there is evidence that shifting the cognitive style of perceivers can be accomplished through practice (Stewart *et al.* 2010). Thus, future researchers might design and test professional development sessions that train teachers using similar approaches to training attributions, though presumably using classroom-based examples. As a complementary activity, teachers (particularly in social studies or literature classes) might experiment with encouraging their students to develop a disposition to always think through ways in which the situation may have caused someone (a historical figure or a protagonist) to behave in the way they did. As teachers develop techniques they think are effective, they can collaborate with researchers to test them experimentally.

One social perspective-taking strategy that has proven successful in helping individuals to make more accurate social inferences has been to consider alternative possibilities or explanations. This approach seems like a particularly promising strategy for helping people overcome the pitfalls of confirmation bias. For instance, in asking subjects to 'consider the opposite', Lord *et al.* (1984) found that they made less-biased social judgments. Liberman *et al.* (2012) found similarly promising reductions in bias by asking subjects to work with a peer (i.e. take into account another perspective) before making their social judgments. However, future research needs to ascertain whether these approaches to reducing bias in social judgments can be applied to the classroom to improve teacher–student relationships.

Other social perspective-taking strategies could be applied to classroom settings and utilized in field experiments as well. Building on the 'wisdom of dyads' idea (Liberman *et al.* 2012), participants in Gehlbach and Brinkworth's study (2012) reported that they employed a *conferring* strategy to take the perspective of others. In other words, subjects reported that they often tried to take the perspective of a focal individual by speaking to a third party (who might be a trusted friend or might be someone who knows the focal individual) to get a different perspective on this person of interest. One way this idea could be operationalized in a school setting is to match a teacher who is trying to improve his or her relationship with a particular student with a 'naïve' colleague who does not know the student in question. The goal of this discussion would be for the naïve teachers to provide their partners with a series of alternative hypotheses or theories about why the student in question was behaving as he or she was. Researchers could then assess whether teachers who participated in this intervention were more willing to entertain alternative explanations of the student's behavior (i.e. engaged in less confirmation bias) and ultimately began to get along better with the focal student. A peer mediation/counseling program could be used to test a similar intervention for students who had strained relationships with particular teachers.

Conclusion

The goal of this chapter was two-fold. First, we sought to describe three of the many perceptual biases that act as barriers to the development of strong, positive teacher–student relationships. We discussed these errors of person perception in light of two motivations that underlie our social cognitions: cognitive efficiency and protecting one's sense of self. Second, we sought to identify ideas for researchers and practitioners to overcome these biases in the future. Though more research in classrooms is needed, we believe that social perspective taking offers tremendous promise as a tool to ameliorate these and other perceptual biases that interfere with the development of teacher–student relationships. It is our hope that the present discussion will instigate future research to evaluate the efficacy of perspective taking as a way to reduce bias in these relationships. The implications of such work would present an exciting next step in the scholarship on interventions for teacher–student relationships.

References

Alexander, K.L., Entwisle, D.R. and Thompson, M.S. (1987) 'School performance, status relations, and the structure of sentiment: bringing the teacher back in', *American Sociological Review*, 52: 665–682.

Allport, G.W. (1979/1954) *The Nature of Prejudice*, Reading, MA: Addison-Wesley.

Ames, D. (2004) 'Inside the mind-reader's toolkit: projection and stereotyping in mental state inference', *Journal of Personality and Social Psychology*, 87: 340–353.

Andre, T., Whigham, M., Hendrickson, A. and Chambers, S. (1999) 'Competency beliefs, positive affect, and gender stereotypes of elementary students and their parents about science versus other school subjects', *Journal of Research in Science Teaching*, 36: 719–747.

Billig, M. and Tajfel, H. (1973) 'Social categorization and similarity in intergroup behaviour', *European Journal of Social Psychology*, 3: 27–52.

Brewer, M.B. and Silver, M. (1978) 'Ingroup bias a function of task characteristics', *European Journal of Social Psychology*, 8: 393–400.

Brinkworth, M.E. (2010, April/May) 'Relatedness in secondary schools: what motivates the development of teacher–student relationships?' Paper presented at the annual meeting of the *American Educational Research Association*, Denver, CO.

Brophy, J.E. and Good, T.L. (1970) 'Teachers' communication of differential expectations for children's classroom performance: some behavioral data', *Journal of Educational Psychology*, 61: 365–374.

Brophy, J.E. and Good, T.L. (1972) 'Teacher expectations: beyond the Pygmalion controversy', *Phi Delta Kappan*, 54: 276–278.

Chang, D.F. and Demyan, A.L. (2007) 'Teachers' stereotypes of Asian, Black, and White students', *School Psychology Quarterly*, 22: 91–114.

Coren, S. (1993) 'When teaching is evaluated on political grounds', *Academic Questions*, 6: 73.

Davis, H.A. (2003) 'Conceptualizing the role and influence of student–teacher relationships on children's social and cognitive development', *Educational Psychologist*, 38: 207–234.

Devine, P. (1995) 'Prejudice and out-group perception', in A. Tesser (ed.) *Advanced Social Psychology* (pp. 466–524), New York: McGraw-Hill.

Driscoll, K.C., Wang, L., Mashburn, A.J. and Pianta, R.C. (2011) 'Fostering supportive teacher–child relationships: intervention implementation in a state-funded preschool program', *Early Education and Development*, 22: 593–619.

Dunning, D. (1999) 'A newer look: motivated social cognition and the schematic representation of social concepts', *Psychological Inquiry*, 10: 1.

Dusek, J.B. and Joseph, G. (1983) 'The bases of teacher expectancies: a meta-analysis', *Journal of Educational Psychology*, 75: 327–346.

Ferguson, R.F. (2003) 'Teachers' perceptions and expectations and the Black–White test score gap', *Urban Education*, 38: 460–507.

Ferreira, M.M. and Bosworth, K. (2001) 'Defining caring teachers: adolescents' perspectives', *Journal of Classroom Interaction*, 36: 24–30.

Festinger, L. (1962) 'Cognitive dissonance', *Scientific American*, 207: 93–107.

Fine, M. (1991) *Framing Dropouts: Notes on the Politics of an Urban Public High School*, Albany, NY: State University of New York Press.

Fisher, C.B., Wallace, S.A. and Fenton, R.E. (2000) 'Discrimination distress during adolescence', *Journal of Youth and Adolescence*, 29: 679–695.

Fiske, S.T. (1995) 'Social cognition', in A. Tesser (ed.) *Advanced Social Psychology* (pp. 145–194), New York: McGraw-Hill.

Galinsky, A.D. and Moskowitz, G.B. (2000) 'Perspective-taking: decreasing stereotype expression, stereotype accessibility, and in-group favoritism', *Journal of Personality and Social Psychology*, 78: 708–724.

Garza, R. (2009) 'Latino and white high school students' perceptions of caring behaviors: are we culturally responsive to our students?', *Urban Education*, 44: 297–321.

Gehlbach, H. and Brinkworth, M.E. (2008) 'Motivated thinkers and the mistakes they make: the goals underlying social cognitions and their consequences for achievement', in M.L. Maehr, S. Karabenick and T. Urdan (eds) *Advances in Motivation and Achievement: Social Psychological Perspective on Motivation and Achievement* (pp. 119–144), Bingley, UK: Emerald.

Gehlbach, H. and Brinkworth, M.E. (2012) 'The social perspective taking process: strategies and sources of evidence in taking another's perspective', *Teachers College Record*, 114.

Gehlbach, H., Brinkworth, M.E. and Harris, A.D. (2012a) 'Changes in teacher–student relationships', *British Journal of Educational Psychology*, 82: 690–704.

Gehlbach, H., Brinkworth, M.E. and Wang, M.-T. (2012b) 'The social perspective taking process: what motivates individuals to take another's perspective?', *Teachers College Record*, 114: 1–29.

Goodman, J.F. (2009) 'Respect-due and respect-earned: negotiating student–teacher relationships', *Ethics and Education*, 4: 3–17.

Graham, S., Bellmore, A. and Mize, J. (2006) 'Peer victimization, aggression, and their co-occurrence in middle school: pathways to adjustment problems', *Journal of Abnormal Child Psychology*, 34: 349–364.

Greenwald, A. and Pratkanis, A. (1984) 'The self', in R.S. Wyer, and T.K. Srull (eds) *Handbook of Social Cognition* (pp. 129–178), Hillsdale, NJ: Erlbaum.

Helker, W.P., Schottelkorb, A.A. and Ray, D. (2007) 'Helping students and teachers connect: an intervention model for school counselors', *Journal of Professional Counseling: Practice, Theory and Research*, 35: 31–45.

Helwig, R., Anderson, L. and Tindal, G. (2001) 'Influence of elementary student gender on teachers' perceptions of mathematics achievement', *The Journal of Educational Research*, 95: 93–102.

Jussim, L. and Eccles, J.S. (1992) 'Teacher expectations II: construction and reflection of student achievement', *Journal of Personality and Social Psychology*, 63: 947–961.

Jussim, L.J., McCauley, C.R. and Lee, Y.-T. (1995) 'Why study stereotype accuracy and inaccuracy?', in Y.-T. Lee, L.J. Jussim and C.R. McCauley (eds) *Stereotype Accuracy: Toward Appreciating Group Differences* (pp. 3–27), Washington, DC: American Psychological Association.

Kahneman, D. (2011) *Thinking, Fast and Slow*, New York: Farrar, Straus and Giroux.

Katz, D. and Braly, K. (1933) 'Racial stereotypes of one hundred college students', *The Journal of Abnormal and Social Psychology*, 28: 280–290.

Liberman, V., Minson, J.A., Bryan, C.J. and Ross, L. (2012) 'Naïve realism and capturing the "wisdom of dyads"', *Journal of Experimental Social Psychology*, 48: 507–512.

Lord, C.G., Lepper, M.R. and Preston, E. (1984) 'Considering the opposite: a corrective strategy for social judgment', *Journal of Personality and Social Psychology*, 47: 1231–1243.

Medway, F.J. (1979) 'Causal attributions for school-related problems: teacher perceptions and teacher feedback', *Journal of Educational Psychology*, 71: 809–818.

Morewedge, C.K. and Kahneman, D. (2010) 'Associative processes in intuitive judgment', *Trends in Cognitive Sciences*, 14: 435–440.

Morris, M.W. and Peng, K. (1994) 'Culture and cause: American and Chinese attributions for social and physical events', *Journal of Personality and Social Psychology*, 67: 949–971.

Muller, C. (1997) 'The minimum competency exam requirement, teachers' and students' expectations and academic performance', *Social Psychology of Education*, 2: 199–216.

Muller, C. (2001) 'The role of caring in the teacher-student relationship for at-risk students', *Sociological Inquiry*, 71: 241–255.

Murdock, T.B. (1999) 'The social context of risk: status and motivational predictors of alienation in middle school', *Journal of Educational Psychology*, 91: 62–75.

Murray, C. and Malmgren, K. (2005) 'Implementing a teacher–student relationship program in a high-poverty urban school: effects on social, emotional, and academic adjustment and lessons learned', *Journal of School Psychology*, 43: 137–152.

Myers, D.G. (2007) *Exploring Social Psychology*, New York: McGraw-Hill.

Nisbett, R.E., Peng, K., Choi, I. and Norenzayan, A. (2001) 'Culture and systems of thought: holistic versus analytic cognition', *Psychological Review*, 108: 291–310.

Pianta, R.C., Hamre, B. and Stuhlman, M. (2003) 'Relationships between teachers and children', in W.M. Reynolds and G.E. Miller (eds) *Handbook of Psychology: Educational Psychology* (pp. 199–234), Hoboken, NJ: John Wiley.

Pianta, R.C., Stuhlman, M.W. and Hamre, B.K. (2002) 'How schools can do better: fostering stronger connections between teachers and students', in J.E. Rhodes (ed.) *A Critical View of Youth Mentoring* (pp. 91–107), San Francisco, CA: Jossey-Bass.

Raudenbush, S.W. (1984) 'Magnitude of teacher expectancy effects on pupil IQ as a function of the credibility of expectancy induction: a synthesis of findings from 18 experiments', *Meta-analysis of Research*, 76: 85–97.

Rosenthal, R. (2002) 'The Pygmalion effect and its mediating mechanisms', in J. Aronson (ed.) *Improving Academic Achievement: Impact of Psychological Factors on Education* (pp. 3–21), San Diego, CA: Academic Press.

Rosenthal, R. and Jacobson, L. (1968) *Pygmalion in the Classroom: Teacher Expectation and Pupils' Intellectual Development*, New York: Holt Rinehart & Winston.

Ross, L., Amabile, T.M. and Steinmetz, J.L. (1977) 'Social roles, social control, and biases in social-perception processes', *Journal of Personality and Social Psychology*, 35: 485–494.

Stewart, T.L., Latu, I.M., Kawakami, K. and Myers, A.C. (2010) 'Consider the situation: reducing automatic stereotyping through situational attribution training', *Journal of Experimental Social Psychology*, 46: 221–225.

Tenenbaum, H.R. and Ruck, M.D. (2007) 'Are teachers' expectations different for racial minority than for European American students? A meta-analysis', *Journal of Educational Psychology*, 99: 253–273.

Turner, J.C., Brown, R.J. and Tajfel, H. (1979) 'Social comparison and group interest ingroup favouritism', *European Journal of Social Psychology,* 9: 187–204.

Vescio, T.K., Sechrist, G.B. and Paolucci, M.P. (2003) 'Perspective taking and prejudice reduction: the mediational role of empathy arousal and situational attributions', *European Journal of Social Psychology,* 33: 455–472.

Wason, P.C. (1960) 'On the failure to eliminate hypotheses in a conceptual task', *The Quarterly Journal of Experimental Psychology,* 12: 129–140.

Wentzel, K.R. (2002) 'Are effective teachers like good parents? Teaching styles and student adjustment in early adolescence', *Child Development,* 73: 287.

19

SOCIAL WITHDRAWAL AND SCHOOLING

Michael Townsend and Pamela Seccombe

The term 'socially withdrawn' appears well understood if judged by its everyday use. Teachers need only a moment's reflection to answer, if asked, whether there are any socially withdrawn children in their classroom, typically identifying a single child or two. Parents, too, appear to have a common understanding of which children in their child's preschool, classroom, or birthday party group are socially withdrawn. These judgments are typically made with relative certainty, common agreement, and little or no discussion of the criteria being applied. But this apparent ease in the application of the term in our everyday social lives stands in marked contrast to the complexity that characterizes research on social withdrawal. A feature of this complexity, discussed in the first section of this chapter, is the large number of subtypes of social withdrawal that can seem overwhelming to parents and teachers concerned about the behavior of a specific child. With the identification of two major subtypes of social withdrawal, shyness and unsociability, the authors then address the important role of social relationships in development and learning, and the evidence of long-term effects of reduced participation in these relationships. Consistent with the social psychological theme of this book, we then examine the classroom practices of teachers; a theme of this section is that the current pedagogical emphasis on classrooms as 'communities' of learners' has encouraged teaching and learning strategies that rely on social interaction techniques that may mitigate some of the effects of social withdrawal. Notwithstanding this possible schooling effect, the chapter then provides some examples of intervention practices, from simple and covert to systematic and directed, available to parents and teachers. The chapter concludes with some cautions about the limits of our understanding of social withdrawal.

The complexity of social withdrawal

Much of the complexity just noted stems from a confusing array of overlapping terms or concepts that elude a single definition with conceptual certainty. One attempt to capture and organize this complexity is the development by Coplan and Rubin (2010) of a taxonomy of 'solitude' (defined as 'being alone in the presence of others') consisting of more than 30 terms related to social withdrawal found in the research literature. Some understanding of the complexity can be seen in a random selection of the included terms: active isolation, passive withdrawal, behavioral inhibition, conflicted shyness, social wariness, solitropy, anxious withdrawal, and peer neglect. The taxonomy is not intended to be an exhaustive list of terms associated with social withdrawal, and readers will be aware of other common terms that are not included in the taxonomy such as coy, timid, diffident, nervous, uneasy, sensitive, and so on. Rather, the purpose of the taxonomy is to demonstrate that underlying the large number of descriptors of social withdrawal there are two motivational or causal processes associated with being alone near others.

Being alone in the presence of others may stem from an external source outside the child, which the authors call active isolation, or an internal source called social withdrawal. Active isolation includes solitude resulting from active peer exclusion, neglect, or rejection. Research has shown that active isolation by peers is frequently a response to a child's overt or externalizing behaviors, lack of social skills, or their socially unacceptable behaviors of aggression and bullying (Nicholson and Townsend 2011; Rubin *et al.* 2006; Townsend 1993). Because such children often draw the attention of others, they are easily recognized by parents and teachers. Social withdrawal, on the other hand, occurs when children remove themselves from social interaction. These children, the subjects of this chapter, are described as having covert or internalizing behavior problems that frequently take longer to recognize, if at all, and are far less likely to be referred for outside assistance than children with externalizing problems (Kauffman and Landrum 2009).

In the taxonomy just noted, children are motivated to withdraw from social situations for one of two reasons. One reason is that they are fearful or wary of being with others in social situations, (we commonly refer to such children as shy, inhibited, anxious, or hovering), which may be an adaptive response to a combination of biological low tolerance for stimulation (Gray and McNaughton 2000) and early experiences of rejection and neglect (Smillie 2008). However, another motive for social withdrawal is simply a preference for being alone, called unsociability or social disinterest. This may also have both a biological and an experiential basis. Unsociable children have been found to have a high temperamental attention span which is associated with a preference for objects rather than people (Coplan and Armer 2007). They may also have had less exposure in their early years to parental modeling and support of behaviors that develop peer relationships. This motivational distinction between shyness and unsociability is explored in this chapter.

The definitional problems just noted make it difficult to estimate the prevalence of social withdrawal. For example, although Zimbardo (1977) found that more than 90 percent of the population have reported experiencing shyness at some time in their lives, more recent estimates are somewhat lower. A diagnostic interview study involving over 10,000 adolescents in the United States found that 62 percent of parents thought their children shy, and this reduced to a self-reported shyness rate of 47 percent among the adolescents themselves (Burnstein *et al.* 2011). The study also reported that only 8 percent of the adolescents met the clinical criteria for 'social phobia', an extreme form of social withdrawal resulting from active isolation. Social phobia increased across ages 13 to 18 but was unrelated to gender, while shyness remained relatively steady across age but was more common in females than males. In a recent Finnish study, Puuraa *et al.* (2010) reported that clinically significant social withdrawal in infants was lower than 3 percent. Within the limits of the definitional problems previously outlined, and the various estimates of shyness just mentioned, it would not be unreasonable for a teacher to assume that in any given classroom there will be two or three students whose social and intellectual development is at some degree of risk from social withdrawal.

The need for social relationships

The importance of social withdrawal to parents and teachers stems from our understanding that the development of any child is dependent on the child's interrelationships with other children. This understanding was explicit in Plato's 'academy' model of schooling in ancient Greece where students (boys only!) were specifically engaged in interactive discussions, perhaps a precursor of the currently popular concept of 'co-constructed learning', and in later Roman models of schooling where Quintilian was an advocate for the inclusion of play activities for young children. However, systematic empirical investigations of the importance of child interrelationships did not begin until the early twentieth century. For example, Charles Cooley's (1902) observations of children at play led him to identify the play group as a 'primary' source of development of the 'looking-glass' model of self-perception and socialization, while Jean Piaget (1926, 1932) concluded from his studies of children that interaction with others is essential in social, moral and intellectual development. From his work on mental illness and loneliness, together with childhood experience of social isolation, the psychiatrist Harry Sullivan (1953) developed an interpersonal theory of mental health in which childhood relationships, particularly those which foster acceptance, are critical for personality development. These early studies were the forerunners of the rapid growth of research over the past 40 years on the effect of social relationships in development and in learning (Asher and Gottman 1981; Asher et al. 1977; Asher and Renshaw 1981; Beaty 2014; Deci and Ryan 1985; Rubin and Asendorpf 1993; Rubin et al. 2006; Rubin and Coplan 2010; Rubin et al. 1989; Ryan and Ladd 2012).

A corollary of the understanding that development is critically influenced by social relationships is that any form of social withdrawal may be a threat to development. Early observational research confirmed this association, especially after the publication of Parten's (1932) taxonomy of sociability which identified several types of withdrawn (nonsocial) behavior in group situations such as unoccupied, onlooking (hovering), and solitary play. Such behaviors had already attracted the attention of researchers in education concerned with the effects of withdrawn behavior on school performance. For example, Dealey (1923) summarized the case histories of 38 children aged 5 to 9 years who were 'misfits' at school, three-quarters of whom were described as timid and/or sensitive. This timidity or super-sensitivity was especially evident in first-born children who were often described as having a very affectionate disposition (i.e. those whom teachers recognize as 'clingy' children), leading Dealey to suggest that parents had given insufficient attention to their older children on the birth of younger siblings. While this remains plausible, Dealey's conclusion that the poor adjustment of these 38 children was largely caused by parental 'extreme ignorance in the most fundamental rules of child training' (1923: 132) seems harsh in the light of more recent research indicating a possible biological or temperamental component of social withdrawal (e.g. Corr 2008).

Teachers, too, attracted criticism from Dealey on two grounds. First, even children recognized by teachers as 'not dull' were still believed to be incapable of achieving at the level of average children. Second, teachers' reports revealed that more than 20 percent of the children were being taught by teachers who actively disliked them. Dealey's concern that these factors may bias a teacher's interactions with the child was prescient of a landmark study almost half a century later which showed that student learning could be influenced by experimentally manipulating the teachers' beliefs about the abilities of the students they taught (Rosenthal and Jacobson 1968). It was this finding that precipitated the more recent research confirming a similar effect for naturally occurring teacher expectations (Jussim et al. 2009; Rubie-Davies et al. 2007). A recent study, for example, found that a negative expectation bias by teachers at the end of primary school predicted lower educational performance five years later (de Boer et al. 2010). To anticipate an issue discussed later in this chapter, it is important that research explore whether teachers hold different beliefs for shy and unsociable children's ability, motivation, and personality, and whether these differences affect the learning and development of the children in the classroom.

Given our current understanding of the importance of social relationships in development generally, as well as within classroom contexts, it seems surprising that research on the effects of social withdrawal was not pursued more vigorously during the middle part of the twentieth century. It has been argued (Coplan and Rubin 2010) that during this time, enthusiasm for research on social withdrawal was affected by the view that it was of limited developmental significance. This conclusion followed research indicating that social withdrawal was both relatively unstable in childhood and not significantly associated with adjustment difficulties in later adolescence and adulthood (Kohlberg *et al.*1972; Robins 1966). Even recently, some researchers have noted that some unsociable behaviors in early childhood settings do not appear to be related to long-term psychosocial maladjustment (Arbeau and Coplan 2007).

The apparent dismissal of the significance of social withdrawal in the past may have been inadvertently reinforced by the classroom teaching practices of the time. It is likely that concern with social relationships in classrooms would have been less likely during a time of relatively rigid, didactic teaching methods (such as rehearsal of multiplication tables, spelling lists, the periodic table, and so on) that discouraged in-class student interaction, and by a curriculum that focused on the absorption and reproduction of prescribed 'factual knowledge' that was both impersonal and relatively unquestioned. It is perhaps no coincidence that the recent resurgence of research interest in social relationships in classrooms has been paralleled by advances in our understanding of how learners construct their own knowledge, particularly within social and cultural frameworks (Vygotsky 1978). This emphasis is captured in common terms heard in today's schools where children are described as 'communities of learners' who interact to produce 'co-constructed knowledge'. This understanding has, in turn, resulted in the development of group-focused teaching strategies such as cooperative learning (Johnson and Johnson 1989; Slavin and Cooper 1999), collaborative discussion (Zhang *et al.* 2013), collaborative reasoning (Fung *et al.* 2008), and reciprocal teaching (Palincsar and Brown 1984; Williams 2011), which have implications for socially withdrawn children because these strategies facilitate group interaction and mutual support to enhance both intellectual and social development in children. Cooperative learning, for example, specifically teaches skills of social interaction that enable children to work together in ways that ensure their classmates gain success in order to gain success themselves. This results in greater inclusion and acceptance of other children, as well as increasing school achievement, motivation to learn, and enjoyment of school (Anderman and Anderman 2014; Jacques *et al.* 1998; Piercy *et al.* 2002).

Effects of social withdrawal

The question of whether childhood social withdrawal has significant long-term effects is of great concern to both parents and teachers. Social isolation can be both a cause and a symptom of disturbed development. Difficulties in interacting in the social world can create an escalating pattern of behaviors that increase isolation, while isolation itself may be an indicator of developmental or psychological health problems such as loneliness or depression. In non-human social species, social isolation is also associated with a range of life-threatening biological outcomes, including reduced lifespan, increased obesity, susceptibility to Type 2 diabetes, and decreased survival of strokes (Cacioppo and Hawkley 2009).

In our current understanding, there is little doubt that social withdrawal can affect both learning and development, particularly for children who are shy or fearful of social interaction. At school, such children may underachieve and show slower language development than their classmates (Evans 2010) as well as experience greater loneliness, depression, and lower self-esteem, which may later find expression in greater substance abuse and antisocial behaviors (Goodwin *et al.* 2004; Marchant *et. al.* 2007; Rubin *et al.* 2010). In one of the relatively rare longitudinal studies of social withdrawal, New Zealand children classified as inhibited at age 3 were characterized more than twenty years later as less socially affiliative, less ambitious, and taking less pleasure in life than other children (Caspi *et al.* 2003; Caspi and Silva 1995).

As noted earlier, a distinction may be drawn between social withdrawal motivated by shyness or fear, and withdrawal motivated by social disinterest (the 'unsociable' child). This difference is easily identifiable, and at a relatively early age. Both kindergarten teachers (Arbeau and Coplan 2007) and children as young as 7 years (Galanaki 2004) are able to distinguish between shy and unsociable children. The shy child, sometimes described as being conflicted between a high social-approach motivation (a desire to be part of the group) and a high social-avoidance motivation (a fear of the group's response), has attracted greater research interest than the unsociable child (Coplan *et al.* 2013) and is more at risk for the outcomes noted above. The unsociable child, on the other hand, although generally affable in the school context and 'socially competent in almost every respect' (Harrist *et al.* 1997: 291), represents a distinct and recognizable form of social withdrawal in which the child prefers solitude but is not resistant to engagement with peers if the circumstances demand it. It is likely that this generally higher level of social competence, together with an acceptance that everyone can benefit from some 'time out' on occasions, has resulted in unsociability being seen as a more benign problem than shyness thus attracting both less research and less concern from teachers and parents. However, the risk remains that frequent loss of social interaction through unsociability may not only result in fewer opportunities to profit from interactions that are vital in the development of language, self-esteem, perspective taking, and the like, but may also become self-sustaining as peers make fewer efforts to include the unsociable child. This suggests that if increased social interaction depends on the willingness of peers to interact socially with the withdrawn child, the shy child may be at less risk than the unsociable child with increasing age.

The role of teachers

In considering the effects of social withdrawal, it is important to consider the role of teachers. As noted earlier, teachers inevitably form beliefs and expectations associated with the children they teach as they interact with them. These beliefs and expectations may cause teachers to act in ways that 'confirm' the beliefs and expectations in the children through a 'self-fulfilling prophecy' of which the teachers may not be aware. (For an interesting discussion of how unconscious processes may affect our behavior, see Mlodinow 2012.) In the original study of teacher expectations (Rosenthal and Jacobson 1968), randomly selected children 'over-achieved' by the end of the school year relative to similar-ability peers when teachers were falsely led to believe that the selected children in the new class were about to 'bloom'. Later research confirmed that teachers behave differently with children for whom they hold different expectations (Jussim *et al.* 2009). For example, a teacher may intervene early to provide assistance to a low-expectation child working on a problem but not to a high-expectation child, thus reducing the personal learning opportunity for the low-expectation child (confirming to the child that he or she lacks the ability to achieve alone, thus influencing the child's effort in future similar activities) and, simultaneously, allowing greater opportunity for the high-expectation child to achieve without assistance (confirming the child's ability). Thus, the expectations of the teachers become self-fulfilling in the performance of the students.

Teacher expectations and behaviors may differ for different kinds of social withdrawal. We might expect, for example, that teachers would be relatively 'warmer' toward shy children who are typically quiet and well-behaved, and 'colder' toward unsociable children who appear less in need of social comfort. This possibility was examined in a study of 200 female kindergarten teachers' beliefs about shy and unsociable children (as well as prosocial and aggressive children, excluded here) (Arbeau and Coplan 2007). These teachers were found to have a 'sophisticated awareness' (311) of fine-grained distinctions between shy and unsociable children which favored the unsociable child. Relative to the shy child, teachers were more tolerant, perceived lower academic and social costs associated with their withdrawal, and were less likely to recommend intervention to increase social interaction for the unsociable child. In particular, the social costs for shy children were seen as being on par with those for aggressive children. These beliefs were influenced by the gender of the child. Shyness was seen as more problematic for boys than girls with the consequence that direct intervention with social skills training was more likely to be recommended for boys.

Are such distinctions and associated beliefs about shyness and unsociability evident in teachers of older children? We explored this question with experienced elementary-school teachers in New Zealand who read one of four vignettes in which a male or a female child was reluctant to participate with peers in class and group activities (Seccombe and Townsend 2013). The vignettes were identical and contained no reference to the cause of the reluctant behavior except for the final sentence, which described the child as 'preferring not to join in with social activities *but doesn't seem anxious when* [he/she] *does so*' (unsociable), or 'preferring not to join in with social activities *and seems anxious when* [he/she] *does so*' (shy). The study used questions similar to those used by Arbeau and Coplan (2007) about the likely causes and the academic and social costs, but also asked teachers to suggest interventions for the child. In addition, teachers in the study rated how likely each of 18 personality adjectives applied to the child in the vignette. These ratings, when taken across both shy and unsociable children, suggested a positive and not unexpected view of socially withdrawn children as intelligent, self-controlled and capable, yet somewhat lacking in assertiveness, self-confidence, and cooperation. However, teachers also differentiated between shy and unsociable children, particularly in relation to gender. For example, the shy female was considered the most intelligent and the most likely to achieve success in school and career, while the unsociable female was rated lowest on these features. Again, although teachers rated self-confidence higher in unsociable children than shy children, this was particularly positive for the unsociable male child. Similarly, the unsociable child was perceived as more resilient than the shy child, especially if male.

An interesting pattern of results emerged when the highest and lowest mean scores for each *withdrawal type* × *gender* group on the eighteen adjectives were examined. These mean scores are shown in Figure 19.1. As may be seen, the great majority (14 of 18) of highest mean scores were shared by the shy female child (8) and the unsociable male child (6), while all but one of the lowest mean scores (17 of 18) were shared by the shy male child (10) and the unsociable female child (7), indicating that teachers were most positive about the shy female and unsociable male child. These results were also supported in teachers' ratings of the academic and social costs of withdrawal. Although teachers perceived greater social costs than academic costs of social withdrawal, especially for shy children, the shy female child was seen as most risk of academic underperformance, while the shy male child was seen as having greater risk associated with social development. As suggested at the beginning of this chapter, teachers frequently reported having taught a child like the one in the vignette, or of having been such a child themselves, and showed an extensive knowledge of strategies or resources to use with socially withdrawn children. The teachers also indicated a responsibility toward these children, to build a 'strong bond' or 'personal relationship' or 'a relationship of trust' and to 'always look at myself first – what have/haven't I done to create a safe classroom culture'. Perhaps paradoxically, the teachers had moderate agreement with the view that the cause of social withdrawal was in the child's nature, yet also agreed that the child may simply be going through a stage and that the social withdrawal was likely to change. Finally, the teachers in this study were positive about the potential for socially withdrawn children to be successful, and were strongly accepting of them: 'Some children are quiet [but are] happy and enjoy school' (female/unsociable); 'Lots of children are like this, and it's okay if they're okay with it' (female/shy); 'Do we all have to be social people? Can't people be different? He may be just an observer of life' (male/unsociable); and 'generally they are perfectly happy children

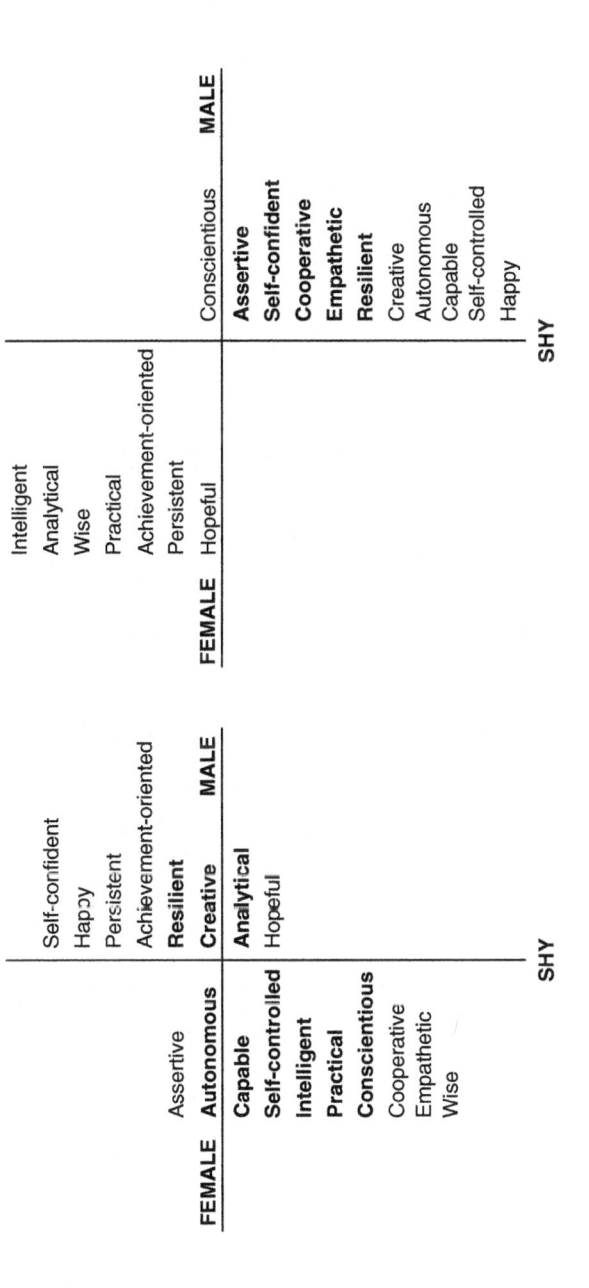

Figure 19.1 Highest and lowest mean scores for ratings of adjectives for types of social withdrawal and gender.

who develop close friendships with one or two others ... as part of their personality trait [and are] quite confident within themselves' (female/unsociable).

Although these results are based on imaginary children, they indicate that teachers both differentiate between shy and unsociable children and hold different beliefs and expectations about these children. If further research was to confirm these results with actual children in classrooms, it would signal a need for greater understanding of the effects of social withdrawal, particularly the long-term consequences of unsociability, about which little is known, before consideration is given to intervention.

Intervention and social withdrawal

It is likely that a teacher or parent who suspects that their child is socially withdrawn will ask several questions: How serious is this problem? Will it affect the long-term development of the child? What can I do to help? Parents may also ask about the cause of the withdrawal, reflecting their concern that they may have contributed to the problem. Unfortunately these questions cannot be answered with certainty. As noted earlier in this chapter, there are some enduring negative effects associated with social withdrawal, particularly withdrawal associated with shyness (Evans, 2001). However, even where effects are known, such as increased loneliness, reduced academic performance, and lower self-esteem, we know little about the magnitude of these effects, or the point at which, for example, a degree of loneliness passes from the normal range to being a problem that needs to be addressed (clinically diagnosed psychopathology such as social phobia excepted). If shyness represents, at least in part, behavioral inhibition caused by a biologically lower tolerance for stimulation (that such children reach social overload or saturation earlier than others) then a lower level of social interaction for a shy child may be just as 'normal' or 'comfortable' as is a slower walking speed for older people. As such, no intervention may be warranted. Nor can we say with any certainty which among the many existing intervention approaches will be most effective. These difficulties of identification and intervention are even more pronounced for unsociable children, a group that has received only a fraction of the research devoted to shy children.

Notwithstanding these problems, researchers typically err on the side of caution, noting the need to provide some form of intervention for children showing early signs of anxious or withdrawn behavior (Asendorpf 2010). A review by Evans (2010) provides an extensive review of simple strategies and suggestions that parents and teachers might use with younger children in ways that do not draw attention to the child. In classrooms, for example, teachers might minimize stress and embarrassment by avoiding direct questions to the withdrawn child during full-class discussions, emphasizing to the class that it is okay to make mistakes, and inconspicuously offering praise to the withdrawn child in a way that links their accomplishment to underlying competence. These same strategies, along with support and encouragement, can easily be adopted by parents within normal family interactions.

For older children and adolescents with symptoms of anxiety disorders, Mychailyszyn *et al.* (2010) provide an overview of the common techniques underlying more overt intervention programs. These include direct social skills training in common social tasks such as making a personal introduction, joining a conversation, or expressing an emotion such as pleasure at group success; psycho-education about the interconnectedness between thoughts, feelings, and behaviors, and how to monitor the symptoms of anxiety; cognitive restructuring which teaches children how to replace negative, anxious thoughts about an experience with more rational alternatives through reflection, decatastrophizing, and reframing; relaxation training of breathing and muscles designed to allow a child to regain a sense of control; and exposure tasks (desensitization) in which children gradually face their fears of anxiety-producing situations they might otherwise avoid (such as school examinations). The authors also provide a description and explanation of a number of commercial intervention programs, along with research evidence of treatment outcomes.

Summary and conclusions

Most children follow normal patterns of social development that allow them to lead successful and fulfilling lives, while a small minority of children exhibit social behavioral problems that put them at some risk of psychological maladjustment. Of this group, those with externalizing behaviors such as bullying and volatility are easily recognized as 'squeaky wheels' and frequently referred for assistance. But those who are socially withdrawn, who do not 'make waves', are often unrecognized or ignored. Within this group, a relatively large and growing research literature has indicated that both shy and unsociable children may be at significant developmental risk with implications for psychological health, school performance, and societal acceptance, as discussed here.

This chapter has suggested that both teachers and parents are rightfully concerned about the learning and development of socially withdrawn children. They are also skillful at differentiating children who are shy from those who are unsociable. Parents can be reassured that current teaching practices create many opportunities for meaningful social interaction during learning that help to mitigate some of the problematic effects of social withdrawal. These practices and opportunities are in the hands of a generation of teachers who are well informed of both the presence and consequences of holding inappropriate, differential expectations for the children they teach. At the same time, teachers and parents have relatively easy access to strategies they can implement themselves (many of which can be found online) and professional programs that can ameliorate problems associated with social withdrawal.

However, some cautions are in order. Our existing knowledge about social withdrawal is made complex by definitional ambiguity, an array of competing and sometimes overlapping terms, and studies that are extremely varied in terms of their populations, methodologies, behaviors of interest, duration, and theoretical underpinnings. Even where we recognize a shy or unsociable child, we have little ability to predict whether the child will experience developmental problems, what those problems will be, how serious the problems are, how long those problems will persist, whether we should intervene, and how much difference an intervention will make. The research evidence suggests that unsociable children have social competencies that may reduce their risk of academic and social risk. But even for shy children who are potentially at greater risk, the relationship between shyness and academic performance is modest at best (Evans 2010) and that many, perhaps the majority, will either outgrow their early shyness, or develop coping strategies (such as using a rehearsed social patter when meeting people, or selecting an occupation that minimizes social interaction) that allow them to lead relatively normal lives. Research on social withdrawal is rich in potential for changing lives but in some ways may still be a literature in search of a purpose. This may lie in connecting social withdrawal more directly with some of the major social problems facing education: underachievement, bullying, alienation, maladaptive motivation, internet overuse, school dropout, and youth suicide.

References

Anderman, E.M. and Anderman, L.H. (2014) *Classroom Motivation*, 2nd edn, Boston: Pearson.
Arbeau, K. and Coplan, R. (2007) 'Kindergarten teachers' beliefs and responses to hypothetical prosocial, asocial, and antisocial children', *Merrill-Palmer Quarterly: Journal of Developmental Psychology*, 53: 291–318.

Asendorpf, J.B. (2010) 'Language performance, academic performance, and signs of shyness', in K. Rubin and R. Coplan (eds), *The Development of Shyness and Social Withdrawal* (pp. 157–178), New York: Guilford Press.

Asher, S.R. and Gottman, J.M. (1981) *The Development of Children's Friendships*, New York: Cambridge University Press.

Asher, S.R., Oden, S.L. and Gottman, J.M. (1977) 'Children's friendships in school settings', in L.G. Katz (ed.), *Current Topics in Early Childhood Education* (Vol. 1, pp. 33–61), Norwood, NJ: Ablex.

Asher, S.R. and Renshaw, P.D. (1981) 'Children without friends: social knowledge and social skill training', in S. Asher and J. Gottman (eds), *The Development of Children's Friendships* (pp. 273–296), New York: Cambridge University Press.

Beaty, J.J. (2014) *Observing Development of the Young Child*, 8th edn, Boston: Pearson.

Burnstein, M., Ameli-Grillon, L. and Marikangas, R. (2011) 'Shyness versus social phobia in US youth', *Pediatrics*, 128: 917–925.

Cacioppo, J.T. and Hawkley, L.C. (2009) 'Perceived social isolates and cognition', *Trends in Cognitive Science*, 13: 447–454.

Caspi, A., Harrington, H., Milne, B., Amell, J., Theodore, R. and Moffitt, T. (2003) 'Children's behavioral styles at age 3 are linked to their adult personality traits at age 26', *Journal of Personality and Social Psychology*, 71: 495–514.

Caspi, A. and Silva, P. (1995) 'Temperamental qualities of at age three predict personality traits in young adulthood: longitudinal evidence from a birth cohort', *Child Development*, 66: 486–498.

Cooley, C.H. (1902) *Human Nature and the Social Order*, New York: Scribner.

Coplan, J. and Armer, M. (2007) 'A multitude of solitude: a closer look at social withdrawal and nonsocial play in early childhood', *Child Development Perspectives*, 1: 26–32.

Coplan, R., Rose-Kransor, L., Weeks, M., Kingsbury, A., Knigsbury, M. and Bullock, A. (2013) 'Alone is a crowd: social motivations, social withdrawal, and socioemotional functioning in later childhood', *Developmental Psychology*, 49: 861–875.

Coplan, R.J. and Rubin, K.H. (2010) 'Social withdrawal and shyness in children: history, theories, definitions and assessment', in R. Coplan and K. Rubin (eds), *The Development of Shyness and Social Withdrawal* (pp. 3–22), New York: Guilford Press.

Corr, P.J. (2008) *The Reinforcement Sensitivity Theory Of Personality*, Cambridge, UK: Cambridge University Press.

Dealey, C.E. (1923) 'Problem children in the early school grades', *Journal of Abnormal Psychology and Social Psychology*, 18: 125–136.

de Boer, H., Bosker, R. and van der Werf, M. (2010) 'Sustainability of teacher expectation bias effects on long-term student performance', *Journal of Educational Psychology*, 102: 168–179.

Deci, E. and Ryan, R (1985) *Intrinsic Motivation and Self-determination in Human Behavior*, New York: Academic Press.

Evans, M. (2001) 'Shyness in the classroom and home', in W.R. Crozier and L.E. Alden (eds), *International Handbook of Social Anxiety: Concepts, Research and Interventions Relating to the Self and Shyness* (pp. 159–183), Chichester, UK: Wiley.

Evans, M. (2010) 'Language performance, academic performance, and signs of shyness: a comprehensive review', in R. Coplan and K. Rubin (eds), *The Development of Shyness and Social Withdrawal* (pp. 179–212), New York: Guilford Press.

Fung, I., Townsend, M. and Parr, J. (2008) 'Essential conditions for effective critical thinking in schools', in C. Rubie-Davies and C. Rawlinson (eds), *Challenging Thinking About Teaching and Learning* (pp. 97–111), Hauppauge, NY: Nova Science.

Galanaki, E. (2004) 'Are children able to distinguish among the concepts of aloneness, loneliness, and solitude?' *International Journal of Behavioral Development*, 28: 435–443.

Goodwin, R., Fergusson, D. and Horwood, L. (2004) 'Early anxious/withdrawn behaviours predict later internalising disorders', *Journal of Child Psychology and Psychiatry*, 45: 874–883.

Gray, J.A. and McNaughton, N. (2000). *The Neuropsychology of Anxiety: An Inquiry into the Functions of the Septo-hippocampal System*, 2nd edn, Oxford: Oxford University Press.

Harrist, A., Zaia, A., Bates, J., Dodge, K. and Pettit, G. (1997) 'Subtypes of social withdrawal in early childhood: sociometric status and social-cognitive differences across four years', *Child Development*, 68: 278–294.

Jacques, N., Wilton, K. M. and Townsend, M.A.R. (1998) 'Cooperative learning and social acceptance of children with mild intellectual disability', *Journal of Intellectual Disability Research*, 42: 29–36.

Johnson, D.W. and Johnson, R.T. (1989) *Cooperation and Competition: Theory and Research*, Edina, MN: Interaction Book Company.

Jussim, L., Robustelli, S. and Cain, T. (2009) 'Teacher expectations and self-fulfilling prophecies', in K. Wentzel and A. Wigfield (eds), *Handbook of Motivation at School* (pp. 349–380), Abingdon, Oxon: Routledge.

Kauffman, J. and Landrum, T. (2009) *Characteristics of Emotional and Behavioral Disorders of Children and Youth*, 9th edn, Upper Saddle River, NJ: Pearson Education.

Kohlberg, L., LaCrosse, L. and Ricks, D. (1972) 'The predictability of adult mental health from childhood behavior', in B.B. Wolman (ed.), *Manual of Child Psychotherapy* (pp. 1217–1284), New York: McGraw-Hill.

Marchant, M., Solano, B., Fisher, A., Caldarella, P., Young, R. and Renshaw, T. (2007) 'Modifying socially withdrawn behavior: a playground intervention for students with internalizing behaviors', *Psychology in the Schools,* 44: 779–794.

Mlodinow, L. (2012) *Subliminal: How Your Unconscious Mind Rules Your Behavior*, New York: Pantheon Books.

Mychailyszyn, M., Cohen, J., Edmunds, J., Crawley, S. and Kendall, P. (2010) 'Treating social anxiety in youth', in K. Rubin and R. Coplan (eds), *The Development of Shyness and Social Withdrawal* (pp. 300–324), New York: Guilford Press.

Nicholson, T. and Townsend, M. (2011) 'Children's friendships: real and imaginary', in C. Rubie-Davies (ed.), *Educational Psychology: Concepts, Research and Challenges* (pp. 200–214), Abingdon, Oxon: Routledge.

Palincsar, A.M. and Brown, A.L. (1984) 'Reciprocal teaching of comprehension-fostering and comprehension-monitoring activities', *Cognition and Instruction*, 1: 117–175.

Parten, M.B. (1932) 'Social participation among preschool children', *Journal of Abnormal Psychology*, 27: 243–269.

Piaget, J. (1926) *The Language and Thought of the Child*, London: Routledge and Kegan Paul.

Piaget, J. (1932) *The Moral Judgement of the Child* (trans. M. Gabain), Glencoe, IL: Free Press.

Piercy, M., Wilton, K., and Townsend, M. (2002) 'Promoting the social acceptance of young children with moderate/severe intellectual disability using cooperative learning techniques', *American Journal of Mental Retardation*, 107: 352–360.

Puuraa, K., Mäntymaab, M., Luomab, I., Kaukonenb, P., Guedeneyc, A., Salmelinb, R. and Tamminen, T. (2010) 'Infants' social withdrawal symptoms assessed with a direct infant observation method in primary health care', *Infant Behavior and Development,* 33: 579–588.

Robins, L.N. (1966) *Deviant Children Grown Up*, Baltimore, MD: Williams and Wilkins.

Rosenthal, R. and Jacobson, L. (1968) *Pygmalion in the Classroom: Teacher Expectations and Student Intellectual Development*, New York: Holt.

Rubie-Davies, C.M., Hattie, J.A.C., Townsend, M.A.R. and Hamilton, R.J. (2007) 'Aiming high: teachers and their students', in V.N. Galwye (ed.), *Progress in Educational Psychology Research* (pp. 65–91), Hauppauge, NY: Nova.

Rubin, K.H. and Asendorpf, J.B. (1993) *Social Withdrawal, Inhibition and Shyness in Childhood*, Hillsdale, NJ: Erlbaum.

Rubin, K.H., Bukowski, W.M. and Parker, J.G. (2006) 'Peer interactions, relationships and groups', in N. Eisenberg (ed.), *The Handbook of Child Psychology*, 6th edn, (pp. 571–645), New York: Wiley.

Rubin, K.H. and Coplan, R.J. (eds). (2010) *The Development of Shyness and Social Withdrawal*, New York: Guilford Press.

Rubin, K.H., Hymel, S. and Mills, R.S.L. (1989) 'Sociability and social withdrawal in childhood: stability and outcomes', *Journal of Personality*, 57: 238–255.

Rubin, K., Root, A. and Bowker, J. (2010) 'Parents, peers and social withdrawal in childhood: a relationship perspective', in H. Gazelle and K. Rubin (eds), *Social Anxiety in Childhood: Bridging Developmental and Clinical Perspectives. New Directions for Child and Adolescent Development* (pp. 79–94), San Francisco: Jossey-Bass.

Ryan, A.M. and Ladd, G.W. (eds) (2012) *Peer Relationships and Adjustment at School*, Charlotte, NC: Information Age Publishing.

Seccombe, P. and Townsend, M. (2013, July) 'Costs of social withdrawal in children', paper presented at the Social Psychology of the Classroom international conference, Auckland, New Zealand.

Slavin, R.E. and Cooper, R. (1999) 'Improving intergroup-group relations: lessons learned from cooperative learning programs', *Journal of Social Issues*, 55: 647–663.

Smillie, L.D. (2008) 'What is reinforcement sensitivity: neuroscience paradigms for approach-avoidance process theories of personality', *European Journal of Personality*, 22: 359–384.

Sullivan, H.S. (1953) *The Interpersonal Theory of Psychiatry*, New York: Norton.

Townsend, M. (1993) *Children's Friendships and Social Development*, Palmerston North, NZ: Dunmore Press.

Vygotsky, L. (1978) *Mind in Society: The Development of Higher Psychological Processes*, Cambridge, MA: Harvard University Press.

Williams, J. (2011) 'Taking on the role of questioner: revisiting reciprocal teaching', *The Reading Teacher,* 64: 278–281.

Zhang, X., Anderson, R., Dong, T., Nguyen-Jahiel, K., Li, Y., Lin, T. and Miller, B. (2013) 'Children's moral reasoning: influence of culture and collaborative discussion', *Journal of Cognition and Culture,* 13: 497–516.

Zimbardo, P.G. (1977) *Shyness: What is It and What to Do About It*, New York: Symphony Press.

20

POWER AND SUBJECTIVITIES

Foucault and Havel on the complexities of the early years classroom

Marek Tesar

Power and subjectivities are essential aspects of the early years classroom. This chapter explores Foucault's and Havel's philosophical work on power and the production of subjectivities in the early years classroom. The chapter uses a theoretical post-structural lens to argue that childhood subjectivities are produced under the complex ideological umbrellas of governing rationalities, through tensions between the multiple, diverse, ever-changing, and competing discourses in the early years classroom. Through this examination, power relations are exposed, and the production of childhood subjectivities within the early years classroom is reconceptualized as those of victims, supporters, and rebels.

At the outset it is important to note that this chapter argues for multiplicity, and historically and locally shaped knowledges and power relations within the early years classroom. This post-structural inquiry into the social psychology of the classroom focuses on language and its capacity to structure and make meaning, as well as to form place/space and subjectivities. The politics of the place/space of the early years classroom are rethought through Foucault's writing, juxtaposed with Havel's thinking of ideology and power. The chapter treats these theorists as neither similar nor opposite, but carefully juxtaposes their arguments in order to share a unique and innovative lens on the early years classroom.

The chapter focuses on particular aspects of Foucault's and Havel's work; however, it does not attempt to merge their thinking into a singular framework. There is an ethical question in working with these theorists and using them in the same chapter, or even within the same sentence. They differ in their approaches, ideas, thinking, and the time and space of conducting their inquiries. However, there is something about their work with ideology, subjectivities, and subject positions that, while it does not justify a singular framework, implicitly brings politics and ethics into the classroom. This chapter focuses on Foucault's notion of the production of subjectivities and Havel's subject positions, and their respective thinking about power and power relations. They think separately and differently, yet somehow together, juxtaposed, in tension, and sometimes even opposed. Their theories form an unstable, ever-changing, and flowing lens that considers power relations, subjectivities and subject positions, and ideology in the classroom. These terms do not sit comfortably alongside each other; however, through Havel's and Foucault's writings, they gain prominence and form an interesting juxtaposition in the early years classroom landscape.

Much of the debate in a range of disciplines focuses on the nature of power, and the way it is exercised, exploited, and harnessed (see e.g. Apple 2013; Foucault 1980; Lukes 2004). These ideas often deal with the notions of authority, social class, charisma, knowledge, social and moral persuasion, and others. In this chapter I focus on ideology and governing rationalities (Rose 1999), and the way they affect the production of childhood subjectivities and power constructions within the early years classroom.

An analysis of complex power relations in the context of silent and invisible technologies of control argues that these forces of control are present in the layers of everyday discourses that position children, and their developing subjectivities, as victims, supporters and rebels in the early years classroom. Often, while the subjectivities of victims and supporters are produced in the public sphere of the classroom, the rebel subjectivity runs counter to the dominant discourse. It can play out both in public and in private, produced by a child's acting, or not acting, upon something. The differing subjective orientations of the victim, supporter and rebel, this chapter argues, are the unintended consequences of the multifaceted power structures that are emblematic of the early years classroom in which such multilayered childhoods occur.

Foucault's and Havel's studies of childhoods

Initially, it is essential to chart the discussion through a genealogy of power relations in terms of how childhood subjectivities are governed and produced. In this chapter, the site of investigation is the early years classroom, and the emphasis is placed on how power relations and classroom ideology produce childhood subjectivities. The chapter only considers ideology as a general binding force in the power relations that produce childhoods. The concern of this chapter is the production of childhood subjectivities in the power-infused classroom, in which teachers aim to educate the children and to protect the innocence of childhoods, while constantly exposing children to some form of ideology through their statements, stories, and educational praxis within a curriculum framework.

Havel's and Foucault's work and ideas were influenced by their own experiences of the political systems they lived in (Marshall 2008; Pontuso 2004). This chapter observes their philosophical conceptualizations as distinctive, sometimes even contradictory, but perceives their juxtaposition useful for the study of the production of childhood subjectivities in the early years classroom. The key points that frame this chapter are the discourse of subjugation and dominance and a genealogy of power relations.

Discourses of subjugation and dominance

Havel and Foucault both argued for a critique of the dominant discourse. With respect to this hegemony, Foucault (2003: 7) promoted the 'insurrection of subjugated knowledges'. What Foucault calls subjugated knowledge is knowledge that is not on the same level as any proven knowledge, but rather knowledge that is not officially approved or recognized, and that has sometimes not even surfaced yet. Foucault (2003: 9) states that 'genealogies are, quite specifically, antisciences'. This argument emphasizes his position on subjugated knowledge as a perspective of thinking of genealogies as not only a means to research subjugated knowledges but to 'fight the power-effects characteristic of any discourse that is regarded as scientific'(2003: 9). So Foucault's relationship with the discourse of dominance takes the perspective of research and knowledges situated at the fringes of officially approved knowledges. In classrooms, the officially approved knowledge is a powerful instrument that shapes the production and the position of the subjugated knowledges, genealogies, and subjectivities of adults and children. Apart from forming victims and supporters of the system, this also leads to the formation of rebel subjectivities.

Rebel subjectivities, and acts of subordination, which are so dangerous in the context of the adult world of power, control, and surveillance, occur in the microcosm of children's worlds, in the playground. With a different intensity and specter of repercussions to the adult world, children also trade subjugated knowledges among themselves in the form of stories that shape their child-hoods and form the child rebel. Subjugated knowledges are not exclusive to adults, but rather, the 'underground' of the playground performs a vital element of resistance that mirrors, or to a certain extent offers, solace and hope to, their adult-rebel counterparts. Theorizing these notions is possible through the concepts of governmentality (Foucault 1982) and genealogy (Foucault 1980), through which the production of childhood subjectivities can be understood. Through Havel's and Foucault's philosophical lenses, the concepts of power and subjectivities, and child-hood counter-cultures prove not only to be vital but also signal the importance of knowledges that are often regarded as 'childish'.

Foucault's genealogy of power relations

Genealogies search for unexpected relationships, and nonlinear, accidental origins, while they focus on complexities and contradictive productions of citizens (and childhoods) through power/knowledge relationships (Ailwood 2004; Dreyfus and Rabinow 1982; Foucault 1980). Foucault reinterprets Nietzsche's concept of genealogy, and it is in this sense that it is used to analyze the power structures which are the subject of inquiry within this chapter (Fitzsimons 2011). Foucault's genealogy or genealogical method has a 'unique interest in the power of practice, not subjects, to determine the form of discourse' (Bastalich 2004). Foucault's notion of governmentality, which Duhn (2006: 21) argues 'emphasises a double focus on large political structures as well as on micro-politics to develop a sense of how political power produces subjects in contemporary society', lies within this framework of genealogy. Genealogical studies thus produce a framework centered on the concept of govermentality, which can be used in readings on power relations in the early years classroom and on the production of childhood subjectivities.

Govermentality allows us to research the alternative, nonlinear ways of how political ration-alities, or classroom agencies, govern childhood subjectivities, and to examine how they administer citizens, teachers, and children (Rose 1993). Rose focuses on 'the forms of power that subject us, the systems of rule that administer us, the types of authority that master us' in neolib-eral society (1993:286), while Larner and Walters (2004: 496) explore governmentality from the position of 'how governing always involves particular representations, knowledges, and expertise'. In this chapter these notions are extended to the early years classroom, as governmentality enables a focus on what Rose (1993: 288) calls 'problematizing life and seeking to act upon it'.

The genealogical explorations of power relations in educational contexts lead back to Foucault's (1980) work on power and its relationship with institutions. The Foucauldian question of 'how' guides this chapter and the examination of techniques and instruments that are indis-pensable to the way classroom agencies operate. The traditional model of a juridical power construct claims that power belongs to someone; that it can be possessed by a class, people, or an institution (Lemke 2002). Within this concept, someone, or an institution at the top of the hier-archy, possesses the power, which is subsequently forced and distributed towards the bottom. Such a distribution of power is therefore punitive, dark, repressive, and usually takes the form of orders and pressure. Foucault (1991) argues that historically the way power was utilized, for example in prisons (and easily stretched to other institutions such as schools), was to punish the prisoners and to discipline their bodies. He rejects this traditional model of power of the individual and group, and introduces it in a new form. Foucault argues for a disciplinary type of power, where power is exercised, and not possessed by any particular group or institution. Foucault's key point is that power is not only repressive but productive by nature, and his claim that power produces knowledge and subjectivities is decisive for the study of the production of childhood subjectivities. The understanding of this productive nature of power then means that power cannot be studied on its own. Power thus needs to be analyzed as linked to institutions such as schools and early years classrooms, political contexts, ideologies, and the government, as the mechanisms of 'visibility' (Arac 1994). As such, the way power shapes the early years classroom through its repressive and productive force is central to this chapter.

Foucault (1991) argues that prison is not the only institution that produces subjectivities, but that it is a part of vast societal networks, which may include schooling, psychological and medical institutions, and military organizations. The characteristics of shifts in the way the prison system operates, such as the constant surveillance and censorship, represent also the power relations that formed other institutions. Foucault's (1991) panopticon was a structure that was originally developed by Jeremy Bentham, and which produced self-discipline and self-governance in prisoners, as they were not certain whether they were being observed or not. This demonstration of disciplinary and productive power has other qualities that are important to analyze in relation to the early years classroom. These qualities involve the central positioning of the panopticon, the teacher, with children at the periphery, demonstrating how only a few individuals can have power over the masses, and the shift to the production of self-governing citizens, teachers, and children. These notions are embedded in the power relations of the early years classroom.

Havel's power relations

To juxtapose Foucault's notion of disciplinary power, and how it operates within the early years classroom, I now briefly analyze Havel's work on power. Havel's (1985) concern is with power relations in a post-totalitarian society, where he distinguished the nature of power from how it operated in a traditional dictatorship. For the purpose of the analysis, these ideas are resituated into a democratic society. The way power operates in society differs in the public and private domains. If citizens (teachers, children) want to live a comfortable life without repercussions they have to accept 'living within a lie' and to publicly conform to the system and its requirements (Havel 1989). Citizens' private lives are undisturbed by the system as long as they do not cross their concerns into the public sphere. So the power relations in the educational sphere such as the early years classroom are bound by a social contract, where teachers and children support the prescribed rules and publicly demonstrate their support of the ideology, regime, and maintenance of the process and classroom, and thus avoid repercussions. In this way, the teachers and children publicly declare their support for the ideology of the early years classroom.

In Havel's analyses of these complex power relations, every teacher and child has access to power in the classroom. He does not necessarily deny the traditional, top-down model of power, as Foucault (1982) tends to, as he notes how some citizens, such as teachers and children, are considered to be powerful and others powerless. Teachers and children can exploit the fluid and free nature of power that they harness and have access to. This 'power of the powerless' creates the possibility of providing pressure and producing an anomaly in the greyness of everyday early years settings. This chapter does not argue the perspectives of either the powerful or the powerless; the focus is on childhoods within both public and private domains that are at the same time a part of the system and outside of it, being neither powerful nor powerless, but experiencing and immersed in the tension in between. The dichotomy of power and the powerless that Havel identifies is further complicated by isolating the subjugating element of power, as exemplified in the official discourse of the early years classroom, with an inherently subversive manipulation of power unique to childhood. This unique form of power is experienced by children in the early years classroom, as teachers guide, teach, learn, and play with them. In this case, the structural nature of power comes from the teacher, through a 'top down' model, creating a reactive polis of 'inbuilt', resistant and secret childhoods. This separation from the adult world is the essential element for the production of multiple childhood subjectivities.

The children in the early years classroom are an example of the effect of such power within childhoods and kindergartens. In this way children are victims and supporters of the panorama of the everyday early years classroom, the hegemonic, public discourse that produces one form of childhood subjectivities. There are, however, also other childhoods, produced outside of the daily routines of education, in a parallel childhood polis (both public and private), where other experiences take precedence. While the hegemonic discourse in early years classrooms where public childhood subjectivities of victim and supporter are formed is powerful, the resistant discourse of the childhood underground is also powerful, and significant in the formation of childhoods and the way children learn and play. Furthermore, children are not passive in these complex classroom power relations, but they are active agents, responding to the hegemonic, dominant public domain.

Havel's and Foucault's power juxtaposition

Focusing on Havel's and Foucault's work on power, Arac (1994) points out the ambiguity of Havel's interpretation of Foucault's perception of power as repressive, and of the productive nature of power. As alluded to already, Foucault (1991) assigned productive power to institutions that produce docile bodies and subjectivities, such as prisons, archives, schools, and early years classrooms. Havel's interpretation of an institution can be considered as a recollection of his own experience of imprisonment, and, while he understands the productive nature of the system, which produces citizens, and therefore childhood subjectivities, he also acknowledges its repressive nature. Havel does not categorically deny the traditional model of the powerful and powerless, but he extends its understanding and implications to conditions in other societies and institutions. Similarly, Hammond and Houston (2001) and Procházka (1993) consider Foucault's and Havel's work on power as parallel, as both argue that power is a productive force, which they interpret in different contexts.

Havel (1985) perceives power as an invisible force that operates through indirect instruments, anonymously, within an ideology that can be adjusted and bent to serve the purpose of the system. Hammond and Houston (2001) argue that it is no longer the distinction between the powerful and the powerless, but the relationship between the individual and society that is central, and in the context of this, system power is exercised through relationships, patterns, and self-organization. Havel's contribution to how power is executed is not only demonstrated in differences and changes, but also in the relationship between the individual and the society, and the responsibility that each citizen, teacher, and child has within the early years classroom system.

Foucault focuses on the question of 'how' in relation to historical perspectives of power and, as Marshall (2000) argues, this represents a question to which governmentality offers an answer. This 'how' is important in this chapter, as it methodologically guides the questioning of how childhood subjectivities are produced in the early years classroom context. Havel's (1985) work on power is concerned with the fate of the human being in particular social and ideological contexts, but can be extended to the early years classroom. In Havel's texts, everyone creates the society and everyone suffers in it; everyone is responsible for, and also a victim of, the social contract. There is no one who is outside the system, and all teachers and children are exposed to the ideology of the early years classroom system. Therefore, there is no free subject for Havel, as all teachers and children are part of a social contract with the system, and as subjects they are formed through complex power relations within the parameters of the early years classroom. Rose (1993: 287) addresses issues of authority and power relations and claims that there is 'no simple distinction between those who have power and who are subject to it' in a modern neo-liberal society. Nor, this chapter argues, does such a distinction exist in the early years classroom.

While the focus is different, Havel's work on power relations complements Foucault's, as both analyze the shift in the construction of power and the way power is exercised. Both examine the shift towards more sophisticated, complex, and calculated forms of discipline and punishment that produce citizens in an ideologically charged context. They claim that power has transitioned away from an idealistic towards a calculated construct, shaped by the shift from direct to complex, nonlinear power relations. Part of this complexity of relations of power is the role that desire plays in upholding certain subjective positions towards power. As Havel (1990: 182) argues:

> The exercise of power is determined by thousands of interactions between the world of the powerful and that of the powerless, all the more so because these worlds are never divided by a sharp line: everyone has a small part of himself in both.

These intersections of power between the 'powerful' and 'powerless' will become evident in the next section, about the child.

The child

To perform and demonstrate how this juxtaposition of Foucault's and Havel's thinking operates, this chapter illustrates the analysis of power relations and the production of childhood subjec-tivities through a story about a child called Tom. By applying their theoretical lenses in the early years classroom, as argued above, childhood subjectivities are produced under the ideological umbrellas of governing rationalities, through tensions between the dominant and resistant discourses in the early years classroom.

Tom publicly behaves as is expected of him; he does not do anything extraordinary, and lives his life expecting that the system, embodied in the teacher-guardians, will take no notice of him. Tom participates in the public domain, attends mat times, does and displays his artwork, and uses ideologically and politically correct language. Tom does all of this to remain untouchable by the system and its teacher-guardians. Tom knows and understands it is only a game, and he accepts its rules and plays his part well. In one particular moment of Tom's being in the early years class-room, he is asked by the head teacher to focus on artwork relevant to the theme of spring. This is not surprising to Tom, as this strong recommendation has been made in various forms before. The recommendation comes with a very simple request: to create this artwork and to display it in a way that everyone, every parent, visiting lecturer, inspector, and visitor to the early years classroom can see it. The artwork does not say anything surprising or new; this theme, this request, has been expressed the year before and the year before that. Tom is in a familiar situation, as he sees the same artwork on the same theme produced by other children. So Tom creates his piece of art, and, together with a teacher, places it next to the notice board, right between the announcement of the increase of fees and the note that each visitor needs to sign.

In both a Focauldian and Havelian sense, the concern is why Tom creates this artwork and why he places it on the notice board. Tom has always done this, because he is aware of the consequences of not displaying it: he would most likely be questioned by a teacher, this incident could be written down, his parents could be notified and Tom could be considered to be a disturbance to the early years classroom system, and furthermore, in addition to being a victim and supporter of the system, he could also become a rebel. Tom could also be labeled as noncooperative and he could be subjected to various psychological or developmental evaluations. So if Tom wants to exist, play, interact, and not be subjected to developmental practices, if he wishes to be unnoticeable by the teacher-guardians, he needs to draw the required picture to fit with the theme of spring and to display it. The 'picture of spring' thus demonstrates that Tom officially, publicly declares that he has accepted the early years classroom system and care, and that he is ready to live in harmony with it and its structures. In the Foucauldian and Havelian argument, the message that Tom conveys as he displays the picture of spring is: 'I, [Tom], learn here, and I know what I must do. I behave in the manner expected of me. I can be depended upon and am beyond reproach. I am obedient and therefore I have the right to be left in peace', in other words to play freely outside of this activity and not to be observed or challenged as to why he has chosen not to follow the teacher's suggestion.

When Tom paints a picture and displays it, he acts *as if* he accepts the meaning of the 'picture of spring'. For Havel (1985), the meaning of his actions lies not in the picture itself but in the performative aspect of responding to the request and placing it on the notice board. This act carries a different message from the semantics of the picture itself. As Tom displays the picture, the message conveyed to all other children walking past the notice board is: 'I am just like you, I play my part in the early years classroom system, I displayed the picture on the notice board just as all of you have done your own little parts. You cannot badmouth me, you cannot tell on me, I am supporting the early years classroom's system. My teachers know that I have fulfilled my part and that I have obeyed the order of it'. Both Foucault and Havel's theories are engaged in this analysis of Tom, and it is their difference and similarity, at the very same time, that juxtaposes their notions of 'power' and 'subjectivities'.

Concluding comments

In this chapter, Havel's and Foucault's power relations have been juxtaposed within the early years classroom. The subjectivities produced, of both victims and supporters of the early years system, are essential, and are interwoven to demonstrate the complexities of the system itself. The system governs children through desires, and children are active agents in this process, as victim and supporter subjects. Furthermore, children actively acquire knowledge and information that is outside the public domain in their childhood underground and unofficial curriculum, where the production of the subjectivity of a child rebel occurs. Havel and Foucault help to shed light on the effect of the public and private discourse, and how it overtly and covertly affects childhood subjectivities through everyday life and systems.

This chapter has argued that Foucault's and Havel's work on power is relevant to children's centrality in power relations within early years classrooms. Everyone, every child, is part of the system, even if they are on the fringes of the early years classroom society or seen and portrayed by the traditional model of power as powerless. In the early years classroom, all children are both the victims and the pillars of the system and of the wider early years educational order, as they struggle with and at the same time support the policies and requirements of early years settings. However, the early years system does not publicly reveal this struggle, and instead presents itself with a public façade of being caring, supportive, and democratic. Foucault's and Havel's critique of society, transposed into early years settings, challenges the official perception of a beautiful, happy, peaceful façade of childhood by exposing the ruthless and selective power that structures it. Tom, the teacher, and the parents are all part of these public structures of the system. They cannot escape them, so they all support the system, as they interact with the ideas that the system outlines; they live within the system, and they behave according to the system's requirements. The early years classroom system regulates and thrives on the power exerted in governing all children in the early years classroom space.

The importance of this chapter lies in uncovering and rethinking the tension between the public and private domain, and serves as a story of hegemony and resistance in early years classrooms. This examination of power relations exposes and reconceptualizes productions of childhood subjectivities within the early years classroom: of a victim, supporter, and rebel. Childhood subjectivities are produced by what Havel and Foucault would perhaps identify as technologies within the early years classroom that affect the self to produce the self. Balancing power through these unmarked categories and uncharted fresh juxtapositions of theories does not challenge traditional forms of power and subjectivities, but adds another layer of complexity and explanation to the toolbox of the social psychology of the classroom.

References

Ailwood, J. (2004) 'Genealogies of governmentality: producing and managing young children and their education', *Australian Educational Researcher*, 31: 19–34.

Apple, M.W. (2013) *Education and Power*, New York: Routledge.

Arac, J. (1994) 'Foucault and central Europe: a polemical speculation', *Boundary*, 21: 197–210.

Bastalich, W. (2004) 'Reading Foucault: genealogy and social science research methodology and ethics', *Sociological Research Online*, 14.

Dreyfus, H.L. and Rabinow, P. (1982) *Michel Foucault: Beyond Structuralism and Hermeneutics*, Chicago: University of Chicago Press.

Duhn, I. (2006) 'Cartographies of childhood: mapping the modern/global child', unpublished doctoral thesis, University of Auckland, New Zealand.

Fitzsimons, P. (2011) *Governing the Self: A Foucauldian Critique of Managerialism in Education*, New York: Peter Lang Publishing.

Foucault, M. (1980) *Power/knowledge: Selected Interviews and Other Writings (1972–1977)*, Brighton, UK: Harvester Press.

Foucault, M. (1982) 'The subject and power', *Critical Inquiry*, 8: 777–795.

Foucault, M. (1991) *Discipline and Punish: The Birth of the Prison*, London: Penguin Books.

Foucault, M. (2003) *Society Must be Defended: Lectures at the Collège de France (1975–1976)*, New York: Picador.

Hammond, S.C. and Houston, R. (2001) 'The prison with symbolic walls: complexity and structuration in Havel's *Power of the Powerless*', *Tamara: Journal of Critical Postmodern Organization Science*, 1: 47–59.

Havel, V. (1985) 'The power of the powerless', in J. Keane (ed.), *The Power of the Powerless: Citizens against the State in Central – Eastern Europe* (pp. 23–96), London: Hutchinson.

Havel, V. (1989) *Living in Truth: Twenty-two Essays Published on the Occasion of the Award of the Erasmus Prize to Václav Havel*, London: Faber & Faber.

Havel, V. (1990) *Disturbing the Peace: A Conversation with Karel Hvížd'ala*, New York: Random House.

Larner, W. and Walters, W. (2004) 'Globalization as governmentality', *Alternatives: Global, Local, Political*, 29: 495–514.

Lemke, T. (2002) 'Foucault, governmentality, and critique', *Rethinking Marxism*, 14: 49–64.

Lukes, S. (2004) *Power: A Radical View*. New York: Palgrave Macmillan.

Marshall, J.D. (2000) 'Thomas Hobbes: education and governmentality', in *Encyclopedia of Philosophy of Educational Theory*. Retrieved from http://www.ffst.hr/ENCYCLOPAEDIA/doku.php?id=hobbes_and_philosophy_of_education

Marshall, J.D. (2008) 'Michel Foucault: discipline, power relations and education', in V. Carpenter, J. Jesson, P. Roberts and M. Stephenson (eds), *Nga Kaupapa Here: Connections and Contradictions in Education* (pp. 88–97), North Shore, New Zealand: Cengage Learning New Zealand.

Pontuso, J.F. (2004) *Václav Havel: Civic Responsibility in the Postmodern Age*, Lanham, MD: Rowman & Littlefield.

Procházka, M. (1993) 'Prisoner's predicament: public privacy in Havel's letters to Olga', *Representations*, 43: 126–154.

Rose, N. (1993) 'Government, authority and expertise in advanced liberalism', *Economy and Society*, 22: 283–299. doi: 10.1080/03085149300000019

Rose, N. (1999) *Governing the Soul: The Shaping of the Private Self*, London: Free Association Books.

PART V

Classroom climate and classroom management

21

THE VALUE OF USING OBSERVATIONAL AND STUDENT REPORT METHODOLOGIES IN CLASSROOM RESEARCH

Erik A. Ruzek and Robert C. Pianta

Social psychologists have pursued two interrelated lines of investigation in classroom research: (1) describing the nature and quality of instructional, interpersonal, and organizational features of classroom processes; and (2) studying the effect of these classroom processes on students' cognitive and social-affective development. Multiple methods exist for assessing the nature and quality of classroom processes as well as multiple sources for gathering this information, and in this chapter we describe classroom environment research conducted using two of the most prevalent methods for understanding classrooms: observations and student surveys. We discuss the advantages of both types of methods, and review selected research on classrooms using the two methods. We make the case that employing both observations *and* student reports can lead to a fuller descriptive understanding of classrooms, as well as illuminating how classroom processes relate to student development. Importantly, combining the information gathered from both methods has great potential for the continued improvement of classroom instruction and the professional development of teachers.

Observations of classroom contexts

Early classroom observational research used a process–product orientation to identify teacher behaviors linked to student achievement (Brophy and Good 1986). These early methods often employed observer checklists to record teachers' instructional behaviors (Turner and Meyer 2000). Although exceptions to the checklist approach existed (e.g. Dunkin and Biddle 1974; Flanders 1970), observation systems measuring dynamics of teacher–student interactions are relatively recent. Here we focus on the Classroom Assessment Scoring System (the CLASS instrument; Pianta *et al.* 2008a) as an example of social psychological research informing the design and use of classroom observations.

A recent line of research on teacher effects (i.e. teacher value-added) demonstrates that teachers matter for student achievement (Hanushek 2002; Kane and Staiger 2012; Sanders and Rivers 1996) and motivation (Ruzek *et al.* 2014a). However, this work often ignores the specific teaching behaviors that produce these outcomes and how these behaviors are organized. The need to articulate theoretical frameworks for teaching is critical to the further development of our knowledge of classroom instruction (Douglas 2009). Here we present one such framework of effective teaching, operationalized through observation, and focusing exclusively on *interactions* between teachers and students. Developmental theory and research support the idea that everyday interactions with adults and peers drive students' learning and development (Bronfenbrenner and Morris 1998).

Drawing from theoretical and empirical work in the educational and psychological literatures (e.g. Brophy 1999; Eccles and Roeser 1999; Pressley *et al.* 2003), our approach specifies a *multilevel latent structure* for organizing teacher–student interactions (Hamre and Pianta 2007). Three domains of teacher–student interaction are hypothesized as important in promoting learning and social development–emotional support, classroom organization, and instructional support. The observational measure assessing teacher–student interactions, the CLASS instrument (Pianta *et al.* 2008), details specific dimensions of teacher–student interaction within each broad domain (see Figure 21.1), which are further specified by explicit behavioral indicators and observable descriptions of interactions. All interaction processes are conceptualized and indexed at the classroom level to describe teachers' average interactional qualities with their students.

In the CLASS instrument, specific observable descriptions are anchored at points along a 7-point rating scale to guide observers' judgments regarding the quality of teacher–student interaction for that dimension. These specific behavioral descriptions of dimensions and indicators shift across grades to be appropriate for students at a given developmental level. Studies examining application of this 3-domain latent structure of teacher–student interactions to samples ranging from preschool through twelfth-grade report some degree of convergence. Although the CLASS instrument measures many types of teacher–student interactions, it is not intended to capture all possible features of teachers' interactive behavior. For example, Domitrovich *et al.* (2009) demonstrated that elements of the emotional environment, such as a teachers' use of emotion words and emotion coaching, were elements of interaction not measured by the CLASS instrument.

Below we highlight the literature supporting the domains of teacher–student interactions included in this model of classroom processes and assessed through the CLASS instrument (see also Hamre and Pianta 2007).

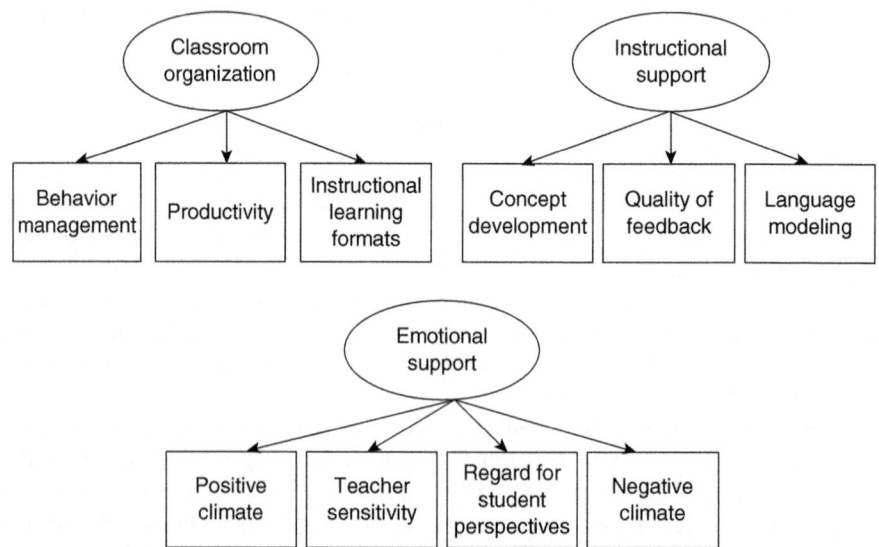

Figure 21.1 The CLASS framework for teacher–student interactions.

Emotional support

Positive facilitation of teacher–student and student–student interactions are key elements of effective classroom practice supported by attachment theory (Bowlby 1969), which posits that adult emotional support (i.e. a predictable, consistent, and safe environment) fosters self-reliance and exploration. Self-determination (or self-systems) theory (Connell and Wellborn 1991) suggests that children are motivated to learn when adults support their need to feel competent, positively related to others, and autonomous.

In the CLASS instrument, emotional support contains three dimensions: positive climate (the nature and quality of relationships within the classroom); teacher sensitivity (attunement and responsiveness to individual cues and needs); and regard for student perspectives (teachers solicit students' ideas, follow students' lead, and allow students to have a *formative* role).

Students with more positive relationships with teachers display greater peer competencies and more positive academic development (Bryk *et al.* 1993; Connell and Wellborn 1991; Crosnoe *et al.* 2004; Roeser *et al.* 2000). From an adolescent's perspective, few things are of greater importance than the degree to which they feel adults are able to respect and support their growing needs for autonomy, within the context of supportive relationships (Eccles *et al.* 1993; Roeser *et al.* 2000). Autonomy can be supported by giving students choices of partners for group projects, types of projects to perform, and so on (Allen *et al.* 1994; Anderman and Midgley 1997). When teachers proactively work with adolescents' developmental push for autonomy, students are more motivated to learn, more engaged, and happier with the school environment (Deci *et al.* 1991; Reeve *et al.* 2004; Ruzek *et al.* 2014b).

CLASS-measured emotional support predicts student performance on tests of early literacy in preschool and first grade (NICHD ECCRN 2003), lower levels of internalizing behaviors reported by mothers in kindergarten and first grade (NICHD ECCRN 2003), and student's behavioral engagement across several elementary grades (NICHD ECCRN 2002); it also appears to help protect children at risk of school failure due to behavioral problems (Buyse *et al.* 2008; Gazelle 2006). The link of emotional support with gains in achievement appears mediated by student engagement (Reyes *et al.* 2012).

Classroom organization and management

Helping students organize their behavior and attention towards the pursuit of academic goals is a second domain of teachers' classroom interactions. Children's self-regulatory and executive functioning skills (Blair 2002; Ponitz *et al.* 2009a) are enhanced in classrooms with clear and consistent routines (e.g. Emmer and Strough 2001; Ponitz *et al.* 2009b). When these aspects of teaching improve, so do children's teacher- and observer-reported self-regulatory skills (e.g. Raver *et al.* 2008).

In the CLASS instrument, organizational features fall under classroom organization and management, which is composed of three dimensions: (1) behavior management practices to promote positive behavior and prevent misbehavior (e.g. clear and consistent expectations, redirecting minor misbehavior, minimal amount of time on behavior management); (2) productivity (teachers' efficient use of time); and (3) instructional learning formats (provision of interesting activities, instruction, work-centers, materials, and activity facilitation for active engagement). Interestingly, one recent report using data from National Longitudinal Study of Adolescent Health suggests that adolescents report feeling more connected to school when they experience positive classroom management (McNeely *et al.* 2002).

Several recent studies suggest that productive teachers spend more time creating efficient routines at the beginning of the school year and that this early investment enables them to spend more time in child-managed activities later in the school year (e.g. Cameron *et al.* 2005). Consistent with constructivist theories (Rogoff 1990; Vygotsky 1980), when teachers provide high-quality learning formats, students are *active* participants in learning. Importantly, students learn more in classrooms in which teachers do a better job managing students' behavior, time, and attention (Ponitz *et al.* 2009a), partly due to children's development of better behavioral and cognitive self-control (Rimm-Kaufman *et al.* 2009). Likewise, student-reported engagement is high when students participate in more active methods such as laboratories and groups and lowest during lectures (Yair 2000). Unfortunately, these more active methods occur only 3 percent of sampled classroom time.

Instructional support

The theoretical foundation for instructional support derives from research on children's cognitive and language development (e.g. Catts *et al.* 2001; Taylor *et al.* 2003) highlighting the distinction between learning facts and learning how facts are interconnected, organized, and conditioned upon one another (Mayer 2002). This type of learning is contingent on the opportunities adults provide to express existing skills, scaffold more complex ones (Skibbe *et al.* 2004), and tie new information to students' background knowledge and to real-world examples (Bransford *et al.* 2000). In addition, effective instruction includes feedback that is immediate, contingent and specific (e.g. Kulik and Kulik 1988). Such feedback serves to control frustration, increase interest and motivation, and promotes higher order thinking (Butler 1987; Good and Brophy 2008; Rogoff 1990).

The instructional support domain of the CLASS instrument is composed of three dimensions of teacher–student interaction: (1) concept development (practices that stimulate students' higher order thinking skills, cognitions, and understanding of content [Pianta *et al.* 2008]); (2) quality of feedback (helps students learn how to arrive at correct answers, loops in back-and-forth exchanges toward a deeper understanding [Pianta *et al.* 2008]); and (3) language modeling (conversational style, including open-endedness, extension, and level of teachers' language use with students).

Bransford *et al.* (2000) termed classrooms high in these features 'knowledge-centered environment(s)', and the presence of such interactions is related to students' achievement gains (Taylor *et al.* 2003) and understanding of information (Barron *et al.* 1998). In classrooms offering higher quality feedback, students display greater gains in literacy and language across the preschool and kindergarten years (Mashburn *et al.* 2006) and feedback contributes to a closing of the achievement gap for disadvantaged first-grade students (Hamre and Pianta 2005). CLASS-measured instructionally supportive interactions predict students' academic functioning (Hamre and Pianta 2005; Howes *et al.* 2008) and behavioral engagement in classroom activities (NICHD ECCRN 2003). Involving high-school students in significant, real-world, voluntary community service, and then discussing it within the classroom in an ongoing way, has been found to reduce failure rates by 50 percent, in randomly controlled trials, with similarly beneficial effects on other behaviors (Allen *et al.* 1997).

In sum, there is ample evidence that, at the classroom-level, teacher–student interaction patterns can be conceptualized and defined, reliably observed, and account for student learning. These processes reflect some compilation of classroom capacity to foster students' learning. An inherent drawback of our approach is the assumption that the interactions we observe (and code) are experienced similarly by all students, and we emphasize that there are also models for observing these very classroom processes in the form of individual teacher–student interaction that could reflect the unique experiences of each child. We describe the *classroom-level* framework and observations of teacher–student interaction processes to suggest that there is evidence for educationally salient processes at the level of the classroom. In the section that follows, we outline survey approaches to conceptualizing and assessing classroom processes from the unique perspective of each student.

Student reports of classroom environments

Understanding students' *unique perceptions* of their classroom experiences is integral to social psychological research on classrooms (Fraser and Walberg 1981; Turner and Meyer 2000; Weinstein 1983), and is commonly assessed through survey methods. Student surveys are a defining feature of educational psychology research on the effects of classroom environments on students' motivation and psychological beliefs. While some work in this area has employed observations to assess instructional climates (e.g. Jang *et al.* 2010; Patrick *et al.* 2001; Spearman and Watt 2013), most studies use student surveys to measure classroom climate. A preference for measuring student perceptions stems from the view that a student's own perspective is the primary determinant of his or her beliefs and behavior (Fraser and Walberg 1981), and is therefore the most salient for predicting student-level outcomes (Ludtke *et al.* 2009).

Educational psychologists employ student surveys to collect data on a variety of classroom phenomena, including teachers' motivational messages (e.g. Ames and Archer 1988; Bong 2005; Lau and Nie 2008; Wolters 2004) and instructional and organizational practices (e.g. Kunter *et al.* 2007; Wang and Holcombe 2010), teacher–student relationships (e.g. Roeser *et al.* 2000; Wentzel 1998), and peer relationships (e.g. Furrer and Skinner 2003). Examples of survey instruments in this line of research include the widely-used Patterns of Adaptive Learning Scales (Midgley *et al.* 2000) and the Student Classroom Survey (Eccles *et al.* 1997). Though each of these instruments contains a variety of personal belief and classroom perception scales, typically student surveys from these measures are used to further the goal of understanding *how* classroom phenomena relate to students' motivation, interest, engagement and learning. Indeed, a long line of research oriented towards this goal (see Weinstein 1983 for an early review) has led to significant insights into the teacher–student relationship qualities as well as the instructional and peer context factors that promote students' adoption of adaptive motivation, engagement, interest, and learning behaviors (Turner and Meyer 2000).

In contrast to the time-stamped snapshots provided by observation instruments such as the CLASS instrument, a benefit of surveys is that students draw on a deep set of personalized experiences to assess their teacher's instructional practices (Wagner *et al.* 2013). While interview methodologies also provide detailed accounts of experiences (Turner and Meyer 2000), surveys are particularly efficient for reaching large numbers of students. Surveys are also employed because researchers view classroom climate as a 'global' or 'quantifiable' state of the learning environment (Babad 2009) that can help explain students' learning and behavioral outcomes. Examples of survey use in educational research include the measurement of the overall classroom climate based on multiple students' reports within the same classroom (Marsh *et al.* 2012) as well as the measurement of differential student experiences both *within* (Kuklinski and Weinstein 2001) and *across* classrooms (Oakes 2005).

Despite strong logic for using student surveys to assess classroom climates, survey research reveals that students in classrooms disagree about the extent to which their teacher engages in measured instructional practices. Significant within-classroom variability in student reports threatens the reliability of surveys for measuring 'average' classroom instruction (Ludtke *et al.* 2008; Miller and Murdock 2007). These reliability problems are partially addressed by using more complicated methodologies to statistically model student surveys for classroom climate research (i.e. multilevel confirmatory factor analysis; Fauth *et al.* 2014; Marsh *et al.* 2012; Wagner *et al.* 2013). Some of these challenges might be better addressed with classroom data that comes from multiple sources and is gathered through multiple methods (e.g. Patrick *et al.* 2001; Turner *et al.* 2002).

Combining classroom observations and student reports to address research and theory

Using aggregated student reports to describe classroom instructional climates is challenged by significant within-classroom student report variability, and might suggest that student surveys only be employed to get at an individual's idiosyncratic experiences in the classroom. Contrastingly, theoretically-driven classroom observations represent a viable method for measuring and understanding classroom processes in aggregate (Pianta and Hamre 2009). We argue that instead of choosing one method or the other, research must move in the direction of incorporating both student-reported and observational measures of classrooms (e.g. Patrick et al. 2001; Reyes et al. 2012; Ruzek et al. 2014b; Turner et al. 2002; Urdan 2004).

Closely tracking student ratings of teachers' practices with independent observers' ratings may provide critical information for addressing three challenges to our understanding of how classroom environments influence student outcomes: (1) nonsignificant (or weakly significant) relations between classroom climate measures and theoretically-linked outcomes (Miller and Murdock 2007); (2) highly variable student reports of the learning climate within the same classroom; and (3) lack of clarity around how teachers' interactions with students influence students' perceptions of the classroom (Turner and Meyer 2000).

Throughout this section we use the classroom construct of teachers' emotionally-supportive interactions to discuss how student reports and observational measures can jointly address the challenges outlined above. Emotional support is a centerpiece of the CLASS observational measure of teacher–student interactions (Pianta et al. 2008), and refers to teachers' efforts to support students' social and emotional functioning in the classroom. In a multimeasure framework, one could ask how observer ratings of a teacher's emotional support correspond to student ratings of that teacher's emotional support, honing in on particular facets of emotionally-supportive interactions that are hypothesized to influence important student outcomes. For example, we paired observations of emotional support with student surveys measuring the prevalence of classroom interactions likely to promote a student's motivation, focusing on student perceptions of teachers' support for autonomy and the degree to which teachers promoted positive relationships among students in the classroom (Ruzek et al. 2014b), thus illuminating how observed instruction corresponds to students' actual experiences in the classroom (Urdan and Schoenfelder 2006).

Perhaps observations are too general to capture a particular student's experiences, and instead, it is necessary to gather information from each student. However, research suggests that observations of teacher–student interactions in a classroom, using the CLASS instrument, can indeed predict individual student learning and behavioral outcomes (e.g. Allen et al. 2011; Hamre and Pianta 2005; Howes et al. 2008; Reyes et al. 2012). For survey researchers, it would be important to know whether certain students are more 'objective' observers of their classroom than others, who might be more apt to report on their own personal experiences. Research to identify particular student characteristics (e.g. motivational orientations, prior achievement, or gender) associated with greater or lesser correspondence to observer ratings would therefore be useful. If one's interest is measuring differential experiences in the classroom, then focusing on survey reports of students mostly likely to report on their individual experiences is optimal. Alternatively, if the interest is using student reports to measure overall classroom climate, one might get a more reliable estimate from the surveys of students less likely to report on their idiosyncratic experiences.

Teachers do not instruct all students in the same ways, sometimes holding different expectations for different groups of students or treating certain groups one way and others differently (Weinstein 2008). Understanding differential experiences is an important area of inquiry for research on classroom environments (Weinstein 2002), and is particularly well-suited to the combined use of observation and student report methods. For example, how might we productively combine observational data about teachers' emotional support in classrooms with student survey data about teacher emotional support to better understand differential student experiences? Student reports can help contextualize observational ratings, allowing us to examine whether in classrooms where students disagree about the nature of emotionally- supportive interactions, observational ratings of emotional support are lower. Describing the extent to which students disagree about emotionally-supportive interactions could help explain why associations between classroom-level constructs and theoretically-linked outcomes (i.e. student motivation) are weaker than expected (Miller and Murdock 2007). One could test whether theoretically-linked outcomes show higher associations with emotional support when there is greater agreement between observer and student ratings of emotional support. In recent work we find that student-reported experiences of opportunities to exercise autonomy and positive relationships with their peers partially *mediate* relations between observed emotional support and academic year gains in students' motivation and engagement. This and other work (e.g. Reyes *et al.* 2012; Spearman and Watt 2013) illuminates the student perceptual *processes* by which observations (CLASS-based or otherwise) affect student outcomes. As a next step in this work, researchers should examine whether these process effects are stronger in classrooms where more students report having these positive experiences.

While we focused on emotional support as a classroom-level construct here, the issues raised are equally salient for other classroom climate variables. Research aimed at addressing the three unknowns of classroom processes, outlined above, may provide clarity as to how students experience instruction, why students' reports of classroom experiences are so variable within a given classroom, and why classroom climate measures often show weak associations with theoretically-linked outcomes.

In practice: Improving classroom instruction

As applied scholars, we are interested in both the theoretical understanding of classroom processes *and* the improvement of those processes in actual classrooms. Our team developed an instructional coaching model for teachers' professional development, MyTeachingPartner, which has repeatedly demonstrated efficacy in multiple large-scale randomized control trials. Ongoing, personalized coaching and feedback around a common instructional framework (the CLASS instrument) improves teacher instruction in preschools (Mashburn *et al.* 2010; Pianta *et al.* 2008) and secondary schools (Allen *et al.* 2011), and is deliverable consistently at scale (Locasale-Crouch *et al.* 2011). In our prior work, coaches have exclusively used observational techniques (largely the CLASS instrument) to assess teachers' instruction and provide the raw material for coaching. However, student reports could be combined with observations to provide complimentary information that enhances the coaching process.

Given that student reports provide unique information about students' perceptions of their experiences (Turner and Meyer 2000), survey data could inform coaches' efforts to help teachers improve interactions with particular students. Armed with survey data on how students' perceived their teacher's fairness, for example, a coach could identify specific students who felt unfairly treated. Recorded classroom videos could help identify interactions that indicate why students might feel that way, which then becomes a focus in subsequent coaching sessions. As subsequent student-reported data arrives, the coach–teacher team examines whether students who initially reported being treated unfairly change their appraisals. The student survey data thus serves as both impetus for improvement *and* as feedback on the effectiveness of improvement efforts with particular students. Observational data helps diagnose and confirm the individual student reports, and helps determine whether changes teachers are implementing with particular students have classroom-level instructional effects. The two methods thus serve as a feedback loop for continual improvement.

Conclusion

Challenges in understanding classroom processes illuminate an important fact about classrooms: they are complex environments not easily understood through one method or one source of information. As researchers we are acutely aware of the limited explanatory power of our measured constructs on any changes we see in student outcomes. For practical and theoretical reasons, researchers often choose a single, well-understood method for measuring classroom constructs because of the difficulty of measuring these constructs well. We believe that using one method to the exclusion of others perpetuates a piecemeal and incomplete understanding of classroom processes (Turner and Meyer 2000; Urdan 2004). Collecting observation *and* student-reported data is expensive and can complicate analysis. However, doing so can enhance not only our understanding of how and why classrooms matter, but also efforts to improve instruction and the professional development of teachers.

References

Allen, J.P., Kuperminc, G., Philliber, S. and Herre, K. (1994) 'Programmatic prevention of adolescent problem behaviors: the role of autonomy, relatedness, and volunteer service in the teen outreach program', *American Journal of Community Psychology*, 22: 617–638.

Allen, J.P., Philliber, S., Herrling, S. and Kuperminc, G.P. (1997) 'Preventing teen pregnancy and academic failure: experimental evaluation of a developmentally based approach', *Child Development*, 68: 729–742.

Allen, J.P., Pianta, R.C., Gregory, A., Mikami, A.Y. and Lun, J. (2011) 'An interaction-based approach to enhancing secondary school instruction and student achievement', *Science*, 333: 1034–1037.

Ames, C. and Archer, J. (1988) 'Achievement goals in the classroom: students' learning strategies and motivation processes', *Journal of Educational Psychology*, 80: 260–267.

Anderman, E.M. and Midgley, C. (1997) 'Changes in achievement goal orientations, perceived academic competence, and grades across the transition to middle-level schools', *Contemporary Educational Psychology*, 22: 269–298.

Babad, E. (2009) *The Social Psychology of the Classroom*, New York: Routledge.

Barron, B.J.S., Schwartz, D.L., Vye, N.J., Moore, A., Petrosino, A., Zech, L. and Bransford, J.D. (1998) 'Doing with understanding: lessons from research on problem- and project-based learning', *Journal of the Learning Sciences*, 7: 271–311.

Blair, C. (2002) 'School readiness: integrating cognition and emotion in a neurobiological conceptualization of children's functioning at school entry', *American Psychologist*, 57: 111–127.

Bong, M. (2005) 'Between- and within-domain relations of academic motivation among middle and high school students: self-efficacy, task value, and achievement goals', *Journal of Educational Psychology*, 93: 23–34.

Bowlby, J. (1969) *Attachment and Loss*, Vol. 1: *Attachment*, New York: Basic Books.

Bransford, J.D., Brown, A.L. and Cocking, R.R. (eds) (2000) *How People Learn: Brain, Mind, Experience, and School* (expanded ed.), Washington, DC: National Academies Press.

Bronfenbrenner, U. and Morris, P.A. (1998) 'The ecology of developmental processes', in A.S. Bryk and M. Driscoll (eds), *The High School as a Community: Contextual Influences and Consequences for Teachers* (pp. 993–1028), Madison: University of Wisconsin, National Center on Effective Secondary Schools.

Brophy, J. (1999) *Teaching*, Geneva: International Academy of Education and International Bureau of Education.

Brophy, J.E. and Good, T.L. (1986) 'Teacher behavior and student achievement', in M.C. Wittrock (ed.), *Handbook of Research on Teaching* (pp. 328–375), New York: Macmillan.

Bryk, A.S., Lee, V.E. and Holland, P.B. (1993) *Catholic Schools and the Common Good*, Cambridge, MA: Harvard University Press.

Butler, R. (1987) 'Task-involving and ego-involving properties of evaluation effects of different feedback conditions on motivational perceptions, interest, and performance', *Journal of Educational Psychology*, 79, 474–482.

Buyse, E., Verschueren, K., Doumen, S., Van Damme, J. and Maes, F. (2008) 'Classroom problem behavior and teacher–child relationships in kindergarten: the moderating role of the classroom climate', *Journal of School Psychology*, 46: 367–391.

Cameron, C.E., Connor, C.M. and Morrison, F.J. (2005) 'Effects of variation in teacher organization on classroom functioning', *Journal of School Psychology*, 43: 61–85.

Catts, H.W., Fey, M.E., Zhang, X. and Tomblin, J.B. (2001) 'Language basis of reading and reading disabilities: evidence from a longitudinal investigation', *Scientific Studies of Reading*, 3: 331–361.

Connell, J.P. and Wellborn, J.G. (1991) 'Competence, autonomy, and relatedness: a motivational analysis of self-system processes', in M.R. Gunnar and L.A. Sroufe (eds), *Self Process and Development: The Minnesota Symposia on Child Development* (Vol. 23, pp. 43–77), Hillsdale, NJ: Erlbaum.

Crosnoe, R., Johnson, M.K. and Elder, G.H., Jr. (2004) 'Intergenerational bonding in school: the behavioral and contextual correlates of student–teacher relationships', *Sociology of Education*, 77: 60–81.

Deci, E.L., Vallerand, R.J., Pelletier, L.G. and Ryan, R.M. (1991) 'Motivation and education: the self-determination perspective', *Educational Psychologist*, 26: 325–346.

Domitrovich, C.E., Gest, S.D., Gill, S., Bierman, K.L., Welsh, J. and Jones, D. (2009) 'Fostering high quality teaching with an enriched curriculum and professional development support: the Head Start REDI program', *American Educational Research Journal*, 46: 567–597.

Douglas, K. (2009) 'Sharpening our focus in measuring classroom instruction', *Educational Researcher*, 38: 518–521.

Dunkin, M. and Biddle, B. (1974) *The Study of Teaching*, New York: Holt.

Eccles, J.S., Lord, S.E., Roeser, R.W., Barber, B.L. and Hernandez Jozefowicz, D.M. (1997) 'The association of school transitions in early adolescence with developmental trajectories through high school', in J. Schulenberg, J.I. Maggs and K. Hurrelmann (eds), *Health Risks and Developmental Transitions During Adolescence* (pp. 283–321), New York: Cambridge University Press.

Eccles, J.S., Midgley, C., Wigfield, A., Buchanan, C.M., Reuman, D., Flanagan, C. and Mac Iver, D. (1993) 'Development during adolescence: the impact of stage-environment fit on young adolescents' experiences in schools and in families', *American Psychologist*, 48: 90–101.

Eccles, J.S. and Roeser, R.W. (1999) 'School and community influences on human development', in M.H. Boorstein and M.E. Lamb (eds), *Developmental Psychology: An Advanced Textbook*, 4th edn (pp. 503–554), Hillsdale: Erlbaum.

Emmer, E.T. and Strough, L. (2001) 'Classroom management: a critical part of educational psychology, with implications for teacher education', *Educational Psychologist*, 36: 103–112.

Fauth, B., Decristan, J., Rieser, S., Klieme, E. and Büttner, G. (2014) 'Student ratings of teaching quality in primary school: dimensions and prediction of student outcomes', *Learning and Instruction*, 29: 1–9.

Flanders, N. (1970) *Analyzing Teacher Behavior*, Reading, MA: Addison-Wesley.

Fraser, B.J. and Walberg, H.J. (1981) 'Psychosocial learning environment in science classrooms: a review of research', *Studies in Science Education*, 8: 67–92.

Furrer, C. and Skinner, E. (2003) 'Sense of relatedness as a factor in children's academic engagement and performance', *Journal of Educational Psychology*, 95: 148–162.

Gazelle, H. (2006) 'Class climate moderates peer relations and emotional adjustment in children with an early childhood history of anxious solitude: a child-by-environment model', *Developmental Psychology*, 42: 1179–1192.

Good, T.L. and Brophy, J.E. (2008) *Looking in Classrooms*, 10th edn, Boston: Pearson Allyn & Bacon.

Hamre, B.K. and Pianta, R.C. (2005) 'Can instructional and emotional support in the first grade classroom make a difference for children at risk of school failure', *Child Development*, 76: 949–967.

Hamre, B.K. and Pianta, R.C. (2007) 'Learning opportunities in preschool and early elementary classrooms', in R. Pianta, M. Cox and K. Snow (eds), *School Readiness and the Transition to Kindergarten in the Era of Accountability* (pp. 49–84), Baltimore, MD: Brookes.

Hanushek, E.A. (2002) 'The Long Run Importance of School Quality', NBER Working Papers 9071, National Bureau of Economic Research.

Howes, C., Burchinal, M., Pianta, R., Bryant, D., Early, D., Clifford, R. and Oscar, B. (2008) 'Ready to learn? Children's pre-academic achievement in pre-kindergarten programs', *Early Childhood Research Quarterly*, 23: 27–50.

Jang, H., Reeve, J. and Deci, E.L. (2010) 'Engaging students in learning activities: it is not autonomy support or structure but autonomy support and structure', *Journal of Educational Psychology*, 102: 588–600.

Kane, T.J. and Staiger, D.O. (2012) 'Gathering Feedback for Teachers: Combining High-quality Observations with Student Surveys and Achievement Gains', policy and practice brief prepared for the Bill and Melinda Gates Foundation.

Kuklinski, M.R. and Weinstein, R.S. (2001) 'Classroom and developmental differences in a path model of teacher expectancy effects', *Child Development*, 72: 1554–1578.

Kulik, J.A. and Kulik, C.L. (1988) 'Timing of feedback and verbal learning', *Review of Educational Research,* 58: 79–97.

Kunter, M., Baumert, J. and Köller, O. (2007) 'Effective classroom management and the development of subject-related interest', *Learning and Instruction,* 17: 494–509.

Lau, S. and Nie, Y. (2008) 'Interplay between personal goals and classroom goal structures in predicting student outcomes: a multilevel analysis of person–context interactions', *Journal of Educational Psychology,* 100: 15–29.

LoCasale-Crouch, J., Kraft-Sayre, M., Pianta, R.C., Hamre, B.K., Downer, J.T., Leach, A., Burchinal, M., Howes, C., La Paro, K. and Scott-Little, C. (2011) 'Implementing an early childhood professional development course across 10 sites and 15 sections: lessons learned', *NHSA Dialog,* 14: 275–292.

Lüdtke, O., Marsh, H.W., Robitzsch, A., Trautwein, U., Asparouhov, T. and Muthén, B. (2008) 'The multilevel latent covariate model: a new, more reliable approach to group-level effects in contextual studies', *Psychological Methods,* 13: 203–229.

Lüdtke, O., Robitzsch, A., Trautwein, U. and Kunter, M. (2009) 'Assessing the impact of learning environments: how to use student ratings of classroom or school characteristics in multilevel modeling', *Contemporary Educational Psychology,* 34: 120–131.

McNeely, C.A., Nonnemaker, J.M. and Blum, R.W. (2002) 'Promoting school connectedness: evidence from the National Longitudinal Study of Adolescent Health', *Journal of School Health,* 72: 138–146.

Marsh, H.W., Lüdtke, O., Nagengast, B., Trautwein, U., Morin, A.J.S., Abduljabbar, A.S. and Köller, O. (2012) 'Classroom climate and contextual effects: conceptual and methodological issues in the evaluation of group-level effects', *Educational Psychologist,* 47: 106–124.

Mashburn, A.J., Downer, J.T., Hamre, B.K., Justice, L.M. and Pianta, R.C. (2010) 'Consultation for teachers and children's language and literacy development during pre-kindergarten', *Applied Developmental Science,* 14: 179–196.

Mashburn, A., Hamre, B., Downer, J. and Pianta, R. (2006) 'Teacher and classroom characteristics associated with teachers' ratings of pre-kindergartners relationships and behaviors', *Journal of Psychoeducational Assessment,* 24: 367–380.

Mayer, R.E. (2002) 'Rote versus meaningful learning', *Theory into Practice,* 41: 226–233.

Midgley, C., Maehr, M.L., Hruda, L.Z., Anderman, E., Anderman, L., Freeman, K.E., Gheen, M., Kaplan, A., Kumar, R., Middleton, M.J., Nelson, J., Roeser, R. and Urdan, T. (2000) *Manual for the Patterns of Adaptive Learning Scales.* Retrieved at http://www.umich.edu/~pals/PALS%202000_V13Word97.pdf

Miller, A.D. and Murdock, T.B. (2007) 'Modeling latent true scores to determine the utility of aggregate student perceptions as classroom indicators in HLM: the case of classroom goal structures', *Contemporary Educational Psychology,* 32: 83–104.

NICHD Early Child Care Research Network (2002) 'The relation of global first-grade classroom environment to structural classroom features and teacher and student behaviors', *The Elementary School Journal,* 102: 367–387.

NICHD Early Child Care Research Network (2003) 'Social functioning in first grade: prediction from home, child care and concurrent school experience', *Child Development,* 74: 1639–1662.

Oakes, J. (2005) *Keeping Track: How Schools Structure Inequality,* New Haven, CT: Yale University Press.

Patrick, H., Anderman, L.H., Ryan, A.M., Edelin, K.C. and Midgley, C. (2001) 'Teachers' communication of goal orientations in four fifth-grade classrooms', *The Elementary School Journal,* 102: 35–58.

Pianta, R.C. and Hamre, B.K. (2009) 'Conceptualization, measurement, and improvement of classroom processes: standardized observation can leverage capacity', *Educational Researcher,* 38: 109–119.

Pianta, R.C., Mashburn, A.J., Downer, J.T., Hamre, B.K. and Justice, L. (2008) 'Effects of web-mediated professional development resources on teacher-child interactions in pre-kindergarten classrooms', *Early Childhood Research Quarterly,* 23: 431–451.

Ponitz, C.C., Rimm-Kaufman, S.E., Brock, L.L. and Nathanson, L. (2009a) 'Contributions of gender, early school adjustment, and classroom organizational climate to first grade outcomes', *Elementary School Journal,* 110: 143–162.

Ponitz, C.C., Rimm-Kaufman, S.E., Grimm, K.J. and Curby, T.W. (2009b) 'Kindergarten classroom quality, behavioral engagement, and reading achievement', *School Psychology Review,* 38: 102–120.

Pressley, M., Roehrig, A., Raphael, L., Dolezal, S., Bohn, C., Mohan, L., Wharton-McDonald, R., Bogner, K. and Hogan, K. (2003) 'Teaching processes in elementary and secondary education', in W. Reynolds and G. Miller (eds), *Handbook of Psychology: Vol. 7, Educational Psychology* (pp. 153–176), Hoboken, NJ: John Wiley.

Raver, C.C., Jones, A.S., Li-Grining, C.P., Metzger, M., Smallwood, K. and Sardin, L. (2008) 'Improving preschool classroom processes: preliminary findings from a randomized trial implemented in Head Start settings', *Early Childhood Research Quarterly,* 23: 10–26.

Reeve, J., Jang, H., Carrell, D., Jeon, S. and Barch, J. (2004) 'Enhancing students' engagement by increasing teachers' autonomy support', *Motivation and Emotion*, 28: 147–169.

Reyes, M.R., Brackett, M.A., Rivers, S.E., White, M. and Salovey, P. (2012) 'Classroom emotional climate, student engagement, and academic achievement', *Journal of Educational Psychology*, 104: 700–712.

Rimm-Kaufman, S.E., Curby, T.W., Grimm, K.J., Nathanson, L. and Brock, L.L. (2009) 'The contribution of children's self-regulation and classroom quality to children's adaptive behaviors in the kindergarten classroom', *Developmental Psychology*, 45: 958–972.

Roeser, R.W., Eccles, J.S. and Sameroff, A.J. (2000) 'School as a context of early adolescents' academic and social-emotional development: a summary of research findings', *The Elementary School Journal*, 100: 443–471.

Rogoff, B. (1990) *Apprenticeship in Thinking: Cognitive Development in Social Context*, New York: Oxford University Press.

Ruzek, E.A., Domina, T., Duncan, G.J., Conley, A.M. and Karabenick, S.A. (2014a) 'Using value-added models to measure teacher effects on students' motivation and achievement', *Journal of Early Adolescence*. doi: 10.1177/0272431614525260

Ruzek, E.A, Hafen, C.A., Allen, J.P., Gregory, A., Mikami, A. and Pianta, R.C. (2014b) 'Teacher–student interactions and student motivation, engagement, and competence beliefs: the mediating roles of autonomy support and peer-relatedness', manuscript in preparation.

Sanders, W. and Rivers, J. (1996) *Cumulative and Residual Effects of Teachers on Future Student Academic Achievement*, Knoxville: University of Tennessee, Value-Added Research and Assessment Center.

Skibbe, L., Behnke, M. and Justice, L.M. (2004) 'Parental scaffolding of children's phonological awareness skills: interactions between mothers and their preschoolers with language difficulties', *Communication Disorders Quarterly*, 25: 189–203.

Spearman, J. and Watt, H.M.G. (2013) 'Perception shapes experience: the influence of actual and perceived classroom environment dimensions on girls' motivations for science', *Learning Environments Research*, 16: 217–238.

Taylor, B.M., Pearson, P.D., Peterson, D.S. and Rodriguez, M.C. (2003) 'Reading growth in high-poverty classrooms: the influence of teacher practices that encourage cognitive engagement in literacy learning', *The Elementary School Journal*, 104: 3–28.

Turner, J.C. and Meyer, D.K. (2000) 'Studying and understanding the instructional contexts of classrooms: using our past to forge our future', *Educational Psychologist*, 35: 69–85.

Turner, J.C., Midgley, C., Meyer, D.K., Gheen, M., Anderman, E.M., Kang, Y. and Patrick, H. (2002) 'The classroom environment and students' reports of avoidance strategies in mathematics: a multimethod study', *Journal of Educational Psychology*, 94: 88–106.

Urdan, T. (2004) 'Using multiple methods to assess students' perceptions of classroom goal structures', *European Psychologist*, 9: 222–231.

Urdan, T. and Schoenfelder, E. (2006) 'Classroom effects on student motivation: goal structures, social relationships, and competence beliefs', *Journal of School Psychology*, 44: 331–349.

Vygotsky, L.S. (1980) *Mind in Society: The Development of Higher Psychological Processes*, Cambridge, MA: Harvard University Press.

Wagner, W., Göllner, R., Helmke, A., Trautwein, U. and Lüdtke, O. (2013) 'Construct validity of student perceptions of instructional quality is high, but not perfect: dimensionality and generalizability of domain-independent assessments', *Learning and Instruction*, 28: 1–11.

Wang, M.-T and Holcombe, R. (2010) 'Adolescents' perceptions of school environment, engagement, and academic achievement in middle school', *American Educational Research Journal*, 47: 633–662.

Weinstein, R.S. (1983) 'Student perceptions of schooling', *The Elementary School Journal*, 83: 286–312.

Weinstein, R.S. (2002) 'Overcoming inequality in schooling: a call to action for community psychology', *American Journal of Community Psychology*, 30: 21–42.

Weinstein, R.S. (2008) 'Schools that actualize high expectations for all youth: theory for setting change and setting creation', in M. Shinn and H. Yoshikawa (eds), *Toward Positive Youth Development: Transforming Schools and Community Programs* (pp. 81–101), Oxford: Oxford University Press.

Wentzel, K.R. (1998) 'Social relationships and motivation in middle school: the role of parents, teachers, and peers', *Journal of Educational Psychology*, 90: 202–209.

Wolters, C.A. (2004) 'Advancing achievement goal theory: using goal structures and goal orientations to predict students' motivation, cognition, and achievement', *Journal of Educational Psychology*, 96: 236–250.

Yair, G. (2000) 'Educational battlefields in America: the tug-of-war over student's engagement with instruction', *Sociology of Education*, 73: 247–269.

22

CLASSROOM MANAGEMENT

Current research in the light of social psychology

Johanna Seiz and Mareike Kunter

In regular classrooms, students are often heterogeneous, with diverse social and academic backgrounds. Disruptive behavior of students in class is a day-to-day reality. Still, teachers need to design lessons in which time is not wasted but that nonetheless allow for all students' needs and abilities to be addressed. Obviously such situations highlight the importance of classroom management. Classrooms are complex environments and their management continues to be one of the greatest challenges for teachers. According to Evertson and Weinstein (2006a: 4), classroom management can be understood as 'the actions teachers take to create an environment that supports and facilitates both academic and social-emotional learning'. This definition subsumes various aspects of teacher behavior. For example, the establishment of a structured classroom environment and the introduction of rules or dealing with students' disruptive behavior are also part of classroom management as teachers aim to build a trustworthy student–teacher relationship (e.g. Marzano *et al.* 2003). Yet there are diverse definitions of classroom management, each putting an emphasis on a different aspect (see Evertson and Weinstein 2006b).

Classroom management can be analyzed using different psychological perspectives. From a psychology of learning perspective, it can be interpreted in terms of how instruction and curriculum standards meet students' interest and how students' motivation can be fostered. From an organizational psychological view, it can mean the way instructional activities involve the whole class. In contrast, we discuss classroom management from a social-psychological perspective. Classrooms represent complex social environments, with the teacher as a ruler and the students as 'citizens'. The class as a social group is affected by its interactions, relationships, roles, and norms (Babad 2009). Additionally, teachers act in this social context and their behavior is influenced by their social-cognitive processes. This raises the question as to which processes and characteristics guide teachers' actions – and lead to differences in teachers' classroom management. Hence, we will discuss the relevance of teachers' beliefs, motivation, and knowledge concerning classroom management as these characteristics may influence teacher behavior (Ajzen 1991). However, before analyzing these characteristics in detail we describe the empirical significance and theoretical development of classroom management.

Relevance of classroom management

Classroom management is regarded as one aspect of effective instruction (Kunter and Voss 2013; Pianta and Hamre 2009) and there is some evidence of its meaningfulness for various groups of students and domains (Wang *et al.* 1993).

Clearly, students show less inappropriate behavior in classes where effective classroom management strategies are enacted (Evertson and Harris, 1999). Various studies show that classroom management is one of the strongest predictors for student achievement (e.g. Wang *et al.* 1993). Additionally, it was found to be related to students' motivational outcomes such as engagement (Marzano *et al.* 2003), subject-related interest (Kunter *et al.* 2007) and students' satisfaction with school (Nie and Lau 2009).

However, teachers often describe classroom management as a challenge – especially beginning teachers, who report not feeling well-prepared by teacher education (Liston *et al.* 2006). Meanwhile, students' disruptive behavior is associated with teacher burnout and emotional exhaustion (Dicke *et al.* 2014). Classroom management not only affects teachers and students separately; a joint effect on their relationship was also shown. Therefore, proactive and sensitive classroom management strategies seem to go with better student–teacher relationships (de Jong *et al.* 2014; Marzano *et al.* 2003).

Research perspectives on classroom management

Classroom management has been approached from different theoretical perspectives. In the 1950s and 1960s, researchers (Kounin and Gump 1958; Thomas *et al.* 1968) explicitly started to focus on classroom management, first under a behavioral and then an ecological perspective. Recent approaches have focused on person-oriented classroom management (Freiberg 1999a).

Behavioral approaches

Following the boom in behaviorist approaches to human behavior, researchers started to transfer this knowledge of behavior modification from laboratory settings to the classroom. Initial research aimed at shaping desired behavior of individual students by reinforcement, and eliminating undesired student actions by ignoring them (see Landrum and Kauffman 2006). Later, modification techniques were further adapted to the classroom by using rules or reminders to induce favorable behavior (see Brophy 2006). For instance, studies show that praise as a form of operant conditioning promotes attentive student behavior (McAllister *et al.* 1969). In spite of the empirical evidence of its effectiveness, teachers often use praise insufficiently and struggle using contingent rewards (e.g. Shores *et al.* 1993). In fact, such behavioral approaches have often been opposed by educators and researchers (Freiberg 1999a). Nowadays, although the philosophy of this approach is not well-liked, its methods are still frequently used, as the behavioral approach is often addressed in school-wide behavior management programs (Landrum and Kaufman 2006). Notably, the behaviorist approach strongly focuses on behavior regulation of the individual student, neglecting important social processes associated with classroom management.

Ecological approaches

The ecological approach conceptualizes classroom management as a constructive regulation process meaning that the flow of instruction is regarded as an activity vector – the stronger the vector, the fewer disruptions occur. The role of the teacher is to secure this vector by establishing environmental conditions for efficient instruction (Doyle 2006). The ecological perspective emerged mainly due to the research of Kounin and Gump (1958) and further conceptual work by Walter Doyle (1986, 2006). Based on research using videotaped classroom situations, Kounin (1970) concluded that it was not the teacher's reaction to a disruption that made a teacher effective at classroom management, but their preventing actions and behaviors. Kounin's studies revealed several key components of teacher behavior which promote adequate student behavior and help to prevent disruptions during instruction (see Doyle 2006; Kounin 1970). The main components are *withitness, overlapping, smoothness, momentum* and *group focus*.

Both withitness and overlapping support the teacher's monitoring activities. Withitness describes the continuous observation of all classroom processes, a process which is noticeable to students. Overlapping is expressed in the ability to perform several tasks simultaneously. Smoothness and momentum are important to the management of transitions in the classroom. Smoothness is expressed by avoiding breaks between segments of instruction and effectively managing changes of tasks. Momentum supports smoothness and is expressed through continuity of signaling. The group focus is maintained when all students are equally approached, knowing they are individually responsible for task performance (Kounin 1970). The relevance of these components was supported by further studies (e.g. Anderson *et al.* 1979). Compared to the behavioral approach, the ecological perspective shifts the focus to preventive activities of teachers and from the individual student to the class as a group (Evertson and Harris 1999). Additionally, the ecological perspective highlights the importance of smooth transitions between several instructional activities, and the use of nonverbal behavior.

Teacher behavior at the beginning of the school year was the research focus of the research group around Emmer and Evertson. With their longitudinal observational studies (e.g. Emmer *et al.* 1980), they revealed the importance of an early and thorough introduction of class rules and procedures. In addition to Kounin's components, effective managers showed quick reactions to disruptive student behavior (Emmer *et al.* 1980). Based on these findings, a well-evaluated program for teachers was developed (the Classroom Organization and Management Program, or COMP), encompassing six key components; for example, arranging the space in the classroom, planning and teaching rules and procedures, managing student work and maintaining good student behavior (for further description, see Evertson and Harris 1999).

Person-centered approaches

In line with a more socio-constructivist view of teaching, and reflecting a shift of paradigms, a person-centered perspective on classroom management has emerged. This means that the active participation of students in classroom management is emphasized (Freiberg and Lamb 2009). Person-centered approaches aim to foster students' motivation and engagement through social-emotional emphasis, school connectedness, a positive climate, and student self-discipline. Based on this theory, the well-evaluated Consistency Management and Cooperative Discipline Program was developed (Freiberg 1999b), incorporating the themes of prevention, caring, cooperation, organization, and community. In a similar vein, further recent approaches have emphasized developmental aspects and the relevance of positive student–teacher relationships and caring communities to classroom management (e.g. Pianta 2006).

Classroom management from a social-psychological perspective

The ecological as well as the recent approaches on classroom management have already incorporated the importance of social group processes and interactions in their understanding.

In addition, social-psychological theories could help to study further relevant classroom management processes. On the one hand, these theories could improve research on social interaction in the classroom and analyze student behavior. On the other hand, a social-cognition framework could be used to analyze processes guiding teacher behavior. We will focus on the latter in this chapter.

Teachers' social-cognitive processes and classroom management

Research has accumulated much knowledge about teacher behaviors and strategies which help to establish structured and caring classrooms, promoting students' academic learning and well-being. Yet not every teacher succeeds at this task. At present, we know little about why teachers differ in their classroom management effectiveness, though such knowledge is important for improving teacher education. Below we will use the theory of planned behavior (Ajzen 1991) to describe research on teacher characteristics associated with classroom management. The theory of planned behavior is an important framework when it comes to understanding, predicting, and changing peoples' social behavior (Ajzen 2012). It assumes that the greater the intention for a certain behavior, the more likely this behavior will occur. Behavior intention, in return, is influenced by attitudes towards the behavior, subjective norms, and perceived and actual behavioral control. Using this theory as a framework, we will discuss research on teachers' attitudes (represented by their beliefs), their motivation, and their knowledge regarding classroom management, as these characteristics may influence the process of behavior implementation.

Teachers' beliefs

The theory of planned behavior assumes that attitudes towards a behavior influence its intention (Ajzen 1991). Teacher research mostly focuses on teacher beliefs instead of attitudes, which can be interpreted as the cognitive aspects of attitudes (Richardson 1996). Thus teacher beliefs can be defined as an understanding of the world perceived to be true (Richardson 1996). Beliefs have several functions. First, they influence teachers' interpretation of events, acting as filters. Further, beliefs shape the way problems are framed (Fives and Buehl 2012) and they influence the implementation of teacher behaviors (Pajares 1992). Researchers have developed various frameworks regarding beliefs about classroom management, using different conceptualizations of control (see Woolfolk Hoy and Weinstein 2006). Despite these different conceptualizations, the purpose has been to analyze whether teacher beliefs affect behavior.

As a first step, researchers have aimed to describe the interindividual differences of teachers in their beliefs concerning classroom management. An early theoretical conception was the *pupil control ideology* (Hoy 2001; Willower *et al.* 1967), which assumed that teachers' control orientations spread on a continuum from custodial (believing that student behavior needs to be rigidly controlled) to humanistic (emphasizing the teacher–student relationship and substituting teacher control with students' self-regulation) (Hoy 2001). Martin and colleagues (1998) proposed a multifaceted approach including instructional, people, and behavioral management and distinguishing three philosophies about the control of classroom interaction: non-interventionist, interactionalist, and interventionist (Glickman and Tamashiro 1980). The non-interventionist believes in humanism, assuming that children have an inner drive for self-expression, whereas the interactionalist aims at finding solutions that are satisfying for the student and the teacher. The interventionist shows the most controlling approach, believing that the environment needs to shape the students' development (Martin *et al.* 1998).

Generally, it seems as if teachers differ considerably in their classroom management beliefs. Beliefs are shaped by context (Fives and Buehl 2012), thus orientation towards management varies within contexts (e.g. Martin and Yin 1999). In addition, several studies have investigated the development of these beliefs, comparing expert and novice teachers, but results are mixed (Martin and Shoho 2000; Woolfolk and Hoy 1990). A study by Ritter and Hancock (2007) helps to interpret these mixed results. In their sample, experienced and novice teachers did not differ in their classroom management orientation – there was only a difference when experience was analyzed in combination with source of certification. Experienced traditionally certified teachers were significantly less interventionist than novice teachers (traditionally certified) and alternatively certified teachers (novice or experienced). In summary, it seems that in traditional settings and towards the beginning of their career, teachers tend to have more controlling beliefs, whereas more experienced teachers seem to afford more freedom to their students.

To analyze whether beliefs affect behavior, the link between the two is of greatest interest. Unfortunately, this link has been investigated less often and results differ (e.g. Fives and Buehl 2012). One recent study explicitly examined the relationship between pupil control orientations of preservice teachers and their discipline strategies used in the classroom as rated by students (de Jong et al. 2013). Results indicate that teachers with more custodial control orientations used more aggressive discipline strategies and fewer sensitive strategies. These results demonstrate that teachers' beliefs might be one aspect influencing teachers' behavior intention, although research has not been systematic. There is also evidence that teachers' beliefs can be changed through intervention (e.g. Rimm-Kaufmann et al. 2006), highlighting the relevance of further research.

Motivational characteristics

In terms of the theory of planned behavior, behavior intention is also assumed to include motivational factors, one relevant factor of teacher motivation being teachers' self-efficacy (Tschannen-Moran et al. 1998). Self-efficacy is explicitly addressed in the theory of planned behavior as it represents perceived behavioral control (Ajzen 2012). There has been research focusing on teachers' self-efficacy regarding classroom management. This efficacy may be defined as 'the teachers' beliefs in their capabilities to organize and execute the courses of action required to maintain classroom order' (Brouwers and Tomic 2000: 242). Hence, just as in their beliefs, teachers differ in their classroom management efficacy. Female teachers seem to feel less efficacious than male teachers and elementary teachers have higher self-efficacy ratings than those teaching other school types (Klassen and Chiu 2010). In the same study, the development of teacher efficacy over the teaching career was analyzed. Interestingly, the pattern across the career was not linear; efficacy increased over about 23 years of experience, after which it started decreasing. Regarding cultural differences, Ho and Hau (2004) compared Australian and Chinese teachers. Here, self-efficacy for classroom management was found to be valid across these two different cultural contexts, although Australian teachers rated their efficacy significantly higher.

Regarding the link between self-efficacy and teachers' classroom management behavior, teachers with higher efficacy prefer behavior strategies in favor of establishing and increasing desired behavior (Emmer and Hickman 1991). Morris-Rothschild and Brassard (2006) showed that efficacious teachers also reported a more positive conflict management style.

Teacher enthusiasm, that is, a manifestation of the intrinsic motivation of teachers, is another aspect of teachers' motivation relevant for classroom management (Kunter et al. 2008). Using student and teacher ratings for instruction, Kunter et al. (2013) showed that teachers scoring high on enthusiasm showed more effective classroom management, even when student characteristics and other teacher characteristics such as knowledge or beliefs were controlled.

Teacher knowledge and expertise

According to the theory of planned behavior, actual behavioral control – the extent to which a person possesses objective skills – mediates the link between intention and behavior. However, research on teacher skills seems to mainly focus on teacher knowledge. There have been few attempts to quantitatively measure knowledge about classroom management (Voss *et al.* 2011). Winitzky and colleagues (1994) analyzed the development of the structure of teachers' classroom management knowledge using concept maps. After one year of teaching, their knowledge showed further differentiation. Needels (1991) showed in her study that experienced teachers had a deeper understanding and knowledge of classroom situations in comparison to novices.

Using think-aloud protocols, Swanson and colleagues (1990) analyzed differences in information processing between expert and novice teachers with regard to classroom discipline situations. Their results seem to indicate differences in the use of heuristics and strategies as well as in the solution of the problem situations. Expert teachers showed detailed analysis of the situations and proposed solutions. Contrastingly, novice teachers defined the problem mostly using possible solutions and lacked a detailed analysis. A further study on differences in information processing was conducted by Sabers and colleagues (1991), comparing novice teachers, advanced beginners and expert teachers. Participants looked at taped classroom situations displayed simultaneously by three monitors showing different perspectives of the classroom. The scanning patterns and the focus differed significantly between the groups: experts were significantly better at handling the simultaneity of the situation, noticing events from all three monitors, whereas novice and beginning teachers mainly focused on the front screen.

The ongoing research on the differences in perception between novices and experts has recently been framed under the term *professional vision* (Goodwin 1994). This term describes the ability of members of a professional group to interpret central phenomena related to their profession. Sherin (2007) transferred this term to teachers and describes their professional vision as the ability to make sense of classroom situations. This complex and interactive process consists of the two subprocesses *selective attention* and *knowledge-based reasoning*.

Van den Bogert and colleagues (2014) used eye tracking in their study to compare differences in the perception of classroom management situations between experienced and novice teachers. Regarding the length and the frequency of vision, results indicate that experienced teachers look at students for a shorter period of time but do so more frequently, whereas novice teachers throw longer glances, but less frequently and extensively. Additionally, the visual focus of experienced teachers in the classroom is more homogenous across situations, whereas novice teachers tend to keep their focus on a problem situation, neglecting other processes in the classroom.

Summing up, teacher novices and experts differ in their knowledge and professional vision. Experts have considerably more knowledge, helping them to adequately interpret classroom situations (e.g. Carter *et al.* 1988) and behave accordingly.

Thus, there is considerable evidence that teachers vary in terms of their individual characteristics such as beliefs, motivational orientations, and knowledge, be it at the time they enter teacher education or as working teachers. Yet these aspects influence behavior intention, as they may promote or prevent effective implementation of classroom management.

Challenges and future directions

The relevance of classroom management to effective instruction is supported by numerous studies. Still, there are some unsolved issues that future research should consider. For example, too little is known as to why some teachers succeed in classroom management and others struggle with it. Taking the theory of planned behavior as a framework, it can be concluded that several aspects influence teacher behavior and that behavioral decisions are based on more than knowledge about classroom management. There is still a need to investigate how teachers' social-cognitive processes translate into action and then, in turn, affect various student outcomes. Therefore different methodological designs need to be implemented, such as combining observational studies with quantitative studies or using experiments to manipulate these processes and discover their trajectories. Further, there is a need for simultaneous assessment of teacher and student data to analyze the significance of teacher behavior to different student outcomes (e.g. Brown *et al.* 2010).

Research would also benefit from better assessment of teacher characteristics; in particular, the instruments assessing beliefs about classroom control need further validation. Rimm-Kaufmann and colleagues (2006) developed a tool for assessing teachers' priorities among their beliefs about classroom management which could be useful for further analyses of the link between beliefs and behavior.

Additionally, classroom management is affected by contextual factors (Shuell 1996); however, this interdependence between classroom management and context has been neglected in research. This is especially important as educational developments often lead to context changes, such as more socio-constructivist or inclusive classroom settings. Accordingly, instructional formats progress and cooperative learning or more individualized learning settings challenge classroom management research (Emmer and Stough 2001). In addition, context is shaped by culture, despite little being known about how classroom management is perceived in different cultures (e.g. Zhou *et al.* 2012). Future research should consider these varying social contexts and potential reciprocal relationships between context and effects of classroom management.

As to the importance of classroom management to students, too little is yet known about potential child-by-instruction interactions, indicating that certain groups of students benefit especially from classroom management; for example, students with functional or demographic risks (Decristan *et al.* in press).

Apart from this, teacher characteristics also depend on context. For example, self-efficacy varies in different classes (Raudenbush *et al.* 1992), so research should address the question as to what kinds of classroom surroundings are supportive for teachers' motivational orientations and beliefs. It is also evident that different individual teacher characteristics interact and, additionally, are influenced by context factors. Longitudinal research would help to address unresolved questions on stability, causality, and reciprocity regarding these aspects. Interestingly, Holzberger *et al.* (2013) showed in their longitudinal study that effective classroom management – rated by students and teachers – led to increased general teachers' self-efficacy one year later.

Only if we know more about how social-cognitive processes translate into teacher classroom management behavior, which characteristics influence these processes and how context relates to them, can teacher education be improved.

The demand for implementing classroom management programs in teacher education has already been made (Emmer and Stough 2001); nevertheless, we would like to highlight this importance again. In this chapter we have outlined that several factors act on teacher behavior, and would like to conclude by saying that in teacher education it is not only necessary to convey knowledge about classroom management but also to actively challenge existing beliefs and motivational orientations. These characteristics are likely to have an effect on behavioral decisions. To initiate reflective processing on these aspects, the use of video tools seems a promising approach that provides opportunities for reflection but also fosters knowledge gain and increasing professional vision (Blomberg *et al.* 2013). If novice teachers enter teacher education with very controlling beliefs towards classroom management or without feeling capable of managing, the mere ability to interpret classroom situations or knowledge of the best techniques will not be sufficient for successful implementation of classroom management.

References

Ajzen, I. (1991) 'The theory of planned behavior', *Organizational Behavior and Human Decision Processes*, 50: 179–211.

Ajzen, I. (2012) 'The theory of planned behavior', in P. Van Lange, A. Kruglanski and E.T. Higgins (eds), *Handbook of Theories of Social Psychology* (Vol. 1, pp. 438–460), London: Sage Publications.

Anderson, L.M., Evertson, C.M. and Brophy, J.E. (1979) 'An experimental study of effective teaching in first-grade reading groups', *The Elementary School Journal*, 79(4): 193–223.

Babad, E. (2009) *The Social Psychology of the Classroom*, New York: Routledge.

Blomberg, G., Renkl, A., Sherin, M.G., Borko, H. and Seidel, T. (2013) 'Five research-based heuristics for using video in pre-service teacher education', *Journal for Educational Research Online*, 5: 90–114.

Brophy, J.E. (2006) 'History of research on classroom management', in C.M. Evertson and C.S. Weinstein (eds) *Handbook of Classroom Management* (pp. 17–43), Mahwah, NJ: Lawrence Erlbaum.

Brouwers, A. and Tomic, W. (2000) 'A longitudinal study of teacher burnout and perceived self-efficacy in classroom management', *Teaching and Teacher Education*, 16: 239–253.

Brown, J., Jones, S., LaRusso, M. and Aber, J.L. (2010) 'Improving classroom quality: teacher influences and experimental impacts of the 4Rs program', *Journal of Educational Psychology*, 102: 153–167.

Carter, K., Cushing, K., Sabers, D., Stein, P. and Berliner, D. (1988) 'Expert-novice differences in perceiving and processing visual classroom information', *Journal of Teacher Education*, 39: 25–31.

de Jong, R., van Tartwijk, J., Wubbels, T., Veldman, I. and Verloop, N. (2013) 'Student teachers' discipline strategies: relations with self-images, anticipated student responses and control orientation', *Educational Studies*, 39: 582–597.

de Jong, R., Mainhard, T., van Tartwijk, J., Veldman, I., Verloop, N. and Wubbels, T. (2014) 'How pre-service teachers' personality traits, self-efficacy, and discipline strategies contribute to the teacher-student relationship', *British Journal of Educational Psychology*, 84: 294–310.

Decristan, J., Kunter, M., Fauth, B., Büttner, G., Hardy, I. and Hertel, S. (in press) 'What role does instructional quality play for elementary school children's science competence – a focus on students at risk', *Journal for Educational Research Online*.

Dicke, T., Parker, P.D., Marsh, H.W., Kunter, M., Schmeck, A. and Leutner, D. (2014) 'Self-efficacy in classroom management, classroom disturbances, and emotional exhaustion: a moderated mediation analysis of teacher candidates', *Journal of Educational Psychology*, 106: 569–583.

Doyle, W. (1986) 'Classroom organization and management', in M.C. Wittrock (ed.) *Handbook of Research on Teaching* (pp. 392–431), New York: Macmillan.

Doyle, W. (2006) 'Ecological approaches to classroom management', in C.M. Evertson and C.S. Weinstein (eds) *Handbook of Classroom Management* (pp. 97–125), Mahwah, NJ: Lawrence Erlbaum.

Emmer, E.T., Evertson, C.M. and Anderson, L.M. (1980) 'Effective classroom management at the beginning of the school year', *The Elementary School Journal*, 80: 219–231.

Emmer, E.T. and Hickman, J. (1991) 'Teacher efficacy in classroom management and discipline', *Educational and Psychological Measurement*, 51: 755–765.

Emmer, E.T. and Stough, L.M. (2001) 'Classroom management: a critical part of educational psychology, with implications for teacher education', *Educational Psychologist*, 36: 103–112.

Evertson, C.M. and Harris, A.H. (1999) 'Support for managing learning-centered classrooms: the Classroom Organization and Management Program', in H. J. Freiberg (ed.) *Beyond Behaviorism: Changing the Classroom Management Paradigm* (pp. 59–74), Boston: Allyn & Bacon.

Evertson, C.M. and Weinstein, C.S. (2006a) 'Classroom management as a field of inquiry', in C.M. Evertson and C.S. Weinstein (eds), *Handbook of Classroom Management* (pp. 3–15), Mahwah, NJ: Lawrence Erlbaum.

Evertson, C.M. and Weinstein, C.S. (eds) (2006b) *Handbook of Classroom Management*, Mahwah, NJ: Lawrence Erlbaum.

Fives, H. and Buehl, M.M. (2012) 'Spring cleaning for the "messy" construct of teachers' beliefs: What are they? Which have been examined? What can they tell us?', *APA Educational Psychology Handbook*, Vol 2. *Individual Differences and Cultural and Contextual Factors* (pp. 471–499), Washington, DC: American Psychological Association.

Freiberg, H.J. (1999a) *Beyond Behaviorism: Changing the Classroom Management Paradigm*, Boston: Allyn & Bacon.

Freiberg, H.J. (1999b) 'Consistency management and cooperative discipline: from tourists to citizens in the classrooms', in H.J. Freiberg (ed.) *Beyond Behaviorism: Changing the Classroom Management Paradigm* (pp. 75–97), Boston: Allyn & Bacon.

Freiberg, H.J. and Lamb, S.M. (2009) 'Dimensions of person-centered classroom management', *Theory into Practice,* 48: 99–105.

Glickman, C.D. and Tamashiro, R.T. (1980) 'Clarifying teachers' beliefs about discipline', *Educational Leadership,* 37: 459–464.

Goodwin, C. (1994) 'Professional vision', *American Anthropologist,* 96: 606–633.

Ho, I.T. and Hau, K.-T. (2004) 'Australian and Chinese teacher efficacy: similarities and differences in personal instruction, discipline, guidance efficacy and beliefs in external determinants', *Teaching and Teacher Education,* 20: 313–323.

Holzberger, D., Philipp, A. and Kunter, M. (2013) 'How teachers' self-efficacy is related to instructional quality: a cross-lagged panel analysis', *Journal of Educational Psychology,* 105: 774–786.

Hoy, W.K. (2001) 'The pupil control studies. a historical, theoretical and empirical analysis', *Journal of Educational Administration,* 39: 424–441.

Klassen, R.M. and Chiu, M.M. (2010) 'Effects on teachers' self-efficacy and job satisfaction: teacher gender, years of experience, and job stress', *Journal of Educational Psychology,* 102: 741–756.

Kounin, J.S. (1970) *Discipline and Group Management in Classrooms,* New York: Holt, Rinehart and Winston.

Kounin, J.S. and Gump, P.V. (1958) 'The ripple effect in discipline', *The Elementary School Journal,* 59: 158–162.

Kunter, M., Baumert, J. and Köller, O. (2007) 'Effective classroom management and the development of subject-related interest', *Learning and Instruction,* 17: 494–509.

Kunter, M., Klusmann, U., Baumert, J., Richter, D., Voss, T. and Hachfeld, A. (2013) 'Professional competence of teachers: effects on instructional quality and student development', *Journal of Educational Psychology,* 105: 805–820.

Kunter, M., Tsai, Y.-M., Klusmann, U., Brunner, M., Krauss, S. and Baumert, J. (2008) 'Students' and mathematics teachers' perceptions of teacher enthusiasm and instruction', *Learning and Instruction,* 18: 468–482.

Kunter, M. and Voss, T. (2013) 'The model of instructional quality in COACTIV: a multicriteria analysis', in M. Kunter, J. Baumert, W. Blum, U. Klusmann, S. Krauss and M. Neubrand (eds) *Cognitive Activation in the Mathematics Classroom and Professional Competence of Teachers. Results from the COACTIV Project* (pp. 97–124), New York, NY: Springer.

Landrum, T.J. and Kauffman, J.M. (2006) 'Behavioral approaches to classroom management', in C.M. Evertson and C.S. Weinstein (eds) *Handbook of Classroom Management* (pp. 47–71), Mahwah, NJ: Lawrence Erlbaum.

Liston, D., Whitcomb, J. and Borko, H. (2006) 'Too little or too much: teacher preparation and the first years of teaching', *Journal of Teacher Education,* 57: 351–358.

McAllister, L.W., Stachowiak, J.G., Baer, D.M. and Conderman, L. (1969) 'The application of operant conditioning techniques in a secondary school classroom', *Journal of Applied Behavior Analysis,* 2(4): 277–285.

Martin, N.K. and Shoho, A. (2000, January) 'Teacher experience, training, and age: the influence of teacher characteristics on classroom management style', paper presented at the annual meeting of the Southwest Educational Research Association, Dallas, TX. (ERIC Document Reproduction Service No. ED 440963)

Martin, N.K. and Yin, Z. (1999) 'Beliefs regarding classroom management style: differences between urban and rural secondary level teachers', *Journal of Research in Rural Education,* 15: 101–105.

Martin, N.K., Yin, Z. and Baldwin, B. (1998) 'Construction validation of the attitudes and beliefs on classroom control inventory', *Journal of Classroom Interaction,* 33(2): 6–15.

Marzano, R.J., Marzano, J.S. and Pickering, D.J. (2003) *Classroom Management that Works – Research-based Strategies for Every Teacher,* Alexandria, VA: Association for Supervision and Curriculum Development.

Morris-Rothschild, B.K. and Brassard, M.R. (2006) 'Teachers' conflict management styles: the role of attachment styles and classroom mangement efficacy', *Journal of School Psychology,* 44: 105–121.

Needels, M.C. (1991) 'Comparison of student, first-year, and experienced teachers' interpretations of a first-grade lesson', *Teaching and Teacher Education,* 7: 269–278.

Nie, Y. and Lau, S. (2009) 'Complementary roles of care and behavioral control in classroom management: the self-determination theory perspective', *Contemporary Educational Psychology,* 34: 185–194.

Pajares, M.F. (1992) 'Teachers' beliefs and educational research: cleaning up a messy construct', *Review of Educational Research,* 62: 307–332.

Pianta, R.C. (2006) 'Classroom management and relationships between children and teachers: implications for research and practice', in C.M. Evertson and C.S. Weinstein (eds) *Handbook of Classroom Management* (pp. 685–709). Mahwah, NJ: Lawrence Erlbaum.

Pianta, R.C. and Hamre, B.K. (2009) 'Conceptualization, measurement, and improvement of classroom processes: standardized observation can leverage capacity', *Educational Researcher,* 38(2): 109–119.

Raudenbush, S.W., Rowan, B. and Cheong, Y.F. (1992) 'Contextual effects on the self-perceived efficacy of high school teachers', *Sociology of Education,* 65: 150–167.

Richardson, V. (1996) 'The role of attitudes and beliefs in learning to teach', in J. Sikula, T. Buttery and E. Guyton (eds) *Handbook of Research on Teacher Education* (2nd edn, pp. 102–106), New York: Macmillan.

Rimm-Kaufmann, S.E., Storm, M.D., Sawyer, B.E., Pianta, R.C. and LaParo, K.M. (2006) 'The teacher belief q-sort: a measure of teachers' priorities in relation to disciplinary practices, teaching practices, and beliefs about children', *Journal of School Psychology,* 44: 141–165.

Ritter, J.T. and Hancock, D.R. (2007) 'Exploring the relationship between certification sources, experience levels, and classroom management orientations of classroom teachers', *Teaching and Teacher Education,* 23: 1206–1216.

Sabers, D.S., Cushing, K.S. and Berliner, D.C. (1991) 'Differences among teachers in a task characterized by simultaneity, multidimensionality, and immediacy', *American Educational Research Journal,* 28: 63–88.

Sherin, M.G. (2007) 'The development of teachers' professional vision in video clubs', in R. Goldman, R. Pea, B. Barron and S.J. Derry (eds) *Video Research in the Learning Sciences* (pp. 383–395), Mahwah, NJ: Lawrence Erlbaum.

Shores, R.E., Jack, S.L., Gunter, P.L., Ellis, D.N., DeBriere, T.J. and Wehby, J.H. (1993) 'Classroom interactions of children with behavior disorders', *Journal of Emotional and Behavioral Disorders,* 1: 27–39.

Shuell, T.J. (1996) 'Teaching and learning in a classroom context', in D.C. Berliner and R.C. Calfee (eds) *Handbook of Educational Psychology* (pp. 726–764), New York: Simon & Schuster.

Swanson, H.L., O'Connor, J.E. and Cooney, J.B. (1990) 'An information processing analysis of expert and novice teachers' problem solving', *American Educational Research Journal,* 27: 533–556.

Thomas, D.R., Becker, W.C. and Armstrong, M. (1968) 'Production and elimination of disruptive classroom behavior by systematically varying teacher's behavior', *Journal of Applied Behavior Analysis,* 1: 35–45.

Tschannen-Moran, M., Woolfolk Hoy, A. and Hoy, W.K. (1998) 'Teacher efficacy: it's meaning and measure', *Review of Educational Research,* 68: 202–248.

van den Bogert, N., van Bruggen, J., Kostons, D. and Jochems, W. (2014) 'First steps into understanding teachers' visual perception of classroom events', *Teaching and Teacher Education,* 37: 208–216.

Voss, T., Kunter, M. and Baumert, J. (2011) 'Assessing teacher candidates' general pedagogical/psychological knowledge: test construction and validation', *Journal of Educational Psychology,* 103: 952–969.

Wang, M.C., Haertel, G.D. and Walberg, H.J. (1993) 'Toward a knowledge base for school learning', *Review of Educational Research,* 63(3): 249–294.

Willower, D.J., Eidell, T.L. and Hoy, W.K. (1967) *The School and Pupil Control Ideology,* University Park, PA: Pennsylvania State University.

Winitzky, N., Kauchak, D. and Kelly, M. (1994) 'Measuring teachers' structural knowledge', *Teaching and Teacher Education,* 10: 125–139.

Woolfolk, A.E. and Hoy, W.K. (1990) 'Prospective teachers' sense of efficacy and beliefs about control', *Journal of Educational Psychology,* 82: 81–91.

Woolfolk Hoy, A. and Weinstein, C.S. (2006) 'Student and teacher perspectives on classroom management', in C.M. Evertson and C.S. Weinstein (eds) *Handbook of Classroom Management* (pp. 181–219), Mahwah, NJ: Lawrence Erlbaum.

Zhou, N., Lam, S.-F. and Chan, K.C. (2012) 'The Chinese classroom paradox: a cross-cultural comparison of teacher controlling behaviors', *Journal of Educational Psychology,* 104: 1162–1174.

23

LEARNING ENVIRONMENT

The influence of school and classroom space on education

Ulrike Stadler-Altmann

This chapter presents an overview of the theoretical and empirical research on the influence of the constructed environment on education. It brings together research from different traditions – the field of architecture as it relates to the design of schools and classrooms and the fields of education and social psychology – and looks at the connections that can be drawn between teacher–student interactions and the surroundings in which those interactions take place.

The chapter first discusses the framework for evaluating learning environments. It then illustrates the influence of school architecture on school design and culture, and on classroom architecture and classroom activities. In particular, it examines teaching and learning in these constructed environments by depicting how teachers and students deal with school buildings and classroom conditions. The most powerful research seeks to display connections between the classroom as a constructed environment and the pedagogy and social psychology that takes place in that environment. The chapter concludes with some questions for future research.

Framework for evaluating learning environments

Is there an influence of school or classroom buildings and space on education? The use of the school and classroom – that is, the relationships between the classroom and its arrangement with the conduct of lessons within that classroom – plays an insignificant role in the international educational research. Rather, the focus is on the teaching and learning activities, and the school space and classrooms in which these activities take place are often not even considered. Only a few educational researchers focus on the relationship between the architecture of the school and classrooms and the learning that takes place within these schools and classrooms (Higgins *et al.* 2005; Woolner 2010).

Among the first studies to discuss the potential influences of the learning environment are those of Moos (1979), Steele (1973) and Bronfenbrenner (1981, 2005). These studies present models of the relationship between environments and students' outcomes, as well as reflecting on the importance of the environment to learning.

The model developed by Moos emphasizes the relevance of the physical setting, as part of the environmental system, to student outcomes. Moos states that 'architecture and physical design can influence psychological states and social behavior' (Moos 1979: 6). Over the years, Moos' model has influenced research on architecture and education that has identified other influences that the physical environment can have on student achievement and behavior.

Steele (1973) analyzes the basic functions of school architecture and classrooms, five of which became important for subsequent educational research (see Weinstein 2007; Weinstein and Mignano 2011). The five functions are security and shelter, pleasure, symbolic identification, task instrumentality, and social contact (for a detailed discussion, see the section on classroom space). According to Steele, these basic functions must be fulfilled for effective teaching and learning, especially in the classroom.

Bronfenbrenner (1981, 2005) sees the social ecological dimension for teaching and learning in schools and classrooms. The benefit of this theory for creating learning arrangements is illustrated by Sacher (2006) in his *Didaktik der Lernökologie*. He shows how the social surrounding could be used for designing teaching and learning in classrooms.

This fundamental research of Bronfenbrenner, Moos and Steele helps to organize and understand existing research and to formulate strategies for further conceptual and practical advances. The following discussion offers an overview of this field of research and presents some interesting aspects for further study in the area of teaching and learning in schools and classrooms.

Higgins *et al.* (2005: 5) use the research questions about the physical conditions of schools and classrooms and the consequences of these physical conditions for teaching and learning for their overview. These questions are modified and used in this chapter to highlight the effect of school and classroom space on teachers' and students' behavior, learning and teaching, and achievement.

Although the work by Moos and Steele discussed above goes some way to understanding current research, nonetheless the research on learning environments is sparse and has no overarching focus, as Gislason (2011) and Higgins *et al.* (2005: 6) have demonstrated:

> The empirical research that exists on the impacts of environment on teaching and learning tends to focus more upon some elements (for example, noise) and to fail to synthesize understandings (for example the implication of noise and temperature research tend to conflict). Cultural and geographical differences also highlight the importance of sensitivity to context. For these reasons it is very difficult to make judgements about which areas are 'worth' focussing on.

Consequently, the next two sections focus on research on school building and classroom design from an architectural point of view. This is followed by a section that approaches the subject from an educational point of view.

School space

The importance of school buildings and classroom spaces for teachers' and students' practice had been ignored for many years (see Martin 2002): most teachers do not think about their school and their classrooms as a built environment for teaching and learning. Rather, they focus on the restrictions of their school building and their classrooms (see Walden 2009; Weinstein 2007; Weinstein and Mignano 2011). Students also see the bad conditions in their classrooms and their schools. However, when asked in more detail – for example in the studies of Woolner *et al.* (2007, 2011, 2012, 2013) – teachers and students were able to communicate the school buildings and classrooms they desired. If we thought about better conditions for teaching and learning in our schools and classrooms, we would realize that a focus on the constructed environment and its possibilities would support teaching and learning. The perspective of teachers and students needs to be seen and included in the research questions.

School architecture

Henry Sanoff (1994, 1996) discusses school design and the possibilities of designing a responsive school and shows that the school building is an important factor for successful schools. Rotraut Walden (2009: 75), in writing about schools for the future, outlines the main aspects for 'a positive educational quality of the learning environment', such as color scheme, form design, lighting, heating, cooling and ventilation, acoustics and noise, furniture, and equipment. Her work also corresponds to Steele's (1973) findings which state that physical settings serve a number of basic functions (see the next section).

As outlined by Gislason (2011), there are many studies on building quality and academic outcomes, which focus on indoor air quality, lighting, noise and acoustics, occupant density, and thermal comfort. The importance of these environmental factors is recognized by architects and building engineers. However, these empirical studies have only considered the surroundings as important factors for well-being in schools, and do not provide any detailed evidence of their importance for teaching and learning. Research has also shown that the quality of facilities influences the citizens' perceptions of schools and thus can serve as a point of community pride and increased support for public education (Uline *et al.* 2007).

School design and culture

School design influences school culture and changes the way of teaching and learning. Or is it the other way round – have the changes in teaching and learning over the past two hundred years changed the school design and school culture? Most of the research in this field postulates changes in teaching and learning which have influenced the school building and classroom design (see Gislason 2011). Both for Europe and for the United States, Gislason finds two developments in school history which have a strong effect on school design and school culture: first, 'the single-grade classroom replaced the multi-grade school-room' (Gislason, 2011: 1) and second, 'a growing interest in non-traditional educational practices has prompted architects to develop a variety of experimental design solutions' (Gislason, 2011: 1).

Pamela Woolner (2010) describes three principles for understanding how schools are judged over time: the value of community recognition, the importance of good design, and the importance of evaluation continuing over time.

The influence of school buildings on education

Higgins *et al.* (2005: 7) provide an overview of the research findings in this field, which are still state-of-the-art:

- There is strong, consistent evidence for the effect of basic physical variables (air quality, temperature, noise) on learning.
- Once minimal standards are attained, evidence of the effect of changing basic physical variables is less significant.
- There is conflicting evidence, but forceful opinions, on the effects of lighting and color.
- Other physical characteristics affect students' perceptions and behavior, but it is difficult to draw definite, general conclusions.
- The interactions of different elements are as important as the consideration of single elements.

Classroom space

Little is known about how teachers and students deal with the school and classroom environment for their teaching and learning (Stadler-Altmann 2013). To describe ideal learning environments, this section will illustrate some relationships between the constructed environment of the classroom and the educational processes that take place within them.

Most of the educational research is based on the work of Steele (1973), who illustrated the function of various classroom settings. He states that the physical environment can influence the way teachers and students feel, think, and behave. Following his considerations, Weinstein (2007; Weinstein and Mignano 2011) argues that five of Steele's functions – security and shelter, pleasure, symbolic identification, task instrumentality, and social contact – are especially important for teaching and learning in classes:

- *Security and shelter:* These are the most fundamental functions of all built environments. Physical security is a precondition that must be satisfied, at least to some extent, before the environment can serve students' and teachers' other, higher-level needs. Additionally, psychological security is also an important precondition; that is, the feeling that school and classrooms are safe and good, comfortable places to be.
- *Pleasure:* Equally important is the fact that teachers and students find their classrooms attractive and pleasing. Some educational studies demonstrate that an aesthetically pleasing environment can influence behavior: attractive classrooms have a positive effect on attendance and feeling of group cohesion (Horowitz and Otto 1973) and on participation in class discussions (Sommer and Olson 1980).
- *Symbolic identification:* This is the so-called personality of classrooms and schools, when they are designed by teachers and students in a daily routine.
- *Task instrumentality:* This function describes the ways in which the environment helps us to carry out the tasks teachers want to accomplish.
- *Social contact:* The arrangements of desks, for example, promote social contact or give space for individual work. So teachers could plan clusters for student interaction. The way students are arranged can also affect the interaction between teachers and students. A number of studies have found that in classrooms where desks are arranged in rows, the teacher interacts mostly with students seated in front and in the center of the classroom. Students in this 'action zone' participate more in class discussions and initiate more question and comments.

These functions of the classroom settings discussed above provide the background theory for many studies and research projects. Other studies concern the design of classroom environments and the effect of these environments on the practice of teachers (Martin 2002).

There is little on the use of the classroom in the empirical educational research. Where it has been considered, one focus has been on the questions of how teachers deal with room conditions, how they position themselves in the classroom, how they move through the classroom and how the teacher's body language, expressed therein, influences lessons. A second focus has been whether changes in classroom architecture (cf. Buddensiek 2008; Rittelmeyer 2010) affect the level of classroom activity (cf. Steele 1973; Weinstein 2007; Weinstein and Mignano 2011). The following discussion examines whether teachers change their teaching in school or classroom spaces that have been changed according to their wishes, on the basis that the classroom, as a constructed environment, influences both well-being and classroom activities (cf. Forster 1997; Rittelmeyer 2010).

However, before crucial aspects of teacher's practice and students' response are outlined, consider the environmental situation in German and English. Most of the European and American classrooms are planned in the same way. As a consequence of the fact that most of our schools were planned and built in the nineteenth century (see Buddensiek 2008; Tanner and Lackney 2006), the governmental guidelines for school architecture are still often based on these traditions (see Rittelmeyer 2010). As Tanner and Lackney (2006) have shown in their *History of Education Architecture*, there was and still is a relevant discussion and critique on school building and classroom design. The progressive movement of the late nineteenth century has had a strong influence on school architecture, with new forms of school buildings being designed. These schools are often private schools; for example the Laboratory School of John Dewey, the Waldorf School of Rudolf Steiner, and the schools in the tradition of Maria Montessori. One can also find influences of the progressive movement in public schools (see Tanner and Lackney 2006). In general, though, traditional classrooms and traditional furniture still prevails, in that most of these traditional classrooms were planned as rooms for teaching in front of the class and for teacher-centered instruction (for more details, see Buddensiek 2008; Montag Stiftung 2011).

Classroom architecture

As Martin (2002: 143) explains,

> the hierarchy of design-ability is a construct that measures the degree of control of change that teachers have over the physical elements of the classroom setting. In examining teacher's use of the classroom space, architectural elements have been classified in terms of hard (fixed features) and soft architecture (semi-fixed, semi-flexible and flexible features).

Teachers generally manipulate the environment for their students in changing the arrangements of desks and chairs to improve their teaching and the students' learning. Martin (2002) shows there is a strong relationship between the pedagogical ideas of the teachers and their dealing with the classroom conditions, but often the teachers have no ideas about how to change classrooms to improve their teaching.

Classroom activities: Teaching and learning

Higgins *et al.* (2005) point out that, despite the fact that we still find traditional classrooms in use,

> at the same time our understanding of learning itself is changing. Research on learning styles, formative assessment, multiple and emotional intelligences, constructivism and so on have combined with the rapid development of technology-enabled, peer-to-peer and self-directed learning to facilitate very different approaches to the 30-students-in-rows model. But despite these changes, we do not yet have a robust research base for integrated and personalized learning environments.
>
> *(Higgins et al. 2005: 3)*

As a result, teachers have to deal with traditional room settings while at the same time they often want to teach in a modern and future-centered way.

Teaching

Teaching is necessarily interactive and people-centered. This interaction is frequently mediated by equipment and materials, and teachers adapt their teaching to supplies and equipment available. In traditional classrooms, teachers have only limited space for their movement and their interaction with their students. As illustrated by Müller (2008), even within bad room conditions there exist some possibilities to activate and to motivate students; for instance, the teacher's movement can produce interaction with and between the students.

All these proxemics are examined by Sacher (2000) in his study of teachers' movement in the classroom. Sacher found relationships between the different ways in which teachers moved around the classroom and their interactions with students. Sacher's examples illustrate the individual use of constructed environments; the different ways in which teachers use classrooms that are poorly designed. However, it needs to be clarified that we cannot say anything about the pedagogical interaction from these observation results.

More detailed are the observations by Martin (2002). She demonstrated in her study that there is a relation between the teaching environment and the teachers' pedagogy. Her focus was on the teacher and on the classroom physical environment. Martin explored the technique of behavioral mapping (see Prosansky *et al.* 1974) and interviews. Her examples are based on extremes in classroom organization, mobility, and degree of centeredness, and illustrate the link to pedagogy. For example, one of the cases is teacher-centered, whereas the other is child-centered, yet both are very much related to how the classroom is organized, and how the teacher moves within this arrangement (for more detail, see Martin 2002: 145).

All these research examples of teachers' movement in classes exemplify that there are interesting findings about the teacher's practice in the classroom and that teaching is necessarily interactive and people centered. This interaction is frequently mediated by the constructed environment.

Learning

The results from most educational empirical research show the teachers' reactions to the constructed environment and the consequences on their practice. Furthermore, the students' action in classroom is initially a reaction to and interaction with the classroom's arrangement and second, with the learning possibilities which these arrangements include.

Teachers talked a lot about where students take their seats in the classroom (for classroom seating location, see Montello, 1988), when they are asked about the students' activities during one lesson. Sacher (2000) shows different positions in the classroom and finds a zone of action, which is also revealed by Martin (2002) and others in their studies. Sacher postulates five reasons for teacher–student interaction related to the teacher's movement in the classroom: support, discipline, confidence, attraction, and indifference. Each reason for the interaction was based on the teacher's movement and instruction. Sacher (2000) also illustrates that teachers give more support and confidence when the classroom arrangement features more space and more possibilities for different working forms.

Tagliacollo *et al.* (2010: 201) also highlight the interaction between performance and room arrangement by stating that:

> students' motivation for learning determines concomitantly students' seat choice and school performance. Therefore, we suggest that displacing students to a frontal seat position in the classroom to improve learning performance is probably not a desirable alternative; instead, the teacher should consider raising the students' motivation.

Classrooms' influence on education

The previous sections have provided an overview of the studies in the field of learning environment. Many educational studies initially focused on the design and the architecture of schools and classrooms. Second, these studies often discussed connections between the school building/classroom architecture and teaching and learning. Only a few studies in the past discussed the influence of school buildings and classrooms architecture on educational processes, shown in teachers' and students' interaction during the lessons. Nowadays, more studies seek information on direct and indirect influences by stating that teachers and students must be part of the research project over the whole research process (see Woolner *et al.* 2010, 2011), not only as objects of the research, but also as subjects.

Martin (2002: 154) states:

> As Moore and Lackney (1993) reflect over their findings, it is not unreasonable to suggest that more positive attitudes and behaviors on the part of both teachers and children may reflect positively on improved academic achievement, therefore the environment seen as having an indirect effect on achievement.

Martin concludes that the training of teachers after and during research projects thus represents a matter of greatest importance in order to understand the effects which the classroom has on teachers.

We (the author and colleagues) examined teachers and students in two school projects which included teacher training in the understanding and planning of learning areas in the teacher training aspect of the projects (see Sacher and Stadler-Altmann 2006; Scheunpflug *et al.* 2012; Stadler-Altmann 2010).[1] This research is discussed next as an example of modern research in the field of learning environment.

When Martin (2002) examined teachers' environmental awareness, she used three types of attitudes which she labeled the *imprisoned*, the *free*, and the *simply confused*. She describes *imprisoned* teachers as 'teachers that do not perceive their surroundings in a constructive way and do not seem to perceive how much impact that setting is having on his/her teaching and class' (Martin, 2002: 53). The *simply confused* teachers are aware of the effect of the setting on themselves and on the students. However, some of these teachers are victims of their own classroom settings, because they knew something was not working well but they were not able to find a solution. The *free* teachers were aware of their surroundings and deliberately used them.

In our projects, most teachers were in the category *simply confused* and some in the category *free*. Both school projects pursued the main goal of improving teaching and learning in the way the teacher preferred. We evaluated the changes in daily school life and daily instruction in the classes. The teachers who participated in the projects suggested that their teaching would be more successful if they were allowed to plan their individual classrooms for the students' learning, a so-called 'Lernraum' ('learning classroom'). When we evaluated this change of teachers' thinking about teaching and of classroom arrangements, we found that teachers now focused more on student-centered lessons, talked more about learning strategies and initiated many more cooperative learning settings (see Martin, 2002; Scheunpflug *et al.* 2012 Woolner *et al.* 2012). The teachers themselves named some useful arrangements and focused on innovative aspects such as:

- a classroom floor plan suitable for various instructional methods;
- furniture that enabled opportunities for small group learning and individual study;
- the stimulation of all senses, without becoming distracted;
- good environmental conditions;
- areas for retreat and individual privacy.

After four years of work on the school project KOMPASS, we have discovered some positive changes (Scheunpflug *et al.* 2012) in teachers' satisfaction with their work in their individual support for students, increased self-efficacy, and better learning atmosphere.

In the SELF school project, we detected that the students' perception of learning atmosphere and class atmosphere exercises an influence on their evaluation of their abilities and their self-concept (see Stadler-Altmann, 2010). This result is not surprising as it replicates similar studies. However, more interesting are some results in the aggregate value of class atmosphere; these effects could be supported by the classroom arrangement, the constructed environment, because these shown classroom arrangements are preconditions for changing teaching and learning.

As illustrated by these examples, the research process must be a part of school and teaching development. As an aspect of school development, the focus on the learning environment has to be part of the communication, both discussions and planning in schools and with teachers and students. These results are also pointed out by Higgins *et al.* (2005: 7) in his research overview of learning environments:

- Much of what is known about student comfort, particularly in terms of furniture, has yet to be translated into actual school/classroom environments.
- Since different room arrangements serve different purposes, it is necessary for classrooms to have some degree of flexibility.
- Some improvements to the classroom environment may save time, which is then available for learning.
- 'Ownership' of space and equipment by both teachers and students is important.
- Ownership and engagement are ongoing elements, so there has to be a balance (in display of student work, for example) between permanent and fresh elements.
- Some physical elements in the classroom improve comfort, well-being, and probably attitude – and so, perhaps, improve achievement.

Most of the educational research found in the field of the learning environment centers more on the perspectives of teachers. Consequently, there is a big challenge for further research to focus on the students' perspective.

Further research

As shown in Blackmore and colleagues' literature review (2011), there are still many gaps in the research on the relationships between school architecture, classroom design, and learning environment; for example:

- in the design phase (ibid.: 11) of new school buildings and/or redesign;
- within the transition phase (ibid.: 19) between teaching and learning in old and new designed learning spaces;
- in the consolidation phase (ibid.: 32–33) in new designed learning spaces;
- in the sustainability/re-evaluation phase (ibid.: 36).

However, there are also some further educational research problems which need to be addressed. As outlined in the previous sections, there needs to be more research which integrates students in the research process. As illustrated by Woolner and others (2010), students could be an important partner in the research about school design/architecture and classrooms. She and others used an interesting research design 'diamond ranking activity' (see Clark *et al.* 2013) to involve students of all ages and teachers.

Based on the class atmosphere model by Eder and Mayr (2000), it is necessary to find a more detailed model which features factors of individual well-being in class as well as the specific interaction between students and teachers in class dealing with classroom and school conditions. Then it could be possible to understand the effectiveness of group competition and cohesion in class, and the effects of the classroom environment. The classroom atmosphere is a very relevant variable in this context and we need more studies which connect the atmosphere and the learning environment.

Finally, as Hattie writes,

> the remarkable feature of the evidence is that the biggest effects of student learning occur when teachers become learners of their own teaching, and when students become their own teachers. When students become their own teachers they exhibit self-regulatory attributes that seem most desirable for learners (self-monitoring, self-evaluation, self-assessment, self-teaching).
>
> *(Hattie, 2009: 22)*

Thus, teachers and students need to be supported in this change of views about their teaching and learning, and in understanding the influence of the constructed learning environment on that.

Conclusion

The educational and social psychology research on learning environment is still growing, but, as Higgins *et al.* state, 'it is extremely difficult to come to firm conclusion about the impact of learning environments because of the multi-faceted nature of environments and the subsequent diverse and disconnected nature of the research literature' (2005: 6). Hence research in this field must take into consideration the complexity of teaching and learning in schools and classes.

Note

1 The two school projects are SELF and KOMPASS. The sample for the SELF project includes 2,873 students in the second year of secondary school, in 87 classes from 24 Bavarian grammar schools. For more details, see Sacher and Stadler-Altmann (2006); Stadler-Altmann (2010). The KOMPASS sample includes 2,100 students in the second year of secondary school, in 77 classes from 20 Bavarian secondary schools. For more details, see Scheunpflug *et al.* (2012).

References

Blackmore, J., Bateman, D., Loughlin, J., O'Mara, J. and Aranda, G. (2011) *Research into the Connection between Built Learning Spaces and Student Outcomes, Literature Review*, Paper No. 22, Melbourne, Australia: Education and Policy Research Division, Department of Education and Early Childhood Development. Available at https://www.deakin.edu.au/arts-ed/efi/pubs/deecd-reports-blackmore-learning-spaces.pdf.

Bronfenbrenner, U. (1981) *Die Ökologie der menschlichen Entwicklung: Natürliche und geplante Experimente* [The Ecology of Human Development: Natural and Planned Experiments], Stuttgart: Klett-Cotta.

Bronfenbrenner, U. (2005) *Making Human Beings Human: Bioecological Perspectives on Human Development*, Thousand Oaks, CA: Sage.

Buddensiek, W. (2008) 'Lernräume als gesundheits- & kommunikationsfördernde Lebensräume gestalten. Auf dem Weg zu einer neuen Lernkultur' [Schoolrooms supporting health and communication. A way to a new learning-culture], in G. Brägger, N. Posse and G. Israel (eds), *Bildung und Gesundheit – Argumente für eine gute und gesunde Schule* (pp. 1-28), Bern: h.e.p.Verlag.

Clark, J., Laing, K., Tiplady, L. and Woolner, P. (2013) *Making Connections: Theory and Practise of Using Visual Methods to Aid Participation in Research*, Newcastle, UK: Research Centre for Learning and Teaching, Newcastle University.

Eder, F. and Mayr, J. (2000) *Linzer Fragebogen zum Schul- und Klassenklima für die 4.– 8. Klassenstufe (LFSK 4–8)* [Linzer Questionnaire for School and Class Conditions], Göttingen: Hogrefe.

Forster, J. (1997) 'Kind und Schulraum – Ansprüche und Wirkungen. Eine interdisziplinäre Annäherung an pädagogische Fragestellungen' [Child and School Environment – Requirements and Impact], in G. Becker, J. Bilstein and E. Liebau (eds), *Räume bilden. Studien zur pädagogischen Topologie und Topographie* (pp. 175–194), Seelze: Kallmayer.

Gislason, N. (2011) *Building Innovation. History, Cases, and Perspectives on School Design*, Big Tancook Island, Canada: Backalong Books.

Hattie, J. (2009) *Visible Learning: A Synthesis of Over 800 Meta-analyses Relating to Achievement*, London: Routledge.

Higgins, S., Hall, E., Wall, K., Woolner, P. and McCaughey, C. (2005) *The Impact of School Environments: A Literature Review*, London: Design Council.

Horowitz, P. and Otto, D. (1973) *The Teaching Effectiveness of an Alternative Teaching Facility*, Alberta, Canada: University of Alberta.

Martin, S.H. (2002) 'The classroom environment and its effects on the practice of teachers', *Journal of Environmental Psychology*, 22: 139–156.

Montag Stiftung Urbane Räume, Montag Stiftung Jugend und Gesellschaft (2011) (eds) *Vergleich ausgewählter Richtlinien zum Schulbau – Kurzfassung* [Comparison of Selected Guidelines for School Buildings], Heft 1, Reihe: Rahmen und Richtlinien für einen leistungsfähigen Schulbau in Deutschland.

Montello, D. R. (1988) 'Classroom seating location and its effects on course achievement, participation, and attitudes', *Journal of Environmental Psychology*, 8: 149–157.

Moos, R. H. (1979) *Evaluating Educational Environments*, San Francisco: Jossey-Bass.

Müller, W. (2008) 'Der Lehrer auf der Bühne des Klassenraums. Wirkungen der Raumregie' [Teacher on Stage of the Classroom. Effects of the Stage Directions], *Pädagogik*, 60: 26–30.

Prosansky, E. and Wolfe, M. (1974) 'The physical setting and open education', *School Review*, 82: 557–574.

Rittelmeyer, C. (2010) 'Wie wirkt Schularchitektur auf Schülerinnen und Schüler? Ein Einblick in Ergebnisse der internationalen Schulbauforschung' [Do school buildings affect students? Results of the international research on school buildings], in *Gestaltung von Schulbauten. Ein Diskussionsbeitrag aus erziehungswissenschaftlicher*, Zürich: Stadt Zurich, Schulamt.

Sacher, W (2000) *Proxemik im Klassenraum. Studien zu Nähe und Distanz im Schulalltag* [Proxemics in the Classroom. Studies of Closeness and Distance in Daily School], SUN-Reihe Nr. 11, Nürnberg.

Sacher, W. (2006) *Didaktik der Lernökologie. Lernen und Lehren in unterrichtlichen und medienbasierten Lernarrangements* [Didactics of Learning-Ecology], Bad Heilbrunn: Klinkhardt.

Sacher, W. and Stadler-Altmann, U. (2006), *SELF – Selbstkonzept fördern durch lehrplankonforme Förderung. Bericht über die Durchführungsphase* [SELF – Improving Self-concept through Encourage. Research Report] 01.10.2005-31.10.2006, unveröffentl. Forschungsbericht, 250 S.

Sanoff, H. (1994) *School Designs*, New York: Wiley.

Sanoff, H. (1996) 'Designing a responsive school', *The School Administrator*, 53: 18 22.

Scheunpflug, A., Stadler-Altmann, U. and Zeinz, H. (2012) *Bestärken und Fördern. Wege zu einer veränderten Lernkultur in der Sekundarstufe I* [Confirm and Encourage. Ways to Change Learning Culture], Seelze: Klett Kallmeyer.

Sommer, R. and Olson, H. (1980) 'The soft classroom', *Environment and Behavior*, 12: 3–16.

Stadler-Altmann, U. (2010) *Das Schülerselbstkonzept. Eine empirische Annäherung* [Students Self-Concept. An empirical Approach], Bad Heilbrunn: Klinkhardt.

Stadler-Altmann, U. (2013) 'Lehren und Lernen in gebauter Umgebung. Anmerkungen zur medialen Nutzung des Klassenraums' [Teaching and Learning in a Constructed Environment], in K. Westphal and B. Jörissen (eds), *Vom Straßenkind zum Medienkind. Raum- und Medienforschung im 21* (pp. 176–196), Jahrhundert: Juventa.

Steele, F. I. (1973) *Physical Settings and Organisation Development*, Reading, MA: Addison-Wesley.

Tagliacollo, V. A., Volpato, G. L. and Pereira Junior, A. (2010) 'Association of student position in classroom and school performance', *Educational Research*, 1: 198–201.

Tanner, C. K. and Lackney, J. A. (2006) *Educational Facilities Planning. Leadership, Architecture, and Management*, Boston: Pearson.

Uline, C. L., Tschannen-Moran, M. and DeVere Wolsey, T. (2007 'The walls still speak: the stories occupants tell', paper presented at the annual meeting of the American Educational Research Association, Chicago.

Walden, R. (2009) *Schools for the Future: Design Proposals from Architectural Psychology*, Cambridge: Hogrefe & Huber.

Weinstein, C.S. (2007) *Middle and Secondary Classroom Management: Lessons from Research and Practice*, New York: McGraw-Hill.

Weinstein, C.S. and Mignano, A.J. (2011) *Elementary Classroom Management: Lessons from Research and Practice*, New York: McGraw-Hill.

Woolner, P. (2010) *The Design of Learning Spaces*, London, New York: continuumbooks.com.

Woolner, P., Clark, J., Hall, E., Tiplady, L., Thomas, U. and Wall, K. (2010) 'Pictures are necessary but not sufficient: using a range of visual methods to engage users about school design', *Learning Environments Research*, 13: 1–22.

Woolner, P., Clark, J., Laing, K., Thomas, U. and Tiplady, L. (2012) 'Changing spaces: preparing students and teachers for a new learning environment', *Children, Youth and Environments,* 22: 52–74.

Woolner, P., Clark, J., Laing, K., Tiplady, L. and Thomas, U. (2013) 'Teachers preparing for changes to learning environment and practices in a UK secondary school', paper presented at the European Conference on Educational Research conference, Istanbul.

Woolner, P., Hall, E., Wall, K. and Dennison, D. (2007) 'Getting together to improve the school environment: user consultation, participatory design and student voice', *Improving Schools*, 10: 233–248. Retrieved from http://imp.sagepub.com/content/10/3/233 November 19, 2013.

Woolner, P., McCarter, S., Wall, K. and Higgins, S. (2011) 'Changed learning through changed space: when can a participatory approach to the learning environment challenge preconceptions and alter practice?', paper presented at the American Educational Research Association annual meeting, New Orleans, Louisiana.

24

THE LINK BETWEEN CLASS CLIMATE AND TEACHER AND STUDENT EMOTIONS

Implications for theory, research, and educational practice

Betty Becker-Kurz and Zoe A. Morris

Emotions in the classroom context

Classrooms are host to a multitude of emotions which evolve within the academic context, all of which are of critical importance for both the students and teachers involved (Frenzel *et al.* 2009a; Pekrun *et al.* 2002; Pekrun and Stephens 2012; Sutton and Wheatley 2003). Literature on the prevalence, effect, and measurement of anxiety in the classroom is well established, particularly in relation to test anxiety (Zeidner 1998). However, classroom emotion requires consideration across the full spectrum of emotional possibilities. For instance, students can experience excitement learning new concepts, but they can also feel frustrated when failing to grasp the learning material. Similarly, teachers are likely to experience a plethora of emotions during the course of their work. These emotions may range from the enjoyment that arises when witnessing their students' progress, to the anger felt when students disrupt their lesson. Such an array of experiences, for both teacher and student, can result in a veritable 'emotional whirlpool' (Erb 2002).

Teachers' emotions contribute to their personal well-being and teaching style, but also relate to students' performance and emotions (Frenzel *et al.* 2009a; Klusmann *et al.* 2008; Radel *et al.* 2010; Sutton and Wheatley 2003). In the same vein, students' emotions relate to a host of other variables which are important within the academic domain. Positive student emotions facilitate setting and achieving goals, foster receptivity for learning material, and promote creative problem solving (Clore and Huntsinger 2007; Fredrickson 2001; Pekrun and Stephens 2012; Pekrun *et al.* 2007; Schutz and Pekrun 2007). Experiencing negative emotions, however, can undermine a student's motivation, limit his or her academic performance, prompt school dropout, and negatively affect health (Pekrun and Stephens 2012; Zeidner 1998, 2007).

One emotion which has attracted considerable interest since the early 1950s, and which has amassed more than 1,000 published studies (Pekrun *et al.* 2002), is anxiety, particularly test anxiety (Zeidner 1998) and achievement-related anxiety. High levels of student anxiety have been found to correlate negatively with classroom academic achievement, due to its ability to interfere with task-focused attention in challenging tasks (Pekrun 2000). The effects of test anxiety are not universal; it has been shown to contribute to a continuum of outcomes, ranging from incapacitation to enhancing effects, depending on a broad range of factors such as self-efficacy, motivation and classroom environment (Zeidner 1998). Test anxiety typically occurs in educational settings in response to concerns of poor performance in evaluative situations, and has also been associated with diminished performance. For example, test anxiety can be heightened in competititive and evaluative classroom environments, which are understood to be detrimental to student motivation (Wentzel and Brophy 2014) particularly for those students who are anxious (Wigfield and Eccles 1990). In this era of high-stakes testing, test anxiety remains a pertinent issue (Segool *et al.* 2013).

Teachers also experience anxiety in the classoom context, particularly when they have the impression that their own competence or effort is insufficient to reach a certain classroom goal (Frenzel *et al.* 2009b; Smith and Lazarus 1993). Teacher anxiety may also be linked to the use of rigid teaching strategies and repetitive exercises, as highly anxious teachers have difficulty engaging flexibility in regards to previously planned lesson scripts (Frenzel *et al.* 2009a).

Despite their important influence, teachers' emotions have thus far received a noticeable lack of research attention (Chang 2013; Pekrun *et al.* 2002). Given the plethora of teachers' and students' emotions as well as the interplay between their emotions within the classroom context (Frenzel *et al.* 2009a), it is important to take both teachers' and students' distinct emotions into account to understand classroom dynamics. A growing number of researchers in emotion also recognize the importance of understanding and harnessing the rich tapestry of emotions present in academic settings (Pekrun *et al.* 2002). Before addressing the research and implications surrounding the topic of emotions within the academic context, the concept of emotion should initially be defined.

The definition of 'emotion'

There appears to be as many definitions of the term emotion as there are researchers interested in the topic (Van Kleef *et al.* 2004b). However, most definitions include cognitive, affective, physiological, motivational, and expressive components (Kleinginna and Kleinginna 1981; Scherer 2009).

There are two related concepts that commonly arise in the emotion literature: *mood* and *affect*. Both terms differ qualitatively from 'emotion' and comprise their own distinctive features, which will be elucidated below. Despite these differences, it is commonplace for the three terms to be used relatively interchangeably. 'Moods' are considered an emotional state that has a longer duration than the experience of a specific emotion (Oatley and Jenkins 1996). Moods are also said to be less discrete (Russell and Barrett 1999), and are not directed at a specific event or object of reference (Frijda 1993; Pekrun and Linnenbrink-Garcia 2014; Russell and Barrett 1999). Although moods show similar qualitative features to emotions and share a similar profile of components (Pekrun and Stephens 2012), they are considered low-intensity emotions (Pekrun *et al.* 2006). 'Affect', on the other hand, is often explained in terms of a superordinate construct; an overarching term that comprises both moods and emotions (Barry and Oliver 1996; Van Kleef *et al.* 2004a). Therefore, positive affect in the classroom may be a combination of postive feelings, thoughts and desires about the task at hand as well as positive mood that is not specific to the task.

It is important that we operationally define the term 'emotion' as distinct to the notions of mood and affect, not only to fully grasp it as a concept, but also to make sense of the research that will be presented below. At the core of the nature of emotion is its multidimensionality. As such, a successful operationalization of the concept must appeal to a model that addresses all facets of its 'multi-component' structure (Pekrun *et al.* 2006). Only in this way can one begin to represent, research, and in turn, understand emotions in their vast complexity.

Pekrun's three-dimensional taxonomy of academic achievement emotions

In the three-dimensional taxonomy of emotions, Pekrun *et al.* (2006) formalize the concept of achievement emotions. By combining the dimensions of (1) valence, (2) activation, and (3) object focus, achievement emotions are arranged into a 3 × 2 taxonomy (Pekrun and Linnenbrink-Garcia 2014; Pekrun and Stephens 2012). In terms of valence, both positive and negative emotions can be distinguished from one another. Regarding activation, physiologically activating emotions can be distinguished from deactivating emotions. For example, anger is activating, whereas boredom is deactivating (Pekrun *et al.* 2006; Pekrun and Stephens 2012). In terms of object focus, achievement emotions are further distinguished as activity emotions or outcome emotions. While activity emotions are experienced during the achievement activity itself, outcome emotions are the emotional reactions in response to the result or outcome of an academic activity or event (Pekrun and Linnenbrink-Garcia 2014; Pekrun and Stephens 2012). Achievement outcomes are typically understood in terms of success or failure. Instances of activity emotions, for example, are those emotions which students experience in the process of doing their homework. Outcome emotions, however, refer to either retrospective emotions (in response to past failure or success) or prospective emotions (in anticipation of upcoming failure or success).

The control–value theory: A framework for achievement emotions

Given the relevance of academic emotions for both students and teachers (Frenzel *et al.* 2009a; Pekrun *et al.* 2002; Pekrun and Stephens 2012; Sutton and Wheatley 2003), it is highly pertinent to acquire knowledge about their antecedents to determine evidence-based techniques to generate and enhance positive emotions and reduce negative emotional states. It is also important to bear in mind the various factors that play a causal and influential role in the emergence of emotions within an individual, such as a student or teacher; for example, genetic predispositions, neurohormonal processes, cognitive appraisals, and sensory feedback from facial, gestural, and postural expression (Lewis *et al.* 2008; Pekrun and Stephens 2012; Scherer 2001; 2009). Cognitive appraisals, in particular, have played an important role in students' performance, persistence, and task choices (Eccles 2011; Watt *et al.* 2012). Furthermore, students' appraisals, especially control and value appraisals, play an important role in connection with their emotions (Pekrun *et al.* 2006; Scherer 2001).

Drawing on these findings, the control–value theory (Pekrun *et al.* 2007) implies that emotions are determined by individuals' experiences of control over the actions and outcomes, as well as their perceived subjective value of the actions and outcomes, of a given achievement situation (Pekrun *et al.* 2006, 2007; Pekrun and Stephens 2012). For example, pride would be conceived as being related to an individual's experience of high perceived control, as well as a high subjective value, over the actions and outcomes of some event. Anxiety, on the other hand, would be identified as an individual's experience of low perceived control and high subjective value toward some set of actions and outcomes. Besides students' emotions, the assumptions of the control–value theory can also be applied to teachers' emotions, which contribute to teachers' professional behavior and instructional practices (Pekrun *et al.* 2006). Researchers have begun to consider the role of teacher emotion in regard to their students at a conceptual level. One model which is also rooted in appraisal theory and links teachers' emotions to students' emotions is the Frenzel and colleagues reciprocal model (2009b).

Causes and effects of teachers' emotions: A reciprocal model

Drawing on the empirical evidence of the links between teacher emotions and behavior (Sutton 2004), the reciprocal model provides a theoretical framework for the causes and effects of teachers' emotions, as proposed by Frenzel and colleagues (2009b). The model illustrates that classroom conditions (e.g. classroom climate) directly influence teacher perceptions of student behavior and teacher goals for student behavior. Further, teacher emotions directly inform instructional behavior (e.g. motivational stimulation). The model is reciprocal in that teacher emotions also influence overarching teacher ideals and goals for their students and their subjective perceptions of student behaviors through a feedback loop mechanism.

In detail, this model postulates that the ways teachers perceive their students' behaviors (e.g. achievement behavior) and the goals they set for their students' behavior are influenced by objective classroom conditions (e.g. competence levels of students). In addition, teachers' overarching teaching ideals (e.g. cognitive growth) have an effect on the goals they have for their students' behavior. Teachers' subjective perceptions of their students as well as their goals for their students' behavior have an effect on teachers' emotions. Teachers' emotions, in turn, are proposed to influence the way teachers perceive their students' behaviors and set goals for their students' future behaviors. In addition, Frenzel *et al.* (2009b) have suggested that teachers' emotions are linked to their instructional behavior (e.g. cognitive and motivational stimulation of students) which again influence the classroom conditions. The reciprocal relationships between teachers' emotions, their instructional behavior, and students' outcomes proposed in this model (Frenzel *et al.* 2009b) have also, through advances in technology and through statistical measures and techniques, been empirically supported (Frenzel *et al.* 2009a).

Social emotions in the classroom

As the reciprocal model highlights, emotions are interactive – they do not occur in a vacuum, but develop within the context of social interactions with other people (Van Kleef *et al.* 2011). The classroom is a typical example of a social setting that is perpetually filled with emotion. Classroom settings are a platform upon which social emotions might develop and arise. Potential interactions range from those between teachers and students to those between colleagues and those between teachers and parents (Pekrun and Linnenbrink-Garcia 2014). The term 'social emotion' comprises both achievement and non-achievement emotions. While social achievement emotions refer to the *success or failure* of others, such as contempt, admiration, empathy or envy, non-achievement emotions refer to the *relationships* with others, such as affection or hate (Weiner 2007).

Several studies in the field of social psychology have emphasized the importance of social emotions in the academic context. Do and Schallert (2004), for example, have shown that the social component of a discussion among undergraduate students changed the interplay between affect and social interaction. Without accounting for the social dynamics of the discussion, positive affect was found to be related to higher engagement and negative affect to lower engagement. However, when factoring these social dynamics into the analysis, students' negative affect displayed the opposite effect: it led students to increase their engagement in the discussion. Furthermore, their findings demonstrated shifts in students' behavior over the course of the discussion, suggesting that affect is dynamic within social interactions.

Given the inherent social nature of the classroom context, the role that affect plays in the development of emotions within educational practice has gained research interest (Linnenbrink-Garcia *et al.* 2011). Specifically, the dynamic interaction between teacher emotions and student emotions, and its effects on teaching and learning outcomes, is of particular relevance to the academic community. However, empirical findings on how these emotions interact, or to what degree they may transmit between pupil and teacher, remain few and far between. One exception is the work by Frenzel *et al.* (2009a), which demonstrated that secondary-school teachers' enjoyment in mathematics classes correlated positively with students' enjoyment of these classes, even when adjusting for students' previous levels of mathematics enjoyment. There exists strong preliminary evidence to suggest that a student's degree of experienced enjoyment in a subject matter is somewhat intertwined with the degree to which their teacher displays enjoyment while teaching (Frenzel *et al.* 2009a).

Teacher and student emotions: The importance of context

Teachers' and students' emotions are also related to the specific context or domain within which they evolve. Studies on the context-specificity of students' emotions (Goetz *et al.* 2006; Goetz *et al.* 2007) reveal that students' experience of each emotion differs depending on the domain in which it was experienced. Similar findings have been reported with regard to teacher emotions; the context, such as the subject taught, plays a crucial role in a teacher's emotional experience within her or his learning environment (Frenzel and Goetz 2007).

One important contextual variable of teacher and student emotions is the climate of the classroom. Although there is no fixed definition of 'classroom climate' (Zullig *et al.* 2010), most scientists describe the term as a multidimensional concept comprising interpersonal, instructional, and organizational characteristics (Loukas and Robinson 2004). In contrast to classroom emotions, class climate has a long history of research in the context of learning and teaching dating back to the 1920s, and interest has grown steadily since. Early researchers focused on the link between leadership and group climate by examining behavioral patterns of 10- and 11-year-old boys (see Lewin *et al.* 1939). One of their main findings was that leadership style had a strong effect on the social climates in groups.

As research progressed, the focus shifted to the development of theoretical and empirical frameworks of classroom climate, though at first the relevance of emotions, and their role in classroom climate, was not recognized. This lack of recognition in relation to emotions was also reflected within the terminology, with Withall (1949) defining 'social-emotional climate' as:

> A general emotional factor which appears to be present in interactions occurring between individuals in face to face groups. It seems to have some relationship to the degree of acceptance expressed by members of a group regarding each other's needs or goals. Operationally defined, it is considered to influence: (1) the inner private world of each individual; (2) the esprit de corps of a group; (3) the sense of meaningfulness of group and individual goals and activities; (4) the objectivity with which a problem is attacked; and (5) the kind and extent of interpersonal interaction in a group.
>
> *(Withall 1949: 348–349)*

Such interactions are typically found in classroom contexts between teachers and students as well as among students. Hence, initially the link between emotions and class climate was considered global. That is, the specific emotions that might lead to a particular class climate were not investigated.

Measuring class climate: What is the role of emotional tone?

As the concept and study of emotional climate advanced, tools to measure the concept were developed. Of note is the observation instrument 'OScAR' (Observation Schedule and Record), which was created to measure classroom climate by observing the classroom social structure, as well as to measure nonverbal behavior in the classroom (Medley and Mitzel 1958). The three scales of the instrument were 'verbal emphasis', 'social organization', and 'emotional climate'. Interestingly, the latter was the best predictor for a number of classroom variables, such as teachers' competence and teacher–student rapport. Applying the OScAR scales, (Morrison 1961 as cited in Chávez 1984) further evidenced that emotional climate was a key element of teacher competence, as well as teacher–student rapport.

Subsequent classroom climate research which utilized observation instruments similar to OScAR also highlighted the importance of including a measure of the 'emotional tone' of a classroom. This can be observed in the Flander's Interaction Analysis System (Amidon and Hough 1967). One of the ten items in this scale (which contribute to a description of teacher and student behavior) is 'acceptance of feelings', which aims to measure the extent to which a teacher accepts and validates the feelings of her or his students in a nonthreatening manner. In other words, this item measures the degree to which a teacher explicitly acknowledges and respects the emotions of her or his students, regardless of whether feelings are positive or negative. Through the development of these observation instruments, and the insights offered by them, researchers grew to recognize and acknowledge the importance of incorporating the emotional tone of a classroom when investigating the multidimensional concept of classroom climate.

From classroom climate to classroom *emotional* climate

Student–teacher interactions are intricate, and current classroom dynamics research recognizes emotion is an influential component warranting investigation. Rather than focusing solely on the social interactions between teachers and students or among students, researchers show more interest in additionally taking the emotional interactions in classrooms into account. This is also reflected in the terminology: research increasingly focuses on the 'classroom *emotional* climate', which is defined as the quality of emotional and social interactions between and among students and teachers (Pianta *et al.* 2008).

One example of this research is Hamre and Pianta's Teaching Through Interactions framework (2007). This framework determines that the emotional climate in classrooms is related to a set of particular characteristics. In classrooms with a positive emotional climate, the following characteristics can be found: teachers show sensitivity towards their students' emotional and academic needs and respect students' perspectives, encourage active participation, and do not use abrasive discipline or cynicism. Such classrooms are characterized by a warm, friendly, respectful, and nurturing teacher–student relationship. In classrooms with negative emotional climates, however, the atmosphere is dominated by mistrust and disrespect and teachers and students share little emotional connection (Reyes *et al.* 2012).

Classroom climate and teachers' and students' discrete emotions

Despite researchers acknowledging the importance of emotional tone and emotional climate when investigating the classroom climate, there remains a lack of research relating these concepts to teachers' and students' *discrete* emotions. However, there are a number of studies which provide important indications on the link between the climate within a group and the discrete emotions of its members.

Drawing upon the findings of the National Institute of Child Health and Human Development Early Child Care Research Network (ECCRN) (2003) on first-grade classrooms with negative versus more positive emotional climates, Gazelle (2006) concluded that an anxiety-provoking classroom context may have a stronger effect on the experience of anxiety within children with pre-existing vulnerability to social anxiety. Furthermore, Schaps and Solomon (1990) reported that students' sense of class community was related to their experience of positive feelings in class.

In addition to the contributions of positive classroom climate on students' emotional outcomes, Jennings and Greenberg have proposed that teachers also benefit from a healthy classroom climate, as outlined in their model of the prosocial classroom (Jennings and Greenberg 2009). They illustrate that the 'improvements in classroom climate may reinforce a teacher's enjoyment of teaching' (2009: 493). However, there is a need to supplement these findings with a larger number of studies, to more thoroughly support this assumption and comprehensively investigate the link between the classroom climate and teachers' and students' concrete emotions.

Challenges and future directions

To further understand the relationship between the dynamics in class climate and teachers' and students' discrete emotions, it is necessary to acknowledge the interplay and interaction between these variables. By connecting these areas of research, a better understanding can be derived with regards to the underlying mechanisms of social interactions between teachers and students, as well as among students.

One critical concern for those attempting to pursue this research goal is acknowledging the level of complexity that exists when trying to identify and isolate discrete emotions arising within the classroom, as well as the different levels of interactions that might occur between and within groups of students and teachers. As such, researchers are recommended to apply methods capable of depicting the nested data structure within classrooms (Raudenbush *et al.* 2002). Applying multilevel modeling allows for simultaneous consideration of the nested data and the specification of each separate structural model at each level. Such models can take account of, for example, teacher factors in order to determine class-level effects (Byrne 2012). Unfortunately, there is a 'substantial research literature into the effects of classroom contexts and climates that has either ignored this multilevel perspective or apparently misunderstood it' (Marsh *et al.* 2012:120). In line with this statement by Marsh and colleagues, we would thus emphasize the importance of analyzing climate effects on the basis of class-averaged aggregates, even when classroom climate measures are based upon individual student responses (see Marsh *et al.* 2012 for comprehensive guidelines).

Beyond the proposed methodological approach of aggregating data at the class level, we recommended that to effectively understand the complexity of classroom emotions, researchers address a wider variety of components which may play important roles in classroom dynamics. In presenting the core components of emotions in the academic context, this chapter has provided insight into some of the significant findings and contributions from previous research. Given that emotions are embedded in the very nature of classrooms and, by extension, teaching and learning, it is essential that researchers and practitioners acknowledge the complexity of academic emotions, and the interplay that exists with the (emotional) class climate in order to shape an academic atmosphere which is conducive to learning. Acknowledging the complexity and interplay of academic emotions, it would be beneficial to create an awareness among teachers that all members of an educational setting, including themselves, influence each other to varying degrees. Further, teachers should be encouraged to remember that their own enjoyment may be transmitted to students and in turn, influence student enjoyment through a positive feedback mechanism, reciprocally inciting more enjoyment in the classroom (Frenzel *et al.* 2009a). Teachers' and students' positive emotions may build a more open and inviting platform upon which to approach challenges. In the same vein, a more negative learning environment risks inciting academic obstacles that may be deemed motivationally thwarting. Considerable merit exists in promoting an emotional class climate in which achievement goals are not only valued, but also addressed in such a way that yields confidence in attaining these goals: these criteria may ultimately translate into a deeper enjoyment toward future learning experiences (Pekrun *et al.* 2006).

Researchers and practitioners are encouraged to consider both teachers' and students' discrete emotions as well as the interplay between their emotions when investigating the classroom climate. Likewise, when designing intervention programs, it seems worthwhile to attend to the dynamic interaction of emotions in the classroom to optimally tailor interventions to target these emotions and improve a positive class climate.

References

Amidon, E.J. and Hough, J. (1967) *Interaction Analysis: Theory, Research, and Application*, Reading, MA: Addison-Wesley.

Barry, B. and Oliver, R.L. (1996) 'Affect in dyadic negotiation: a model and propositions', *Organizational Behavior and Human Decision Processes*, 67: 127–143.

Byrne, B.M. (2012) *Structural Equation Modeling with Mplus: Basic Concepts, Applications, and Programming*, New York: Routledge.

Chang, M.-L. (2013) 'Toward a theoretical model to understand teacher emotions and teacher burnout in the context of student misbehavior: appraisal, regulation and coping', *Motivation and Emotion*, 37: 799–817. doi: 10.1007/s11031-012-9335-0

Chávez, R.C. (1984) 'The use of high-inference measures to study classroom climates: a review', *Review of Educational Research*, 54: 237–261. doi: 10.3102/00346543054002237

Clore, G.L. and Huntsinger, J.R. (2007) 'How emotions inform judgment and regulate thought', *Trends in Cognitive Sciences*, 11: 393–399. doi: 10.1016/j.tics.2007.08.005

Do, S.L. and Schallert, D.L. (2004) 'Emotions and classroom talk: toward a model of the role of affect in students' experiences of classroom discussions', *Journal of Educational Psychology*, 96: 619–634. doi: 10.1037/0022-0663.96.4.619

Eccles, J. (2011) 'Gendered educational and occupational choices: applying the Eccles *et al.* model of achievement-related choices', *International Journal of Behavioral Development*, 35: 195–201. doi: 10.1177/0165025411398185

Erb, C.S. (2002) 'The emotional whirlpool of beginning teachers' work', paper presented at the annual meeting of the Canadian Society of Studies in Education, Toronto, Canada.

Fredrickson, B.L. (2001) 'The role of positive emotions in positive psychology: the broaden-and-build theory of positive emotions', *American Psychologist*, 56: 218–226. doi: 10.1037/0003-066x.56.3.218

Frenzel, A.C. and Goetz, T. (2007) 'Emotionales erleben von lehrkräften beim unterrichten', *Zeitschrift für Pädagogische Psychologie/German Journal of Educational Psychology*, 21: 283–295. doi: 10.1024/1010-0652.21.3.283

Frenzel, A.C., Goetz, T., Lüdtke, O., Pekrun, R. and Sutton, R.E. (2009a) 'Emotional transmission in the classroom: exploring the relationship between teacher and student enjoyment', *Journal of Educational Psychology*, 101: 705–716. doi: 10.1037/a0014695

Frenzel, A.C., Goetz, T., Stephens, E.J. and Jacob, B. (2009b) 'Antecedents and effects of teachers' emotional experiences: an integrated perspective and empirical test', in P.A. Schutz and M. Zembylas (eds) *Advances in Teacher Emotion Research: The Impact of Teachers' Lives* (pp. 129–152), New York: Springer.

Frijda, N.H. (1993) 'Moods, emotion episodes, and emotions', in M. Lewis and J.M. Haviland (eds) *Handbook of Emotions* (pp. 381–403), New York: Guilford Press.

Gazelle, H. (2006) 'Class climate moderates peer relations and emotional adjustment in children with an early history of anxious solitude: a child × environment model', *Developmental Psychology*, 42: 1179–1192. doi: 10.1037/0012-1649.42.6.1179

Goetz, T., Frenzel, A.C., Pekrun, R. and Hall, N.C. (2006) 'The domain specificity of academic emotional experiences', *Journal of Experimental Education*, 75: 5–29. doi: 10.3200/jexe.75.1.5–29

Goetz, T., Frenzel, A.C., Pekrun, R., Hall, N.C. and Lüdtke, O. (2007) 'Between- and within-domain relations of students' academic emotions', *Journal of Educational Psychology*, 99: 715–733.

Hamre, B.K. and Pianta, R.C. (2007) 'Learning opportunities in preschool and early elementary classrooms', in R.C. Pianta, M.J. Cox and K.L. Snow (eds) *School Readiness and the Transition to Kindergarten in the Era of Accountability* (pp. 49–83), Baltimore, MD: Brookes.

Jennings, P.A. and Greenberg, M.T. (2009) 'The prosocial classroom: teacher social and emotional competence in relation to student and classroom outcomes', *Review of Educational Research*, 79: 491–525. doi: 10.3102/0034654308325693

Kleinginna, P.R. and Kleinginna, A.M. (1981) 'A categorized list of emotion definitions, with suggestions for a consensual definition', *Motivation and Emotion*, 5: 345–379.

Klusmann, U., Kunter, M., Trautwein, U., Lüdtke, O. and Baumert, J. (2008) 'Teachers' occupational well-being and the quality of instruction: the important role of self-regulatory patterns', *Journal of Educational Psychology*, 100: 702–715.

Lewin, K., Lippitt, R. and White, R.K. (1939) 'Patterns of aggressive behavior in experimentally created "social climates"', *The Journal of Social Psychology*, 10: 271–299. doi: 10.1080/00224545.1939.9713366

Lewis, M., Haviland, J.M. and Feldman Barrett, L. (2008) *Handbook of Emotions*, 3rd edn, New York: Guilford.

Linnenbrink-Garcia, L., Rogat, T.K. and Koskey, K.L.K. (2011) 'Affect and engagement during small group instruction', *Contemporary Educational Psychology*, 36: 13–24. doi: 10.1016/j.cedpsych.2010.09.001

Loukas, A. and Robinson, S. (2004) 'Examining the moderating role of perceived school climate in early adolescent adjustment', *Journal of Research on Adolescence*, 14: 209–233. doi: 10.1111/j.1532-7795.2004.01402004.x

Marsh, H.W., Lüdtke, O., Nagengast, B., Trautwein, U., Morin, A.J.S., Abduljabbar, A.S. and Köller, O. (2012) 'Classroom climate and contextual effects: conceptual and methodological issues in the evaluation of group-level effects', *Educational Psychologist*, 47: 106–124. doi: 10.1080/00461520.2012.670488

Medley, D.M. and Mitzel, H.E. (1958) 'A technique for measuring classroom behavior', *Journal of Educational Psychology*, 49: 86–92. doi: 10.1037/h0040378

National Institute of Child Health and Human Development Early Child Care Research Network (ECCRN) (2003) 'Social functioning in first grade: associations with earlier home and child care predictors and with current classroom experiences', *Child Development*, 74: 1639–1662.

Oatley, K. and Jenkins, J.M. (1996) *Understanding Emotions*, Cambridge, MA: Blackwell.

Pekrun, R. (2000) 'A social-cognitive, control-value theory of achievement emotions', in J. Heckhausen (ed.) *Motivational Psychology of Human Development* (pp. 143–164), Amsterdam: Elsevier Science B.V.

Pekrun, R., Elliot, A.J. and Maier, M.A. (2006) 'Achievement goals and discrete achievement emotions: a theoretical model and prospective test', *Journal of Educational Psychology*, 98: 583–597. doi: 10.1037/0022-0663.98.3.583

Pekrun, R., Frenzel, A.C., Goetz, T. and Perry, R.P. (2007) 'The control-value theory of achievement emotions: an integrative approach to emotions in education', in P.A. Schutz and R. Pekrun (eds), *Emotion in Education* (pp. 13–36), San Diego, CA: Elsevier Academic Press.

Pekrun, R., Goetz, T., Titz, W. and Perry, R.P. (2002) 'Academic emotions in students' self-regulated learning and achievement: a program of qualitative and quantitative research' [Emotionen im bereich des selbstgesteuerten lernens und der leistung von schülern und studenten: ein programm für qualitative und quantitative forschung], *Educational Psychologist*, 37: 91–105.

Pekrun, R. and Linnenbrink-Garcia, L. (2014) 'Introduction to emotions in education', in R. Pekrun and L. Linnenbrink-Garcia (eds) *Handbook of Emotions and Education* (pp. 1–10), New York: Routledge.

Pekrun, R. and Stephens, E.J. (2012) 'Academic emotions', in K.R. Harris, S. Graham, T. Urdan, S. Graham, J.M. Royer and M. Zeidner (eds), *APA Educational Psychology Handbook*, Vol. 2, *Individual Differences and Cultural and Contextual Factors* (pp. 3–31), Washington, DC: American Psychological Association.

Pianta, R.C., Belsky, J., Vandergrift, N., Houts, R. and Morrison, F. (2008) 'Classroom effects on children's achievement trajectories in elementary school', *American Educational Research Journal*, 45: 365–397. doi: 10.3102/0002831207308230

Radel, R., Sarrazin, P., Legrain, P. and Wild, T.C. (2010) 'Social contagion of motivation between teacher and student: analyzing underlying processes', *Journal of Educational Psychology*, 102: 577–587. doi: 10.1037/a0019051

Raudenbush, S.W., Bryk, A.S. and Congdon, R. (2002) *Hierarchical Linear Models: Applications and Data Analysis Methods*, 2nd edn, Newbury Park, CA: Sage.

Reyes, M.R., Brackett, M.A., Rivers, S.E., White, M. and Salovey, P. (2012) 'Classroom emotional climate, student engagement, and academic achievement', *Journal of Educational Psychology*, 104: 700–712. doi: 10.1037/a0027268

Russell, J.A. and Barrett, L.F. (1999) 'Core affect, prototypical emotional episodes, and other things called emotion: dissecting the elephant', *Journal of Personality and Social Psychology*, 76: 805–819. doi: 10.1037/0022-3514.76.5.805

Schaps, E. and Solomon, D. (1990) 'Schools and classrooms as caring communities', *Educational Leadership*, 48: 38–42.

Scherer, K.R. (2001) 'Appraisal considered as a process of multilevel sequential checking', in K.R. Scherer, A. Schorr and T. Johnstone (eds), *Appraisal Processes in Emotion: Theory, Methods, Research* (pp. 92–120), New York: Oxford University Press.

Scherer, K.R. (2009) 'The dynamic architecture of emotion: evidence for the component process model', *Cognition and Emotion,* 23: 1307–1351.

Schutz, P.A. and Pekrun, R. (2007) 'Introduction to emotion in education', in P.A. Schutz and R. Pekrun (eds) *Emotion in Education* (pp. 3–10), San Diego, CA: Elsevier Academic Press.

Segool, N.K., Carlson, J.S., Goforth, A.N., Von Der Embse, N. and Barterian, J.A. (2013) 'Heightened test anxiety among young children: elementary school students' anxious responses to high-stakes testing', *Psychology in the Schools,* 50: 489–499. doi: 10.1002/pits.21689

Smith, C.A. and Lazarus, R.S. (1993) 'Appraisal components, core relational themes, and the emotions', *Cognition and Emotion,* 7: 233–269.

Sutton, R.E. and Wheatley, K.F. (2003) 'Teachers' emotions and teaching: a review of the literature and directions for future research', *Educational Psychology Review,* 15: 327–358. doi: 10.1023/a:1026131715856

Van Kleef, G.A., De Dreu, C.K.W. and Manstead, A.S.R. (2004a) 'The interpersonal effects of anger and happiness in negotiations', *Journal of Personality and Social Psychology,* 86: 57–76. doi: 10.1037/0022-3514.86.1.57

Van Kleef, G.A., De Dreu, C.K.W. and Manstead, A.S.R. (2004b) The interpersonal effects of emotions in negotiations: a motivated information processing approach', *Journal of Personality and Social Psychology,* 87: 510–528. doi: 10.1037/0022-3514.87.4.510

Van Kleef, G.A., Van Doorn, E.A., Heerdink, M.W. and Koning, L.F. (2011) 'Emotion is for influence', *European Review of Social Psychology,* 22: 114–163. doi: 10.1080/10463283.2011.627192

Watt, H.M.G., Shapka, J.D., Morris, Z.A., Durik, A.M., Keating, D.P. and Eccles, J.S. (2012) 'Gendered motivational processes affecting high school mathematics participation, educational aspirations, and career plans: a comparison of samples from Australia, Canada, and the United States', *Developmental Psychology.* doi: 10.1037/a0027838

Weiner, B. (2007) 'Examining emotional diversity on the classroom: an attribution theorist considers the moral emotions', in P.A. Schutz and R. Pekrun (eds), *Emotion in Education* (pp. 73–88), San Diego, CA: Academic Press.

Wentzel, K.R. and Brophy, J.E. (2014) *Motivating Students to Learn* (4th edn), New York: Routledge.

Wigfield, A. and Eccles, J.S. (1990) 'Expectancy-value theory of achivement motivation', *Contemporary Educational Psychology,* 25: 68–81. doi: 10.1006/ceps.1999.1015

Withall, J. (1949) 'The development of a technique for the measurement of social-emotional climate in classrooms', *Journal of Experimental Education,* 17: 347–361.

Zeidner, M. (1998) *Test Anxiety: The State of the Art,* New York: Plenum.

Zeidner, M. (2007) 'Test anxiety in educational contexts: concepts, findings, and future directions', in P.A. Schutz and R. Pekrun (eds), *Emotion in Education* (pp. 165–184), San Diego, CA: Elsevier Academic Press.

Zullig, K.J., Koopman, T.M., Patton, J.M. and Ubbes, V.A. (2010) 'School climate: historical review, instrument development, and school assessment', *Journal of Psychoeducational Assessment,* 28: 139–152. doi: 10.1177/0734282909344205

25

TEACHER AUTHORITY IN DIVERSE HIGH-SCHOOL CLASSROOMS

Anne Gregory and Amori Yee Mikami

Teachers in secondary schools face the challenge of compelling large groups of adolescents to follow instructions and engage with material that may feel only tangentially relevant to their everyday lives. The challenge of eliciting cooperation is partially due to developmental needs of adolescents, whereby it is normative for teens to assert their individuality and autonomy. As a result, power struggles between students and teachers are common in secondary classrooms (Vavrus and Cole 2002). Power struggles can culminate in teachers issuing discipline referrals for 'defiance', 'insubordination', 'disruption' – the most common reasons teachers send students out of the classroom (Fabelo *et al.* 2011; Gregory and Weinstein 2008). Teacher and student conflict in the classroom, however, is not evenly distributed across student subgroups. In numerous countries, including the United States, Canada, and Great Britain, research has documented that certain students (specifically racial/ethnic minorities, indigenous youth, males, students in special education) disproportionately receive exclusionary discipline referrals, whereby they are asked to leave the classroom and receive formal sanctions for their behavior (Blair 2001; Gazeley 2010; Greflund *et al.* 2013; Gregory *et al.* 2010a). Disparities in school discipline point to the need for an in-depth understanding of the dynamics of power and authority in diverse classrooms.

Given the complex interplay among individuals in classrooms, an examination of teacher power and authority requires a systems framework (Pianta 1998) which takes into account numerous interacting influences – the teacher with individual students, with the group as a whole, and with subgroups of students (i.e. low achieving versus high achieving). Also important to consider are ways in which teacher demonstrations of power and authority may influence respectful interactions among peers themselves. Drawing on a systems framework, the current chapter presents research on the varying ways teachers use authority in the classroom, how such variation may depend on characteristics of students and classrooms, and how teacher authority can affect the quality of peer interactions. The synthesis of research also points to conceptual and empirical challenges and areas for future research.

Research background on teacher authority

Variations in teachers' use of power in the classroom

Secondary teachers differ in how they embody their positions of authority and how they elicit student cooperation. To conceptualize such differences, broad sociological theories have been used to create a typology of teachers: teachers relying on *traditional* authority expect student cooperation because of custom and their position of power. Teachers with *charismatic* authority elicit cooperation through their passion and commitment, which inspires students' emotional attachment. Teachers using *legal–rational* authority depend on their position in the bureaucracy and their right to reward or punish behavior. Finally, teachers drawing on *professional* authority gain cooperation through instructional skills and their expertise in their subject area (Durkheim 1956; Metz 1978; Weber 1947; for a review, see Pace and Hemmings 2007). The typology itself sheds light on how some teachers simply *expect* student compliance given their professional role or subject matter expertise. By contrast, other teachers believe they need to earn legitimacy in their authority (and subsequent student cooperation) through the treatment of students.

The differing ways teachers exert power in the classroom likely relate to their underlying values about the role of schooling and beliefs about students' need for external constraint. Hoy (2001) distinguishes teachers by their 'pupil control ideology', which juxtaposes a custodial orientation with a humanistic orientation. Teachers with a custodial orientation believe students benefit from an autocratic approach and from punishment for their wayward behavior. In contrast, teachers with a humanistic orientation see a need for student self-determination and for student-driven norms and rules in the classroom. Similar to underlying beliefs about student needs, teacher values likely play a central role in how teachers exert power in classrooms. Apple and Beane (2007) described teachers and administrators whose behavior was largely guided by their valuing of 'democratic schooling'. Such core values guided how these individuals negotiated power in the schools; namely, decisions were made through a participatory process, which included the honoring of student perspectives on rules in classrooms.

Teachers' varying approaches to authority are also exhibited through differing classroom management practices. The old adage 'never smile before Christmas' suggests that teachers need to present themselves as stern and uncompromising in the first months of the school year. It is the case that the beginning weeks of the school year can be crucial in setting norms for behavior (Everston and Emmer 1982). Yet, teachers vary in the degree to which they collaborate with their students in setting those norms. Recently, teachers have been trained in restorative approaches to school discipline, whereby they engage youth in taking ownership for prosocial norms in the classroom community (McCluskey *et al.* 2008; Zehr 2002). Instead of establishing classroom rules in advance, teachers might ask students to sit in a circle and take turns in identifying their own expectations for behavior. Similarly, when conflict arises, teachers might facilitate a discussion to engage in group problem solving to repair the harm (Wachtel *et al.* 2009).

Whereas there appears to be a variety of ways teachers enact their authority in the classroom, some ways may be more likely to occur in specific classroom contexts and with specific groups of students than others. Oakes (1985) documented the use of authority in lower-track classrooms, which in many regions of the United States tend to be composed of a majority of low-income students, and African American and Latino students. In her ethnographic study, Oakes (1985) found that teachers rigidly applied the rules and tightly controlled student movement, perhaps reflecting the teachers' fear of losing authority or distrust in students' ability to self-regulate. A more complex portrait of how teachers use authority in low-track classrooms has been observed in other in-depth case studies. Page (1991) observed a low-track teacher who relinquished some of his authority through humor and teasing which ultimately compromised the classroom's academic focus. Similarly, Pace (2003) documented that teachers of more remedial classes were 'ambiguous' about their authority – they emphasized building rapport and eliciting compliance without the emphasis on academic standards. She observed that they did not demonstrate clear and high expectations for behavior and academic engagement. A striking contrast has been observed in honors level (or high-track) classrooms. Wing (2006) documented how honors teachers clearly communicated expectations for advanced academic work yet also tended to relax the rules, operating on an implicit assumption that high-achieving students are appropriately self-governing.

How educators exercise their authority may also be a function of student characteristics. Specifically, perceptions of students and subsequent punishments for rule infractions may depend on students' gender, race/ethnicity, academic level, disability status, and sexual or gender identity. Evidence of differential treatment in school discipline has accrued. In the United States, a statewide, longitudinal study showed that, for first-time offenders, African American students received harsher discipline sanctions for similar behaviors compared to European American students (Fabelo *et al.* 2011). In a United States nationally-representative sample of tenth graders, Latino students were twice as likely as European American students to be issued out-of-school suspension, after accounting for student- and teacher-reported misbehavior (Finn and Servoss 2015). This means that Latino students were excluded from instruction more than European American students with similar patterns of misbehavior. Similarly, after accounting for family poverty and school urbanicity, American Indian girls were twice as likely as European American girls to be issued suspension or expulsion (Wallace *et al.* 2008). New evidence from a national study in the United States suggests that lesbian, gay, bisexual, and gender non-conforming youth also experience harsh sanctions for behavior compared to their heterosexual peers (Himmelstein and Bruckner 2011). Harsher discipline sanctions typically result in more days suspended out of school. Lost instructional time can accumulate for suspended students, further contributing to gaps in achievement across racial groups (Gregory *et al.* 2011).

Student responses to teacher authority

Student responses to teacher power may depend on whether students perceive they received procedural justice. Tyler (1997) has shown that adults tend to comply with police and judges if they perceive they were treated in a fair manner. Without this sense of procedural justice, adults are less likely to comply. Similar processes have been found in schools, whereby students tend to cooperate when they feel fairly treated by teachers (Gregory and Ripski 2008; Sheets 1996). However, when students feel unfairly treated, they may respond to educators with resistance. In other words, students may exert their own power and actively defy authority figures to stand against perceived injustice. Willis (1977) documented this kind of resistance in his ethnography of low-income boys in England. Willis interpreted what others might regard as 'acting out' behavior as the students' attempts to maintain their own integrity in the face of an oppressive system. Giroux (1986) argued this kind of resistance arises from students who are in less powerful positions in schools and in society.

In his cultural ecological theory of ethnic-minority student responses to schooling, Ogbu (1985, 1991) argues that some youth engage in survival strategies to cope with conditions in school. After experiencing academic failure and conflict with the teacher, students may adopt defiant behavior to preserve self-esteem (Steele 1997). A sense of competence may be derived from resisting teachers' authority and disidentifying from academic tasks (Steele 1997). Internalizing the role of 'class clown' could further foster the development of an anti-school identity, which could then manifest itself in negative interactions with other school personnel who are not limited to the classroom teacher (Spencer *et al.* 2006). It is important to note that although resistance is one possible reaction to adults' harsh or arbitrary use of power, some students may also react with emotional withdrawal and behavioral disengagement from teachers and schooling altogether (Fine 1991; Strambler and Weinstein 2010).

How teachers use their authority may affect peer dynamics

Thus far this chapter has discussed the range of ways teachers exert authority and implications for students' likelihood of compliance with rules in the future. However, teacher–student authority negotiations may also have ripple effects extending beyond the teacher–student dyad directly involved in the experience. Rather, teacher–student interactions may affect the classroom climate as a whole, including shaping the interactions that students have with one another. This perspective is supported by systems theory, which holds that interpersonal transactions between any two members of the classroom system (e.g. a teacher and student) will necessarily have consequences for the rest of the system (Pianta 1999; Tseng and Seidman 2007).

Specifically, teachers who have respectful and productive authority negotiations with students may encourage students to similarly work collaboratively with one another and to find an appropriate balance between asserting their own opinions and listening to peers' differing points of view. By contrast, teachers who assert authority in an autocratic manner and who rely on punitive discipline practices with students, or show differential treatment of students, may contribute to students' adopting a status hierarchy with one another. In these classrooms, students may be likely to devalue peers who are different from themselves and criticize or ostracize peers who make mistakes (Mikami *et al.* 2010).

There are several potential processes through which the tenor of teacher–student authority negotiations may influence peer interactions in the classroom as described above. One hypothesized process is that the teacher's actions instruct students in behaviors to model with one another. Past research has demonstrated the importance of observational learning (Bandura *et al.* 1961). When students observe an authority negotiation between their teacher and one student, even if these observers are not directly involved in the transaction, they gain a salient example of how to handle conflict and how to negotiate disagreements. If the teacher demonstrates courteousness and respect at the same time as maintaining appropriate assertiveness during the authority negotiation, then the observing students learn how to use these techniques. The teacher's behavior has instructed students in positive conflict resolution strategies, and students may then be better equipped to model these types of strategies in their own conflicts with their classmates.

Another hypothesized process through which teacher–student authority negotiations influence students' peer interactions is through indirect communication of the teacher's values. The teacher's behavior sends a message about what the teacher considers to be appropriate in that classroom, shaping the classroom climate. As such, a teacher's response to one student in a hierarchical, authoritarian fashion, or a teacher's differential treatment of students, implicitly communicates to all the classroom peers the acceptability of a status hierarchy where some individuals are considered to be above others. One possible result is that observing peers may devalue and reject the same student that the teacher has put down, because the teacher has communicated that this student has lower worth. However, it is important to note that the teacher's personal hierarchy may differ from the hierarchy that the students adopt, especially in secondary classrooms where students who are disliked by the teacher may receive accolades from their peers as a result. The point is that teachers who handle an authority negotiation with a student in an autocratic fashion will communicate implicitly that some type of hierarchical social structure in the classroom is acceptable. By contrast, teachers who approach authority negotiations respectfully set the expectation that everyone deserves respect, regardless of personal differences (Mikami *et al.* 2010). The teacher's behavior creates a tolerant classroom climate, which then encourages students to conform to this norm during their interactions with peers.

In sum, the ways in which teachers negotiate authority with students may have ramifications that extend beyond the relationship between the teacher and student involved. Therefore, teachers who use productive, respectful authority negotiation strategies may be helping not only their own relationship with that particular student, but also be affecting classroom climate and the social-emotional competence of all students.

Major empirical findings

Ideally, teachers exert their authority in a manner that successfully elicits student trust, cooperation, and engagement in academic tasks. However, to date there are no large-scale studies which have pinpointed the optimal manner for teachers to use their authority in secondary-school classrooms which apply across geographic region, grade level, and composition of the classroom (e.g. percentage low-achieving students or racial/ethnic-minority students). Large-scale studies that focus on teacher use of authority as it influences a range of behavioral and academic student outcomes are rare.

Studies in related areas (teacher classroom management and instructional practices) are also informative. In middle and high schools, there is some evidence that an authoritative approach to rule setting is linked to positive student behavior and reduced use of school discipline (e.g. Wentzel 2002). In a statewide study in the United States, Gregory *et al.* (2011) measured teacher and student perception of structure (fair and consistent application of rules) and support (adult care and accessible help), two dimensions of an authoritative approach to school discipline. Authoritative schools (high on structure and support) had lower bullying, teasing, and victimization for both teachers and students (Gregory *et al.* 2010b, 2012). They also found that schools low on structure and support had the highest rates of suspension and the largest racial disparities in suspensions (e.g. African American students were referred at much higher rates than European American students).

Also supporting the premise that an authoritative approach is beneficial, Wentzel (2002) found that reports from sixth-grade students of teachers' infrequent negative feedback and frequent high expectations (an authoritative teaching style) predicted pursuit of student-reported responsibility goals. In turn, these social goals predicted less irresponsible behavior as reported by the teacher. Taken together, the studies suggest that educators who offer support, consistent and fair follow-through on rules, and who also hold high academic expectations, will be more likely to have positive norms of behavior in their classrooms and throughout the school. Authoritative teachers might be able to leverage trusting relationships to exert their authority. In fact, Gregory and Ripski (2008) showed that teachers who reported that they systematically build relationships with students as their explicit classroom management approach tended to build trust with students (as reported by students) and also elicited their cooperation more than teachers who placed less emphasis on relationship building. One related meta-analysis is worth noting: Cornelius-White (2007) synthesized findings from 119 studies and found that person-centered teacher characteristics (nondirectivity, empathy, warmth) were associated with a range of affective and behavioral student outcomes.

Developing positive relationships as a way to earn legitimacy in teacher authority may be particularly important for students from groups who have traditionally been underserved in education. Teens at risk for drop-out who report having a close and supportive relationship with a teacher are more likely succeed in school compared to similar peers (Resnick *et al.* 1997). When relationships function well, the resulting increase in motivation to comply with basic school norms also appears likely to lead to reductions in problematic behavior (Bryant *et al.* 2000). Pianta, Hamre and Stuhlman (2002) conclude that for adolescents, the dimensions of closeness, connection, and affiliation are critical features of classrooms in which students follow teachers' directives and actively engage with course material.

Intervention research can also shed light on contributors to teachers' use of their authority in diverse classrooms. A recent randomized-control trial of a teacher professional development coaching program, MyTeachingPartner-Secondary, showed that program teachers sent African American and all other student racial/ethnic groups out of their classroom for misbehavior at similarly low rates (Gregory *et al.* 2015). The control teachers, in contrast, had a large racial gap in discipline referrals. The intervention focused on building more positive teacher–student relationships and helped teachers integrate opportunities for higher-level problem solving, student choice, leadership, and peer sharing. The positive and motivating way the program teachers led students through instruction may have resulted in increased positive interactions with African American students and their teachers, which, in turn, could have prevented escalating power struggles.

Research documenting the implications of teacher–student interactions for peer interactions is considerably more extensive in the elementary-school grades (Chang *et al.* 2007; McAuliffe *et al.* 2009; Mikami *et al.* 2012) relative to in secondary classrooms. However, two studies at the secondary level have found that interventions to improve teacher–student interactions (specifically, teachers being emotionally in tune with students, treating students with respect, and incorporating student perspectives into instructional activities) have been found to have positive effects on students' peer interactions on self-report (Mikami *et al.* 2005) as well as observational (Mikami *et al.* 2011) measures. Another study of the MyTeachingPartner-Secondary professional development intervention (mentioned above) suggested that the positive effects of improving teacher–student interactions may have the most benefit for the peer relationships of secondary school students who are high on disruptive behavior problems (Mikami *et al.* 2011) – a population of students who are at high risk for conflicts with both teachers and peers (Stormont 2001).

Challenges and future directions

Many questions remain about how teachers effectively exert their authority in diverse secondary classrooms. Few large-scale studies have linked variations in teacher 'type' of authority figure (Metz 1978) or teacher beliefs about student need for external control (Hoy 2001) to the frequency of power struggles, or the likelihood of cooperation, between teachers and adolescents. Future research on teacher authority should also consider complex issues related to diversity. Effective ways to express authority and elicit cooperation may require that teachers shift their approach in response to cultural norms. As of yet, however, it is unknown whether the way teachers enforce rules and elicit cooperation needs to be in synch with students' familial and cultural experiences outside of school. Weinstein et al. (2004) argue that culturally-responsive approaches to eliciting student cooperation would benefit students. Teachers could modify how they interact with students based on students' cultural needs or forms of expression but also equip students to thrive within the norms of schools (mutual accommodation). Recognition of differing culturally-based ways of expressing power may minimize what Gay (2006) calls communicative tensions which arise through cultural difference – and ultimately reduce power conflicts in the classroom. That said, the theory about the benefits of culturally-responsive approaches to teacher authority has outpaced empirical studies in this area.

The field also knows little about what drives student reactivity to teachers' use of power. Future research might examine secondary students' aversive reactions to procedural injustice (being treated unfairly). It would be especially informative to ascertain whether student perceptions of unfairness predicts student resistance, above and beyond other known student characteristics that fuel opposition against adult authority such as student deficits in social information processing (Dodge *et al.* 2013) and learned patterns of relating with others (Dishion and Patterson 2006). Also from the student perspective, it would be informative to unpack power dynamics based on race and gender. For instance, it is unknown whether European American teachers or male teachers are more likely to be seen as legitimate authority figures given racial and gender stereotypes about their 'being in charge'. Alternatively, European American students may be less willing to automatically imbue teachers of color with a right to assert power (Rodriguez 2009). Also related are examinations of how teachers may express their authority differently depending on student characteristics, including students' reputation, achievement level, race, and parents' influence (or lack thereof) in the school. This area of research is particularly pressing given findings from many countries that harsher sanctions are applied to more marginalized student groups (Blair 2001; Gazeley 2010; Greflund *et al.* 2013).

Finally, intervention and basic process research should be conducted from a systems perspective (Pianta 1998). Teachers may be unaccustomed to thinking about implications of their authority negotiations that extend outside their relationship with the particular student involved in the transaction. However, when students have difficulty working collaboratively and respectfully with their peers, this is of significant concern to teachers because it disrupts the learning environment for everyone. Interventions to improve authority negotiations between teachers and students may therefore have important downstream benefits on all students' productivity and learning.

In sum, the field would benefit from ecologically-rich investigations of teacher authority in diverse high-school classrooms. Understanding how to prevent and diffuse power struggles could help schools ultimately increase engagement and cooperation while reducing disparities in school discipline. Despite the many unknowns, research and theory on classroom management and teacher professional development have provided some initial insights into promising practices. Teachers connecting with students in a supportive manner may help teachers earn legitimacy of their authority and gain student cooperation. Student experience of teachers' high expectations and consistent and fair application of rules also seems key for teachers' ability to effectively manage student behavior. This way of negotiating power with students appears to have ripple effects on how peers interact among themselves. In addition, increasing access to supportive, consistent, fair teachers with high expectations is an issue of equity. Students and classrooms comprising historically-underserved students (e.g. low achieving, ethnic minority, low income) need greater access to teachers who approach authority in this manner.

References

Apple, M.W. and Beane, J.A. (eds) (2007) *Democratic Schools: Lessons in Powerful Education* (2nd edn), Portsmouth, NH: Heinemann.

Bandura, A., Ross, D. and Ross, S.A. (1961) 'Transmission of aggression through imitation of aggressive models', *The Journal of Abnormal and Social Psychology*, 63: 575–582.

Blair, M. (2001) *Why Pick on Me? School Exclusion and Black Youth*, Stoke-on-Trent, UK: Trentham Books.

Bryant, A.L., Schulenberg, J., Bachman, J.G., O'Malley, P.M. and Johnston, L.D. (2000) 'Understanding the links among school misbehavior, academic achievement, and cigarette use: a national panel study of adolescents', *Prevention Science*, 1: 71–78.

Chang, L., Liu, H., Fung, K.Y., Wang, Y., Wen, Z., Li, H. and Farver, J.A.M. (2007) 'The mediating and moderating effects of teacher preference on the relations between students' social behaviors and peer acceptance', *Merrill-Palmer Quarterly: Journal of Developmental Psychology*, 53: 603–630.

Cornelius-White, J. (2007) 'Learner-centered teacher–student relationships are effective: a meta-analysis', *Review of Educational Research*, 77: 113–143.

Dishion, T.J. and Patterson, G.R. (2006) 'The development and ecology of antisocial behavior', in D. Cicchetti and D. Cohen (eds), *Developmental Psychopathology*. Vol. 3: *Risk, Disorder, and Adaptation* (rev. edn, pp. 503–541), New York: John Wiley.

Dodge, K.A., Godwin, J. and Conduct Problems Prevention Research Group (2013) 'Social-information-processing patterns mediate the impact of preventive intervention on adolescent antisocial behavior', *Psychological Science*, 24: 456–465.

Durkheim, E. (1956) *Education and Sociology* (S. D. Fox, trans.), New York: Free Press.

Everston, C.M. and Emmer, E.T. (1982) 'Effective management at the beginning of the school year in junior high classes', *Journal of Educational Psychology*, 74: 485–498.

Fabelo, T., Thompson, M.D., Plotkin, M., Carmichael, D., Marchbanks, M.P. III and Booth, E.A. (2011) *'Breaking Schools' Rules: A Statewide Study of How School Discipline Relates to Students' Success and Juvenile*

Justice Involvement, Washington, DC: Council of State Governments. Retrieved from http://justicecenter. csg.org/resources/juveniles

Fine, M. (1991) *Framing Drop Outs: Notes on the Politics of an Urban Public High School*, Albany: State University of New York Press.

Finn, J.D. and Servoss, T.J. (2015) 'Misbehavior, suspensions, and security measures in high school: racial/ ethnic and gender differences', in D. Losen (ed.) *Closing the Discipline Gap* (pp. 44–58), New York: Teachers College Press.

Gay, G. (2006) 'Connections between classroom management and culturally responsive teaching', in C.M. Evertson and C.S. Weinstein (eds) *Handbook of Classroom Management* (pp. 343–370), Mahwah, NJ: Lawrence Erlbaum Associates.

Gazeley, L. (2010) 'The role of school exclusion processes in the re-production of social and educational disadvantage', *British Journal of Educational Studies*, 1: 1–17.

Giroux, H.A. (1986) 'Authority, intellectuals, and the politics of practical learning', *Teachers College Record*, 88: 22–40.

Greflund, S., McIntosh, K., Mercer, S.H. and May, S.L. (2013) 'Examining disproportionality in school discipline practices for native American students in Canadian schools implementing PBIS', paper presented at the Center for Civil Rights Remedies national conference, Closing the School to Research Gap: Research to Remedies Conference, Washington, DC.

Gregory, A., Allen, J., Mikami, A., Hafen, C. and Pianta, R. (2015) 'The promise of a teacher professional development program in reducing the racial disparity in classroom exclusionary discipline', in D. Losen (ed.) *Closing the Discipline Gap* (pp. 166–179), New York: Teachers College Press.

Gregory, A., Cornell, D. and Fan, X. (2011) 'The relationship of school structure and support to suspension rates for Black and White high school students', *American Educational Research Journal*, 48: 904–934.

Gregory, A., Cornell, D. and Fan, X. (2012) 'Teacher safety and authoritative school climate in high schools', *American Journal of Education*, 118: 1–25.

Gregory, A., Cornell, D., Fan, X., Sheras, P.L., Shih, T. and Huang, F. (2010b) 'Authoritative school discipline: high school practices associated with lower student bullying and victimization', *Journal of Educational Psychology*, 102: 483–496.

Gregory, A. and Ripski, M. (2008) 'Adolescent trust in teachers: implications for behavior in the high school classroom', *School Psychology Review*, 37: 337–353.

Gregory, A., Skiba, R.J. and Noguera, P.A. (2010a) 'The achievement gap and the discipline gap: two sides of the same coin?', *Educational Researcher*, 39: 59–68.

Gregory, A. and Weinstein, S.R. (2008) 'The discipline gap and African Americans: defiance or cooperation in the high school classroom', *Journal of School Psychology*, 46: 455–475.

Himmelstein, K.E.W. and Bruckner, H. (2011) 'Criminal justice and school sanctions against non-heterosexual youth: a national longitudinal study', *Pediatrics*, 127: 49–57.

Hoy, W.K. (2001) 'The pupil control studies: a historical, theoretical, and empirical analysis', *Journal of Educational Administration*, 39: 424–444.

McAuliffe, M., Hubbard, J. and Romano, L. (2009) 'The role of teacher cognition and behavior in children's peer relations', *Journal of Abnormal Child Psychology*, 37: 665–677.

McCluskey, G., Lloyd, G., Stead, J., Kane, J., Riddell, S. and Weedon, E. (2008) 'I was dead restorative today': from restorative justice to restorative approaches in school', *Cambridge Journal of Education*, 38: 199–216.

Metz, M.H. (1978) *Classrooms and Corridors: The Crisis of Authority in Desegregated Secondary Schools*, Berkeley: University of California Press.

Mikami, A.Y., Boucher, M.A. and Humphreys, K. (2005) 'Prevention of peer rejection through a classroom-level intervention in middle school', *The Journal of Primary Prevention*, 26: 5–23.

Mikami, A.Y., Gregory, A., Allen, J.P., Pianta, R.C. and Lun, J. (2011) 'Effects of a teacher professional development intervention on peer relationships in secondary classrooms', *School Psychology Review*, 40: 367–385.

Mikami, A.Y., Griggs, M.S., Reuland, M.M. and Gregory, A. (2012) 'Teacher practices as predictors of children's classroom social preference', *Journal of School Psychology*, 50: 95–111.

Mikami, A.Y., Lerner, M.D. and Lun, J. (2010) 'Social context influences on children's rejection by their peers', *Child Development Perspectives*, 4: 123–130.

Oakes, J. (1985) *Keeping Track: How Schools Structure Inequality*, New Haven, CT: Yale University Press.

Ogbu, J. (1985) 'Cultural-ecological influences on minority education', *Language Arts*, 62: 860–869.

Ogbu, J. (1991) 'Minority coping responses and school experience', *Journal of Psychohistory*, 18: 433–456.

Pace, J.L. (2003) 'Revisiting classroom authority: theory and ideology meet practice', *Teachers College Record*, 105: 1559–1585.

Pace, J.L. and Hemmings, A. (2007) 'Understanding authority in classrooms: a review of theory, ideology, and research', *Review of Educational Research*, 77: 4–27.

Page, R.N. (1991) *Lower-track Classrooms: A Curricular and Cultural Perspective*, New York: Teachers College Press.

Pianta, R.C. (1998) *Enhancing Relationships Between Teachers and Students*, Washington DC: American Psychological Association Press.

Pianta, R.C. (1999) 'How the parts affect the whole: systems theory in classroom relationships', in R.C. Pianta (ed.) *Enhancing Relationships Between Children and Teachers* (pp. 23–43), Washington, DC: American Psychological Association.

Pianta, R.C., Hamre, B.K., and Stuhlman, M. (2002) 'How schools can do better: fostering stronger connections between teachers and students', in J.E. Rhodes (ed.) *New Directions for Youth Development: A Critical View of Youth Mentoring* (pp. 91–107), San Francisco: Jossey-Bass.

Resnick, M.D., Bearman, P.S., Blum, R.W., Bauman, K., Harris, K.M., Jones, J., Tabor, J. *et al.* (1997) 'Protecting adolescents from harm: findings from the National Longitudinal Study of Adolescent Health', *Journal of the American Medical Association*, 278: 823–832.

Rodriguez, D. (2009) 'The usual suspect: negotiating White student resistance and teacher authority in a predominantly white classroom', *Cultural Studies – Critical Methodologies*, 9: 483–508.

Sheets, R.H. (1996) 'Urban classroom conflict: student–teacher perception ethnic integrity, solidarity and resistance', *Urban Review*, 28: 165–183.

Spencer, M.B., Harpalani, V., Cassidy, E., Jacobs, C., Donde, S., Goss, T. *et al.* (2006) 'Understanding vulnerability and resilience from a normative development perspective: implications for racially and ethnically diverse youth', in D. Chicchetti and E. Cohen (eds) *Handbook of Developmental Psychopathology* (Vol. 1, pp. 627–672), Hoboken, NJ: John Wiley.

Steele, C. (1997) 'A threat in the air: how stereotypes shape intellectual identity and performance', *American Psychologist*, 52: 613–629.

Stormont, M. (2001) 'Social outcomes of children with AD/HD: contributing factors and implications for practice', *Psychology in the Schools*, 38: 521–531.

Strambler, M.J. and R.S. Weinstein (2010) 'Psychological disengagement among ethnic minority children in elementary school', *Journal of Applied Developmental Psychology*, 31: 155–165.

Tseng, V. and Seidman, E. (2007) 'A systems framework for understanding social settings', *American Journal of Community Psychology*, 39: 217–228.

Tyler, T.R. (1997) 'The psychology of legitimacy', *Personality Social Psychology Review*, 323–344.

Vavrus, F. and Cole, K.M. (2002) '"I didn't do nothing": the discursive construction of school suspension', *Urban Review*, 34: 87–111.

Wachtel, T., Costello, B. and Wachtel, J. (2009) *The Restorative Practices Handbook for Teachers, Disciplinarians and Administrators*, Bethlehem, PA: International Institute of Restorative Practices.

Wallace, J.M. Jr., Goodkind, S., Wallace, C.M. and Bachman, J.G. (2008) 'Racial, ethnic, and gender differences in school discipline among U.S. high school students: 1991–2005', *The Negro Educational Review*, 59: 47–62.

Weber, M. (1947) *The Theory of Social and Economic Organization* (A.M. Henderson and T. Parsons, trans.), New York: Free Press. (Original work published 1925.)

Weinstein, C.S., Tomlinson-Clarke, S. and Curran, M. (2004) 'Toward a conception of culturally responsive classroom management', *Journal of Teacher Education*, 55: 25–38.

Wentzel, K. (2002) 'Are effective teachers like good parents? Teaching styles and student adjustment in early adolescence', *Child Development*, 73: 287–301.

Willis, P. (1977) *Learning to Labour: How Working-class Kids Get Working-Class Jobs*, Farnborough, UK: Saxon House.

Wing, J.Y. (2006) 'Integration across campus, segregation across classrooms: a close-up look at privilege', in P. Noguera, and J.Y. Wing, *Unfinished Business: Closing the Racial Achievement Gap in Our Schools* (pp. 87–120), San Francisco: John Wiley.

Zehr, H. (2002) *The Little Book of Restorative Justice*, Intercourse, PA: Good Books.

PART VI

Teacher expectations, judgment, and differentiation

26

HOW I SPENT MY LAST 50-YEAR VACATION

Bob Rosenthal's lifetime of research into interpersonal expectancy effects

Robert Rosenthal and Christine M. Rubie-Davies

This chapter provides a comprehensive history of the beginnings of research in the area of the interpersonal expectancy effect and in particular of the application of expectation effects to education. It is drawn from a pre-recorded video presentation given by Professor Robert Rosenthal at the Social Psychology of the Classroom International Conference held in Auckland, New Zealand in 2013. The chapter is a transcription completed by Christine Rubie-Davies and checked by Professor Rosenthal for accuracy. The transcription has been changed to a third-person report to suit the written chapter format; nevertheless the words and voice are those of Professor Robert Rosenthal. Thus, the body of the chapter presents Professor Rosenthal's summary of his work across his career as well as some allied research and findings. This is a career that Professor Robert Rosenthal has enjoyed so much that he describes it as his 50–year vacation.

Introduction to expectancy-effects research

What we expect of each other is often what we actually get from each other. This phenomenon is referred to as the interpersonal expectancy effect or the interpersonal self-fulfilling prophecy. The idea of the interpersonal power of expectations is an idea that began intriguing Robert Rosenthal in 1956 when he was doing his dissertation at University of California at Los Angeles (UCLA), where he admits to ruining the results of the dissertation because he somehow nonverbally leaked information to his research participants about what he wanted them to do and they obligingly did it. He had shown that the behavior of one person (the perpetrator) could be interpreted by a target person such that the target complied with what they believed the perpetrator expected of them – the interpersonal expectancy effect.

This accidental early interest evolved from the dissertation into a life's work. In 1957 Rosenthal began a program of research at the University of North Dakota that continued for many years at Harvard and which now continues at the University of California at Riverside (UCR) where he is currently based. It is a program of research on interpersonal expectancy effects. The first part of that research program was to learn whether and how other behavioral researchers might ruin the results of their experiments as well by unintentionally treating their research subjects or participants in such a way as to cause the expected behavior.

The early ideas related to this field were anecdotal but came from a very rich data base. Robert Merton (1948), a prominent sociologist at Columbia University, discussed the self-fulfilling prophecy effect that occurred within the context of the economy. Merton wrote about the conception that if many people believed that the bank in their small town was failing and they all got in line at the same time to withdraw all of their money, because banks do not keep all their money on hand, the bank would fail. Hence, the belief that a prosperous bank would fail makes it happen. Thus, in economics the concept of the self-fulfilling prophecy is well-understood and is an old idea first brought into reality in the pages of the *Antioch Review*.

Gordon Allport (1937), a founding father of social and personality psychology, believed that interpersonal self-fulfilling prophecies were among the causes of war. He argued that when one country gained the impression that another country was building up its arsenal, as in the Cold War, for example, then the first country would become anxious that the second country might have a larger weapons stockpile than they did and so they would increase their warfare armaments. Then the second country would realize that the first was catching up to their military might and so would decide that they had better commit to increasing their armaments further. The first country would then realize the other country was trying to get ahead, and decide that they had better develop even more weapons, and so on. Pretty soon there would be an escalating arms race which could lead to war.

A further example of the self-fulfilling prophecy effect, a particularly interesting case from business, was reported by Joseph Jastrow (1900). This is a story that came from the Census Bureau. People in the Census Bureau had to punch holes in Hollerith tabulating cards (similar to IBM cards) and the Hollerith cards were then used to select a sample from the population for studying. Samples could be achieved by sticking knitting needles through the holes in order to get the sample you wanted, for example, fathers aged 25–30 who had two children, a boy and a girl. Clerks employed to punch these tabulating cards could punch around 700 cards a day; that was considered the limit possible in 8 hours. The Secretary of the Interior who headed the Census Bureau requested that all managers tell the card punchers they should aim to complete 700 of these cards a day and so when fresh batches of Hollerith card punchers came in the clerks were to be told that 700 was the upper limit. And that was what the card punchers achieved. However, in one group when new clerks were being trained, the person admitting the new group forgot to tell them that 700 was the upper limit of human endurance. Within three days, the new people were punching 2,000 cards a day and were managing this without stress. This is an example of an interpersonal expectancy that worked in the business context.

An example within the academic context, again in this anecdotal domain, is that of a first-year course in advanced research methods that Rosenthal himself has taught for the past 40 years. For the past 35 years, as part of this course the undergraduate students have been asked to come up with an original research idea, collect all the data related to their question, and complete all of their statistical analyses based on those data. Their work then has to be written up as though it were going to be published in one of the American Psychological Association journals using the APA publication manual as a guide. The undergraduates have to do all that in one quarter of the academic year. Professors cannot do that; graduate students cannot do that. Undergraduate students can do it. They do not know it cannot be done! For the past 35 years, undergraduate students have been completing all these tasks in one academic quarter in Rosenthal's class, and some of their papers have been published in psychological journals.

Possibly the most famous case in the history of experimental psychology within the self-fulfilling prophecy field and still in the anecdotal domain relates to Clever Hans (Rosenthal 1998), the horse. At the turn of the twentieth century there were lots of very clever animals: reading pigs, clever chimpanzees, talking dogs. The thing that made Clever Hans so different from all the other chimpanzees, dogs, pigs, and other clever animals was that with all of the other animals, the owner had to be around when you asked the dog a question, or the pig a question, or the chimpanzee a question. Mr Von Osten, a German mathematics instructor, the owner of Clever Hans, would let people ask the horse mathematics questions in the owner's absence. So that made him a very different kind of animal, literally. There was a famous commission called the Hans Commission made up of circus experts, zoo keepers, comparative psychologists, veterinarians, and other experts in animal behavior who studied the horse to see whether or not this horse had special abilities. They decided that the horse's abilities were genuine, that no fraud was occurring. The owner did not have to be there and the horse would still correctly answer the mathematics problems a large percentage of the time. Oscar Pfungst, a graduate student at the time, and Carl Stumpf, his professor, together undertook a program of research into the abilities of this animal. For example, they began to experimentally manipulate the distance from the horse that people stood. The further the experimenters were from the horse when they asked the horse the question, the less accurate the horse was; he would make more mistakes the further experimenters were away. Then Pfungst and Stumpf did some experiments on ocular occlusion where they put blinders on the horse and the more of the visual field that was blinded that Clever Hans could not see out of, the less accurate was the horse. Pfungst and Stumpf found that visibility was an important variable; there were visual cues. As a further step in their research, they did a blind type of questioning through which they found that if they sent somebody in to ask the question who did not know the answer, there was much less chance that the horse would be correct. This did not completely solve the problem but it was an interesting result. What Pfungst and Stumpf eventually found out was based on the ecology of the questioner–horse relationship. When people approached the horse they would look up at him to ask their question and then drop their head to watch him tap out his answer with his hoof. What the researchers discovered was that the horse did not need to be asked a question at all. All that needed to be done was for a person to look the horse in the eye and then drop their head. That was the signal for the horse to commence tapping. But how did he know when to stop tapping? Provided the questioner knew the answer, when the horse reached the answer the questioner knew he was going to stop tapping and so moved his head or eyes upwards or dilated a nostril (something that Pfungst conjectured). The very subtle cue was read by the horse and the horse was right again, having been made correct by the expectation of the questioner.

Laboratory experiments

This anecdotal research underpinned Rosenthal's growing interest in expectancy effects. His work for his doctoral dissertation involved a photo-rating task based on some earlier work by Henry Murray who created the Thematic Apperception Test. The basic paradigm of the research was to have photographs of people, cut from news magazines. Rosenthal developed a rating scale that went from minus 10 to plus 10, where minus 10 meant extreme failure and plus 10 meant extreme success. In one of the experiments from Rosenthal's dissertation (Rosenthal 1956), there were three groups of participants: college men, college women, and paranoid schizophrenic patients (because a hallmark of schizophrenia was very high projection). One-third of each group had a success experience, one-third had a failure experience, and one-third had a neutral experience. The hypothesis was that on examining the ratings of the photos, if the participant had had a failure experience they would rate people in the photos as being more failing and if they had had a success experience they would rate them as being more successful. In a further set of experiments involving sophomore participants (Rosenthal and Fode 1961), this same task was used but a larger number of experimenters were recruited (approximately 16).

The experimenters were told that the research involved standardization of an empathy test in which they would ask their participants to decide from photos how much success or failure they believed the people in the photos had experienced. Half of the randomly assigned experiment-ers were told that their participants were success-perceivers, that is, that they were likely to give report ratings above 5, and the other randomly chosen half of the experimenters were told that they had been given a sample of failure-perceivers. The results showed that if experimenters had been led to expect high photo ratings, they recorded high photo ratings, whereas if they expected low photo ratings, they got low photo ratings. Because the researchers found it difficult to believe the results, the experiment was repeated several times with the same result although not all were statistically significant; however, later meta-analyses did show the results becoming progressively more significant, even when studies were included that were not significant in and of themselves. The experimenters were also filmed to ensure that they read exactly the same instructions to each of their participants. Indeed, they were all reading the same instructions and hence it did not appear to be verbal communication that was acting as a mediating variable in portraying what was expected. This led to the conjecture that experimenters could be com-municating their expectations through nonverbal communication. Hence, further experiments were conducted in which, in some studies, half the experimenters had a screen between the experimenter and the subject so they could talk and be heard but they could not see each other. That procedure eliminated the visual cues and it was found that the experimenter effect did reduce but it was not completely eliminated.

A few years later, at the University of Manitoba, Adair and Epstein (1968) added understand-ings to this emerging field of research. They conducted their experiments in two stages. Stage 1 was a basic replication of the studies previously undertaken by Rosenthal and his colleagues and outlined above. That is, half the experimenters were led to believe they would get positive ratings, the other half were led to believe they would get negative ratings from their participants. Indeed, that was what the results showed. However, Stage 2 involved no experimenters at all. The subjects arrived at the psychology department and were directed to follow the signs to the laboratory down the hall. Upon reaching the laboratory, there was a further sign inviting the participants to enter. Once inside, participants found an audio recorder and a further sign that directed them to push the start button on the recorder. What they heard was the audiotaped voices of the experi-menters from the first two experiments. In this second phase, where participants only heard the voice of the experimenters but did not meet them, Adair and Epstein found that they achieved almost the same magnitude of difference. That is, the difference remained when participants were directed by either the voices of experimenters who had been led to believe their participants were success-perceivers, versus those experimenters who believed their participants were failure-perceivers. Thus the expected difference remained even when only the voices were present. Hence, the message was being transmitted through the voices.

Verbal and nonverbal interaction

This experiment further ignited Rosenthal's nascent interest in nonverbal behavior and nonver-bal communication, mostly in relation to experimenter–subject interaction but more generally as well. However, about this time, Rosenthal was at the University of North Dakota and had done maybe eight or ten studies, none of which had been accepted for publication. Colleagues of Rosenthal's believed that the reason his studies were being rejected was because they were threat-ening to the establishment and experimenters. Another group of colleagues who were 'rat runners' suggested that human participants would comply with what they believed was expected, whereas rats would not. This challenge led Rosenthal to embark on a further series of studies with rats. At the time, Robert Tryon was at the University of California at Berkeley (UCB). He was a behavioral psychologist who began to inbreed generations of rats to determine if their intelligence for particular tasks could be increased (Hall and Halliday 1998). Using a complicated 17-joint T-maze, he interbred the male and female rats who had learnt the most quickly how to obtain the food at the end of the maze (maze-bright rats) and also interbred those who took the longest to learn (maze-dull rats). Having done this over several generations he ultimately obtained nonoverlapping distributions. Every rat that was in the maze-bright strand was smarter at learning to go through the 17-joint T-maze than any of the rats that had been bred for dullness. Rosenthal and Fode (1963) claimed to have obtained some of these rats but actually used only locally available rats that had never been selected for their maze-running ability. Rosenthal and his graduate student Fode randomly placed notices on the rats' cages to indicate that the rats were (supposedly) either maze-bright or maze-dull. The experiment took place over one week. At the end of the first day of rat-running, the randomly assigned rats, that is, those that had been alleged to be maze-bright, ran better, ran faster, and learnt in fewer trials how to get to the food than those rats that had been labeled dull. Rosenthal hypothesized that the experimenters may have handled the rats differently depending on whether they believed the rats were maze-bright or maze-dull and that this differential handling possibly resulted in the randomly assigned rats learning more quickly or more slowly since the type of maze they were using required the experimenters to carry the rats from their cages to the beginning point of the maze and then to carry them back once they had completed their trials for the day.

Shortly afterwards, Rosenthal was invited to deliver a seminar on the social psychology of the psychological experiment at Ohio State University. Reed Lawson, who was in the audience, challenged the findings and suggested that the same results would not be found if the rats were in Skinner boxes. This led to Rosenthal and Lawson (1964) conducting an experiment over a whole quarter of an academic year. Almost from the beginning, for the experimenters who had been led to believe that their rats were Skinner-box bright, the rats learnt more quickly than did the rats of those experimenters who had been led to believe that their rats were Skinner-box dull. Hence, the handling of the rats no longer appeared to be a plausible explanation for why rats learnt more quickly when experimenters were told their rats were bright, since in the Skinner boxes, there was almost no handling of the rats. There had to be some other kind of explanation and the explanation seemed to be that it had to do with the reinforcement pattern. The same behavior among rats believed to be bright or dull was interpreted differently and rewarded when the experimenter believed the rat was bright but not when the experimenter believed the rat was dull.

Interpersonal expectancy effects in education

Because Rosenthal initially had difficulty getting his studies published and had accumulated approximately a dozen studies including the animal studies and the human studies, these studies were subsequently synthesized into an overview article which was published in *American Scientist* (Rosenthal 1963), a journal for scientists across disciplinary boundaries. This meant that the article needed to be written in a broadly communicative fashion. The article ended by implying that if rats learned better when they were expected to, then perhaps children, too, would learn better if they were expected to.

Soon after the article was published, Rosenthal received a letter from South San Francisco from school principal, PhD candidate at UCB, and education scholar Leonore Jacobson which said, 'Let me know when you ever graduate from rats to children because have I got a school for you'. This resulted in Rosenthal's flying to San Francisco to meet the boundlessly energetic educator and scholar. Rosenthal and Jacobson met with the school superintendent, who had to give permission for the study and did. At the end of that academic year Rosenthal and Jacobson administered to all of the children in the school a test called the Harvard Test of Inflected Acquisition. They told the teachers that the Harvard Test of Inflected Acquisition could predict academic 'blooming'. That is, it would be possible to tell from these test results which children were going to make substantial gains in IQ the following academic year. The test was, in fact, a standardized but not well-known IQ test, the Flanagan Test of General Ability, an IQ test that was not reliant on students' reading and therefore did not require high levels of language. The test contained both verbal and reasoning items, with students being asked, for example, to locate the item that could be eaten from a series of pictures or to identify which in a series of pictures did not belong with the rest (the items were read aloud to students). It was a multiple-choice test which could be delivered to a whole class at a time and which contained more and more complicated questions as students worked through it.

All the students were tested at the end of the school year. At the beginning of the following school year, teachers were informed which of their new students had been identified by the Test of Inflected Acquisition as those likely to suddenly bloom intellectually that year. Teachers were given the names of between three and five students in every class who had, in fact, been selected using a table of random numbers. Students were then re-tested using the same test after one semester and then again at the end of the school year. In summary, the students who had been alleged to bloom, bloomed; they gained more IQ points than those about whom nothing was said. Because Rosenthal and Jacobson did not use a negative expectation, the comparison was of no expectation versus an enhanced expectation (see Rosenthal and Jacobson 1968 for further findings).

One concern has been that there may be something unethical in telling a teacher that certain students are going to suddenly achieve more intellectually, because it might detract attention from all the others as teachers focus on those they have been manipulated to believe will suddenly do well. Whether this did occur cannot be addressed because the teachers were not closely observed. However, one interesting counterintuitive finding was that the greater the gain of the identified children in a particular classroom, the greater the gain of the control group children. It therefore did not seem as though there were any negative consequences for the control group, based on that finding. Because of the previous animal and human studies, it was perhaps not surprising that the results were replicated in the schooling setting.

However, there was one finding that was most unexpected. The school in which this study was based had tracking and so each grade level had a fast track, a medium track, and a slow track. Hence, the experimental design of the study was a 6 × 3 × 2 factorial analysis of variance. This was because there were 6 grades, 3 tracks and students randomly assigned to the 2 conditions: experimental or control. Many of the students who were not in the experimental group also gained a lot in IQ scores over the time of the experiment. However, the teachers were unaware of the student gains since, because they were blind to the purpose of the study, they were not given the student scores. An unsettling finding was that the more students gained in IQ, if they were not in the experimental group, and especially if they were in the slow track, the more unfavorably they were viewed by their teachers.

Unfortunately, this finding has been replicated in other contexts. For example, Al Shore (1969), who was working at the time at Pasadena City College, found that students who were doing better than expected in IQ were rated lower by their teachers for their personality and psychological adjustment. Pamela Rubovitz and Martin Maehr (1973) in their research at the University of Illinois found that African American students who had been labelled as gifted were criticized more and praised less than other students by their teachers whereas white students labeled as gifted were criticized less and praised more. Complementary studies in other fields found similar results. Eleanor Leacock (1969) in her ethnographic work, *Teaching and Learning in City Schools*, also wrote about how among white students, teachers prefer the brighter ones, whereas among the African American students, they prefer the duller students. It would be easy to assume that this was simply white racism. However, this finding applied to both African American as well as European American teachers. It seemed as though the African American students who achieved contrary to the pervasive stereotypes were rejected socioemotionally by their teachers. They were treated worse in the emotional domain. This is an understudied area in social psychology and warrants further investigation.

Using video tapes of teacher–student interaction from their own laboratories as well as from those around the States and overseas, Monica Harris and Robert Rosenthal (1985) conducted a meta-analysis to determine the mediating variables in the teacher expectation–student achievement process. That is, what do the teachers do differently for the students for whom they have a more favorable expectation when compared with how they interact with students for whom their views are less favorable? Earlier, Rosenthal (1974) had proposed a four-factor theory as identifying the differential mediation in teacher–student interactions depending on whether teachers expected students to do well or not. These four factors were: climate, feedback, input, and output. Climate related to the warmer socioemotional climate that teachers created for those they favored. Feedback referred to the differential types of feedback that low- and high-expectation students received. Rosenthal suggested that teachers spent more time teaching students they expected to do well and presented them with more material and more difficult learning experiences than were experienced by those students for whom the teachers had low expectations. This was the type of interaction Rosenthal labeled 'input'. Finally, output referred to providing the favored students with more opportunities to respond to questions than were offered to other students, providing support when they were having difficulty, and giving them more wait time than students who were less favored.

However, the meta-analysis of Harris and Rosenthal (1985) suggested that the four-factor theory should be adjusted to a two-factor theory: climate and effort. Climate was found to have the most effect on student achievement. The second factor, effort was a combination of input and output. Teachers interacted more frequently and for longer periods with the students they believed would learn more, presented them with more difficult materials, and taught them at a faster pace. Feedback was found to have only small effects in the mediation of teacher expectation effects and therefore was dropped as a major factor.

Application of interpersonal expectancy effects research to other areas

Interpersonal expectancy effects have not only been studied within the elementary-school domain, however. There has been other work related to the doctor–patient interaction, to interactions of teachers within the tertiary- and secondary-school environments and to the interactions of judges with juries. Those that are particularly interesting were extensions of the nonverbal communication which came from the studies of teacher–student interaction in elementary school and experimenter–participant interactions which had been studied earlier (see above). For instance, in a study conducted in the mid-1960s (Milmoe *et al.* 1967), a series of admitting doctors at Massachusetts General Hospital , which was affiliated with the Harvard Medical School, agreed to participate in the research. The responsibilities of these admitting physicians included diagnosing alcoholism among patients who came to the clinic, and trying to get the alcoholic patients into an alcoholism treatment program. At the time of the study, a new alcoholism treatment program had just been set up. All the admitting doctors were audiotaped and interviewed about how they felt about alcoholic patients. They were all asked the question: 'What's been your experience with alcoholic patients?' The researchers isolated a one-minute audio clip from these interviews. The one-minute audio clips were run through a low-pass-band filter which removes the frequencies that permit understanding of the words (content-filtered speech). Removal of the actual speech in which the researchers were less interested enabled them to concentrate on tone of voice for determining how the doctors felt about alcoholic patients. There were very large negative correlations ($r > -0.65$) of independent raters between the ratings of hostility of the tone of voice of the doctors in talking about alcoholic patients and their success with alcoholic patients in effectively getting them referred to the treatment program that had been freshly set up.

A further study related to the ratings that students give to their teachers in college. At Harvard, there was a center established to improve teaching ability within the university. As part of their work, people working at the center videotaped teachers teaching all kinds of courses: history, English, psychology, mathematics, and so on. Ambady and Rosenthal (1993) took short clips of 30 seconds of video tape, made a master tape of them, and then showed them to sophomore raters who rated the teachers on variables such as active, confident, enthusiastic, likable, optimistic, dominant, and warm. What was found was that in 30 seconds of a view of a teacher teaching, where not a word that they were saying could be heard, and where the raters did not know what the teachers were teaching, the statistically significant correlations between the sophomore students' ratings and the teaching evaluations of those faculty members from their own students at the end of the semester were large, ranging from $r = 0.56$ to $r = 0.84$. Another study was conducted with secondary school teachers where independent raters again rated the teachers on similar variables to those in the first study. This time the principals rated the teachers, and then relationships between the assessments of raters who did not know the teachers, and principals' ratings were conducted. Again, very short video clips could predict principals' assessments of teachers. Clearly, a lot of nonverbal communication is taking place in these situations.

Further studies (Blanck *et al.* 1985, 1990) related to the criminal justice system. Peter Blanck videotaped 34 trials. He was interested in whether or not there were nonverbal cues in the judge instructing the jury that could lead to an accurate prediction of how the jury would find. The researchers (Blanck *et al.* 1985) found that the content-filtered tone of voice in which juries were instructed could predict the verdict that juries would return. Further, judges expecting a guilty verdict were perceived by independent raters as being less warm and more anxious in their summing up to juries. However, this was an observational study rather than an experimental one. In a second study (Blanck *et al.* 1990), Allan Hart gained permission to use a large room in the Cambridge Massachusetts Court House where people awaiting jury service were assigned as if they were an actual jury to watch a video of a complete trial. At the end of the trial, rather than hearing the instructions from the judge related to the particular trial that they had just viewed, they were played the instructions from judges in completely different trials who had been previously filmed by Blanck. Half of the jurors were randomly assigned to hear instructions from a judge who had expected that the defendant was guilty, and half of the jurors heard a judge's instructions when the judge believed the defendant to be innocent, so the subjects of this experiment were whole juries. The randomization involved receiving instructions from a judge who had a completely different defendant, one who had nothing to do with the trial they had just viewed. The juries then had to decide whether they thought the defendant in the trial they had viewed was guilty or innocent. Almost frighteningly, there was a 30 percent increase in guilty verdicts if the jury heard instructions from a judge giving instructions in a case where the judge thought the proper verdict would have been guilty – even though the actual trial they had watched was completely different. The percentage of guilty verdicts went from 49 percent to 64 percent.

In a more recent study (Ambady *et al.* 2002), the researchers conducted a study of surgeons and primary-care physicians. The doctors were audiotaped interacting with their patients. From 30-second clips, undergraduate students rated the surgeons and primary-care physicians on variables such as hostility, friendliness, enthusiasm, bossiness, nastiness, and condescension. From the content-filtered speech contained in these audio clips, the researchers were able to predict the number of times that a doctor had been sued. For surgeons, the variable that most strongly predicted being sued was bossiness. Surgeons who were perceived by independent raters to be bossy were more likely to get sued than nonbossy surgeons. In the case of the primary-care physicians, those who were judged as being more concerned for their patients were sued less often than those perceived as being less concerned.

In her senior honors thesis, Sarah Heschtman (Heschtman and Rosenthal 1991) conducted a study in which male and female teachers were teaching male and female students and they were teaching both verbal (female sex-typed) and mechanical/quantitative (male sex-typed) material. Raters viewed videos in which there was no sound and so watched teachers teaching the girls and boys quantitative/ mechanical concepts and material related to verbal learning. The teachers were judged as more hostile in their demeanor when they were teaching material not sex-typed for them rather than when they were teaching material that was appropriately sex-typed. This discrimination, of which the teachers almost certainly were not aware, was less true of female teachers than it was of male teachers and it was less true for androgynous teachers. (Androgynous teachers are those who are classified as a psychological personality in which they are both high on warmth which is traditionally thought of as more feminine and high on being business-like, task-oriented, task-focused, and competent.) It appears that in many walks of life nonverbal behavior influences interactions and outcomes. There is clearly a rich future in pursuing such research.

Nonverbal research has also been applied to personality research. Harrigan et al. (2004) conducted a meta-analysis to determine how anxiety is perceived. They examined trait anxiety (a generalized trait in which some people are determined to be more anxious than others in many situations) and state anxiety (a state of being anxious in a particular moment, for example, if a snake is seen slithering across the room) to determine if there were different nonverbal behaviors that communicated trait anxiety versus state anxiety. They found that state anxiety, the current state of the organism, can be better detected through the audio channel (i.e. content-filtered speech) whereas trait anxiety, the more enduring characteristic of a person, can be better diagnosed through the video channel alone, with no sound. This initial research in the field of personality psychology indicates a way forward for future research in which many different personality variables could be examined to determine how they are communicated.

Finally, while this chapter has concentrated on the psychological and educational literature, there is a large body of work related to Pygmalion in business and industry. An example is a paper by Sterling Livingston (1969) entitled 'Pygmalion in Management'. Livingston was a professor at Harvard Business School who made a movie about the concept of Pygmalion. He believed that if managers *expected* more from their workers, they would *get* more from them – and higher quality work.

Dov Eden, an Israeli researcher, has conducted several randomized experiments in which he did quite a different thing. He used intact groups. In most of the earlier research, a subset was selected and they were singled out as showing some potential blooming. In Eden's studies with military groups (e.g. Eden and Ravid 1982; Eden and Shani 1982), his samples were whole platoons. In these studies, the platoon leaders, were told that they were fortunate that the new batch coming in were an amazing group, and the virtues of the new recruits were listed. Of course, these were randomly assigned labels. But it turned out that the platoon as a whole did gain more when platoon leaders were led to expect more of them. Further, Eden and his graduate students and colleagues have been very productive in relation to studying the expectancy effect in relation to business and management.

Hence, while the Pygmalion effect was first recognized in laboratory experiments and then in elementary classroom environments, it has also been applied to the business setting, to non-verbal behavior in courtrooms, to doctor's offices, to university and secondary-school teachers, and to personality research. Clearly this is an important and productive area of research with still many exciting possibilities for future research. In closing, a quotation from Johann Wolfgang Goethe seems appropriate: 'If you treat a person as they are, they will stay as they are. But if you treat a person as if they were what they ought to be and could be they will become what they ought to be and could be.'

References

Adair, J.G. and Epstein, J.S. (1968) 'Verbal cues in the mediation of experimenter bias', *Psychological Reports* 22: 1045–1053.

Allport, G.W. (1937) *Personality: A psychological interpretation*, New York: Holt, Rinehart and Winston.

Ambady, N., Laplante, D., Nguyen, T., Rosenthal, R., Chaumeton, N. and Levinson, W. (2002) 'Surgeons' tone of vioice: a clue to malpractice history', *Surgery* 132: 5–9.

Ambady, N. and Rosenthal, R. (1993) 'Half a minute: Predicting teacher evaluations from thin slices of nonverbal behavior and physical attractiveness', *Journal of Personality and Social Psychology* 64: 431–441.

Blanck, P.D., Rosenthal, R. and Cordell, L.H. (1985) 'The appearance of justice: judges' verbal and nonver-bal behavior in criminal jury trials', *Stanford Law Review* 38: 89–164.

Blanck, P.D., Rosenthal, R., Hart, A.J. and Bernieri, F. (1990) 'The measure of the judge: an empirically based framework for exploring trial judges' behavior', *Iowa Law Review*, 75: 653–684.

Eden, D. and Ravid, G. (1982) 'Pygmalion versus self-expectancy: effects of instructor- and self-expectancy on trainee performance', *Organizational Behavior and Human Performance*, 30: 351–364.

Eden, D. and Shani, A.B. (1982) 'Pygmalion goes to boot camp: expectancy, leadership, and trainee perfor-mance', *Journal of Applied Psychology*, 67: 194–199.

Hall, M. and Halliday, T. (1998) *Behavior and Evolution*, New York: Springer-Verlag.

Harrigan, J.A., Wilson, K. and Rosenthal, R. (2004) 'Detecting state and trait anxiety from visual and audi-tory cues: a meta-analysis', *Personality and Social Psychology Bulletin*, 30: 56–66.

Harris, M.J. and Rosenthal, R. (1985) 'Mediation of interpersonal expectancy effects: 31 meta-analyses', *Psychological Bulletin*, 97: 363–386.

Heschtman, S. and Rosenthal, R. (1991) 'Teacher sex and nonverbal behavior in the teaching of sexually stereotyped materials', *Journal of Applied Social Psychology*, 21: 446–459.

Jastrow, J. (1900) *Fact and Fable in Psychology*, Boston, MA: Houghton Mifflin.

Leacock, E. (1969) *Teaching and Learning in City Schools: A Comparative Study*, New York: Basic Books.

Livingston, J.S. (1969) 'Pygmalion in management', *Harvard Business Review*, 47: 81–89.

Merton, R.K. (1948) 'The self-fulfilling prophecy', *The Antioch Review*, 8: 193–210.

Milmoe, S., Rosenthal, R., Blane, H.T., Chafetz, M.E. and Wolf, I. (1967) 'The doctor's voice: postdictor of successful referral of alcoholic patients', *Journal of Abnormal Psychology*, 72: 78–84.

Rosenthal, R. (1956) 'An attempt at experimental induction of the defense mechanism of projection', unpublished doctoral dissertation, University of California at Los Angeles, Los Angeles.

Rosenthal, R. (1963) 'On the social psychology of the psychological experiment: the experimenter's hypothesis as unintended determinant of experimental results', *American Scientist*, 51: 268–283.

Rosenthal, R. (1974) 'On the social psychology of the self-fulfilling prophecy: further evidence for Pygmalion effects and their mediating mechanisms', *MSS Modular Publications, Module*, 53: 1–28.

Rosenthal, R. (1998) 'Covert communication in classrooms, clinics and courtrooms', *Eye on Psi Chi*, 3: 18–22.

Rosenthal, R. and Fode, K.L. (1961) 'The problem of experimenter outcome-bias', in D.P. Ray (ed.) *Series Research in Social Psychology*, Symposia studies series, No. 8, Washington, DC: National Institute of Social and Behavioral Research.

Rosenthal, R. and Fode, K.L. (1963) 'The effect of experimenter bias on the performance of the albino rat', *Behavioral Science*, 8: 183–189.

Rosenthal, R. and Jacobson, L. (1968) *Pygmalion in the Classroom: Teacher Expectation and Pupils' Intellectual Development*, New York: Holt, Rinehart and Winston.

Rosenthal, R. and Lawson, R. (1964) 'A longitudinal study of the effects of experimenter bias on the operant learning of laboratory rats', *Psychiatric Research*, 2: 61–72.

Rubovitz, P. and Maehr, M. (1973) 'Pygmalion Black and White', *Journal of Personality and Social Psychology*, 25: 210–218.

Shore, A.L. (1969) 'Confirmation of expectancy and changes in teachers' evaluations of student behavior', doctoral dissertation, available from *Dissertation Abstracts*, 30: 1878–1879.

27

TEACHER EXPECTATIONS AND WITHIN-CLASSROOM DIFFERENTIATION

Eddie Denessen and Alaster Scott Douglas

There are a number of different possible perspectives with regard to differentiation in school teaching. When considering differentiation as a pedagogical practice, the focus is on the teacher adapting to individual students' needs in order to contribute to students' knowledge and skills. But differentiation also occurs as part of daily practice because different students are treated differently when interacting with teachers. This often depends on the perspectives teachers have of their students' needs. However, differentiation may also be considered an aspect of a more global approach to pedagogical practice in the way it can help us understand how teachers can create adaptive learning opportunities for different groups of students, thereby meeting the needs of a group of learners, yet at the same time enabling individuals within that group to meet their own goals. This latter perspective is of particular interest when considering effective differentiation practices within school classrooms where class sizes are often more than 20 students. This chapter considers each of these perspectives: perceptions teachers have of their students' strengths and needs (in the literature often referred to as 'teacher expectations') and instructional perspectives on differentiation, which are acquired based on the knowledge teachers have of their students. We discuss the objectives of differentiation and the conditions that are needed for teachers to attend to classroom diversity. Such foci, we believe, will open up new ways for researching differentiation with regard to teaching and learning in the classroom.

Theoretical background of within-classroom differentiation

In past decades, within-classroom differentiation has been acknowledged as a pedagogy that teachers can apply to address the needs of all learners in their classrooms. Many argue that across the globe, student populations have become increasingly diverse because of migration and the inclusion of students with disabilities in mainstream schools (Subban 2006) and it has become commonly accepted by educators that whole-classroom teaching is not the best pedagogy to address diverse learning needs, and that there is a need for tailored, personalized, adaptive, and differentiated classroom practices to provide an optimal learning context for all learners (Roiha 2014; Sarrazin et al. 2006). Since students bring specific knowledge, skills, personalities, interests, and preferences to the classroom, whole-classroom teaching is becoming an increasingly less attractive pedagogical practice, because it is assumed to serve only a small part of the student population and it leads to frustration and ineffective learning (Gregory and Chapman 2013; Roy *et al.* 2013; Tomlinson *et al.* 2003).

Within-classroom differentiation as rational and deliberate practice

In a context of increased awareness of within-classroom diversity, teachers are thus expected to differentiate among their students to attend to the needs of any individual student in the classroom (see e.g. Gregory and Chapman 2013). According to Tomlinson *et al.* (2003: 121) differentiation is:

> an approach to teaching in which teachers proactively modify curricula, teaching methods, resources, learning activities, and student products to address the diverse learning needs of individual students and small groups to maximize the learning opportunity for each student in the classroom.

Teachers can differentiate among students in several ways; for example by providing students with different tasks at different levels, by adapting the pace of instruction to individual students, or by providing differential cognitive and/or emotional support to individual students (Tomlinson *et al.* 2003).

Theoretically, the current emphasis on differentiation is grounded in constructivist theories regarding teaching and learning. Specifically, differentiated instruction finds a basis in Vygotsky's theory of cognitive development, and the concept of the zone of proximal development (ZPD) is considered the key to differentiated instruction (see e.g. Subban 2006). Vygotsky (1978: 86) defines the zone of proximal development as 'the distance between the actual developmental level as determined by independent problem solving and the level of potential development as determined through problem solving under adult guidance or in collaboration with more capable peers'. For teacher–student interactions to lead to meaningful learning activities, teachers should frame their teaching in each student's zone of proximal development, and because this zone is considered to differ among students, teachers need to differentiate to adapt to student diversity.

From the literature on differentiated instruction, within-classroom differentiation reads as a *rational* and *deliberate* teacher practice (George 2005; Ginsberg 2005). Simply stated, differentiation means that teachers choose from a repertoire of pedagogies to adapt their teaching to their students based on their knowledge of each students' specific learner characteristics (abilities, interest, preferences). As Moon (2005: 227) states: 'differentiation requires decision making'. In addition to the fundamental issue of whether differentiation is a rational and deliberate practice, some interesting questions can be asked about this decision-making process, related to types of decisions that are made and sources of information on which these decisions are based.

First, the decisions that are made concerning differentiation are related to learning activities that teachers expect from their students. Teachers can differentiate, for example, by adapting the curriculum content, the way of required processing of new information, the learner pace, the type and complexity of assignments, and the required learning products (Gregory and Chapman 2013). In a differentiated classroom, students can work individually or in small groups on their own topics, at their own level and speed, and in their own way. Teachers guide these classroom activities by designing or facilitating differentiated activities. For example, they can give some additional instruction to some students while others work indepentently, they can monitor and coach some students more closely than others, or they can give more challenging assignments to talented students in their classroom.

To be beneficial for students, decisions regarding how to differentiate need valid assessments of students' abilities (knowledge, skills, attitudes, competences), interest (what motivates this student), and learning profiles (the way the student seems to learn best). Valid assessments are essential for teachers to adapt their teaching to their students (Clayton 2011). For teaching to be meaningful and adaptive, it should be matched to students' individually different ability and interest and teachers should be aware – or should be made aware – of those individual differences within classrooms.

To gain insight into student differences within classrooms that are relevant for teachers' differentiation decisions, teachers can either rely on the knowledge they have obtained about their students from daily interactions and observations or they can use specific assessements. Although the accuracy of teachers' perceptions of students' abilities is moderately high (Damaray and Elliott 1998; Jussim *et al.* 2009); bias has been observed in teacher ratings of student abilities (see e.g. Ready and Wright 2011). Teachers tend to underestimate the ability levels of students from low socioeconomic and cultural-ethnic minority backgrounds in particular.

To overcome these biased perceptions, the literature suggests that standardized formative assessments are the means par excellence to provide valid input for instructional decisions such as scaffolding and classroom differentiation (Black *et al.* 2004; Brimijoin *et al.* 2003; Moon 2005; Shepard 2005). Based on these assessments, decisions can be made regarding the curriculum content and the learning activities that are expected from students. Teachers should be equipped with valid assessment tools that form a solid diagnostic basis for classroom differentiation. In sum, based on the approach of within–classroom differentiation as a deliberate, proactive, rational teacher practice that is adaptive to students, valid assessments and sound differentiation strategies seem to be beneficial for the learning processes of all students in a classroom.

It can be argued, however, that within–classroom differentiation is more than proactive, rational, and deliberate and that it is not only based on valid assessments of student needs. There are numerous indicators that point to the existence of reactive, unconscious, and intuitive differentiating teacher practices that are based on biased perceptions of students' needs. Classroom differentiation need not only be a proactive teacher behaviour, but may also be related to unintended differentiation behaviours that are not planned in advance but can be observed in classrooms. Teachers may differentiate between students in a rather subtle way (Beaman *et al.* 2006; Harrop and Swinson 2011; Smith 2013); for example, by providing some students with more elaborate feedback and emotional support than others in their daily classroom interactions with their students.

Empirical findings of reactive and implicit differentiation

Based on years of research in this area, Rosenthal (1994) identified four factors of teachers' differential treatment of their students, including climate (creating a warmer socioemotional learning climate for some students), input (teach more and more challenging material to some students), output (giving some students more opportunities for responding), and feedback (giving some students more elaborate feedback). These differential behaviours are verbal and nonverbal and teachers may not be aware of their differential treatment of the students in their classrooms (Babad 2005; Rosenthal 1994).

Since 1968, when Rosenthal and Jacobson published *Pygmalion in the Classroom*, the subject of differential teacher treatment of students based on expectations teachers have of their students has been extensively studied (for reviews, see Jussim *et al.* 2009; McKown and Weinstein 2008). Teacher expectations are teacher cognitions concerning students' future performance that are based on teachers' perceptions of their students. It can be argued that teachers do not rely only on valid assessments or diagnostics to form expectations of their students (Babad 2005; Jussim *et al.* 2009; Rubie-Davies 2009). False expectations are formed when teachers hold group ste-reotyped attitudes towards students. McKown and Weinstein (2008), for example, claim that expectations are partly determined by the cultural-ethnic minority background of students, leading to systematically lower expectations for minority students.

Van den Bergh *et al.* (2010) found that teachers who hold group-stereotyped attitudes towards ethnic minority students rated the ability level of minority students lower compared with teach-ers with less biased attitudes. These results imply that teachers may underestimate their students when they hold group stereotyped attitudes towards these students. This may not only be the case when it comes to students from minority ethnic backgrounds; girls or boys, students from lower social classes, and students with special educational needs may also be subject to group stereotyp-ing by their teachers (Beaman *et al.* 2006; Harrop and Swinson 2011; Hornstra *et al.* 2010; Smith 2013). In previous studies, relationships between group stereotyping, teacher expectations and students' outcomes have been assessed that illustrate how stereotyped attitudes may lead to reac-tive and intuitive within-classroom differentiation practices that increase rather than reduce educational inequalities.

Future directions: Introducing sociocultural classroom contexts of within-classroom differentiation

To overcome negative consequences for educational opportunities because of invalid and biased assessment of students' strengths and needs, it is important that teachers differentiate based on accurate assessment of student needs, and acknowledge that these needs affect and are affected by the social situation. In looking at how the learning opportunities in school classrooms could afford or constrain student learning, learning can be considered in terms of the changing rela-tionship a learner has with their social situation of development: 'The social situation of development is . . . a system of relations between the child of a certain age and social reality' (Vygotsky 1978: 199).

Returning to Vygotsky's notion of the zone of proximal development, in terms of classroom learning, its focus is on the relationship between thinking and the social organization of instruc-tion. A sociocultural perspective accepts that the social system within which students learn is mutually and actively created by the teacher and the students together. The zone of proximal development provides a unit of study that integrates the student with the social environment and overcomes viewing students as separate elements in isolation. This perspective encourages obser-vation of students' interaction with their environments: 'Learning is dependent on several factors but most vital is the engagement of the learner with the environment, that is a psychological engagement with the setting in which the learning takes place' (Jacobs and Harvey 2010: 195).

Rather than considering differentiation in terms of teachers' reaction to group stereotypes, some current research on teachers' differential behavior focuses on the learning setting and uses the zone of proximal development to emphasize the importance of social conditions in under-standing students' thinking and development. This idea of analyzing the learning setting as students experience it is taken up by Hotam and Hadar (2013) in their discussion of their concept of *pedagogy in practice*. The interplay between a teacher's way of teaching and the students' experi-ence of this acknowledges the idea of a hidden curriculum: 'the concealed moral, social, cultural or political meanings that teachers tacitly channel to students' (Hotam and Hadar 2013: 390). Through this concept, hidden messages may bias, for example gender issues. Yet in pedagogy in practice, the focus, rather than being on messages conveyed by a school system, is on the students' perspectives and interpretation of such messages: 'what actually happened in class, and how it differed from teachers' expectations is an aspect that remains understudied' (393).

Accessing the student voice in relation to researching differential teacher behavior in the classroom is also the focus of research based on deaf children's recollections of their school experiences of learning (Smith 2013). Smith's study provides new insights contrary to some preconceived notions about deaf students; for example, when a student feels it nice that his teacher more freely gave answers to him as a deaf student, he then finds that 'when he faced the difficulties of being outside on his own, he realized this teacher had never taught him the skills he needed to be independent' (Smith 2013: 681).

An emphasis on descriptive analysis in some of the literature on teacher expectations and within-classroom differentiation does not get to the heart of how or why differentiation practices are realized. For example, Howe and Abedin (2013: 325), in their review of research into classroom dialogue, note that in four decades 'more is known about how classroom dialogue is organized than about whether certain modes of organization are more beneficial than others'. It is well documented that, on average, boys play more focal roles than girls in the classroom and are more likely to gain more feedback from teachers. Howe and Abedin note that boys are also chosen proportionately more often from students with their hands up (2013: 337). Also, high attainers receive more feedback, which is also more likely to be positive compared to negative feedback, which is more frequently observed with low attainers (2013: 338). Findings across the decades have been clearly replicated with little change in results. Howe and Abedin conclude that future research would benefit from a more extensive exploration of culture in different classroom situations.

An activity theory perspective on within-classroom differentiation

The focus of analysis in activity theory first considers the social situation (rather than the individual). Activity theorists view activities at work as the basis of learning. Looking at opportunities for systemic learning changes the focus of the research to the social context, and shifts attention from the individual to the setting. A study by Douglas (2014) addresses teachers' differential behavior and follows one class of Year 8 students (12- and 13-year-olds) being taught by five teachers in different subjects in one secondary school in London. The research explores how teachers differentiate among their students and the findings consider why the differences regarding classroom differentiation exist between the five subject teachers. The research questions ask how teachers use differentiation in the classroom and how teaching activity tools are used by the teachers in the lessons.

The analysis in this study focuses on the social and cultural practices in school classrooms and uses a cultural historical and activity theory (CHAT) analysis (Engeström 2008). This focuses attention on learning as a social phenomenon, a process that takes place within social systems that have evolved culturally and historically and that offer participants in those systems certain tools with which to work on a shared object. For example, lesson plans, instruction techniques, behavior management strategies, and teaching tasks can all be seen as tools used in lessons. However, material tools (such as lesson plans) and nonphysical tools (such as speech and the use of language) can take on varying significance and use by different teachers. When analyzing the significance and use of these tools, and how they are inherently situated culturally, institutionally and historically, the researcher can consider a number of claims that characterize them in the context of the school classroom's cultural history.

In considering how the use of tools differed between teachers, one aim was to get further insight into how teachers' differential behavior creates learning opportunities for students. In this study, differentiation behaviors that teachers displayed towards their students assigned a mediating role in translating expectations to the students. Several categories of teachers' differentiating behavior were identified and these were related to teachers' perceptions of the student's socioemotional teacher–student relationship, student feedback, classroom interactions, and the type of teaching activities planned.

Where teachers identified concerns in their lessons that were to do with influences from outside the classroom (the school's reputation, family backgrounds or parental upbringing) there was less onus on differentiation beyond the different expected student outcomes from the lessons' tasks and more attention given to behavior management. When discussing the importance of the curriculum subject, those teachers who identified specific skills in relation to the curriculum specification tended to relate learning with identified subject-specific assessment levels. Those who described learning with a more holistic definition saw students' learning as being on a learning trajectory which related to their ongoing maturity and development. These teachers also tended to value pupils learning from one another, and from the social situation of their development (Vygotsky 1978), sharing their ideas and drawing on their own experiences. Examples of differentiation practices illustrate the importance of culture and context in classroom settings, which on a broader scale have been identified in studies across Europe (see Osborn *et al.* 2003).

How students are categorized in classroom policy dominates the way students are constructed in 'terms of rather simplistic, mono-conceptual and evaluative categorizations such as socioeconomic status and ethnicity [which] are insensitive to local contexts' (Waite *et al.* 2010:70). Results of statistical analyses based on these categorizations in relation to large-scale quantitative-style data analysis do not offer explanations that would help teachers adjust their differential behaviors. Such analyses, which may use ethnicity data, for example, to identify individual qualities, locate problems such as underachievement within the individual rather than within institutional practices (Crozier and Davies 2007) and also 'fail to account to the fact that multiple aspects of diverse identity often coexist within one individual' (70). A paper by Waite *et al.* (2010) warns of analysis purely at the individual rather than societal level, but advocates sensitivity to subjective experience in social contexts as 'ethnic grouping or attainment levels does not allow for the lived experience or situated cultural identity of individuals' (71).

This then suggests that large-scale quantitative research, although valuable in how it has helped to form a picture of teachers' differential behavior in classrooms, may not consider social and peer interaction implications from the students' perspectives. This has been addressed in a small-scale qualitative study in a primary school in Finland (Vehkakoski 2012). While looking at teachers' use of differentiation as a pedagogical tool in their teaching practices, the study found that students' own knowledge of the differentiated instruction helped them construct an understanding of their abilities in relation to others in the class. To avoid students' energy going into competing with their classmates or to protecting their own image, the study advocates making differential classroom policies (and therefore behaviors) visible by having teachers discussing these openly with students. 'This may result in students becoming familiar with diversity, and the difference of assignments becoming a natural part of everyday classroom practices' (167). This study, as well as a number of the small-scale qualitative studies mentioned above, start to bring the different strands of research on teacher expectations and within-classroom differentiation together.

Concluding comments

In this chapter, we have addressed links between teacher expectations of their students and their differentiated classroom practice. From an overview of the literature and empirical research, at least five conditions can be derived for effective differentiation practices (Brimijoin *et al.* 2003; Damaray and Elliott 1998; George 2005; Gregory and Chapman 2013; Jussim *et al.* 2009; Moon 2005; Subban 2006; Tomlinson *et al.* 2003). These are:

1   diagnostic skills of teachers (their ability to identify student needs);
2   availability of tools and materials to enable differentiation;
3   teacher differentiation competencies;
4   conduciveness of the classroom context to differentiation practices (climate, group norms regarding different treatments of students);
5   school context (school leadership and vision with regard to differentiation practices).

The concept of 'teacher expectations' refers to the first condition. This is a first step in creating meaningful differentiated learning environments. However, sociocultural theory helps us to understand the role of teachers' expectations in the broader context of classroom differentiation. This wider context is considered in the other four conditions listed above. Appreciating the value of different research traditions and perspectives when considering within-classroom differentiation is important for further developing an appreciation of the concept. Developing the research on within-classroom differentiation can also be achieved, we believe, by incorporating a sociocultural perspective to gain an integrated understanding of the conditions influencing differentiation practices.

References

Babad, E. (2005) 'Guessing teachers' differential treatment of high- and low-achievers from thin slices of their public lecturing behavior', *Journal of Nonverbal Behavior*, 29: 125–134.

Beaman, R., Wheldall, K. and Kemp, C. (2006) 'Differential teacher attention to boys and girls in the classroom', *Educational Review*, 58: 339–366.

Black, P., Harrison, C., Lee, C., Marshall, B. and William, D. (2004) 'Working inside the black box: assessment for learning in the classroom', *Phi Delta Kappan*, 86: 9–21.

Brimijoin, K., Marquissee, E. and Tomlinson. C.A. (2003) 'Using data to differentiate instruction', *Educational Leadership*, 60: 70–73.

Clayton, J. (2011) 'Changing diversity in U.S. schools: the impact on elementary student performance and achievement', *Education and Urban Society*, 43: 671–695.

Crozier, G. and Davies, J. (2007) 'Hard to reach parents or hard to reach schools? A discussion of home-school relations, with particular references to Bangladeshi and Pakistani parents', *British Educational Research Journal*, 33: 295–314.

Damaray, M.K. and Elliott, S.N. (1998) 'Teachers' judgments of students' academic functioning: a comparison of actual and predicted performances', *School Psychology Quarterly*, 13: 8–24.

Douglas, A.S. (2014) 'Addressing diverse learning needs: differentiation behaviours of five teachers towards the same class of students', in L. Daniela, I. Luka, L. Rutka and I. Zogla (eds) *The Teacher of the 21st Century: Quality Education for Quality Teaching* (pp. 28–39), Newcastle, UK: Cambridge Scholars Publishing.

Engeström, Y. (2008) *From Teams to Knots: Activity-Theoretical Studies of Collaboration and Learning at Work*, Cambridge: Cambridge University Press.

George, P. (2005) 'A rationale for differentiating instruction in the regular classroom', *Theory into Practice*, 44: 185–193.

Ginsberg, M. (2005) 'Cultural diversity, motivation, and differentiation', *Theory into Practice*, 44: 218–225.

Gregory H.H. and Chapman, C. (2013) *Differentiated Instructional Strategies: One Size Doesn't Fit All*, Thousand Oaks, CA: Corwin Press.

Harrop, A. and Swinson, J. (2011) 'Comparison of teacher talk directed to boys and girls and its relationship to their behaviour in secondary and primary schools', *Educational Studies*, 37: 115–125.

Hornstra, L., Denessen, E., Bakker, J., van den Bergh, L. and Voeten, M. (2010) 'Teacher attitudes toward dyslexia: effects on teacher expectations and the academic achievement of students with dyslexia', *Journal of Learning Disabilities*, 43: 515–529.

Hotam, Y. and Hadar, L. (2013) 'Pedagogy in practice: the pedagogy of a learning setting as students experience it', *Oxford Review of Education*, 39: 385–399.

Howe, C. and Abedin, M. (2013) 'Classroom dialogue: a systematic review across four decades of research', *Cambridge Journal of Education*, 43: 325–356.

Jacobs, N. and Harvey, D. (2010) 'The extent to which teacher attitudes and expectations predict academic achievement of final year students', *Educational Studies*, 36: 195–206.

Jussim, L., Robustelli, S.L. and Cain, T.R. (2009) 'Teacher expectations and self-fulfilling prophecies', in K.R. Wentzel and A. Wigfield (eds) *Handbook of Motivation in School* (pp. 349–380), New York: Routledge.

McKown, C. and Weinstein, R.S. (2008) 'Teacher expectations, classroom context and the achievement gap', *Journal of School Psychology*, 46: 235–261.

Moon, T.R. (2005) 'The role of assessment in differentiation', *Theory into Practice*, 44: 226–233.

Osborn, M., Broadfoot, P., McNess, E., Planel, C., Ravn, B. and Triggs, P. (2003) *A World of Difference? Comparing Learners across Europe*, Milton Keynes, UK: Open University Press.

Ready, D.D. and Wright, D.L. (2011) 'Accuracy and inaccuracy in teachers' perceptions of young children's cognitive abilities: the role of child background and classroom context', *American Educational Research Journal*, 48: 335–360.

Roiha, A. (2014) 'Teachers' views on differentiation in content and language integrated learning (CLIL): perceptions, practices and challenges', *Language and Education*, 28: 1–18.

Rosenthal, R. (1994) 'Interpersonal expectancy effects: a 30-year perspective', *Current Directions in Psychological Science*, 3: 176–179.

Rosenthal, R. and Jacobson, L. (1968) *Pygmalion in the Classroom*, New York: Holt, Rinehart, and Winston.

Roy, A., Guay, F. and Valois, P. (2013) 'Teaching to address diverse learning needs: development and validation of a differentiated instruction scale', *International Journal of Inclusive Education*, 17: 1186–1204.

Rubie-Davies, C.M. (2009) 'Teacher expectations and labeling', in L.J. Saha and A.G. Dworkin (eds) *International Handbook of Research on Teachers and Teaching* (pp. 695–707), New York: Springer Science.

Sarrazin, P., Tessier, D., Pelletier, L., Trouilloud, D. and Chanal, J. (2006) 'The effects of teachers' expectations about students' motivation on teachers' autonomy-supportive and controlling behaviors', *International Journal of Sport and Exercise Psychology*, 4: 283–301.

Shepard, L. (2005) 'Linking formative assessment to scaffolding', *Educational Leadership*, 63: 66–71.

Smith, D. (2013) 'Deaf adults: retrospective narratives of school experiences and teacher expectations', *Disability and Society*, 28: 674–686.

Subban, P. (2006) 'Differentiated instruction: a research basis', *International Education Journal*, 7: 935–947.

Tomlinson, C.A., Brighton, C., Hertberg, H., Callahan, C.M., Moon, T.R., Brimijoin, K., Conover, L.A. and Reynolds, T. (2003) 'Differentiating instruction in response to student readiness, interest, and learning profile in academically diverse classrooms: a review of literature', *Journal for the Education of the Gifted*, 27: 119–145.

van den Bergh, L., Denessen, E., Hornstra, L., Voeten, M. and Holland, R.W. (2010) 'The implicit prejudiced attitudes of teachers: relations to teacher expectations and the ethnic achievement gap', *American Educational Research Journal*, 47: 497–527.

Vehkakoski, T. (2012) '"More homework for me, too": meanings of differentiation constructed by elementary-aged students in classroom interaction', *European Journal of Special Needs Education*, 27: 157–170.

Vygotsky, L.S. (1978) *Mind in Society*, Cambridge, MA: Harvard University Press.

Waite, S., Boyask, R. and Lawson, H. (2010) 'Aligning person-centred methods and young people's conceptualizations of diversity', *International Journal of Research and Method in Education*, 33: 69–83.

28

TEACHER JUDGMENT AND STUDENT MOTIVATION

Detlef Urhahne and Mingjing Zhu

How well can teachers assess student achievement? How do students feel when teachers do not believe in their abilities and expect a much lower performance than justified? How does it affect students' motivation, emotions, and future achievement? These and similar questions were at the start of an educational research project, which tried to elucidate the relationship between teachers' achievement judgments and students' motivation and emotions. The aim was to find out whether erroneous teacher judgments are related to students' strivings and feelings and what will be the conditions and consequences of teachers' appraisals.

Teachers' judgments about students are of exceptional importance. They enable teachers to adapt their instruction to students' skills (Clark and Peterson 1986; Helmke and Schrader 1987). They are vital in recognizing students with specific performance deficits or giftedness (Auger 2004; Hoge and Cudmore 1986; Sommer *et al.* 2008). Teacher judgments give students access to special opportunities for promotion (Neber 2004) and provide the basis for many educational and career decisions (de Boer *et al.* 2010; Hinnant *et al.* 2009). Therefore, it is important that teachers' judgments are accurate because incorrect judgments may have far-reaching consequences for the students concerned.

This chapter begins by introducing theoretical information about the accuracy of teacher judgment of student characteristics. It then summarizes six studies that focused on the relationship between teachers' judgments of student achievement and students' motivation and emotions. If teachers get a false impression and mistakenly assess student achievement, the judgment error may be reflected in students' motivation, emotions, and future achievement (Brophy 1983). The first study shows that incorrect teacher judgments about student achievement are related to students' motivation and emotions. The second study demonstrates the generalizability of the effects for extreme groups of misjudged students and the similarity of findings in Europe and Asia. The third and fourth studies reveal the stability of the relationship between teacher judgment and student motivation when more sophisticated measures are applied to enhance the internal validity of the investigations. The fifth study sheds light on the mechanism of how teachers' misperceptions of student abilities are reflected in students' motivational and affective outcomes. Finally, the sixth study discloses that false teacher judgments affect student achievement in the long run in terms of a Pygmalion effect. The chapter concludes with some remarks about how the effect of false teacher judgments can be reduced and what research questions require further clarification.

Theoretical background

Accuracy of teacher judgment

Although teacher judgments should be as accurate as possible, previous studies show a different picture. In two historical studies, Starch and Elliot (1912, 1913) found that judgments of different teachers on the same examination papers in English and mathematics that had been copied and sent to schools varied considerably. For work that was average, gradings ranged from very good to fail. Mathematics thereby offered no more certainty in grading than English. Greater reliability and validity are gained when standardized achievement tests or curriculum-based measures are used to examine the accuracy of teacher judgment. Teachers are asked to predict the number of solved tasks for each student in class or rate their test performance on a Likert-type scale. The accuracy of teacher judgment is indicated by three components—rank, level, and differentiation—that compare teacher prediction and student performance (Cronbach 1955).

The rank component shows the extent to which the teacher is able to predict the rank order of students in terms of criteria such as achievement or motivation. The rank component is the mean within-class Pearson correlation between teacher judgments and student characteristics (Helmke and Schrader 1987). It is the most commonly used criterion for indicating the accuracy of teacher judgment (Madelaine and Wheldall 2005).

The level component is calculated as the difference between teacher judgment and student characteristic. Overestimation of student characteristics results in values greater than zero, whereas underestimation leads to values less than zero. Teacher overestimation of student achievement is most common (Bates and Nettelbeck 2001; Begeny *et al.* 2008; Demaray and Elliott 1998; Feinberg and Shapiro 2003, 2009; Hamilton and Shinn 2003), perhaps because teachers judge potential rather than performance.

The differentiation component shows teachers' tendency to over- or underestimate the variability of student characteristics. The differentiation component is mean within-class variance of teacher judgments divided by the variance of the student characteristics. A ratio greater than one indicates overestimation, and a ratio less than one indicates an underestimation of the variability of the criterion (Helmke and Schrader 1987).

The three components of judgment accuracy are not completely independent of each other. When teachers greatly overestimate student characteristics, the variance of teacher judgment is reduced and underestimation of the variability of the student characteristics is more likely. Overall, however, correlations among the three judgment components are weak (Karing *et al.* 2011; Spinath 2005; Südkamp *et al.* 2008). It can be concluded that there is little evidence for understanding the accuracy of teacher judgment as a unitary construct.

Teacher judgment of student characteristics

According to Funder (1995), four categories are important to make accurate judgments about student characteristics: judge, target, trait, and information. His model suggests that there are differences in the diagnostic competence of teachers, that students can be assessed differently, that a trait and its accompanying behavior can be easier or harder to judge, and that teachers need appropriate information to make accurate judgments. Whether teachers are accurate in judging thus depends not only on their own abilities, but also on how long they have known the students and if they are well-informed about student characteristics.

The vast majority of studies on the accuracy of teacher judgments have dealt with teachers' abilities to assess student achievement (Bates and Nettelbeck 2001; Begeny *et al.* 2008, 2011; Demaray and Elliott 1998; Feinberg and Shapiro 2003; Jussim 1989; Jussim and Eccles 1992; Madon *et al.* 1997;

Urhahne *et al.* 2010, 2011). An early meta-analysis of 16 studies by Hoge and Coladarci (1989) yielded a median correlation of 0.66 between teacher judgment about student achievement and student actual achievement in a standardized test. However, the judgment/criterion correlations varied between 0.28 and 0.92. A newer meta-analysis by Südkamp *et al.* (2012) of 75 more recent studies confirmed these findings, with a mean effect size of 0.63 and a varying range of correlations. Overall, however, teachers prove to be accurate judges of student achievement. The quality of their assessments is high because school primarily aims at promoting students' cognitive abilities to which teachers attach great importance. In addition, teachers get much information on student achievement by interacting with students in class and correcting their class work.

Other investigations have focused on the accuracy of teacher judgments about students' motivation and emotions. Teachers typically show a high predictive accuracy when asked about students' expectancy for success—that is, how students expect to perform in the next exam—with correlations higher than 0.60 (Urhahne *et al.* 2010, 2011). Teachers can predict students' academic self-concept with medium accuracy and correlation coefficients usually range between 0.30 and 0.60 (Marsh and Craven 1991; Praetorius *et al.* 2013; Spinath 2005). Correlations of about 0.30 were found for such constructs as achievement-goal orientation, level of aspiration, interest, enjoyment, or test anxiety (Boehnke *et al.* 1986; Dicke *et al.* 2012; Givvin *et al.* 2001; Karing *et al.* in press; Spinath 2005; Urhahne *et al.* 2010, 2011). The closer the hypothetical construct is related to student achievement, the easier for teachers to correctly assess students' self-perceptions. This suggests a halo effect (Thorndike 1920) as teachers seem to generalize their judgments about student achievement to other student characteristics.

One difficulty in judging students' motivation and emotions lies in the absence of relevant information available to the teachers, and if it is available, it needs to be detected and utilized appropriately (Funder 1995). This explains why mental states, which are not always clearly reflected in student behavior and therefore require a higher level of observer inference, can be diagnosed with less accuracy. Ultimately, judgment error does not have to be ascribed to teachers' missing sensitivity. Insufficient intelligibility of the hypothetical constructs and a lack of good information might be plausible reasons why teachers fail to assess students' motivation and emotions accurately.

Theoretical explanations for misjudging students

To elucidate the concordances between teacher judgments and student characteristics from a theoretical point of view, it is worth referring to theories of self-fulfilling prophecies. These theories explain why students develop towards the direction that teachers expect. In particular, the six-stage model of Brophy (1983) provides a good explanation of the relationship between teacher judgments and students' motivational-affective characteristics. Teachers' naturalistic expectations for different students can develop into a self-fulfilling prophecy as follows:

1 Teachers form different expectations about student performance.
2 Teachers behave differently towards students in accordance with their expectations.
3 Teachers' differential behavior provides students with information about how to behave in class and to do what is expected of them at school.
4 Consistent teacher behavior over time is likely to affect student self-concept, achievement motivation, level of aspiration, and interactions with the teacher.
5 These changes in student behavior confirm and reinforce teacher expectations.
6 Finally, student achievement and other outcomes are affected, which is the central idea of a self-fulfilling prophecy.

According to this model of Brophy (1983), students' motivation and emotions may develop differently because of differential teacher expectations. Combining steps 1 and 4, the following statement can be derived: Overestimating students' achievement has a positive effect, and underestimating students' achievement has a negative effect on students' motivation and emotions. This theoretical assumption was tested in the first two studies. The third and fourth studies clarified whether other factors, such as different measures of teacher judgment or self-assessment of student motivation, affected the findings.

Brophy's model (1983) contains two additional implications that were tested in the fifth and sixth studies. First, the model implies that students acquire information on how the teacher is implicitly thinking about them through the teacher's differential behavior. Differential teacher behavior has long been assumed to work as the link between differential teacher expectations and student outcomes (Brattesani *et al.* 1984; Braun 1976; Brophy 1983; Kuklinski and Weinstein 2000, 2001; McKown and Weinstein 2008). Harris and Rosenthal (1985) summarized 135 studies that explored the relationships between teacher expectations and teacher behavior as well as between teacher behavior and student outcomes. They showed that teachers favor high-expectancy students in the following manner compared to low-expectancy students: teachers provide them with a warmer socioemotional climate, give them more differentiated feedback, give them more input in the form of additional and more sophisticated materials, and open up more opportunities for output by asking questions and interacting with the preferred students. Furthermore, they found that positive teacher behavior was associated with better performance of high-expectancy students, which supported the hypothesis of a self-fulfilling prophecy. When students adapt to the teacher's behavior, it will influence their motivational and affective characteristics. Consequently, differential teacher behavior should act as a mediator between different teacher expectations and students' motivation and emotions.

Second, the model suggests that students in the long term develop in different ways because of teachers' differential expectations. Underestimated students should therefore no longer show the same performance as their overrated classmates, but after some time fall behind those in a standardized achievement test. It would support the applicability and credibility of the self-fulfilling prophecy model if these predictions could be substantiated.

Empirical findings

Motivation and emotions of misjudged students

The purpose of the first study was to examine the relationship between teacher judgment and students' motivation and emotions (Urhahne *et al.* 2011). As much was already known about the rank component, the investigation focused more strongly on the level component of teachers' diagnostic competence. Prior studies have shown that teachers tended to appraise students' skills too optimistically (Bates and Nettelbeck 2001; Begeny *et al.* 2008; Demaray and Elliott 1998; Feinberg and Shapiro 2003, 2009; Hamilton and Shinn 2003). What difference does it make if teachers judge students too negatively or too positively? The hypothesis was that students whose achievement is underestimated show different motivation and emotions than students whose achievement is overestimated.

The investigation was conducted in 14 elementary-school classes in Austria and the German-speaking part of Italy, South Tyrol. Students worked on a standardized mathematics test and answered self-assessment items on learning-goal orientation, academic self-concept, test anxiety, expectancy for success, and level of aspiration. The teachers assessed the same six aspects for each student in their class. Teachers were asked to estimate how many tasks the students would correctly solve in the mathematics test and to rate students' motivational and emotional characteristics in comparison to other students of the same age.

As expected, teachers largely overestimated students' achievement in the standardized test. Repeated measures analyses of variance were used to compare teacher judgments and student characteristics, with underestimation versus overestimation as a between-subjects variable. Underestimated students, whose achievement was underrated by the teachers, showed the same test performance as overestimated students but differed from those students in terms of motivation and emotions. Underestimated students had a lower self-concept of mathematical ability, a lower expectancy for success, and more test anxiety than overestimated students. Teachers ascribed a lower expectancy for success and a lower self-concept to the underestimated students. In addition, they assessed their level of aspiration and learning-goal orientation as lower, which was incongruous with the underestimated students' highly motivated self-descriptions. Overall, the first study demonstrated that students, whose achievement was underestimated, could perform on the same level as overestimated students. However, they expressed lower self-confidence, and teachers also shared this view.

External validity of the findings

In psychology, research findings sometimes cannot be replicated (Asendorpf *et al.* 2013). Therefore, a second study was conducted to show the extent to which the motivational tendencies of misjudged students could be replicated and generalized to other populations (Urhahne *et al.* 2010). For the investigations, eight elementary-school classes in Germany and China were selected.

Both Chinese and German elementary-school teachers were able to predict students' test performance, motivation, and emotions well. High correlations between teachers' judgments and student characteristics were detected for test performance and expectancy for success, which was measured as the expected grade in the next mathematics test. Low correlations in both countries, however, were found for such constructs as self-concept of ability, level of aspiration, learning-goal orientation, and test anxiety.

The level component, measuring the average difference between teacher and student scores, showed that teachers of both countries tended to overestimate student achievement. Repeated measures analyses of variance were used to compare teacher judgments and student characteristics with underestimation versus overestimation as a between-subjects variable. Underestimated students displayed in each case the same test performance but had a significantly lower expectancy for success, a lower self-concept of ability, and higher test anxiety than overestimated students. Teachers judged underestimated students significantly worse than overestimated students in terms of test performance, motivation, and emotions. This effect remained robust even when only those student groups were compared with each other whose test performance differed from teachers' estimated scores by half a standard deviation.

All in all, the second study showed that the relationship between teacher judgment and student motivational-affective characteristics can be transferred to other student groups and is not bound to national borders or to the method of grouping students. The smaller group of students, whose test performance was underestimated by the teachers, was particularly affected by the misperceptions. Underestimated students had no performance deficit but lacked confidence in their own abilities and the belief to accomplish the same as overestimated students.

Internal validity of the findings

Replicated findings may be an artifact of methodological consistency across studies, and not necessarily the result of a consistently replicable phenomenon. To check whether the type of measurement had an effect on the apparently robust findings, the research method was varied in two conditions. In the third study, a semi-projective test was used instead of self-report scales to measure students' motivation (Urhahne *et al.* 2013). In the fourth study, teachers assessed student characteristics not only by single items but by three-item scales that exactly matched the wording of the student items (Zhu and Urhahne 2014). With these two changes, the internal validity of the research methodology should be improved and previous research findings thoroughly reconsidered.

The use of self-report scales to measure student motivation is a major methodological problem as it permits students to present themselves in a positive light and affirm a greater motivation than is true. If these data are compared with teachers' estimates of student motivation, differences are inevitable. Ultimately, it cannot be determined whether teachers are wrong with their statements that underestimated students are less motivated than overestimated students. It might be that underestimated students simply report a high level of motivation, but one which is not accurate. This disadvantage is inherent to self-report scales for the assessment of student motivation.

Another option to measure student motivation is the use of a semi-projective test. This method can be traced back to Murray (1943), who presented ambiguous images to his subjects and asked them to write a story about them. The images were intended to stimulate the subjects' unconscious motives, such as achievement, power or affiliation, so that the motives would be expressed in the story told. To compensate for the disadvantages of the picture stories, such as low reliability, semi-projective tests have been developed. They still contain images to stimulate the unconscious motives but use standardized items instead of made-up stories, whereby subjects' motivation can be measured with markedly higher reliability.

The third study applied Lehwald's semi-projective test (2009). It measured students' achievement motivation by the use of three school-related images and 75 items with satisfactory reliability. In the test, students empathized with the person in the image and reflected on the person's thoughts and feelings by answering items such as 'I often work without stopping' or 'Perseverance has never been my strong suit'. Seven sixth-grade classes participated in the mathematics study. The result was that teachers overestimated the performance of their students, leading to a smaller proportion of underestimated students and a larger proportion of overestimated students. A comparison of the two student groups in terms of achievement motivation showed that underestimated students were slightly more motivated than overestimated students. However, the mathematics teachers predicted the opposite and perceived achievement motivation of underestimated students as lower. A repeated measures analysis of variance, in which teacher judgment versus student self-assessment was the within-subjects factor and group membership the between-subjects factor, revealed a significant interaction effect. It can thus be shown that even with the use of a semi-projective motivation test, which provides no incentive for positive self-presentation, the findings remained the same. Teachers underestimated the motivation of students whose performance exceeded teachers' expectations in the mathematics test.

Another problem is the use of single-item measures for teacher judgments about students' characteristics. Single items lack important psychometric properties. They capture a hypothetical construct with less accuracy by not compensating for measurement error. Statements about reliability and validity can only be made to a limited extent (Jordan and Turner 2008). On the other hand, single-item measures are much more economical than multiple-item rating scales. The question was whether various motivational and emotional constructs can be as accurately measured as with multiple items. Teachers' predictions might be more accurate when they can assess students on the exact same items as those the students are asked to answer. Possible misjudgments by the teacher in the use of single items may not be due to the appraiser, but to the method of appraisal.

In the fourth study, Chinese teachers of 16 sixth-grade classes were asked to assess students' motivation and emotions in two different ways (Zhu and Urhahne 2014). First, they used single items combined with a 9-point Likert scale to judge students' academic self-concept, learning effort, test anxiety, and enjoyment of learning English. Second, teachers assessed the same constructs that described students' motivation and emotions with three items, adapted from the student questionnaire, on 4-point Likert scales. Both sets of teacher data were correlated with the items from the student questionnaire. No differences were detected when comparing the two methods in terms of correlations and percentage agreement between teacher and student assessment. The rank component revealed high correlations for academic self-concept, moderate correlations for learning effort and enjoyment, and zero correlations for the assessment of test anxiety. This applied both to the use of single and multiple items.

The fourth study provided further evidence for the validity of the research results. It suggested that the use of single items to assess hypothetical constructs is just as well suited as the use of multiple-item rating scales. It can also be concluded that if teachers were found to judge underestimated students' motivation and emotions low, it is not likely to be because of the assessment method.

The fifth study investigated the function of differential teacher behavior in more detail to clarify whether teacher behavior works as a mediator in the relationship between false teacher expectations and students' motivation and emotions (Urhahne 2015). In addition to the materials commonly used, such as a standardized language test or motivational-affective scales, four scales from the Students' Ratings of Teachers Questionnaire of Babad *et al.* (2003) were selected. A total of 13 German sixth-grade classes and their foreign language teachers participated in the study with a special focus on the subject English.

The statistical analyses were carried out in three steps. In the first step, differences in student characteristics were examined in multiple analyses of variance. The second step was to check whether students differ in their perception of teacher behavior. In the third step, the mediating role of differential teacher behavior was investigated with multilevel mediation analyses.

Again, it was found that teachers generalized their achievement expectations to other evaluation areas. Although underestimated students had significantly higher test scores than overestimated students, English teachers judged them lower in terms of motivation and emotions. Underestimated students had a lower expectancy for success, a lower self-concept of English ability, were less learning-goal oriented, and experienced less enjoyment in learning English. In addition, students perceived differences in teachers' behavior. Underestimated students reported more difficulties in talking to the English teachers and managing well with them than overestimated students did. Thus, they perceived a less conducive socioemotional climate—one of the factors that Rosenthal (1973) also pronounced in his four-factor theory about the mediation of teacher expectancy effects. Multilevel mediation analyses showed that teachers' differential emotional support mediated the effect of teacher expectations on students' learning-goal orientation and enjoyment of learning. The findings supported the assumptions that have been derived from Brophy's model of self-fulfilling prophecy. Apparently, differential teacher behavior is a source from which the students get information about how the teacher is judging them, and this behavior has implications for students' motivation to learn.

Long-term effects of teacher judgment on student achievement

Another prediction derived from Brophy's model (1983) is the occurrence of a self-fulfilling prophecy. After some time, teacher expectations towards certain students should be reflected in students' behavior. Students may develop in line with teacher expectations when teachers misperceive their true capabilities. They may internalize teachers' expectations successively into their self-concept and behave accordingly. Underestimated students with relatively low teacher expectations should therefore develop poorly in comparison to overestimated students with relatively high teacher expectations.

The sixth study tested the hypothesis of a self-fulfilling prophecy (Zhou and Urhahne 2013). The eight classes of Chinese students in the second study (Urhahne *et al.* 2010) were retested in the following school year. In the fourth grade, no differences were found in the mathematics achievement of underestimated and overestimated students. In the fifth grade, however, hierarchical multiple regression analysis showed that underestimated students did significantly worse in the standardized mathematics test than overestimated ones. Thus, as expected on the basis of Brophy's model, a Pygmalion effect has been documented.

Interestingly, not all students were equally affected by the self-fulfilling prophecy. A drop in performance was found especially for those students who attributed success to chance and failure to their own ability. This is consistent with research suggesting that a different pattern of attributions is associated with academic success. Specifically, students tend to be more successful when they attribute success to ability or effort and failure to chance or lack of effort (Weiner 1986). The outcome suggests that the occurrence of a Pygmalion effect does not solely depend on teachers' expectations, but also on students' processing of information. Students with an optimistic attribution style are far less affected by self-fulfilling prophecies.

Conclusions and future directions

Numerous studies on the accuracy of teacher judgment of students' achievement have revealed that teachers are able to assess student achievement with satisfying accuracy (Hoge and Coladarci 1989; Südkamp *et al.* 2012). However, a systematic bias of teacher judgment can be detected as teachers tend to overestimate student achievement. The fact that teachers are not completely accurate in estimating students' level of performance does not necessarily mean that they have to be less optimistic in the future. A slight overestimation is beneficial as it requires students to achieve more than they currently do. In this respect, a small overestimation of students' achievement is educationally desirable.

However, teachers should also be concerned about the consequences for individual students when they misjudge their achievement. The relations between teacher judgment and students' motivation, emotions, and future performance were examined in six discrete but evolutionary studies. It was found that underestimated students indeed had at least the same test performance as overestimated students, but a lower self-concept of ability, a lower expectancy for success, more test anxiety, and less enjoyment in learning. Teachers thought quite similarly about these students and assumed lower motivation and less favorable achievement emotions for underestimated students. The findings remained stable when further studies were carried out in another culture with a different educational system, such as China, when more extreme groups of misjudged students were considered, and different measures for students and teachers were applied. Furthermore, it was found that students received evidence how the teacher is thinking about them through observing teacher's behavior. Misjudging student achievement did have consequences and affected students' future performance so that underestimated students in the next year performed worse on a standardized test than overestimated students.

How can this undesirable trend of erroneous teacher expectations affecting students' motivation, emotions, and future performance be counteracted? One option might be for teachers to have high expectations for all students (Rubie-Davies 2008;Weinstein 2002). Rubie-Davies (2006) has shown that high-expectancy students developed more favorable self-perceptions than low-expectancy students. Therefore, it might be useful that teachers hold higher expectations for student achievement than those students are currently able to achieve. Teachers should challenge students, but they should also try to stay realistic and not drastically over- or underestimate what students can achieve. Frequent gathering of feedback helps teachers to offer challenging learning tasks that fit with the skills of the learners (Rakoczy *et al.* 2008). Training preservice and inservice teachers in a computer simulation of an instructional situation may improve teachers' competency in making accurate judgments (Kaiser *et al.* 2013). Another way to avoid negative judgment effects is concerned with students' causal attributions. The sixth study has shown that only those students who made unfavorable attributions were influenced by negative teacher judgments (Zhou and Urhahne 2013). Reattribution training could help those vulnerable students gain more self-confidence. In the training, they could learn that they do not need to blame themselves for false teacher expectations, but to attribute the cause to external factors (Haynes *et al.* 2009).

Teacher expectations and student characteristics seem to develop in an interactive process and changes may be attributed to both sides. Students are not helplessly exposed to false teacher expectations, but have the opportunity to convince teachers of their skills. Teachers are able to adjust their minds and reassess student achievement after some significant student changes. It is important that teachers keep the necessary openness and do not stick to their prejudices. Fortunately, many teachers can correct themselves, as effects of self-fulfilling prophecies do not accumulate over time, but slowly disappear (Jussim *et al.* 2009). Underestimation, however, is likely to discourage students, and if consistently shown over time, students may regard themselves as unmotivated and disinterested, thereby confirming teachers' expectations (Brophy 1983). Teachers should therefore continuously pay attention to all students' motivation and emotions (Givvin *et al.* 2001) to break the vicious cycle.

This raises the question of whether student over- and underestimation can be viewed as a stable student trait or a temporary phenomenon. For a trait, students would need to be continuously misjudged in one subject or be misperceived in other subjects as well. If a student's misperception turns out to be a constant feature, other personality traits might be identified that favor student's over- or underestimation. Student characteristics such as socioeconomic status, language, clothing, appearance, or behavior should be thoroughly re-examined in future studies.

In addition, there could be testing for teacher characteristics that predispose the teacher to misperceptions about student achievement. Teacher training is often cited as an important predictor of accuracy (Gear 1978; Pin-ten Cate *et al.* 2014; Trittel *et al.* 2014), but there is no convincing evidence of this. More important may be cognitive factors such as teachers' intelligence. Kaiser *et al.* (2012) found in an experimental setting with teacher education students that participants' intelligence had a significant influence on the validity of diagnostic judgments. Other important features might be sought in teachers' openness to new experiences or their pedagogical content knowledge (Shulman 1986).

Overall, research on teacher judgment and student motivation shows that conceptual models from self-fulfilling prophecy research can be used to illuminate the understanding of the relationships between constructs. The six studies reported in this chapter have laid the necessary foundations and provide evidence for the correctness of the assumptions, but the entire model needs to be tested at least once in an encompassing longitudinal study. Ultimately, more systematic work is warranted to shed light on the relations between teacher judgment and student motivation.

References

Asendorpf, J.B., Conner, M., De Fruyt, F., De Houwer, J., Denissen, J.J.A., Fiedler, K., Fiedler, S., Funder, D.C., Kliegl, R., Nosek, B.A., Perugini, M., Roberts, B.W., Schmitt, M., Vanaken, M.A.G., Weber, H. and Wicherts, J.M. (2013) 'Recommendations for increasing replicability in psychology', *European Journal of Personality*, 27: 108–119.

Auger, R.W. (2004) 'The accuracy of teacher reports in the identification of middle school students with depressive symptomatology', *Psychology in the Schools*, 41: 379–389.

Babad, E., Avni-Babad, D. and Rosenthal, R. (2003) 'Teachers' brief nonverbal behaviors in defined instructional situations can predict students' evaluations', *Journal of Educational Psychology*, 95: 553–562.

Bates, C. and Nettelbeck, T. (2001) 'Primary school teachers' judgements of reading achievement', *Educational Psychology*, 21: 177–187.

Begeny, J.C., Eckert, T.L., Montarello, S.A. and Storie, M.S. (2008) 'Teachers' perceptions of students' reading abilities: an examination of the relationship between teachers' judgments and students' performance across a continuum of rating methods', *School Psychology Quarterly*, 23: 43–55.

Begeny, J.C., Krouse, H.E., Brown, K.G. and Mann, C.M. (2011) 'Teacher judgments of students' reading abilities across a continuum of rating methods and achievement measures', *School Psychology Review*, 40: 23–38.

Boehnke, K., Silbereisen, R.K., Reynolds, C.R. and Richmond, B.O. (1986) 'What I think and feel – German experience with the revised form of the Children's Manifest Anxiety Scale', *Personality and Individual Differences*, 7: 553–560.

Brattesani, K.A., Weinstein, R.S. and Marshall, H.H. (1984) 'Student perceptions of differential teacher treatment as moderators of teacher expectation effects', *Journal of Educational Psychology*, 76: 236–247.

Braun, C. (1976) 'Teacher expectation: sociopsychological dynamics', *Review of Educational Research*, 46: 185–213.

Brophy, J.E. (1983) 'Research on self-fulfilling prophecy and teacher expectations', *Journal of Educational Psychology*, 75: 631–661.

Clark, C.M. and Peterson, P.L. (1986) 'Teachers' thought processes', in M.C. Wittrock (ed.) *Handbook of Research on Teaching*: 255–296, New York: Macmillan.

Cronbach, L.J. (1955) 'Processes affecting scores on "understanding others" and "assumed similarity"', *Psychological Bulletin*, 52: 177–193.

de Boer, H., Bosker, R. and van der Werf, M.P.C. (2010) 'Sustainability of teacher expectation bias effects on long-term student performance', *Journal of Educational Psychology*, 102: 168–179.

Demaray, M.K. and Elliott, S.N. (1998) 'Teachers' judgments of students' academic functioning: a comparison of actual and predicted performances', *School Psychology Quarterly*, 13: 8–24.

Dicke, A.-L., Lüdtke, O., Trautwein, U., Nagy, G. and Nagy, N. (2012) 'Judging students' achievement goal orientations: are teacher ratings accurate?', *Learning and Individual Differences*, 22: 844–849.

Feinberg, A.B. and Shapiro, E.S. (2003) 'Accuracy of teacher judgments in predicting oral reading fluency', *School Psychology Quarterly*, 18: 52–65.

Feinberg, A.B. and Shapiro, E.S. (2009) 'Teacher accuracy: an examination of teacher-based judgments of students' reading with differing achievement levels', *Journal of Educational Research*, 102: 453–462.

Funder, D.C. (1995) 'On the accuracy of personality judgment: a realistic approach', *Psychological Review*, 102: 652–670.

Gear, G.H. (1978) 'Effects of training on teachers' accuracy in the identification of gifted children', *Gifted Child Quarterly*, 22: 90–97.

Givvin, K.B., Stipek, D.J., Salmon, J.M. and MacGyvers, V.L. (2001) 'In the eyes of the beholder: students' and teachers' judgments of students' motivation', *Teaching and Teacher Education*, 17: 321–331.

Hamilton, C. and Shinn, M.R. (2003) 'Characteristics of word callers: an investigation of the accuracy of teachers' judgments of reading comprehension and oral reading skills', *School Psychology Review*, 32: 228–240.

Harris, M.J. and Rosenthal, R. (1985) 'Mediation of interpersonal expectancy effects – 31 meta-analyses', *Psychological Bulletin*, 97: 363–386.

Haynes, T.L., Perry, R.P., Stupinsky, R.H. and Daniels, L.M. (2009) 'A review of attributional retraining treatments: fostering engagement and persistence in vulnerable college students', in J.C. Smart (ed.) *Higher Education: Handbook of Theory and Research*: 227–272, Dordrecht: Springer.

Helmke, A. and Schrader, F.-W. (1987) 'Interactional effects of instructional quality and teacher judgement accuracy on achievement', *Teaching and Teacher Education*, 3: 91–98.

Hinnant, J.B., O'Brien, M. and Ghazarian, S.R. (2009) 'The longitudinal relations of teacher expectations to achievement in the early school years', *Journal of Educational Psychology*, 101: 662–670.

Hoge, R.D. and Coladarci, T. (1989) 'Teacher-based judgments of academic achievement: a review of literature', *Review of Educational Research*, 59: 297–313.

Hoge, R.D. and Cudmore, L. (1986) 'The use of teacher-judgment measures in the identification of gifted pupils', *Teaching and Teacher Education*, 2: 181–196.

Jordan, J.S. and Turner, B.A. (2008) 'The use of teacher-judgment measures in the identification of gifted pupils', *Measurement in Physical Education and Exercise Science*, 12: 237–257.

Jussim, L. (1989) 'Teacher expectations: self-fulfilling prophecies, perceptual biases, and accuracy', *Journal of Personality and Social Psychology*, 57: 469–480.

Jussim, L. and Eccles, J. (1992) 'Teacher expectations II: construction and reflection of student achievement', *Journal of Personality and Social Psychology*, 63: 947–961.

Jussim, L., Robustelli, S.L. and Cain, T.R. (2009) 'Teacher expectations and self-fulfilling prophecies', in K.R. Wentzel and A. Wigfield (eds) *Handbook of Motivation at School*: 349–380, New York: Routledge.

Kaiser, J., Helm, F., Retelsdorf, J., Südkamp, A. and Möller, J. (2012) 'Zum Zusammenhang von Intelligenz und Urteilsgenauigkeit bei der Beurteilung von Schülerleistungen im Simulierten Klassenraum [On the relation of intelligence and judgment accuracy in the process of assessing student achievement in the simulated classroom]', *Zeitschrift für Pädagogische Psychologie*, 26: 251–261.

Kaiser, J., Retelsdorf, J., Südkamp, A. and Möller, J. (2013) 'Achievement and engagement: how student characteristics influence teacher judgments', *Learning and Instruction*, 28: 73–84.

Karing, C., Dörfler, T. and Artelt, C. (in press) 'How accurate are teacher and parent judgements of lower secondary school children's test anxiety?', *Educational Psychology: An International Journal of Experimental Educational Psychology*.

Karing, C., Matthäi, J. and Artelt, C. (2011) 'Genauigkeit von Lehrerurteilen über die Lesekompetenz ihrer Schülerinnen und Schüler in der Sekundarstufe I – Eine Frage der Spezifität? [Lower secondary school teacher judgment accuracy of students' reading competence – A matter of specifity?]', *Zeitschrift für Pädagogische Psychologie*, 25: 159–172.

Kuklinski, M.R. and Weinstein, R.S. (2000) 'Classroom and grade level differences in the stability of teacher expectations and perceived differential treatment', *Learning Environments Research*, 3: 1–34.

Kuklinski, M.R. and Weinstein, R.S. (2001) 'Classroom and developmental differences in a path model of teacher expectancy effects', *Child Development*, 72: 1554–1578.

Lehwald, G. (2009) *Beiträge zur Motivationsdiagnostik und Motivförderung in der Schule (5.–12. Schulstufe)* [Contributions to motivation diagnostics and motive training in school (grades 5 to 12)], Salzburg: Österreichisches Zentrum für Begabtenförderung und Begabungsforschung (öbzf).

Madelaine, A. and Wheldall, K. (2005) 'Identifying low-progress readers: comparing teacher judgment with a curriculum-based measurement procedure', *International Journal of Disability, Development and Education*, 52: 33–43.

Madon, S., Jussim, L. and Eccles, J.S. (1997) 'In search of the powerful self-fulfilling prophecy', *Journal of Personality and Social Psychology*, 72: 791–809.

Marsh, H.W. and Craven, R.G. (1991) 'Self-other agreement on multiple dimensions of preadolescent self-concept: inferences by teachers, mothers, and fathers', *Journal of Educational Psychology*, 83: 393–404.

McKown, C. and Weinstein, R.S. (2008) 'Teacher expectations, classroom context, and the achievement gap', *Journal of School Psychology*, 46: 235–261.

Murray, H.A. (1943) *Thematic Apperceptive Test Manual*, Cambridge, MA: Harvard University Press.

Neber, H. (2004) 'Lehrernominierungen für ein Enrichment-Programm als Beispiel für die Talentsuche in der gymnasialen Oberstufe [Teacher nomination for an enrichment program as an example of talent search in college prep courses]', *Psychologie in Erziehung und Unterricht*, 51: 24–39.

Pit-ten Cate, I., Krolak-Schwerdt, S., Glock, S. and Markova, M. (2014) 'Improving teachers' judgments: obtaining change through cognitive processes', in S. Krolak-Schwerdt, S. Glock and M. Böhner (eds) *Teachers' Professional Development: Assessment, Training, and Learning*: 45–61, Rotterdam: Sense Publishers.

Praetorius, A.-K., Berner, V.-D., Zeinz, H., Scheunpflug, A. and Dresel, M. (2013) 'Judgment confidence and judgment accuracy of teachers in judging academic self-concepts', *Journal of Educational Research*, 106: 64–76.

Rakoczy, K., Klieme, E., Bürgermeister, A. and Harks, B. (2008) 'The interplay between student evaluation and instruction: grading and feedback in mathematics classrooms', *Journal of Psychology*, 216: 111–124.

Rosenthal, R. (1973) 'On the mediation of Pygmalion effects: a four factor "theory"', *Papua New Guinea Journal of Education*, 9: 1–12.

Rubie-Davies, C.M. (2006) 'Teacher expectation and student self-perceptions: exploring relationships', *Psychology in the Schools*, 43: 537–552.

Rubie-Davies, C.M. (2008) 'Teacher expectations', in T. Good (ed.) *21st Century Education: A Reference Handbook*: 254–262, Thousand Oaks, CA: Sage Publications.

Shulman, L. (1986) 'Those who understand: knowledge growth in teaching', *Educational Researcher*, 15: 4–14.

Sommer, U., Fink, A. and Neubauer, A.C. (2008) 'Detection of high ability children by teachers and parents: psychometric quality of new rating checklists for the assessment of intellectual, creative and social ability', *Psychology Science Quarterly*, 50: 189–205.

Spinath, B. (2005) 'Akkuratheit der Einschätzung von Schülermerkmalen durch Lehrer und das Konstrukt der diagnostischen Kompetenz [Accuracy of teacher judgments on student characteristics and the construct of diagnostic competence]', *Zeitschrift für Pädagogische Psychologie*, 19: 85–95.

Starch, D. and Elliot, E.C. (1912) 'Reliability of grading high school work in English', *School Review*, 20: 442–457.

Starch, D. and Elliot, E.C. (1913) 'Reliability of grading high school work in mathematics', *School Review*, 21: 254–259.

Südkamp, A., Kaiser, J. and Möller, J. (2012) 'Accuracy of teachers' judgments of students' academic achievement: a meta-analysis', *Journal of Educational Psychology*, 104: 743–762.

Südkamp, A., Möller, J. and Pohlmann, B. (2008) 'Der simulierte Klassenraum: Eine experimentelle Untersuchung zur diagnostischen Kompetenz [The simulated classroom: an experimental study on diagnostic competence]', *Zeitschrift für Pädagogische Psychologie*, 22: 261–276.

Thorndike, E.L. (1920) 'A constant error on psychological rating', *Journal of Applied Psychology*, 4: 25–29.

Trittel, M., Gerich, M. and Schmitz, B. (2014) 'Training prospective teachers in educational diagnostics', in S. Krolak-Schwerdt, S. Glock and M. Böhner (eds) *Teachers' Professional Development. Assessment, Training, and Learning*: 63–78, Rotterdam: Sense Publishers.

Urhahne, D. (2015) 'Teacher behavior as a mediator of the relationship between teacher judgment and students' motivation and emotion', *Teaching and Teacher Education*, 45: 73–82.

Urhahne, D., Chao, S.-H., Florineth, M.L., Luttenberger, S. and Paechter, M. (2011) 'Academic self-concept, learning motivation, and test anxiety of the underestimated student', *British Journal of Educational Psychology*, 81: 161–177.

Urhahne, D., Timm, O., Zhu, M.J. and Tang, M. (2013) 'Sind unterschätzte Schüler weniger leistungsmotiviert als überschätzte Schüler [Are underestimated students less achievement motivated than overestimated students?]', *Zeitschrift für Entwicklungspsychologie und Pädagogische Psychologie*, 45: 34–43.

Urhahne, D., Zhou, J., Stobbe, M., Chao, S.-H., Zhu, M.J. and Shi, J.N. (2010) 'Motivationale und affektive Merkmale unterschätzter Schüler. Ein Beitrag zur diagnostischen Kompetenz von Lehrkräften [Motivational and affective characteristics of underestimated students: a contribution to the diagnostic competence of teachers]', *Zeitschrift für Pädagogische Psychologie*, 24: 275–288.

Weiner, B. (1986) *An Attributional Theory of Motivation and Emotion*, New York: Springer.

Weinstein, R.S. (2002) *Reaching Higher: The Power of Expectations in Schooling*, Cambridge, MA: Harvard University Press.

Zhou, J. and Urhahne, D. (2013) 'Teacher judgment, student motivation, and the mediating effect of attributions', *European Journal of Psychology of Education*, 28: 275–295.

Zhu, M.J. and Urhahne, D. (2014) 'Assessing teachers' judgments of students' academic motivation and emotions across two rating methods', *Educational Research and Evaluation*, 20: 411–427.

29

EXPECTING MORE

Teacher differences as moderators of expectancy effects

Christine M. Rubie-Davies

Pygmalion in the Classroom (Rosenthal and Jacobson 1968) ushered in a new field of educational and social psychological research, interpersonal expectancy effects, and, in particular, teacher expectations. Teacher expectation effects are associated with student achievement or behavior such that when a teacher expects a student to achieve at high or low levels, the teacher interacts with the student in ways that cause the student to achieve or behave in line with the teacher's expectations. The implications of Rosenthal and Jacobson's findings were profound and yet the study left many questions unanswered. For example, how do teachers portray their expectations? On what bases do regular teachers in regular classrooms form their expectations? Are students aware of teachers' expectations? Hence the seminal work in the field led to a plethora of studies that endeavored to answer the many unanswered questions.

The current chapter begins by briefly exploring researcher findings in relation to the questions above. It presents research related to teacher behaviors that portray teacher expectations, discusses the bases on which teachers form their expectations – that is, the student characteristics that influence teachers' expectations – and introduces work which has shown how students ascertain whether their teacher has high or low expectations for them.

However, the primary focus of the chapter is on how differences in teacher beliefs can moderate expectancy effects; that is, how, because of teacher beliefs, the expectation effects of some teachers on student outcomes are much greater than they are in other teachers' classes. The chapter discusses the findings related to biased and no-bias teachers, high and low differentiating teachers, and high and low expectation teachers; presents findings from the first-year of the Teacher Expectation Project which I conducted (see Rubie-Davies 2014a); and concludes with some areas for future research in the field.

Expectation effects: Research on teacher behaviors, student characteristics, and student understandings

The seminal work in teacher expectations (Rosenthal and Jacobson, 1968) suggested that teachers must portray their expectations to their students through the ways they interact with students. The following section presents research that identified differential teacher behaviors towards students for whom teachers had either high or low expectations.

Teacher behaviors

Brophy and Good (1970) and Cooper and Good (1983), as well as others, conducted several studies in an effort to determine the behaviors teachers exhibited towards students for whom they had high versus low expectations. Later, Brophy (1985) provided a synthesis of the findings and showed, for example, that teachers paid more attention to students for whom they had high expectations, waited longer for them to respond to questions, smiled at them more, and praised them more than they did in their interactions with students for whom they had low expectations. However, a measurement of which behaviors had the most effect on student achievement was not completed at the time. Harris and Rosenthal (1985) in a meta-analysis showed that the most salient behaviors were climate and effort. Teachers created a warmer classroom climate for students for whom they had high expectations and they made more effort in their teaching of students whom they judged to be high achievers. That is, they taught such students more concepts, more difficult concepts, and at a faster pace than they did the students for whom they had low expectations. This created differentiation in learning opportunities. Hence, one reason that ultimately low achievers learnt less than they may have been capable of, was because they were taught less – the self-fulfilling prophecy.

Student characteristics

Another group of researchers investigated student characteristics that might influence their teachers' expectations. For example, controlling for achievement, teachers appeared to have higher expectations for European rather than for minority group students (Alexander and Entwisle 1988) and this finding has been confirmed in more recent work (e.g. Tenenbaum and Ruck 2007; van den Bergh *et al.* 2010). When achievement is controlled, it is possible to determine whether teachers' expectations for particular groups are biased. Studies have provided evidence that teachers have higher expectations for girls in the language arts (e.g. Peterson 2000) and for boys in mathematics and science (Archambault *et al.* 2012). A further consistent finding has been that teachers have higher expectations for middle-class students than for students from poor socioeconomic backgrounds (Baron *et al.* 1985; Rist 1970; Sorhagen 2013), again controlling for achievement. Hence, teachers have lower expectations for students from poorer communities than they do for middle-class students even when their achievement is the same. Similarly, in experimental studies (e.g., Batzle *et al.* 2010; Stinnett *et al.* 2001), teachers have been shown to assess those without diagnostic labels more positively than they do students who have been assigned a label (e.g. ADHD) even though the described behaviors and achievement of students with or without the label are identical.

Student understandings

A further productive area of research in the teacher expectation field has been in examining whether students understand their teachers' expectations for them and how they determine whether or not their teachers have high or low expectations for them (e.g. Babad 1990a, 1998, 2009; Cooper and Good 1983; Weinstein 1983, 1989, 1993, 2002; Weinstein *et al.* 1982; Weinstein and Middlestadt 1979). When teachers have high expectations for some students and low for others, they provide differential learning opportunities for students in relation to their expectations – advanced activities for those students for whom teachers have high expectations and repetitive low level tasks for those for whom they have low expectations. Hence, the expectation effects are mediated through the teacher behaviors which create differential opportunities to learn. Students interpret the kinds of learning opportunities they are given as reflecting their capabilities and this shapes their own expectations about what they can achieve. Students are acutely aware of teacher discrimination; even young students are perceptive of differentiation in how they or others are treated. Students can offer critical incidents that poignantly portray their teachers' expectations for them, often with negative overtones (Weinstein 2002). Students have been shown (Babad 1998) to be particularly adept at noting differentiation from teachers in learning and emotional support depending on whether their teacher has high or low expectations for them.

The moderation of teacher expectancy effects

However, the large body of research cited above in relation to teacher differential behaviors, teacher formation of expectations, and student perceptions, aggregated data at the teacher level in order for conclusions to be drawn. Many of these studies took account of student difference but did not take account of teacher difference. Clearly teachers also differ. Some teachers are likely to be more easily influenced by particular student characteristics, some will portray their expectations to students more obviously, some will be influenced more by stereotyping than others, and so on.

A relatively small group of researchers (Babad 2009; Rubie-Davies 2014a; Weinstein 2002) has examined teacher characteristics as potential moderators of teacher expectation effects. This means that differences in teachers may alter the strength of the expectancy effects depending on their beliefs. Babad identified teachers he labeled biased and no-bias teachers. Those who were biased teachers were more easily influenced by false information about their students, were more predisposed to stereotyping, and were more dogmatic and autocratic in their beliefs (Babad *et al.* 1982). Teachers such as this differentiated in their treatment of students for whom they had high or low expectations, not just in the learning support provided to students, but more particularly in their emotional support. Hence, they favored students they thought would do well academically and Babad (1998) found that while younger students were accepting of teachers who provided more learning support for students who were having academic difficulties, they were resentful of teachers who showed greater warmth towards high achievers (Babad 1990b, 1995).

Weinstein and colleagues (Brattesani *et al.* 1984; Weinstein 1993, 2002; Weinstein *et al.* 1982) have identified high and low differentiating teachers. This has enabled Weinstein (2002) to describe two very different classroom contexts. High differentiating teachers are those who discriminate in the ways in which they treat those students for whom they have high and low expectations, whereas low differentiating teachers treat all students similarly. As a result, expectancy effects are much more likely to occur in the classes of high differentiating teachers than they are with low differentiating teachers. For example, in a study by McKown and Weinstein, in classes where students reported high differentiation, teachers' expectations were 0.75 to 1.00 of a standard deviation higher for American European and Asian students than they were for African American and Latino students with similar records of achievement. In classes in which there was low differentiation, teacher expectations were similar for all ethnic groups whose achievement was similar. By the end of the year, high differentiating teachers contributed $d = 0.29$ to exacerbating the ethnic achievement gap, whereas the effect size in classes of low differentiating teachers was only $d = -0.003$.

In her book, Weinstein (2002) has identified six major areas in which high and low differentiating teachers differ in their pedagogical practices: grouping, learning experiences, evaluation, motivation, student autonomy, and relationships. Each of these will be explained in the following sentences. High differentiating teachers have students seated in ability groups and differences in ability are regularly made salient, whereas low differentiating teachers seat students in mixed-ability groupings and rarely make reference to differences in student achievement. Similarly, students in high- and low-ability groups in the classes of high differentiating teachers are given learning experiences that are quite different, whereas those with low differentiating teachers all complete similar tasks. In terms of evaluation, high differentiating teachers enable input from high achievers in their classes (that is, they frequently ask them questions) and give students clear, often public, feedback regarding the grades they have received or on the standard of their work. Again, such differences are not made salient in the classes of low differentiating teachers, and low differentiating teachers are much more equitable in involving students in their contributions to the class. With regard to motivation, high differentiating teachers emphasize extrinsic motivation for students, whereas the weight is placed on intrinsic motivation among low differentiating teachers; they concentrate on individual growth and the development of skills. Comparisons between students are minimal. High differentiating teachers also maintain greater control of students giving them little autonomy, especially those for whom they have low expectations. Special responsibilities and privileges are accorded to those they consider high achieving. On the other hand, low differentiating teachers provide students with more autonomy and greater responsibility for their learning, and all students are offered opportunities for leadership. Finally, high differentiating teachers do not encourage relationships and support among students and are wary of parents who are mostly used to threaten students when they are perceived not to be putting in sufficient effort. In contrast, low differentiating teachers build a classroom community in which warm teacher–student and student–student relationships are encouraged and students are made to feel part of the school community. Moreover, parents are welcomed into the classroom and encouraged to support their children. Hence, overall, it can be seen that the student learning experience in classes of high differentiating teachers is likely to be quite different from that of students in classrooms of low differentiating teachers.

High expectation teachers

Much of the research on teacher expectancy effects has looked at differential expectations and treatment within classrooms, for example as affecting high and low expectation students. Given teacher differences in the propensity to differentiate their expectations, with some treating all students equally, it is important to learn more about these equitable teachers. Can they be identified with regard to their expectations at a whole-class level, with some holding high expectations for all students (high expectation teachers) and some whose expectations are low for all students (low expectation teachers)? Teacher expectations at the class level have been little studied.

I (Rubie-Davies 2006, 2007, 2008) have identified high and low expectation teachers and have shown that not only do such teachers differ in their pedagogical beliefs and instructional practices but that student outcomes differ depending on which classroom students find themselves located. In classes of high expectation teachers, all students make large academic gains ($d = 0.50$) whereas those with low expectation teachers make limited progress ($d = 0.02$) (Rubie-Davies *et al.* 2007). Further, I (Rubie-Davies, 2006) have shown that over one academic year, the self-perceptions of students with high expectation teachers (beliefs that they are competent in mathematics and reading) remain at high levels across the year whereas the self-perceptions of students with low expectation teachers drop considerably. Students also seem to be aware of their teachers' expectations because those with high expectation teachers report that their teachers have high expectations of them while those with low expectation teachers are able to identify that their teachers' expectations are low (Rubie-Davies 2006).

Through classroom observations and interviews (Rubie-Davies 2014a; Rubie-Davies and Peterson 2011), high and low expectation teachers have been shown to differ substantially in relationship to three main areas: grouping and learning experiences, class climate, and goal setting (student motivation, engagement, and autonomy, and teacher evaluation and feedback). The explanations below of the differences between the classrooms of high and low expectation teachers come from my recent book (Rubie-Davies, 2014a).

Grouping and learning experiences

Low expectation teachers form within-class ability groups for core curriculum areas such as reading and mathematics. Students are taught separately in these groups and are assigned activities specific to each ability group. However, high expectation teachers operate what might be termed flexible grouping. That is, they have a range of activities available that all students can select from. Students are neither confined to particular activities nor to a particular level of activity. Some high expectation teachers maintain instructional ability groups but none restrict students to only completing activities 'at their level'. Students are given choice about which activities they wish to complete and with whom, or students work in mixed-ability groups on their learning experiences. Other high expectation teachers draw out students needing to learn particular skills as and when needed such that there is no consistency to the students meeting together to learn specific skills. At times, high expectation teachers incorporate whole-class activities as part of their core curriculum programs which require all students to work together to complete an end product (e.g. a mural) or alternatively, all students complete the same activity (e.g. creating a poster or advertising a book and describing why others should read it). The point is that all activities are available for all students; there is no discrimination. Achievement differences are never made salient and all students are completing challenging learning experiences.

Class climate

The class climate of low expectation teachers is characterized by negative class management, frequent reminders about routines and procedures, and a lack of positive peer relationships across the classroom. In contrast, the classrooms of high expectation teachers are warm, supportive environments. Teachers mostly manage student behavior positively and pre-emptively (Rubie-Davies 2007) and are supportive of students. Further, not only do teachers develop constructive relationships with all their students, they also encourage students to develop affirmative relationships with each other by frequently changing seating groups and actively encouraging collaborative learning. This leads to a network of positive relationships throughout the class.

Goal setting

The overarching heading 'goal setting' includes a range of strategies that high expectation teachers use that in one way or another relate to goal setting. Low expectation teachers do not include goal setting as an approach they incorporate into their classroom practice. One strategy high expectation teachers employ relates to student motivation. In the classes of low expectation teachers, there is little time spent on trying to motivate students; students are given work and expected to complete it. High expectation teachers set individual goals with students based on both formative and summative assessments. Students are given a degree of autonomy related to what they want to learn next and teachers then closely monitor student achievement of their goals (evaluation) so that a student's goals can be reset as the student progresses. High expectation teachers also provide students with clear feedback about their learning and the progress they are making in mastering specific skills. They are provided with information about the next steps in their learning. High expectation teachers incorporate activities into core curriculum areas that are based on student interests. This helps to ensure that students are actively and cognitively engaged in their learning. Further, the focus on achieving specific goals relevant to each individual also helps to ensure that students are on-task and engaged. As a consequence student disruptive or off-task behavior is minimal. A further strategy used by high expectation teachers relates to the promotion of student autonomy. Students are encouraged to take responsibility for their learning. The clear feedback about and specific goals they have for their learning enables them to be focused and to monitor their own progress. The provision of choice related to the activities students complete, most of which contained various levels within one task, mean that students determined the level of challenge they wanted. For example, a reading task might be that students could choose to read a book from a theme box, perhaps dinosaurs. There would be a range of reading levels among the books and students could select those they wished. Hence, although those at lower reading levels may choose to read easier texts, differentiation between students was not being made explicit.

Effectiveness of high expectation teachers' practices

These practices of high expectation teachers have some basis in other literature. While the research reported above relates to the New Zealand context, Weinstein (2002) has found similar results in the United States for teachers who treat all students equitably. They, too, use mixed-ability grouping, they create a classroom community, promote student motivation and engagement, provide students with clear directions for their learning, encourage autonomy, and monitor student progress regularly.

Further, the pernicious effects of ability grouping have been documented by many scholars (e.g. Gamoran *et al.* 1995; Ireson *et al.* 2005; Oakes 1990), although there is a perception that high achievers are disadvantaged by heterogeneous grouping (Hornby *et al.* 2011). However, negative effects on student self-efficacy and other self-beliefs have been shown for both high achievers as well as low (Liem *et al.* 2013). Hence, flexible grouping has benefits that cannot be obtained using within-class ability grouping. For example, teachers do have the flexibility to keep some students together for instruction if they wish but students choose their activities and who they complete them with. This results in all students being exposed to challenging learning activities and enables them to benefit from high-level peer modeling. Because students are challenged and not confined to specific activities, they make rapid progress; they are motivated and engaged. Moreover, children are seated in mixed-ability groupings and groups are changed regularly. This practice facilitates students forming relationships across the classroom, rather than just among those in their ability groups as often happens (Pellegrini and Blatchford 2000). In turn then, flexible grouping is one aspect that serves to enhance the class climate because the high expectation teacher encourages and promotes relationships among all students.

Classrooms of high expectation teachers are managed positively (Rubie-Davies and Peterson 2011) and the teacher enjoys supportive relationships with students, thus also contributing to the positive classroom community that results. Students learn better in environments in which they feel supported and enjoy positive relationships with their teacher and their peers (Boivin and Bégin 1989; Boivin and Hymel 1997; Wentzel 2009). Finally, because high expectation teachers use flexible grouping, they work with students on goal setting. Flexible grouping does result in teachers having less ownership of what tasks students are completing but this simply means that they monitor student progress frequently (Rubie-Davies 2008) which, in turn, provides students with clear directions for their learning. Students understand the skills they have already mastered and know what the next steps are in their learning. They become motivated and engaged in their learning. Goal setting is a practice that is well understood to have benefits for student learning (Hastie 2013; Hattie 2009).

Overall, high expectation teachers differ quite substantially from low expectation teachers in the ways in which they instruct their students and in the relationships they develop with and among their students. These practices appear to have support in the literature outside of the expectation field and may be one explanation for why students with high expectation teachers make substantially more progress both academically and socially than those with low expectation teachers across one year. The practices and beliefs of high expectation teachers formed the basis of an experimental study which will be described in the following paragraphs.

Can high expectation practices be taught? The Teacher Expectation Project

The Teacher Expectation Project (Rubie-Davies 2014a) which I recently completed was a three-year, large-scale teacher expectation intervention, a randomized control trial designed to teach teachers the beliefs and practices of high expectation teachers and to show them how these practices might be incorporated into their classrooms. It was hoped that when teachers integrated the practices of high expectation teachers into their classrooms that their students' achievement would noticeably improve and that they would then also raise their expectations of their students as they came to realize that the students could achieve more than perhaps they had previously envisaged.

In all, 90 teachers were randomly assigned into intervention and control groups. In the first year of the project, those in the intervention group attended four day-long workshops at which they were taught the practices of high expectation teachers in each of the three major areas. Teachers collaboratively planned how they would implement the strategies into their classrooms with the research team on hand to ensure the integrity of the original design. The research team also visited the intervention group three times during the first year to provide support and a forum for discussion related to the success of the implementation, and again to be assured of the integrity of the intervention. The intervention group were videotaped both before and after the intervention and again once in each successive year so that they could monitor changes in their own verbal and nonverbal behavior that could give students messages about what was expected of them. Teachers in the control group took part in their school's regular professional development through-out the first year of the intervention. In the second year of the intervention, the control group were taught the practices of high expectation teachers by the intervention teachers and in the final year, to evaluate the sustainability of the practices, the researchers simply monitored outcomes for both teachers and students across all classes. Teacher expectations and beliefs as well as student achievement and beliefs were measured at regular intervals throughout the project.

In the first year, changes in teacher beliefs and expectations were measured throughout the year and student academic achievement and changes in beliefs were also monitored. Teachers self-analyzed their own DVDs. A Bayesian latent growth curve model showed that students in the intervention group gained approximately 28 percent in their mathematics scores over the year above what was gained by the control group students, although there were no differences in the groups at the beginning of the year (Rubie-Davies et al. 2015). This equated to almost three months additional learning for students in the intervention group. Further, a meta-analysis of the effect of the intervention across schools, grade levels, socioeconomic levels, sex, and ethnicity (Rubie-Davies et al. 2014) showed that the intervention was equally effective for all students in terms of improving student achievement in mathematics.

Preliminary analyses (Rubie-Davies 2014b) using a latent growth curve model also appeared to show effects on teachers' expectations. Expectations were regressed on achievement to gain a residual indicating the extent to which teachers expected their students' to make significant achievement gains over the year. During the first year of the project, intervention teachers' expectations, relative to achievement, became much more positive between the first and second measurement and continued to rise slightly into the second year of the project. Hence the intervention teachers' expected student achievement trajectories to increase markedly while in their classes. On the other hand, the residuals of the control group teachers declined significantly between the first and second measurement and then dropped further into the beginning of the second year. The control teachers were not expecting that their students' would make any steep gains. Hence, the pattern of expectations for intervention and control group teachers can be represented by two opposing curves, one with a steep rise and then a slowing growth and the other with a steep decline and a slowing deterioration.

The data collection also included tracking teacher and student beliefs. Very few analyses have yet been carried out on these data. Some preliminary analyses of the first-year data showed that intervention teachers, compared with the control group teachers, increased in their teaching efficacy over the year, focused less on performance goals, became less anxious, and considered that they were more in control of decisions related to their class. Students showed similar patterns in some of their beliefs. Compared with students whose teachers were in the control group, those whose teachers were in the intervention group increased in their self-concept related to mathematics, their perceptions of academic competence, and their beliefs that mathematics was a useful subject, and they became less performance-oriented.

Hence, although data for the Teacher Expectation Project are still being analyzed, the outcomes are promising. Teachers reported changed practices in accordance with what they had been taught in the workshops and shared their achievements with the researchers and each other. It appears that the intervention did affect teacher practices and beliefs and that these instructional changes were reflected in improvements in student achievement and beliefs. This suggests that when teachers are taught the practices of high expectation teachers, this results in gains for their students. It is to be remembered that these gains were seen in a rigorous randomized control trial, of which there are few in educational research, and therefore claims can be made about causality.

Future directions

Results from the Teacher Expectation Project (mostly the first year only at this stage) suggest that the practices of high expectation teachers can be taught. But, can teachers teach these practices to other teachers? To test this hypothesis, in the second year of the project, intervention teachers taught the practices to the control group teachers. When we have analyzed these data, we will be able to assess how effective this transfer was in spreading the effects of the teacher expectation intervention.

Nevertheless, the findings of Babad (2009), Weinstein (2002), and Rubie-Davies (2014a) all strongly suggest that in conducting research into teacher expectations, an important consideration is individual difference among teachers. This is important not only for conducting research on this phenomenon but most importantly for understanding the phenomenon. An examination of teacher differences (e.g. the degree to which teachers believe they can alter a student's achievement trajectory, or beliefs that all students should be given equitable learning opportunities) allows us to see where these effects are operative and whether the more negative practices can be changed. Teacher difference needs to be taken account of in generalizing results from teacher expectation research. Claims have been made that teacher expectations have only small effects on student achievement (Jussim *et al.* 2009), and when teacher data are aggregated this does appear to be the case. It could be, however, that combining teacher data is masking teacher expectation effects. When data are analyzed taking account of teacher difference, there are some substantial differences found for student outcomes (e.g. Li forthcoming; McKown and Weinstein 2008; Rubie-Davies, 2006; Rubie-Davies *et al.* 2007). My work (Rubie-Davies *et al.* 2012), for example, has shown that across a variety of samples, approximately one-quarter of teachers are high expectation teachers and approximately one-eighth are low expectation. The majority of teachers fall in the middle of the spectrum. Hence, when all data are aggregated, this is likely to mask the contrasts in outcomes for students when they are placed with particular teachers. Future work in the teacher expectation field needs to account for teacher difference.

A further area that is well worth exploration is school-level effects. Class-level effects have been described above but school-level teacher expectation effects have not yet been explored. It would seem probable that high expectation schools would raise achievement even more substantially than high expectation teachers. In a high expectation school, the principal would be leading the focus on teachers having high expectations for all students; teachers would be working together to implement the practices of high expectation teachers. The practices would be accepted and promoted among all staff. The effects could then be expected to be even more powerful than occurs when teachers work in isolation, possibly in contradiction to school or government policies. For example, within the Teacher Expectation Project, some teachers reported (McDonald *et al.* 2014) that their principal or senior management did not support the implementation of flexible grouping into their classes. This meant that although the intervention teachers could see benefits and had noticed increases in their students' achievement beyond what they had seen with previous classes, they did not always have the support of others more senior in the school. They had to work in opposition to accepted practice in their school. New Zealand has a long tradition of within-class ability grouping; it also has the largest disparity between the highest and lowest achievers of any OECD country (Tunmer *et al.* 2004). Finland has one of the smallest gaps and has a policy of heterogeneous grouping at all levels of schooling (OECD 2007). Yet despite the negative consequences of ability grouping cited above, New Zealand ministerial policy endorses the practice. However, working at the school level does enable innovative and effective practices to be implemented. Principal leadership becomes critical.

It can be seen that although much work has already been completed in relation to teacher expectations and much is already known, there are still some large gaps in knowledge, particularly in relation to whole-class and school-level effects. Because of the potential of high teacher expectations to raise achievement for all students, when accompanied by effective, empirically-supported practices, further exploration of class-level and school-level teacher expectation effects is warranted. These are likely to be exciting and thought-provoking areas of future research which can potentially enhance the achievement of all students.

References

Alexander, K.L. and Entwisle, D.R. (1988) 'Achievement in the first 2 years of school: patterns and processes', *Monographs of the Society for Research in Child Development,* 53: 1–157, Serial No. 218.

Archambault, I., Janosz, M. and Chouinard, R. (2012) 'Teacher beliefs as predictors of adolescents' cognitive engagement and achievement in mathematics', *The Journal of Educational Research,* 105: 319–328.

Babad, E. (1990a) 'Calling on students: how a teacher's behavior can acquire disparate meanings in students' minds', *Journal of Classroom Interaction,* 25: 1–4.

Babad, E. (1990b) 'Measuring and changing teachers' differential behavior as perceived by students and teachers', *Journal of Educational Psychology,* 82: 683–690.

Babad, E. (1995) 'The "teacher's pet" phenomenon, teachers' differential behavior, and students' morale', *Journal of Educational Psychology,* 87: 361–374.

Babad, E. (1998) 'Preferential affect: the crux of the teacher expectancy issue', in J. Brophy (ed.) *Advances in Research on Teaching: Expectations in the Classroom,* Greenwich, CT: JAI Press.

Babad, E. (2009) *The Social Psychology of the Classroom,* New York: Routledge.

Babad, E., Inbar, J. and Rosenthal, R. (1982) 'Pygmalion, Galatea and the Golem: investigations of biased and unbiased teachers', *Journal of Educational Psychology,* 74: 459–474.

Baron, R.M., Tom, D.Y.H. and Cooper, H.M. (1985) 'Social class, race and teacher expectations', in J. B. Dusek (ed.), *Teacher Expectancies,* Hillsdale, NJ: Lawrence Erlbaum.

Batzle, C.S., Weyandt, L.L., Janusis, G.M. and DeVietti, T.L. (2010) 'Potential impact of ADHD with stimulant medication label on teacher expectations', *Journal of Attention Disorders,* 14: 157–166.

Boivin, M. and Bégin, G. (1989) 'Peer status and self-perception among early elementary school children: the case of the rejected children', *Child Development,* 60: 591–596.

Boivin, M. and Hymel, S. (1997) 'Peer experiences and social self-perceptions: a sequential model', *Developmental Psychology,* 33: 135–145.

Brattesani, K.A., Weinstein, R.S. and Marshall, H.H. (1984) 'Student perceptions of differential teacher treatment as moderators of teacher expectation effects', *Journal of Educational Psychology,* 76: 236–247.

Brophy, J.E. (1985) 'Teacher–student interaction', in J.B. Dusek (ed.) *Teacher Expectancies* (pp. 303–338), Hillsdale, NJ: Lawrence Erlbaum.

Brophy, J.E. and Good, T.L. (1970) 'Teachers' communication of differential expectations for children's classroom performance: some behavioral data', *Journal of Educational Psychology,* 61: 365–374.

Cooper, H.M. and Good, T.L. (1983) *Pygmalion Grows Up: Studies in the Expectation Communication Process,* New York: Longman.

Gamoran, A., Nystrand, M., Berends, M. and LePore, P.C. (1995) 'An organizational analysis of the effects of ability grouping', *American Educational Research Journal,* 32: 687–715.

Harris, M.J. and Rosenthal, R. (1985) 'Mediation of interpersonal expectancy effects: 31 meta-analyses', *Psychological Bulletin,* 97: 363–386.

Hastie, S. K. (2013) 'Setting academic achievement goals in primary schools', unpublished doctoral thesis, University of Auckland, New Zealand.

Hattie, J. (2009) *Visible Learning: A Synthesis of over 800 Meta-Analyses Relating to Achievement,* London: Routledge.

Hornby, G., Witte, C. and Mitchell, D. (2011) 'Policies and practices of ability grouping in New Zealand intermediate schools', *Support for Learning,* 26: 92–96.

Ireson, J., Hallam, S., and Hurley, C. (2005) 'What are the effects of ability grouping in GCSE attainment?', *British Educational Research Journal,* 31: 443–458.

Jussim, L., Robustelli, S.L. and Cain, T.R. (2009) 'Teacher expectations and self-fulfilling prophecies', in K.R. Wentzel and A. Wigfield (eds) *Handbook of Motivation in School* (pp. 349–80), New York: Routledge.

Li, Z. (forthcoming) 'Teachers matter: expectation effects in foreign language classrooms at university', unpublished doctoral thesis, University of Auckland, New Zealand.

Liem, G.A.D., Marsh, H.W., Martin, A.J., McInerney, D.M., and Yeung, A.S. (2013) 'The big-fish-little-pond effect and a national policy of within-school ability streaming: alternative frames of reference', *American Educational Research Journal,* 50: 326–370.

McDonald, L., Flint, A., Rubie-Davies, C.M., Peterson, E.R., Watson, P. and Garrett, L. (2014) 'Using an intervention to change teacher expectations and associated beliefs and practices' (under review).

McKown, C. and Weinstein, R.S. (2008) 'Teacher expectations, classroom context and the achievement gap', *Journal of School Psychology,* 46: 235–261.

Oakes, J. (1990) *Multiplying Inequalities: The Effects of Race, Social Class, and Tracking on Opportunities to Learn Mathematics and Sciences,* Santa Monica, CA: Rand Corporation.

OECD (2007) *PISA 2006 Science Competencies for Tomorrow's World,* Vol. 1: *Analysis,* Paris: OECD.

Pellegrini, A.D. and Blatchford, P. (2000) *The Child at School: Interactions with Peers and Teachers,* London: Arnold.

Peterson, S. (2000) 'Grades four and eight students' and teachers' perceptions of girls' and boys' writing competencies', *Reading Horizons,* 40: 253–271.

Rist, R. C. (1970) 'Student social class and teacher expectations: the self-fulfilling prophecy in ghetto education', *Harvard Educational Review,* 40: 411–451.

Rosenthal, R., and Jacobson, L. (1968) *Pygmalion in the Classroom: Teacher Expectation and Pupils' Intellectual Development,* New York: Holt, Rinehart and Winston.

Rubie-Davies, C.M. (2006) 'Teacher expectations and student self-perceptions: exploring relationships', *Psychology in the Schools,* 43: 537–552.

Rubie-Davies, C.M. (2007) 'Classroom interactions: exploring the practices of high and low expectation teachers', *British Journal of Educational Psychology,* 77: 289–306.

Rubie-Davies, C.M. (2008) 'Teacher beliefs and expectations: relationships with student learning', in C.M. Rubie-Davies and C. Rawlinson (eds), *Challenging Thinking about Teaching and Learning* (pp. 25–40), Hauppauge, NY: Nova.

Rubie-Davies, C.M. (2014a) *Becoming a High Expectation Teacher: Raising the Bar*, London: Routledge.

Rubie-Davies, C.M. (2014b) 'Tracking changes in teacher expectations over time: can teachers' expectations be changed?' (in progress).

Rubie-Davies, C.M., Flint, A. and McDonald, L. (2012) 'Teacher beliefs, teacher characteristics and school contextual factors: what are the relationships?', *British Journal of Educational Psychology,* 82: 270–288.

Rubie-Davies, C.M., Hattie, J., Townsend, M.A.R. and Hamilton, R.J. (2007) 'Aiming high: teachers and their students', in V.N. Galwye (ed.) *Progress in Educational Psychology Research* (pp. 65–91), Hauppauge, NY: Nova.

Rubie-Davies, C.M. and Peterson, E.R. (2011) 'Teacher expectations and beliefs: influences on the socioemotional environment of the classroom', in C.M. Rubie-Davies (ed.) *Educational Psychology: Concepts, Research and Challenges* (pp. 134–49), London: Routledge.

Rubie-Davies, C.M., Peterson, E.R., Sibley, C.G. and Rosenthal, R. (2015) 'A teacher expectation intervention: modelling the practices of high expectation teachers', *Contemporary Educational Psychology,* 40: 72–85. doi: 10.1016/j.cedpsych.2014.03.003

Rubie-Davies, C.M., Rosenthal, R., Flint, A., Garrett, L., McDonald, L., and Watson, P. (2014) 'Evaluating a teacher expectation intervention: a meta-analytic approach', poster presented at the American Educational Research Association Annual Meeting, Philadelphia, PA.

Sorhagen, N.S. (2013) 'Early teacher expectations disproportionately affect poor children's high school performance', *Journal of Educational Psychology,* 105: 465–477.

Stinnett, T.A., Crawford, S.A., Gillespie, M.D., Cruce, M.K. and Langford, C.A. (2001) 'Factors affecting treatment acceptability for psychostimulant medication versus psychoeducational intervention', *Psychology in the Schools,* 38: 585–591.

Tenenbaum, H.R. and Ruck, M.D. (2007) 'Are teachers' expectations different for racial minority than for European American students? A meta-analysis', *Journal of Educational Psychology,* 99: 253–273.

Tunmer, W.E., Chapman, J.W. and Prochnow, J.E. (2004) 'Why the reading achievement gap in New Zealand won't go away: evidence from the PIRLS 2001 international study of reading achievement', *New Zealand Journal of Educational Studies,* 39: 127–145.

van den Bergh, L., Denessen, E., Hornstra, L., Voeten, M.J. and Holland, R.W. (2010) 'The implicit prejudiced attitudes of teachers: relations to teacher expectations and the ethnic achievement gap', *American Educational Research Journal,* 47: 497–527.

Weinstein, R.S. (1983) 'Student perceptions of schooling', *The Elementary School Journal,* 83: 286–312.

Weinstein, R.S. (1989) 'Perceptions of classroom processes and student motivation: children's views of self-fulfilling prophecies', in R. Ames and C. Ames (eds) *Research on Motivation in Education* (Vol. 3, pp. 187–221), New York: Academic Press.

Weinstein, R.S. (1993) 'Children's knowledge of differential treatment in school: implications for motivation', in T.M. Tomlinson (ed.) *Motivating Students to Learn: Overcoming Barriers to High Achievement* (pp. 197–224), Berkeley, CA: McCutchan.

Weinstein, R.S. (2002) *Reaching Higher: The Power of Expectations in Schooling*, Cambridge, MA: Harvard University Press.

Weinstein, R.S., Marshall, H.H., Brattesani, K.A. and Middlestadt, S. E. (1982) 'Student perceptions of differential teacher treatment in open and traditional classrooms', *Journal of Educational Psychology,* 74: 678–692.

Weinstein, R.S. and Middlestadt, S.E. (1979) 'Student perceptions of teacher interactions with male high and low achievers', *Journal of Educational Psychology,* 71: 421–431.

Wentzel, K.R. (2009) 'Students' relationships with teachers as motivational contexts', in K.R. Wentzel and A. Wigfield (eds) *Handbook of Motivation at School* (pp. 301–322), New York: Routledge.

30

TEACHER EXPECTATION EFFECTS IN THE COLLEGE FOREIGN LANGUAGE CLASSROOM

Zheng Li and Christine M. Rubie-Davies

Since the middle of the last century, teacher expectation effects have attracted great interest from a large number of researchers. Rooted in the sociological concept of self-fulfilling prophecy effects (Merton 1948), Rosenthal and Jacobson's classic Pygmalion experiment (1968) ignited vigorous research about the self-fulfilling effects of teacher expectations in the educational realm. After heated debate about the Pygmalion experiment (Rosenthal and Jacobson 1968), researchers confirmed the existence of teacher expectation effects in classrooms (Raudenbush 1984; Rosenthal 1968, 1974, 1976, 1985; Rosenthal and Rubin 1971, 1978). Subsequently, researchers explored the mediating mechanisms of teacher expectation effects (e.g. Brophy and Good 1974; Rosenthal 1974; Rubie-Davies 2008a; Weinstein 2002), explaining the way teacher expectations are developed, conveyed, perceived and confirmed. Further investigations were conducted regarding the magnitude of teacher expectation effects (e.g. Babad 2009; Jussim *et al.* 1998; Kuklinski and Weinstein 2001; Madon *et al.* 1997; Rubie-Davies 2008b), suggesting that stronger teacher expectancy effects were related to individual differences in teachers, students, and contexts.

Though related research has been fruitful, there still remain some areas in the expectancy field which have not been fully explored. For example, a plethora of research has focused on teacher expectation effects in relation to student learning at elementary and secondary levels (e.g. Babad *et al.* 1982a; Brophy and Good 1974; Rosenthal 1968; Rubie-Davies 2007, 2010; Sorhagen 2013; Weinstein and McKown 1998), while little about teacher expectation effects has been located in tertiary settings. In addition, much research has studied teacher expectation effects in specific curriculum areas such as reading (Rubie-Davies 2008a), mathematics (Riegle-Crumb and Humphries 2012), and physical education (Babad *et al.* 1982a), but little has been conducted in the foreign language classroom. The marked absence of research on teacher expectancy effects in the curriculum of foreign language and tertiary settings await further exploration. Studies are needed to find out if teacher expectancy is a contributing factor to student academic and social outcomes in these new contexts. The results would shed light on a broader understanding of teacher expectation effects, and more importantly provide some insights into enhancing student outcomes in higher education and in learning foreign languages.

As a primary goal, the current study was designed to focus on university teachers and first-year undergraduate students, and examine the existence of teacher expectation effects in foreign language classrooms at university. The relationship between teacher expectations and student academic gains was investigated. Furthermore, the current study explored the mediating process of teacher expectation effects in specific contexts, trying to account for how teacher expectations were developed, communicated, and interpreted.

Research background

This section provides the background to the current study. First, studies of teacher expectation effects in tertiary settings and in the foreign language curriculum are critically reviewed, which identifies research gaps in the existing literature. Second, the conceptual basis of the current study is included, which delineates the theoretical perspective the study adopted.

Teacher expectation effects in tertiary settings

To our knowledge, only a few studies (e.g. Haynes and Johnson 1983; Minner and Prater 1984) have examined teacher expectation effects in tertiary settings, and so far no intensive investigation has been conducted on university teachers and students. For example, Haynes and Johnson's study (1983) manipulated teacher expectations by providing lists purporting to indicate students who were likely to improve in performance. Their study induced teachers' expectations in an experimental setting, but had limited implications for teacher–student dynamic interactions in a naturalistic classroom. Minner and Prater (1984) documented college teachers' biased expectations of students with learning disabilities' which merely indicated the influence of student labeling information on teacher expectations. A more recent thesis by Kim (2003) only discussed how the cultural backgrounds of university teachers and students may affect the formation and interpretations of their expectations. The three studies to date investigated varying teacher expectations for students at university, and went no further with whether those varying teacher expectations were related to student academic gaps. The current study aimed to examine the relationship between teachers' initial expectations and students' later academic achievement in naturalistic tertiary education settings. Research in the expectancy field has collectively focused on elementary- and secondary-school levels; one possible reason may be that it has been widely argued and acknowledged that younger students are more likely to be affected by teacher expectations than older ones (see Brophy 1983; Jussim et al. 1998 for reviews). However, a systematic exploration is needed to confirm whether teacher expectations have an effect on student outcomes in tertiary settings.

Teacher expectation effects in a foreign language curriculum

As noted earlier, previous research on teacher expectation effects has mostly been in specific common curriculum areas, such as reading (Rubie-Davies 2008a), mathematics (Riegle-Crumb and Humphries 2012), or physical education (Babad et al. 1982a). With only one exception (Taguchi 2006), no empirical study could be located that explored expectation effects in the subject of learning foreign languages. Taguchi's study (2006) was designed to investigate the relationship between student motivation and students' foreign language learning. The results showed that the most powerful predictors of language gains were found in more implicit teachers' beliefs about their students' capacities and their expectations of their students' achievement. However, this study had a very limited sample size, four teachers and their 61 students, so that care needs to be taken in generalizing the evidence of teacher expectation effects from the results in the specific curriculum of foreign language learning.

Existing literature has documented that the likelihood and magnitude of teacher expectation effects are a function of the academic subject (Braun 1976; Brophy 1983; Cooper 1985;

Rubie-Davies 2008a; Smith 1980; Sorhagen 2013). It seems necessary to extend teacher expectancy effects research into curriculum subjects other than the subjects that have been commonly explored to date.

The current study

The current study was designed to explore more generalized teacher expectation effects rather than dyadic mechanisms. More generalized teacher expectation effects have become a new interest in the expectancy field (e.g. Archambault *et al.* 2012; Diamond *et al.* 2004; Rubie-Davies 2008a; Rumberger and Palardy 2005), which has developed on the concept that teachers, compared with students, play a more crucial role in generating teacher expectation effects. Researchers have found that it is the individual differences in teachers that probably strengthen or weaken the relationship between teacher expectations and student outcomes. For example, Babad and colleagues (Babad 1979; Babad and Inbar 1981; Babad *et al.* 1982a, 1982b) distinguished teachers with high bias from those with no bias, with the former being more susceptible to student biasing information and more likely to produce teacher expectation effects than the latter. Weinstein and colleagues (Brattesani *et al.* 1984; Weinstein *et al.* 1982) have reported evidence of high differentiating teachers who are perceived by students to treat students differentially and low differentiating teachers who tend to treat students in an undifferentiated way. Their work has shown that the initial expectations of high differentiating teachers are more likely to be confirmed by student academic performance.

More recently, based on the argument that teacher expectation effects are more likely to be related to teacher characteristics than to student characteristics, researchers have proposed that teachers may form uniform expectations towards all the students in the classes and those expectations may be related to the overall class achievement later. Rubie-Davies' work (Rubie-Davies 2006, 2007, 2008a, 2008b) provided empirical evidence which supported that proposal. She identified high expectation and low expectation teachers, those who held uniformly high or low class-level expectations towards all the students in their classes at the beginning of the school year, and such expectation disparity was confirmed by the overall achievement gap between classes at the end of the school year. Therefore the researcher argued that class-level teacher expectation effects were salient; teacher expectations were shaped by teacher characteristics, and consequently so were instructional activities, learning opportunities, and overall student academic gains.

The current study adopted the research perspective of generalized teacher expectation effects, and shifted to the new context of university foreign language classrooms. The study did not focus on teacher expectation effects in relation to individual students; nor did it focus on dyadic teacher–student interactions, because university teachers tend to adopt whole-class instructional methods, and minimize individual differential treatment to different students.

Major empirical findings

This section reports the evidence for teacher expectation effects in college foreign language classrooms and the potential mechanisms. The major findings are also discussed in this section.

Teacher expectation effects in college foreign language classrooms

The study recruited 50 teachers and their more than 4,600 first-year undergraduate students from two universities in China. All the teachers and students came from classrooms where English was taught and learnt as a foreign language (College English classrooms). Teachers and students were randomly assigned to each class. Student characteristics, including gender, socioeconomic status, and prior achievement, were similarly distributed across classes. The teacher participants were made up of teachers with different gender, age, work experience, and educational experience. Student scores for English in the College Entrance Examination were collected at the beginning of the 2011–12 school year, and their scores in another examination, College English Test, were collected at the end of the school year. Both examinations are national standardized tests which are held annually. At the beginning of the school year, all the teachers were asked to complete a Teacher Expectation Scale in the third week, predicting the College English Test score for each student in their class.

The student entrance scores were compared by class and no statistically significant differences between classes were found. Further analysis of each teacher's expectations for multiple classes showed that the teacher held similar expectations for different classes; that is, if a teacher held high expectations for one class, he or she appeared to hold normatively high expectations for other classes, and likewise, teachers who held low expectations for one class held low expectations for all their classes. This is an important finding as the examination of one teacher's expectations across multiple classes has not previously been tested in the literature. The pervasiveness of teacher expectations suggests that generalized teacher expectations may go beyond the boundary of an individual class, which lays a foundation for exploring the relationship between normative teacher expectations and overall student achievement.

However, statistically significant differences in expectations were found between teachers, which was consistent with previous literature (e.g. Rubie-Davies 2008a). For all classes where students had similar demographic characteristics and prior achievement, some teachers had either substantially higher or lower expectations for student future achievement in the College English Test at the end of school year. Hence, three teacher groups were identified: high expectation teachers who had high expectations for all their students relative to initial achievement; medium expectation teachers who had medium level expectations for all their classes; and low expectation teachers who had comparatively lower expectations for all their students' future performance. It appeared that teachers' expectations were not always dependent on student information (i.e. achievement), which suggests that teacher expectations are a teacher-centered variable and not necessarily closely related to student characteristics.

More importantly, it seemed that normative teacher expectations were strongly related to overall student achievement in the year-end examination. Regardless of students' similar previous performance at the beginning of the school year, students' achievement at the end of the school year varied in line with what their teachers expected. Students whose teachers had higher normative expectations at the beginning of the year, tended to score more highly in the standardized English test at the end of the school year than did students with lower expectation teachers. The findings suggest that teachers' normatively high or low expectations may correspond accordingly with their students' academic outcomes; and students appear to benefit or be restricted depending on the teacher type with whom they happen to be placed. Students' differential learning outcomes indicate a considerable effect at the teacher level, rather than the student level. Moreover, the study provides evidence that teacher expectation effects probably are a function of teacher variables and teachers perhaps carry more weight in the formation of expectations and the production of expectancy effects than other factors, such as student characteristics. This finding is consistent with previous research, which highlighted the teacher's role in generating expectancy effects (e.g. Babad 2009; Rubie-Davies 2008a; Weinstein 2002).

Mechanisms for teacher expectation effects

After the identification of teacher expectation groups, 20 teachers from high, middle, and low expectation groups and their 200 students were randomly selected for interviews and focus groups. The teachers were interviewed separately twice: the first interview was at the beginning of the school year and the second was in the middle of the school year. The student focus groups were organized for the middle of the school year. Generally, the teachers were interviewed about the development and expression of their expectations, while the students talked about their perception and interpretation of teachers' expectations.

Teachers' self-report and student focus group data appeared to account for the possible mechanisms of normative teacher expectation effects for all the students in the College English classrooms. Teachers with different normative expectations were found to differ in their beliefs about teaching and learning, their instructional practices, and the climate that they created within their classrooms. It seemed that those variations in beliefs and behaviors between teacher expectation groups communicated teacher expectations and consequently led to expectancy effects in the foreign language classrooms within tertiary settings.

The data showed that teachers' expectations seemed to vary in line with their pedagogical beliefs and self-efficacy. It was found that low expectation teachers believed in their role as instructor and supervisor, deciding what and how the students should learn and spending time in classroom management; the teachers with medium and high expectations viewed themselves as a guide for student learning, and they emphasized learner autonomy in instruction. Only the high expectation teachers believed in the significance of the classroom climate for student learning, and regarded it as their responsibility to create a favorable climate within the classrooms. These findings of variation in teacher beliefs have confirmed Rubie-Davies' studies (Rubie 2004; Rubie-Davies 2007, 2008a, 2008b) about elementary-school teachers that low expectation teachers are likely to take a directive role in instruction but high expectation teachers tend to take a facilitative role. Furthermore, the teachers' teaching efficacy appeared to increase with a rise in teacher expectations, suggesting that low expectation teachers may have had lower teaching efficacy while high expectation teachers may have had greater efficacy. These findings suggest that teacher expectations are closely related to teacher characteristics.

High expectation and low expectation teachers tended to maintain their initial expectations, but medium expectation teachers were likely to adjust their expectations according to the latest information they received about student performance during teacher–student interactions. Furthermore, high and low expectation teachers tended to continue with the same instructional activities even when there was contradictory evidence of student performance, while medium expectation teachers were likely to make changes to the instruction in accordance with students' actual performance and needs.

Just as the related research (Babad *et al.* 1989a, 1989b, 1991, 2003) has pointed out that students are sensitive to teacher expectations, the current study found that students were able to precisely perceive teachers' actual expectations, even though the teachers tried to conceal their negative expectations. The students reported that instructional practices were the major channel through which they perceived and interpreted their teachers' normative expectations. The low expectation teachers seemed to provide easier learning materials, gave overstated feedback, and set readily accomplished goals for their students; the high expectation teachers appeared to choose difficult learning materials, gave business-like feedback, and set challenging goals for student learning. Teachers with different normative expectations differed in their instructional practices, which may have resulted in differing learning opportunities for their students. Existing literature (Rubie-Davies 2007, 2008a; Weinstein 2002) has argued that varying learning opportunities may contribute to differences in student academic outcomes. Given differing learning opportunities, it appears that in the current study the students' academic gains were enhanced or restricted in accordance with the expectations their teachers held.

Therefore, the following mechanism for normative teacher expectation effects is proposed: teachers form normative expectations for all students, teachers deliver instruction, students perceive teacher expectations, and student performance and achievement conform to teacher expectations. During the mediation process, individual differences in teachers seem to shape teachers' normative expectations that may lead to different instructional practices and learning opportunities, which, in turn, may consequently cause student outcomes to confirm teacher expectations accordingly. It can be seen that teacher factors play a key role in the self-fulfillment of normative teacher expectations. It is the individual differences in teachers, rather than student differences, that make the difference in student outcomes, and this adds weight to the argument that teacher expectation effects are more likely to be a function of teacher characteristics (Weinstein 2002; Rubie-Davies 2008a; Babad 2009).

Teacher expectation effects in the foreign language classroom at university

The current study found that teachers' initial expectations were closely related to student later achievement in learning a foreign language at university. Despite similar prior grades, students' year-end achievement varied depending on teacher expectation groups, which indicates an effect of teacher expectations on student outcomes in the tertiary foreign language classrooms.

It seems that the findings of the current study provide evidence that is contradictory to previous research which argued that younger students are more likely to be affected by teacher expectations than older ones (see Brophy 1983; Jussim *et al.* 1998 for reviews). However, existing literature (Eden and Shani 1982; Jussim 1986; Jussim *et al.* 1998; Raudenbush 1984; Swann and Ely 1984; Weinstein and McKown 1998) has found that people, including students and adults, are more susceptible to expectancy effects when they are transferred from familiar situations to new ones, such as entering a new school level, because they may feel less self-aware, less self-confident, and more dependent on teachers' perceptions and expectations. This may also apply to students in tertiary institutions. The current study targeted first-year undergraduate students who were just beginning university. Freshmen at university may find themselves in a brand new situation, because tertiary education is different in many ways from the education they experienced before; for example, there are differences in instructional arrangements, learning methods, assessments, personal interaction, and so on. As a result of inexperience and less clear and confident self-perceptions, first-year undergraduate students are probably more reliant on their teachers' judgments and help. They may have been more likely to accept their teachers' expectations and behave in the way the teacher expected, and consequently their achievement appeared to confirm what the teacher predicted at the beginning of the school year. Hence the findings of the current study have added new evidence of the 'new situation' factor in generating teacher expectation effects.

The foreign language curriculum also seems to be a contributing factor to teacher expectation effects identified in the current study. Teacher expectation effects in foreign language classrooms seem highly probable. One reason may be because of the pedagogical characteristics of the foreign language curriculum where instructional practice mainly consists of dialog, conversation, or discussion. There are more frequent and direct interactions between the teacher and students than in other curriculum areas where lecturing and listening are the major classroom activities (Johnson 2008). Previous research in the expectancy area (e.g. Babad 2009; Babad *et al.* 1989a) has found that teachers may demonstrate substantial leakage effects, namely discrepancy between messages being transmitted through different channels, suggesting that more positive expectations may be transmitted in more controllable channels such as verbal content but that more negative expectations may be leaked in less controllable channels such as nonverbal behaviors. Although teachers believe they can control their affective transmissions and conceal their feelings from their students, students' perceptions of teachers' expectancy-related behaviors appear to be quite accurate (Babad *et al.* 1991), even in a cross-cultural, foreign language context (Babad and Taylor 1992). Therefore, teachers may be less able to conceal or disguise their expectations and beliefs during the frequent and direct interactions with their students in the foreign language classrooms, while students could perceive teachers' expectation cues more easily than they do in other learning contexts, which probably results in more pronounced effects on student learning.

Furthermore, the teaching content may be another situation factor that could account for teacher expectation effects in the current study. Previous research has suggested that self-fulfilling effects of teacher expectations are highly probable, especially when students are dependent on their teachers as limited sources of the new content (Braun 1976; West and Anderson 1976). It has also been proposed that with learning tasks of unfamiliar content and unpredictable difficulty level, self-fulfilling effects of teacher expectations are more likely (Brophy, 1983). There is comparatively little chance for students to learn a tertiary curriculum from sources other than school teachers, because tertiary curricula are more academic than those in elementary and secondary schools. It is probable that students, especially first-year students, are more dependent on teachers and schools for learning opportunities when they are learning unfamiliar tasks. Specifically, the current study focused on the foreign language class in China. There are limited sources in China for students to learn a foreign language outside of a school, because China is located far from English-speaking areas and has a different political ideology from the western world. Therefore it is probable that students in China are more dependent on teachers and schools for learning opportunities when they are learning a foreign language. Their learning opportunities and experiences may be largely shaped by what the teacher provides and creates, which consequently may intensify the relationship between teacher expectations and student academic gains.

The combination of contextual factors of a tertiary setting and a foreign language curriculum seems to buffer the moderation effects of student age, and increases first-year undergraduate students' susceptibility to teacher expectancy effects in learning a foreign language. The findings of the current study suggest that contextual factors play an important role in teacher expectation effects, and more extensive explorations into specific contexts are needed.

Challenges and future directions

The current study has identified the influence of contextual factors on the self-fulfillment of teacher expectancies. It seems that teacher expectation effects are significant in the foreign language curriculum and on students in higher education, especially first-year undergraduates.

The particular curriculum area of foreign language has not been empirically studied in the expectancy field; however, the findings have provided evidence to link teacher expectations to student academic achievement in learning English as a foreign language. That may have some implications for teaching and learning foreign languages. Special attention should be paid to teacher expectations, teacher beliefs, instructional practice, and socioemotional climate in foreign language classrooms so as to improve foreign language learning of students.

What is also worth noting is the new situation that first-year undergraduates may face in tertiary schools. Freshmen may be more susceptible to teacher expectations due to being unfamiliar with the instructional and socioemotional environment of university or college. Understanding of the 'new situation' factor can be integrated into tertiary educational practice. By creating positive teacher expectation effects, first-year undergraduates may achieve at higher levels and more positively adjust to tertiary institutions.

Since the current research has integrated the curriculum and school-level contexts, it cannot be concluded that either the foreign language curriculum or the tertiary education system can solely strengthen or weaken the effects of normative teacher expectations on student outcomes. Future research could focus more particularly on a specific context and identify the contextual moderators by comparing these with their counterparts. For example, normative teacher expectation effects could be explored in different curriculum areas within the same school level, or in the same curriculum but at different school levels. The results may provide more convincing evidence for whether or not the curriculum or the school level moderate teacher expectation effects (or whether both do) and implications for educational practice in a certain subject or a schooling system.

The current study identifies teachers' high, medium, and low expectations for all their students, and suggests that teacher normative expectations are a teacher-centered variable. Further investigation into the distinction of the teacher types is needed. Because of the limited sample size of teacher participants ($n = 50$) and the research design, the current research did not identify the characteristics of teachers who held normatively high or low expectations. Some demographic characteristics of teachers may be related to their expectancies, such as age, gender, and educational and professional experience, and these could be identified in future studies. In addition, the current research found that teacher expectations may be linked to teacher pedagogical beliefs and self-efficacy, but no definite conclusions can be made because the findings were derived from teachers' self-report in a qualitative study. Future empirical work could further explore teacher moderators of their normative expectations for all their students. The identification of the personal characteristics of teachers who hold normatively high or low expectations may help to distinguish the teacher types and enable the implementation of intervention programs for teachers' professional development which hence will help to enhance students' academic achievement.

References

Archambault, I., Janosz, M. and Chouinard, R. (2012) 'Teacher beliefs as predictors of adolescents' cognitive engagement and achievement in mathematics', *The Journal of Educational Research*, 105: 319–328.

Babad, E. (1979) 'Personality correlates of susceptibility to biasing information', *Journal of Personality and Social Psychology*, 37: 195–202.

Babad, E. (2009) *The Social Psychology of the Classroom*, New York: Routledge.

Babad, E., Avni-Babad, D. and Rosenthal, R. (2003) 'Teachers' brief nonverbal behaviors in defined instructional situations can predict students' evaluations', *Journal of Educational Psychology*, 95: 553–562.

Babad, E., Bernieri, F. and Rosenthal, R. (1989a) 'Nonverbal communication and leakage in the behavior of biased and unbiased teachers', *Journal of Personality and Social Psychology*, 56: 89–94.

Babad, E., Bernieri, F. and Rosenthal, R. (1989b) 'When less information is more informative: diagnosing teacher expectations from brief samples of behaviour', *British Journal of Educational Psychology*, 59: 281–295.

Babad, E., Bernieri, F. and Rosenthal, R. (1991) 'Students as judges of teachers' verbal and nonverbal behavior', *American Educational Research Journal*, 28: 211–234.

Babad, E. and Inbar, J. (1981) 'Performance and personality correlates of teachers' susceptibility to biasing information', *Journal of Personality and Social Psychology*, 40: 553–561.

Babad, E., Inbar, J. and Rosenthal, R. (1982a) 'Pygmalion, Galatea, and the Golem: investigations of biased and unbiased teachers', *Journal of Educational Psychology*, 74: 459–474.

Babad, E., Inbar, J. and Rosenthal, R. (1982b) 'Teachers' judgment of students' potential as a function of teachers' susceptibility to biasing information', *Journal of Personality and Social Psychology*, 42: 541–547.

Babad, E. and Taylor, P.J. (1992) 'Transparency of teacher expectancies across language, cultural boundaries', *Journal of Educational Research*, 86: 120–125.

Brattesani, K.A., Weinstein, R.S. and Marshall, H.H. (1984) 'Student perceptions of differential teacher treatment as moderators of teacher expectation effects', *Journal of Educational Psychology*, 76: 236–247.

Braun, C. (1976) 'Teacher expectations: sociopsychological dynamics', *Review of Educational Research,* 46: 185–213.

Brophy, J. (1983) 'Research on the self-fulfilling prophecy and teacher expectations', *Journal of Educational Psychology,* 75: 631–661.

Brophy, J. and Good, T.L. (1974) *Teacher–Student Relationships: Causes and Consequences,* New York: Holt, Rinehart and Winston.

Cooper, H.M. (1985) 'Models of teacher expectation communication', in J.B. Dusek, V. Hall and W. Meyer (eds) *Teacher Expectancies* (pp. 135–158), Hillsdale, NJ: Lawrence Erlbaum.

Diamond, J.B., Randolph, A. and Spillane, J.P. (2004) 'Teachers' expectations and sense of responsibility for student learning: the importance of race, class, and organizational habitus', *Anthropology and Education Quarterly,* 35: 75–98.

Eden, D. and Shani, A.B. (1982) 'Pygmalion goes to boot camp: expectancy, leadership, and trainee performance', *Journal of Applied Psychology,* 67: 194–199.

Haynes, N.M. and Johnson, S.T. (1983) 'Self- and teacher expectancy effects on academic performance of college students enrolled in an academic reinforcement program', *American Educational Research Journal,* 20: 511–516.

Johnson, K. (2008) *An Introduction to Foreign Language Learning and Teaching,* Harlow: Pearson Longman.

Jussim, L. (1986) 'Self-fulfilling prophecies: a theoretical and integrative review', *Psychological Review,* 93: 429–445.

Jussim, L., Smith, A., Madon, S. and Palumbo, P. (1998) 'Teacher expectations', in J. Brophy (ed.) *Advances in Research on Teaching: Expectations in the Classroom* (pp. 1–48), Greenwich: JAI Press.

Kim, Y.S. (2003) 'Classroom interaction in university settings: a case study of language teaching and learning', unpublished doctoral thesis, Central Queensland University.

Kuklinski, M.R. and Weinstein, R.S. (2001) 'Classroom and developmental differences in a path model of teacher expectancy effects', *Child Development,* 72: 1554–1578.

Madon, S., Jussim, L. and Eccles, J. (1997) 'In search of the powerful self-fulfilling prophecy', *Journal of Personality and Social Psychology,* 72: 791–809.

Merton, M. N. (1948) 'The self-fulfilling prophecy', *Antioch Review:* 193–201.

Minner, S. and Prater, G. (1984) 'College teachers' expectations of LD students', *Intervention in School and Clinic,* 20: 225–229.

Raudenbush, S.W. (1984) 'Magnitude of teacher expectancy effects on pupil IQ as a function of the credibility of expectancy induction: a synthesis of findings from 18 experiments', *Journal of Educational Psychology,* 76: 85–97.

Riegle-Crumb, C. and Humphries, M. (2012) 'Exploring bias in math teachers' perceptions of students' ability by gender and race/ethnicity', *Gender and Society,* 26: 290–322.

Rosenthal, R. (1968) 'Experimenter expectancy and the reassuring nature of the null hypothesis decision procedure', *Psychological Bulletin Monograph Supplement,* 70: 30–47.

Rosenthal, R. (1974) *On the Social Psychology of the Self-Fulfilling Prophecy: Further Evidence for Pygmalion Effects and Their Mediating Mechanisms,* New York: MSS Modular Publications.

Rosenthal, R. (1976) *Experimenter Effects in Behavioral Research,* New York: Irvington.

Rosenthal, R. (1985) 'From unconscious experimenter bias to teacher expectancy effects', in J.B. Dusek, V. Hall and W. Meyer (eds) *Teacher Expectancies* (pp. 37–65), Hillsdale, NJ: Lawrence Erlbaum.

Rosenthal, R. and Jacobson, E.S. (1968) *Pygmalion in the Classroom: Teacher Expectation and Pupils' Intellectual Development,* New York: Holt, Rinehart and Winston.

Rosenthal, R. and Rubin, D.B. (1971) 'Pygmalion reaffirmed', in J.D. Elashoff and R.E. Snow (eds) *Pygmalion Reconsidered* (pp. 139–155), Worthington, MN: Jones.

Rosenthal, R. and Rubin, D.B. (1978) 'Interpersonal expectancy effects: the first 345 studies', *Behavioral and Brain Sciences,* 1: 377–386.

Rubie, C.M. (2004) 'Expecting the best: instructional practices, teacher beliefs and student outcomes', unpublished doctoral thesis, University of Auckland, New Zealand.

Rubie-Davies, C.M. (2006) 'Teacher expectations and student self-perceptions: exploring relationships', *Psychology in the Schools,* 43: 537–552.

Rubie-Davies, C.M. (2007) 'Classroom interactions: exploring the practices of high- and low-expectation teachers', *British Journal of Educational Psychology,* 77: 289–306.

Rubie-Davies, C.M. (2008a) *Expecting Success: Teacher Beliefs and Practices that Enhance Student Outcomes,* Saarbrücken: VDM Verlag.

Rubie-Davies, C.M. (2008b) 'Teacher beliefs and expectations: relationships with student learning', in C.M. Rubie-Davies and C. Rawlinson (eds) *Challenging Thinking about Teaching and Learning* (pp. 25–39), New York: Nova Science.

Rubie-Davies, C.M. (2010) 'Teacher expectations and perceptions of student attributes: is there a relationship?', *British Journal of Educational Psychology,* 80: 121–135.

Rumberger, R. and Palardy, G. (2005) 'Does segregation still matter: the impact of student composition on academic achievement in high school', *The Teachers College Record,* 107: 1999–2045.

Smith, M.L. (1980) 'Meta-analysis of research on teacher expectation', *Evaluation in Education,* 4: 53–55.

Sorhagen, N.S. (2013) 'Early teacher expectations disproportionately affect poor children's high school performance', *Journal of Educational Psychology,* 105: 465–477.

Swann, W.B. and Ely, R.J. (1984) 'A battle of wills: self-verification versus behavioral confirmation', *Journal of Personality and Social Psychology,* 46: 1287–1302.

Taguchi, K. (2006) 'Is motivation a predictor of foreign language learning', *International Education Journal,* 7: 560–569.

Weinstein, R.S. (2002) *Reaching Higher: The Power of Expectations in Schooling,* Cambridge: Harvard University Press.

Weinstein, R.S. and McKown, C. (1998) 'Expectancy effects in "context": listening to the voices of students and teachers', in J. Brophy (ed.) *Advances in Research on Teaching: Expectations in the Classroom* (pp. 215–242), Greenwich: JAI Press.

Weinstein, R.S., Marshall, H.H., Brattesani, K.A. and Middlestadt, S.E. (1982) 'Student perceptions of differential teacher treatment in open and traditional classrooms', *Journal of Educational Psychology,* 74: 678–92.

West, C.K. and Anderson, T.H. (1976) 'The question of preponderant causation in teacher expectancy research', *Review of Educational Research*: 613–630.

PART VII

Teacher motivation, professionalism, and well-being

31

RECENT ADVANCES IN RESEARCH ON TEACHER MOTIVATION AND EMOTIONS

Robert Klassen and Tracy Durksen

Research on teacher motivation and emotions has shown considerable growth over the past decades, with much attention paid to building a theoretical understanding of the relationships of motivation, emotions, and various teacher and student outcomes, but with modest effect on practice (e.g. Wheatley 2005). We know teachers' motivation and emotions are influenced by specific forms of professional development (Durksen and Klassen 2013), and we know that teachers' motivation changes over time, from preservice training to later career stages (e.g. Durksen and Klassen 2012). However, we have not yet moved from a foundational knowledge of teacher motivation and emotions to applying that knowledge to practice. In this chapter, we examine the current state of knowledge of teachers' motivation – especially efficacy beliefs – and teacher emotions, and consider new advances in research that applies knowledge to important problems in education.

Conceptual model

Figure 31.1 presents a conceptual model, influenced by the job demands–resources (JD-R) model, whereby workers' well-being is influenced by the balance of job demands that induce stress and burnout, and job resources, characterized by the psychological, social, or organizational aspects of work that reduce job demands and increase personal development (Bakker *et al.* 2011).

Job resources act as buffers that alleviate the influence of job demands on work motivation, emotions, and engagement. The demands of teaching may be universal and unavoidable, but the job resources that are provided – the internal and external supports, including autonomy, social support, coaching, and feedback – change the motivational and emotional responses to demands. Job resources can be fostered through careful attention to professional support groups, open communication from administrators, and opportunities for autonomy-building through professional development (e.g. Bakker *et al.* 2011). In the conceptual model, student achievement emotions reciprocally influence teacher emotions and motivation, which in turn influence teachers' engagement, effectiveness, and eventually educational outcomes.

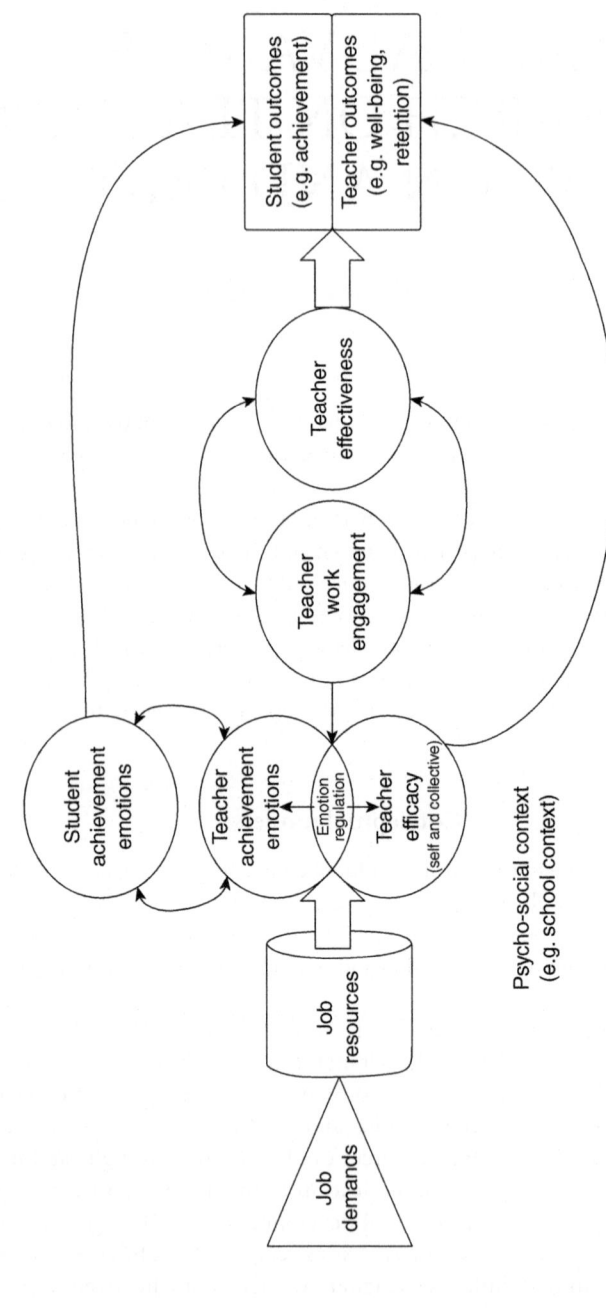

Figure 31.1 Jobs demands–resources model.

Research and findings

Teachers' self-efficacy

Teacher self-efficacy – a teacher's beliefs in the capability to influence student outcomes – continues to attract research attention because it is associated with positive outcomes to a degree that other teacher variables, such as personality, fail to achieve. Klassen and Tze (2014) conducted a meta-analysis of 43 studies representing 9,216 participants, investigating the link between teachers' psychological characteristics and externally measured teaching effectiveness. The overall effect size for the relationship between teachers' psychological characteristics (self-efficacy and personality) and teaching effectiveness was significant but small ($r = .10$, equivalent to Cohen's d of .21). However, the relationship between teachers' self-efficacy and observed teaching performance was much stronger ($r = .28$, equivalent to Cohen's d of .58). As evidence has continued to build about how teacher efficacy is associated with teaching and learning, some new areas of focus are emerging.

Teachers' collective efficacy

Teaching is a collaborative endeavor, in spite of traditions of teacher autonomy symbolized by closed classroom doors (Hargreaves and Fullan 2012). Collaborating with colleagues is crucial in almost all professions – and teaching is no exception – but observation of teachers' practice shows us that collaboration is not always embraced by teachers, nor is it a guarantee of effective practice. The advantages of collaborating with colleagues are multiplied by building *collective efficacy*; that is, the beliefs in the capabilities to accomplish valued goals by working collectively (Bandura 1997). Important educational outcomes are influenced by the degree to which teachers develop and nurture their collective efficacy.

Why has research investigating teachers' collective efficacy grown more slowly than research exploring teachers' self-efficacy? Part of the answer lies in educational psychology's reliance on individual constructs at the expense of conceptions of communal conceptions of selfhood (Martin 2007). Psychology in general has emphasized the study of individual human behavior, but the consequences of the focus on individuals' results is a poorer understanding of 'self-in-relation-to-others' that characterizes most social contexts.

The study of teachers' psychological characteristics – motivation and emotions   has begun to dip into collaborative contexts. Three studies in diverse contexts underscored the importance of teachers' collective efficacy. In Canada, a recent study examined how teachers' professional development activities influenced teachers' self- and collective efficacy (Durksen and Klassen 2013). With data collected from more than 800 teachers over a two-year period, the authors found that teachers' self-efficacy was strongly influenced by teacher-initiated or self-selected professional development opportunities. Collective efficacy beliefs were most influenced by collaborative activities in the form of discussion groups, networking, or through collaborative projects. Traditional conference-type professional development had little effect on either self- or collective efficacy, whereas collaborative and teacher-directed activities had a strong effect.

In Norway, Sørlie and Torsheim (2011) used a two-wave longitudinal study to examine how collective efficacy was related to teacher perceptions of problem behaviors over time. Time 1 school-level collective efficacy predicted severe and less severe problem behaviors at Time 2 (6 months later), with a reciprocal relationship whereby problem behaviors at Time 1 also predicted Time 2 collective efficacy. Promoting perceptions of collective capability in schools was suggested as an important way to positively influence school culture and lessen the negative influence of problem student behaviors. The authors further recommended additional longitudinal studies focused on interventions aimed at raising teachers' collective efficacy beliefs.

In the United Kingdom, Gibbs and Powell (2011) investigated the relationship between teachers' self-efficacy, collective efficacy, and the rate of student expulsion. The authors found that none of the teacher self-efficacy variables was related to expulsion rate, but teachers' collective efficacy was significantly (inversely) related to the number of students excluded during the school year. These two studies suggest that teachers' collective efficacy is associated with school-wide student behavior patterns. Professional development programs that target building school-level efficacy beliefs, rather than teachers' individual beliefs, may provide a productive way to address whole-school student behavior issues.

Recent research has examined cultural influences on teacher motivation. Klassen *et al.* (2008) examined the collective efficacy and job satisfaction of teachers in Canada and Singapore, finding that collective efficacy was a stronger predictor of positive educational outcomes than individual efficacy in both settings. In a subsequent study, Klassen *et al.* (2010) tested the relationship between collective efficacy, job satisfaction, and cultural beliefs (i.e. collectivism) in teachers in Canada, Korea, and the United States. The results of the study showed that teachers' collective efficacy was positively related to job satisfaction across all settings, but that teachers' collectivism beliefs were more strongly associated with job satisfaction for Korean teachers than for North American teachers. Comparative research conducted in additional cultural settings would help clarify the conditions and processes by which cultural values interact with individual and group-oriented motivation.

Developmental trends in teacher motivation

Anyone who has spent time in a workplace for an extended period knows that motivation and emotions fluctuate over time. Teaching is no exception, and teachers' motivation can change as demands increase and energy wanes. Cognitive and emotional responses to student behavior, policy changes, and the daily demands inherent in the act of teaching evolve and change as careers progress (Huberman 1989). According to Huberman, the typical reaction of novice teachers to early classroom experiences combines feelings of survival ('Can I actually do this job?') with discovery ('I really love/hate this job'). However, teachers in later career phases experience the classroom very differently, with end-of-career stages characterized by a gradual disengagement, marked either by serenity, or less optimally, by bitterness (Huberman 1989).

The cognitive and emotional states experienced by teachers may be influenced by career stage, but much of the research on teachers' emotional and motivational states has tended to ignore the age and career stage of respondents, or to focus primarily on teachers at the beginning stages of their careers (e.g. Richardson *et al.* 2013). Recent research has been built on Huberman's work, with Day and Gu (2010) finding that a majority of teachers in mid-career (i.e. 8–23 years of teaching) experience increases in motivation and commitment (i.e. psychological attachment to their profession), whereas teachers in later career stages (24-plus years of experience) report declining levels of motivation (i.e. feeling disenchanted, fatigued, trapped). Career stage investigations of teachers' motivation and emotions have not yet adequately explained differences in teachers' experiences as careers progress.

Interestingly, research into age-related changes in the workplace is more established outside of education, with the suggestion that age interacts with emotional and motivational states over the course of a career (Kooij *et al.* 2008). However, it is not clear how and why these changes occur. Kooij *et al.* found that certain age-related factors (i.e. chronological age, physical health, self-perception, social perception, skill obsolescence, and life stage) played a negative role in the motivation beliefs of older workers, and that motivation and emotions were influenced by an interaction of age-related psychosocial factors.

Although physical and mental health-related declines may be associated with a deterioration of one's self-concept or lead to changes in weighting of work- and leisure-related values, peers' stereotyped perceptions of aging may play a role in lowering affect, reducing skills, motivation, and opportunities for promotion. Lower levels of older teachers' motivation beliefs may be influenced not only by biological and psychological changes related to chronological age, but by student and peer perceptions of declining competence influenced by stereotyped beliefs about aging. An important consideration when researching teachers' age-related changes in motivation and emotions is that observed changes may be influenced not only by chronological age, but by the psychosocial environments in schools.

Particular focus has been paid to changes in teachers' self-efficacy over time. Bandura (1997) hypothesized that self-efficacy remains relatively stable once established, but teacher efficacy is also influenced by the passage of time, just as the motivation of workers in other fields changes over the career span. Research examining the relationship between teaching experience and teachers' self-efficacy has been rare and has yielded mixed results. Wolters and Daugherty (2007) found modest positive effects of experience on self-efficacy for instructional strategies and self-efficacy for classroom management, but no effect of experience on self-efficacy for student engagement. Knoblauch and Woolfolk Hoy (2008) found that self-efficacy increased for novice teachers in rural, suburban, and urban settings. Most of the research, however, has focused on motivational differences of teachers in training or in the early stages of their career, with no attempt to understand motivation changes in teachers with greater than 10 years of experience.

The self-efficacy of preservice teachers changes rapidly during the teaching practicum. Klassen and Durksen (2014) examined the patterns of 150 preservice teachers' self-efficacy and stress over eight weeks during a final teaching practicum and analyzed the data using latent growth curve analysis coupled with qualitative analysis of multiple collective cases. The results revealed a pattern of significantly increasing self-efficacy and significantly decreasing stress, although the trajectories were independent of each other. Qualitative analysis of multiple collective cases highlighted the variability of self-efficacy and stress patterns within the practicum experience, and underscored the critical influence of relationships with mentor teachers on self-efficacy and stress. The findings revealed how context and individual variations interact to influence perceptions of motivation (self-efficacy) and emotions (stress) for people going through the same experience, but whose cognitive processing of the experience results in notable differences and outcomes.

Research on teachers' emotions

Many people recall experiences of strong emotions in classroom settings, either as students or teachers. Teaching is an emotional act, with a great range of positive and negative emotions experienced (and sometimes expressed) by teachers, often leading to strong emotions in students. Teachers experience the whole range of emotions – joy, fear/anxiety, anger, sadness, disgust, and surprise – during the teaching day, but research investigating how teachers experience, express, and regulate these emotions has been relatively rare. Research on teacher emotions has increased in the last decade, adding to the emphasis on teacher burnout conducted in the 1980s (e.g. Kyriacou 1987), recently reviewed by Chang (2009), who proposed a renewed emphasis on antecedents of burnout and a greater focus on emotion regulation. Earlier work on teachers' emotions focused on relatively simple models of burnout, but the recent surge in research represents a more complex and contextualized view of emotions emerging from stronger explanatory frameworks. Recent developments investigating the transmission of emotions from teacher to student provide a pathway to influence student outcomes through teacher emotional states and behaviors.

Recent teacher emotions research has focused on enjoyment, anger, anxiety, and enthusiasm in the classroom. Frenzel *et al.* (2009a) conceptualized teachers' emotions as achievement emotions that result from judgments of perceived success or failure in relation to perceptions of attainment of teaching goals. Frenzel and colleagues focused particularly on three emotions – enjoyment, anger, and anxiety – that are most experienced in daily life and equally prominent in teacher emotion research. They found that enjoyment was experienced more often than either anger or anxiety, and primary school teachers experienced higher mean levels of enjoyment than teachers in secondary schools. Emotions experienced during teaching can be potent influences on the effectiveness of instruction, especially when the emotions are repeatedly experienced.

Emotions can be transmitted from teacher to student. Frenzel *et al.* (2009b) examined the ways in which the enjoyment teachers experience while teaching mathematics is related to the enjoyment students experience in the mathematics class. Working within a social cognitive framework, the authors suggested a social perception model in which teachers communicate value and enjoyment of tasks through teaching enthusiasm, but also through implicit hints about motivational orientation. The researchers studied emotions transmission using a sample of early adolescent mathematics students, and observed that teacher enthusiasm was mediated by the relationship between teacher and student enjoyment. This suggests that teachers' expressed emotions make a difference in student emotional experiences. But emotions are complex: teacher enthusiasm may not operate as a unidimensional construct. Kunter *et al.* (2011) tested the dimensionality and context specificity of teacher enthusiasm, and found two dimensions – enthusiasm for teaching and enthusiasm for the subject – that varied according to contextual classroom variables. Importantly, teaching enthusiasm may be a better predictor of teaching success than subject enthusiasm (Kunter *et al.*).

Teacher engagement

Researchers are beginning to study how teacher engagement develops and is fostered in diverse school settings. Defined as a 'positive, fulfilling, work-related state of mind that is characterized by vigor, dedication, and absorption' (Schaufeli *et al.* 2006: 702), work engagement emerged as an important research focus in general workplace settings over the past decade. Engaged workers devote energy, time, and effort to work tasks (the *vigor* component), view their work as significant and meaningful (the *dedication* component), and fully concentrate on tasks when at work (the *absorption* component).

Research conducted in schools shows that teachers who are engaged are more likely to display higher teaching performance (Bakker and Bal 2010) and to have students who are engaged in learning (Roth *et al.* 2007). Teachers with high levels of engagement are less prone to the health problems associated with burnout (Hakanen *et al.* 2006), thus linking level of engagement inversely with teacher attrition. Engaged teachers are less likely to quit the profession or to require costly support for health-related problems. Teachers' engagement is linked with productivity and workplace participation, meaning that engaged teachers are more likely to contribute to the life of the school and to take on additional duties beyond the classroom (Parker and Martin 2009).

Recent research has focused on contextualizing work engagement scales for use in school settings. The Utrecht Work Engagement Scale is the most frequently used measure of work engagement (Bakker *et al.* 2011); a recent cross-cultural validation study (Klassen *et al.* 2012) found the Utrecht scale was related to teachers' job satisfaction across five countries – Australia, Canada, China, Indonesia, and Oman – but that the three-factor structure of the measure was not invariant across settings. Shuck's recent review of work engagement (2011) concluded that the construct remains in a state of evolution, with disciplinary bridges needed between disparate communities of research. We questioned the fit of business-oriented work engagement models and measures in educational contexts, and responded by creating and testing the Engaged Teacher Scale (Klassen *et al.* 2013). This scale provides a valid measure of contextualized teacher (i.e. classroom) engagement, with the four dimensions of cognitive, emotional, and social engagement (with students and teachers) forming teachers' overall engagement.

The findings from our scale validation provide support for the reliability and validity of the scale. In particular, the item statistics and reliabilities of the scale were very good, and the four factors represented appropriate measures of the internal structure of teacher engagement. Furthermore, the psychometric analyses showed that the scale's factors are discrete, reliable, and valid. From a theoretical perspective, the findings showed that social engagement with students and with colleagues should be considered as important dimensions of teacher engagement, alongside cognitive and emotional dimensions of engagement.

Future directions

Researchers are increasingly interested in making the move from a theoretical understanding of constructs to practical application. We are gaining insight into how teacher motivation plays out in school settings, but we have not yet toiled very long in Pasteur's quadrant (Stokes 1997 – the space where fundamental understanding and application intersect (i.e. use-inspired basic research) – in a way that brings benefit to the education community and society at large. Much progress has been made in our understanding of teacher motivation and emotions in the past 20 years, but there is little evidence of effect on the field (Klassen *et al.* 2011). A multifaceted attempt to extend theory *and* provide guidance for enhancing teaching and learning is clearly needed.

The challenge inherent in making educational and psychological theories relevant to practice and practitioners is not new; even William James was able to offer only modest counsel to teachers regarding the application of psychology to teaching (Pajares 2003). The gap between teacher motivation research and practice may, in fact, be growing, as research designs grow more sophisticated yet more distant from the big problems of education, with many educational psychology researchers continuing to neglect how research findings relate to practice within the local setting, let alone in a global context. The next generation of teacher motivation research needs to address the 'really important problems' (Calfee 2006: 35) that exist in our schools and broader education communities.

Links between motivation and effectiveness

Researchers in education, psychology, and economics have begun to call for research linking teachers' motivation profiles to effective teaching (e.g. Klassen *et al.* 2012; Rimm-Kaufman and Hamre 2010). Teachers' motivational characteristics are related to occupational engagement, level of stress, and commitment to teaching (e.g. Klassen and Chiu 2011), and quality of relationships with students (Rimm-Kaufman and Hamre 2010). Borman *et al.* (2003) reviewed personnel selection research and recommended a research focus on motivation variables rather than personality variables be used in the selection process. Rimm-Kaufman and Hamre (2010) recommended research on how motivation predicts teachers' day-to-day engagement and teaching quality. Rockoff *et al.* (2008) noted that motivation variables such as self-efficacy were more strongly related to teacher quality than personality traits – a finding replicated in a recent meta-analysis. The strength of relationship between teacher characteristics and teaching effectiveness may prove useful for practical applications of motivation research.

Practical application of teacher motivation and emotions research

One project we are currently pursuing that applies theory to practice is using motivation and emotion theories to help select the best possible candidates for teacher training. Two arguments can be made regarding the selection of teachers and teacher training candidates. First, a strong case can be made that the effectiveness of teachers varies widely within cohorts entering the profession (Rockoff 2004). Although most novice teachers tend to show marked increases in effectiveness over the first years of their careers, their *relative* effectiveness (i.e. in relation to other teachers in their cohort) tends to be stable (Atteberry *et al.* 2013). Selecting initial teacher training candidates who will develop into the best teachers is socially and economically important, because the most effective teachers tend to remain in the top rank throughout their careers, and less effective teachers tend to remain less effective, relative to their peers, throughout their careers (Atteberry *et al.*).

The second and more contentious argument – that effective teachers might share common psychological characteristics – is borrowed from a long history of research in vocational psychology on the links between personality and effective workplace behavior. A comprehensive review published by Barrick *et al.* (2001) showed a reliable relationship between *some* personality characteristics, especially conscientiousness, and specific workplace performance criteria. However, much less research has been conducted on the topic in education settings. Rimm-Kaufman and Hamre (2010) rued the lack of attention in educational research paid to connections between recent personality theoretical frameworks such as the Big Five framework and teaching effectiveness, and emphasized the need for an application of psychological science to answering the question of variability in teachers' behavior and interactions with pupils. Recent attention paid to the psychological characteristics of teacher trainees is based on the notion that teachers have an important influence on student outcomes, that there is considerable between-teacher variation in the degree of that influence, that noncognitive attributes matter for effective teaching, and that noncognitive attributes can be reliably measured.

Can motivation research be used for teacher selection?

We propose that teacher motivation and emotion research can be applied to teacher selection practices. Psychological attributes have recently been highlighted as an area of particular importance in the selection of teacher candidates in the United Kingdom: the House of Commons Education Committee (2012) has indicated that a formal assessment of psychological attributes should be one of the criteria to select candidates for initial teacher training. Currently available noncognitive assessment instruments are based on existing vocational personality measures that have been adapted for initial teacher training selection, and are claimed to be relevant for the selection of such candidates; however, the evidence base for the predictive validity of the commercial measures for use in education is lacking.

We are currently designing and testing ways to measure important psychological attributes, including motivation and emotions, of prospective teachers. Our current project is using *situational judgment tests* to evaluate psychological attributes for selection of teachers (Klassen *et al.* 2014). The choice of such tests for selection is because of the effectiveness of the method for predicting future job performance in other domains (e.g. Patterson *et al.* 2013). Situational judgment tests have been shown to be better predictors of job performance than conventional personality tests (e.g. Shultz and Zedeck 2012). In addition, situational judgment tests tend to display stronger face and content validity than conventional psychological measures due to their close correspondence to the work-related situations that they describe (Whetzel and McDaniel 2009).

Situational judgment tests tap an applicant's procedural knowledge about context-specific situations, and are based on the notion that situation-specific judgments and responses reflect implicit personality traits that have a causal effect on job performance. A theoretical foundation for such tests can be found in concept of Motowildlo *et al.* (2006) of *implicit trait policy*, which proposes that we can gain insight into personality traits implicitly, by asking an individual to judge the effectiveness of responses to situations designed to elicit targeted traits. In contrast, conventional personality tests ask individuals to describe themselves (e.g. 'Are you good at encouraging others?'), allowing for the likelihood that candidates will choose responses that portray their personality in the best possible light, but possibly inaccurately.

Situational judgment tests can be built using a bottom-up approach (i.e. from job analysis of teachers) and top-down (theory-driven) approaches which build on research on teacher motivation and emotions. By testing procedural knowledge and implicit knowledge rather than self-reported behavioral tendencies, situational judgment tests avoid the same level of social desirability bias inherent in other psychological assessments. Situational judgment tests can be considered a measurement method, and as such can be designed to capture noncognitive domains – such as teacher emotions, resilience, professional integrity, and empathy – derived from a careful job analysis of workplace demands. A meta-analysis by McDaniel and Nguyen (2001) found situational judgment tests to be significantly related to measures of psychological attributes, especially emotional stability, agreeableness, and conscientiousness. Furthermore, test competence domains can be created through top-down (deductive) or bottom-up (inductive) approaches, resulting in a test with practical and theoretical rigor. A bottom-up approach to establishing competency domains could be carried out through a job analysis of teaching activities; a top-down approach could involve operationalizing relevant theories that have been posited to explain effective teaching practices.

Conclusions

Recent research investigating teachers' motivation and emotions has made considerable progress in building a fundamental understanding of the inner lives of teachers, but the field has yet to have a strong effect on practice and policy. As much as researchers have perhaps rightfully avoided the 'motivation-in-a-kit' approach to applying simple solutions to complex situations, the field needs to begin to provide answers – not just insight – into the important problems noted by Calfee (2006). To remain a vital and valued research quest, those who conduct research in teachers' motivation and emotions must make at least cautious forays into applying the theoretical and empirical knowledge that has been gained in the last decades.

References

Atteberry, A., Loeb, S. and Wyckoff, J. (2013) 'Do first impressions matter? Improvement in early career teacher effectiveness', National Center for the Analysis of Longitudinal Data in Education Research (Calder) working paper 90, Washington, DC: American Institutes for Research. Available at www.caldercenter.org

Bakker, A.B., Albrecht, S.L. and Leiter, M.P. (2011) 'Key questions regarding work engagement', *European Journal of Work and Organizational Psychology,* 20: 4–28. Available at http://dx.doi.org/10.1080/13594 32X.2010.485352

Bakker, A.B. and Bal, P.M. (2010) 'Weekly work engagement and performance: a study among starting teachers', *Journal of Occupational and Organizational Psychology,* 83: 189–206. doi:10.1348/096317909X402596

Bandura, A. (1997) *Self-efficacy: The Exercise of Control,* New York: Freeman.

Barrick, M.R., Mount, M.K. and Judge, T.A. (2001) 'Personality and performance at the beginning of the new millennium: what do we know and where do we go next?', *International Journal of Selection and Assessment,* 9: 9–30. doi: 10.1111/1468–2389.00160

Borman, W.C., Hedge, J.W., Ferstl, K.L., Kaufman, J.D., Farmer, W.L. and Bearden, R.M. (2003) 'Current directions and issues in personnel selection and classification', *Research in Personnel and Human Resources Management,* 22: 287–355. doi:10.1016/S0742–7301(03)22007–7

Calfee, R. (2006) 'Educational psychology in the 21st century', in P.A. Alexander and P.H. Winne (eds) *Handbook of Educational Psychology,* 2nd edn (pp. 29–42), Mahwah, NJ: Lawrence Erlbaum.

Chang, M.-L. (2009) 'An appraisal perspective of teacher burnout: examining the emotional work of teachers', *Educational Psychology Review,* 21: 193–218. doi: 10.1007/s10648–009–9106–y

Day, C. and Gu, Q. (2010) *The New Lives of Teachers,* New York: Taylor & Francis.

Durksen, T.L. and Klassen, R.M. (2012) 'Pre-service teachers' weekly commitment and engagement during a final practicum: a longitudinal mixed methods study', *Educational and Child Psychology,* 29: 32–46. Retrieved from http://www.bps.org.uk/content/educational-child-psychology-vol-29-no-4-december-2012–teachers-well-being

Durksen, T.L. and Klassen, R.M. (2013, April) 'From isolation to inspiration: the development of self- and collective efficacy through teachers' professional learning activities', paper presented at the annual American Educational Research Association conference, San Francisco, CA.

Frenzel, A.C., Goetz, T., Lüdtke, O., Pekrun, R. and Sutton, R.E. (2009b) 'Emotional transmission in the classroom: exploring the relationship between teacher and student enjoyment', *Journal of Educational Psychology,* 101: 705–716. doi:10.1037/a0014695

Frenzel, A.C., Goetz, T., Stephens, E.J. and Jacob, B. (2009a) 'Antecedents and effects of teachers' emotional experiences: an integrated perspective and empirical test', in P.A. Schutz and M. Zembylas (eds) *Advances in Teacher Emotion Research* (pp. 129–151), Dordrecht: Springer.

Gibbs, S. and Powell, B. (2011) 'Teacher efficacy and pupil behaviour: the structure of teachers' individual and collective beliefs and their relationship with numbers of pupils excluded from school', *British Journal of Educational Psychology,* 82: 564–584. doi:10.1111/j.2044–8279.2011.02046.x

Hakanen, J.J., Bakker, A.B. and Schaufeli, W.B. (2006) 'Burnout and work engagement among teachers', *Journal of School Psychology,* 43: 495–513. doi:10.1016/j.jsp.2005.11.001

Hargreaves, A. and Fullan, M. (2012) *Professional Capital,* New York: Teachers College.

House of Commons Education Committee (2012) *Great Teachers: Attracting, Training and Retaining the Best: Government Response to the Committee's Ninth Report of Session 2010–2012,* London: House of Commons.

Huberman, M. (1989) 'The professional life cycle of teachers', *Teachers College Record,* 91: 31– 57. Available from http://www.tcrecord.org

Klassen, R.M., Al-Dhafri, S., Mansfield, C.F., Purwanto, E., Siu, A., Wong, M.W. and Woods-McConney, A. (2012) 'Teachers' engagement at work: an international validation study', *Journal of Experimental Education,* 80: 1–20. doi: 10.1080/00220973.2012.678409

Klassen, R.M. and Chiu, M.M. (2011) 'The occupational commitment of experienced and novice teachers: influence of self-efficacy, job stress, and teaching context', *Contemporary Educational Psychology,* 36: 114–129. doi: 10.1016/j.cedpsych.2011.01.002

Klassen, R.M., Chong, W.H., Huan, V.S., Wong, I., Kates, A. and Hannok, W. (2008) 'Motivation beliefs of secondary school teachers in Canada and Singapore: a mixed methods study', *Teaching and Teacher Education,* 24: 1919–1934. doi:10.1016/j.tate.2008.01.005

Klassen, R.M. and Durksen, T.L. (2014) 'Weekly self-efficacy and work stress during the final teaching practicum: a mixed methods study', *Learning and Instruction,* 33: 158–169. Retrieved from http://dx.doi.org/10.1016/j.learninstruc.2014.05.003

Klassen, R.M. and Tze, V.M.C. (2014) 'Teachers' self-efficacy, personality, and teaching effectiveness: a meta-analysis', *Educational Research Review,* 12: 59–76. Retrieved from http://dx.doi.org/10.1016/j.edurev.2014.06.001, UK.

Klassen, R.M., Durksen, T.L., Rowett, E. and Patterson, F. (2014) 'Applicant reactions to a Situational Judgment Test used for selection into Initial Teacher Training', *International Journal of Educational Psychology,* 3: 104–125. Retrieved from http://www.hipatiapress.com/hpjournals/index.php/ijep

Klassen, R.M., Tze, V.M.C., Betts, S.M. and Gordon, K.A. (2011) Teacher efficacy research 1998–2009: signs of progress or unfulfilled promised?', *Educational Psychology Review,* 23: 21–43. doi: 10.1007/s10648–010–9141–8

Klassen, R.M., Usher, E.L. and Bong, M. (2010) 'Teachers' collective efficacy, job satisfaction, and job stress in cross-cultural context', *Journal of Experimental Education,* 78: 464–486. doi:10.1080/00220970903292975

Klassen, R.M., Yerdelen, S. and Durksen, T.L. (2013) 'Measuring teacher engagement: the development of the Engaged Teacher Scale (ETS)', *Frontline Learning Research,* 1: 33–52. Retrieved from http://journals.sfu.ca/flr/index.php/journal/article/view/44/37

Knoblauch, D. and Woolfolk Hoy, A. (2008) '"Maybe I can teach *those* kids": the influence of contextual factors on student teachers' efficacy beliefs', *Teaching and Teacher Education*, 24: 166–179. doi:10.1016/j.tate.2007.05.005

Kooij, D., de Lange, A., Jansen, P. and Dikkers, J. (2008) 'Older workers' motivation to continue to work: five meanings of age', *Journal of Managerial Psychology*, 23: 364–394. doi: 10.1108/02683940810869015

Kunter, M., Frenzel, A., Nagy, G., Baumert, J. and Pekrun, R. (2011) 'Teacher enthusiasm: dimensionality and context specificity', *Contemporary Educational Psychology*, 36: 289–301. doi:10.1016/j.cedpsych.2011.07.001

Kyriacou, C. (1987) 'Teacher stress and burnout: an international review', *Educational Research*, 29: 146–152. doi: 10.1080/0013188870290207

Martin, J. (2007) 'The selves of educational psychology: conceptions, contexts, and critical considerations', *Educational Psychologist*, 42: 79–89. doi: 10.1080/00461520701263244

McDaniel, M.A. and Nguyen, N.T. (2001) 'Situational judgment tests: a review of practice and constructs assessed', *International Journal of Selection and Assessment*, 9: 103–113. doi: 10.1111/1468–2389.00167

Motowildlo, S.J., Hooper, A.C. and Jackson, H.L. (2006) 'A theoretical basis for situational judgment tests', in J.A. Weekley and R.E. Ployhart (eds) '*Situational Judgment Tests: Theory, Measurement and Application* (pp. 57–81), Mahwah, NJ: Lawrence Erlbaum Associates.

Pajares, F. (2003) 'William James: our father who begat us', in B.J. Zimmerman and D.H. Schunk (eds) *Educational Psychology: A Century of Contributions* (pp. 41–64), Mahwah, NJ: Erlbaum.

Parker, P. D. and Martin, A.J. (2009). Coping and buoyancy in the workplace: understanding their effects on teachers' work-related well-being and engagement. *Teaching and Teacher Education*, 25: 68–75.

Patterson, F., Lievens, F., Kerrin, M., Munro, N., and Irish, B. (2013) 'The predictive validity of selection for entry into postgraduate training in general practice: evidence from three longitudinal studies', *British Journal of General Practice*, 63: e734–e741. doi: 10.3399/bjgp13X667196

Richardson, P.W., Watt, H.M.G. and Devos, C. (2013) 'Types of professional and emotional coping among beginning teachers', in M. Newberry, A. Gallant and P. Riley (eds) *Advances in Research on Teaching*, (pp. 229–253), Bingley, UK: Emerald.

Rimm-Kaufman, S.E. and Hamre, B.K. (2010) 'The role of psychological and developmental science in efforts to improve teacher quality', *Teachers College Record*, 112: 2988–3023. Available from http://www.tcrecord.org

Rockoff, J. E. (2004) 'The impact of individual teachers on student achievement: evidence from panel data', *AEA Papers and Proceedings*, 94: 247–252.

Rockoff, J.E., Jacob, B.A., Kane, T.J. and Staiger, D.O. (2008) 'Can you recognize an effective teacher when you recruit one?', National Bureau of Economic Research Working Paper 14485, Cambridge, MA: NBER.

Roth, G., Assor, A., Kanat-Maymon, Y. and Kaplan, H. (2007) 'Autonomous motivation for teaching: how self-determined teaching may lead to self-determined learning', *Journal of Educational Psychology*, 99: 761–774. doi: 10.1037/0022–0663.99.4.761

Schaufeli, W.B., Bakker, A.B., and Salanova, M. (2006) 'The measurement of work engagement with a short questionnaire', *Educational and Psychological Measurement*, 66: 701–716. doi: 0.1177/0013164405282471

Shuck, M.B. (2011) 'Four emerging perspectives of employee engagement: an integrative literature review', *Human Resource Development Review*, 10: 304–328. doi:10.1177/1534484311410840

Shultz, M.M. and Zedeck, S. (2012) 'Admission to law school: new measures', *Educational Psychologist*, 47: 51–65. doi: 10.1080/00461520.2011.610679

Sørlie, M-A. and Torsheim, T. (2011) 'Multilevel analysis of the relationship between teacher collective efficacy and problem behaviour in school', *School Effectiveness and School Improvement: An International Journal of Research, Policy and Practice*, 22: 175–191. doi: 10.1080/09243453.2011.563074

Stokes, D. E. (1997) *Pasteur's Quadrant: Basic Science and Technological Innovation*, Washington, DC: The Brookings Institute.

Wheatley, K.F. (2005) 'The case for reconceptualizing teacher efficacy research', *Teaching and Teacher Education*, 21: 747–766. doi:10.1016/j.tate.2005.05.009

Whetzel, D.L. and McDaniel, M.A. (2009) 'Situational judgment tests: an overview of current research', *Human Resource Management Review*, 19: 188–202. doi:10.1016/j.hrmr.2009.03.007

Wolters, C.A. and Daugherty, S.G. (2007) 'Goal structures and teachers' sense of efficacy: their relation and association to teaching experience and academic level', *Journal of Educational Psychology*, 99: 181–193. doi: 10.1037/0022–0663.99.1.181

32

TEACHER SELF-EFFICACY

A thriving area of research

Sindu George, Paul Richardson, and Jeffrey Dorman

Self-efficacy is a progressively active area of theory and research within several disciplines. Literature suggests that self-efficacy is securely situated within the psychological branch of social psychology, with two lines of development: motivational theories that conceptualize self-efficacy in motivational terms; and cognitive theories which conceptualize self-efficacy in terms of expectancies and perceptions of control (Gecas 1989). At the same time, Gecas points out that self-efficacy is increasingly prominent within the sociological branch of social psychology, which interprets and explains how different social phenomena influence people and how people interact with others. Researchers agree that the effect of self on society is the most important connection within social psychology (Coleman 1986; Turner 1988), which assumes that the interaction between the individual and the situation plays a decisive role on the behavioral outcome. This dynamic interaction among personal factors (cognitive, affective, and biological events), environmental factors, and behavior is the key concept of Bandura's (1989) social cognitive theory, within which the construct of self-efficacy was developed.

Self-efficacy: The cornerstone of social cognitive theory

Since Bandura introduced the concept of self-efficacy[1] more than thirty years ago as an important factor in human motivation, many researchers have focused on the role of self-efficacy in human agency. Self-efficacy is not just the ability to make choice and action plans, but the ability to give shape to appropriate courses of action and the ability to initiate and regulate these actions (Bandura 2006). The definition of self-efficacy as people's beliefs about their abilities to produce designated levels of performance that has significant influence over their lives (Bandura 1994) reflects the important role of self-efficacy in human agency.

According to Bandura's social cognitive theory (1986, 1989) the self-referent thought of an individual acts as a mediator between her or his knowledge and actions, and individuals often evaluate their own experiences and thought processes through self-reflection. Pajares (1996) argues that Bandura views people as self-organizing, proactive, self-reflecting, and self-regulating rather than as reactive organisms. From this perspective, human functioning can be explained as the product of a dynamic interaction between personal, behavioral, and environmental influences. In other words, how people interpret the results of their own behavior will inform and alter their self-beliefs, as well as their environment, which in turn will alter their subsequent behavior. This is the foundation of Bandura's (1986) concept of *reciprocal determinism*, in which behavior, personal factors, and environmental factors generate interactions resulting in a *triadic reciprocality*.

Bandura's social cognitive model considers self-reflection as a unique human capability through which an individual evaluates and alters her or his behavior as well as her or his perceptions of self-efficacy. Bandura (1997: 3) defined self-efficacy as an 'individual's confidence in her or his ability to organize and execute a course of action to solve a problem or accomplish a task'. He suggested that some people have a strong sense of self-efficacy and others do not; some have self-efficacy that covers many situations, whereas others have narrow self-efficacy; and some believe they have high self-efficacy to do the most difficult task, while others do not. Bandura's key contention regarding the role of self-efficacy beliefs in human functioning is that individuals' motivation to carry out a particular task and their actions may be based on what they believe they can do, rather than their real ability.

Accordingly, individuals' behavior can often be better predicted by the beliefs they hold about their capabilities than by what they actually are capable of accomplishing. Thus, Bandura concludes that self-efficacy perceptions can help to determine what individuals do with the knowledge and skills they have. He also acknowledges that beliefs and reality are seldom perfectly matched, and individuals are typically guided by their beliefs as they engage with the world around them. As a consequence, people's accomplishments are generally better predicted by their self-efficacy beliefs than by their previous achievements, knowledge, or skills (Bandura 1997).

Bandura (1994, 1997) has proposed four main sources of self-efficacy beliefs: (1) mastery experiences; (2) vicarious experiences; (3) social persuasion; and (4) emotional states. He considers mastery experiences as the most effective way of creating a strong sense of efficacy. Vicarious experiences provided by social models also generate and strengthen self-efficacy beliefs. As such, individuals who observe people similar to themselves succeeding will have an enhanced level of belief that they too are capable of achieving. At the same time, there is a reciprocal effect: observing others' failure may lower the judgment of one's own capabilities. A third source of self-efficacy is social persuasion. Although it is true that positive appraisals are helpful in building confidence to engage in activities and achieve success, there is a possibility of unrealistic boosting of self-efficacy, which will be undermined once confronted with failure. The fourth antecedent to self-efficacy is one's own emotional state, so that stress, tension, and mood also affect one's judgment of self-efficacy. Bandura proposes that it may not be the intensity of the emotional reactions that counts, but the way it is perceived and interpreted. He suggests that reducing one's stress and changing one's negative emotional tendencies will result in improved self-efficacy.

This general model of self-efficacy is highly relevant to teachers. Extensive research supports the claim that self-efficacy has an important influence on human achievement in a variety of settings, including educational achievement (Pajares and Miller 1994; Ross 1992; Skaalvik and Skaalvik 2007; Tschannen-Moran and Woolfolk Hoy 2001). Pintrich and Schunk (1995) pointed out that the attention the construct has received in the field of educational research was mainly in motivation studies. In an extensive review, Pajares (1997) classified self-efficacy research in education into three categories: (1) research exploring the link between self-efficacy and career choice (e.g. Lent and Hackett 1987); (2) research exploring the link between teacher self-efficacy and their classroom behaviors and various student outcomes (e.g. Ashton and Webb 1986); and (3) exploration of the association between students' self-efficacy and other motivation constructs such as goals, as well as their academic performance and achievement.

Teacher self-efficacy

Research on teacher self-efficacy dates back to the studies carried out by the RAND organization in 1970s (Tschannen-Moran *et al.* 1998), and a remarkable growth of teacher self-efficacy research has occurred since Bandura published his influential work, 'Self-efficacy: Toward a Unifying Theory of Behavioral Change' (1977). Teacher self-efficacy researchers since the early 1980s claimed to 'develop a potentially powerful paradigm, on the basis of the construct of teacher self-efficacy' (Ashton 1984: 28). It was Tschannen-Moran et al. (1998) who emphasized the context-specific nature of teacher self-efficacy, in accordance with Bandura's theory, putting forward an integrated model of teacher self-efficacy. They proposed that teachers would not feel equally efficacious in all teaching situations and in relation to all aspects of their role. For instance, one may feel efficacious teaching a particular subject or teaching a particular group of students, and one may feel more or less efficacious under different circumstances such as using a new method for teaching instead of the traditional method. Thus, Tschannen-Moran and Woolfolk Hoy argued that when judging teachers' self-efficacy, it is necessary to consider two broad dimensions; *teaching task and context*, which is related to the resources available to facilitate the learning process, and *personal competence*, which is related to the skills, knowledge, and personality traits of the individual (Tschannen-Moran et al. 1998). The interaction of these two dimensions results in a judgment about one's self-efficacy.

Many well-crafted studies have been conducted in the area of teacher self-efficacy with researchers interested in the practical application of their work. For example, Ross (1998) identified some links between teachers' self-efficacy and teachers' classroom behaviors, especially when using new approaches and strategies for teaching, promoting student autonomy, catering to the individual difference of students, and persisting in the face of student failures. Constructivist views of learning require a classroom environment that encourages students to become active, self-motivated, or mastery-oriented learners (Deemer 2004). Teachers' beliefs are important in creating such environments. For example, it has been reported that teachers with high self-efficacy beliefs are likely to adopt more student-centered approaches than teacher-centered approaches in classrooms (Swars 2005). A considerable amount of research demonstrates that teachers' self-efficacy is related to important educational outcomes such as student achievement and motivation (Caprara et al. 2006; Deemer 2008; Klassen and Chiu 2010; Labone 2004; Pajares 1996; Schunk 1991).

Teachers' self-efficacy beliefs have been found to be associated with their instructional behaviors (Holzberger et al. 2013; Morris-Rothschild and Brassard 2006; Wolters and Daugherty 2007); their well-being (Betoret 2006; Brouwers and Tomic 2000; Fernet et al. 2012); and their job satisfaction (Caprara et al. 2003; Collie et al. 2012; Moè et al. 2010; Skaalvik and Skaalvik 2007). It has been observed that teachers with higher self-efficacy provide more effective feedback, show openness to innovation, re-teach, and communicate effectively with different groups of students in the classroom (Emmer and Aussiker 1990; Emmer and Hickman 1991); exhibit greater levels of planning and enthusiasm (Allinder 1994); are more open to new ideas and more willing to experiment with innovative methods that meet the needs of the students (Cousins and Walker 1995); and persist in following up on students' wrong answers (Ashton and Webb 1986). In addition, it has been reported that teachers who expressed greater self-efficacy work longer with struggling students (Gibson and Dembo 1984); attend to the special needs of children by working with parents (Soodak and Podell 1993); and make less negative predictions about students (Tournaki and Podell 2005). As Woolfolk Hoy et al. (2009) point out, teachers' behaviors in the classroom, including planning, communication, monitoring, and interactions with students, are shaped in part by their self-efficacy. They suggest that self-efficacy of teachers would have direct, indirect, and relational consequences, although these are sometimes overlapping. Direct consequences include instructional decisions and actions; indirect consequences include verbal and nonverbal communications about expectation and motivation; and relational consequences include interpersonal and emotional dynamics of the classroom. Thus, it can be seen that research over the past thirty years has documented solid evidence supporting the relationship between teachers' self-efficacy and their behavioral outcomes.

Major issues in teacher self-efficacy research

Teacher self-efficacy, the confidence that teachers hold about their individual capabilities to influence student learning, is considered one of the key motivation beliefs influencing teachers' professional behaviors and student learning. In recent years, teacher self-efficacy research has been described as being 'on the verge of maturity' (Tschannen-Moran *et al*. 1998: 242) and 'ready to move beyond adolescent angst' (Henson 2002: 148). However, although the volume of teacher self-efficacy research has increased, it is widely accepted that questions remain about the direction, quality, and influence of this research (Klassen *et al*. 2011). Many critiques have highlighted issues that need attention for teacher self-efficacy research to attain maturity (Goddard *et al*. 2004; Henson 2002; Pajares 1997; Wheatley 2005), although it is unclear what effect these suggestions have had on the self-efficacy research (Klassen *et al*. 2011). The major areas of concern are summarized below.

Misinterpretation of the construct

There are other variables that share conceptual similarity with self-efficacy. Constructs such as teachers' self-efficacy, self-concept, and self-esteem are sometimes used interchangeably (Schunk and Pajares 2009). Self-concept is a multidimensional construct which refers to one's collective perceptions formed through experiences, and influenced by others' reinforcements and evaluations (Shavelson and Bolus 1982). Compared to self-efficacy, self-esteem is a more general affective evaluation of oneself and often includes the judgment of self-worth (Schunk and Pajares 2005). Bandura has stated that self-efficacy is a context assessment of competency to do something specific, which is a stronger predictor of behavior than self-concept or self-esteem. Similarly, it should be noted that ability beliefs refer to individuals' evaluations of their competence or ability (Wigfield and Eccles 2000), and is conceptually a different construct from self-efficacy. Schunk and Pajares (2009) also warn about the tendency to use self-confidence, a general capability belief, synonymously with self-efficacy. They observe that although self-confident people are often self-efficacious, there is no automatic relationship between these variables.

Measurement dilemmas

Klassen *et al*. (2011: 36) have argued that 'the use of conceptually troubled measures plagues teacher self-efficacy research', while others (Henson 2002; Pajares 1997; Zimmerman 1996) have called attention to the use of problematic measures in self-efficacy research. Klassen and colleagues reviewed 218 teacher self-efficacy studies conducted from 1998 to 2009 and found that over one-third of them used variations of the Gibson and Dembo (1984) Teacher Efficacy Scale. The major conceptual difficulty with this scale is that the focus of the questionnaire is on teachers' beliefs about their control of students' outcomes, rather than on their capabilities to effectively teach the students (Klassen *et al*. 2011). Beliefs about control of students' outcomes originated from the locus of control theories (Rotter 1966), not from the social cognitive theory. Gibson and Dembo's (1984) measure consists of two factors: *personal teaching efficacy* and *general teaching efficacy*. Henson *et al*. (2001) have pointed out that most of the items in the general teaching efficacy factor focus not on teachers' beliefs about capabilities, but on external constraints that can influence student outcomes. An example item is 'The amount a student can learn is primarily related to family background'. Henson and colleagues have questioned the construct validity of the general teaching efficacy subscale and have raised concerns regarding the continued use of this scale in the field. The issue of conceptual discrepancy is not only confined to the global measure, but is also there with domain-specific measures such as the Science Teaching Efficacy Belief Instruments - STEBI (Riggs and Enochs 1990), which is founded on Gibson and Dembo's Teacher Efficacy Scale.

There are many other scales used in self-efficacy research which are conceptually incongruent with Bandura's concept of self-efficacy. For example, Tournaki and Podell asked teachers to reflect on their past teaching experiences to assess their self-efficacy, rather than focusing on forward-looking capabilities. An example item is 'When a student does better than usual, many times it is because I exerted a little extra effort' (2005: 303). The review of self-efficacy studies by Klassen *et al.* (2011) reveals that out of the 218 studies conducted in self-efficacy research during 1998–2009, half used measures which were not congruent with Bandura's theory of self-efficacy, which raised concerns for Klassen and colleagues about the misleading conclusions that may be derived from these studies.

The use of global measures, which assess teachers' classroom self-efficacy as a single construct, has also been a cause for concern. Bandura cautioned researchers that 'self-efficacy belief should be measured in terms of particularized judgment of capability that may vary across realms of activity, different levels of task demands within a given activity domain, and under different situational circumstances' (1997: 6). Despite this explicit warning, there are self-efficacy measures, such as the Classroom and School Context Teacher Self-efficacy Scale (Friedman and Kass 2002), which assess teachers' classroom self-efficacy as a single construct. Although Bandura specifies the multifaceted and context-specific nature of self-efficacy, researchers have differed in defining an optimal level of specificity. Pajares (1997) instructs that development of domain specific self-efficacy measures should not be interpreted as development of self-efficacy measures with extreme situational specificity. Such a scenario would reduce efficacy assessment to atomistic proportions. He agrees with Lent and Hackett (1987) who maintain that micro-level assessment of self-efficacy results in loss of practical utility and external validity. Tschannen-Moran *et al.* (1998) also caution against developing extremely specific self-efficacy measures.

The Teacher Sense of Efficacy Scale (TSES) developed by Tschannen-Moran and Woolfolk Hoy (2001) is considered one of the most congruent measures with self-efficacy theory, and the most widely used measure in the field. The TSES includes three factors: self-efficacy for classroom management; self-efficacy for student engagement; and self-efficacy for instructional strategies. This scale addresses the two issues mentioned earlier: (a) context specificity, as the judgments are to be made based on specific outcomes; and (b) focus on capabilities to carry out a particular course of action. These researchers suggest that since in second-order factor analysis these three subscales form a single factor, these can be combined as a single measure (Tschannen-Moran and Woolfolk Hoy 2001: 801).

A recently developed measure of teachers' self-efficacy, the Teachers' Efficacy Belief System–Self Form (TEBS–Self) proposes that the existing measures of teacher efficacy do not reflect self-efficacy theory (Dellinger *et al.* 2008). These authors distinguish between *teacher efficacy* and *teacher self-efficacy beliefs*, arguing the need for measures of teachers' self-efficacy grounded in the context of classrooms. They defined teacher self-efficacy as 'teachers' individual beliefs in their capabilities to perform specific teaching tasks at a specified level of quality in a specified situation' (Dellinger *et al.* 2008: 752). The TEBS–Self scale has six components: communication/clarification; management/climate; accommodating individual differences; motivation of students; managing learning routines; and higher-order thinking skills.

Dominance of quantitative and cross-sectional studies

Klassen and colleagues (2011) compared the self-efficacy research conducted in two twelve-year periods: 1986–1997 and 1998–2009. They observe that there was an increase in the volume of published research during 1998–2009 with a total of 218 articles published (an average of 18.2 articles per year), while only 68 articles were published during the period 1986–1997, (an average of 5.7 articles per year). They also analyzed the diverse methodologies used in papers published during 1998–2009, and concluded that the majority of studies were quantitative. Klassen *et al.* also highlighted another methodological drawback: the dominance of cross-sectional research, which has delimited the scope of studies, especially in terms of warranting causal inference. They point out that of the 167 quantitative studies conducted during the years 1998–2009, only 19 studies (8.7 percent) were longitudinal (Klassen *et al.* 2011: 29), allowing researchers to gain insights into many issues such as changes in self-efficacy with experience.

Causal predominance of self-efficacy

Whether feeling confident about one's ability to perform a particular task is primarily responsible for the desired outcome or successful performance is largely responsible for stronger self-efficacy remains a thorny issue. Pajares (1997) observes that this 'chicken-or-egg' question, prevalent in self-concept studies, is relevant in self-efficacy research as well. There is a large volume of correlational studies in self-efficacy research, but these studies do not solve the problem of causal ordering. Pajares (1997) has suggested that because of the reciprocal nature of human behavior and motivation (Bandura 1986), it may be difficult to give a precise answer to such a question. However, it is possible to develop knowledge about the conditions under which self-efficacy beliefs operate as causal factors of human behavior. Marsh (1993: 76) offered 'a 2-wave, 2-variable design' as a possible solution to this question, emphasizing the need for longitudinal studies in the field. He suggested the following procedure: (a) infer the latent constructs on the basis of multiple indicators, using a large and diverse sample to justify the use of confirmatory factor analysis (CFA); (b) fit the data to a variety of CFA models that incorporate measurement error; and (c) test for likely residual covariation among measured variables.

Teacher self-efficacy: Stable or malleable?

Although Bandura (1997) proposed that self-efficacy, once established, will be relatively stable, researchers have noted that 'little evidence exists about how teachers' self-efficacy solidifies or changes across stages of a career' (Tschannen-Moran *et al.* 1998: 238). The number of studies on the relationship between teaching experience and self-efficacy is limited and the studies that have been conducted have yielded varied results. A study conducted by Ross *et al.* (1996) observed mixed results for the influence of teaching experience on teachers' self-efficacy, while a study by Ghaith and Yaghi (1997) revealed a negative correlation between experience and self-efficacy among teachers. A study by Woolfolk Hoy and Burke Spero (2005) investigated teachers' self-efficacy during the early years of teaching, showing a decline in self-efficacy through the first year of teaching. This longitudinal study collected data from teachers ($N = 29$) using four different self-efficacy measures at three time points; twice during their teacher training program, and once at the end of their first year of teaching. A significant rise of self-efficacy was reported during the teacher training program, followed by a decline at the end of their first year of teaching, which could be attributed to the conflict between the idealistic teaching conceptualization of novice teachers and the challenges of classroom teaching.

An online study (Wolters and Daugherty 2007) with a large sample of teachers ($N = 1,024$) from the United States examined the influence of teaching experience on teachers' self-efficacy. These researchers classified teachers into four groups based on years of teaching experience: <1 year, 1–5 years, 6–10 years, and 11–plus years of experience. They employed the Teachers' Sense of Efficacy Scale (Tschannen-Moran and Woolfolk Hoy 2001) and analyzed the influence of experience on self-efficacies for classroom management, instructional strategies and student engagement. A positive influence of teaching experience was observed for self-efficacies for classroom management and instructional strategies; in other words, teachers with more experience expressed higher levels of management and instructional efficacies than teachers with less teaching experience. However, there was no experience-related difference reported in the case of self-efficacy for student engagement, which the researchers highlight as an area for further exploration. In this study teachers with more than 11 years of experience were included under one group, resulting in a lack of differentiation among the most experienced teachers which 'may mask the changes in self-efficacy that may occur toward the end of the teachers' careers' (Wolters and Daugherty 2007: 189).

In a cross-sectional study of 1,430 teachers, Klassen and Chiu (2010) observed a nonlinear relationship between teachers' self-efficacies for classroom management, instructional strategies and student engagement, and years of teaching experience; there was a positive correlation between teachers' experience and their self-efficacy among teachers with experience from 0 to 23 years, and then a decline in self-efficacy as years of experience increased. To be more precise, the study revealed that teachers gain in confidence in their teaching skills through their early years and into the mid-career years, but these levels of confidence were found to decline as the teachers enter their late-career stage.[2] All three facets of self-efficacy followed the same pattern of increase and decrease, which was not reflected in the study conducted by Wolters and Daugherty (2007). Klassen and Chiu partially agree with Bandura's contention of the stable nature of self-efficacy by pointing out that this stability may be true only within a specific career stage. These diverse findings underscore the need for more longitudinal studies to investigate the effect of teaching experience on teachers' self-efficacy so as to arrive at a more general conclusion in relation to this much debated issue.

Outlook and future directions

It has been proposed that meaningful and engaging professional development opportunities are the most effective methods to enhance teachers' self-efficacy (Henson 2002). There have been efforts (e.g. Ross 1995) to increase teacher self-efficacy and to improve student achievement which have yielded mixed results, both regarding increasing teacher self-efficacy and the influence of increased self-efficacy on student achievement. Ross and Bruce (2007) designed a professional development program to increase the self-efficacy of mathematics teachers that explicitly addresses the four sources of teacher self-efficacy identified in Bandura's social cognitive theory: mastery experiences, vicarious experiences, social persuasion, and physiological and emotional states. Despite the fact that treatment teachers outperformed the control group teachers on the three components of self-efficacy (self-efficacy for instructional strategies, classroom management, and student engagement), results were statistically significant only for self-efficacy for classroom management. The researchers justify this finding by declaring that the professional development program gave priority to discussions related to management of classroom. It has been observed that self-efficacy is relatively more malleable in the beginning years of a teaching career when mastery experiences are the most effective sources of self-efficacy (Mulholland and Wallace 2001), and teachers' self-efficacy, once established, resists change even if teachers are exposed to workshops and new teaching methods (Ross 1995). Thus, professional development programs to enhance self-efficacy that are implemented in teachers' early career years might yield maximum results.

Two major issues in self-efficacy research are yet to be resolved: first the issue of causal ordering; and second, the malleability of self-efficacy. Longitudinal studies and the application of more sophisticated statistical techniques such as structural equation modeling are likely to assist in the resolution of these enduring issues.

Conclusion

Teacher efficacy is a self-perception, not an objective measure of teaching effectiveness, and it is hard to evaluate the extent to which teacher self-efficacy has an effect on the student outcomes. Although many studies have revealed that teachers with high efficacy beliefs generate stronger student achievement than teachers with lower teacher efficacy (see Woolfolk Hoy *et al.* 2009 for a review), the mechanisms through which teachers' self-efficacy beliefs might influence their actions and decisions are not investigated in detail. While researchers believe undoubtedly that teacher self-efficacy matters (Ross 1998), there are many unanswered questions such as when, how, and how much does it matter. Wheatley (2005: 759) observes that 'teachers' beliefs about their self-efficacy are not merely results of complex interpretations, but are themselves complex interpretations, and, teacher goals, beliefs about teachers, students, and teaching methods are often irreducible parts of teachers' self-efficacy belief'. Wheatley insists on the need to reconceptualize teacher self-efficacy research in order to be constructive and its practical fruits to be more obvious to teachers and teacher educators.

Self-efficacy researchers (e.g. Klassen *et al.* 2011; Wheatley 2005) call for a collaborative approach where expert teachers, novice teachers, and researchers work together to be aware of the issues in real classroom teaching, and to identify the kind of self-efficacy beliefs needed to face such situations. Along with designing professional development programs for inservice teachers, it would be relevant to explore how teacher education programs can contribute to the development of self-efficacy. Collaboration of teacher educators and researchers is recommended to understand the demands of teacher education from the perspectives of teacher educators and to analyze how self-efficacy research can contribute to improving preservice teacher's self-efficacy beliefs. To conclude, the suggestion made by Peterson *et al.* (1996) of a backward mapping from teaching demands to teaching prerequisites might be helpful in reducing the gap between research and practice, and in turn making the practical fruits of self-efficacy research clearer and more useful to teachers and teacher educators.

Notes

1 Many authors have used the terms self-efficacy, sense of efficacy, teacher efficacy, teachers' sense of efficacy, sense of self-efficacy, perceived self-efficacy, and efficacy beliefs interchangeably in the literature. The terminology 'self-efficacy' will be followed throughout this chapter.
2 Klassen and Chiu refer to the career stages outlined by Huberman (1989) in defining the early, mid- and late career stages. Huberman defines four distinct stages in the professional life of teachers: early career stage (1–6 years), mid-career years (7–18 years), late-career phase I (19–30), and late-career phase II (31–40 years).

References

Allinder, R. (1994) 'The relationships between efficacy and instructional practices of special education teachers and consultants', *Teacher Education and Special Education*, 17: 86–95.
Ashton, P. (1984) 'Teacher efficacy: a motivational paradigm for effective teacher education', *Journal of Teacher Education*, 35: 28–32.
Ashton, P. and Webb, R.B. (1986) *Making a Difference: Teachers' Sense of Efficacy and Student Achievement*, New York: Longman.

Bandura, A. (1977) 'Self-efficacy: toward a unifying theory of behavioral change', *Psychological Review,* 84: 191–215.

Bandura, A. (1986) *Social Foundations of Thought and Action: A Social Cognitive Theory,* Englewood Cliffs, NJ: Prentice-Hall.

Bandura, A. (1989) 'Social cognitive theory', in R. Vasta (ed.) *Annals of Child Development: Six Theories of Child Development* (Vol. 6, pp. 1–60), Greenwich, CT: JAI Press.

Bandura, A. (1994) 'Self-efficacy', in V.S. Ramachaudran (ed.) *Encyclopedia of Human Behavior* (Vol. 4, pp. 71–81), New York: Academic Press.

Bandura, A. (1997) *Self-efficacy: The Exercise of Control,* New York: W.H. Freeman.

Bandura, A. (2006) 'Towards a psychology of human agencies', *Perspectives on Psychological Sciences,* 1: 164–180.

Betoret, F.D. (2006) 'Stressors, self-efficacy, coping resources, and burnout among secondary school teachers in Spain', *Educational Psychology,* 26: 519–539.

Brouwers, A. and Tomic, W. (2000) 'A longitudinal study of teacher burnout and perceived self-efficacy in classroom management', *Teaching and Teacher Education,* 16: 239–253.

Caprara, G.V., Barbaranelli, C., Borgogni, L., and Steca, P. (2003) 'Efficacy beliefs as determinants of teachers' job satisfaction', *Journal of Educational Psychology,* 95: 821–832.

Caprara, G.V., Barbaranelli, C., Steca, P., and Malone, P. (2006) 'Teachers' self-efficacy beliefs as determinants of job satisfaction and students' academic achievement: a study at the school level', *Journal of School Psychology,* 44: 473–490.

Coleman, J.S. (1986) 'Social theory, social research, and a theory of action', *American Journal of Sociology,* 91: 1309–1335.

Collie, R.J., Shapka, J.D., and Perry, N.E. (2012) 'School climate and social-emotional learning: predicting teacher stress, job satisfaction, and teaching efficacy', *Journal of Educational Psychology,* 104: 1189–1204.

Cousins, J.B. and Walker, C. (1995) 'Personal teacher efficacy as a predictor of teachers' attitude toward applied educational research', paper presented at the annual meeting of Canadian Association for the Study of Educational Administration, Montreal.

Deemer, S.A. (2004) 'Classroom goal orientation in high school classrooms: revealing links between teacher beliefs and classroom environments', *Educational Research,* 46: 73–90.

Deemer, S.A. (2008) 'Review of teaching and learning outside the box: inspiring imagination across the curriculum', *Journal of Educational Research,* 101: 190–191.

Dellinger, A.B., Bobbett, J.J., Olivier, D.F., and Ellet, C.D. (2008) 'Measuring teachers' self-efficacy beliefs: development and use of the TEBS-Self', *Teaching and Teacher Education,* 24: 751–766.

Emmer, E.T. and Aussiker, A. (1990) 'School and classroom discipline programs: how well do they work?', in O.C. Moles (ed.) *Student Discipline Strategies: Research and Practice* (pp.129–165), Albany: State University of New York Press.

Emmer, E.T. and Hickman, J. (1991) 'Teacher efficacy in classroom management and discipline', *Educational and Psychological Measurement,* 51: 755–765.

Fernet, C., Guay, F., Senécal, C., and Austin, S. (2012) 'Predicting intraindividual changes in teacher burnout: the role of perceived school environment and motivational factors', *Teaching and Teacher Education,* 28: 514–525.

Friedman, I.A. and Kass, E. (2002) 'Teacher self-efficacy: a classroom-organization conceptualization', *Teaching and Teacher Education,* 18: 675–686.

Gecas, V. (1989) 'The social psychology of self-efficacy', *Annual Review of Psychology,* 15: 291–316.

Ghaith, G. and Yaghi, H. (1997) 'Relationship among experience, teacher efficacy and attitudes toward the implementtaion of instructional innovation', *Teaching and Teacher Education,* 13: 451–458.

Gibson, S. and Dembo, M. (1984) 'Teacher efficacy: construct validation', *Journal of Educational Psychology,* 76: 569–582.

Goddard, R.D., Hoy, W.K., and Woolfolk Hoy, A. (2004) 'Collective efficacy beliefs: theoretical developments, empirical evidence, and future directions', *Educational Researcher,* 33: 3–13.

Henson, R.K. (2002) 'From adolescent angst to adulthood: substantive implications and measurement dilemmas in the development of teacher efficacy research', *Educational Psychologist,* 37: 137–150.

Henson, R.K., Kogan, L.R., and Vacha-Haase, T. (2001) 'A reliability generalization study of the teacher efficacy scale and related instruments', *Educational and Psychological Measurement,* 61: 404–420.

Holzberger, D., Philipp, A. and Kunter. M. (2013) 'How teachers' self-efficacy is related to instructional quality: a longitudinal analysis', *Journal of Educational Psychology,* 105: 774–786.

Huberman, M. (1989) 'The professional life cycle of teachers', *Teachers College Record,* 91: 31–57.

Klassen, R.M., Al-Dhafri, S., Hannok, W., and Betts, S.M. (2011) 'Investigating pre-service teacher motivation across cultures using the Teachers' Ten Statements Test', *Teaching and Teacher Education,* 27: 579–588.

Klassen, R.M. and Chiu, M.M. (2010) 'Effects on teachers' self-efficacy and job satisfaction: teacher gender, years of experience, and job stress', *Journal of Educational Psychology*, 102: 741.

Labone, E. (2004) 'Teacher efficacy: maturing the construct through reserach in alternative paradigms', *Teaching and Teacher Education*, 20: 341–359.

Lent, R.W. and Hackett, G. (1987) 'Career self-efficacy: empirical status and future directions', *Journal of Vocational Behaviour*, 30: 347–382.

Marsh, H.W. (1993) 'Academic self-concept: theory, measurement and research', in J. Suls (ed.) *Psychological Perspectives on the Self* (Vol. 4, pp. 59–98), Hillsdale, NJ: Lawrence Erlbaum.

Moè, A., Pazzaglia, F., and Ronconi, L. (2010) 'When being able is not enough: the combined value of positive affect and self-efficacy for job satisfaction in teaching', *Teaching and Teacher Education*, 26: 1145–1153.

Morris-Rothschild, B.K. and Brassard, M.R. (2006) 'Teachers' conflict management styles: the role of attachment styles and classroom management efficacy', *Journal of School Psychology*, 44: 105–121.

Mulholland, J. and Wallace, J. (2001) 'Teacher induction and elementatry science teaching: enhancing self-efficacy', *Teaching and Education*, 17: 243–261.

Pajares, F. (1996) 'Self-efficacy beliefs in academic settings', *Review of Educational Research*, 66: 543–578.

Pajares, F. (1997) 'Current directions in self-efficacy research', in M. Maehr and P. R. Pintrich (eds) *Advances in Motivation and Achievement* (Vol. 10, pp. 1–49), Greenwich, CT: JAI Press.

Pajares, F. and Miller, M. (1994) 'Role of self-efficacy and self-concept beliefs in mathematical problem solving: a path analysis', *Journal of Educational Psychology*, 86: 193–203.

Peterson, P.L., McCarthey, S.J. and Elmore, R.F. (1996) 'Learning from school restructuring', *American Educational Research Journal*, 33: 119–153.

Pintrich, P.R. and Schunk, D.H. (1995) *Motivation in Education: Theory, Research, and Applications*, Englewood Cliffs, NJ: Prentice Hall.

Riggs, I.M. and Enochs, L.G. (1990) 'Toward the development of an elementary teacher's science teaching efficacy belief instrument', *Science & Education*, 74: 625–637.

Ross, J.A. (1992) 'Teacher efficacy and the effect of coaching on student achievement', *Teaching and Teacher Education*, 10: 381–394.

Ross, J.A. (1995) 'Strategies for enhancing teachers' beliefs in their effectiveness: research on a school improvement hypothesis', *Teachers College Record*, 97: 227–250.

Ross, J.A. (1998) 'The antecedents and consequences of teacher efficacy', in J. Brophy (ed.) *Advances in Research on Teaching* (Vol. 7, pp. 49–73), Greenwich, CT: JAI Press.

Ross, J.A. and Bruce, C. (2007) 'Professional development effects on teacher efficacy: results of randomized field trial', *The Journal of Educational Research*, 101: 50–60.

Ross, J.A., Cousins, J.B., and Gadalla, T. (1996) 'Within-teacher predictors of teacher efficacy', *Teaching and Teacher Education*, 12: 385–400.

Rotter, J.B. (1966) 'Generalized expectancies for internal versus external control of reinforcement', *Psychological Monographs*, 80: 1–28.

Schunk, D.H. (1991) 'Self-efficacy and academic motivation', *Educational Psychologist*, 26: 207–231.

Schunk, D.H. and Pajares, F. (2005) *Competence Perceptions and Academic Functioning*, New York, NY: Guilford Publications.

Schunk, D.H. and Pajares, F. (2009) 'Self-efficacy theory', in K.R. Wentzel and A. Wigfield (eds) *Handbook of Motivation at School* (pp. 35–53), New York, NY: Routledge.

Shavelson, R. and Bolus, R. (1982) 'Self-concept: the interplay of theory and methods', *Journal of Educational Psychology*, 74: 3–17.

Skaalvik, E.M. and Skaalvik, S. (2007) 'Dimensions of teacher self-efficacy and relations with strain factors, perceived collective teacher efficacy, and teacher burnout', *Journal of Educational Psychology*, 99: 611–625.

Soodak, L.C. and Podell, D.M. (1993) 'Teacher efficacy and student problem as factors in special education referral', *Journal of Special Education*, 27: 66–81.

Swars, S.L. (2005) 'Examining perceptions of mathematics teaching effectiveness along elementary preservice teachers with differing levels of mathematics teacher efficacy', *Journal of Instructional Psychology*, 32: 139–147.

Tournaki, N. and Podell, D.M. (2005) 'The impact of student characteristics and teacher efficacy on teachers' predictions of student success', *Teaching and Teacher Education*, 21: 299–314.

Tschannen-Moran, M. and Woolfolk Hoy, A. (2001) 'Teacher efficacy: capturing an elusive construct', *Teaching and Teacher Education*, 17: 783–805.

Tschannen-Moran, M., Woolfolk Hoy, A., and Hoy, W.K. (1998) 'Teacher efficacy: its meaning and measure', *Review of Educational Research*, 68: 202–248.

Turner, R.H. (1988) 'Personality in society: social psychology's contribution to sociology', *Social Psychology Quarterly,* 51: 1–10.

Wheatley, K.F. (2005) 'The case for reconceptualizing teacher efficacy research', *Teaching and Teacher Education,* 21: 747–766.

Wigfield, A. and Eccles, J. (2000) 'Expectancy-value theory of achievement motivation', *Contemporary Educational Psychology,* 25: 68–81.

Wolters, C. and Daugherty, S.G. (2007) 'Goal structures and teachers' sense of self-efficacy: their relation and association to teaching experience and academic level', *Journal of Educational Psychology,* 99: 181–193.

Woolfolk Hoy, A.E. and Burke Spero, R. (2005) 'Changes in teacher efficacy during the early years of teaching: a comparison of four measures', *Teaching and Teacher Education,* 21: 343–356.

Woolfolk Hoy, A. E., Hoy, W.K., and Davis, H.A. (2009) 'Teachers' self-efficacy beliefs', in K. R. Wentzel and A. Wigfield (eds) *Handbook of Motivation at School* (pp. 627–653), New York: Routledge.

Zimmerman, B.J. (1996) 'Measuring and mismeasuring academic self-efficacy: dimensions, problems and misconceptions', paper presented at the annual meeting of the American Educational Research Association, New York.

33

TEACHERS' EMOTIONAL SKILLS, MOTIVATION, AND WELL-BEING

Shane T. Harvey and Amanda Naus

Peter[1] sat in my office, downcast and holding his head in his hands. He was not long out of training, having just completed his teaching registration. He had been a top student and was described as someone who would have a glittering career in education. Through furrowed brows he stammered: 'I love this work. I love the kids. I just don't think I can sustain it emotionally. I'm giving out like an emotional ATM every day at school and right now, I'm giving out 50 percent more than I have'.

Two years after I had contact with a middle school where I had worked with a gifted teacher to integrate a highly challenging student, I made contact with one of the senior managers again. 'How is Sandy?' I enquired. 'She is no longer teaching' was the reply. 'Her family asked her to change career because of the emotional cost on her and her family. She was exceptional and teaching was her life. Unfortunately it had become detrimental to her and her family.'

Teaching is an emotional career. As these very real experiences illustrate, an emotional fee is attached to those wanting to be an effective teacher (Hargreaves 1998, 2000). Teaching draws on one's own emotional reserves and skills, and support is often required to sustain it. It is not uncommon for us to witness teachers initially managing a successful balance between class structure and emotional connectedness, only to gradually distance themselves from students in their care and rely increasingly on structure and routine to manage this emotional toll. As the teacher's emotional withdrawal occurs, so too, it seems, does the students' affection towards one another, their curiosity about learning, and their attitude towards school.

This observation is not new. Hargreaves (1998) argued emotions were central to teaching and shaped teachers' relational connections with students. To be effective, teachers require awareness of emotion, understanding of emotional information, to be able to emotionally regulate, and to provide well placed empathic responses to students' emotions. Sustaining this requires intensive emotional labor (see Çukar 2009; Hochschild 1983), which in turn requires a high degree of emotional skill (Cheung and Tang 2009).

The purpose of this chapter is to focus on the significance of teachers' emotional skills to teaching and the importance these skills have for the social psychology of the classroom and outcomes with students. Understanding the conceptual foundations for teachers' emotional skills and their relationship to motivation and well-being are covered first. We then turn to empirical studies, theoretical models, and applications related to these ideas.

Conceptual foundations

Definitions of emotional intelligence contain concepts such as the ability to observe one's own and other people's feelings and emotions, to differentiate between them, and to use them to direct one's thinking and actions (Salovey and Mayer 1990), the ability to motivate oneself, persist in frustrating situations, control impulses and delay gratifications, and to regulate one's mood (Goleman 1996). Emotional competence includes the four abilities mentioned in Salovey and Mayer's definition of emotional intelligence, but adds social abilities related to emotional expression, empathy, relationships, and self-efficacy (Saarni 1999). Emotional intelligence and competencies carry the unfortunate connotation that these worthwhile attributes are innate to an individual. For this reason, we prefer to use the term emotional skills, in that it implies these same qualities can be learned through instruction, practice and everyday experiences.

Motivation is considered to be an important feature of emotional intelligence (Goleman 1996). In education, motivation has been channeled into two concepts: motivational factors and motivated behavior. Teachers' motivational factors are thought to include self-efficacy, value (goals and interest in the task), and teachers' feelings about their work in general (Thoonen *et al.* 2011). Motivational factors determine motivated behavior (Maehr and Braskamp 1986), which is behavior driven by either intrinsic or extrinsic motivation (Ryan and Deci 2000). Given the link emotion has to motivation, the assumption is that teachers' emotional well-being is also related to their motivation. Low mood or emotional exhaustion, for instance, could lower teachers' beliefs about their capability to perform, alter how they value their role, invade their feelings toward their profession, and reduce the amount of energy and behavior invested in teaching. Important ideas detailing teacher well-being have highlighted resilience to strain, mental health and 'burnout' (Howard and Johnson 2004), and well-being has also been linked to the concepts of morale and job satisfaction (Burke and Greenglass 1995). Teacher burnout is defined here as the feelings of exhaustion, lack of energy, and depletion of mental resources as a result of overwork and unobtainable demands as a teacher (Babad 2009; Friedman and Farber 1992). Van Petegem *et al.* (2005) defined well-being for teachers as a positive affective state resulting from a healthy balance between teachers' personal needs and organizational requirements. As evidenced thus far, a substantial overlap in ideas exist behind concepts related to emotional skills, motivation and well-being. For the purposes of this review, we have afforded a degree of separation in order to understand the contributions of each to empirical research, theoretical models, and their applications for practice.

Descriptive empirical studies

If emotions are linked to motivation and social interactions, then it stands to reason that teachers' use of social and emotional skills could influence students' emotions, social interactions, and motivation to learn. Conversely, teachers' motivation to use emotions skillfully could in turn be influenced by their own context and emotional well-being. This section will review the empirical evidence linking the use of social emotional skills to student outcomes and the factors sustaining teachers' motivation and emotional well-being.

Emotional skills

Teachers' emotional skills have consequences not only for students, but also for teachers and parents themselves. These skills are linked to teachers' emotional well-being, regulation of emotions, higher job satisfaction, and general positive affect (Brackett *et al.* 2010). Likewise, teachers' emotional and instructional support are related to increased positive interpersonal behavior and fewer intrapersonal behavior problems in students (Perry *et al.* 2007) and higher levels of both teacher-reported and independently observed social competence and teacher-reported self-control (Wilson *et al.* 2007). Others have found teachers' emotionally supportive interactions fostered students' social competence, behavioral self-control, emotional intelligence, emotion regulation, and lower levels of aggression (Evans and Harvey 2012; Harvey 2004; Mashburn *et al.* 2008; Merritt *et al.* 2012). Competent social-emotional practices have resulted in academic benefits for students (e.g. Connor *et al.* 2005; Curby *et al.* 2009), better early mathematics and learning behaviors in children (Son *et al.* 2013), and was a better predictor of academic outcome than teacher training and the teacher–student ratio (Mashburn *et al.* 2008).

Given the potential benefits to students, researchers planning interventions targeting students' social and emotional learning will be well-advised to account for teachers' emotional skills. Teachers lacking emotional skills are ill-equipped to take on the pressures and challenges of the classroom, leading to emotional distress (Jennings *et al.* 2011a). Emotional distress impairs teachers' performance and can also lead to burnout (Montgomery and Rupp 2005). Models depicting which emotional skills are necessary for developing the social-emotional classroom environment and the pathway to emotional distress and burnout when these are absent have been presented below in the following two sections: Motivation and well-being and Theoretical models.

Motivation and well-being

Most research on school effectiveness focuses on structural and policy issues rather than psychological factors like motivation (Thoonen *et al.* 2011). Unsurprisingly, teachers' motivation has been found to be affected by principals' leadership style and undesirable emotions (Geijsel *et al.* 2003; Pekrun *et al.* 2002). According to Bass and Avolio (1994), the two types of leadership affecting teachers' motivation are transformational and transactional. Transformational principals nurture teachers' needs, provide a model to follow, and foster creative thinking. Conversely, transactional principals focus on compliance with organization rules and policies and maintaining efficiency (Bass and Avolio 1994). Geijsel *et al.* (2003) found transformational leadership directly enhanced teachers' motivation (see also Thoonen *et al.* 2011) and decreased the likelihood of teachers' burnout, a relationship partially mediated by intrinsic motivation (Eyal and Roth 2011). Transactional leadership had a contrasting effect; it was linked to burnout and partially mediated by controlled or external motivation. The effect of teachers' motivation on their professional practice is clear. Intrinsic motivation buffered against burnout and promoted self-actualization, whereas controlled motivation was linked to burnout and decreased self-actualization (Roth *et al.* 2007). Although these studies do not explain *how* these leadership styles influence motivation, it is conceivable that undesirable emotions arise from transactional styles of management, thus undermining dynamics sustaining teachers' intrinsic motivation. Certainly, undesirable emotion per se has been linked to decreased intrinsic motivation, pleasure, and interest in teaching (Pekrun *et al.* 2002). With the onset of undesirable emotion and without the emotional skills and leadership support necessary to manage them, frustration and emotionally exhaustion are likely, leading to burnout.

Burnout is a common problem among teachers (Farber 1984) and is associated with decreased job satisfaction (Kantas and Vassilaki 1997). Emotional demands in education are a considerable source of job-related stress (Zapf 2002), which in turn affects teachers' job satisfaction (Borg *et al.* 1991), effectiveness with pupils (Blase 1986), physical and mental illness (Kyriacou 1987), and emotional exhaustion (Bauer *et al.* 2007). Sadly, teachers are said to experience more work-related stress and burnout than many other occupational groups (Johnson *et al.* 2005). Burnout can manifest as heightened anxiety, depression, nervousness, apathy, and exhaustion as well as lowered self-efficacy, self-esteem, and a loss of control (Babad 2009). Predictors of teacher burnout include being under stress for a prolonged period of time (Blase 1986; Farber 1984), difficult classes, behavior problems, shortages of equipment, demands on after-school time (Abel and Sewell 1999; Bauer *et al.* 2007; Kyriacou and Sutcliffe 1978), work–family conflict (Cinamon *et al.* 2007), teacher–student relations (Babad 2009), and the classroom climate (Bryne 1994). Insufficient rewards, status, high administrative demands, and lack of promotional opportunities are other sources of stress thought to lead to burnout (Babad 2009; Kyriacou and Sutcliffe 1978). Retelsdorf *et al.* (2009), for example, found external restrictions, imposed reforms and standards, and multiple goals were associated with teachers' quality and intensity of motivation, affect, and burnout. Higher levels of burnout have been found in urban teachers compared with rural teachers (Abel and Sewell 1999), and in teachers who perceive their job as demanding and lacking control (Santavirta *et al.* 2007). Babad (2009) also attributed teacher training as a source of burnout, as he argued that an idyllic and ideological view of teaching was often presented, without consideration or preparation for the severe challenges teachers are likely to encounter.

Teachers' job-related stress is negatively correlated to the length of time they have been employed as a teacher (Bradley 2007; Kahn *et al.* 2006). Bradley (2007) argued this could be explained by Karasek's (1979) demand–control–support model of job stress, which theorizes that strain is created by high demands, low control, and low social support. Presumably, the longer someone is employed, the more established their collegial relationships are, the better teachers adapt to job demands, and the higher their levels of autonomy. This argument might not be so valid for workplace demands, however, as often additional responsibilities are placed on senior teachers. Indeed, job demands negatively predicted job satisfaction and positively predicted somatic complaints and burnout, whereas job control was a positive predictor of job satisfaction (e.g. Pascual *et al.* 2003; Pomaki and Anagnostopoulou 2003). Furthermore, the size of the relationship was small between social support and job strain (Bradley 2007; Burke and Greenglass 1995; Sheffield *et al.* 1994).

As expected, a negative association exists between burnout and well-being (Milfont *et al.* 2008). Whenever teachers experience burnout, it affects not only them, but students, colleagues, and the wider school community. Students of burnt-out teachers are less motivated in their learning (Kyriacou and Sutcliffe 1978) and these teachers are less effective in meeting educational goals. Taken together, the above findings highlight the importance of guarding against burnout amongst teachers while promoting their emotional health and well-being to enable pedagogical success.

Theoretical models

Within the classroom, teachers and students express emotions in everyday conversations and actions that set the tone of the class, or class climate (Meyer and Turner 2006). In turn, the emotional class climate colors emotional experience, emotions expressed, and the quality of emotional behavior (Harvey 2004). Two balancing principles in many models of class climate appear to be relationship/support (e.g. Brand *et al.* 2003; Matsumura *et al.* 2008; Moos 1979; Wubbels *et al.* 1991) and class organization/structure (e.g. Brand *et al.* 2003; Moos 1979; Pianta *et al.* 2008; Wubbels *et al.* 1991). Other models also include variants of behavior management and pedagogy (Anderson and Walberg 1974; Brand *et al.* 2003; Fraser *et al.* 1982; Pianta *et al.* 2008). Two key points must be noted here. The first is that many models extend beyond the emotional world of the teacher, choosing features instead that better manage and teach pupils. The second point is that many models allude to the presence of emotion through concepts like relationships, behavior management, and formal teaching, without directly identifying it

(Evans *et al.* 2009). We found two models, the Harvey and Evans model of the classroom emotional environment (Evans and Harvey 2012; Harvey and Evans 2003; Harvey *et al.* 2012) and the Jennings and Greenberg prosocial classroom model (2009) that predominantly focused on the emotional skills of the teacher.

The Harvey and Evans classroom emotional environment model identifies six key social-emotional skills teachers require that benefit students emotionally (Harvey *et al.* 2012, see Figure 33.1): emotional relationships, emotional awareness, emotion management, emotional intrapersonal beliefs, emotional interpersonal guidelines, and emotion contagion. Concepts typically fall along two general axes, intrapersonal and interpersonal, with emotional relationships positioned as the central organizing principle. Each concept is subdivided into subordinate concepts. By way of example, *emotion management* contains two subordinate concepts that relate to teachers' *emotion regulation* and *emotion coaching* of students (see Harvey *et al.* 2012 for more details).

In a similar vein to Harvey and Evans' model, Jennings and Greenberg (2009) developed the prosocial classroom model, whereby teachers' social and emotional competence and well-being produces a healthy classroom climate through healthy student–teacher relationships, effective classroom management, and effective implementation of social and emotional learning. In turn, the resulting healthy classroom climate enhances students' academic, social, and emotional outcomes. Jennings and Greenberg also describe the downward spiral or 'burnout cascade' that occurs when teachers lack social and emotional skills. They argue that teachers unskilled in emotional areas are less able to tackle the social and emotional challenges that occur within the classroom, and thus students' performance and on-task behavior declines. This leads to a deterioration in the classroom climate, and an increase in challenging behavior from students. Teachers, in turn, become emotionally exhausted and the strain on them leads them to increasingly rely on punitive punishment practices. This causes a further deterioration of the classroom climate and the strain of the teacher increases.

Therefore, to foster emotional skills in students, teachers require the effective use of emotional skills themselves. One shortcoming associated with both models is that they tend to locate the source of emotional skills and emotional climate within the teacher. In light of the previous research, it would seem likely that these skills find their expression best within an emotionally supportive network. Furthermore, even if beneficial emotional skills are present in a teacher's behavioral repertoire, the state of teachers' own emotional health and energy will potentially influence the likelihood of them drawing on these skills in their practice.

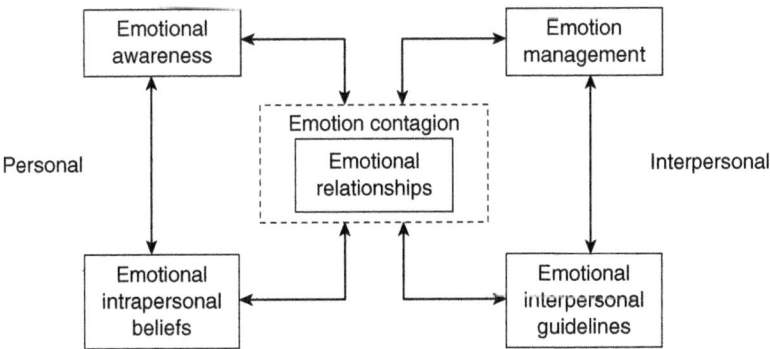

Figure 33.1 Harvey and Evans' model of the classroom emotional environment (Evans and Harvey, 2012; Harvey *et al.* 2012). Used with permission from the authors.

Applications for practice

In light of the empirical evidence and conceptual models linking teachers' emotional well-being and emotional skills to effective practice, research is required to establish whether these can be formally taught. The following section identifies and reviews interventions aimed at fostering these emotional skills in teachers.

Emotional skills

The majority of emotional skills training focuses on improving student's social and emotional competencies by training teachers to deliver an emotion-based curriculum (see, for example, the Caring School Community, formerly the Child Development Project, Battistich *et al.* 2000; Domitrovich *et al.* 2007; Promoting Alternative THinking Strategies (PATHS), Greenberg and Kusché 1993; Social and Emotional Aspects of Learning, Department for Children, Schools and Families 2007), but very few concentrate on improving the emotional skills of teachers. Given teachers are likely to learn about emotion by participating in and delivering social and emotional learning-based programs, it is plausible that participation will be of indirect benefit. For instance, teachers who implemented the PATHS (Domitrovich *et al.* 1999) curriculum received additional support from project staff. Moreover, they were noted to improve their discipline techniques, emotional communication and support, social awareness, problem solving, and the prevention of misbehavior. Rivers *et al.* (2013) included training for teachers that supported them to deliver their literacy-based social and emotional learning program for students (RULER). Observational and teacher report (but not student) suggested that their joint approach benefited the classroom emotional climate. Although exciting, these programs still focus on teachers explicitly and formally teaching emotional competencies to children. Studies are needed to investigate how teachers' emotional skills per se influence students' emotional development.

Several intervention programs and pilot studies have recently emerged in the past three years that aim to promote teachers' emotional skills. Ulloa (2011) for instance, found emotional training involving mindfulness and emotion focused reflective practice significantly increased teachers' emotional competence. Following the completion of the Emotional Intelligence Based Instructional Package (EIBIP) for teachers, Joshith (2012) reported a significant increase in teachers' emotional intelligence and a strengthening relationship between emotional intelligence and teacher competency. Finally, teachers' social and emotional learning knowledge, knowledge application, and well-being were found to increase for those who underwent the Teacher Effectiveness Training (TET) (Gordon Training International 2012) program, which includes active listening and I-messages designed to enhance teachers' empathy, understanding, and social awareness (Talvio *et al.* 2013).

The findings from these three interventions signify the importance teachers' emotional skills have to teaching. However, no effects on students were reported in these studies. Evans and Harvey (2012) measured the effects on students as a result of teachers undergoing an emotional skills intervention. They observed that post-treatment, teachers significantly increased their use of emotion coaching, emotional awareness, and positive relationship strategies, while decreasing their use of undesirable behavior management techniques. Teachers who made improvements in their emotional behavior were noted by students as being comparatively better in leadership, helpfulness/friendliness, understanding, and student responsibility/freedom, and significantly lower in strictness, compared to teachers who had not. Moreover, students in the change group of teachers indicated comparatively better prosocial behavior and positive emotions, and lower negative emotions, bullying, and victimization than students of teachers in non-change group.

When Harvey *et al*'s (2012) emotional concepts were applied within a whole school context, improvements were reported in supportive collegial behavior, collegial relationships, and teachers positive comments, remarks, and observations (Evans and Harvey 2012).

Results from these social-emotional interventions indicate that teachers' emotional skills are related to teaching competency and collegial support, and are likely to have spin-offs for students' own emotional well-being. Although results are promising, more evidence is needed to validate and extend on these initial studies. Data on students' academic and behavioral changes resulting from changes to teachers' emotional skills are also lacking. Given the indirect manner by which teachers emotional skills are imparted to students using this approach, longitudinal studies may be useful to capture changes.

Professional well-being

Several interventions have aimed to promote teacher well-being and reduce burnout by developing emotional awareness, emotion regulation, and mindfulness. Jennings and colleagues have published two programs based on these principles: The Cultivating Emotional Balance program (Jennings *et al.* 2011a) and their more recent intensive program, Cultivating Awareness and Resilience in Education (CARE, Jennings *et al.* 2011b, 2013). Combining meditation practices with emotional understanding, regulation, and compassion-building techniques, they reported improvements in depression, anxiety, rumination, negative and positive affect, general well-being, efficacy, burnout, and mindfulness in teachers.

The use of mindfulness as an emotional well-being technique has recently been gaining in popularity. Jennings *et al.* (2013) argued that by fostering mindfulness, emotion regulation and emotional awareness during stressful situations is enhanced. This has the effect of minimizing the effect of stress, which in turn, improves overall well-being. Indeed, by using mindfulness and self-compassion training, Roeser *et al.* (2013) reported improvements in teachers' mindfulness and self-compassion, occupational stress, burnout, depression, and anxiety. These studies illustrate the usefulness of mindfulness, awareness, regulation, and understanding of emotions in increasing teachers' resilience against stressful situations and minimizing burnout. By enabling teachers to conserve energy through the use of these skills, energy can be reinvested in managing students, teaching effectively, and maintaining general well-being.

Summary

While research on teachers' emotional skills, motivation, and well-being has increased in recent years, much remains to be done. A shortfall is that the majority of studies formally teach students about emotions, while neglecting the contribution teachers' own emotional skills have. This is important as evidence implies teachers' emotional skills are related to students' social and emotional competence, self-control, behavior, and academic outcomes. Furthermore, teachers' emotional skills are related to their happiness and job satisfaction. Research suggests teachers' motivation is context-driven. Principals' leadership style and negative emotions influence levels of motivation, which in turn, is linked to their engagement in professional development and overall well-being.

Teaching involves high emotional labor, which can be stressful and result in burnout. When teachers are unable to manage and self-regulate their emotions, they can become overwhelmed by stress. This leads to deterioration in their classroom climate, and to further stress and burnout (Jennings and Greenberg 2009). Burnout has been linked to stresses such as time pressure, lack of resources, and difficult classes. The high levels of stress and burnout in the teaching profession have significant implications for both teachers and students, as well as the education profession as a whole.

Some promising interventions are emerging aimed at cultivating teachers' emotional skills. These include techniques based on emotional awareness, regulation, coaching, support, reflection, understanding, and mindfulness. The incorporation of mindfulness into training is an important development, and one which is likely to be seen increasingly throughout education. One consideration on this could be offered, however. Mindfulness per se emphasizes the acceptance of feelings. Within this notion of acceptance, is the tendency to sit with the emotion rather than act on it. However, emotion can also be used as a tool to enhance teaching practice. Undesirable emotions, such as sadness, anger and fear, can enable teachers to reflect on practice, consider barriers to achieving outcomes, and motivate both teachers and students. The skill comes in understanding how emotion can best be managed given the circumstances and resources available. A second consideration regarding mindfulness training with educators is that most work to date has examined the effects of mindfulness on teacher self-reported outcomes. It would be important to investigate how this particular skill translates into teachers' practice and the social-emotional climate of the classroom. Furthermore, the result on students' social-emotional skills – particularly how this varies for students with different needs – requires further investigation.

Teachers' emotional skills, motivation, and well-being (or lack of them) are important features underlying the successful education of students, overall emotional health, and job satisfaction, and the number of teachers leaving the teaching profession. Highlighting this issue is the first step to improving emotional skills and well-being and enabling much-needed research and training. Perhaps in the future, practitioners like Peter and Sandy could be partnered with effective evidence-based practices that enable them to be successfully supported and trained to manage the high emotional demands facing them.

Note

1   Identifying information has been altered.

References

Abel, M.H. and Sewell, J. (1999) 'Stress and burnout in rural and urban secondary school teachers', *Journal of Educational Research*, 92: 287–293.

Anderson, G.J. and Walberg, H.J. (1974) 'Learning environments', in H.J. Walberg (ed.), *Evaluating Educational Performances* (pp. 81–98), Berkeley, CA: McCutchan.

Babad, E. (2009). *The Social Psychology of the Classroom*, New York, NY: Routledge.

Bass, B.M. and Avolio, B.J. (1994) *Improving Organizational Effectiveness Through Transformational Leadership*, Thousand Oaks, CA: Sage.

Battistich, V., Schaps, E., Watson, M.S., Solomon, D.H. and Lewis, C. (2000) 'Effects of the Child Development Project on students' drug use and other problem behaviors', *Journal of Primary Prevention*, 17: 75–99.

Bauer, J., Unterbrink, T., Hack, A., Pfeifer, R., Buhl-Griesshaber, V., Muller., Wesche, H., Frommhold, M., Seibt, R., Scheuch, K. and Wirsching, M. (2007) 'Working conditions, adverse events and mental health problems in a sample of 949 German teachers', *International Archives of Occupational and Environmental Health*, 80: 442–449.

Blase, J.J. (1986) 'A qualitative analysis of sources of teacher stress: consequences for performance', *American Educational Research Journal*, 23: 13–40.

Borg, M.G., Riding, R.J. and Falzon, J.M. (1991) 'Stress in teaching: a study of occupational stress and its determinants, job satisfaction and career commitment among primary schoolteachers', *Educational Psychology: An International Journal of Experimental Educational Psychology*, 11: 59–75.

Brackett, M.A., Palomera, R., Mojsa, J., Reyes, M. and Salovey, P. (2010) 'Emotion regulation ability, job satisfaction, and burnout among British secondary school teachers', *Psychology in the Schools*, 47: 406–417.

Bradley, G. (2007) 'Job tenure as a moderator of stressor–strain relations: a comparison of experienced and new-start teachers', *Work and Stress,* 21: 48–64.

Brand, S., Felner, R., Shim, M., Seitsinger, A. and Dumas, T. (2003) 'Middle school improvement and reform: development and validation of a school-level assessment of climate, cultural pluralism, and school safety', *Journal of Educational Psychology,* 95: 570–588.

Bryne, B.M. (1994) 'Burnout: testing for the validity, replication, and invariance of causal structure across elementary, intermediate, and secondary teachers', *American Educational Research Journal,* 31: 645–673.

Burke, R.J. and Greenglass, E.R. (1995) 'A longitudinal study of psychological burnout in teachers', *Human Relations,* 48: 187–202.

Cheung, F.Y. and Tang, C.S. (2009) 'The influence of emotional intelligence and affectivity on emotional labor strategies at work', *Journal of Individual Differences,* 30: 75–86.

Cinamon, R.G., Rich, Y. and Westman, M. (2007) 'Teachers' occupation-specific work–family conflict', *Career Development Quarterly,* 55: 249–261.

Connor, M.C., Son, S., Hindman, A.H. and Morrison, F.J. (2005) 'Teacher qualifications, classroom practices, family characteristics, and preschool experience: complex effects on first graders' vocabulary and early reading outcomes', *Journal of School Psychology,* 43: 343–375.

Çukar, C.Ş. (2009) 'The development of the Teacher Emotional Labor Scale (TELS): validity and reliability', *Educational Sciences: Theory and Practice,* 9: 559–574.

Curby, T.W., Rimm-Kaufman, S.E. and Ponitz, C.C. (2009) 'Teacher–child interactions and children's achievement trajectories across kindergarten and first grade', *Journal of Educational Psychology,* 101: 912–925.

Department for Children, Schools and Families (2007) *Social and Emotional Aspects of Learning for Secondary Schools,* Nottingham: DCSF Publications.

Domitrovich, C.E., Corest, R.C. and Greenberg, M.T. (2007) 'Improving young children's social and emotional competence: a randomized trial of the preschool PATHS curriculum', *The Journal of Primary Prevention,* 28: 67–91.

Domitrovich, C.E., Greenberg, M.T., Kusche, C. and Cortes, R. (1999) *Manual for the Preschool PATHS Curriculum,* South Deerfield, MA: Channing-Bete Company.

Evans, I.M. and Harvey, S.T. (2012) *Warming the Emotional Climate of the Primary School Classroom,* Wellington, New Zealand: Dunmore Publishing.

Evans, I.M., Harvey, S.T., Buckley, L. and Yan, E. (2009) 'Differentiating classroom climate concepts: academic, management, and emotional environment', *Kōtuitui: New Zealand Journal of Social Sciences Online,* 4: 131–146.

Eyal, O. and Roth, G. (2011) 'Principals' leadership and teachers' motivation: self-determination theory analysis', *Journal of Educational Administration,* 49: 256–275.

Farber, B.A. (1984) 'Teacher burnout: assumptions, myths, and issues', *Teachers College Record,* 86: 321–338.

Fraser, B.J., Anderson, G.J. and Walberg, H.J. (1982) *Assessment of Learning Environments: Manual for Learning Environment Inventory (LEI) and My Class Inventory (MCI),* Perth, Australia: Western Australian Institute of Technology.

Friedman, I.A. and Farber, B.A. (1992) 'Professional self-concept as a predictor of teacher burnout', *Journal of Educational Research,* 86: 28–35.

Geijsel, F., Sleegers, P., Leithwood, K. and Jantzi, D. (2003) 'Transformational leadership effects on teachers' commitment and effort toward school reform', *Journal of Educational Administration,* 41: 228–256.

Goleman, D. (1996) *Emotional Intelligence: Why It can Matter More Than IQ,* London: Bloomsbury.

Gordon Training International. (2012) *T.E.T. Teacher Effectiveness Training.* Available at http://www.gordon-training.com/teachertrainingprogram.html

Greenberg, M.T. and Kusché, C.A. (1993) *Promoting Social and Emotional Development in Deaf Children: The PATHS Project,* Seattle, WA: University of Washington Press.

Hargreaves, A. (1998) 'The emotional practice of teaching', *Teaching and Teacher Education,* 14: 835–854.

Hargreaves, A. (2000) 'Mixed emotions: teachers' perceptions of their interactions with students', *Teaching and Teacher Education,* 16: 811–826.

Harvey, S.T. (2004) 'Understanding the emotional environment of the classroom', unpublished doctoral dissertation, Waikato University, Hamilton, New Zealand.

Harvey, S.T., Bimler, D., Evans, I.M., Kirkland, J. and Pechtel, P. (2012) 'Mapping the classroom emotional environment', *Teaching and Teacher Education,* 28: 628–640.

Harvey, S.T. and Evans, I.M. (2003) 'Understanding the emotional environment of the classroom', in D. Fraser and R. Openshaw (eds), *Informing our Practice* (pp. 182–195), Palmerston North, NZ: Kanuka Grove Press.

Hochschild, A.R. (1983) *The Managed Heart: Commercialization of Human Feeling*, Berkeley, CA: University of California Press.

Howard, S. and Johnson, B. (2004) 'Resilient teachers: resisting stress and burnout', *Social Psychology of Education*, 7: 399–420.

Jennings, P.A., Foltz, C., Snowberg, K.E., Sim, H. and Kemeny, M. (2011a) 'The influence of mindfulness and emotional skills training on teachers' classrooms: the effects of the cultivating emotional balance training' [online submission]. Available at http://www.eric.ed.gov/?id=ED518584

Jennings, P.A., Frank, J.L., Snowberg, K.E., Coccia, M.A. and Greenberg, M.T. (2013) 'Improving classroom learning environments by cultivating awareness and resilience in education (CARE): results of a randomized controlled trial', *School Psychology Quarterly*, 28: 374–390.

Jennings, P.A. and Greenberg, M.T. (2009) 'The prosocial classroom: teacher social and emotional competence in relation to student and classroom outcomes', *Review of Educational Research*, 79: 491–525.

Jennings, P.A., Snowberg, K.E., Coccia, M.A. and Greenberg, M.T. (2011b) 'Improving classroom learning environments by cultivating awareness and resilience in education (CARE): results of two pilot studies', *Journal of Classroom Interactions*, 46: 37–48.

Johnson, S., Cooper, C., Cartwright, S., Donald, I., Taylor, P. and Millet, C. (2005) 'The experience of work-related stress across occupations', *Journal of Managerial Psychology*, 5: 2–5.

Joshith, V.P. (2012) 'Emotional intelligence as a tool for innovative teaching', *Journal on Educational Psychology*, 5: 54–60.

Kahn, J.H., Schneider, K.T., Jenkins-Henkelman, T.M. and Moyle, L.L. (2006) 'Emotional social support and job burnout among high school teachers: Is it all due to dispositional affectivity?', *Journal of Organizational Behavior*, 27: 793–807.

Kantas A. and Vassilaki, E. (1997) 'Burnout in Greek teachers: main findings and validity of the Maslach Burnout Inventory', *Work and Stress*, 11: 94–100.

Karasek, R.A. (1979) 'Job demands, job decision latitude, and mental strain: implications for job redesign', *Administrative Science Quarterly*, 24: 285–308.

Kyriacou, C. (1987) 'Teacher stress and burnout: an international review', *Educational Research*, 29: 146–152.

Kyriacou, C. and Sutcliffe, J. (1978) 'Teacher stress: prevalence, sources, and symptoms', *British Journal of Educational Psychology*, 48: 159–167.

Maehr, M.L. and Braskamp, L.A. (1986) *The Motivation Factor: A Theory of Personal Investment*, Lexington, MA: Lexington Books.

Mashburn, A.J., Pianta, R.C., Hamre, B.K., Downer, J.T., Barbarin, O.A., Bryant, D., Burchinal, M., Early, D.M. and Howes, C. (2008) 'Measures of classroom quality in prekindergarten and children's development of academic, language, and social skills', *Child Development*, 79: 732–749.

Matsumura, L.C. Slater, S.C. and Crosson, A. (2008) 'Classroom climate, rigorous instruction and curricula, and students' interactions in urban middle school classrooms', *Elementary School Journal*, 108: 293–312.

Merrit, E.G., Wanless, S.E., Rimm-Kaufman, S.E., Cameron, C. and Peug, J.L. (2012) 'The contribution of teachers' emotional support to children's social behaviors and self-regulatory skills in first grade', *School Psychology Review*, 41; 141–159.

Meyer, D.K., and Turner, J.C. (2006) 'Re-conceptualizing emotion and motivation to learn in classroom contexts', *Educational Psychology Review*, 18: 377–390.

Milfont, T.L., Denny, S., Ameratunga, S., Robinson, E. and Merry, S. (2008) 'Burnout and wellbeing: testing the Copenhagen Burnout Inventory in New Zealand teachers', *Social Indicators Research*, 89: 169–177.

Montgomery, C. and Rupp, A.A. (2005) 'A meta-analysis for exploring the diverse causes and effects of stress in teachers', *Canadian Journal of Education*, 28: 458–486.

Moos, R.H. (1979) *Evaluating Educational Environments*, San Francisco, CA: Jossey-Bass.

Pascual, E., Perez Jover, V., Mirambell, E., Ivanez, G. and Terol, M.C. (2003) 'Job conditions, coping and wellness/health outcomes in Spanish secondary school teachers', *Psychology and Health*, 18: 511–521.

Pekrun, R., Goetz, T., Titz, W. and Perry, R.P. (2002) 'Academic emotions in students' self- regulated learning and achievement: a program of qualitative and quantitative research', *Educational Psychology*, 37: 91–106.

Perry, K.E., Donohue, K.M. and Weinstein, R.S. (2007) 'Teaching practices and the promotion of achievement and adjustment in first grade', *Journal of School Psychology*, 45: 269–292.

Pianta, R.C., La Paro, K.M. and Hamre, B.K. (2008) *Classroom Assessment Scoring System*, Baltimore, MD: Paul H. Brookes Publishing Company.

Pomaki, Y. and Anagnostopoulou, T. (2003) 'A test and extension of the demand/control/social support model: prediction of health- and work-related outcomes in Greek teachers', *Psychology and Health*, 18: 537–550.

Retelsdorf, J., Butler, R., Streblow, L. and Schiefele, U. (2009) 'Teachers' goal orientations for teaching: associations with instructional practices, interest in teaching, and burnout', *Learning and Instruction,* 20: 1–17.

Rivers, S.E., Brackett, M.A., Reyes, M.R., Elbertson, N.A. and Salovey, P. (2013) 'Improving the social and emotional climate of classrooms: a clustered randomized controlled trial testing the RULER approach', *Prevention Science,* 14: 77–87.

Roeser, R.W., Schonert-Reichl, K.Z., Jha, A., Cullen, M., Wallace, L., Wilensky, R., Oberle, E., Thomson, K., Taylor, C. and Harrison, J. (2013) 'Mindfulness training and reductions in teacher stress and burnout: results from two randomized, waitlist-control field trails', *Journal of Educational Psychology,* 105: 787–804.

Roth, G., Assor, A., Kaplan, H. and Kanat-Maymon, Y. (2007) 'Perceived autonomy in teaching: how self-determined teaching may lead to self-determined learning', *Journal of Educational Psychology,* 99: 761–774.

Ryan, R. M. and Deci, E. L. (2000) 'Intrinsic and extrinsic motivations: classic definitions and new directions', *Contemporary Educational Psychology,* 25: 54–67.

Saarni, C. (1999) *The Development of Emotional Competence,* New York, NY: Guilford.

Salovey, P. and Mayer, J.D. (1990) 'Emotional intelligence', *Imagination, Cognition, and Personality,* 9: 185–211.

Santavirta, N., Solovieva, S. and Theorell, T. (2007) 'The association between job strain and emotional exhaustion in a cohort of 1,028 Finnish teachers', *British Journal of Educational Psychology,* 77: 213–228.

Sheffield, D., Dobbie, D. and Carroll, D. (1994) 'Stress, social support, and psychological and physical wellbeing in secondary school teachers', *Work and Stress,* 8: 235–243.

Son, S-H.C. Kwon, K-A., Jeon, H-J. and Hong, S-Y. (2013) 'Head Start classrooms and children's school readiness benefit from teachers' qualifications and ongoing training', *Child Youth Care Forum,* 42: 525–553.

Talvio, M., Lonka, K., Komulainen, E., Linunen, T. and Kuusela, M. (2013) 'Revisiting Gordon's Teacher Effectiveness Training: an intervention study on teacher's social and emotional learning', *Electronic Journal of Research in Educational Psychology,* 11: 693–716.

Thoonen, E.E.J., Sleegers, P.J.C., Oort, F.J., Peetsma, T.T.D. and Geijsel, F.P. (2011) 'How to improve teaching practices: the role of teacher motivation, organizational factors, and leadership practices', *Educational Administration Quarterly,* 47: 496–536.

Ulloa, M.L. (2011) 'Teaching to care: emotionally intelligent teachers support preschool children's emotional intelligence', unpublished doctoral dissertation, Massey University, Palmerston North, New Zealand.

Van Petegem, K., Creemers, B.P.M., Rossel, Y. and Aelterman, A. (2005) 'Relationships between teacher characteristics, interpersonal behavior and teacher wellbeing', *Journal of Classroom Interaction,* 40: 34–43.

Wilson, H.K., Pianta, R.C. and Stuhlman, M. (2007) 'Typical classroom experiences in first grade: the role of classroom climate and functional risk in the development of social competencies', *The Elementary School Journal,* 108: 81–96.

Wubbels, T., Brekelmans, M., and Hooymayers, H.P. (1991) 'Interpersonal teacher behavior in the classroom', In B.J. Fraser and H.J. Walberg (eds), *Educational Environments and Effects: Evaluation, Antecedents and Consequences* (pp. 141–169), London: Pergamon.

Zapf, D. (2002) 'Emotion work and psychological wellbeing: a review of the literature and some conceptual considerations', *Human Resource Management Review,* 12: 237–268.

34

CONTEMPORARY PROFESSIONAL BOUNDARIES AND THEIR RELATIONSHIP WITH TEACHER AND STUDENT WELL-BEING

Zoe A. Morris

Over the past 10–15 years, effort has been made internationally to professionalize teaching, particularly in the areas of certification, licensure, and regulation (Dinham 2013). Teachers are expected to uphold high social standards in their work with young people and these obligations are in addition to the moral expectations for any lay person (Campbell 2003). Recently, rapid advances in social media and digital communication have created new spaces for learning and relationships (e.g. social networking sites such as EdModo and Facebook). In this developing arena, standards of behavior evolve somewhat more slowly than the technology itself, creating a degree of risk for students and teachers alike. Combined with the pressure of high-stakes test regimes and teacher accountability for learning outcomes, the expectations placed on teachers appear to be contributing negatively to their well-being (Valli and Buese 2007). The professional boundaries of the teacher–student relationship are largely underexplored. In this chapter, contemporary professional boundaries for teachers and their students are examined in the context of knowledge from other helping professions such as medicine and psychology. The outcomes for teacher and student well-being and implications for teacher education and training are considered.

Boundaries of the teacher–student relationship: What can be learned from other professions?

Humans, even those with extensive professional training, are not infallible. Teaching licensure boards and regulation bodies have increasingly invested in the development of codes of conduct which have formalized the behavioral expectations of teachers. Such documents have aimed to define the boundaries of appropriate and inappropriate teacher practice (e.g. The Victorian Institute of Teaching 2008). This is inherently challenging; professional boundaries are not static, nor do they have neatly defined 'lines' and 'edges' (Riley 2013). Boundaries are therefore difficult for teachers to negotiate, for researchers to quantify, and for formal regulators to define clearly. With inevitable social and technological change, codes may need to be revisited in order to maintain relevance over time.

Boundary *violations* are behaviors which deviate from the professional role and cause harm to the student (e.g. sexual harassment). Boundary *crossings* are more difficult to define as they involve more minor departures from commonly accepted practice (Australian Psychological Society 2012). Figures suggest that less than 1 percent of registered teachers engage in serious misconduct; for example, sexual relationship with a student (Morris *et al.* 2012). Less is known about the frequency of boundary crossings (Page 2013). Yet, such events are significant, as minor transgressions can have a devastating effect on an individual teacher's personal well-being and professional standing. Further, there can be a significant effect on the student/s and school communities involved.

Despite holding equal importance in education, the arena of professional behavior appears somewhat more advanced in the fields of psychology and medicine (Buchberger *et al.* 2000). These two professions have a rich tradition of creating and applying research-based knowledge to develop, support, and enhance competent and responsible practice. As a result, there is less 'infrastructure' available to teachers compared with other occupations (Cohen 2011: 57). For example, the Australian Psychological Society (APS) periodically releases detailed ethical guidelines (APS 2012) in addition to its code of ethics (APS 1997, 2007) on issues such as physical contact, managing professional boundaries and working with young people. These detailed guidelines support ethical decision making by providing questions for self-reflection and practical suggestions to avoid negative outcomes for the client and the professional (e.g. it is recommended that a third party be in the vicinity for interventions involving physical contact). In discussing boundary crossings, practitioners are asked to reflect whether they are acting uncharacteristically with the client, or if they are self-disclosing more than usual.

This guiding approach is in contrast to some of the teacher codes of conduct available. For example, The Institute's code of conduct (Victorian Institute of Teaching 2008) states in Principle 1.5: 'Teachers are always in a professional relationship with the students in their school, whether at school or not'. The code lists five behaviors to illustrate how a teacher would violate a professional relationship relating to: sexual relationship with a student; physically touching a student; using sexual innuendo or inappropriate language/materials; accepting gifts; and holding conversations of a personal nature through written or electronic means. The notion of the behavior occurring within a 'valid context' or being motivated by a 'valid reason' is emphasized in relation to touching and conversations with students, yet a definition of 'valid' is not explicitly provided. Internationally, codes of conduct have been critically received, and described as general and ambiguous (Barrett *et al.* 2012). The resources available in psychology, medicine, and related professions appear to support ethical decision making in greater depth, and for a broader range of situations.

Psychological perspectives on the teacher–student relationship and well-being

Over the past decade, psychology and education have become interested in the relationship between emotion and other well-studied processes such as cognition, motivation, and decision making (Woolfolk Hoy 2013). In something of a boom, emotions-focused research has yielded aspirational teacher characteristics such as 'care' (Wentzel 1997, 2010), 'enthusiasm' (Kunter *et al.* 2011), 'relatedness' (Klassen *et al.* 2012), 'relational goals' (Butler 2012) and various elements of 'emotional support' (Hamre and Pianta 2008). Generally, it is agreed that teachers who are socially and emotionally competent develop supportive and encouraging relationships with their students (Jennings and Greenberg 2009). Research on the social-emotional context of the classroom has been influential, but has tended to focus on the student emotions and outcomes and the characteristics of teachers that can enhance positive outcomes for students (Split *et al.* 2011). For example, positive teacher–student relationships have been linked to positive social and academic outcomes (Wentzel 2010), whereas relationships characterized by conflict and mistrust are linked with poor learning outcomes (Hamre and Pianta 2001). Conversely, teachers report that maintaining positive teacher–student relationships is one of their major stressors (Liston *et al.* 2006). The teacher–student relationship might also influence teacher well-being, yet less research has investigated this outcome (Split *et al.* 2011).

The positive psychology movement has led to gains in the interest in, and broader understanding of, teacher well-being. Day and Qing (2009) define well-being as both a psychological and a social construct, and it is believed to be shaped by social experiences. In the context of teacher well-being, the teacher–student relationship is therefore an important component to consider. Teacher well-being encompasses both personal and professional elements, possibly because teaching requires a significant level of personal investment (Day 2013). There is a very strong connection between teachers' lives and their work, perhaps more than other helping professions because of the frequent and prolonged engagement with students and their education. For example, it would be rare for a doctor or psychologist to spend up to 5 hours in a day with a client for up to 40 weeks of a year. Indeed, 'being a teacher seems to involve a special relationship with other people that you don't find' in many other professions (Robertson 1997, as cited in Trier 2001: 35). As Robertson (1997) suggests, the teacher–student relationship is riddled with complicated and sometimes hidden psychodynamics that – while often cited as some of the most rewarding aspects of the role, are also an important source of teacher motivation (Hargreaves 2000). Therefore this relationship has a powerful potential in shaping teacher-well-being, yet it can also be a source of stress if the teacher–student relationship is found to be challenging.

There is growing acknowledgment of the effect of emotional labor on teachers, as well as international concern over rates of teacher retention and burnout (Richardson *et al.* 2013). Emotional labor refers to modifying one's emotional expression by enhancement, falsification, and/or suppression (Isenbarger and Zembylas 2006). This process is often embedded in the creation and maintenance of teacher–student relationships. The intense involvement with students' individual and social needs can therefore be emotionally and mentally draining for teachers (Newberry 2013). Robust professional boundaries may be a protective factor for teacher well-being, as the teacher is required to acknowledge that his or her responsibility for student needs is limited, and it is sometimes necessary to delegate to others. For example, a student who may be having significant mental health issues should be referred to a psychologist for additional assistance, rather than the teacher attempting to engage in therapeutic interactions. In turn, this has a positive effect on the student as boundaries denote the limit of a given professional relationship and they enable a sense of trust, safety, and predictability (Hammond 2010).

Antecedents to boundary violations:
The slippery-slope effect

In the main, teachers do not generally set out to violate boundaries with their students. The 'slippery-slope effect' relates to the argument that boundary violations are often preceded by a chain of minor erosions (Hammond 2010). Research has focused on the slippery-slope effect within the context of doctor–patient relationships (Galletly 2004), therapist–client relationships (Barnett *et al.* 2007), clinical supervision (Plaut 1993), and faculty–student relationships in academic settings (Biaggio *et al.* 1997). Numerous terms are used to describe minor transgressions (e.g. boundary 'excursions', 'crossings', or 'blurring') and they are collectively agreed to occur more frequently than boundary violations and often without formal penalties (Simon 1999). However, these minor transgressions can cause harm to those involved and are thought to increase the risk of boundary violations, and the development of inappropriate relationships between a professional and those in their care (Galletly 2004).

Unlike medicine and psychology, educational research has seldom considered the slippery-slope effect in the context of teacher misconduct (Shakeshaft 2004). Potentially, it is a difficult area to gain access to because of the ethical issues involved in investigating potential sexual misbehavior involving minors. This is an important phenomenon to understand in teaching as the frequency of contact with students is generally much higher than that between doctors and patients, and psychologists and clients. In addition, professional standards in education are less clear-cut than those for psychology and medicine where enforceable codes of ethics are long established (Barrett *et al.* 2006). Thus, the 'slope' is not only slippery but dimly lit, as registration authorities and research have neglected to illuminate the issue for teaching professionals.

Research on the slippery-slope effect has tended to concentrate on inappropriate sexual relationships (Russell and Peterson 1998). From a risk management perspective, in order to prevent sexual boundary violations the professional should be stopped from entering the slippery slope at the outset (Barnett *et al.* 2007). Contemporary approaches acknowledge that conceptions of boundaries are always evolving and, thus, are complex. Teachers work across a multitude of contextual combinations; for example, school type (primary, secondary, or tertiary) and setting (rural, suburban). Further, they simultaneously interact with students from a range of cultural backgrounds who may also identify as gay/lesbian/bisexual/transgender. Fromuth and colleagues (2010) highlight that contextual factors are influential in deciding where boundaries lie, a difficult task for teachers perhaps, considering the range of factors above.

The slippery slope for teachers often comprises nonsexual behaviors and interactions as teachers negotiate multiple types of boundaries simultaneously. Based on a literature review, Aultman *et al.* (2009) identified eleven boundaries in the teacher–student relationship; for example, institutional (e.g. driving a student home), financial (e.g. loaning money to a student), communication (e.g. high level of self-disclosure which may not benefit the student), and emotional (e.g. controlling teacher emotions). Aultman and colleagues concluded that teachers need to be mindful of these boundaries whilst also balancing the elements of care and control in their relationship with students. An area which is not overtly highlighted in the proposed boundaries is the tension between 'public' and 'private' aspects of the teacher, particularly in relation to online communication.

Teacher behavior online: Where private meets public

Technological advancements have created a further emergent context for teacher–student relationships. Social media platforms (e.g. social networking sites such as Facebook and Instagram) have also allowed personal social interactions to be documented, redistributed, and made available to a broader audience online. Research has begun evaluating the value of using social media in teaching and learning (Alvermann *et al.* 2013). Split and colleagues (2011) also suggest that technology may be a means by which teachers can build a personal connection to students and negate the alienation of secondary school structure. Social networking presents as a double-edged sword, elevating communication to a global level, with unprecedented speed and accessibility. However, communications are relatively permanent, vulnerable to misinterpretation, and without due care can lack security and confidentiality (DeJong 2014). Thus, this technology has also provided new avenues for breaches of professional boundaries, for which little formal guidance is available (DeJong 2014).

I propose three key areas of concern in the use of social networking by teaching professionals:

1   *Blurring boundaries of the teacher–student relationship.* In terms of boundaries, teachers need to be mindful that their interactions with students online remain professional and learning-focused (regardless of interactions being public or private). Between 2011 and 2013, transcripts of formal discipline hearings regarding teacher misconduct in Victoria, Australia, indicated a slippery-slope effect involving both online and offline behaviors such as text messages, gift giving, and hugging (Victorian Institute of Teaching 2014).

2   *Online representation of teachers.* Coutts *et al.* (2007) reported that 82 percent of the 385 pre-service elementary teachers surveyed were registered on Facebook, yet less than half had restricted profile access to their 'friends' only. Increasingly, teachers are being faced with negative repercussions of unbecoming online postings as students, parents, employers, or prospective employers view, report, or disseminate information or images from personal profiles. Teachers should enable strict privacy settings so that their personal social media profiles are not accessible without their approval.

3   *Duty of care responsibilities.* If teachers interact with, or befriend, students on social media, even in the context of a school-related/professional profile, they may be privy to sensitive information from their students' profiles (e.g. relating to risky behavior or mental health issues). Depending on the jurisdiction, teachers may have a duty of care to report or act upon such information where the safety of a student is compromised.

These three factors all pose risks for both the teacher and student individually, and may cause the teacher–student relationship to be compromised, exploited, or harmed. Research is yet to uncover the effect of such events on the teacher or student's well-being.

In the absence of clear formal expectations, teachers have been increasingly held accountable by the media and general public for their behaviors beyond the classroom as they are represented and documented online (Barrett *et al.* 2012). The misbehavior of teachers is under-researched and thus the public tend to rely on information based on sensationalist reports as opposed to empirical research (Knoll 2010; Page 2013). Teaching has historically been viewed as a role that is undertaken 24 hours a day, 7 days a week, 365 days a year. Technology has further blurred the boundaries between teachers' public and private lives, and professional expectations are placed on teachers online as well as outside of the workplace and online. Internationally, the media has reported on cases of teachers' online posts and photos which are seen to be discordant with the teacher in terms of the sexual and racial undertones or religious vilification conveyed by the posts. Even legal behaviors such as alcohol consumption and wearing fancy dress costumes have proved problematic when represented online. The media reports on misbehavior of other professional groups, yet teachers appear to be over-represented (Burke 2014), leading to a degree of 'scrutiny stress' within the profession (Lasalvia 2011).

Teaching is considered an inherently emotional moral and ethical activity (Campbell 2003) that involves high levels of interpersonal contact with often vulnerable young people (Zembylas and Schutz 2009); thus, high expectations have been, and continue to be, ascribed to members of the teaching profession. In 1872, the Ontario Common Rules for Teachers declared that female teachers would be dismissed if they married or engaged in unbecoming conduct. Further, restrictions were placed on the number of evenings male teachers could 'court' a female per week, and those who were seen smoking, drinking liquor, attending pool or public halls, or being shaved in a barbershop were assumed to have suspect intentions, integrity, and honesty (Richter 2006). It is interesting to consider these antiquated expectations of teachers whilst acknowledging that teacher behavior has been, and continues to be, held to higher expectations than others. It is unknown whether attitudes towards social media postings will relax over time as the attitudes about appropriate conduct did for teachers in Ontario. Regardless, this example provides a historical context for the tensions which continue to exist between the public and private lives of teachers.

Profiling those who cross boundaries: Naivety, unconscious motivations, and good intentions

Teaching is a highly autonomous role, and thus teachers need to regulate and take responsibility for their own behavior. While the vast majority of teachers succeed in abiding with professional expectations, there may be characteristics which increase the risk of boundary crossings and violations. Little is known about the profiles of teachers who cross professional boundaries, whether it is an isolated event or a more engrained interaction style. At the extreme end of boundary crossing, research by Knoll (2010) revealed that teachers who engaged in sexual misconduct ranged from mediocre to outstanding in their teaching skills. This is in contrast to the stereotype that those who fail to maintain appropriate boundaries are 'bad' teachers. Because of a lack of formal documentation, there is less knowledge about the kinds of teachers who engage in minor boundary crossings. Inexperience is an influential factor as early career teachers may be particularly vulnerable to errors of judgment (Cattley 2007). This is further compounded by age, as such teachers can be as young as 20 or 21 years, when research suggests the brain is still developing in terms of executive functioning (Steinberg 2011).

Individuals who engage in minor boundary crossings may also be well-meaning in their motives to support, connect, or engage their students, yet they demonstrate poor judgment in their choice of actions (Barnett *et al.* 2007). Regretfully, such situations can cause shame, humiliation, and loss of face, and can even lead to the termination of employment of otherwise well-performing teachers. Formal codes of professional expectations should optimize professional relationships by supporting and guiding teachers to create and maintain appropriate boundaries with their students. In this way, standards will be largely developmental rather than judgmental or a pathway to dismissal (Dinham 2013).

Examples of less desirable motivations for engaging with students are those that are self-indulgent (Hargreaves 2000) or self-serving (Riley 2011), and these are often unconscious. Based on a psychodynamic approach, Riley (2011) suggests that some insecurely attached individuals may seek teaching as a profession to gain care from others and create a corrective emotional experience. Further, from the perspective of self-determination theory, Klassen and colleagues (2012) demonstrated that 'teacher relatedness' with students may fulfil basic psychological needs for the teacher and promote teacher engagement and positive emotions. Butler (2012) highlighted that teachers' goals reflect not only personal, but interpersonal needs. Relational goals were found to positively predict teacher social support and mastery instruction. Thus, unconscious motivations and goals may be underlying drivers of boundary crossing behavior in the teacher–student relationship. This body of research may see teacher selection methodology shift from an academic focus to a more holistic selection process, akin to that in medicine, where personal characteristics are also taken into account (Wilson *et al.* 2012) – an example being the web-based survey tool 'Teacher Selector' (Melbourne Graduate School of Education 2013), which was developed based on an ongoing large-scale research study with the aim of identifying the attributes of effective teachers, and is currently being trialed.

Mindful navigation of the intersecting complexities of boundaries, motivation, and emotion

The recent emphasis on teacher emotional profiles and qualities such as teacher care and relatedness has created powerful conversations about the importance of the teacher–student relationship in learning and well-being for both parties. Hargreaves urges the consideration that 'more emotion is not always better' (2000: 813). This prompts consideration of two questions: how much teacher care is too much and can a teacher relate too intensely with students? Research is highlighting numerous encouraging aspects of positive teacher–student emotions and interactions, yet they are without boundaries. The complexity lies in the teacher being mindful of when the 'optimal dosage' is reached, so that a balance is found between elements of care and professionalism.

Teachers must therefore actively self-regulate their behavior to promote balance in their relationships with students. Ludmerer (1999) highlighted three essential characteristics of medical professionals which are relevant for teachers: (1) expert knowledge; (2) self-regulation; and (3) responsibility to place the needs of the client (the student) ahead of the self-interest of the practitioner (the teacher). By extension, this triad of skills acknowledges the importance of training, self-awareness, self-management, and an understanding of one's motivations. Woolfolk Hoy (2013) further emphasizes the notion of 'the self-regulating professional' (265) and highlights other critical skills such as relationship skills, responsible decision making, and self-awareness, all of which receive little attention in preservice teacher training.

Teachers also need to be mindful that the provision of care and emotional support does not negatively affect their own well-being, or contribute to a path of burnout. In his discussion of appropriate boundaries within the context of mental health professionals, Plaut (2010) recommends the practice of self-care, and nurturing systems of support such as personal relationships. Self-care is the process of maintaining well-being and personal health through positive actions and attitudes. Mindfulness is one technique which has received recent empirical and practitioner attention and is demonstrating usefulness in a range of health settings, including stress reduction and enhanced clinical performance in medical students and doctors (Hassed et al. 2009). The premise of mindfulness, which has ties to meditative techniques, is to regulate attention with aim to direct awareness to the present moment, rather than dwelling on the past (Hassed 2008). Mindfulness training is beginning to be used in educational contexts and may have the potential to assist teachers in managing the demanding social-emotional terrain of the classroom (Roeser et al. 2012). Teacher education programs currently provide little guidance or instruction on creating, navigating, and maintaining relationships (Richardson et al. 2013). It is essential that teacher education acknowledges the importance of emotional self-regulation (Woolfolk Hoy 2013) to encourage the development of positive and professional teacher–student relationships.

Teacher education and ethics instruction: The black box?

Despite the importance of ethical skills, ethical training in teacher education remains something of a black box. Very little research has quantified teacher education students' perceptions of, and satisfaction with, preservice ethical training in education. Tobias and Boon (2009) reported that nearly three-quarters of Australian preservice primary teachers' wanted more overt instruction and clarification of teacher ethics. Morris and colleagues (2012) found that only 3 percent of preservice secondary teachers regarded their ethical training as 'very adequate' on a four-point scale from 'not at all adequate' to 'very adequate'. Further, 70 percent of these preservice secondary teachers were 'not at all' familiar with the formal teacher code of conduct in their state. Glanzer and Ream (2007) studied the curriculum of 151 religious colleges and universities in the United States. Of those that offered a major in education, only 6 percent required students to complete an ethics course. Of the seven disciplines surveyed, the education discipline was the least likely to include a compulsory ethics component. A greater percentage of universities offering business (46%), nursing (43%), and social work/criminal justice (39%) majors were likely to include a compulsory ethics unit. Taken together, these results do not paint a favorable picture of ethics training in education.

Education has become a somewhat 'battered profession' (Scott and Dinham 2002), with a high level of external critique evident in the fabric of society. This has placed growing pressure on training providers to produce quality graduates who not only are effective teachers, but also possess the internal awareness, ethical knowledge, and decision-making skills to operate professionally and ethically (Boon 2011). Despite the importance placed on ethics training in education, there remains much scope for research in the area. Largely unknown are the *attitudinal outcomes* of the ethics training received; that is, how are contemporary boundaries currently understood? For example, what types of student–teacher interactions are considered to be appropriate by teachers (e.g. adding a student as a friend on Facebook, giving a student a hug as a means of consolation, driving a student in their car, attending student social events outside of school)? Do contextual factors such as age, gender, experience, school setting (remote, suburban), student age (primary, secondary) play a role in defining how boundaries are interpreted? Are particular teachers at greater risk of boundary crossing? Can this be profiled based on individual characteristics and motivations? The answers may provide important feedback on the current state of ethics training in teacher education and assist in improving the curriculum to meet specific teacher needs.

Challenges and future directions

While it is the minority of professionals who find themselves in professional disrepute, it is important that *all* teachers hold the ethical element of practice constantly in the background of their work so that it can become easily activated (Campbell 2003). In this way, professionals are able to self-regulate their behavior by becoming aware of inner messages and 'red flags' which signal the approach of a professional boundary or potential slippery slope (Plaut 2010: 24). From the small amount of research available, we can see that the ethical component of preservice training requires improvement to assist teachers in this goal. Teachers require supportive and clear professional behavioral guidelines and explicit training in ethical decision making and other relevant skills such as mindfulness. In this way they will be equipped to face novel situations that present, particularly in navigating the complex interpersonal terrain of teaching. Such training would also be supportive of both teacher and student well-being, which can be affected by inappropriate, negative, or unprofessional relationships.

It is hoped that this important, yet often neglected, area of research is fertile in the future. In assisting teachers to both become and remain ethical teachers, we first need to better understand the nature of contemporary teacher professional boundaries. In building this program of research, multiple perspectives and methodologies are required and encouraged to create valid and reliable measures of constructs. Research and practice in the disciplines of psychology and medicine provide an encouraging model for education; nevertheless the teacher–student relationship has unique qualities to be examined and understood.

Acknowledgments

With gratitude to Paul W. Richardson, Helen M.G. Watt and Philip Riley, for their earlier draft comments.

References

Alvermann, D.E., Hutchins, R.J. and McDevitt, R. (2013) 'Adolescents' engagement with web 2.0 and social media: research, theory, and practice', *Research in Schools,* 19: 33–44.

Aultman, L.P., Williams-Johnson, M.R. and Schutz, P.A. (2009) 'Boundary dilemmas in teacher–student relationships: struggling with "the line"', *Teaching and Teacher Education,* 25: 636–646. doi:10.1016/j.tate.2008.10.002

Australian Psychological Society (1997) *Code of Ethics,* Melbourne, Vic: Author.

Australian Psychological Society (2007) *Code of Ethics,* Melbourne, Vic: Author.

Australian Psychological Society (2012) *Ethical Guidelines: Complementing the APS Code of Ethics,* 11th edn, Melbourne, Vic: Author.

Barnett, J.E., Lazarus, A., Vasquez, M.J.T., Moorehead-Slaughter, O. and Johnson, W.B. (2007) 'Boundary issues and multiple relationships: fantasy and reality', *Professional Psychology: Research and Practice,* 38: 401–410. doi: 10.1037/0735–7028.38.4.401

Barrett, D.E., Casey, J.E., Visser, R.D. and Headley, K.N. (2012) 'How do teachers make judgments about ethical and unethical behaviors? Toward the development of a code of conduct for teachers', *Teaching and Teacher Education,* 28: 890–898. doi: 10.1016/j.tate.2012.04.003

Barrett, D.E., Headley, K.N., Stovall, B. and Witte, J.C. (2006) 'Teachers' perceptions of the frequency and seriousness of violations of ethical standards', *The Journal of Psychology,* 140: 421–433. doi: 10.3200/JRLP.140.5.421–433

Biaggio, M., Paget, T.L. and Chenoweth, M.S. (1997) 'A model for ethical management of faculty – student dual relationships', *Professional Psychology: Research and Practice,* 28: 184. doi: 10.1037/0735–7028.28.2.184

Boon, H.J. (2011) 'Raising the bar: ethics education for quality teachers', *Australian Journal of Teacher Education,* 36: 76–93.

Buchberger, F., Campos, B.P., Kallos, D. and Stephenson, J. (eds) (2000) *Green Paper on Teacher Education in Europe,* Sweden: Thematic Network on Teacher Education in Europe (TNTEE). Available at: http://www.iperbole.bologna.it/iperbole/adi/XoopsAdi/uploads/PDdownloads/tntee_green_paper_on_teacher_education_in_europe.pdf

Burke, R.J. (2014) 'Human frailties in the workplace: their nature, consequences and remedy', in R.J. Burke, S. Fox and C.L. Cooper (eds), *Human Frailties: Wrong Choices on the Drive to Success* (pp. 3–52), Farnham, UK: Gower.

Butler, R. (2012) 'Striving to connect: extending an achievement goal approach to teacher motivation to include relational goals for teaching', *Journal of Educational Psychology,* 104: 726. doi: 10.1037/a0028613

Campbell, E. (2003) *The Ethical Teacher,* Maidenhead, UK: Open University Press.

Cattley, G. (2007) 'Emergence of professional identity for the pre-service teacher', *International Education Journal,* 8: 337–347.

Cohen, D.K. (2011) *Teaching and Its Predicaments,* Cambridge: Harvard University Press.

Coutts, J., Boyer, J., Dawson, K. and Ferdig, R. (2007) 'Will you be my friend? Prospective teachers' use of Facebook and implications for teacher education', paper presented at the Proceedings of Society for Information Technology and Teacher Education International Conference, Chesapeake.

Day, C. (2013) 'The new lives of teachers', in M.A. Flores, A.A. Carvalho, Ferreira, F.I. and M.T. Vilaça (eds), *Back to the Future* (pp. 57–74), Rotterdam: Sense Publishing.

Day, C. and Qing, G. (2009) 'Teacher emotions: wellbeing and effectiveness', in P.A. Schutz and M. Zembylas (eds), *Advances in Teacher Emotion Research: The Impact on Teachers Lives* (pp. 15–32), London: Springer.

DeJong, S. (2014) *Blogs and Tweets, Texting and Friending: Social Media and Online Professionalism in Health Care,* San Diego: Academic Press.

Dinham, S. (2013) 'The quality teaching movement in Australia encounters difficult terrain: a personal perspective', *Australian Journal of Education,* 57: 91–106. doi: 10.1177/0004944113485840

Fromuth, M.E., Mackey, A.L. and Wilson, A. (2010) 'Effect of student vulnerability on perceptions of teacher–student sexual involvement', *Journal of Child Sexual Abuse,* 19: 419–433. doi: 10.1080/10538712.2010.495700

Galletly, C.A. (2004) 'Crossing professional boundaries in medicine: the slippery slope to patient sexual exploitation', *Medical Journal of Australia,* 181: 380–383.

Glanzer, P.L. and Ream, T.C. (2007) 'Has teacher education missed out on the "ethics boom"? A comparative study of ethics requirements and courses in professional majors of Christian colleges and universities', *Christian Higher Education,* 6: 271–288.

Hammond, S. (2010) 'Boundaries and multiple relationships', in A. Allan and A. Love (eds), *Ethical Practice in Psychology: Reflections from the Creators of the APS Code of Ethics* (pp. 135–147), Oxford: John Wiley.

Hamre, B.K. and Pianta, R.C. (2001) Early teacher–child relationships and the trajectory of children's school outcomes through eighth grade', *Child Development,* 72: 625–638. doi: 10.1111/1467–8624.00301

Hamre, B.K. and Pianta, R.C. (2008) 'Can instructional and emotional support in the first-grade classroom make a difference for children at risk of school failure?' *Child Development,* 76: 949–967. doi: 10.1111/j.1467–8624.2005.00889.x

Hargreaves, A. (2000) 'Mixed emotions: teachers' perceptions of their interactions with students', *Teaching and Teacher Education,* 16: 811–826.

Hassed, C. (2008) *The Essence of Health: The Seven Pillars of Wellbeing,* Sydney: Random House.

Hassed, C., de Lisle, S., Sullivan, G. and Pier, C. (2009) 'Enhancing the health of medical students: outcomes of an integrated mindfulness and lifestyle program', *Advances in Health Science Education,* 14: 387–398. doi: 10.1007/s10459–008–9125–3

Isenbarger, L. and Zembylas, M. (2006) 'The emotional labour of caring in teaching', *Teaching and Teacher Education,* 22: 120–134. doi: 10.1016/j.tate.2005.07.002

Jennings, P.A. and Greenberg, M.T. (2009) 'The prosocial classroom: teacher social and emotional competence in relation to student and classroom outcomes', *Review of Educational Research,* 79: 491–525. doi: 10.3102/0034654308325693

Klassen, R.M., Perry, N.E. and Frenzel, A. (2012) 'Teachers' relatedness with students: an underemphasized component of teachers' basic psychological needs', *Journal of Educational Psychology,* 104: 150–165. doi: 10.1037/a0026253

Knoll, J. (2010) 'Teacher sexual misconduct: grooming patterns and female offenders', *Journal of Child Sexual Abuse,* 19: 371–386. doi: 10.1080/10538712.2010.495047

Kunter, M., Frenzel, A., Nagy, G., Baumert, J., and Pekrun, R. (2011) Teacher enthusiasm: dimensionality and context specificity', *Contemporary Educational Psychology,* 36: 289–301. doi: 10.1016/j.cedpsych.2011.07.001

Lasalvia, A. (2011) *Handbook of Stress in the Occupations,* Cheltenham, UK: Edward Elgar.

Liston, D., Whitcomb, J. and Borko, H. (2006) 'Too little or too much: teacher preparation and the first years of teaching', *Journal of Teacher Education,* 57: 351–358. doi: 10.1177/0022487106291976

Ludmerer, K.M. (1999) 'Instilling professionalism in medical education', *The Journal of the American Medical Association,* 282: 881.

Melbourne Graduate School of Education (2013) Teacher Selector Website. Available at: https://teacherselector.com.au/

Morris, Z.A., Richardson, P.W. and Watt, H.M.G. (2012) 'What is popular is not always right: measuring teacher professional behaviour', in J. Wright (ed.), *Proceedings Joint Australian Association of Research in Education (AARE) Annual Conference and Asia Pacific Education Research Association Conference,* Sydney, December 2–6.

Newberry, M. (2013) 'The demand of multiplicity in the classroom: emotion regulation and cognitive load', in M. Newberry, A. Gallant and P. Riley (eds), *Emotion and School: Understanding How the Hidden Curriculum Influences Relationships, Leadership, Teaching, and Learning* (Advances in Research on Teaching, Vol. 18, pp. 25–48), Bingley, UK: Emerald Group Publishing.

Page, D. (2013) 'Teacher misbehaviour: an analysis of disciplinary orders by the General Teaching Council for England', *British Educational Research Journal,* 39: 545–564. doi: 10.1080/01411926.2012.674103

Plaut, S.M. (1993) 'Boundary issues in teacher–student relationships', *Journal of Sex and Marital Therapy,* 19: 210–219.

Plaut, S.M. (2010) 'Understanding and managing professional–client boundaries', in S.B. Levine, C.B. Risen and S.E. Althof (eds), *Handbook of Clinical Sexuality for Mental Health Professionals,* 2nd edn (pp. 21–38), New York: Brunner-Routledge.

Richardson, P.W., Watt, H.M.G. and Devos, C. (2013) 'Types of professional and emotional coping among beginning teachers', in M. Newberry, A. Gallant and P. Riley (eds), *Emotion and School: Understanding How the Hidden Curriculum Influences Relationships, Leadership, Teaching, and Learning* (Advances in Research on Teaching, Vol. 18, pp. 229–254), Bingley, UK: Emerald Group Publishing.

Richter, B. (2006, October) 'It's elementary: a brief history of Ontario's public elementary teachers and their federations part two: early 1800's to 1944', *EFTO Voice.* Available from http://www.etfo.ca/SiteCollectionDocuments/About%20ETFO%20Documents/ETFO%20History%20Documents/history-pt2.pdf

Riley, P. (2011) *Attachment Theory and the Teacher–Student Relationship,* London: Routledge.

Riley, P. (2013) 'The complexities of school leadership: many boundaries to cross', in J. Langan-Fox and C.L. Cooper (eds) *Boundary-Spanning in Organizations: Network, Influence, and Conflict* (pp. 187–205), New York: Routledge.

Robertson, J.P. (1997) 'Screenplay pedagogy and the interpretation of unexamined knowledge in preservice primary teaching', *TABOO: A Journal of Culture & Education,* 1 (Spring): 25–60.

Roeser, R.W., Skinner, E., Beers, J. and Jennings, P.A. (2012) 'Mindfulness training and teachers' professional development: an emerging area of research and practice', *Child Development Perspectives,* 6: 167–173. doi: 10.1111/j.1750–8606.2012.00238.x

Russell, C.S. and Peterson, C.M. (1998) 'The management of personal and professional boundaries in marriage and family therapy training programs', *Contemporary Family Therapy,* 20: 457–470.

Scott, C. and Dinham, S. (2002) 'The beatings will continue until quality improves: carrots and sticks in the search for educational improvement', *Teacher Development,* 6: 15–31.

Shakeshaft, C. (2004, June) *Educator Sexual Misconduct: A Synthesis of Existing Literature,* Washington, DC: US Department of Education.

Simon, R.I. (1999) 'Therapist–patient sex: from boundary violations to sexual misconduct', *Psychiatric Clinics of North America,* 22: 31–47.

Split, J.L., Koomen, H.M.Y. and Thijs, J.T. (2011) 'Teacher wellbeing: the importance of teacher–student relationships', *Educational Psychology Review,* 23: 467–477. doi: 10.1007/s10648–011–9170–y

Steinberg, L. (2011) 'Demystifying the adolescent brain', *Educational Leadership,* 68: 42–46.

Tobias, S. and Boon, H. (2009, November) 'Codes of conduct and ethical dilemmas in teacher education', paper presented at the Australian Association for Research in Education Annual Conference, Canberra, November 29–December 3.

Trier, J.D. (2001) 'The cinematic representation of the personal and professional lives of teachers', *Teacher Education Quarterly,* 28: 127–147.

Valli, L. and Buese, D. (2007) 'The changing roles of teachers in an era of high-stakes accountability', *American Educational Research Journal,* 44: 519–558. doi: 10.3102/0002831207306859

Victorian Institute of Teaching (2008) 'Victorian Teaching Profession Code of Conduct'. Available at: http://www.vit.vic.edu.au/SiteCollectionDocuments/PDF/1543_Code-of-Conduct-June-2008.pdf

Victorian Institute of Teaching (2014) 'Formal hearing decisions'. Available at: http://www.vit.vic.edu.au/conduct/formal-hearing/formal-hearing-decisions/Pages/default.aspx

Wentzel, K.R. (1997) 'Student motivation in middle school: the role of perceived pedagogical caring', *Journal of Educational Psychology,* 89: 411–419.

Wentzel, K.R. (2010) 'Students' relationships with teachers', in J.L. Meece and J.S. Eccles (eds), *Handbook of Research on Schools, Schooling, and Human Development* (pp. 75–91), New York: Routledge.

Wilson, I.G., Roberts, C., Flynn, E.M. and Griffin, B. (2012) 'Only the best: medical student selection in Australia', *The Medical Journal of Australia,* 196: 377–388. doi: 10.5694/mja10.11388

Woolfolk Hoy, A. (2013) 'A reflection on the place of emotion in teaching and teacher education', in M. Newberry, A. Gallant and P. Riley (eds) *Emotion and School: Understanding How the Hidden Curriculum Influences Relationships, Leadership, Teaching, and Learning* (Advances in Research on Teaching, Vol. 18, pp. 255–270), Bingley, UK: Emerald Group Publishing.

Zembylas, M. and Schutz, P.A. (2009) 'Research on teachers' emotions in education: findings, practical implications and future agenda', in P.A. Schutz and M. Zembylas (eds), *Advances in Teacher Emotion Research: The Impact on Teachers' Lives* (pp. 367–377), London: Springer.

PART VIII

The final word

35

THE SOCIAL PSYCHOLOGY OF THE CLASSROOM

Reflections about past, present, and future

Elisha Babad

Social psychology of the classroom as an independent domain

I was honored that the title of my 2009 book *The Social Psychology of the Classroom* was adopted as the general theme for the 2013 Social Psychology of the Classroom International Conference in New Zealand. I share the vision of the conference organizers and book co-editors that the social psychology of the classroom should be recognized as an independent domain in educational psychology. In fact, I have been a social psychologist of the classroom throughout my professional career of more than four decades.

On a personal note, I am sorry that I was not able to attend the conference in person. I have never been an avid conference-goer, even when events were held much closer than half a globe away from Jerusalem.

In a broad definition, the social psychology of the classroom can cover a wide array of topics and phenomena. This is clearly indicated by the range of topics in the 2013 conference program and the table of contents of this book. But in my mind, the definition of the social psychology of the classroom is narrower and more focused, dealing more exclusively with teachers and students, with the interactions between teachers and students and the interactions among students. The social psychology of the classroom should be focused directly on classroom processes, their antecedents, and their outcomes.

With regard to the major criterion outcome of the social psychology of the classroom, however, I do have one issue with the book editors. In the introductory chapter, they quote Hattie's (2009) book, which reports a synthesis of more than 800 meta-analyses examining contributions to students' learning, as a second stimulus for the 2013 conference and the current book. To quote from the introductory chapter, 'a major thrust is ... to dedicate a book to providing evidence for the importance of caring for students, to interacting positively with them, and to the corresponding benefits for their learning that result'.

The issue of 'caring for students' and 'interacting positively with them' is discussed later in this chapter. However, in principle, I consider that learning achievements should constitute a lesser criterion of social psychological forces in the classroom. Numerous background variables, students' attributes and abilities, teaching methods, and the quality of teaching contribute to learning, but the *social psychology* of the classroom also contributes to social outcomes such as well-being, satisfaction, motivation, and a positive climate (and the point the editors make is that these factors may, in turn, contribute to learning benefits as well).

I believe that teaching and learning specialists should be concerned about learning outcomes and achievements, whereas social psychologists should be concerned about social outputs and outcomes. In the field of students' evaluation of teachers in higher education (the focus of my current research), there was a widespread illusion that scholastic achievements constitute the relevant outcomes of effective teaching. We know today that assessing student satisfaction rather than learning outcomes is a more effective measure of course quality – satisfaction serving as a 'conceptual proxy' for achievement.

Social psychology within educational psychology: Past and present

My objective in this chapter is to make meaning of the social psychology of the classroom from a historical perspective, analyzing the past, the present, and the projected future in educational psychology and in social psychology. I will next examine social psychological phenomena within the wider perspective of educational psychology, to trace changes and turns that took place in the past decades. Topics and phenomena that disappeared or changed considerably over the years can provide clues for deciphering the underlying zeitgeist that can explain the present status, and the future of the social psychology of the classroom.

The following list presents a subjective account of social psychology within educational psychology as I have known and experienced the field since the 1960s, and emphasizes the turns and changes that occurred over the decades:

1   *Behaviorism and behavior modification* played a central role in educational psychology and in teacher training in the 1960s and 1970s. It was presented both as a theoretical perspective and as a collection of applied techniques for dealing with a variety of educational problems, and even as a major approach to teaching. The behavioral approach disappeared almost completely from textbooks in educational psychology, following a paradigm shift (Freiburg 1999). Today, its practical replacement – classroom management – is based on an approach that emphasizes more affective (perhaps 'softer') teacher–student relationships.

2   *The human relations movement* bloomed in the 1960s and 1970s (see Babad 2009). It promoted psychological change through experiential group methods for emotional self-inquiry. Educational applications of this approach included several editions of the popular book *Group Processes in the Classroom* by Schmuck and Schmuck (1975), and numerous applications for teachers and students such as 'the magic circle'. This approach disappeared from educational psychology over the years. Its current replacement perhaps includes self-reflection and meta-cognition, based on a different set of assumptions about psychological change.

3   In earlier decades, textbooks in educational psychology used to include chapters covering an array of *social psychological intergroup phenomena* such as stereotyping, prejudice, authoritarianism, dogmatism, cultural inter-group conflict, segregation, underprivileged groups, and so on. Such chapters changed considerably over the years, replaced by softer discourse about multicultural-ism, containment of those who are different, and so on.

4   In the earlier years, *motivation* was discussed in personal, social, and emotional terms. Today, achievement goal theory is more dominant (see Harackiewicz *et al.* 2002; Butler 2007), focus-ing on more cognitive elements influencing students' learning.

5   The social psychology of the classroom and the characterization of the classroom society were measured by *sociometric measurement* 40 years ago, and this type of measurement evoked great

enthusiasm among teachers and educators. Sociometric measurement disappeared over the decades, and today measurement of *classroom climate* is dominant (see Babad 2009).

6 Past coverage of the *measurement of intelligence* in educational psychology textbooks was heavily laden with bitter social and sociological disputes and controversies, despite the purely cognitive and intellectual nature of intelligence. The entire domain is quite out of focus today in educational psychology.

7 *Computer technologies* sparked an eternal and ongoing revolution in all aspects of education. Early on in my career, the major concern was how to develop and implement programmed instruction and how to develop computer literacy. Today, teachers can learn computer literacy from their young students, and the revolution has affected education in numerous dramatic ways. Great and amazing advances, most of them yet unimaginable, lie ahead for the entire field of education. In terms of social psychological aspects in and out of the classroom, I think that we are yet unable to deal with the utilization of technological advances by students and with social networks and their immense influence on students, on the world of children, and on the classroom and school societies.

8 Finally, the *Pygmalion research, teacher expectations,* and *teachers' differential behavior in the classroom* constitute what I consider as the core and essence of the social psychology of the classroom, and here the historical changes are dramatic. The publication of *Pygmalion in the Classroom* (Rosenthal and Jacobson 1968) was clearly a dramatic breakthrough in research in educational psychology. The book (which followed earlier Rosenthal research on effects of experimenters' expectations), has caused immense controversies since its publication (see e.g. Wineburg 1987) and served as an impetus for hundreds of studies and numerous meta-analyses (e.g. Harris and Rosenthal 1985). The Pygmalion research demonstrated that (fabricated) expectations in teachers' minds about hidden potential of particular students could lead to improvement in these students' intellectual performance. Rich subsequent lines of research investigated over two decades the formation of teacher expectations; the transmission of differential teacher expectations to students in subtle verbal and nonverbal ways; student perceptions of teachers' expectations and their evaluations of the teachers; and the social outcomes of teacher differential behavior on individual students and on whole classrooms (Babad *et al.* 1982; Babad 1995; Babad *et al.* 2003). Additional studies examined personality attributes of teachers susceptible to biasing information (Babad 1979) and a whole set of related phenomena such as the teachers' pet phenomenon (Babad 1995).

Pygmalion and teacher expectations became hot issues in the social psychology of the classroom and in educational psychology in general in the 1970s and 1980s, and self-fulfilling prophecy (no less than Pygmalion) became a household term and a widely known cultural phenomenon. I have spent much of my research career investigating various aspects and phenomena within this domain in school and in college classrooms (see Babad 2009), and later also in the public media, by examining how differential nonverbal behavior of a television interviewer can influence viewers' impressions of the interviewed politician (Babad 2005).

Three years ago I decided to check how current textbooks in educational psychology presented Pygmalion and teacher expectation phenomena to teachers in training. In my scrutiny of numerous educational psychology and general psychology introductory textbooks, I was dumbfounded to discover that Robert Rosenthal, Pygmalion, teacher expectations, and teacher differential behavior had disappeared almost completely, and the few existing citations were scanty and superficial. (Some new expectation research is included in a few introductory texts, see later discussion.) If the collection of current textbooks in educational psychology represents the body of educational psychology transmitted to future teachers, then the sad conclusion must be that prospective teachers are taught very little about teacher expectation phenomena and how to deal with these phenomena in the classroom.

Another salient and illuminating example of this trend to ignore teacher expectation phenomena emerged out of the scrutiny of the influential *Handbook of Classroom Management: Research, Practice, and Contemporary Issues*, published in 2006 by Carolyn Evertson and Carol Weinstein. This voluminous book (1,346 pages) included 47 chapters by 91 authors, including a chapter on 'Classroom management and relationships between children and teachers' by Robert Pianta, and a chapter on 'History of research on classroom management' by the late Jere Brophy.

I assume that nobody could or would claim that, within its broad definition, classroom management should not include phenomena focused on teacher–student interaction, teachers' self-fulfilling prophecies, expectation-based teacher differential behavior in the classroom, or the 'teacher's pet' phenomenon. And yet, none of these phenomena are mentioned at all in the 2006 handbook, which was claimed to be *the* authoritative statement on contemporary classroom management. Robert Rosenthal was cited only once in this book, and this citation did not refer to Pygmalion but to earlier work on the experimenter effect. Brophy's chapter on the history of classroom management made no reference at all to Pygmalion and teacher expectation phenomena, although Brophy himself was one of the most salient and productive researchers of teacher expectations in the 1970s and the 1980s, and published numerous influential articles (e.g. Brophy 1983, 1985), review chapters, and even edited a book on expectations in the classroom (Brophy 1998). In this 2006 history chapter, Brophy even omitted any reference to his own work on teacher expectations.

I must admit that I found this trend surprising, and as a long-time researcher of teachers, students and their classroom interaction, even somewhat insulting. Even if contemporary writers thought that the multitude of studies and findings on teacher expectations were invalid, they should not ignore a research body with hundreds of studies, and should at least have acknowledged it and discussed the relevant issues in current books.

To make sense of the trends described above and to understand the zeitgeist in educational psychology, I propose next a well-known conceptual historical framework that can explain the disappearance of Pygmalion and teacher expectations from educational psychology introductory textbooks and from the classroom management literature. The conceptualization relates to the global history of psychology, and particularly to clinical psychology, and its application to educational psychology can explain quite clearly the current status of the social psychology of the classroom and its projected future.

Positive psychology versus corrective psychology: A long historical struggle

It is commonly held that the roots of modern psychology stem from Freud's work on psychoanalysis as a theory of personality and as a method of psychotherapy. Freud was criticized incessantly over decades for a variety of issues and aspects. In the past 70 years, one of the major challenges to Freudian psychology came from humanistic psychology (with figures such as Maslow and Rogers) and in later decades from positive psychology (Seligman and Csikszentmihalyi 2000). This became a cultural struggle between two movements, or basic philosophies, in the practice of psychology – positive psychology and corrective psychology. (I use the term 'corrective' for lack of an agreed-upon title, and 'negative' as opposed to 'positive' is a bit too negative!)

Freudian psychodynamic theory viewed the internal psyche as a constant battleground between strong dynamic forces, some of which are negative and destructive. 'The imagination of a man's heart is evil from his youth' (Genesis 8:21), and it is better that the person would remain unconscious of many ideas and wishes lying deep inside. In contrast, positive psychology is optimistic, focusing on internal powers and resources that lead people to prosper in the face of adversity. The old psychology deals with inherent neuroticism and sickness and seeks the means for overcoming these forces (hence the title 'corrective'), whereas positive psychology seeks to enhance the healthy resources. The common overall objective of both psychologies is to reach the best possible outcomes of mental health, sanity, well-being, and self-efficacy. Perhaps they are similar to each other and the difference is only in the framing of the main ideas – but it seems that the difference between the two views is more critical and substantive to the practice of psychology.

In corrective psychology, the person must learn in the healing process to overcome the inner conflicts and the pathologies, and the *Diagnostic and Statistical Manual of Mental Disorders* (American Psychiatric Association 2013) is the symbolic banner of this perspective. In positive psychology, the goal is to develop the healthy and positive inner forces through humanistic, positive, and encouraging education and training.

Movements in neighboring nonclinical domains reflected the same ideas as positive psychology. The human relations movement originated in the birth of the sensitivity training group with Kurt Lewin in the late 1940s and eventually led to the development of organizational psychology. Some of its known slogans were personal growth, a spirit of inquiry, and collaborative relations and conduct; its banner book was *The Planning of Change* (Bennis et al. 1985), which appeared in several editions over three decades.

I believe that early behavior therapy of half a century ago also represented a certain aspect of positive psychology as opposed to the Freudian model, because it was practical and direct in its approach to behavior modification and change, without dealing with deep psychodynamic constructs and inherent psychopathology. But the behavioral approach was too mechanistic to be considered humanistic, and I believe that its acceptance of punishment as being as effective as positive reinforcement made it non-kosher for believers of positive psychology.

Probably the most dramatic shift from a negative perspective to a positive perspective – a shift in which the very same researchers were involved in both stages, and the same experimental studies were reinterpreted – occurred in a rigorously experimental cognitive domain, focused on information processing, bias, and decision making. Kahneman and Tversky (Kahneman et al. 1982) led a strong area of research on human information processing, and presented a set of heuristics (or biases), which were common mistaken ways of thinking that led people to deviate from rational thinking.

I was Kahneman's undergraduate student, and later his junior colleague. Every researcher of bias made use of Kahneman and Tversky's ideas. For 20–25 years, the image of man in that approach was negative – people are biased, wrong, and can almost never process information correctly. Instead of thinking logically and rationally, they use intuitive shortcuts (heuristics) that lead to biased solutions. This is what I taught my students for decades, when I was involved in the investigation of teachers' biases and self-fulfilling prophecies and voters' wishful thinking in predicting election results.

And then, in the last 20 years, the conception of information processing flipped and shifted dramatically to a positive psychological perspective, while still maintaining the strict experimental methodology (and Kahneman received the Nobel Prize in 2002; Tversky unfortunately died of cancer earlier). The revised approach dominates the fields of decision making and economic psychology as strongly today as the previous perspective did before. The same two systems of information processing are posited – the fast, intuitive and emotional System 1, and the slower, more deliberate and more logical System 2 – but now Kahneman exalts the extraordinary capabilities of fast thinking, praises the pervasive influence of intuition, and encourages people to trust their intuition (Kahneman 2011). In recent years he wrote about well-being (Kahneman and Diener 2003) and about 'happiness by design' (Dolan and Kahneman 2014). The field is flourishing with experimental research, and salient books such as those by Dan Ariely (2008, 2010) praise the intuitive and the irrational. Intuition had been a liability in the early years, and now it has become a virtue. I think that this is the most extreme example of the shift from corrective psychology to positive psychology, led by the same person with the same kind of experimental studies, and the new perspective was worthy of the Nobel prize!

Paradigm shift in the social psychology of the classroom

The current state of the social psychology of the classroom can be explained in relation to the background of the struggle between positive psychology and corrective psychology, and of the shifts and changes that took place in theory and research in clinical psychology and in experimental psychology. The two pivots in this examination of the social psychology of the classroom are the area of teacher expectations and the field of classroom management.

The Pygmalion experiment emerged from a background of negative, corrective psychology, despite the fact that it examined the effect of positive expectations only. Rosenthal's previous research on experimenters' effects and the influence of their expectations on experimental results exposed a deeply rooted bias phenomenon which implied that the results of controlled laboratory experiments should be suspected and could not be counted upon. *Pygmalion in the Classroom* was born out of those previous studies when Lenore Jacobson, a Californian school principal, urged Rosenthal to apply his expectation research ideas in education, within the classroom.

The study (Rosenthal and Jacobson 1968) examined the effects of planting in teachers' minds expectations about hidden, yet unrealized, intellectual potential of certain (randomly selected) students in the classroom. And indeed self-fulfilling prophecy effects were recorded for some late blooming students in some classrooms. Despite the barrage of sharp criticisms over the years, the probability of finding self-fulfilling prophecy effects was established following numerous replication studies and meta-analyses. The debates and controversies lasted from the 1960s to the 1980s – some were focused on experimenter effects (e.g. Barber and Silver 1968); some dealt exclusively with Pygmalion (e.g. Elashoff and Snow 1971); and numerous others dealt with expectation effects in all domains (e.g. Rosenthal and Rubin's article in *The Behavioral and Brain Sciences* journal in 1978, followed by 29 open peer commentaries). At the same time, the issue of teacher expectations evoked a tremendous interest among researchers, and hundreds of expectation studies were published in the two decades following the publication of Pygmalion.

For obvious ethical reasons, the Pygmalion study examined only the influence of positive expectations and avoided the manipulation of negative expectations. (Effects of negative expectations can be examined in a non-experimental method by asking the investigated teachers to nominate high expectation and low expectation students in their classrooms, and subsequently observe the teachers' behaviors towards those students.) But the untested implications about negative effects of teachers' low expectations always dominated in the debate over the Pygmalion effect, and strongly affected critics' views. If fabricated positive expectations can improve students' intellectual performance following an implicit and complex process of mediation, it stands to reason that teachers' real negative expectations may well hinder the performance of students viewed by teachers as having low potential. Such negative effects would constitute a grave threat to the reputation of school teachers, as they would be blamed for being responsible for school failure (see Wineburg 1987). In those decades, school failure was one of the most salient and painful issues in American education. Rosenthal argues until this day that his main objective in the Pygmalion research was to investigate the potential contributions of teachers' positive expectations (personal communication 2012).

The central topic in the numerous teacher expectation studies in the 1970s and 1980s was teachers' differential behavior towards high and low expectation students in the classroom. Teacher differential behavior is the main link in the behavioral mediation of expectations, from information in the teacher's head in the first stage all the way to student's actual performance. The early mediation studies were based on actual behavioral observations in the classroom. In later studies, researchers used a variety of methods, from students' reports of teacher behavior to the analysis of teachers' nonverbal behaviors in thin slices of videotaped clips.

Because it was not possible (for ethical reasons) to manipulate negative expectations in teachers' minds, the evidence of harmful consequences of teachers' negative expectations emerged from studies of teacher differential behavior (Babad 1993). And indeed substantial documentation delineating teachers' conduct toward their low expectation students was published (e.g. Brophy 1983, 1985; Harris and Rosenthal 1985). In 1982, we published the study 'Pygmalion, Galatea, and the Golem' (Babad *et al.* 1982) that demonstrated clearly that biased teachers (as contrasted with unbiased teachers) behaved negatively and hindered the performance of their low expectation students. The negative effects were even more strongly demonstrated in the investigation of thin slices of videotaped teachers' nonverbal behavior (Babad *et al.* 2003), where teachers' differentiality was correlated negatively with students' morale and satisfaction.

My own research (alone and in collaboration with Rosenthal) until a decade ago indeed represented the perspective of corrective psychology, calling attention to negative outcomes of teacher expectations. But many other researchers and authors tried – in the spirit of positive psychology – to protect teachers' professional status and to minimize the implications of the negative findings. The overall growth of positive psychology was reflected in educational research and practice (e.g. see Noble and McGrath 2008; Park and Peterson 2008).

The growing field of contemporary classroom management was certainly based on principles of positive psychology – strengthening personal resources; empowering students and teachers; encouraging teachers' positive emotionality; and fostering emotional relations with students – in addition to paying extra attention to the characterization and development of excellent teachers (see various authors in Evertson and Weinstein 2006; the review in Babad 2009). According to the above historical analysis presented in the last few paragraphs, contemporary classroom management was, and is, very likely to succeed and to gain many supporters among researchers, educational administrators, teachers, and book publishers.

The late Jere Brophy himself, in person, served as a salient demonstration of the paradigm shift in educational psychology. Brophy and Good were among the most productive researchers of teacher expectations in the 1970s. In his 1983 and 1985 publications, Brophy provided a list of teacher differential behaviors that summarized his own research and findings of other colleagues. Many of the listed behaviors were negative in characterizing teacher behavior toward low expectation students. But even then Brophy argued that such differential behaviors characterize only a small fraction of teachers and do not reflect a global process. He wrote several times that 'teacher expectations are generally accurate, reality-based, and open to corrective feedback' (Brophy 1985: 304).

Over the years, Brophy became one of the leaders of the classroom management movement, and wrote the chapter on the history of research on classroom management in the *Handbook of Classroom Management: Research, Practice, and Contemporary Issues* (Brophy 2006). As stated earlier, there was no reference at all to teacher expectations in Brophy's chapter, and he did not mention his past long-time involvement in that area. We can only speculate about Brophy's reasons(s) for such an omission (because he could not have thought that teacher expectations and teacher–student expectation-based interaction do *not* constitute classroom management events).

Another party that has a critical influence on the shape of the field must be considered, and that is the group of book publishers. Textbook publishers do not exert much direct influence on the research in any field, but they sit in a critical junction, controlling the dissemination of psychological knowledge to the students and to the field. They determine which books will be published and reach their prospected audiences, and which books will not! In the case of educational psychology, the largest readership consists of students in teacher training in almost all institutions of higher education, and who will be the teachers of the next generation. Editors' selection of authors and book plans determine the kind of psychology that will be learned by future teachers.

Book companies want to increase sales and to win over other companies in the market. I presume that books that present a more positive outlook and are more encouraging of new teachers will have a higher chance of being adopted than books that emphasize negative phenomena and pitfalls of which teachers must beware. Because the domain of teacher expectations and teacher differential behavior has negative implications and teachers are criticized indirectly through negative research results, this entire domain may well damage book sales. Book editors may therefore prefer positive and optimistic psychology that is based on a solid rationale and supported by a wide body of research. Such books may be preferable to both the instructors who adopt the books and to the students who learn from these books and subsequently evaluate their teachers. Therefore, the disappearance of Pygmalion and teacher expectation research from textbooks, and the concurrent increase in the popularity of positive books presenting the contemporary philosophy of classroom management makes a lot of sense.

A final note: Positive social psychology of the classroom

Despite the gloomy discussion in the previous pages, this reflective chapter can end on a positive note, because at least one subfield in expectation research represents the optimistic spirit of positive psychology. Over 25 years ago, my good friend Dov Eden, an expectation researcher from Tel Aviv University, developed applications of the Pygmalion research and the self-fulfilling prophecy domain into organizational psychology and manager training. Eden wrote a book entitled: *Pygmalion in Management: Productivity as a Self-fulfilling Prophecy* (1990), and spoke about "harnessing Pygmalion" (Eden 1992) and using the self-fulfilling prophecy as a management tool. The idea was to foster a positive ideology and to train managers with an optimistic vision who would believe in (all) their workers and transmit positive expectations to them. Eden's conceptual shift was that instead of dealing with expectations as held differentially toward individuals, he defined positive expectations as an overall state of mind of successful managers, and developed training methods to foster this view and its relevant behavioral strategies. Eden's work fitted positive psychology perfectly, and was well in line with contemporary ideas about how psychology should be applied.

A similar trend is now being developed and tested within the framework of the social psychology of the classroom. Christine Rubie-Davies, a relative newcomer to expectation research, has developed a conceptualization and training methods to foster teachers' positive beliefs and expectations towards *all* students in the classroom, and has examined student outcomes in the classrooms of 'Pygmalion teachers' (Rubie-Davies 2014; Rubie-Davies *et al.* in press). This promising direction is harmonious with the philosophy of positive psychology and fits with the framework of contemporary classroom management, and is therefore projected to be a promising feature of the social psychology of the classroom in the future.

Indeed, this volume alone attests to a bright future for the social psychology of the classroom. It is pleasing to note the wide range of researchers who have contributed. The area of the social psychology of the classroom is clearly one that is active and vibrant. It augurs well for the well-being, satisfaction, motivation, and resulting positive classroom climate that future generations of students are likely to enjoy.

References

American Psychiatric Association (2013) *Diagnostic and Statistical Manual of Mental Disorders: DSM-5*, 5th edn, Washington, DC: American Psychiatric Association.

Ariely, D. (2008) *Predictably Irrational: The Hidden Forces that Shape Our Decisions*, Toronto: HarperCollins.

Ariely, D. (2010) *The Upside of Irrationality: The Unexpected Benefits of Defying Logic at Work and at Home*, Toronto: HarperCollins.

Babad, E. (1979) 'Personality correlates of susceptibility to biasing information', *Journal of Personality and Social Psychology*, 37: 195–202.

Babad, E. (1993) 'Teachers' differential behavior', *Educational Psychology Review*, 5: 347–376.

Babad, E. (1995) 'The "teacher's pet" phenomenon, teachers' differential behavior, and students' morale', *Journal of Educational Psychology*, 87: 361–374.

Babad, E. (2005) 'The psychological price of media bias', *Journal of Experimental Psychology: Applied*, 11: 245–255.

Babad, E. (2009) *The Social Psychology of the Classroom*, New York: Routledge.

Babad, E., Avni-Babad, D. and Rosenthal, R. (2003) 'Teachers' brief nonverbal behaviors can predict certain aspects of students' evaluations', *Journal of Educational Psychology*, 95: 553–562.

Babad, E., Inbar, J. and Rosenthal, R. (1982) 'Pygmalion, Galatea, and the Golem: investigations of biased and unbiased teachers', *Journal of Educational Psychology*, 74: 459–474.

Barber, T. and Silver, M. (1968) 'Fact, fiction, and the experimenter bias effect', *Psychological Bulletin Monographs Supplement*, 70: 1–29.

Bennis, W.G., Benne, K. D. and Chin, R. (1985) *The Planning of Change*, 4th edn, New York: Holt, Rinehart and Winston.

Brophy, J. (1983) 'Research on the self-fulfilling prophecy and teacher expectations', *Journal of Educational Psychology*, 75: 631–661.

Brophy, J. (1985) 'Teacher–student interaction', in J. Dusek (ed.) *Teacher Expectancies* (pp. 303–328), Hillsdale, NJ: Erlbaum.

Brophy, J. (1998) (ed.) *Advances in Research on Teaching*, Vol. 7: *Expectations in the Classroom*, Greenwich, CO: JAI Press.

Brophy, J. (2006) 'History of research on classroom management', in C. Evertson and C. Weinstein (eds) *Handbook of Classroom Management: Research, Practice and Contemporary Issues* (pp. 17–43), Mahwah, NJ: Erlbaum.

Butler, R. (2007) 'Teachers' achievement goal orientations and associations with teachers' help-seeking: examination of a novel approach to teacher motivation', *Journal of Educational Psychology*, 99: 241–252.

Dolan, P. and Kahneman, D. (2014) 'Happiness by Design: Change What You Do, Not How You Think', Harmondsworth, UK: Penguin.

Eden, D. (1990) *Pygmalion in Management: Productivity as a Self-fulfilling Prophecy*, Lexington, MA: Lexington Books.

Eden, D. (1992) 'Self-fulfilling prophecy as a management tool: harnessing Pygmalion', *Academy of Management Review*, 9: 64–73.

Elashoff, J. and Snow, R. (eds) (1971) *Pygmalion Reconsidered*, Worthington, OH: Charles A. Jones.

Evertson, C. and Weinstein, C. (eds) (2006) *Handbook of Classroom Management: Research, Practice and Contemporary Issues*, Mahwah, NJ: Erlbaum.

Freiberg, H. (ed.) (1999) *Beyond Behaviorism: Changing the Classroom Management Paradigm*, Needham Heights, MA: Allyn & Bacon.

Harackiewicz, J., Barron, K., Pintrich, P., Elliott, A. and Thrash, T. (2002) 'Revision of achievement goal theory: necessary and illuminating', *Journal of Educational Psychology*, 94: 638–645.

Harris, M. and Rosenthal, R. (1985) 'Mediation of interpersonal expectancy effects: 31 meta-analyses', *Psychological Bulletin*, 97: 363–386.

Hattie, J. (2009) *Visible Learning: A Synthesis of Over 800 Meta-analyses Relating to Achievement*, London: Routledge.

Kahneman, D. (2011) *Thinking Fast and Slow*, New York: Farrar, Straus and Giroux.

Kahneman, D. and Diener, E. (eds) (2003) *Well-being: Foundations of Hedonic Psychology*, New York: Russell Sage Foundation.

Kahneman, D., Slovic, P. and Tversky, A. (eds) (1982) *Judgment Under Uncertainty: Heuristics and Biases*, New York: Cambridge University Press.

Noble, T. and McGrath, H. (2008) 'The positive educational practices framework: a tool for facilitating the work of educational psychologists in promoting pupil wellbeing', *Educational and Child Psychology*, 25: 119–134.

Park, N. and Peterson, C. (2008) 'Positive psychology and character strengths: application to strengths-based school counseling', *Professional School Counseling*, 12: 85–92.

Pianta, R. (2006) 'Classroom management and relationships between children and teachers: implications for research and practice', in C. Evertson and C. Weinstein (eds.) *Handbook of Classroom Management: Research, Practice and Contemporary Issues* (pp. 685–710), Mahwah, NJ: Erlbaum.

Rosenthal, R. and Jacobson, L. (1968) *Pygmalion in the Classroom*, New York: Holt, Rinehart and Winston.

Rosenthal, R. and Rubin, D. (1978) 'Interpersonal expectancy effect: the first 345 studies', *The Behavioral and Brain Sciences*, 3: 377–415.

Rubie-Davies, C.M. (2014) *Becoming a High Expectation Teacher: Raising the Bar*, London: Routledge.

Rubie-Davies, C.M., Peterson, E.R., Sibley, C.G. and Rosenthal, R. (in press) 'A teacher expectation intervention: modelling the practices of high expectation teachers', *Contemporary Educational Psychology*. doi: 10.1016/j.cedpsych.2014.03.003

Schmuck, R. and Schmuck, P. (1975) *Group Processes in the Classroom*, 2nd edn, Dubuque, IA: Wm. C. Brown.

Seligman, M. and Csikszentmihalyi, M. (2000) 'Positive psychology: an introduction', *American Psychologist*, 55: 5–14.

Wineburg, S. (1987) 'The self-fulfillment of the self-fulfilling prophecy', *Educational Researcher*, 16: 28–44.

INDEX